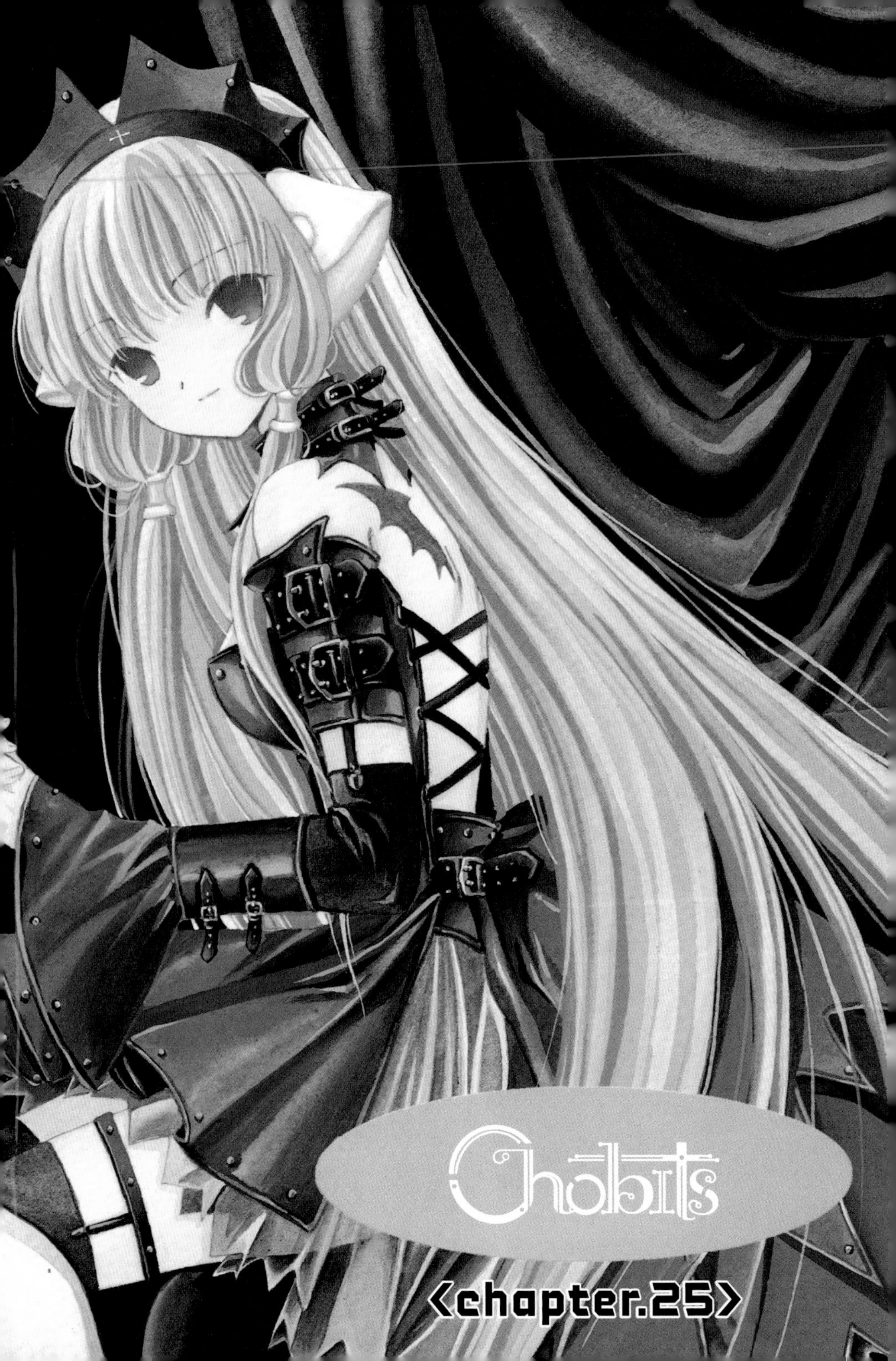
Chobits
<chapter.25>

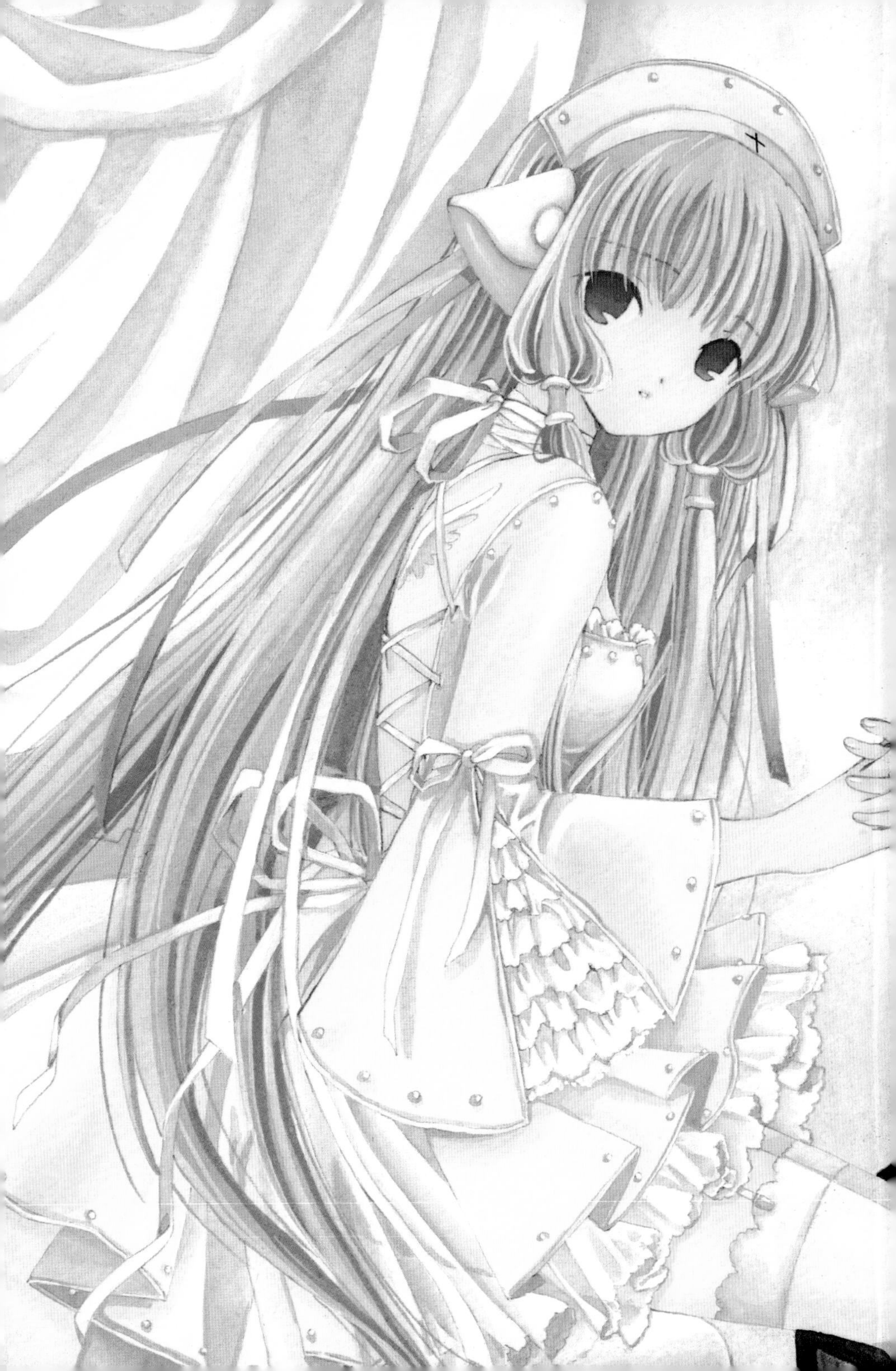

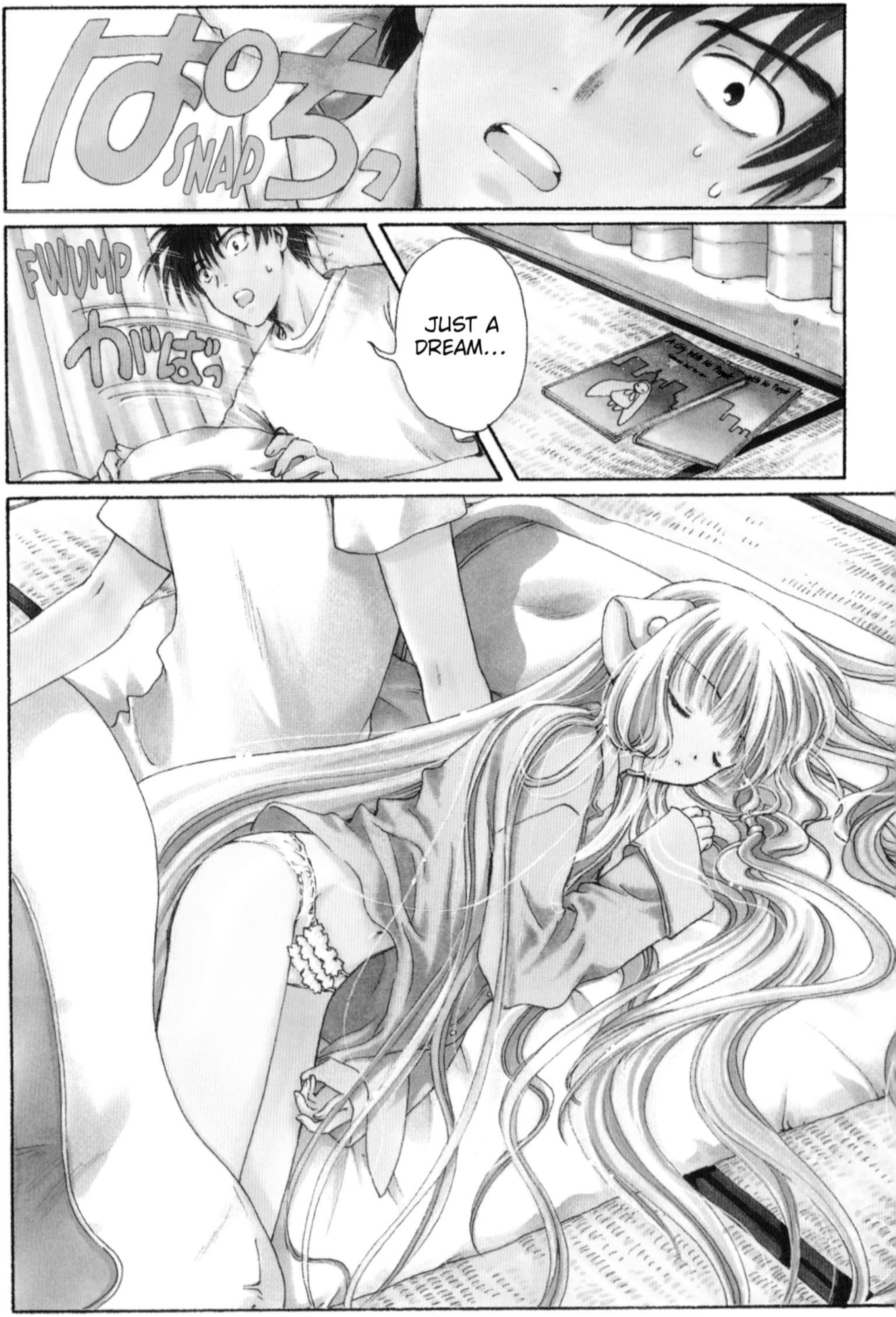
ぱちっ
SNAP
JUST A DREAM...
FWUMP
がばっ

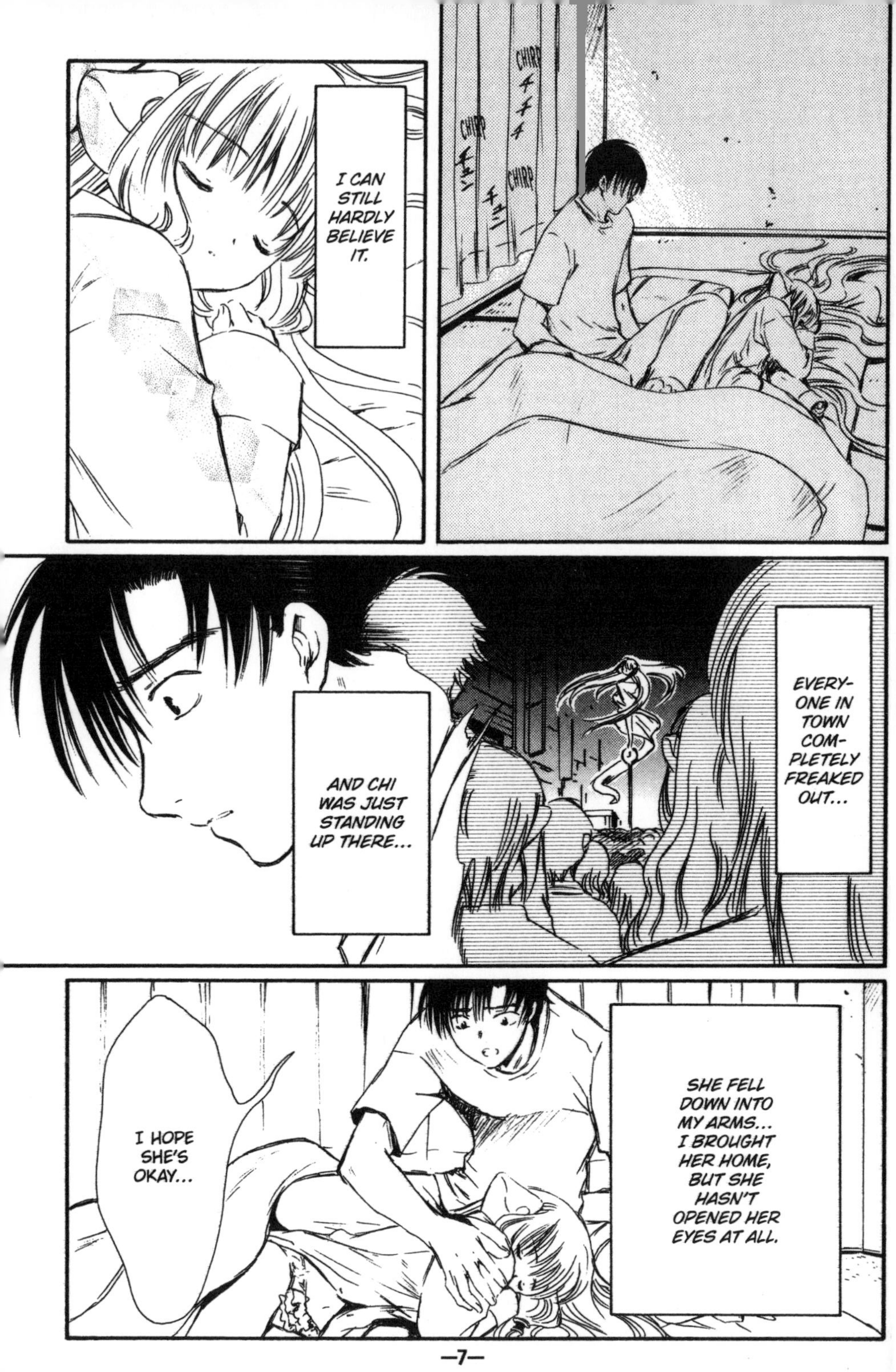

CHIRP
チチチ
CHIRP
チュン
CHIRP
チュン
I CAN STILL HARDLY BELIEVE IT.
EVERY-ONE IN TOWN COM-PLETELY FREAKED OUT…
AND CHI WAS JUST STANDING UP THERE…
SHE FELL DOWN INTO MY ARMS… I BROUGHT HER HOME, BUT SHE HASN'T OPENED HER EYES AT ALL.
I HOPE SHE'S OKAY…

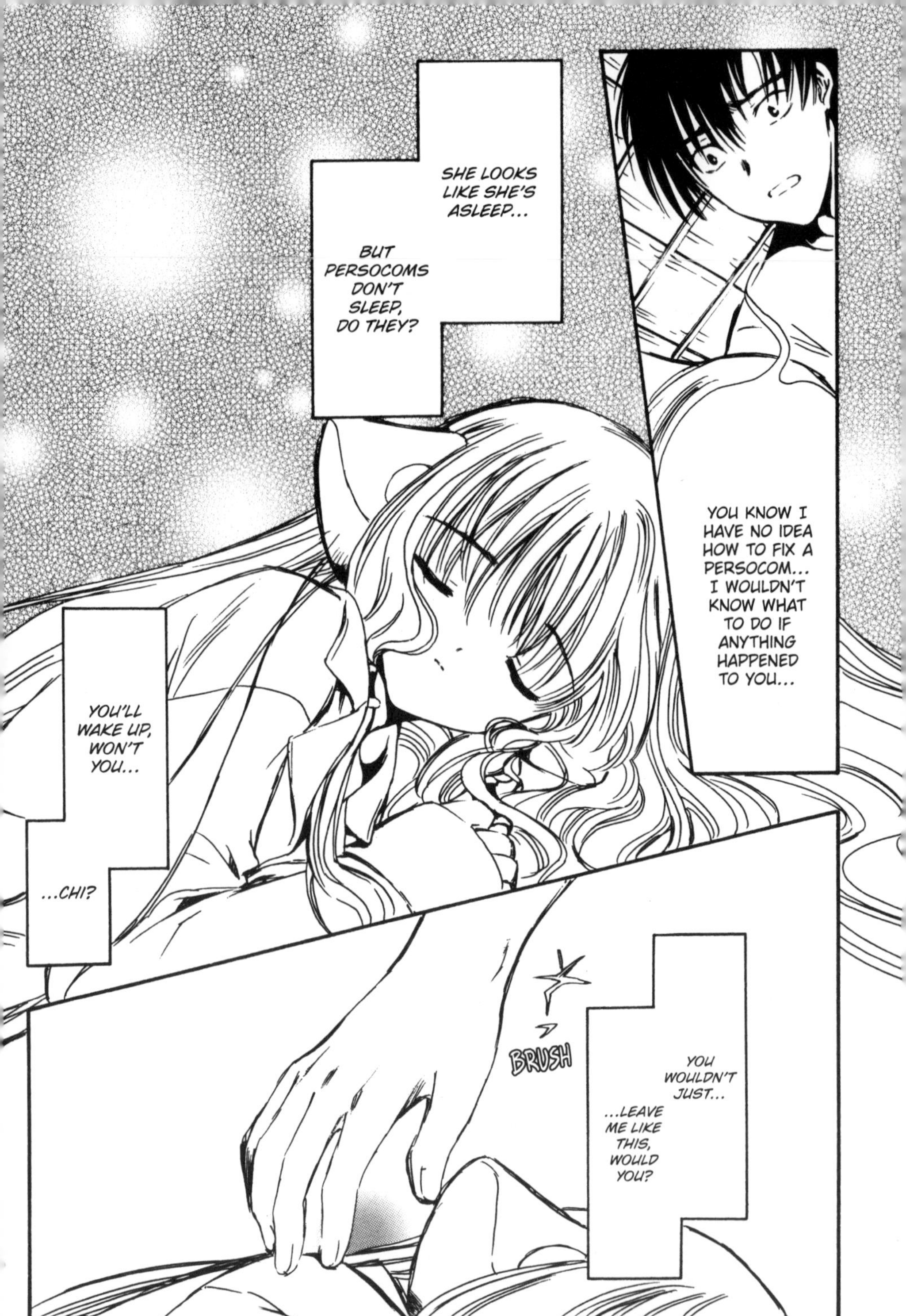
SHE LOOKS LIKE SHE'S ASLEEP...
BUT PERSOCOMS DON'T SLEEP, DO THEY?
YOU KNOW I HAVE NO IDEA HOW TO FIX A PERSOCOM... I WOULDN'T KNOW WHAT TO DO IF ANYTHING HAPPENED TO YOU...
YOU'LL WAKE UP, WON'T YOU...
...CHI?
BRUSH
YOU WOULDN'T JUST...
...LEAVE ME LIKE THIS, WOULD YOU?

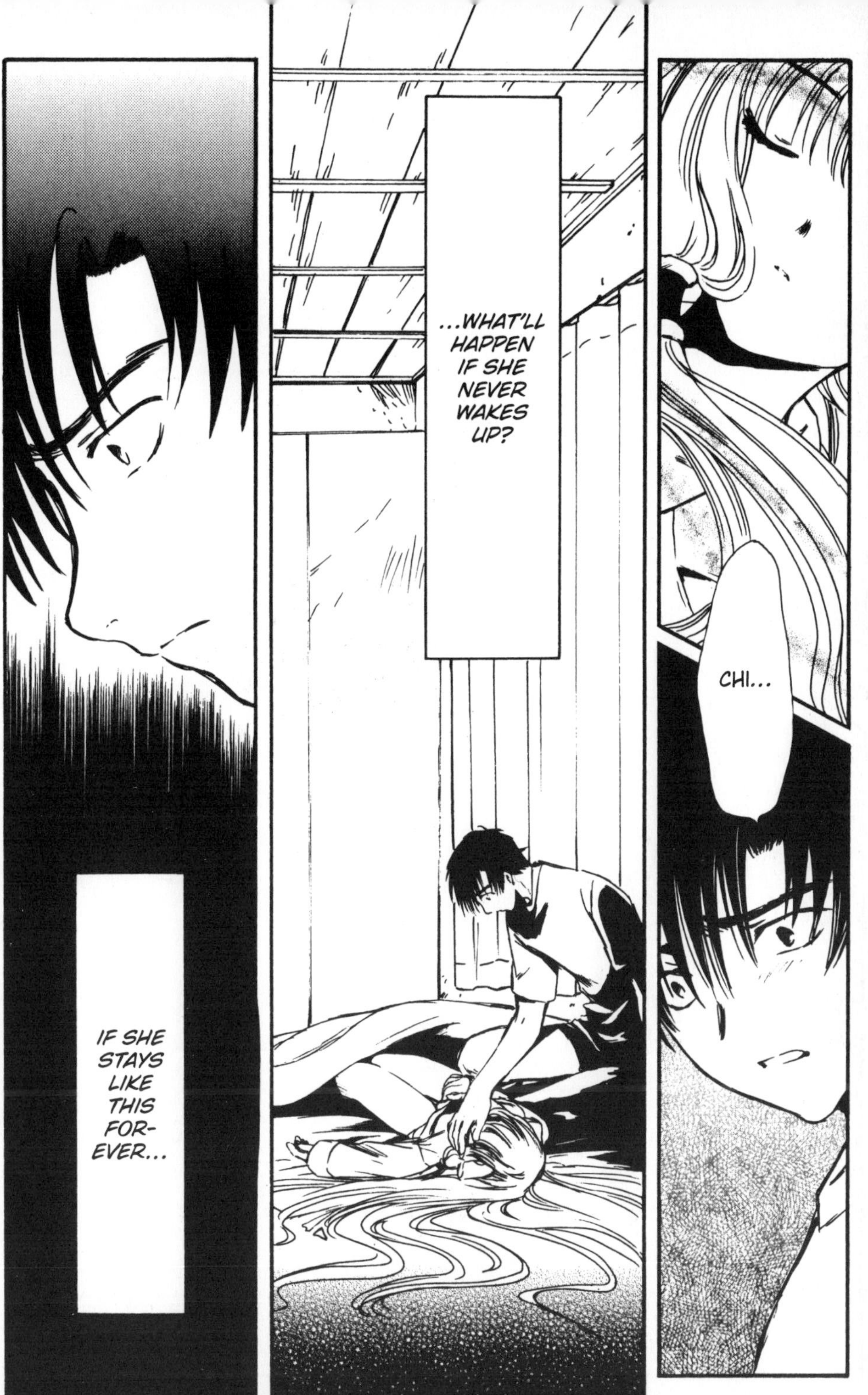
CHI...
...WHAT'LL HAPPEN IF SHE NEVER WAKES UP?
IF SHE STAYS LIKE THIS FOR-EVER...

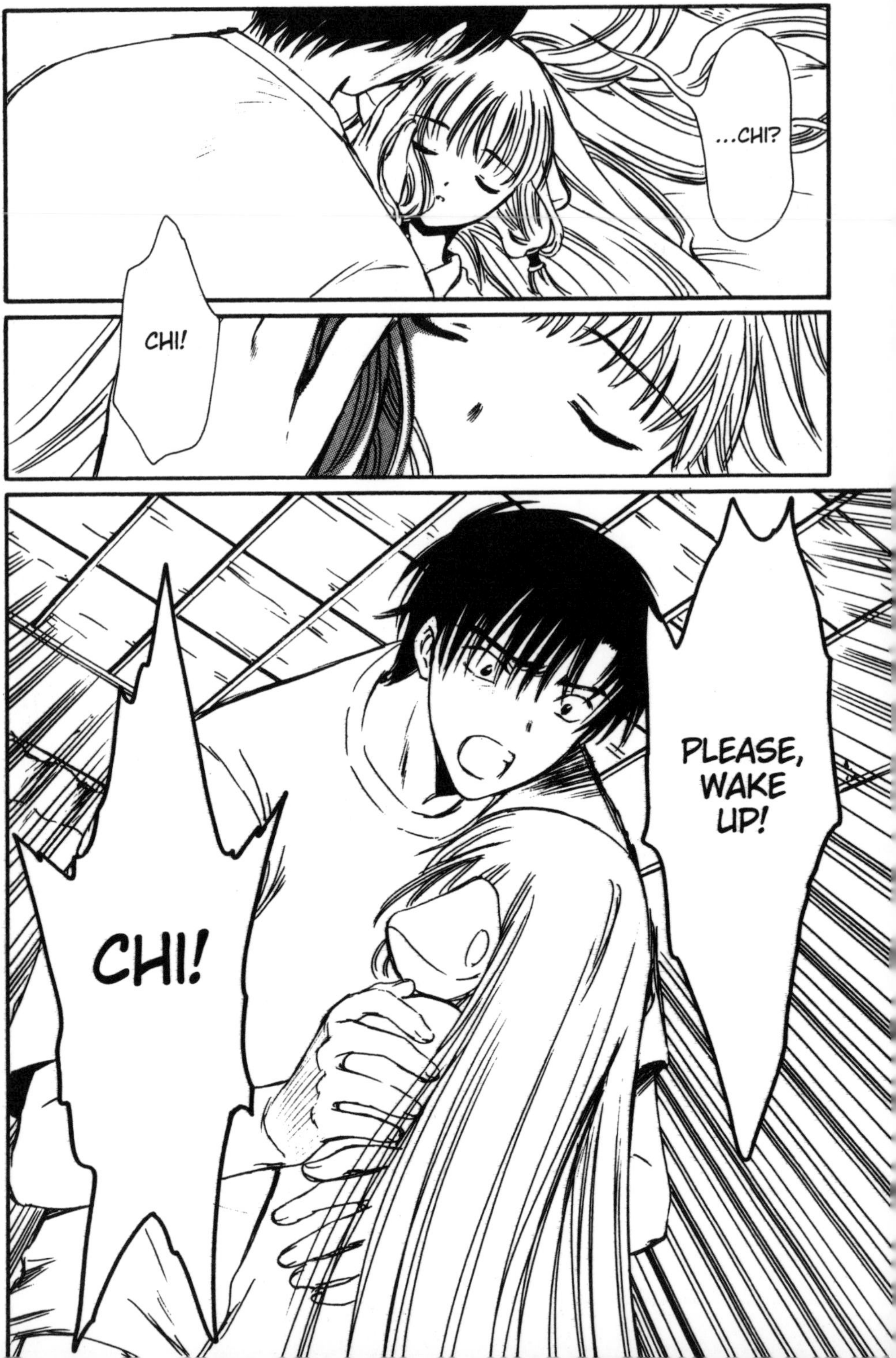
...CHI?
CHI!
PLEASE, WAKE UP!
CHI!

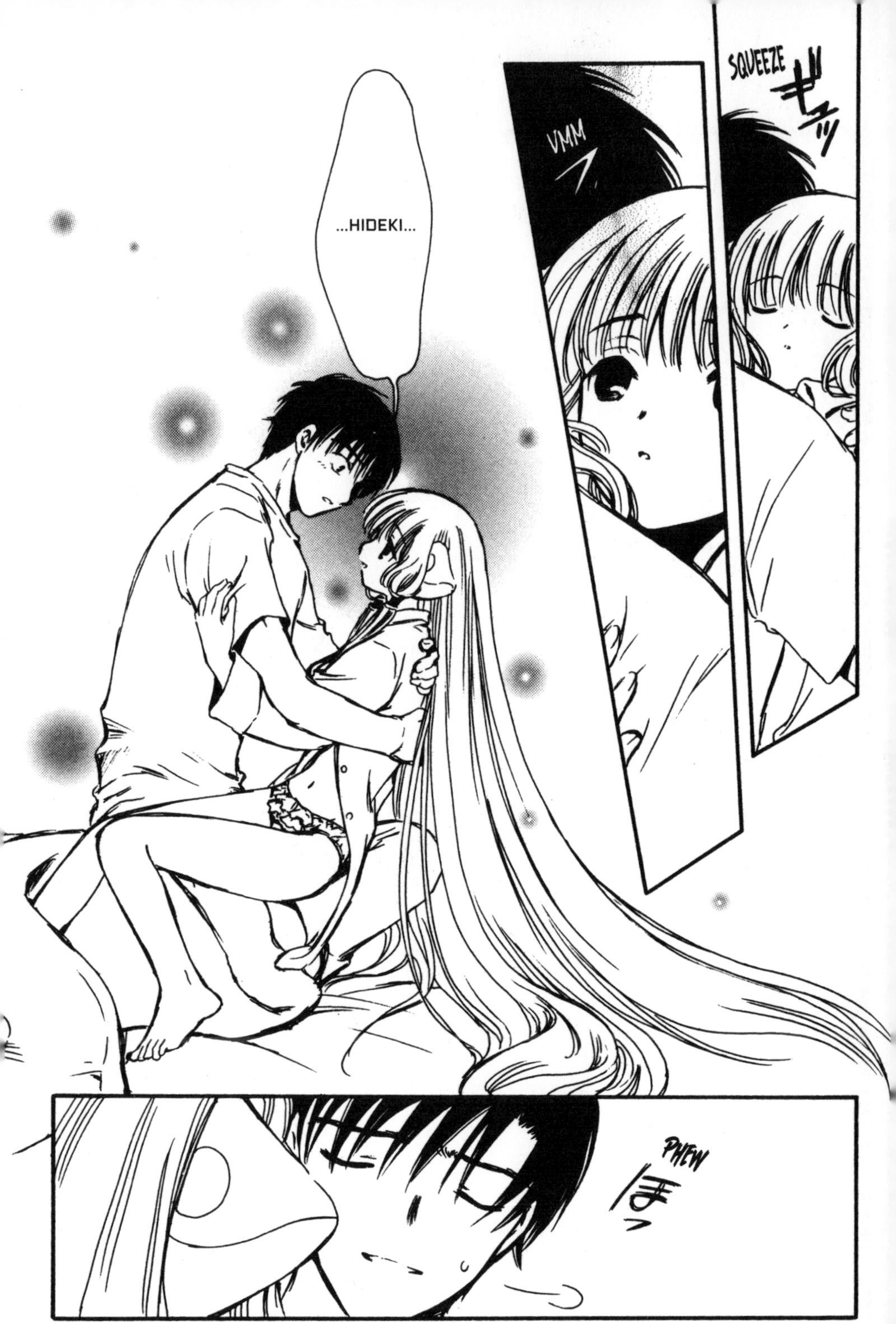
SQUEEZE
ギュッ
VMM
...HIDEKI...
PHEW
ほっ

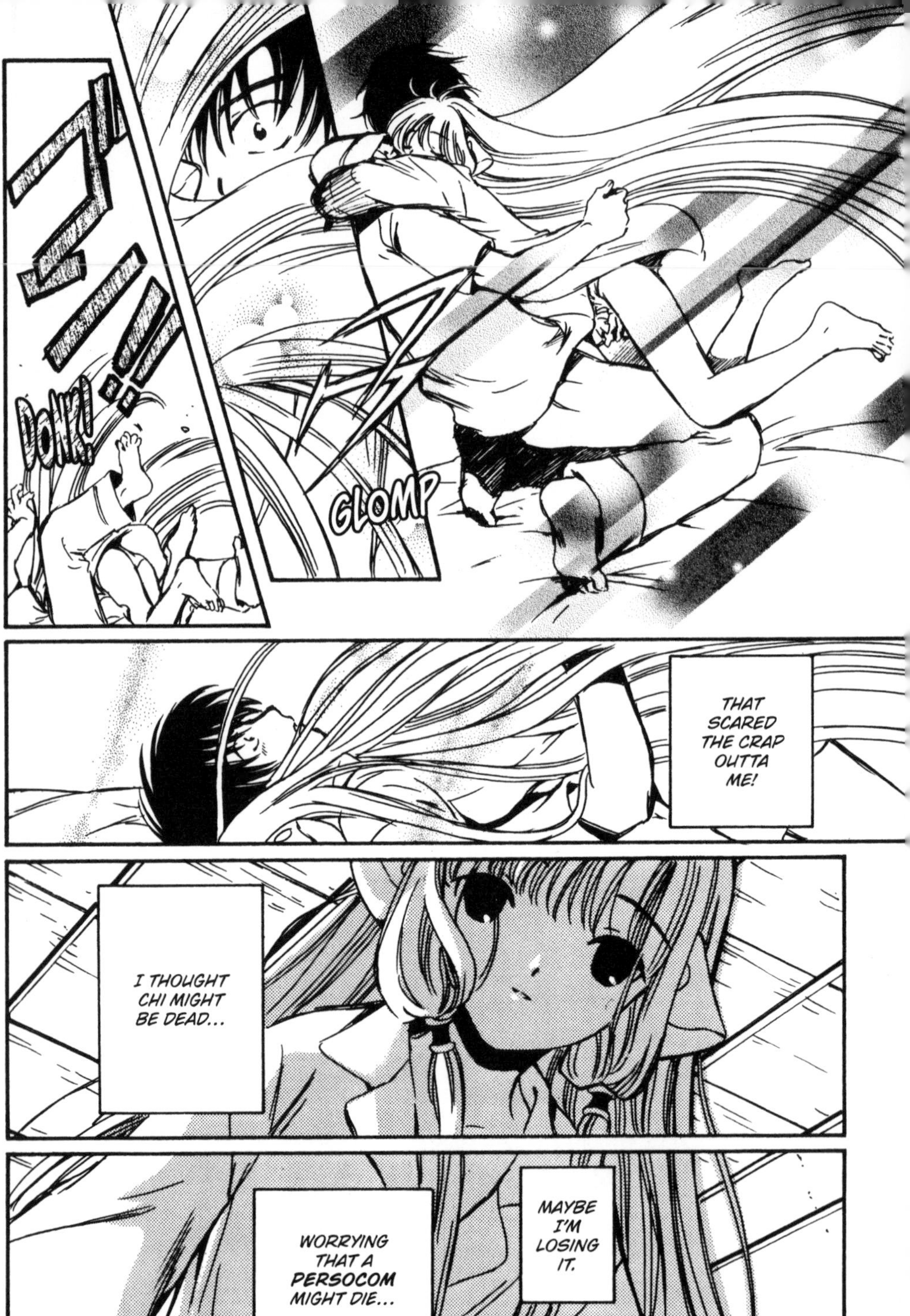
GLOMP
DOHZ!
THAT SCARED THE CRAP OUTTA ME!
I THOUGHT CHI MIGHT BE DEAD...
MAYBE I'M LOSING IT.
WORRYING THAT A **PERSOCOM** MIGHT DIE...

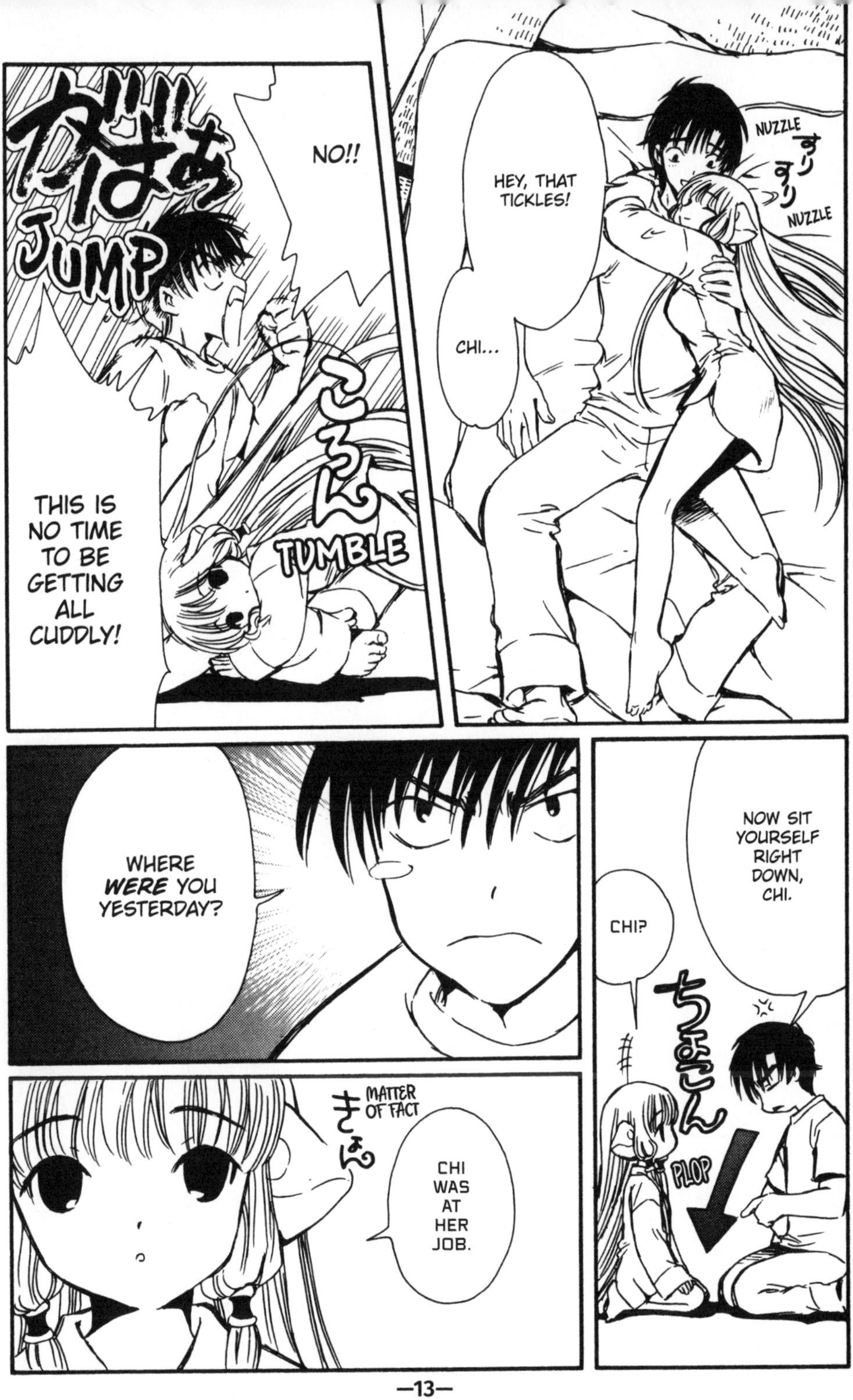
すり すり
NUZZLE NUZZLE
HEY, THAT TICKLES!
CHI...
NO!!
がばぁ
JUMP
ころん
TUMBLE
THIS IS NO TIME TO BE GETTING ALL CUDDLY!
NOW SIT YOURSELF RIGHT DOWN, CHI.
CHI?
ちょこん
PLOP
WHERE *WERE* YOU YESTERDAY?
きょん
MATTER OF FACT
CHI WAS AT HER JOB.

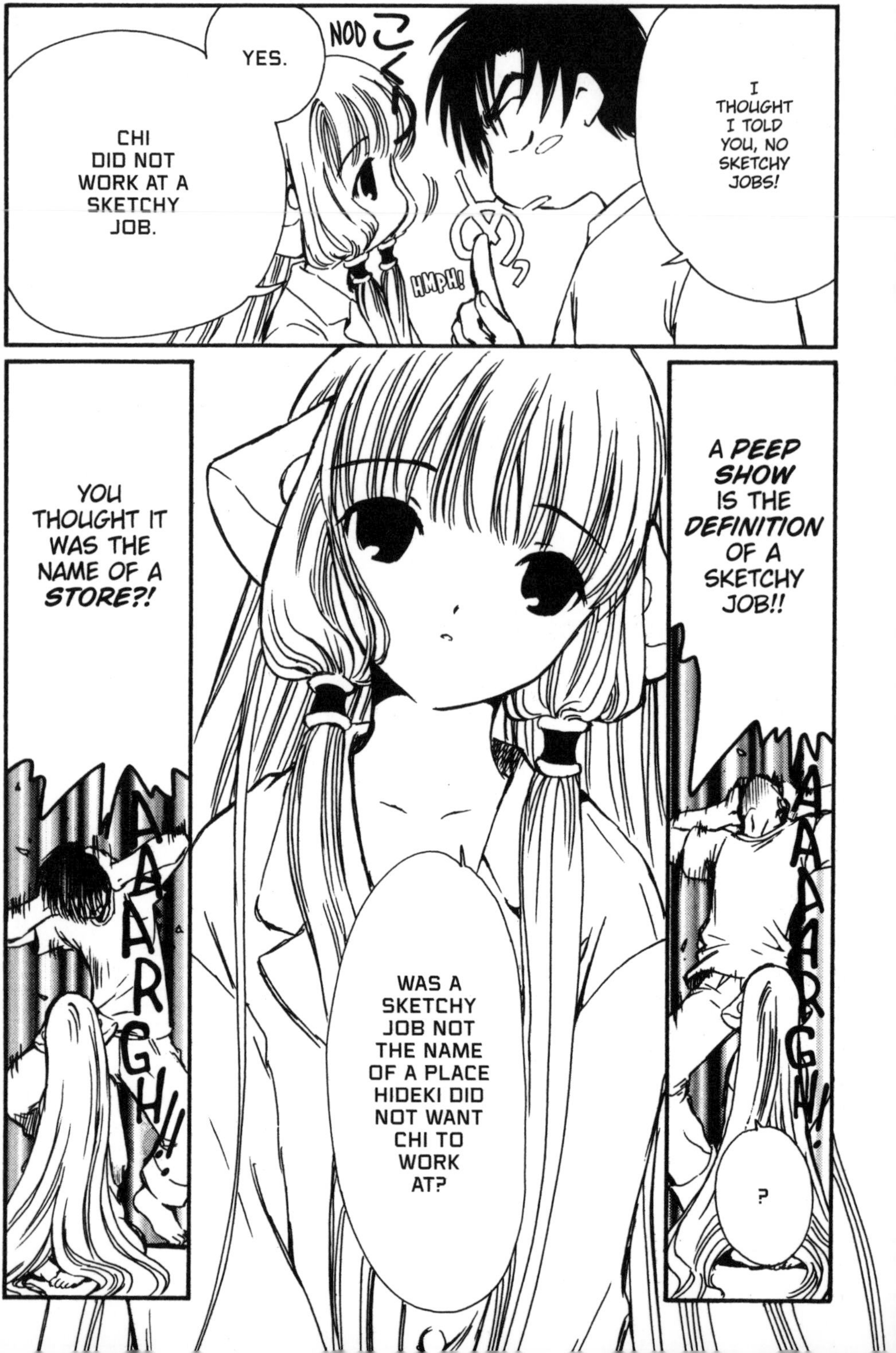

I THOUGHT I TOLD YOU, NO SKETCHY JOBS!
NOD
YES.
HMPH!
CHI DID NOT WORK AT A SKETCHY JOB.
A PEEP SHOW IS THE DEFINITION OF A SKETCHY JOB!!
AAAARGH!!
?
WAS A SKETCHY JOB NOT THE NAME OF A PLACE HIDEKI DID NOT WANT CHI TO WORK AT?
YOU THOUGHT IT WAS THE NAME OF A STORE?!
AAARGH!!

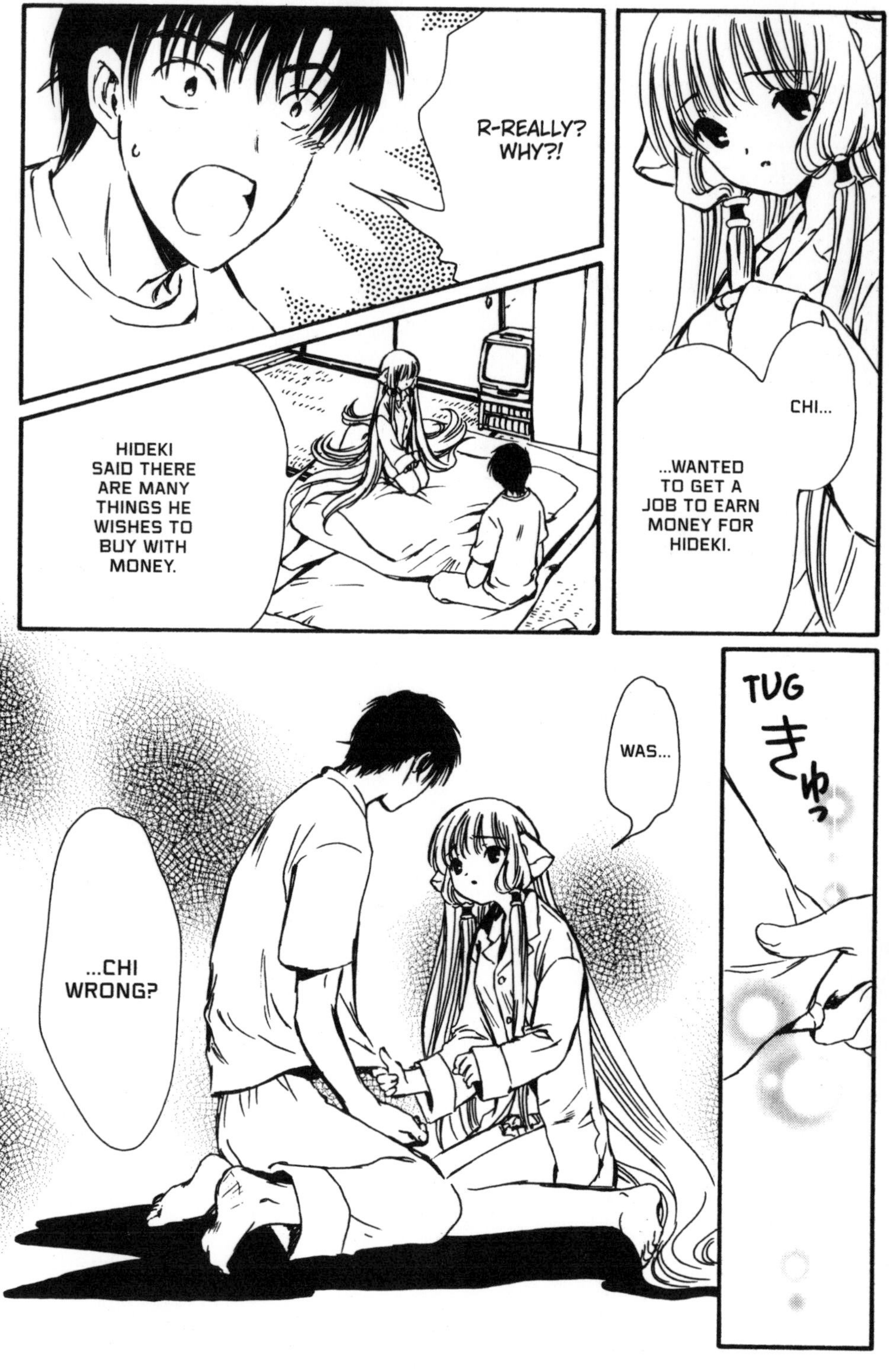
CHI...
...WANTED TO GET A JOB TO EARN MONEY FOR HIDEKI.
R-REALLY? WHY?!
HIDEKI SAID THERE ARE MANY THINGS HE WISHES TO BUY WITH MONEY.
TUG
きゅっ
WAS...
...CHI WRONG?

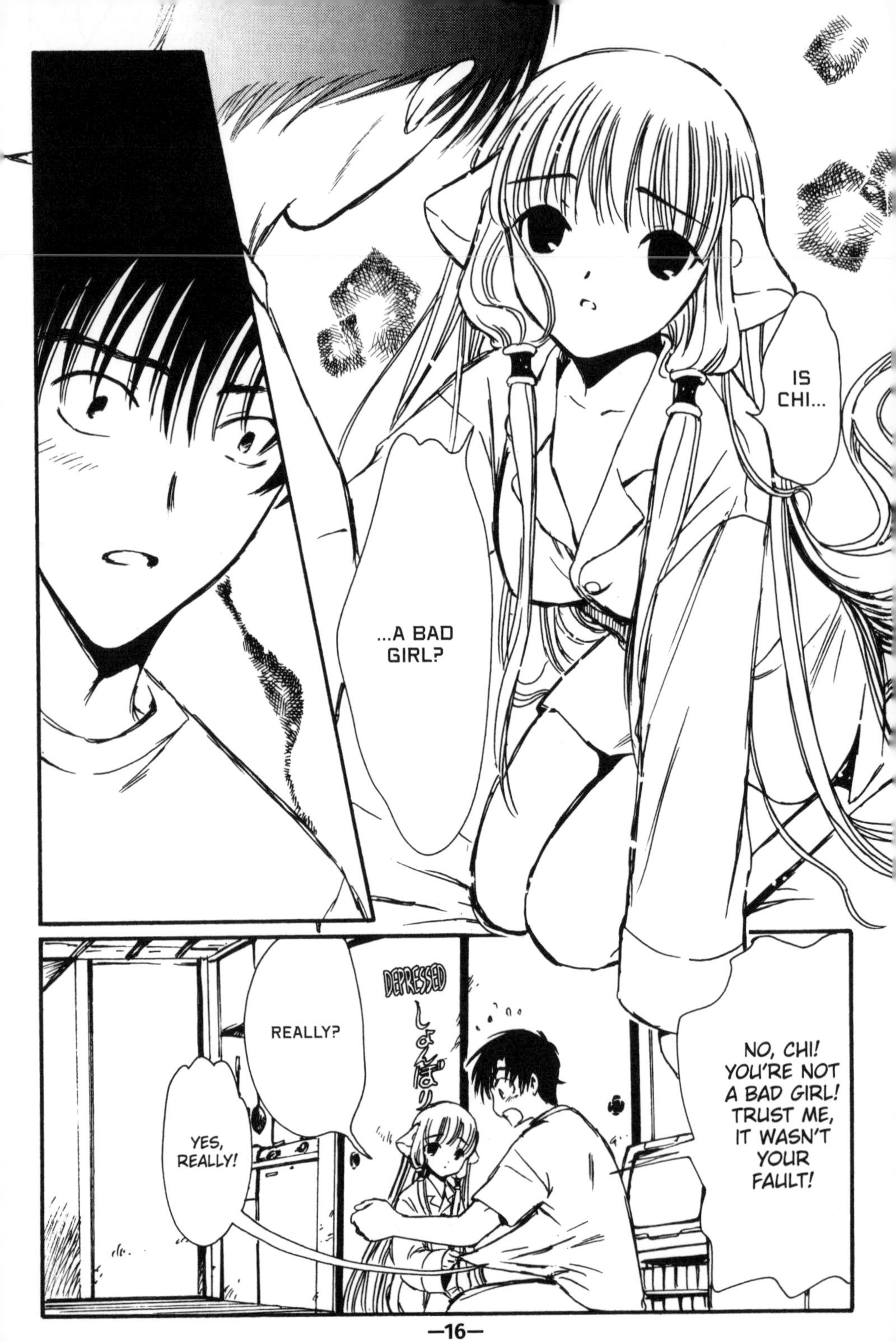
IS CHI...
...A BAD GIRL?
NO, CHI! YOU'RE NOT A BAD GIRL! TRUST ME, IT WASN'T YOUR FAULT!
DEPRESSED
しょんぼり
REALLY?
YES, REALLY!

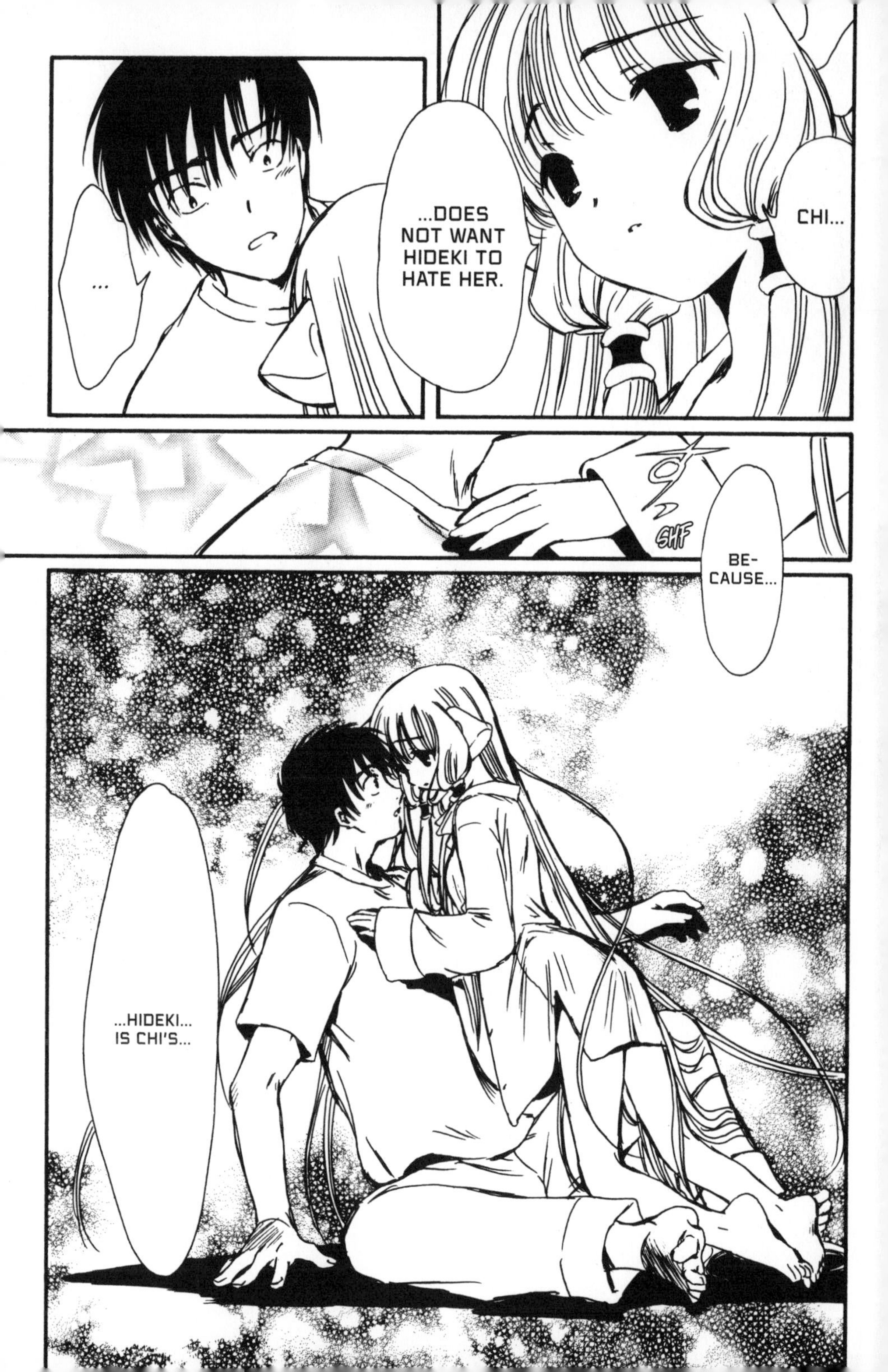
CHI...
...DOES NOT WANT HIDEKI TO HATE HER.
...
SHF
BE-CAUSE...
...HIDEKI... IS CHI'S...

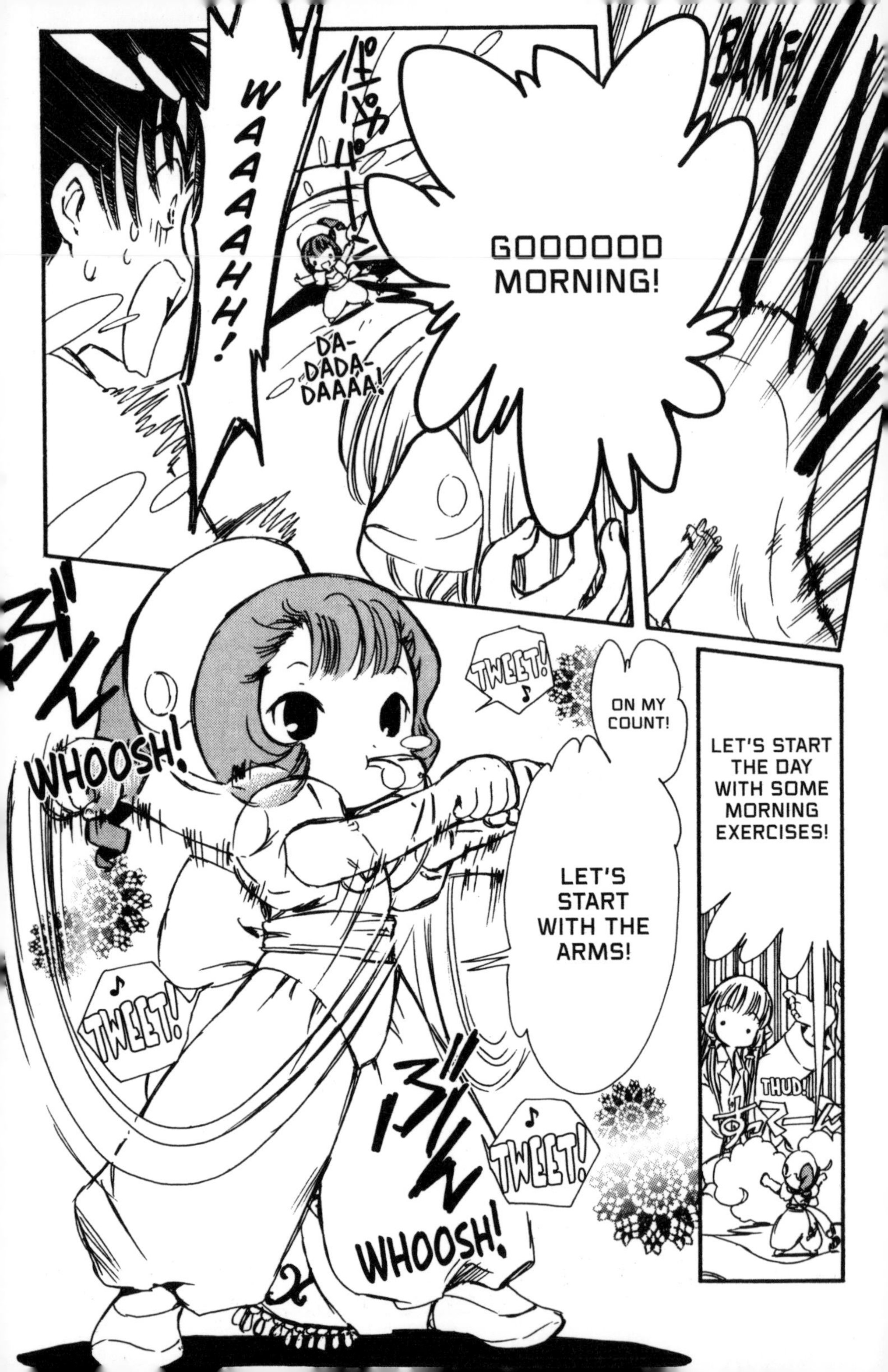
BAM!
GOOOOOD MORNING!
WAAAAAAHH!
DA-DADA-DAAAA!
LET'S START THE DAY WITH SOME MORNING EXERCISES!
THUD!
TWEET!
ON MY COUNT!
LET'S START WITH THE ARMS!
WHOOSH!
TWEET!
TWEET!
WHOOSH!

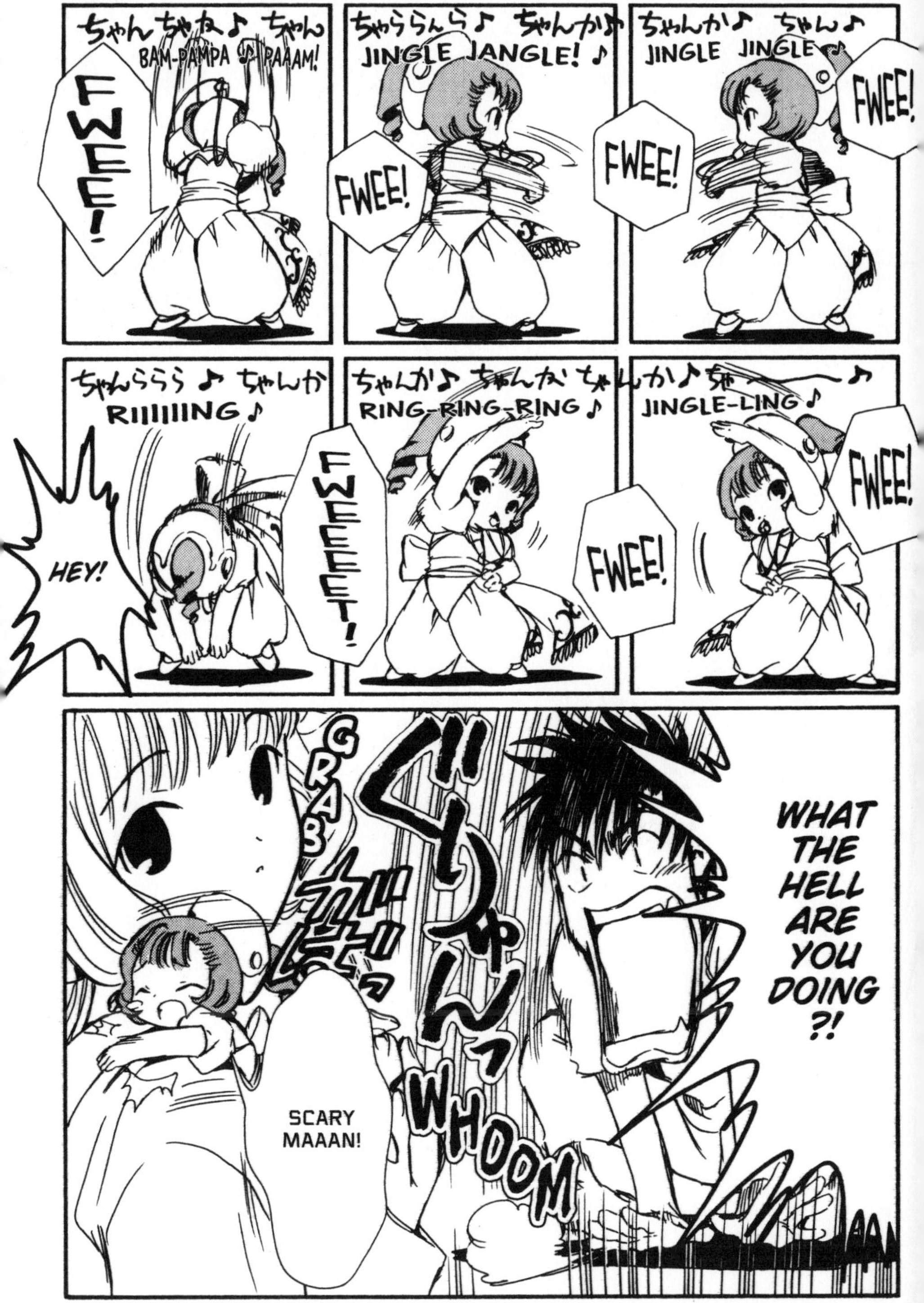
ちゃんか♪ ちゃん♪
JINGLE JINGLE ♪
FWEE!
FWEE!
ちゃららんら♪ ちゃんか♪
JINGLE JANGLE! ♪
FWEE!
FWEE!
ちゃんちゃね♪ ちゃん
BAM-PAMPA ♪ PAAAM!
FWEE!
JINGLE-LING ♪
FWEE!
FWEE!
ちゃんか♪ ちゃんか ちゃんか♪ちゃ～～～♪
RING-RING-RING ♪
FWEE!
FWEEEEET!
ちゃんららら ♪ ちゃんか
RIIIIIIING ♪
HEY!
WHAT THE HELL ARE YOU DOING ?!
WHOOM
GRAB
SCARY MAAAN!

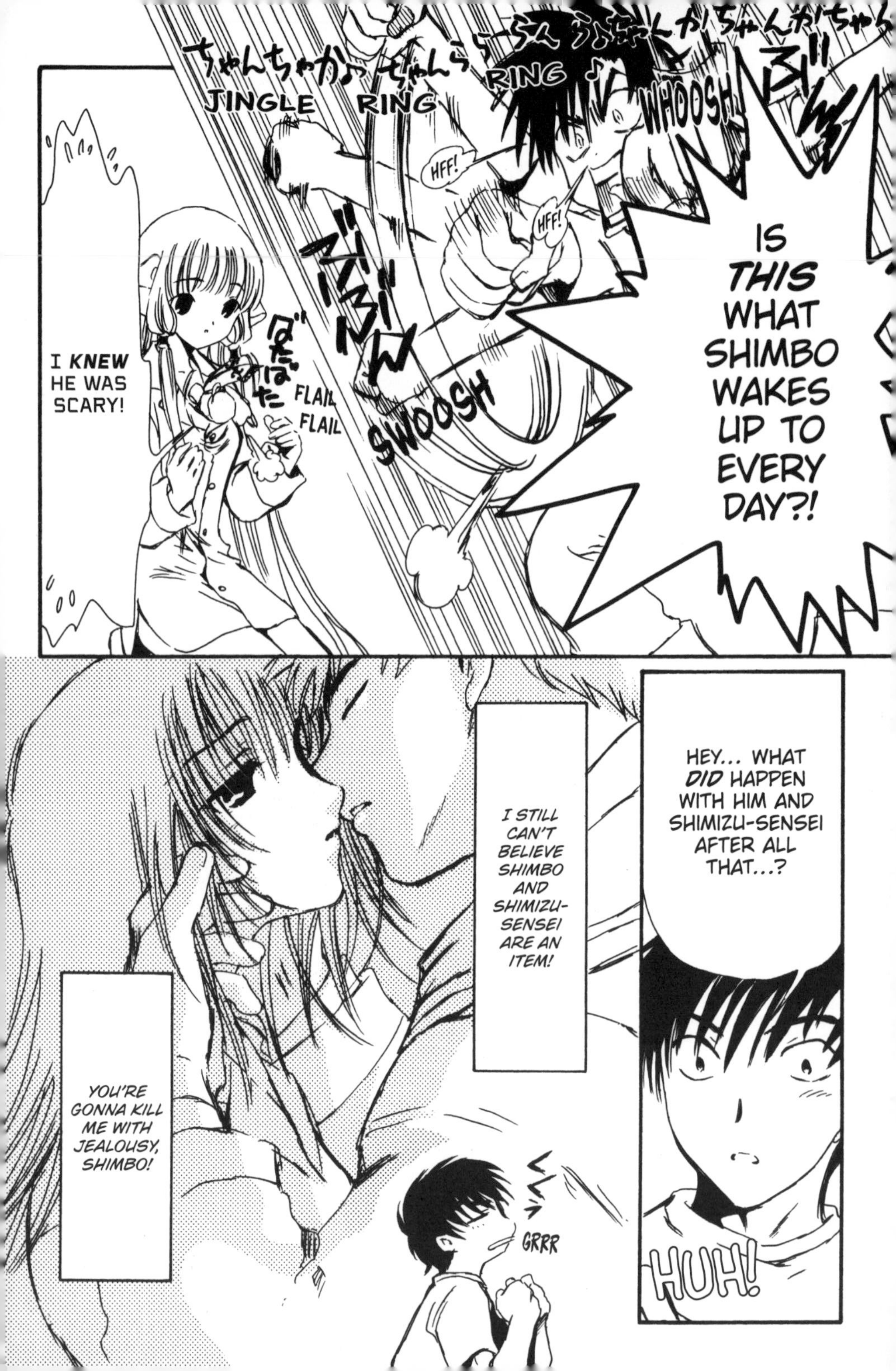

RING ♪
WHOOSH
JINGLE RING
HFF!
HFF!
IS *THIS* WHAT SHIMBO WAKES UP TO EVERY DAY?!
SWOOSH
FLAIL FLAIL
I *KNEW* HE WAS SCARY!
HEY... WHAT *DID* HAPPEN WITH HIM AND SHIMIZU-SENSEI AFTER ALL THAT...?
HUH!
I STILL CAN'T BELIEVE SHIMBO AND SHIMIZU-SENSEI ARE AN ITEM!
GRRR
YOU'RE GONNA KILL ME WITH JEALOUSY, SHIMBO!

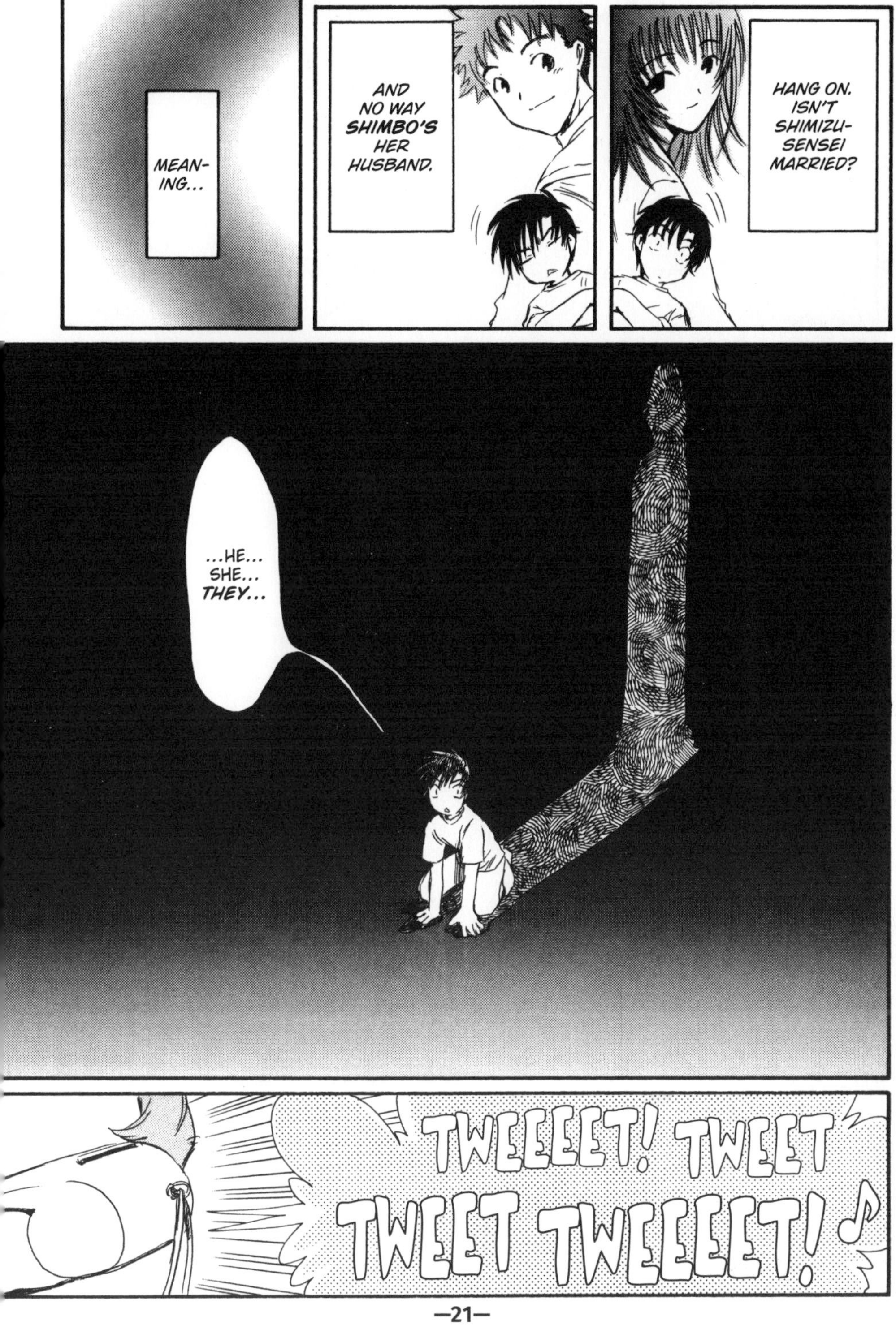
HANG ON. ISN'T SHIMIZU-SENSEI MARRIED?
AND NO WAY SHIMBO'S HER HUSBAND.
MEAN-ING...
...HE... SHE... THEY...
TWEEEET! TWEET TWEET TWEEEET! ♪

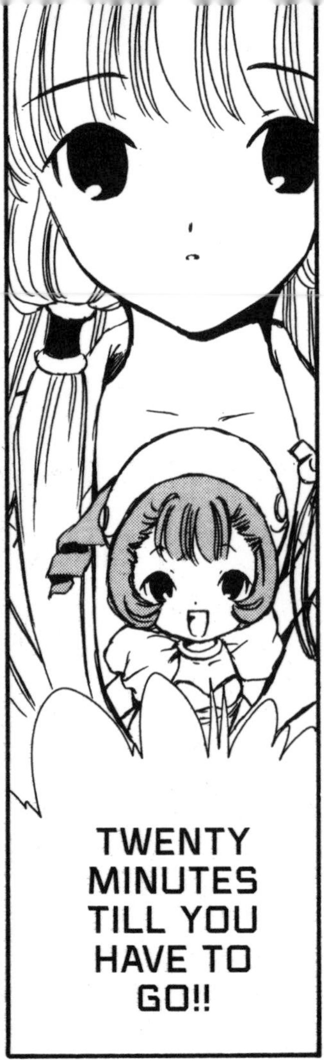
TWENTY MINUTES TILL YOU HAVE TO GO!!

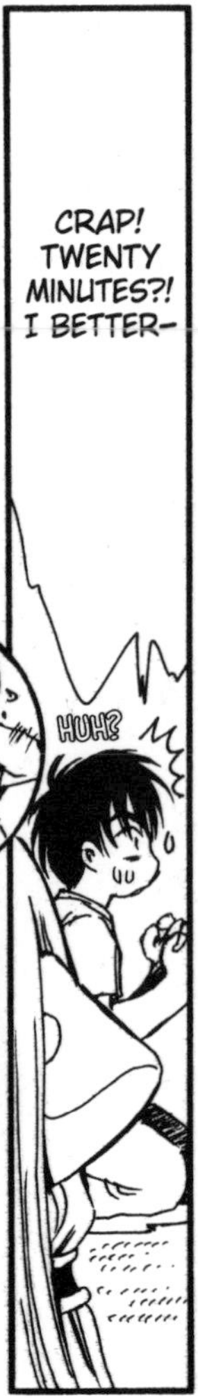
CRAP! TWENTY MINUTES?! I BETTER–
HUH?

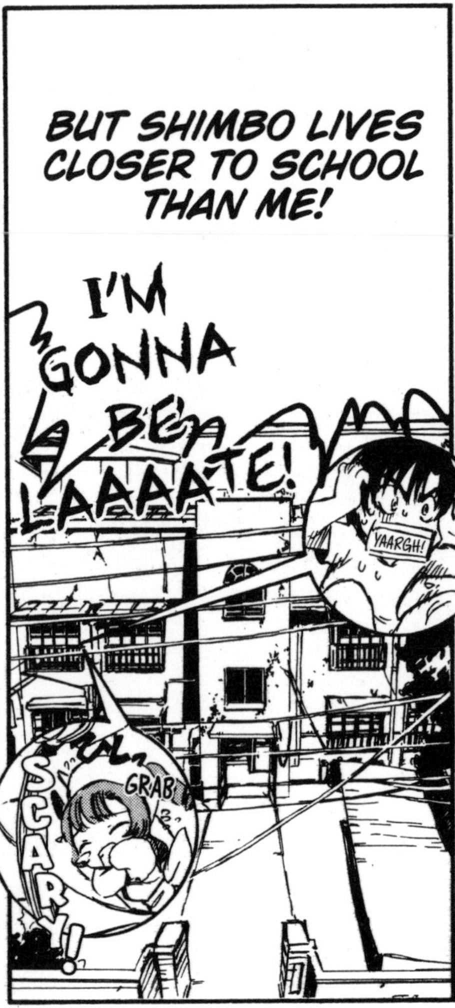
BUT SHIMBO LIVES CLOSER TO SCHOOL THAN ME!
I'M GONNA BE LAAAATE!
YAARGH!
GRAB!
SCARY!

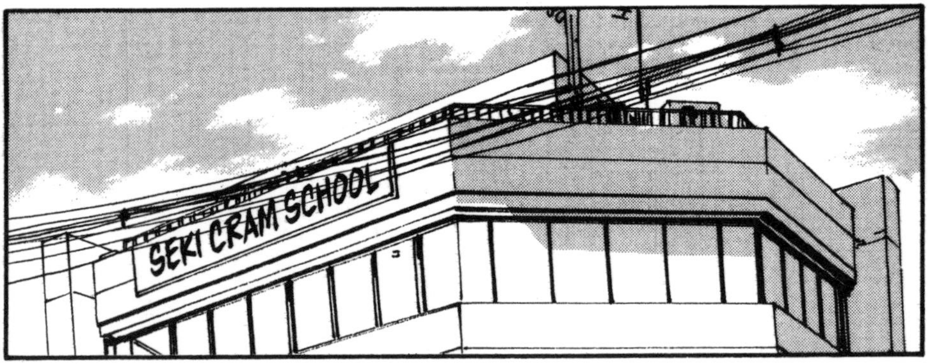
SEKI CRAM SCHOOL

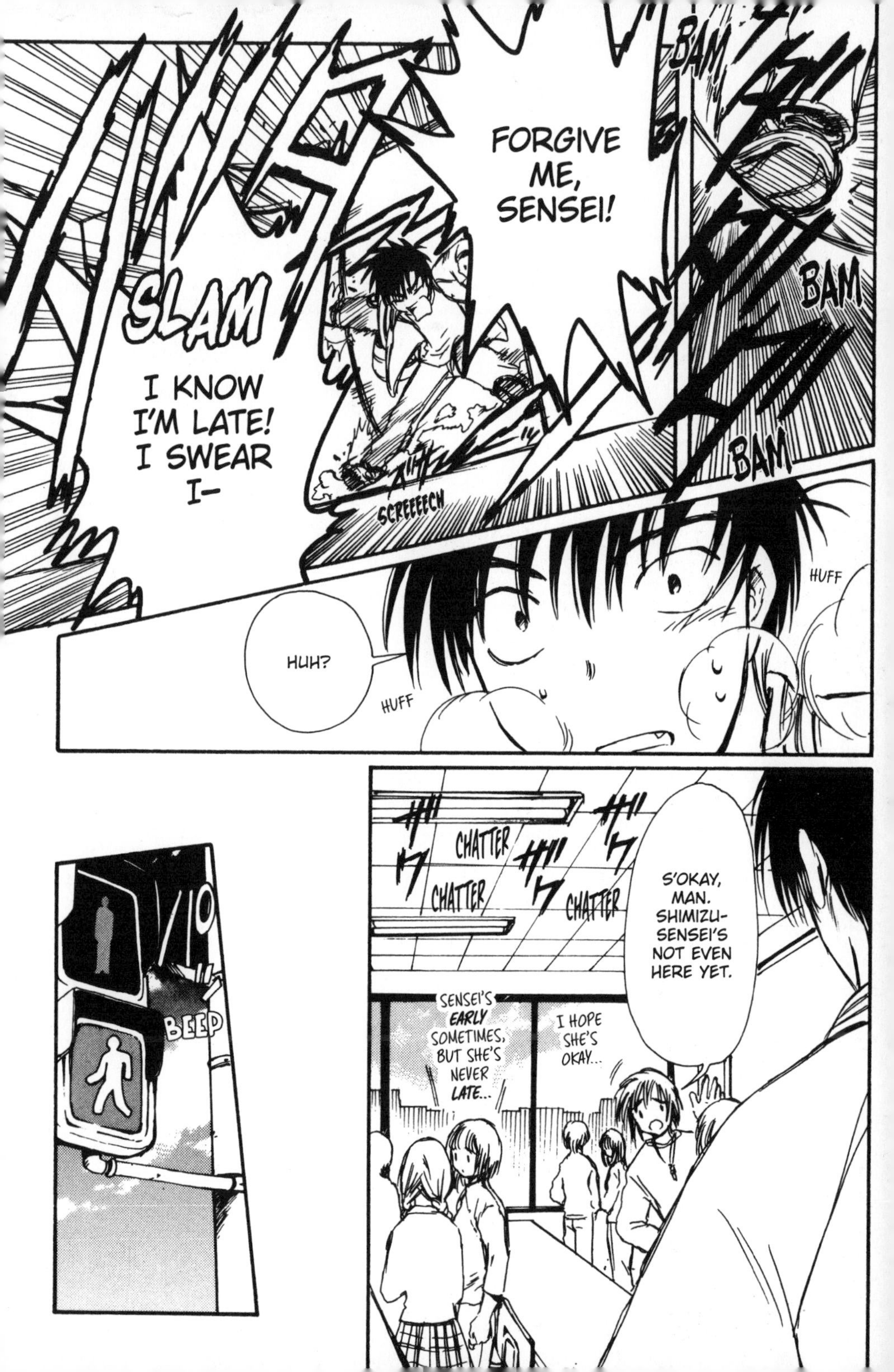
BAM
BAM
BAM
FORGIVE ME, SENSEI!
SLAM
I KNOW I'M LATE! I SWEAR I-
SCREEEECH
HUFF
HUH?
HUFF
S'OKAY, MAN. SHIMIZU-SENSEI'S NOT EVEN HERE YET.
CHATTER
CHATTER
CHATTER
I HOPE SHE'S OKAY...
SENSEI'S EARLY SOMETIMES, BUT SHE'S NEVER LATE...
BEEP

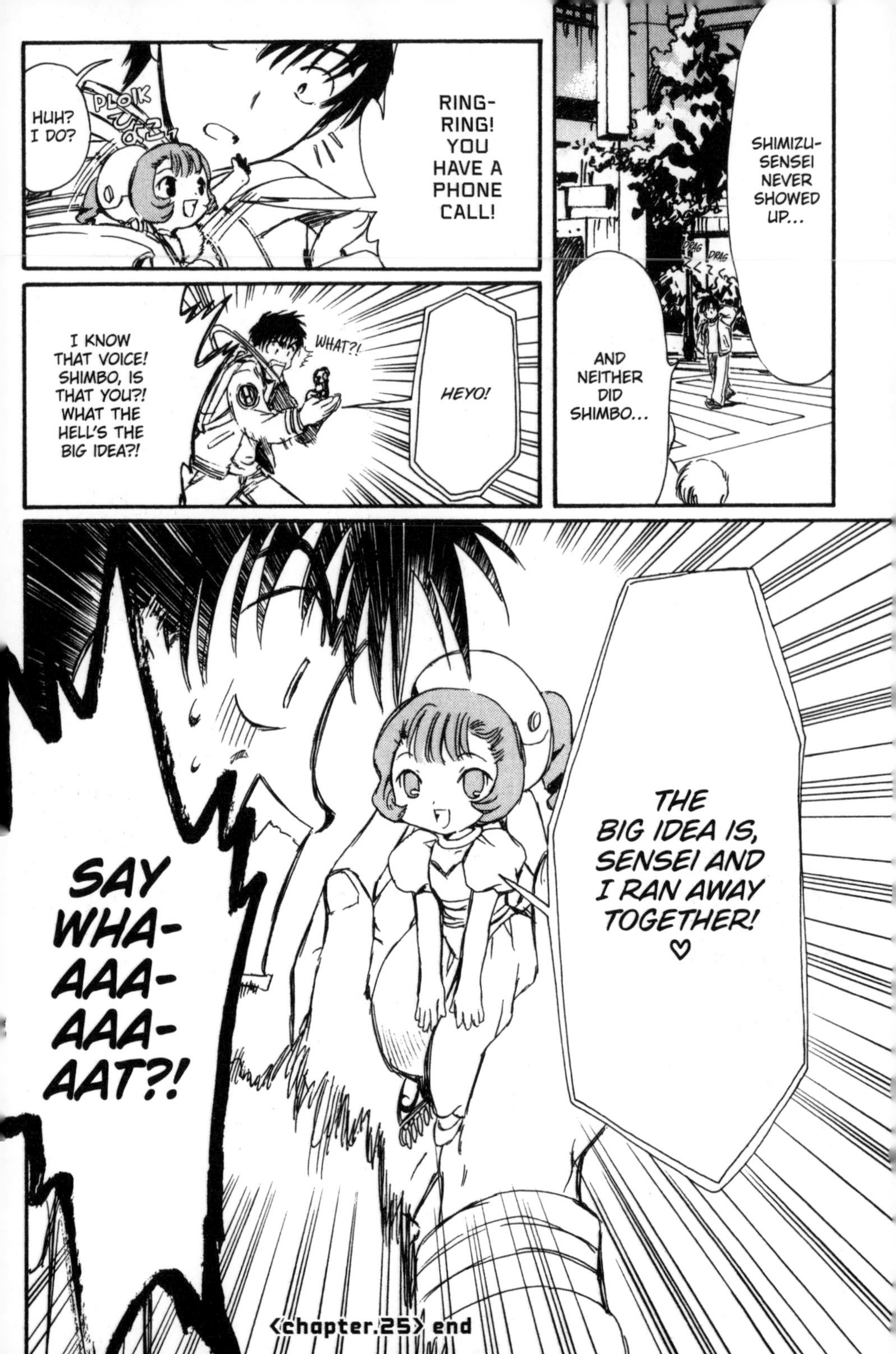
SHIMIZU-SENSEI NEVER SHOWED UP...
DRAG DRAG
AND NEITHER DID SHIMBO...
RING-RING! YOU HAVE A PHONE CALL!
PLOIK
HUH? I DO?
HEYO!
WHAT?!
I KNOW THAT VOICE! SHIMBO, IS THAT YOU?! WHAT THE HELL'S THE BIG IDEA?!
THE BIG IDEA IS, SENSEI AND I RAN AWAY TOGETHER! ♡
SAY WHA-AAA-AAA-AAT?!
‹chapter.25› end

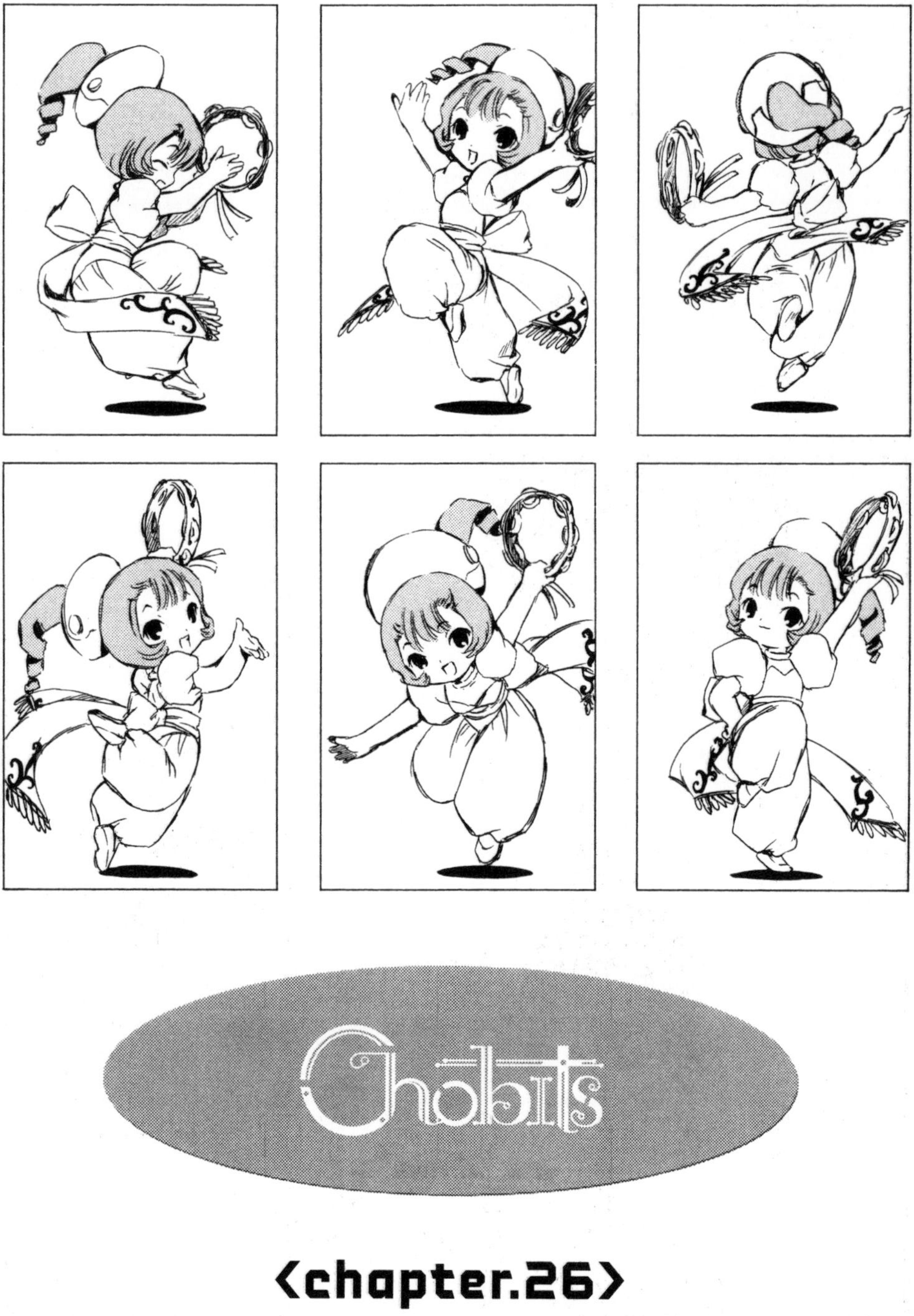

Chobits

<chapter.26>

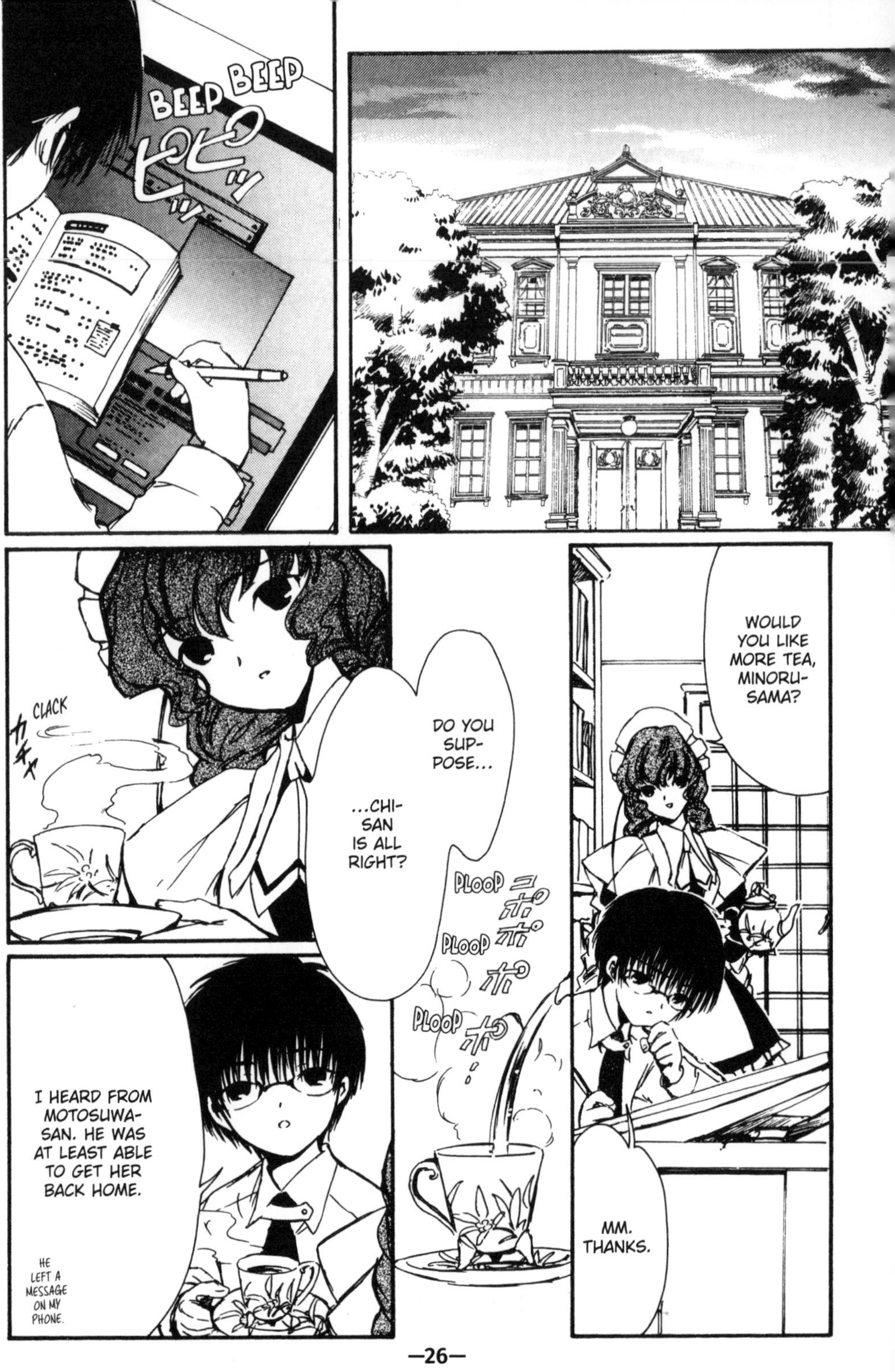
BEEP BEEP
ピピッ
ピッ
WOULD YOU LIKE MORE TEA, MINORU-SAMA?
PLOOP
コポ
PLOOP
ポ
PLOOP
ポ
MM. THANKS.
CLACK
カチャ
DO YOU SUP-POSE...
...CHI-SAN IS ALL RIGHT?
I HEARD FROM MOTOSUWA-SAN. HE WAS AT LEAST ABLE TO GET HER BACK HOME.
HE LEFT A MESSAGE ON MY PHONE.

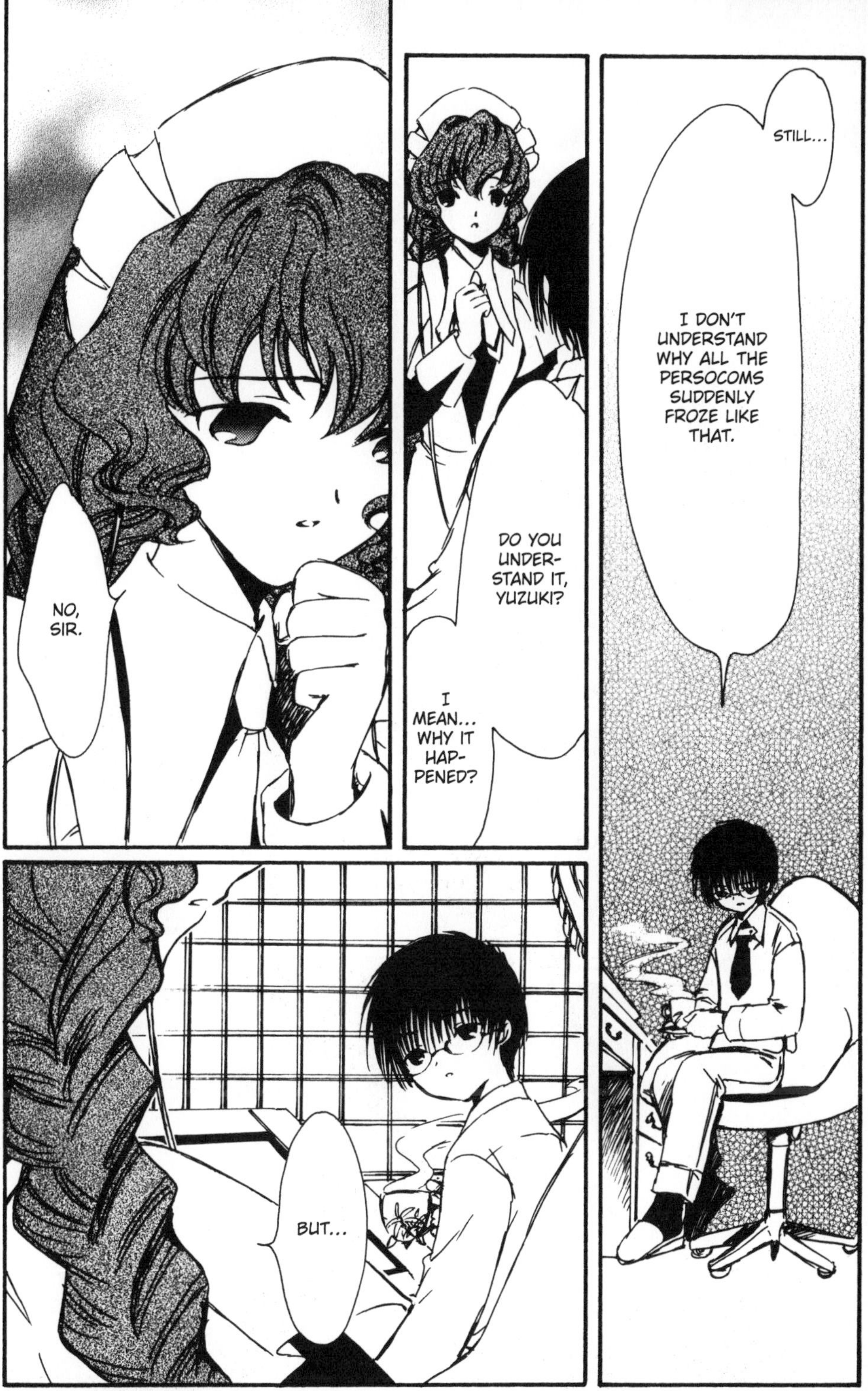
STILL...
I DON'T UNDERSTAND WHY ALL THE PERSOCOMS SUDDENLY FROZE LIKE THAT.
DO YOU UNDER-STAND IT, YUZUKI?
I MEAN... WHY IT HAP-PENED?
NO, SIR.
BUT...

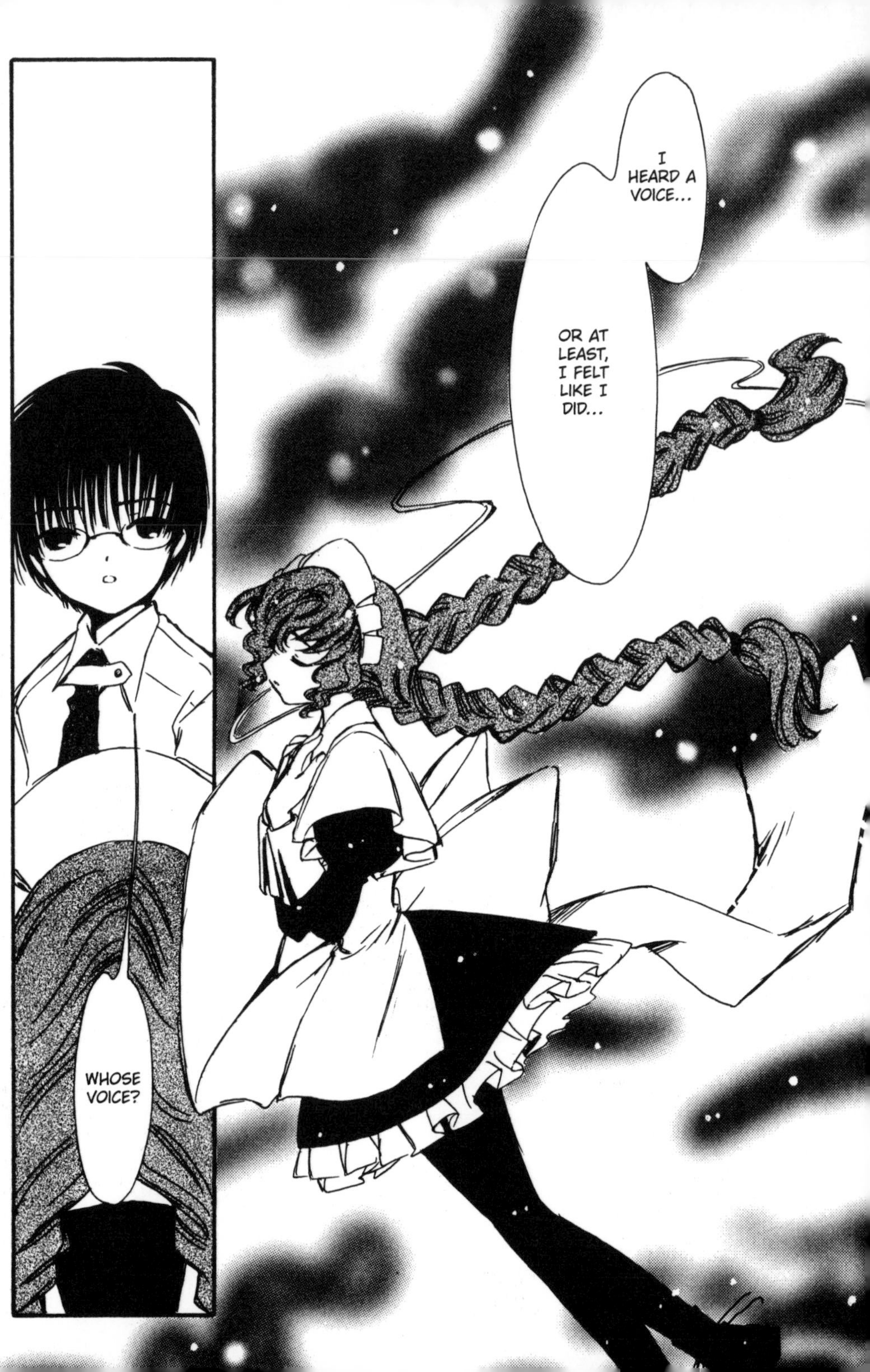
I HEARD A VOICE...
OR AT LEAST, I FELT LIKE I DID...
WHOSE VOICE?

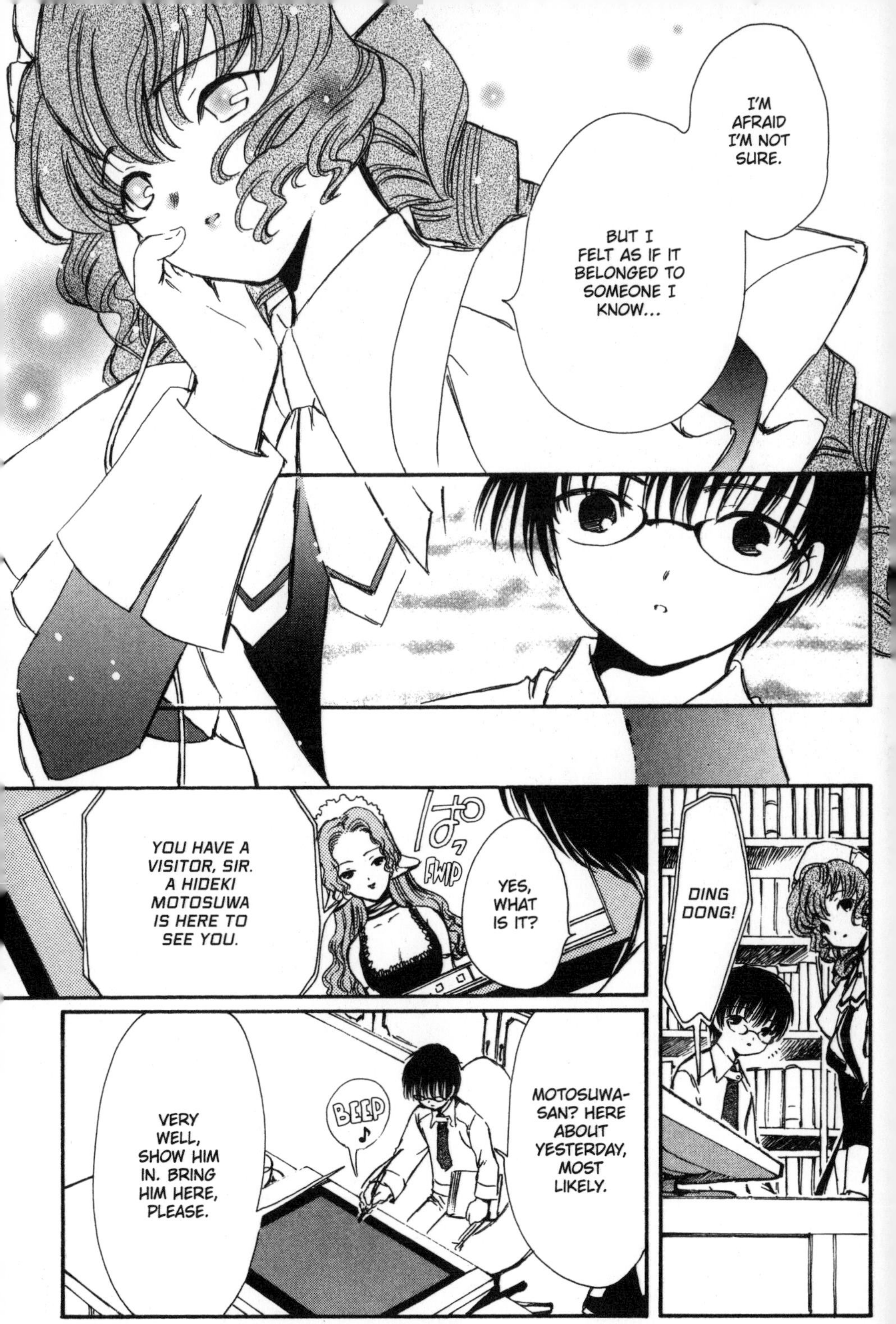
I'M AFRAID I'M NOT SURE.
BUT I FELT AS IF IT BELONGED TO SOMEONE I KNOW...
DING DONG!
YES, WHAT IS IT?
FWIP
YOU HAVE A VISITOR, SIR. A HIDEKI MOTOSUWA IS HERE TO SEE YOU.
MOTOSUWA-SAN? HERE ABOUT YESTERDAY, MOST LIKELY.
BEEP ♪
VERY WELL, SHOW HIM IN. BRING HIM HERE, PLEASE.

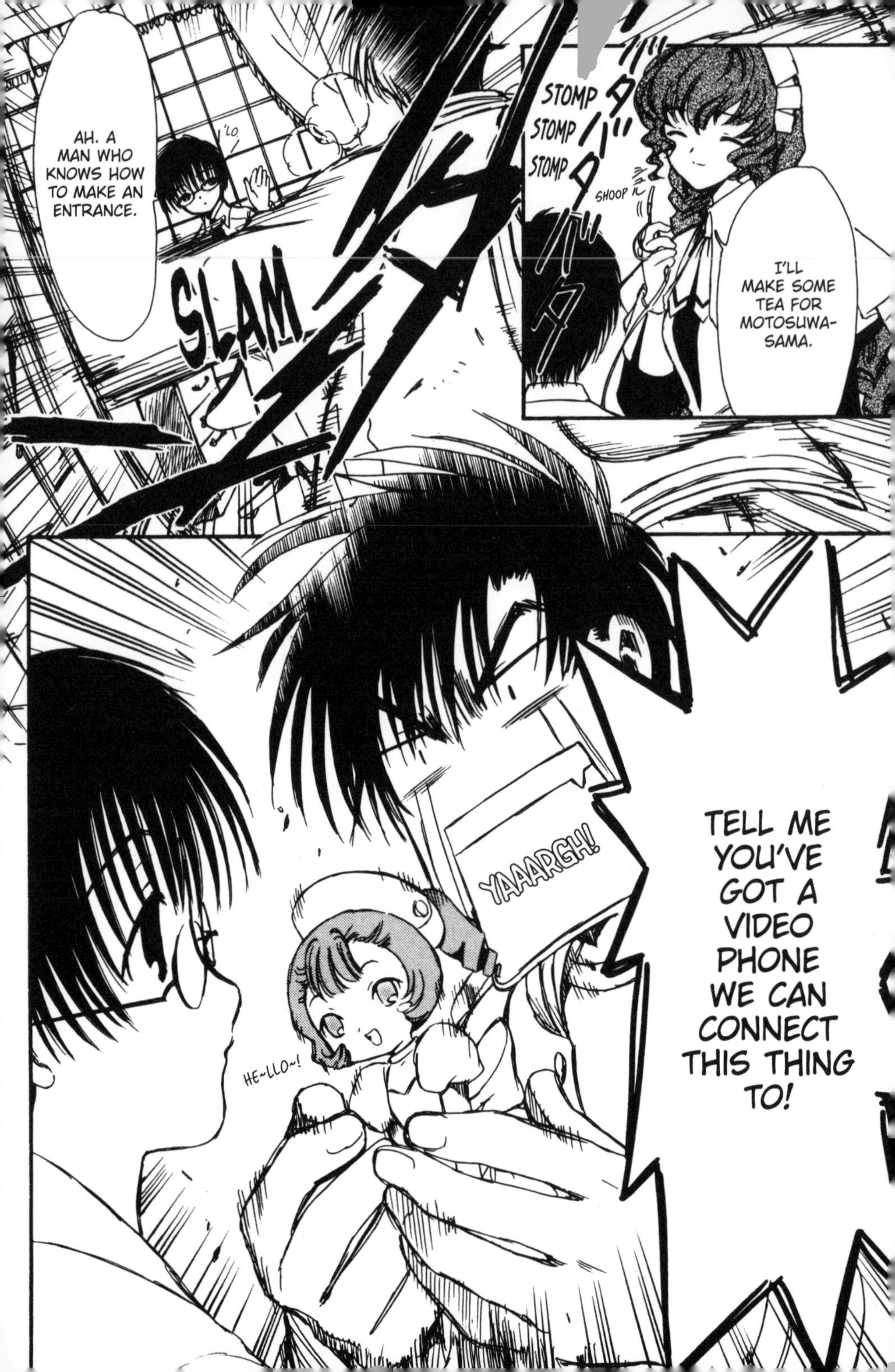
STOMP
STOMP
STOMP
SHOOP
I'LL MAKE SOME TEA FOR MOTOSUWA-SAMA.
'LO
AH. A MAN WHO KNOWS HOW TO MAKE AN ENTRANCE.
SLAM
TELL ME YOU'VE GOT A VIDEO PHONE WE CAN CONNECT THIS THING TO!
YAAARGH!
HE~LLO~!

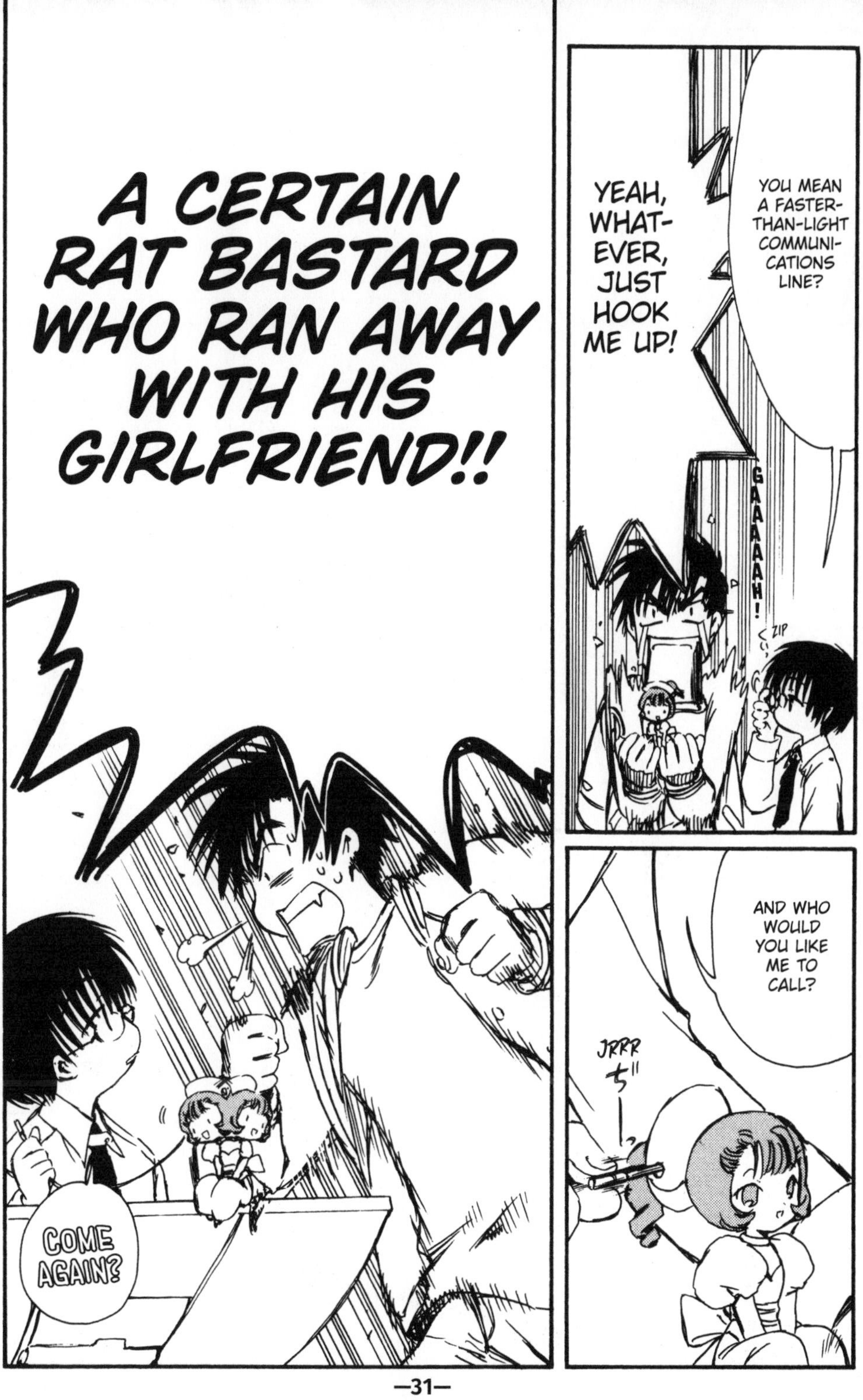
YOU MEAN A FASTER-THAN-LIGHT COMMUNI-CATIONS LINE?
YEAH, WHAT-EVER, JUST HOOK ME UP!
GAAAAAAH!
ZIP
AND WHO WOULD YOU LIKE ME TO CALL?
JRRR
A CERTAIN RAT BASTARD WHO RAN AWAY WITH HIS GIRLFRIEND!!
COME AGAIN?

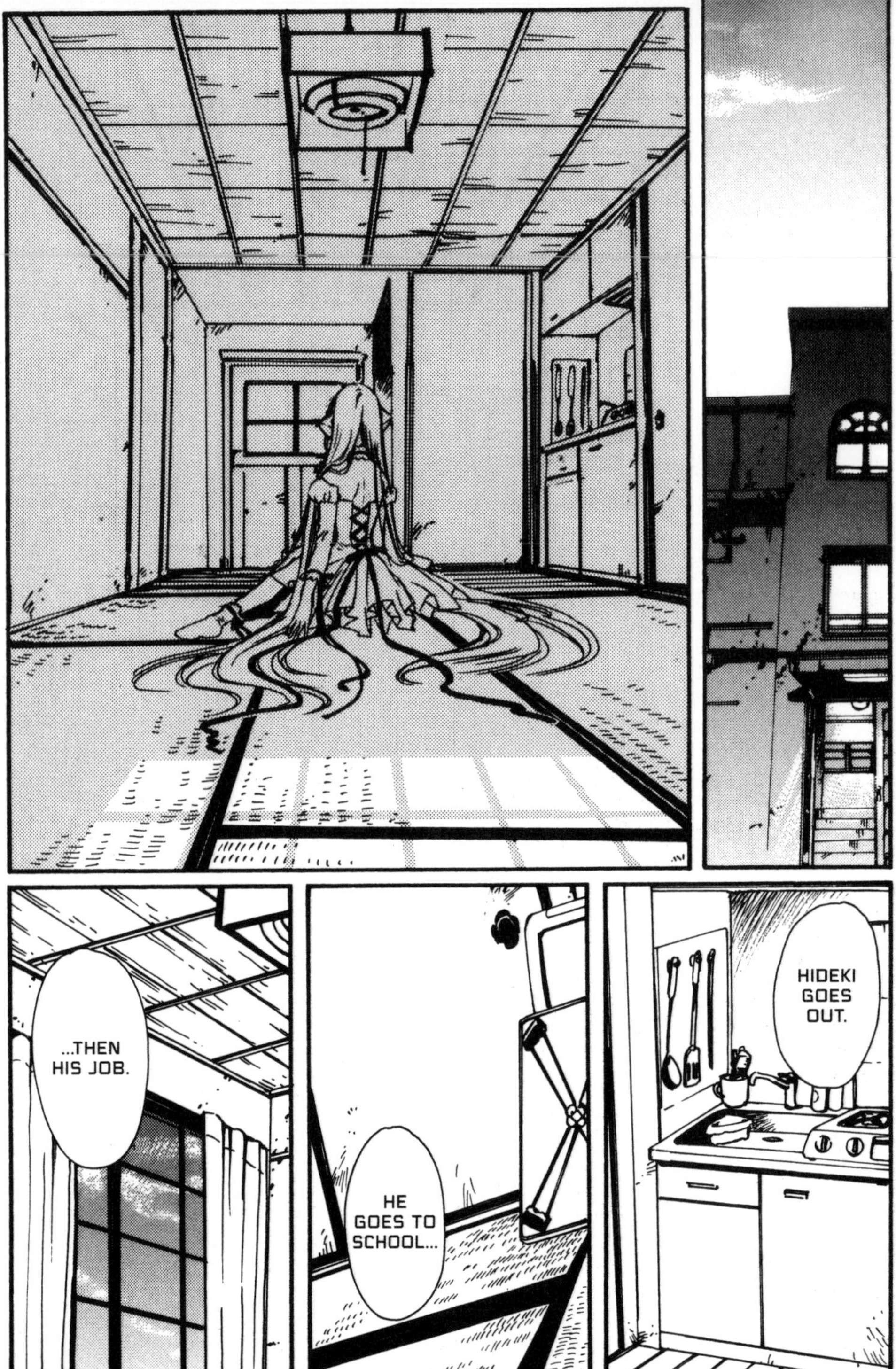
HIDEKI GOES OUT.
HE GOES TO SCHOOL...
...THEN HIS JOB.

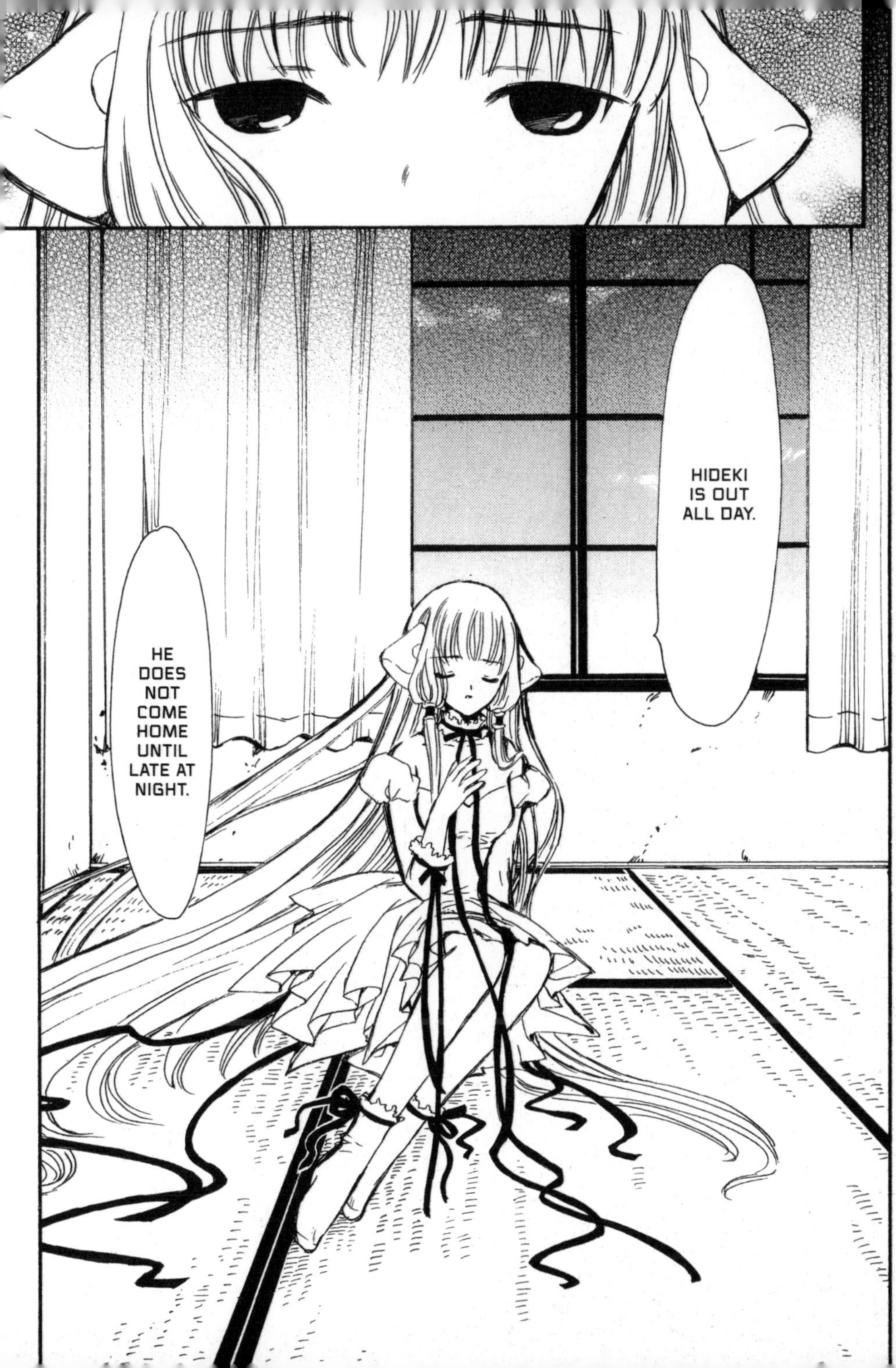
HIDEKI IS OUT ALL DAY.
HE DOES NOT COME HOME UNTIL LATE AT NIGHT.

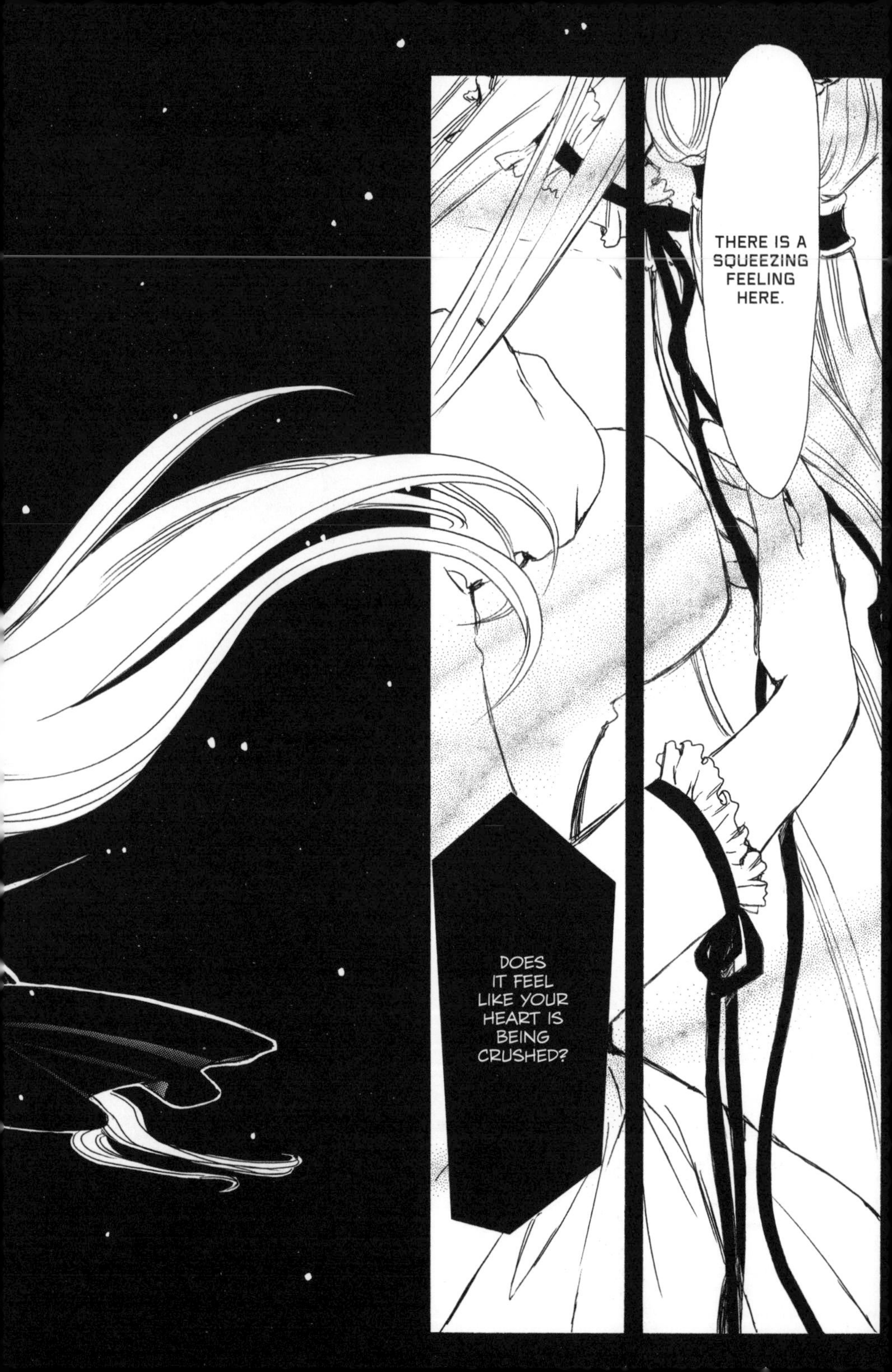
THERE IS A SQUEEZING FEELING HERE.
DOES IT FEEL LIKE YOUR HEART IS BEING CRUSHED?

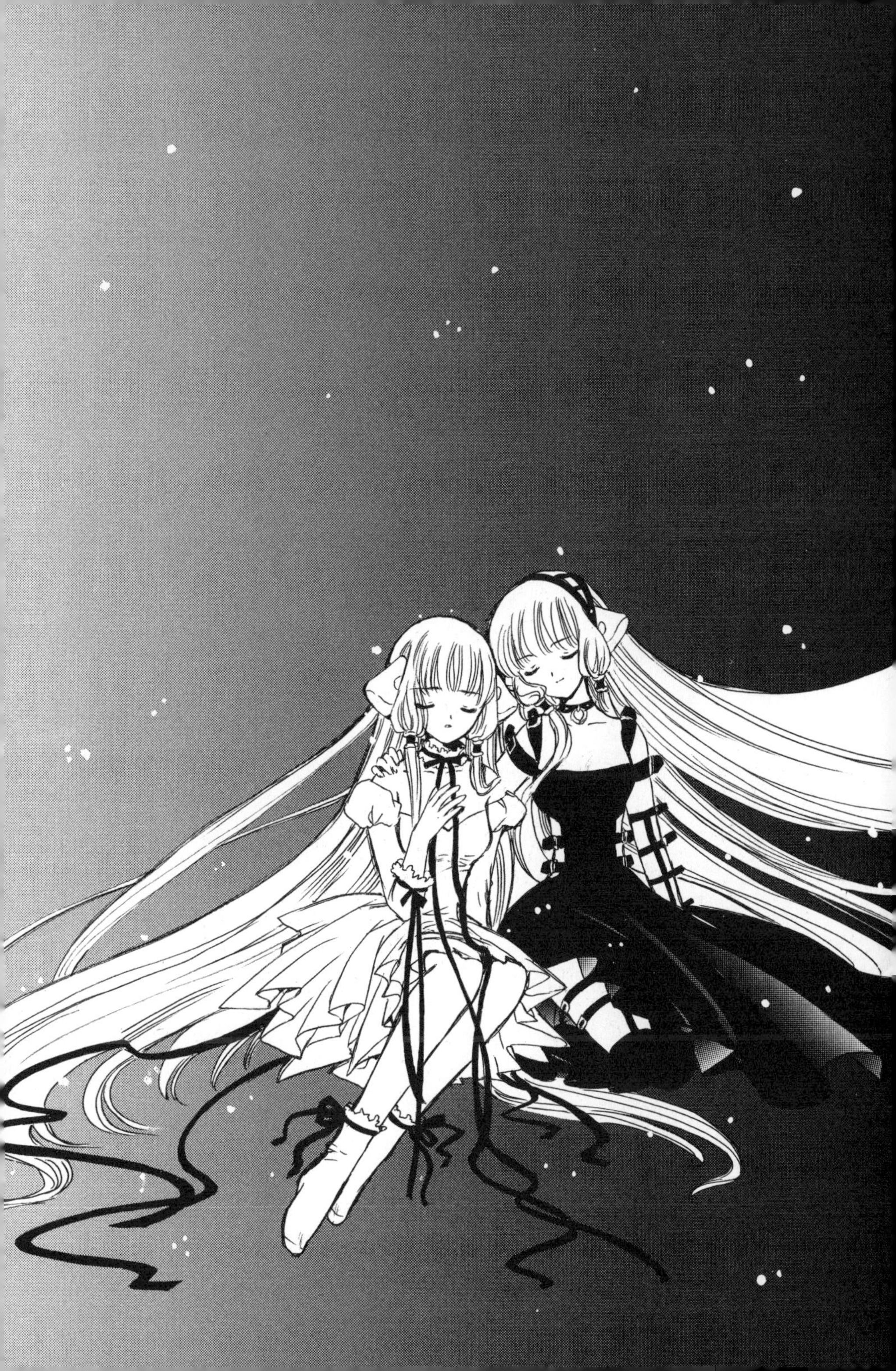

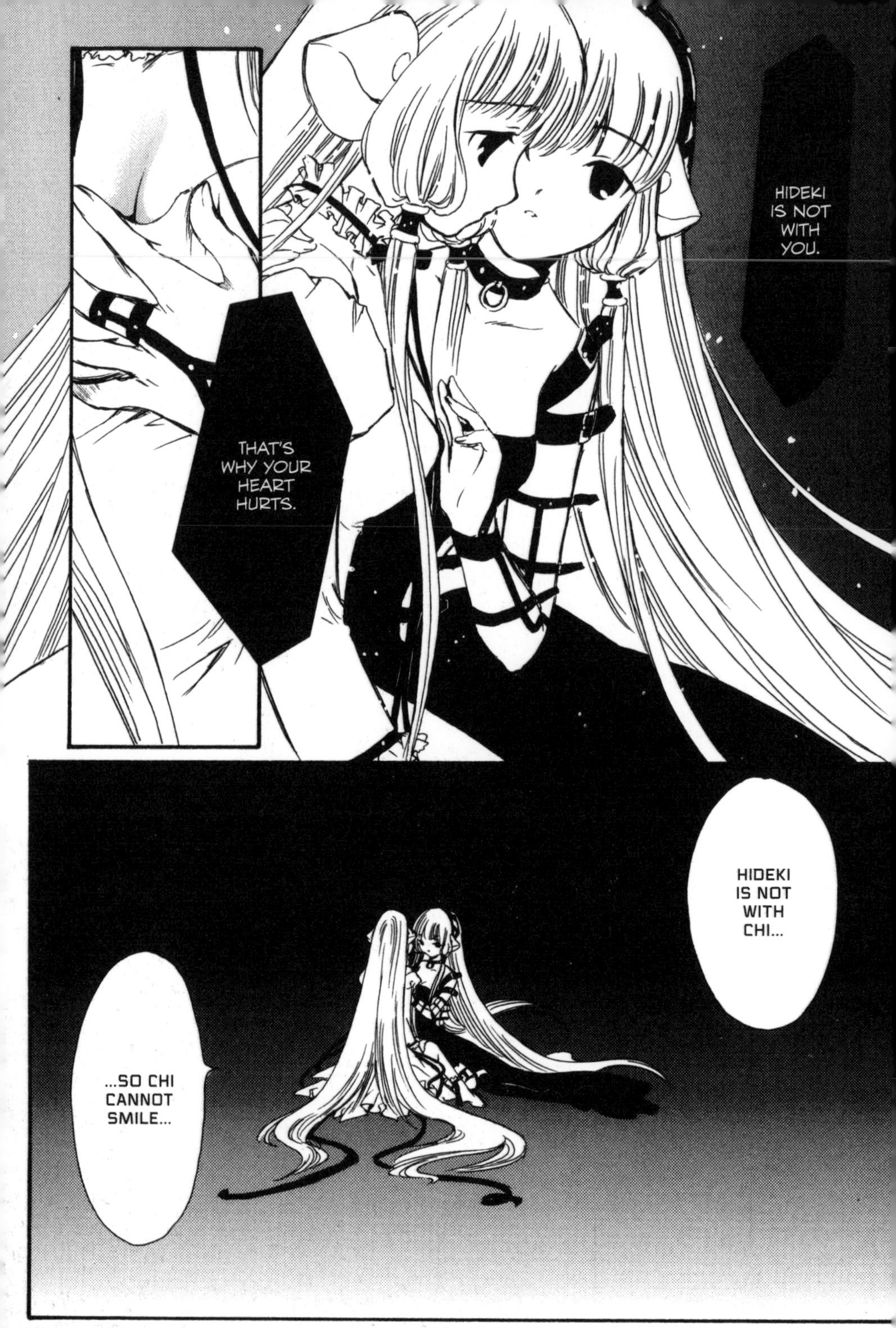
HIDEKI IS NOT WITH YOU.
THAT'S WHY YOUR HEART HURTS.
HIDEKI IS NOT WITH CHI...
...SO CHI CANNOT SMILE...

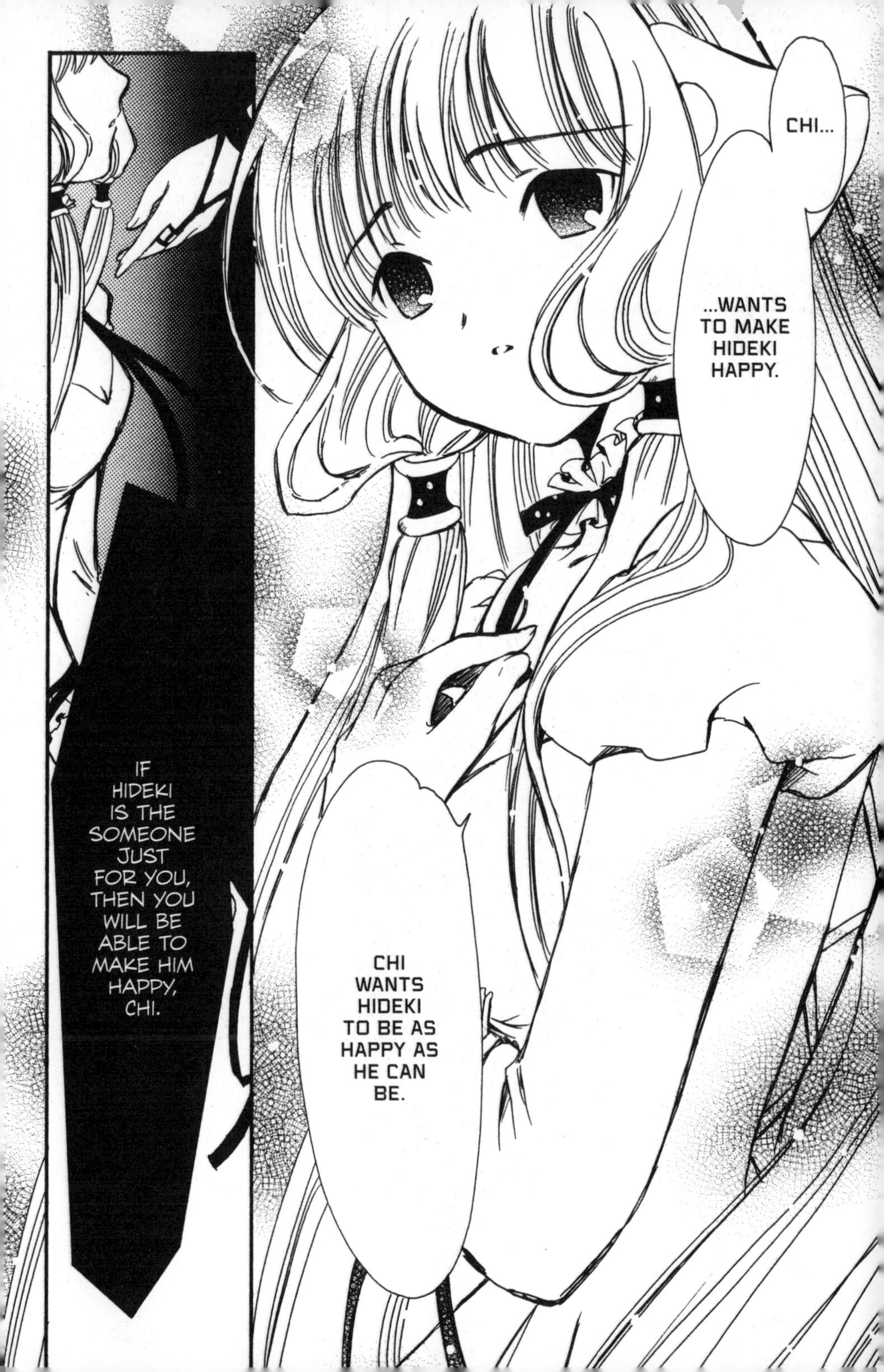
CHI...
...WANTS TO MAKE HIDEKI HAPPY.
CHI WANTS HIDEKI TO BE AS HAPPY AS HE CAN BE.
IF HIDEKI IS THE SOMEONE JUST FOR YOU, THEN YOU WILL BE ABLE TO MAKE HIM HAPPY, CHI.

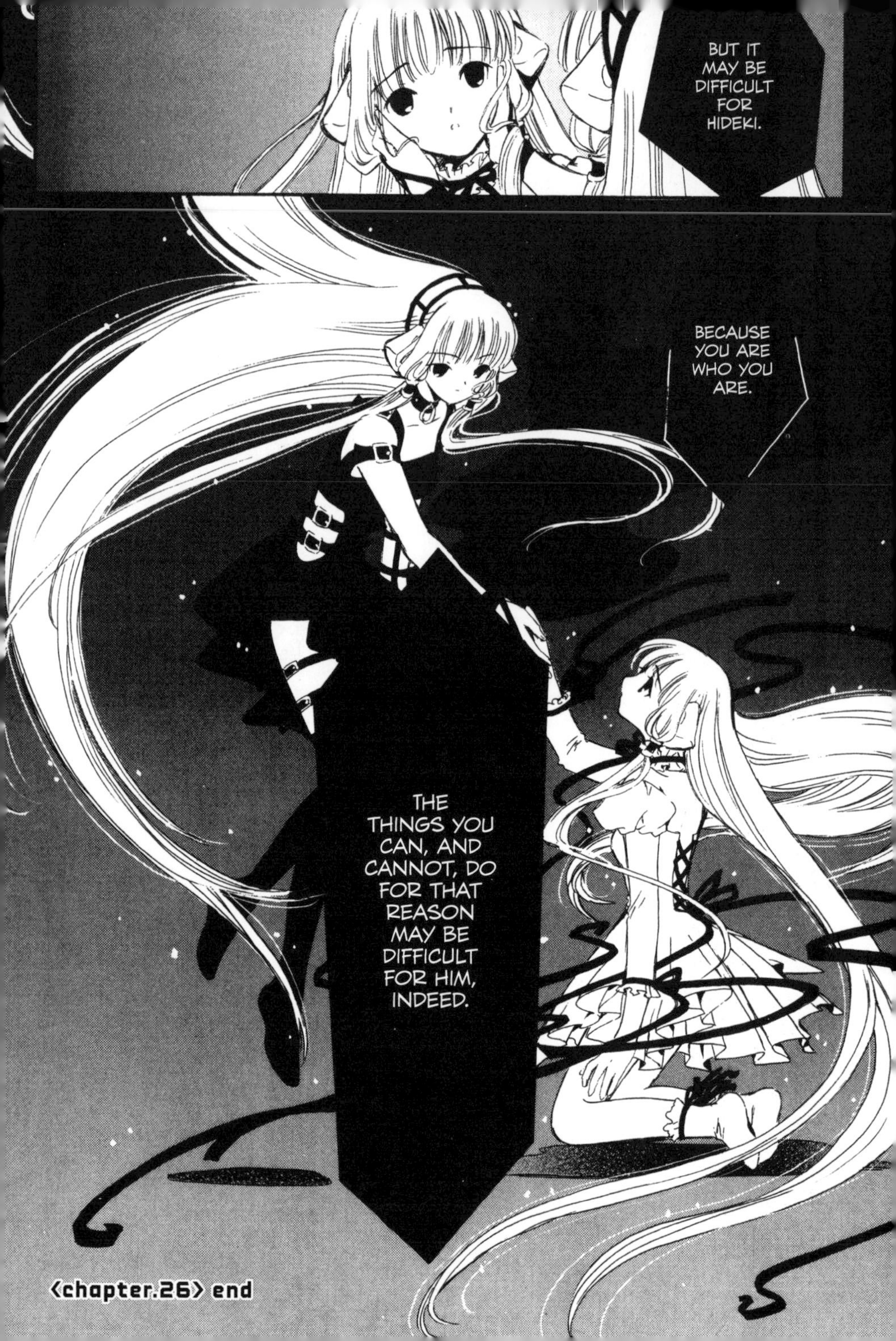
BUT IT MAY BE DIFFICULT FOR HIDEKI.
BECAUSE YOU ARE WHO YOU ARE.
THE THINGS YOU CAN, AND CANNOT, DO FOR THAT REASON MAY BE DIFFICULT FOR HIM, INDEED.
<chapter.26> end

〈chapter.27〉

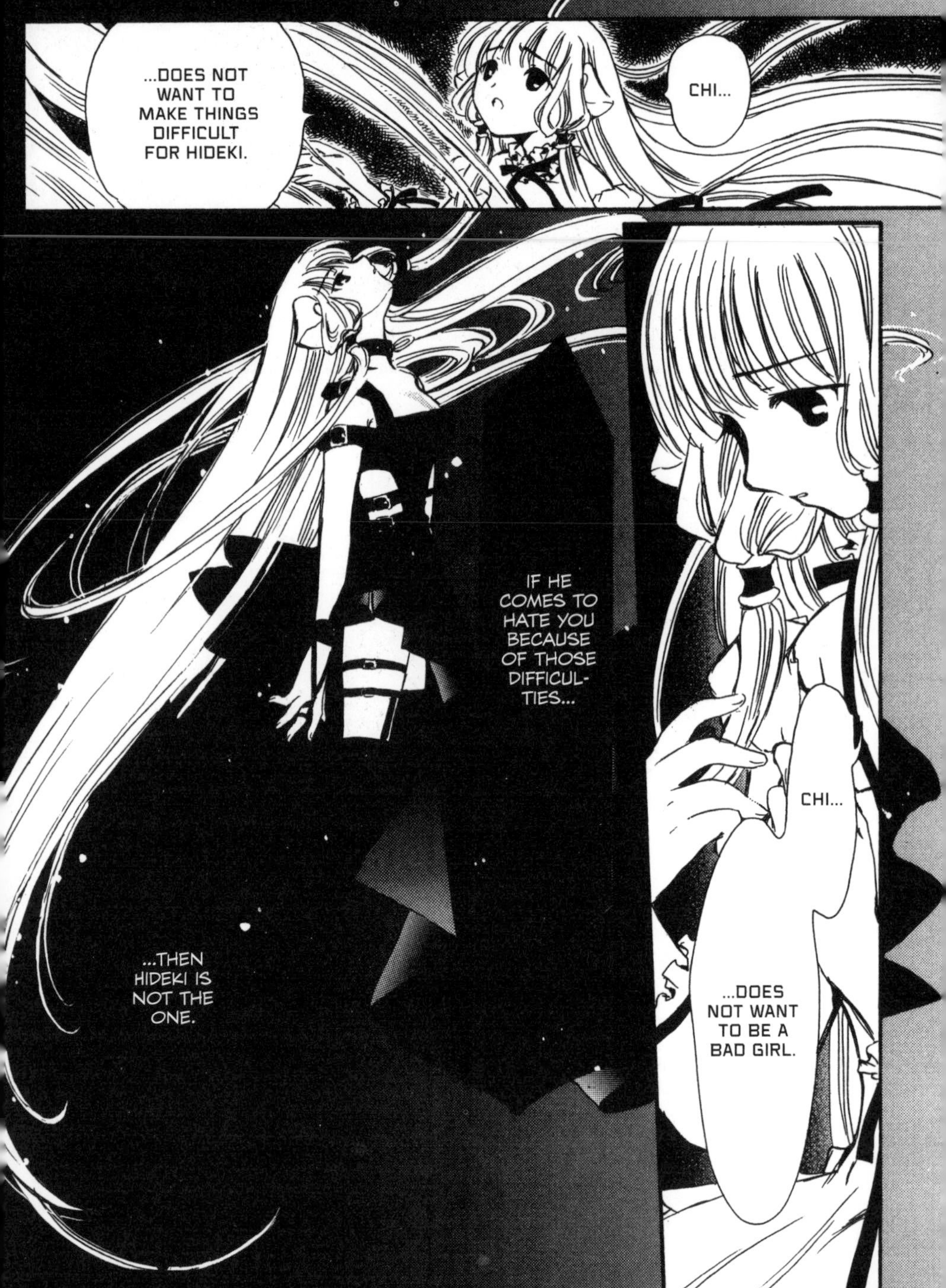
CHI...
...DOES NOT WANT TO MAKE THINGS DIFFICULT FOR HIDEKI.
CHI...
...DOES NOT WANT TO BE A BAD GIRL.
IF HE COMES TO HATE YOU BECAUSE OF THOSE DIFFICUL-TIES...
...THEN HIDEKI IS NOT THE ONE.

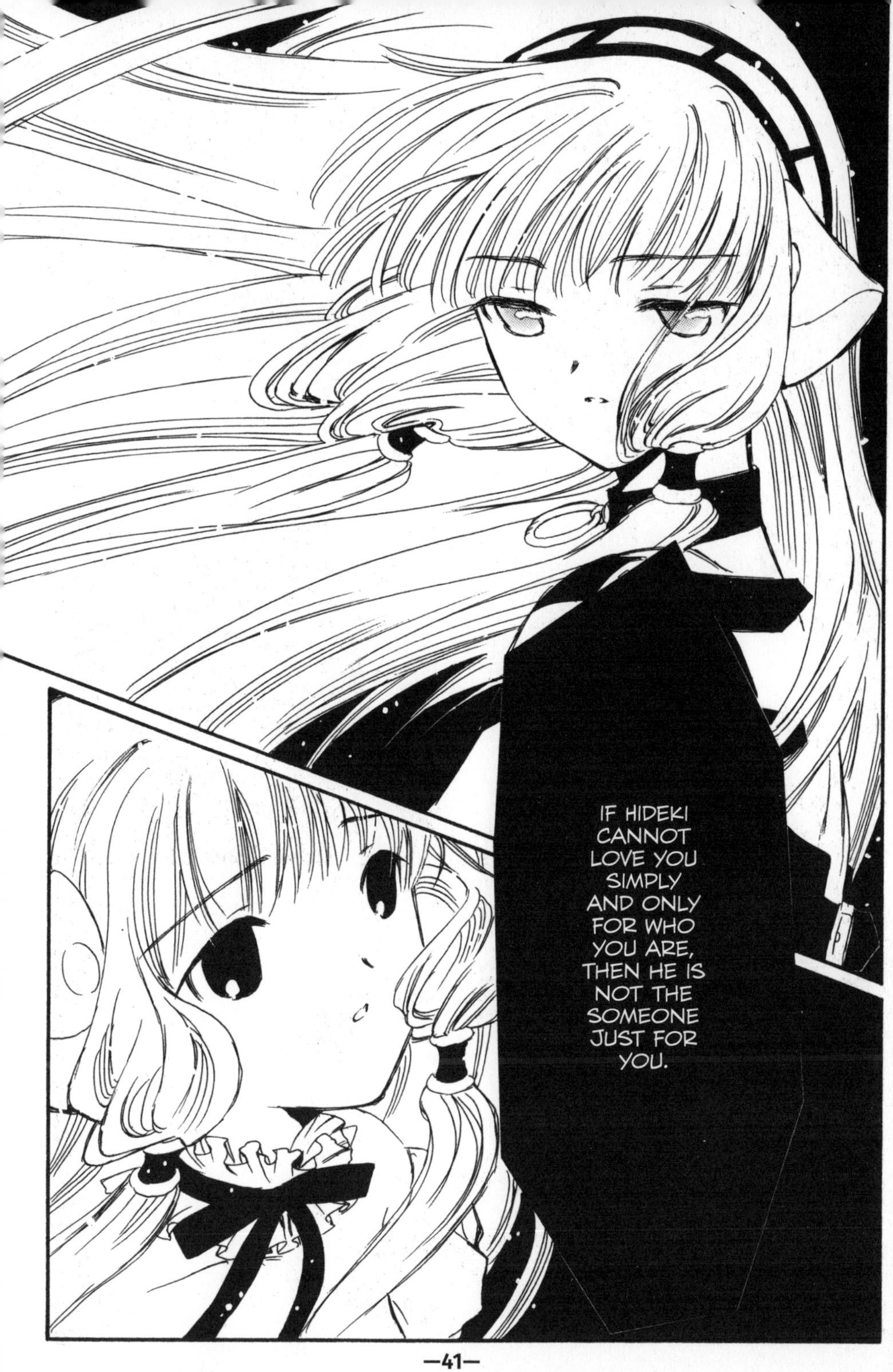
IF HIDEKI CANNOT LOVE YOU SIMPLY AND ONLY FOR WHO YOU ARE, THEN HE IS NOT THE SOMEONE JUST FOR YOU.

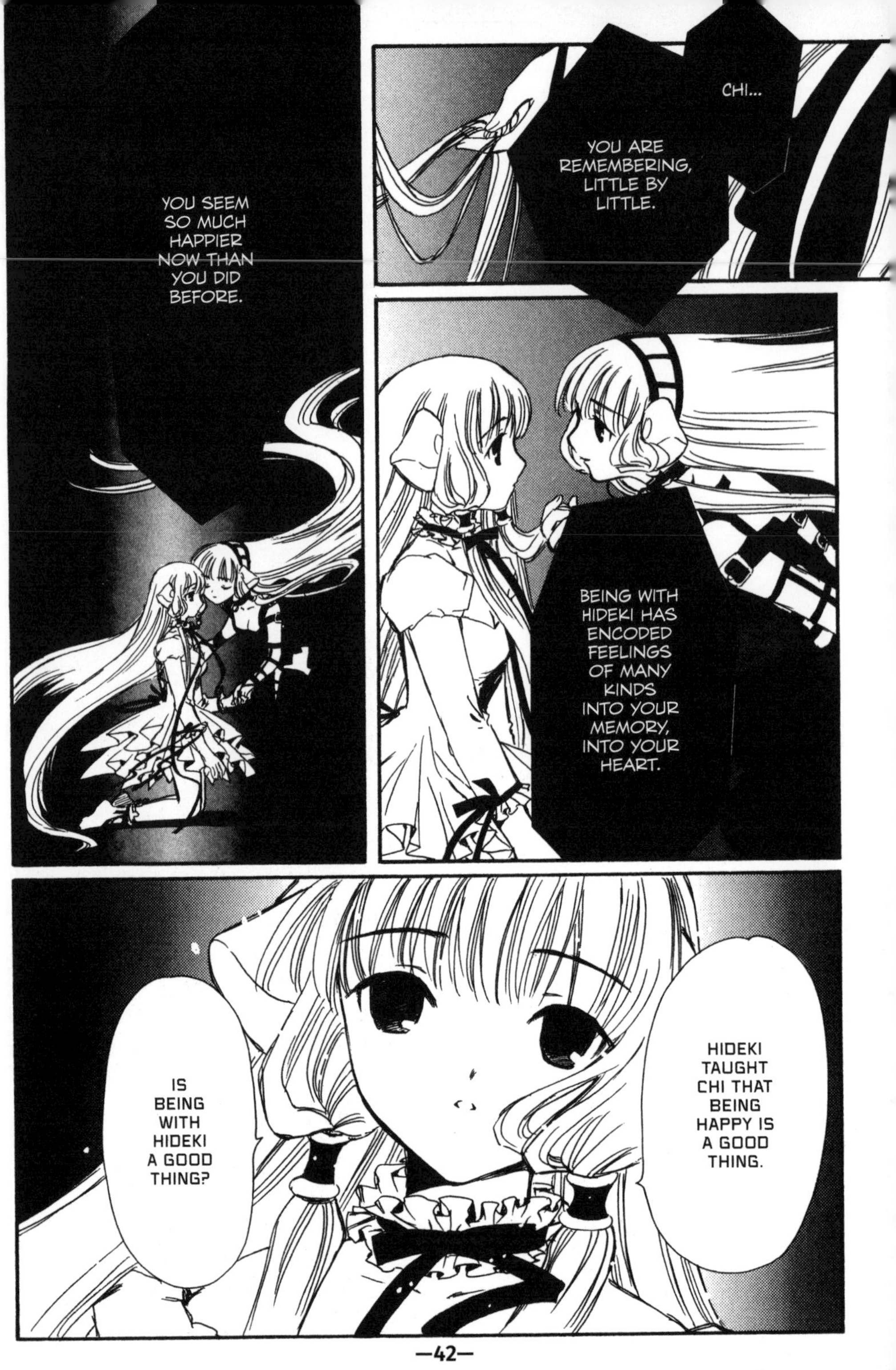
CHI...
YOU ARE REMEMBERING, LITTLE BY LITTLE.
BEING WITH HIDEKI HAS ENCODED FEELINGS OF MANY KINDS INTO YOUR MEMORY, INTO YOUR HEART.
YOU SEEM SO MUCH HAPPIER NOW THAN YOU DID BEFORE.
HIDEKI TAUGHT CHI THAT BEING HAPPY IS A GOOD THING.
IS BEING WITH HIDEKI A GOOD THING?

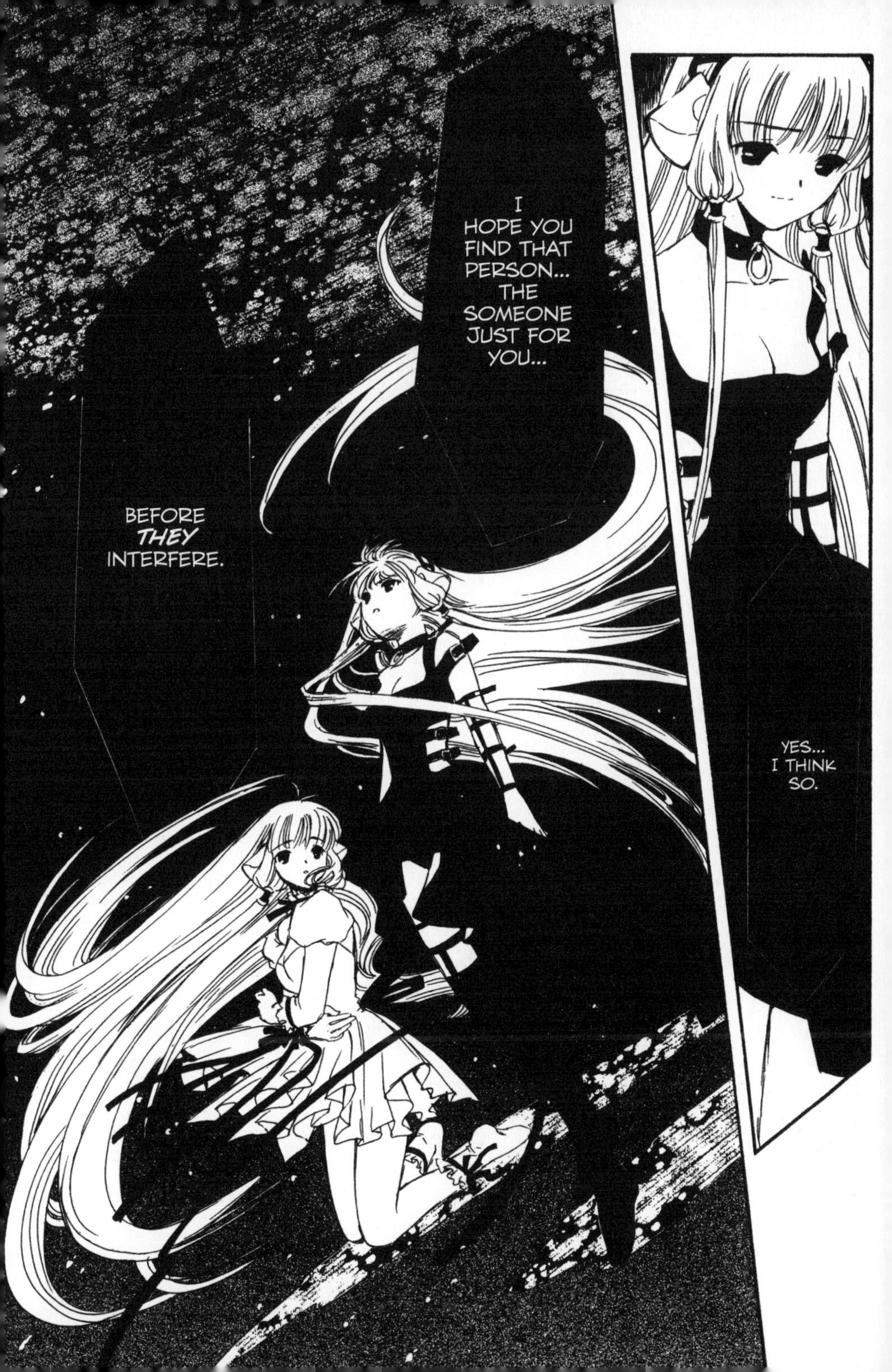
YES... I THINK SO.
I HOPE YOU FIND THAT PERSON... THE SOMEONE JUST FOR YOU...
BEFORE *THEY* INTERFERE.

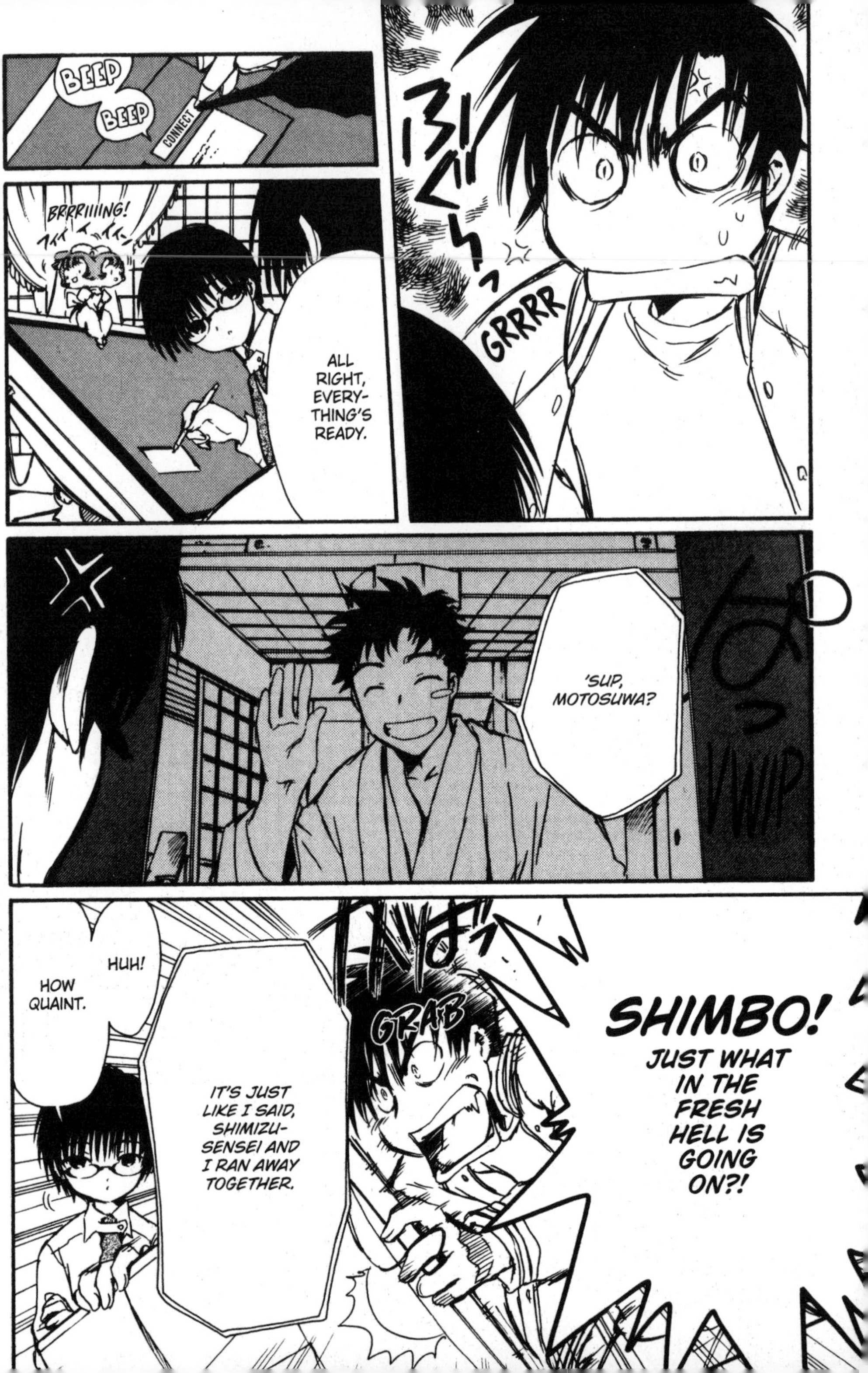
GRRRR
BEEP
BEEP
CONNECT
BRRRIIIING!
ALL RIGHT, EVERY-THING'S READY.
VWIP
'SUP, MOTOSUWA?
GRAB
SHIMBO! JUST WHAT IN THE FRESH HELL IS GOING ON?!
IT'S JUST LIKE I SAID, SHIMIZU-SENSEI AND I RAN AWAY TOGETHER.
HUH!
HOW QUAINT.

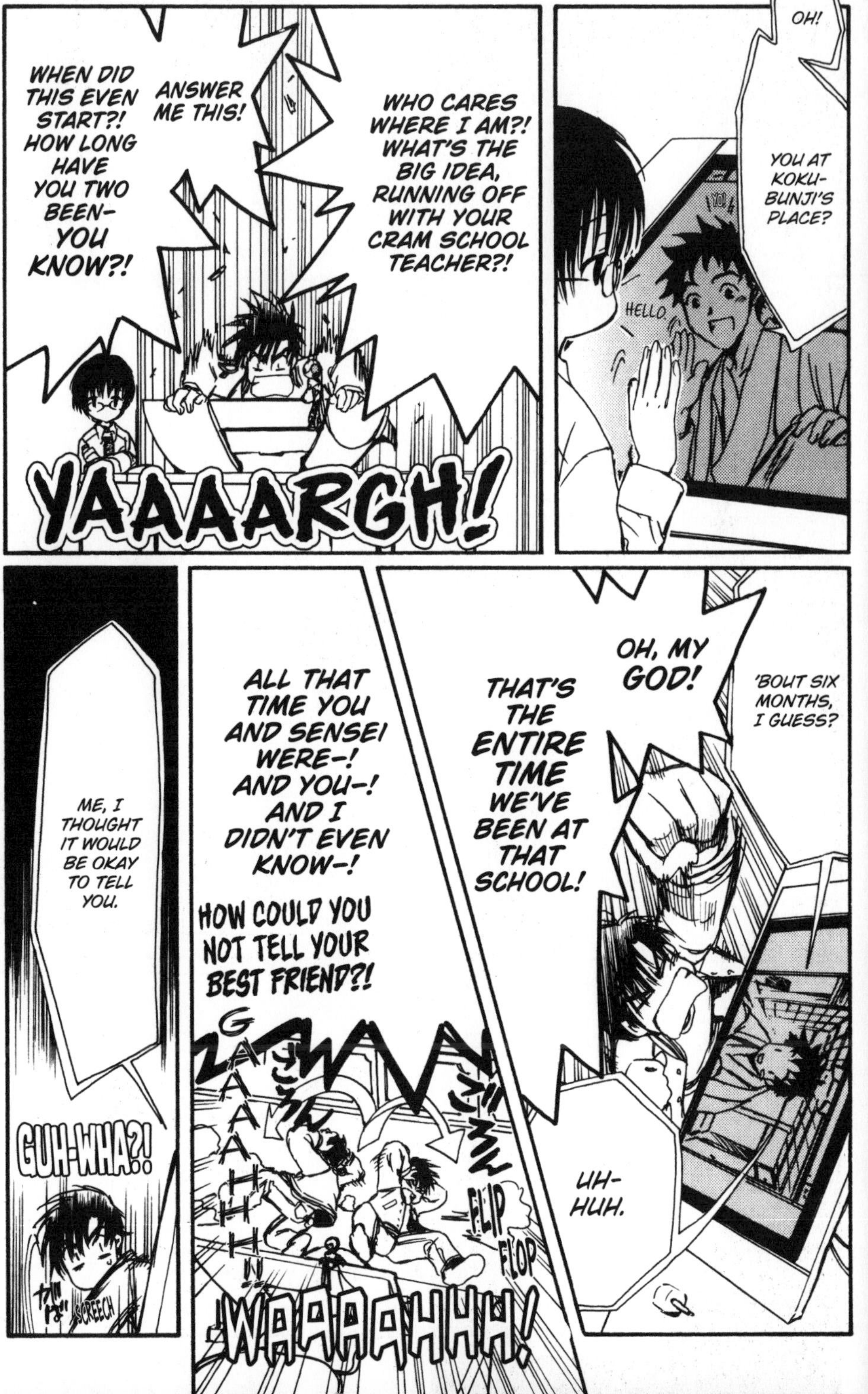
OH!
YOU AT KOKU-BUNJI'S PLACE?
YO!
HELLO
WHO CARES WHERE I AM?! WHAT'S THE BIG IDEA, RUNNING OFF WITH YOUR CRAM SCHOOL TEACHER?!
ANSWER ME THIS!
WHEN DID THIS EVEN START?! HOW LONG HAVE YOU TWO BEEN- YOU KNOW?!
YAAAARGH!
'BOUT SIX MONTHS, I GUESS?
OH, MY GOD!
THAT'S THE ENTIRE TIME WE'VE BEEN AT THAT SCHOOL!
UH-HUH.
ALL THAT TIME YOU AND SENSEI WERE-! AND YOU-! AND I DIDN'T EVEN KNOW-!
HOW COULD YOU NOT TELL YOUR BEST FRIEND?!
GAAAAHHHH!!
FLIP
FLOP
WAAAAHHHH!
ME, I THOUGHT IT WOULD BE OKAY TO TELL YOU.
GUH-WHA?!
SCREECH

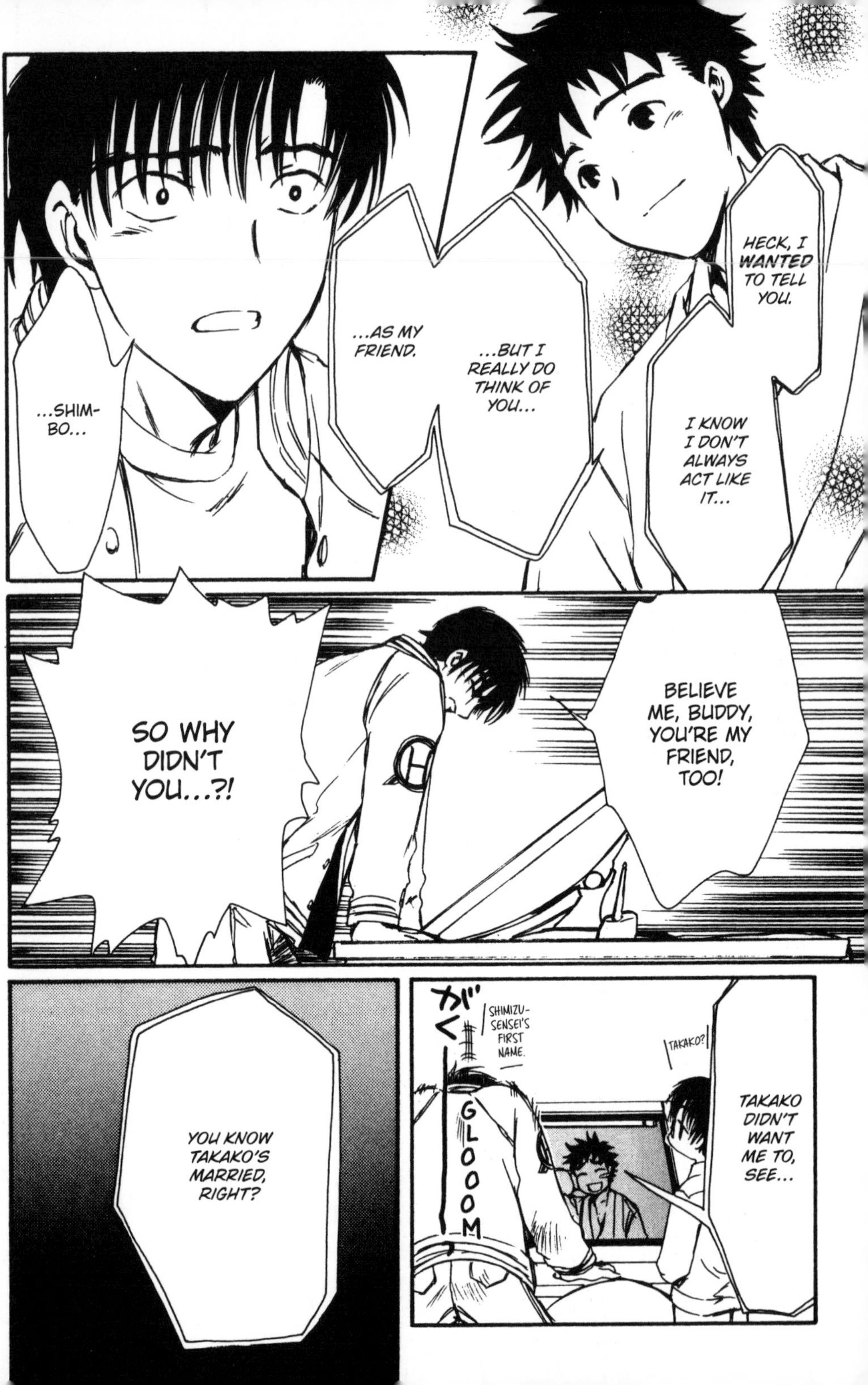
HECK, I WANTED TO TELL YOU.
I KNOW I DON'T ALWAYS ACT LIKE IT...
...BUT I REALLY DO THINK OF YOU...
...AS MY FRIEND.
...SHIM-BO...
BELIEVE ME, BUDDY, YOU'RE MY FRIEND, TOO!
SO WHY DIDN'T YOU...?!
TAKAKO?
TAKAKO DIDN'T WANT ME TO, SEE...
SHIMIZU-SENSEI'S FIRST NAME.
がく
GLOOOM
YOU KNOW TAKAKO'S MARRIED, RIGHT?

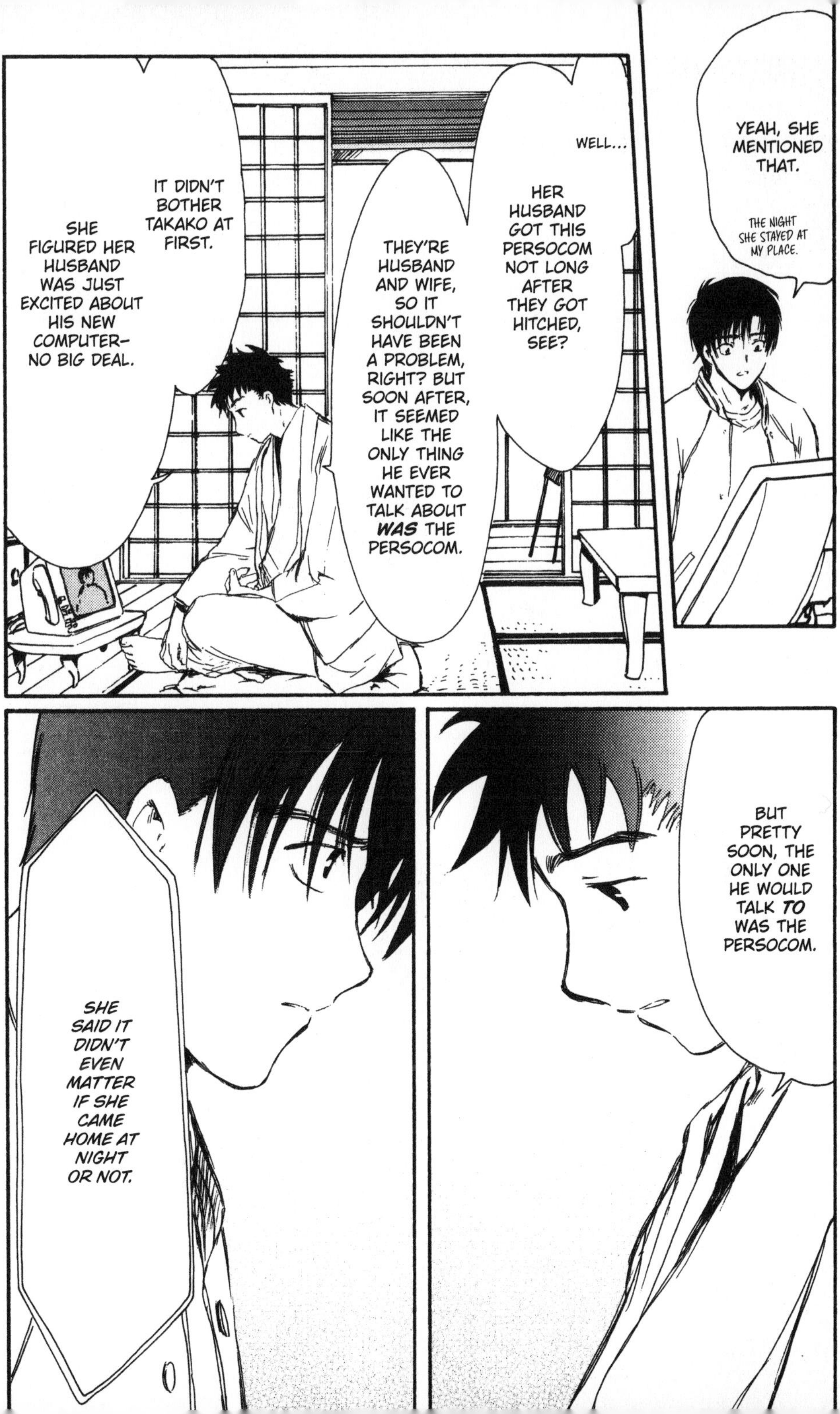
YEAH, SHE MENTIONED THAT.
THE NIGHT SHE STAYED AT MY PLACE.
WELL...
HER HUSBAND GOT THIS PERSOCOM NOT LONG AFTER THEY GOT HITCHED, SEE?
THEY'RE HUSBAND AND WIFE, SO IT SHOULDN'T HAVE BEEN A PROBLEM, RIGHT? BUT SOON AFTER, IT SEEMED LIKE THE ONLY THING HE EVER WANTED TO TALK ABOUT ***WAS*** THE PERSOCOM.
IT DIDN'T BOTHER TAKAKO AT FIRST.
SHE FIGURED HER HUSBAND WAS JUST EXCITED ABOUT HIS NEW COMPUTER—NO BIG DEAL.
BUT PRETTY SOON, THE ONLY ONE HE WOULD TALK ***TO*** WAS THE PERSOCOM.
SHE SAID IT DIDN'T EVEN MATTER IF SHE CAME HOME AT NIGHT OR NOT.

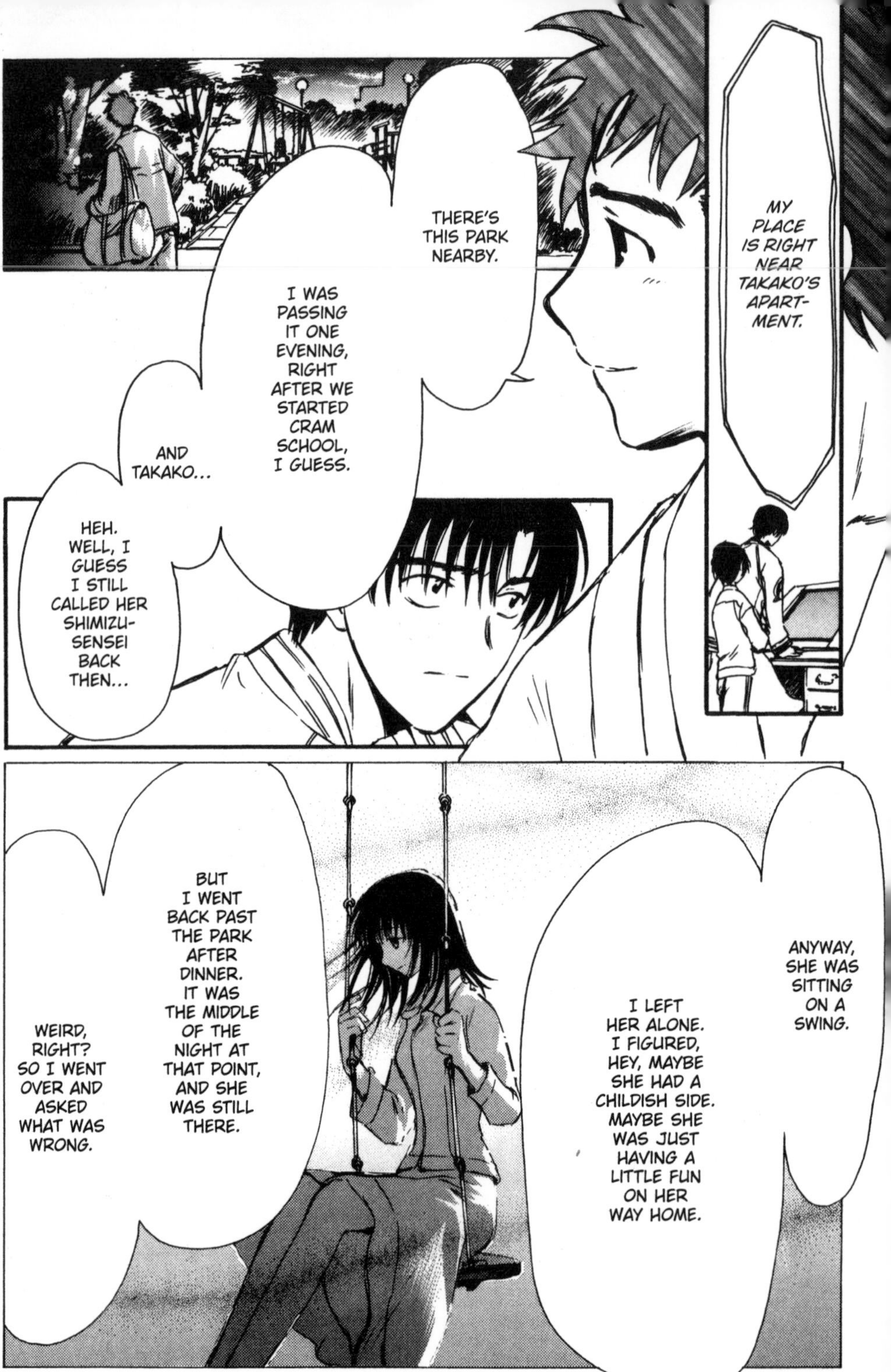
MY PLACE IS RIGHT NEAR TAKAKO'S APARTMENT.
THERE'S THIS PARK NEARBY.
I WAS PASSING IT ONE EVENING, RIGHT AFTER WE STARTED CRAM SCHOOL, I GUESS.
AND TAKAKO...
HEH. WELL, I GUESS I STILL CALLED HER SHIMIZU-SENSEI BACK THEN...
ANYWAY, SHE WAS SITTING ON A SWING.
I LEFT HER ALONE. I FIGURED, HEY, MAYBE SHE HAD A CHILDISH SIDE. MAYBE SHE WAS JUST HAVING A LITTLE FUN ON HER WAY HOME.
BUT I WENT BACK PAST THE PARK AFTER DINNER. IT WAS THE MIDDLE OF THE NIGHT AT THAT POINT, AND SHE WAS STILL THERE.
WEIRD, RIGHT? SO I WENT OVER AND ASKED WHAT WAS WRONG.

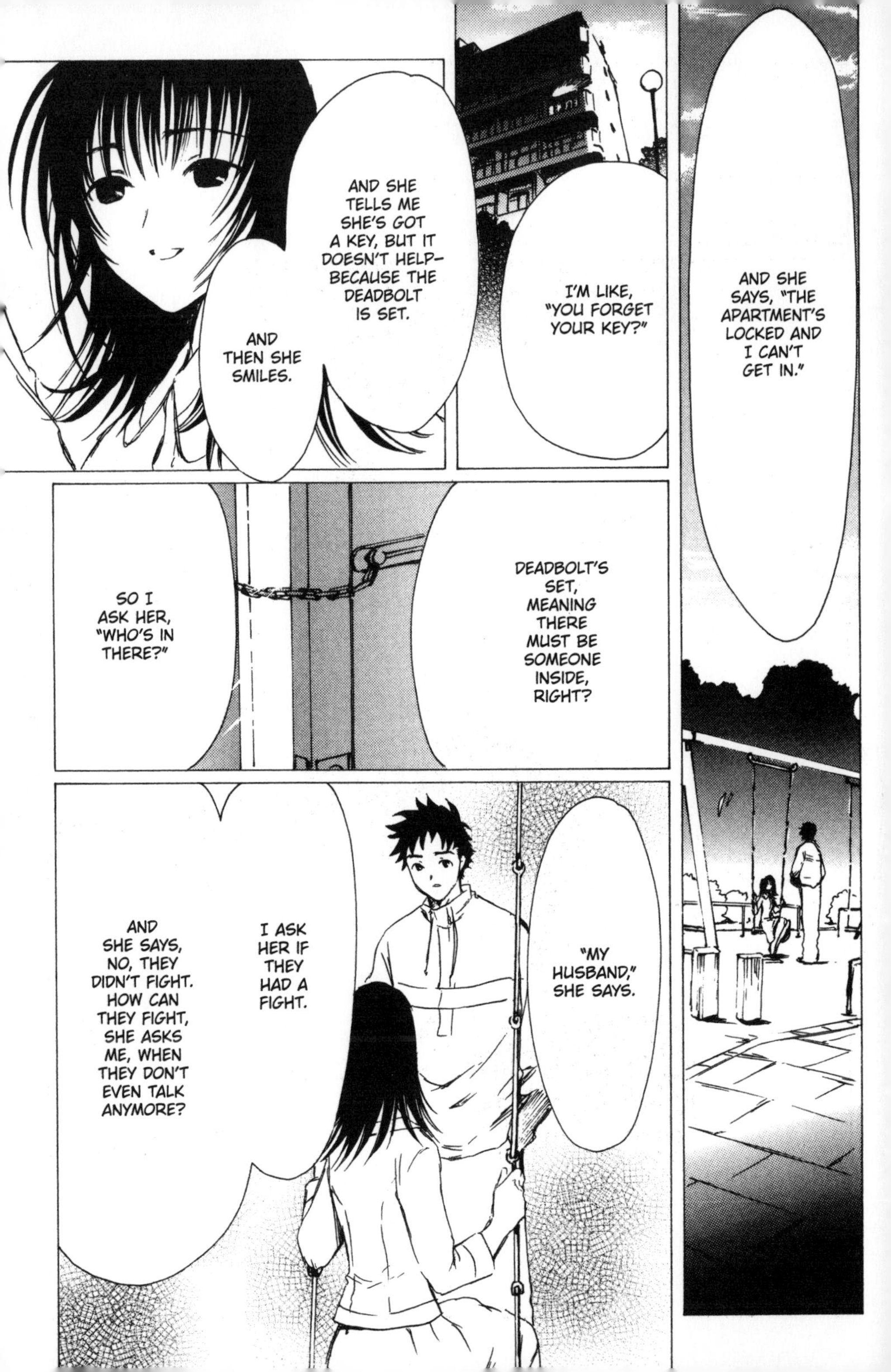
AND SHE SAYS, "THE APARTMENT'S LOCKED AND I CAN'T GET IN."
I'M LIKE, "YOU FORGET YOUR KEY?"
AND SHE TELLS ME SHE'S GOT A KEY, BUT IT DOESN'T HELP-BECAUSE THE DEADBOLT IS SET.
AND THEN SHE SMILES.
DEADBOLT'S SET, MEANING THERE MUST BE SOMEONE INSIDE, RIGHT?
SO I ASK HER, "WHO'S IN THERE?"
"MY HUSBAND," SHE SAYS.
I ASK HER IF THEY HAD A FIGHT.
AND SHE SAYS, NO, THEY DIDN'T FIGHT. HOW CAN THEY FIGHT, SHE ASKS ME, WHEN THEY DON'T EVEN TALK ANYMORE?

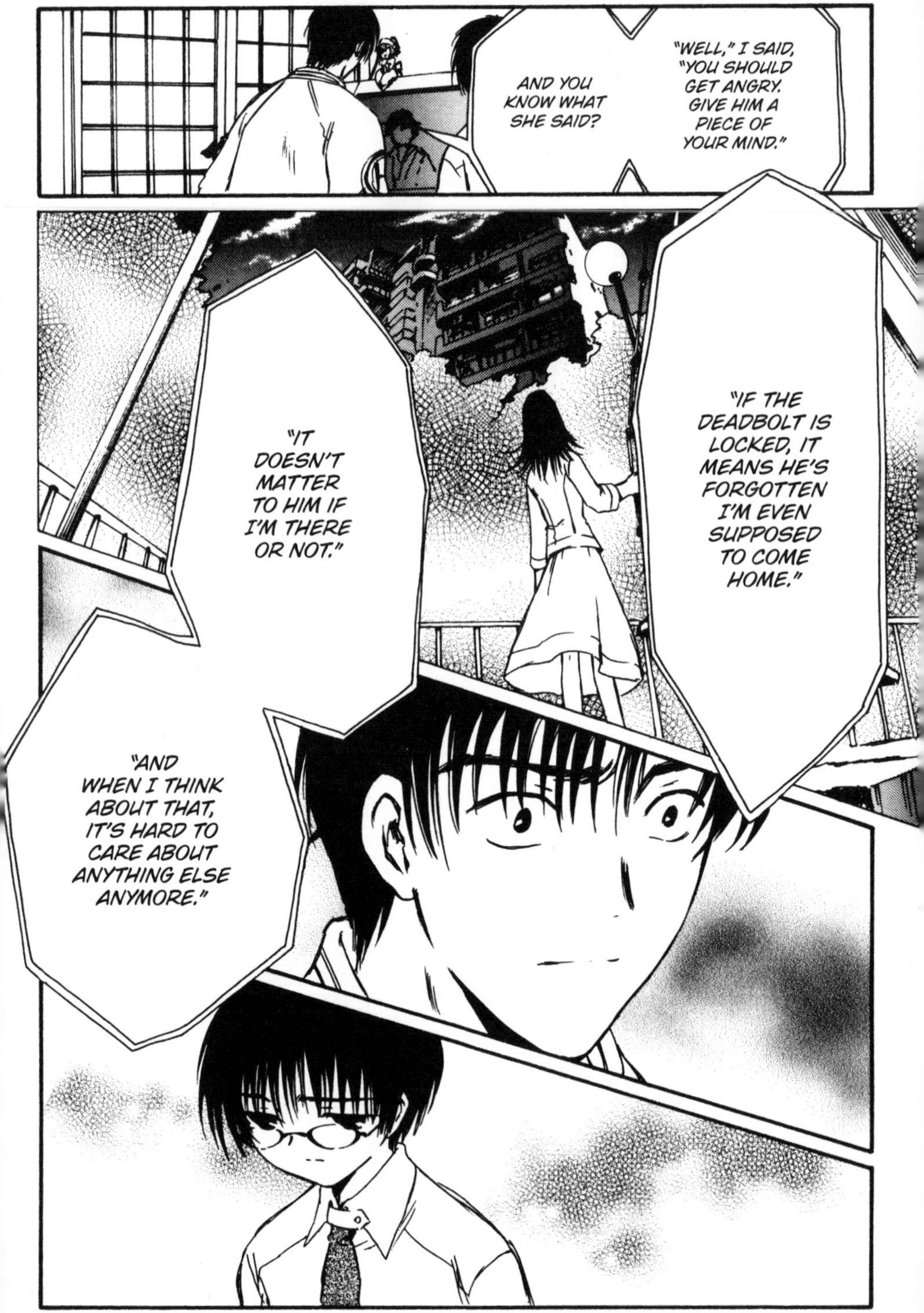
"WELL," I SAID, "YOU SHOULD GET ANGRY. GIVE HIM A PIECE OF YOUR MIND."
AND YOU KNOW WHAT SHE SAID?
"IF THE DEADBOLT IS LOCKED, IT MEANS HE'S FORGOTTEN I'M EVEN SUPPOSED TO COME HOME."
"IT DOESN'T MATTER TO HIM IF I'M THERE OR NOT."
"AND WHEN I THINK ABOUT THAT, IT'S HARD TO CARE ABOUT ANYTHING ELSE ANYMORE."

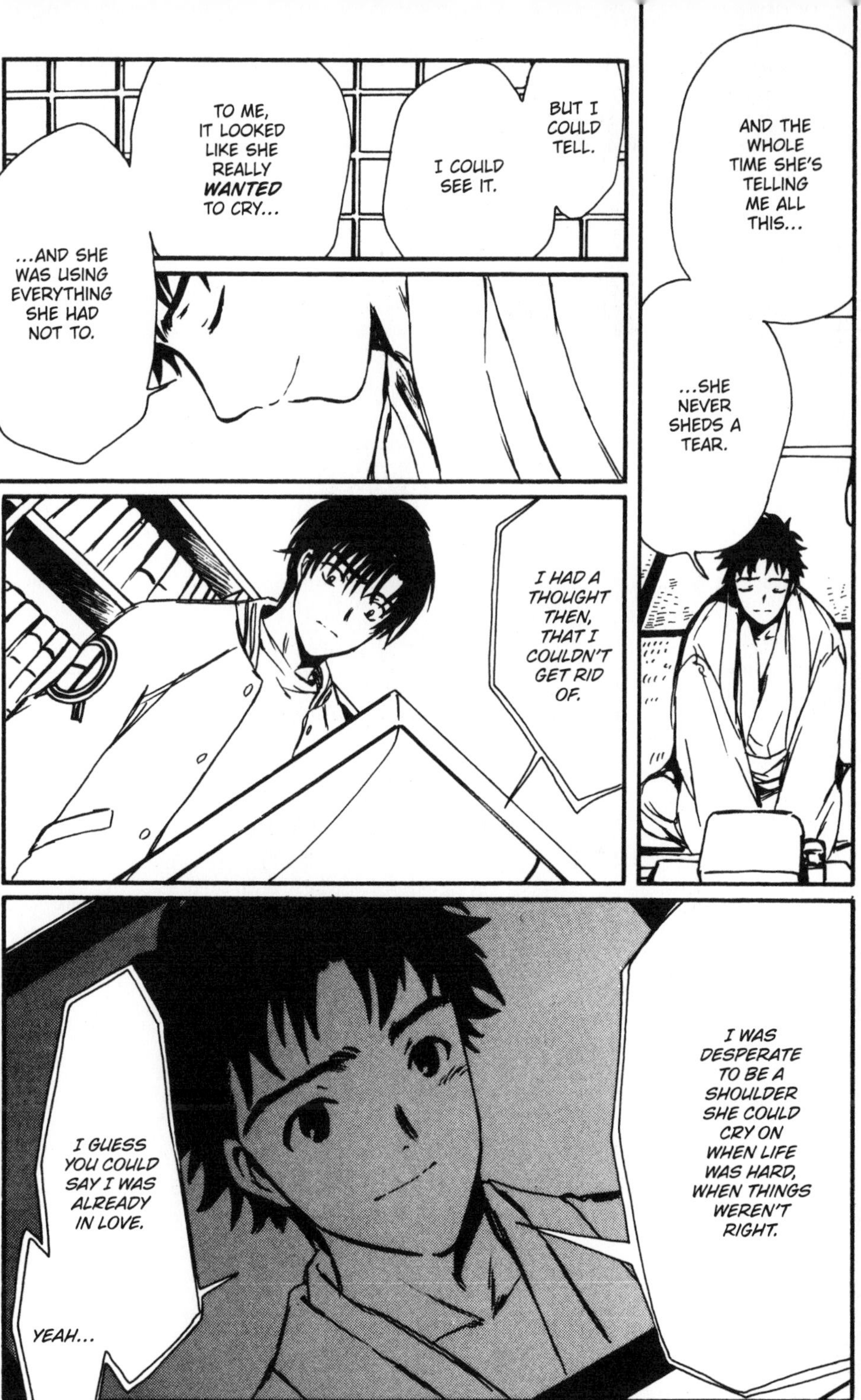
AND THE WHOLE TIME SHE'S TELLING ME ALL THIS...
...SHE NEVER SHEDS A TEAR.
BUT I COULD TELL.
I COULD SEE IT.
TO ME, IT LOOKED LIKE SHE REALLY **WANTED** TO CRY...
...AND SHE WAS USING EVERYTHING SHE HAD NOT TO.
I HAD A THOUGHT THEN, THAT I COULDN'T GET RID OF.
I WAS DESPERATE TO BE A SHOULDER SHE COULD CRY ON WHEN LIFE WAS HARD, WHEN THINGS WEREN'T RIGHT.
I GUESS YOU COULD SAY I WAS ALREADY IN LOVE.
YEAH...

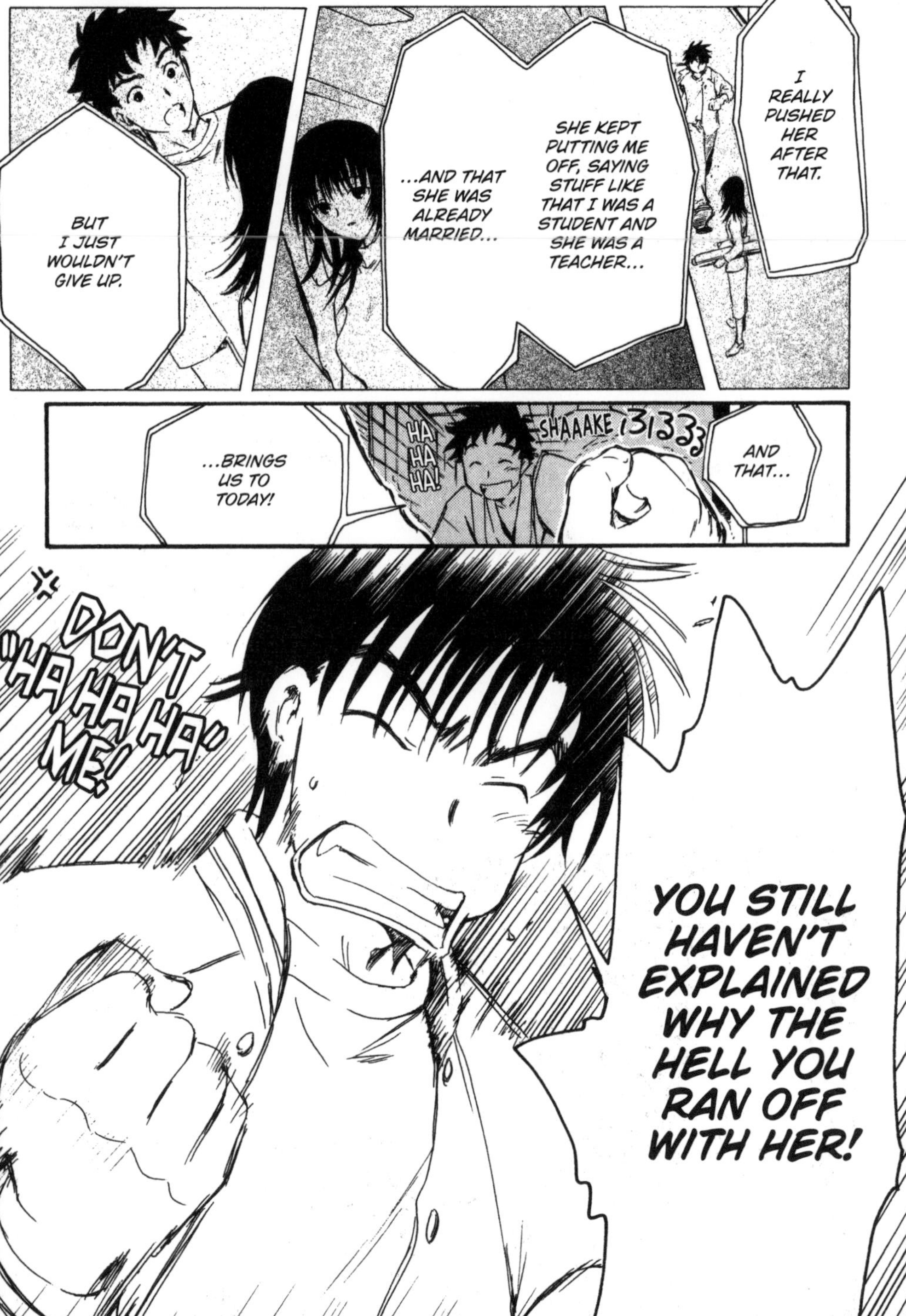
I REALLY PUSHED HER AFTER THAT.
SHE KEPT PUTTING ME OFF, SAYING STUFF LIKE THAT I WAS A STUDENT AND SHE WAS A TEACHER...
...AND THAT SHE WAS ALREADY MARRIED...
BUT I JUST WOULDN'T GIVE UP.
AND THAT...
SHAAAKE
HA HA HA!
...BRINGS US TO TODAY!
YOU STILL HAVEN'T EXPLAINED WHY THE HELL YOU RAN OFF WITH HER!
DON'T "HA HA HA" ME!
<chapter.27> end

OMURA

Chobits

<chapter.28>

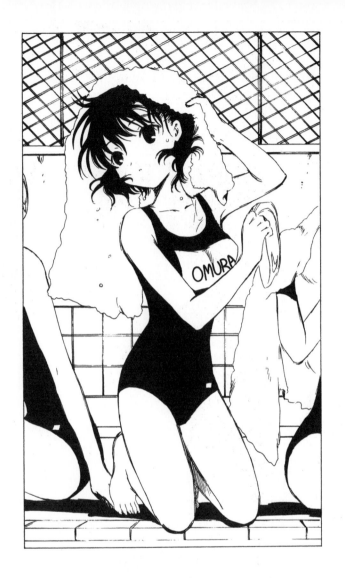

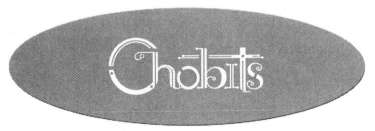

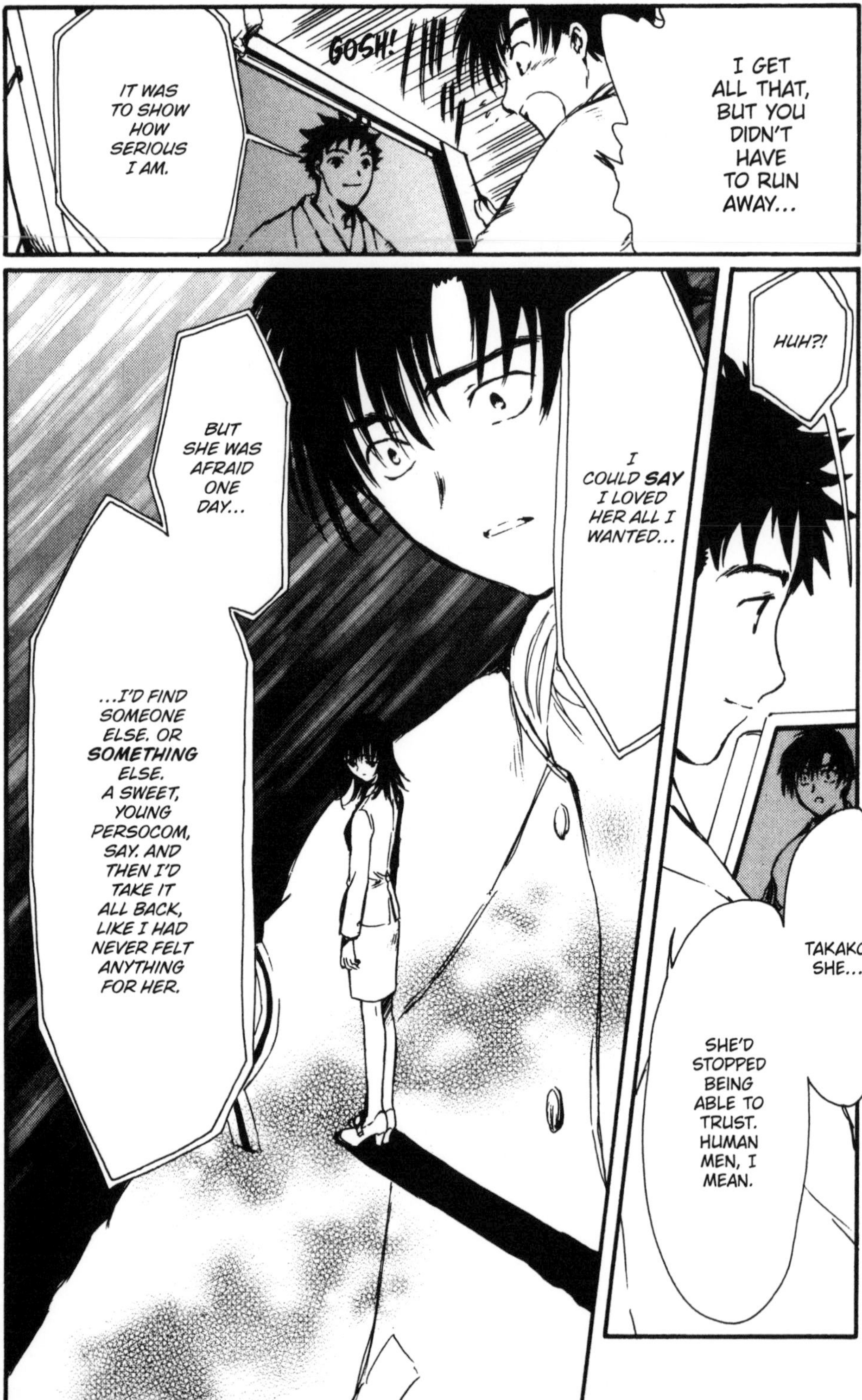

I GET ALL THAT, BUT YOU DIDN'T HAVE TO RUN AWAY...
GOSH!
IT WAS TO SHOW HOW SERIOUS I AM.
HUH?!
TAKAKO, SHE...
SHE'D STOPPED BEING ABLE TO TRUST. HUMAN MEN, I MEAN.
I COULD **SAY** I LOVED HER ALL I WANTED...
BUT SHE WAS AFRAID ONE DAY...
...I'D FIND SOMEONE ELSE. OR **SOMETHING** ELSE. A SWEET, YOUNG PERSOCOM, SAY. AND THEN I'D TAKE IT ALL BACK, LIKE I HAD NEVER FELT ANYTHING FOR HER.

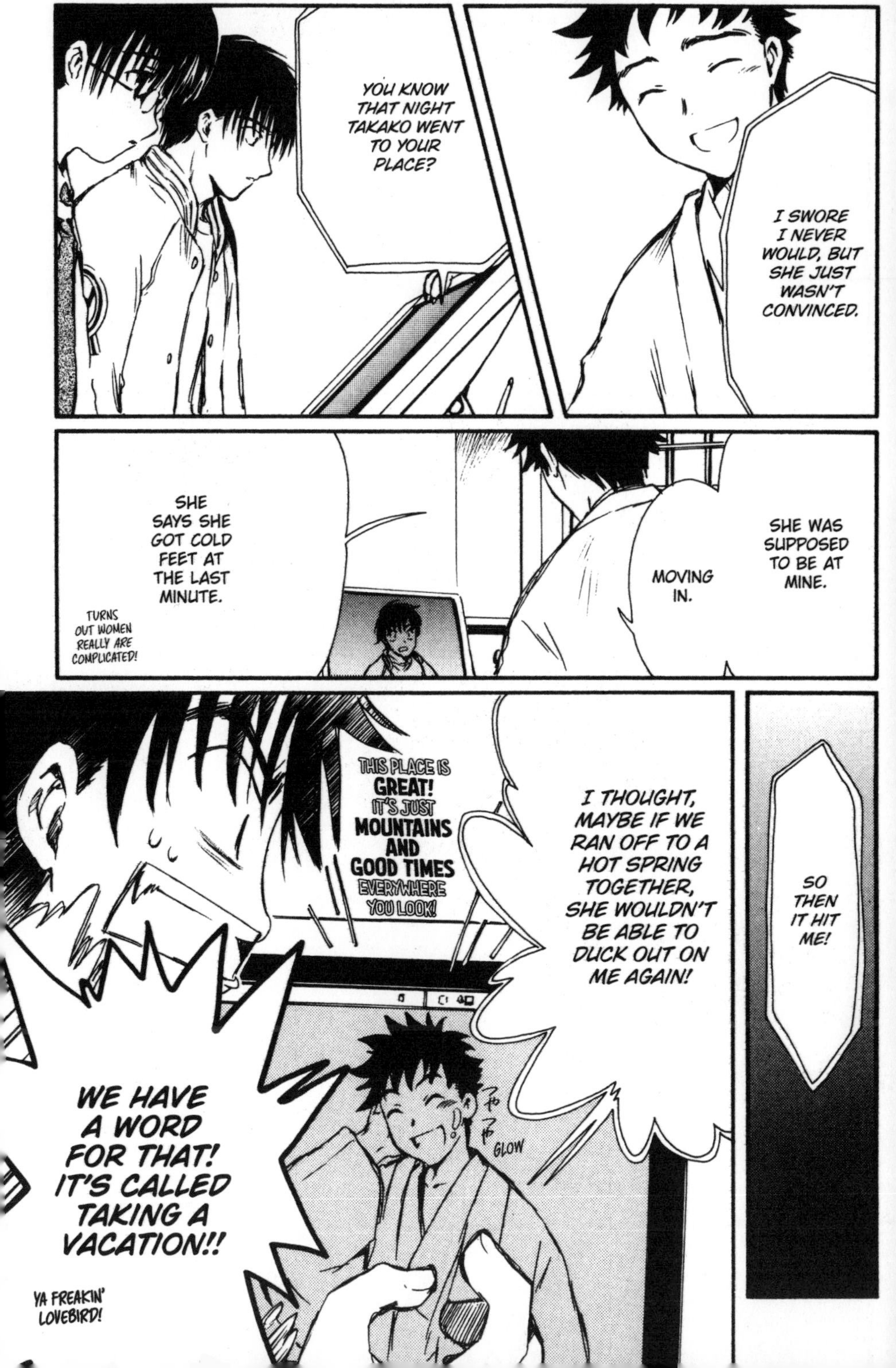
I SWORE I NEVER WOULD, BUT SHE JUST WASN'T CONVINCED.
YOU KNOW THAT NIGHT TAKAKO WENT TO YOUR PLACE?
SHE WAS SUPPOSED TO BE AT MINE.
MOVING IN.
SHE SAYS SHE GOT COLD FEET AT THE LAST MINUTE.
TURNS OUT WOMEN REALLY ARE COMPLICATED!
SO THEN IT HIT ME!
I THOUGHT, MAYBE IF WE RAN OFF TO A HOT SPRING TOGETHER, SHE WOULDN'T BE ABLE TO DUCK OUT ON ME AGAIN!
THIS PLACE IS GREAT! IT'S JUST MOUNTAINS AND GOOD TIMES EVERYWHERE YOU LOOK!
GLOW
WE HAVE A WORD FOR THAT! IT'S CALLED TAKING A VACATION!!
YA FREAKIN' LOVEBIRD!

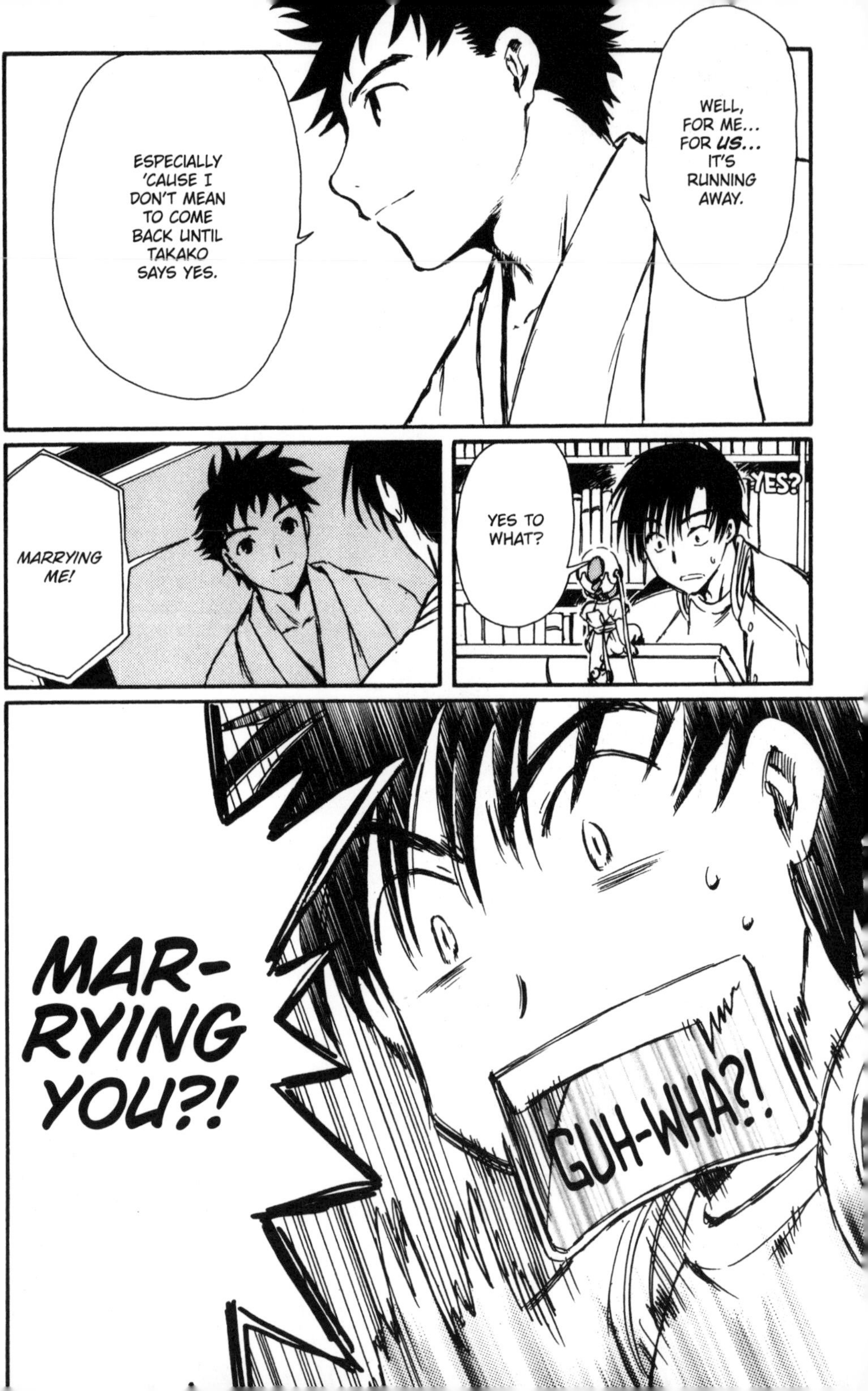
WELL, FOR ME... FOR *US*... IT'S RUNNING AWAY.
ESPECIALLY 'CAUSE I DON'T MEAN TO COME BACK UNTIL TAKAKO SAYS YES.
YES?
YES TO WHAT?
MARRYING ME!
GUH-WHA?!
MAR-RYING YOU?!

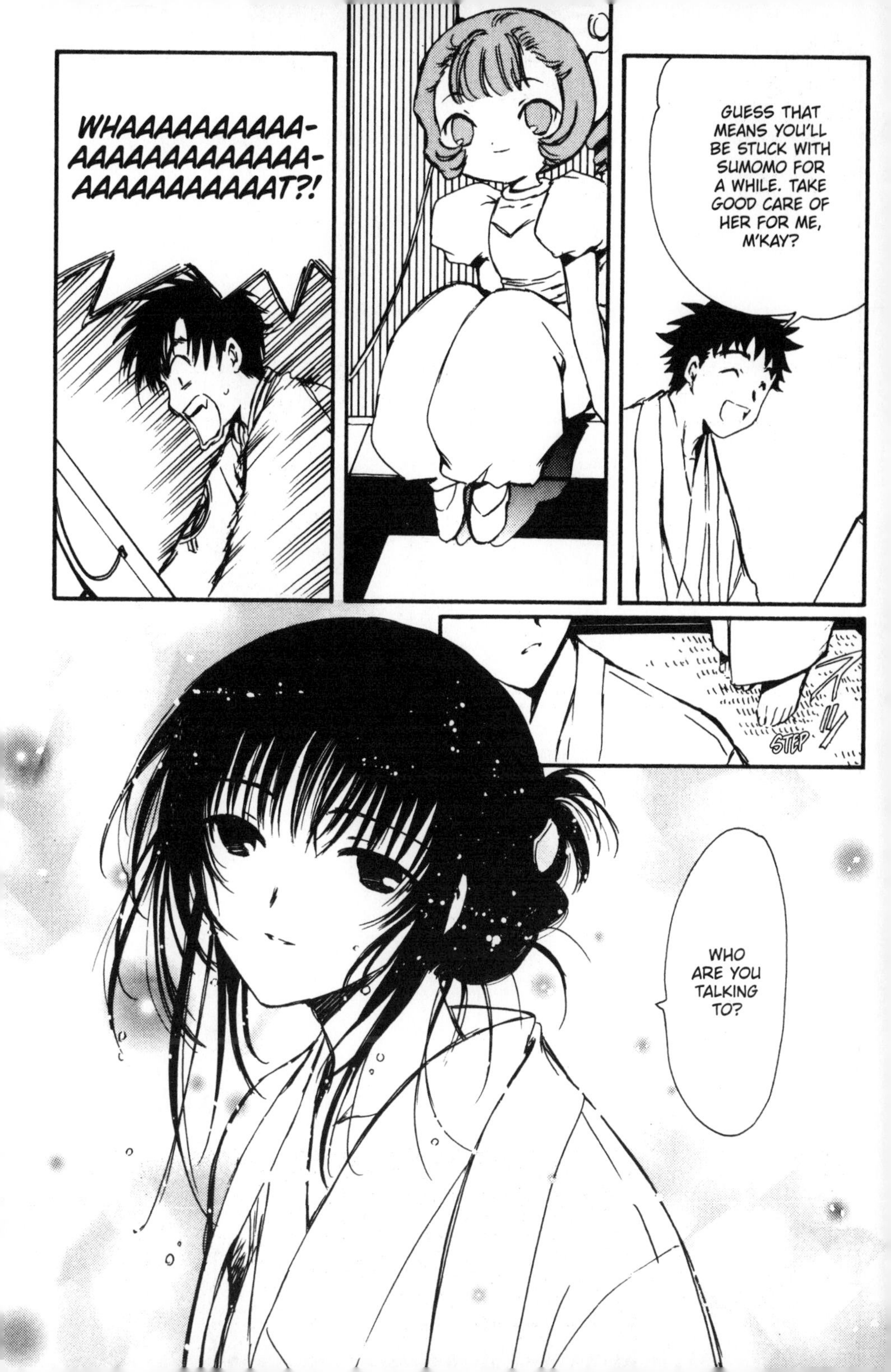
GUESS THAT MEANS YOU'LL BE STUCK WITH SUMOMO FOR A WHILE. TAKE GOOD CARE OF HER FOR ME, M'KAY?
WHAAAAAAAAAA-AAAAAAAAAAAAA-AAAAAAAAAAAT?!
STEP
WHO ARE YOU TALKING TO?

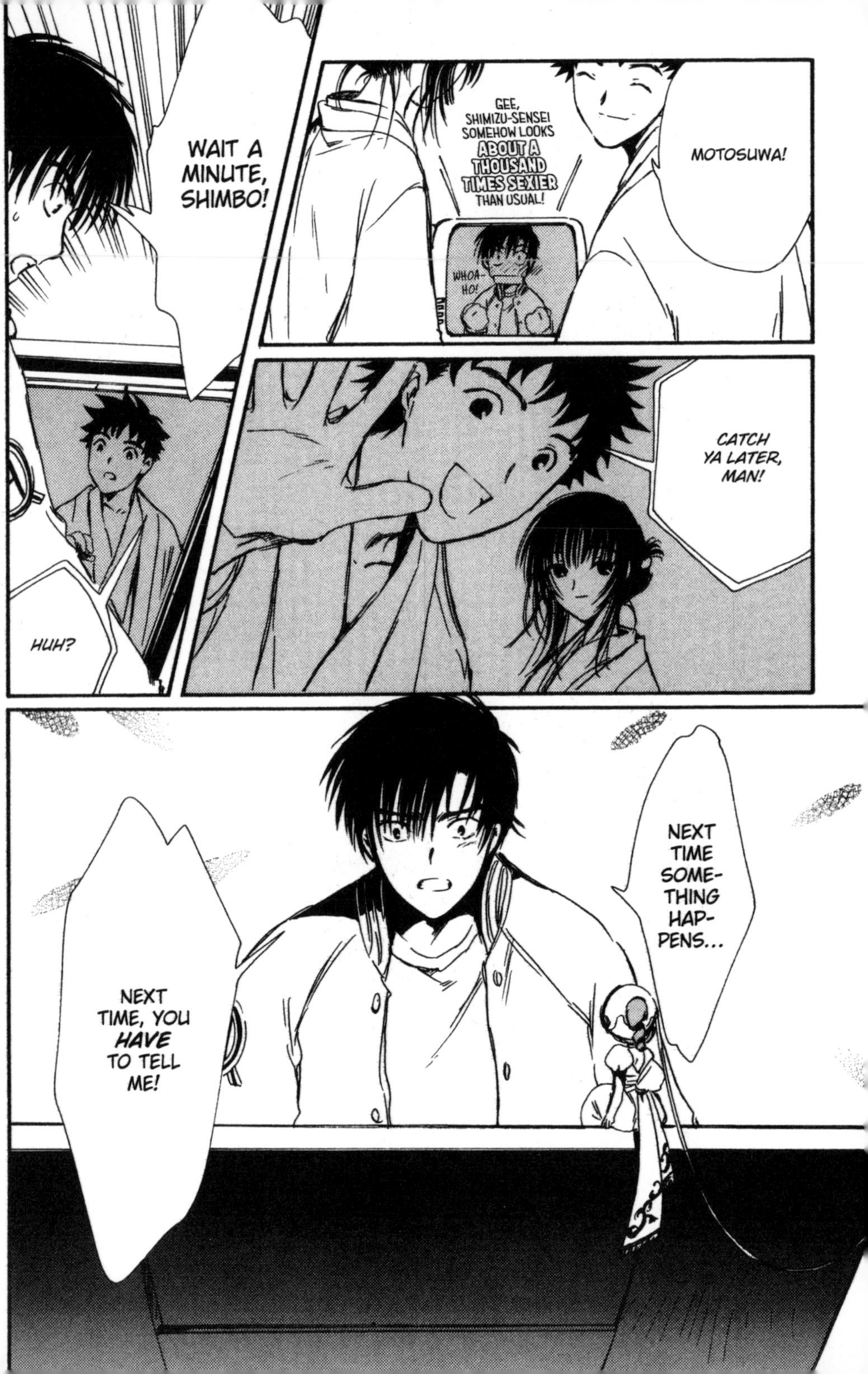
MOTOSUWA!
GEE, SHIMIZU-SENSEI SOMEHOW LOOKS ABOUT A THOUSAND TIMES SEXIER THAN USUAL!
WHOA-HO!
CATCH YA LATER, MAN!
WAIT A MINUTE, SHIMBO!
HUH?
NEXT TIME SOME-THING HAP-PENS...
NEXT TIME, YOU ***HAVE*** TO TELL ME!

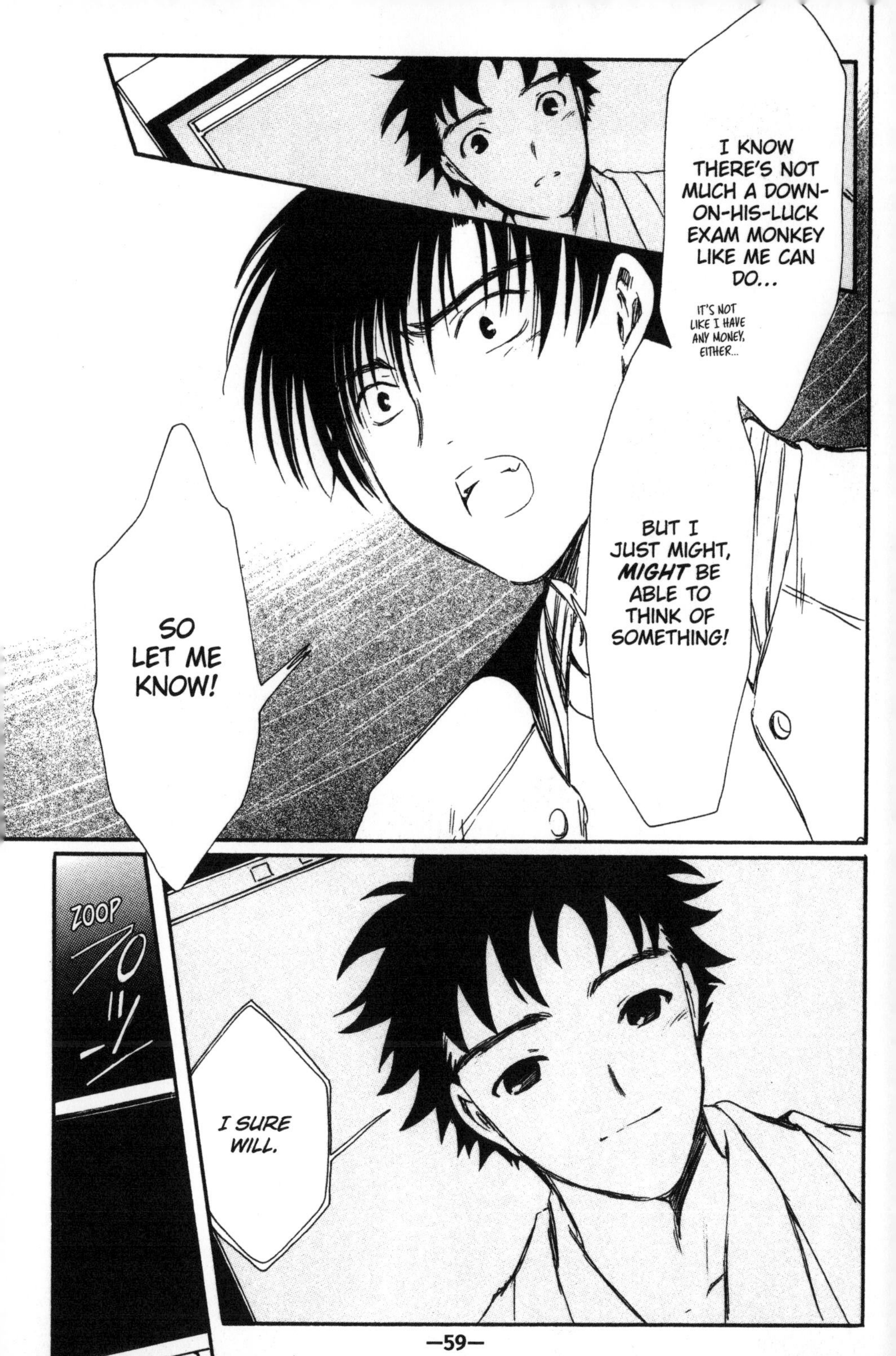
I KNOW THERE'S NOT MUCH A DOWN-ON-HIS-LUCK EXAM MONKEY LIKE ME CAN DO...
IT'S NOT LIKE I HAVE ANY MONEY, EITHER...
BUT I JUST MIGHT, MIGHT BE ABLE TO THINK OF SOMETHING!
SO LET ME KNOW!
ZOOP
I SURE WILL.

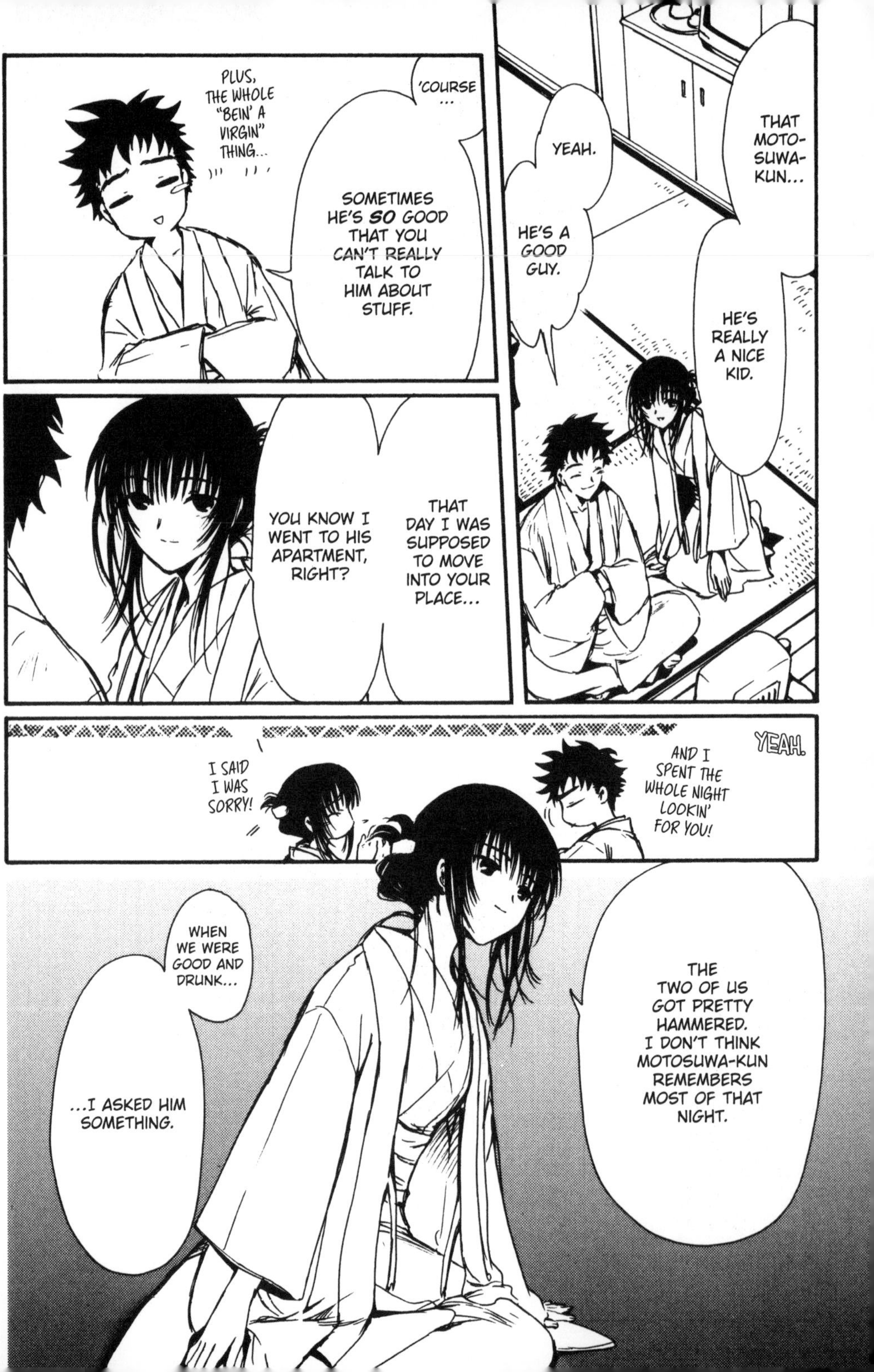

THAT MOTO-SUWA-KUN...
HE'S REALLY A NICE KID.
YEAH.
HE'S A GOOD GUY.
'COURSE...
SOMETIMES HE'S **SO** GOOD THAT YOU CAN'T REALLY TALK TO HIM ABOUT STUFF.
PLUS, THE WHOLE "BEIN' A VIRGIN" THING...
THAT DAY I WAS SUPPOSED TO MOVE INTO YOUR PLACE...
YOU KNOW I WENT TO HIS APARTMENT, RIGHT?
YEAH.
AND I SPENT THE WHOLE NIGHT LOOKIN' FOR YOU!
I SAID I WAS SORRY!
THE TWO OF US GOT PRETTY HAMMERED. I DON'T THINK MOTOSUWA-KUN REMEMBERS MOST OF THAT NIGHT.
WHEN WE WERE GOOD AND DRUNK...
...I ASKED HIM SOMETHING.

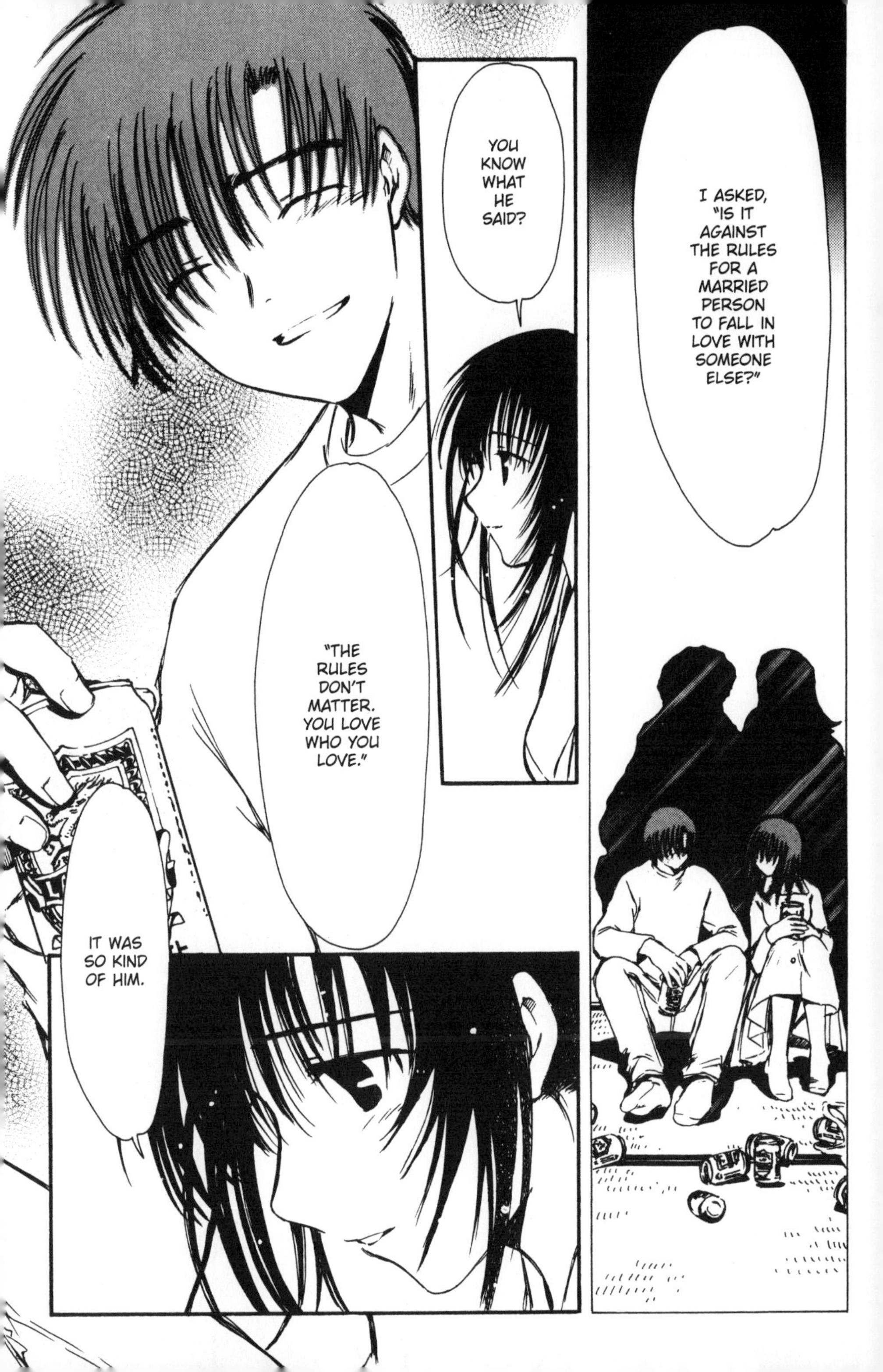
I ASKED, "IS IT AGAINST THE RULES FOR A MARRIED PERSON TO FALL IN LOVE WITH SOMEONE ELSE?"
YOU KNOW WHAT HE SAID?
"THE RULES DON'T MATTER. YOU LOVE WHO YOU LOVE."
IT WAS SO KIND OF HIM.

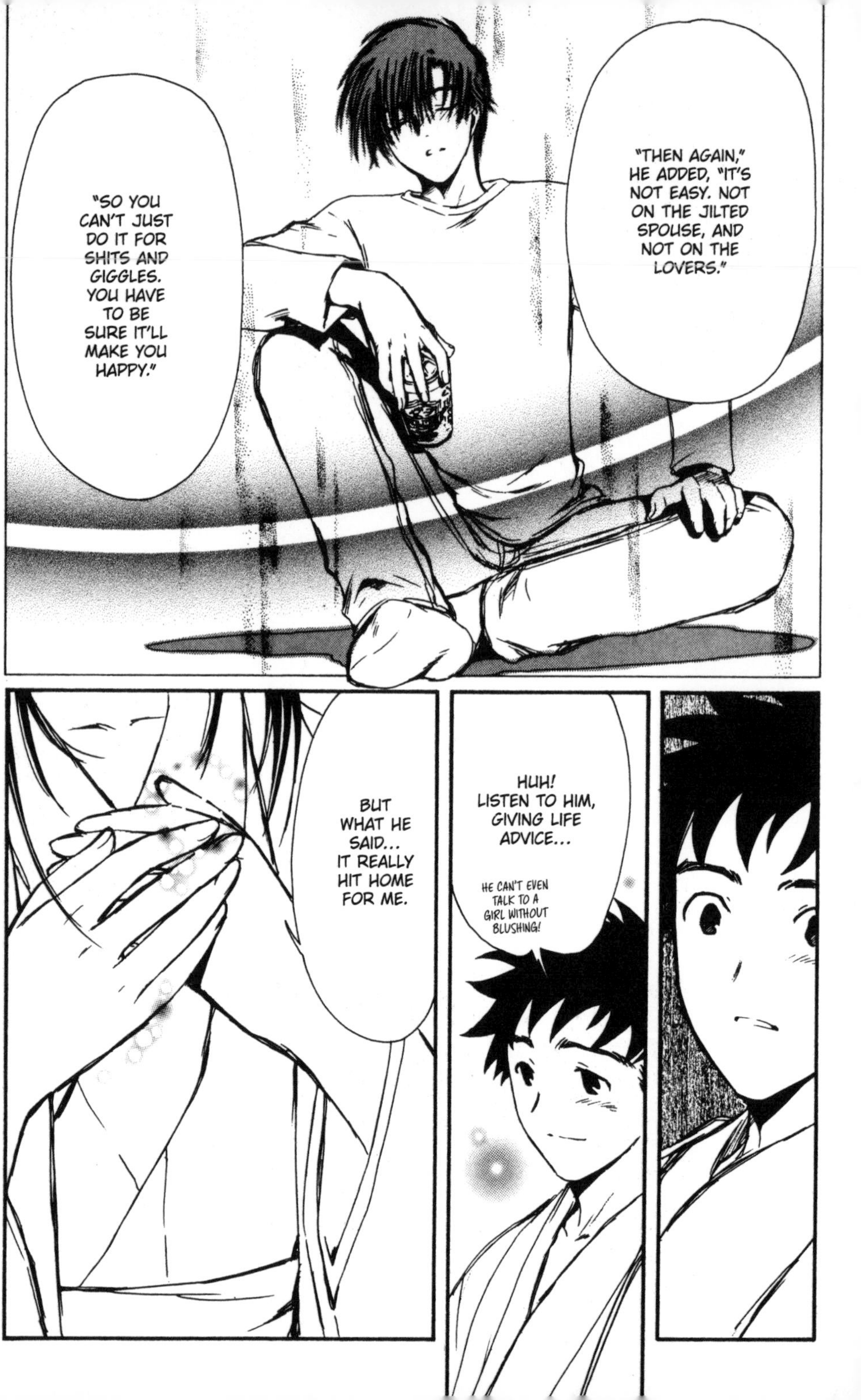
"THEN AGAIN," HE ADDED, "IT'S NOT EASY. NOT ON THE JILTED SPOUSE, AND NOT ON THE LOVERS."
"SO YOU CAN'T JUST DO IT FOR SHITS AND GIGGLES. YOU HAVE TO BE SURE IT'LL MAKE YOU HAPPY."
HUH! LISTEN TO HIM, GIVING LIFE ADVICE...
HE CAN'T EVEN TALK TO A GIRL WITHOUT BLUSHING!
BUT WHAT HE SAID... IT REALLY HIT HOME FOR ME.

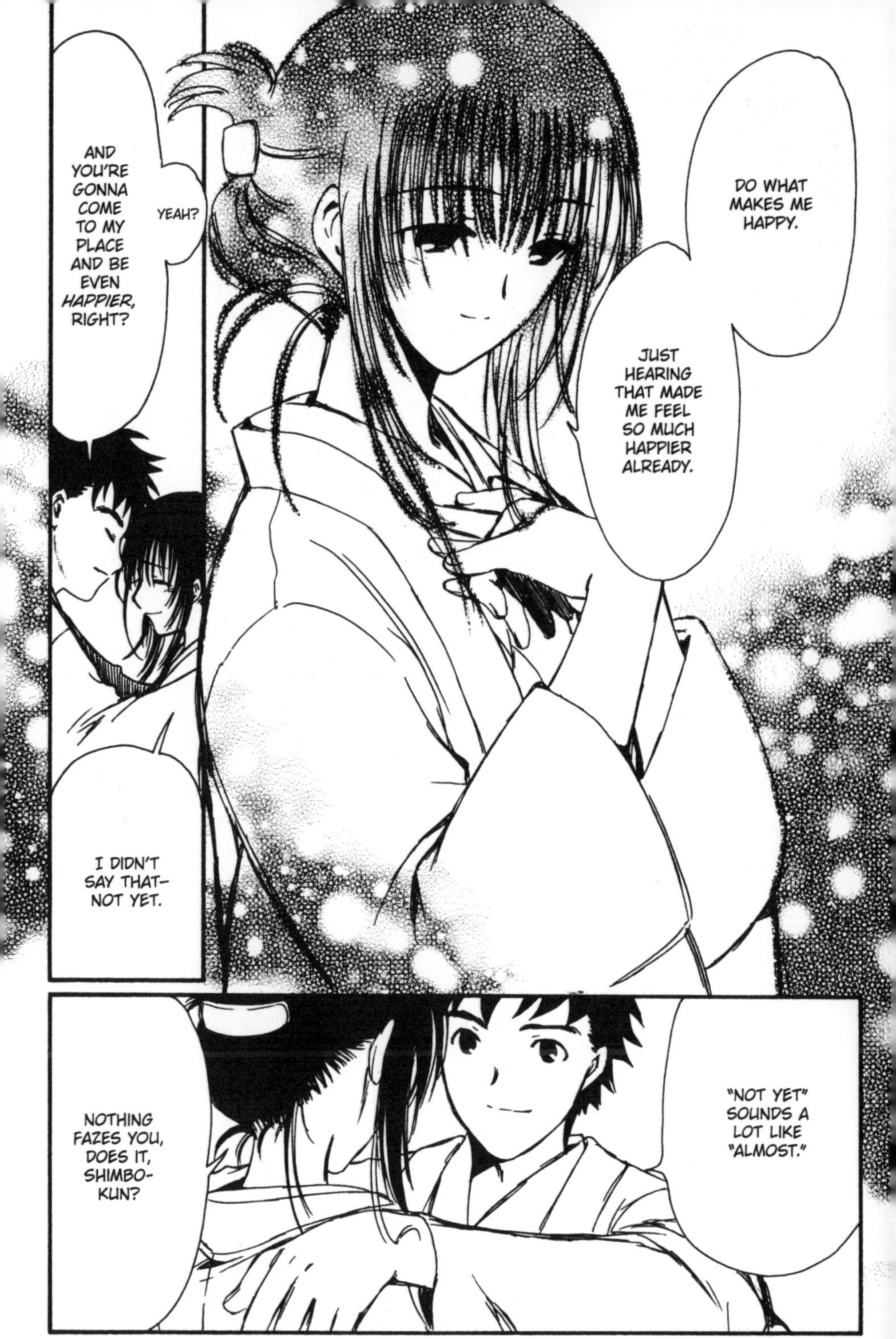
DO WHAT MAKES ME HAPPY.
JUST HEARING THAT MADE ME FEEL SO MUCH HAPPIER ALREADY.
AND YOU'RE GONNA COME TO MY PLACE AND BE EVEN *HAPPIER*, RIGHT?
YEAH?
I DIDN'T SAY THAT—NOT YET.
"NOT YET" SOUNDS A LOT LIKE "ALMOST."
NOTHING FAZES YOU, DOES IT, SHIMBO-KUN?

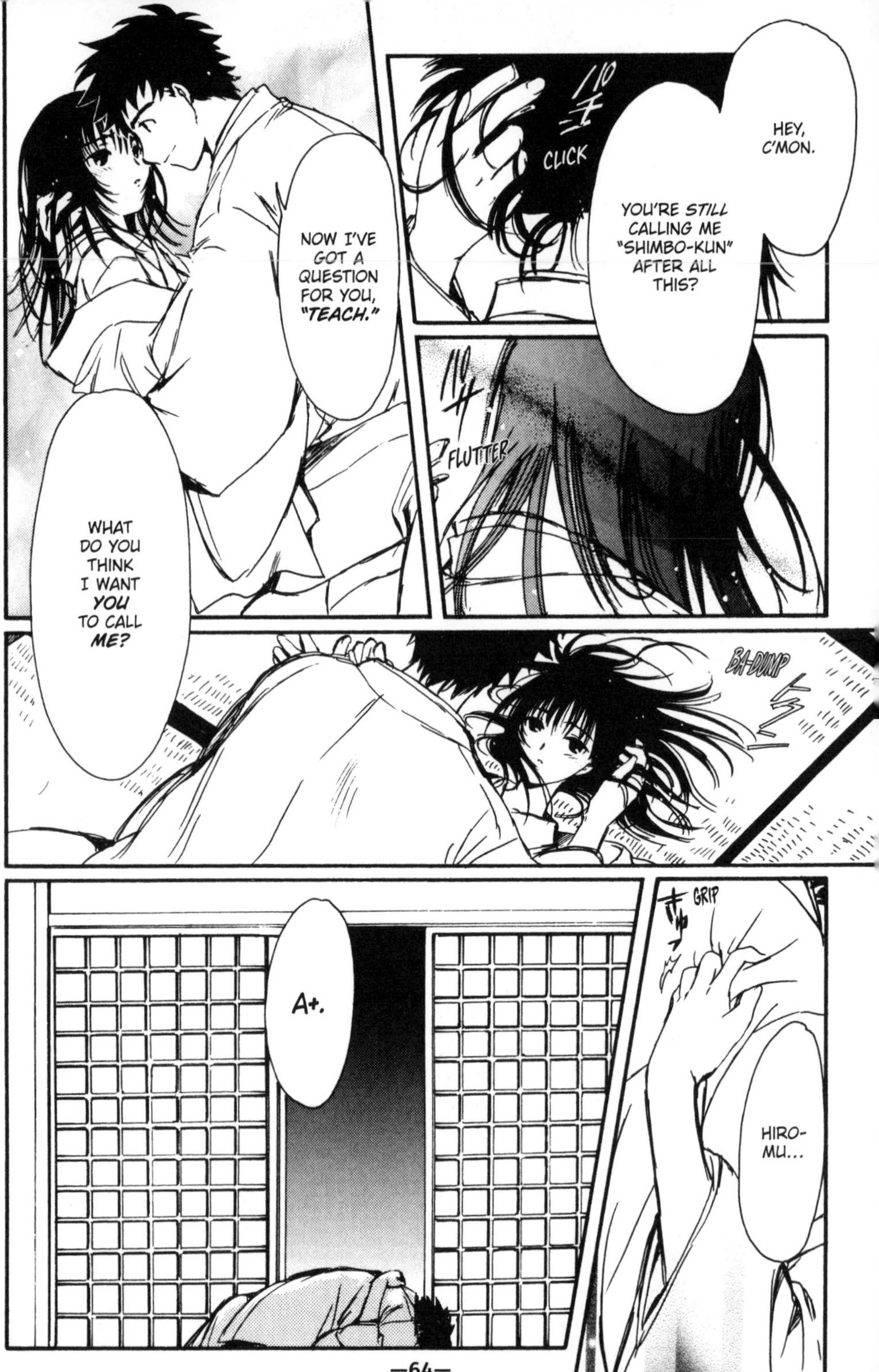
CLICK
HEY, C'MON.
YOU'RE STILL CALLING ME "SHIMBO-KUN" AFTER ALL THIS?
FLUTTER
NOW I'VE GOT A QUESTION FOR YOU, "TEACH."
WHAT DO YOU THINK I WANT YOU TO CALL ME?
BA-DUMP
GRIP
HIRO-MU...
A+.

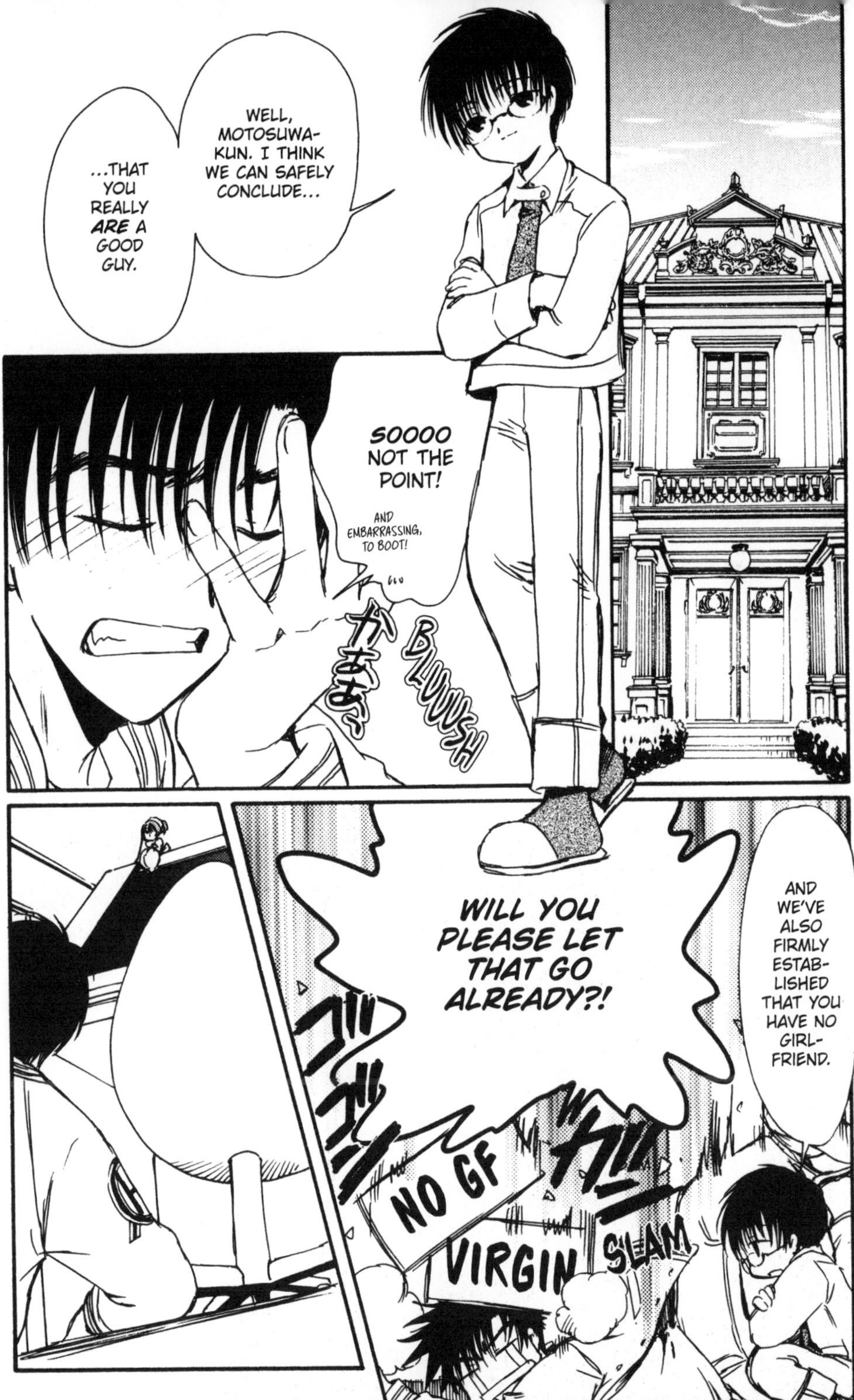
WELL, MOTOSUWA-KUN. I THINK WE CAN SAFELY CONCLUDE...
...THAT YOU REALLY ARE A GOOD GUY.
SOOOO NOT THE POINT!
AND EMBARRASSING, TO BOOT!
BLUUSH
AND WE'VE ALSO FIRMLY ESTABLISHED THAT YOU HAVE NO GIRLFRIEND.
WILL YOU PLEASE LET THAT GO ALREADY?!
NO GF
VIRGIN
SLAM

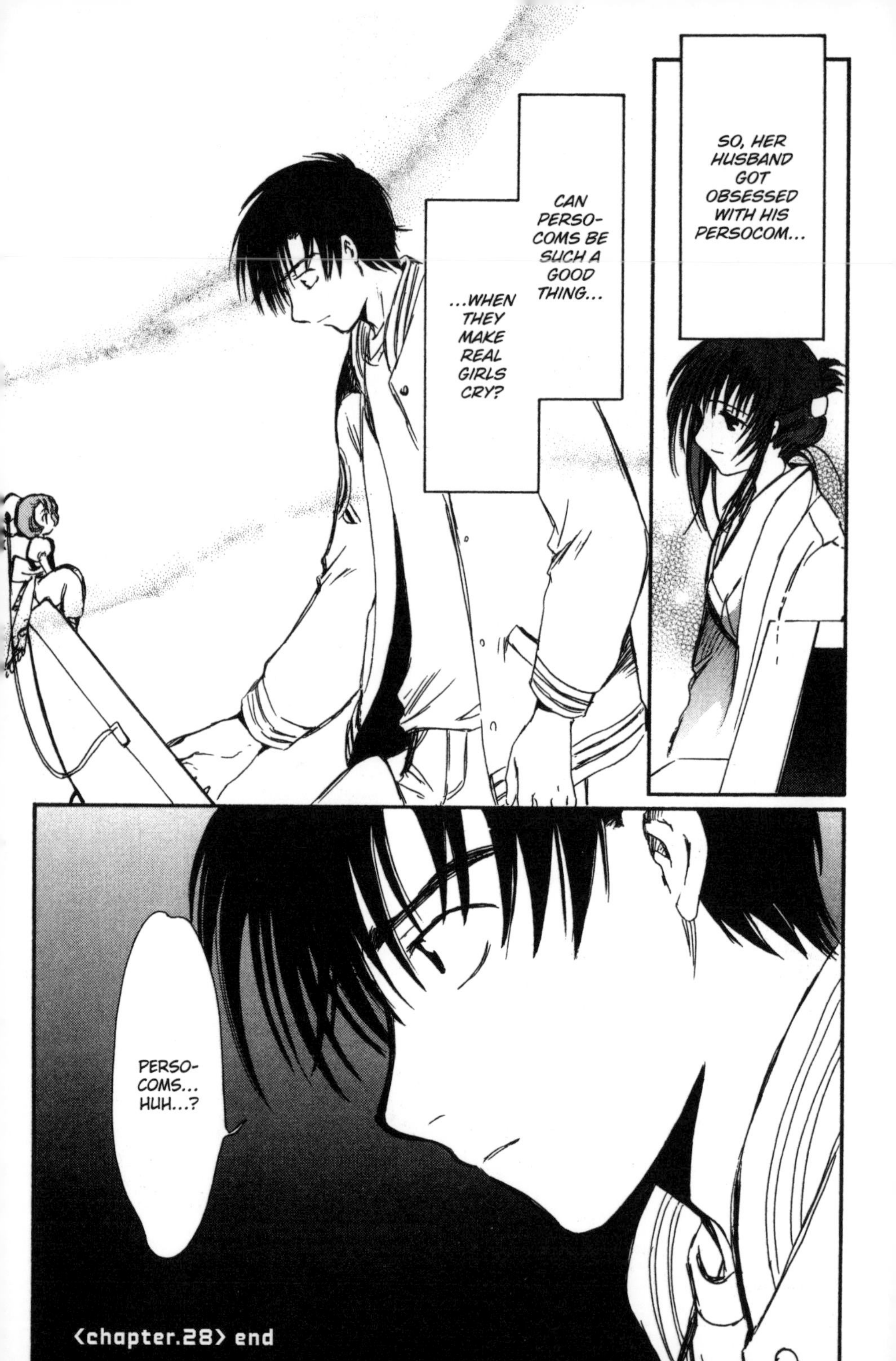
SO, HER HUSBAND GOT OBSESSED WITH HIS PERSOCOM...
CAN PERSO-COMS BE SUCH A GOOD THING...
...WHEN THEY MAKE REAL GIRLS CRY?
PERSO-COMS... HUH...?

<chapter.28> end

〈chapter.29〉

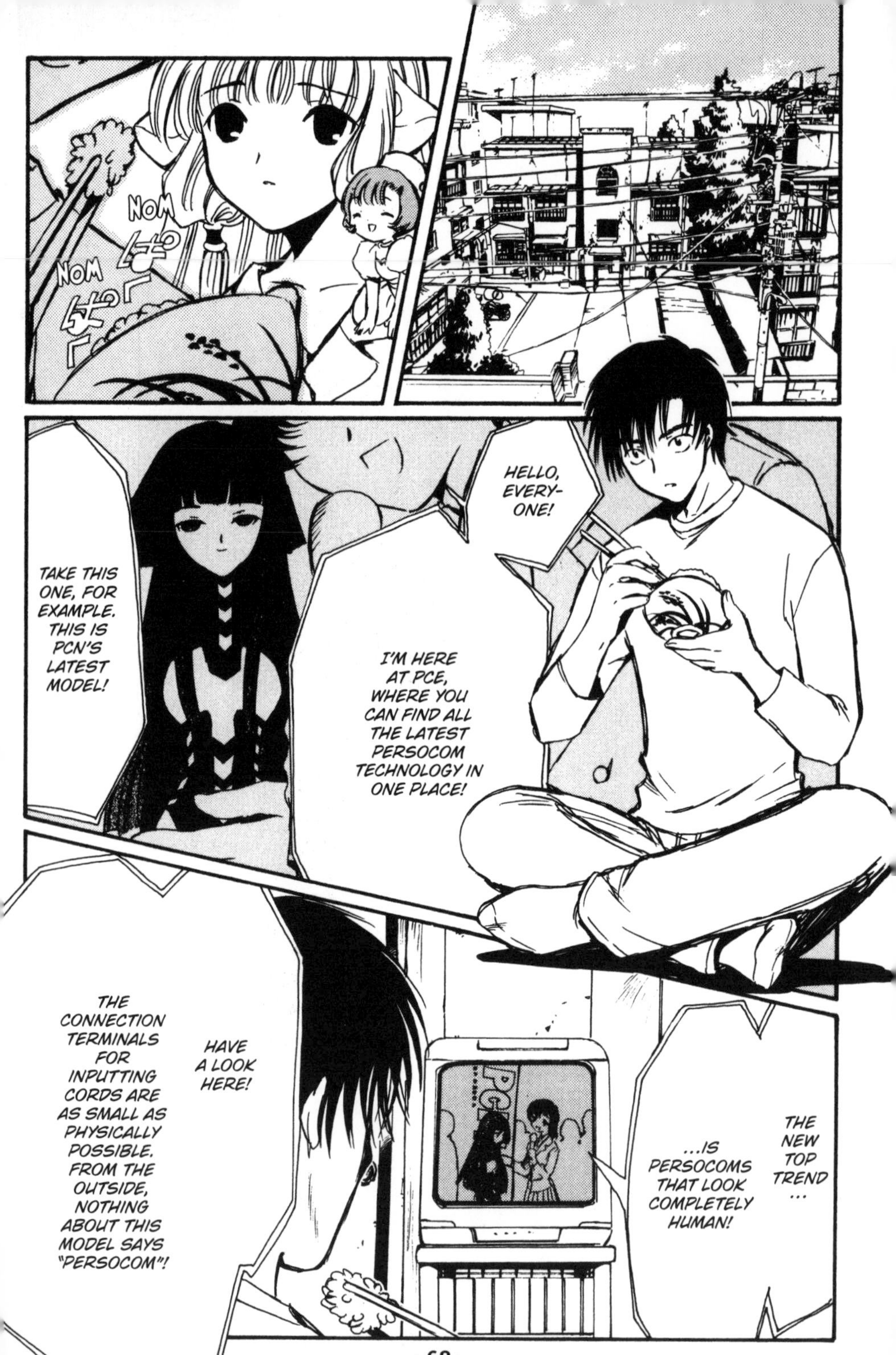
NOM
NOM
HELLO, EVERY-ONE!
I'M HERE AT PCE, WHERE YOU CAN FIND ALL THE LATEST PERSOCOM TECHNOLOGY IN ONE PLACE!
TAKE THIS ONE, FOR EXAMPLE. THIS IS PCN'S LATEST MODEL!
THE NEW TOP TREND...
...IS PERSOCOMS THAT LOOK COMPLETELY HUMAN!
HAVE A LOOK HERE!
THE CONNECTION TERMINALS FOR INPUTTING CORDS ARE AS SMALL AS PHYSICALLY POSSIBLE. FROM THE OUTSIDE, NOTHING ABOUT THIS MODEL SAYS "PERSOCOM"!

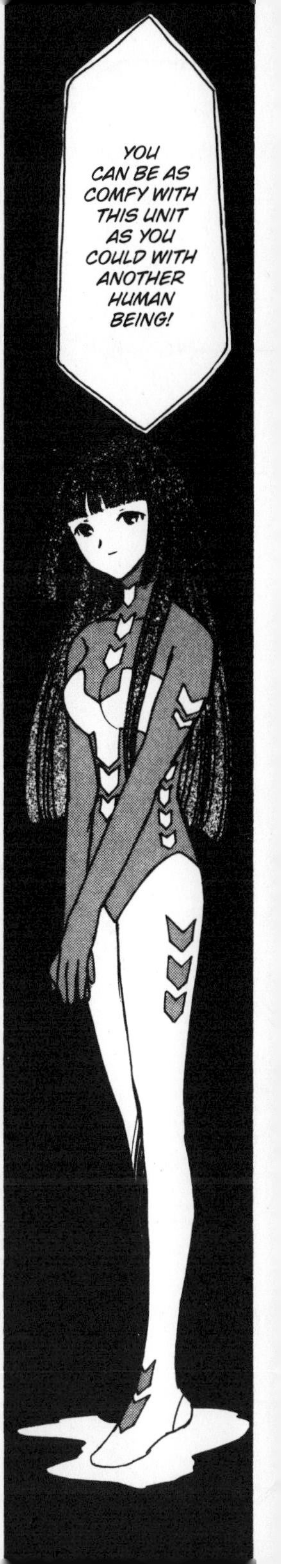
YOU CAN BE AS COMFY WITH THIS UNIT AS YOU COULD WITH ANOTHER HUMAN BEING!
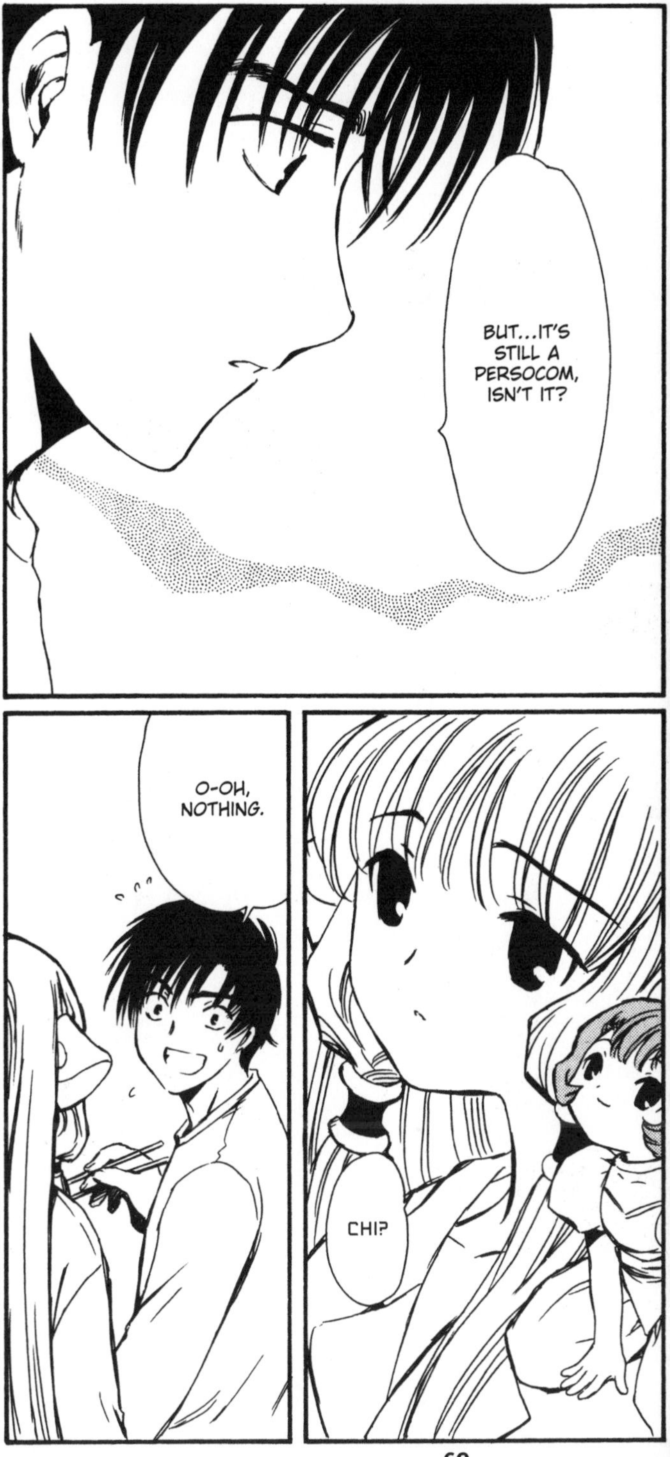
BUT...IT'S STILL A PERSOCOM, ISN'T IT?
CHI?
O-OH, NOTHING.

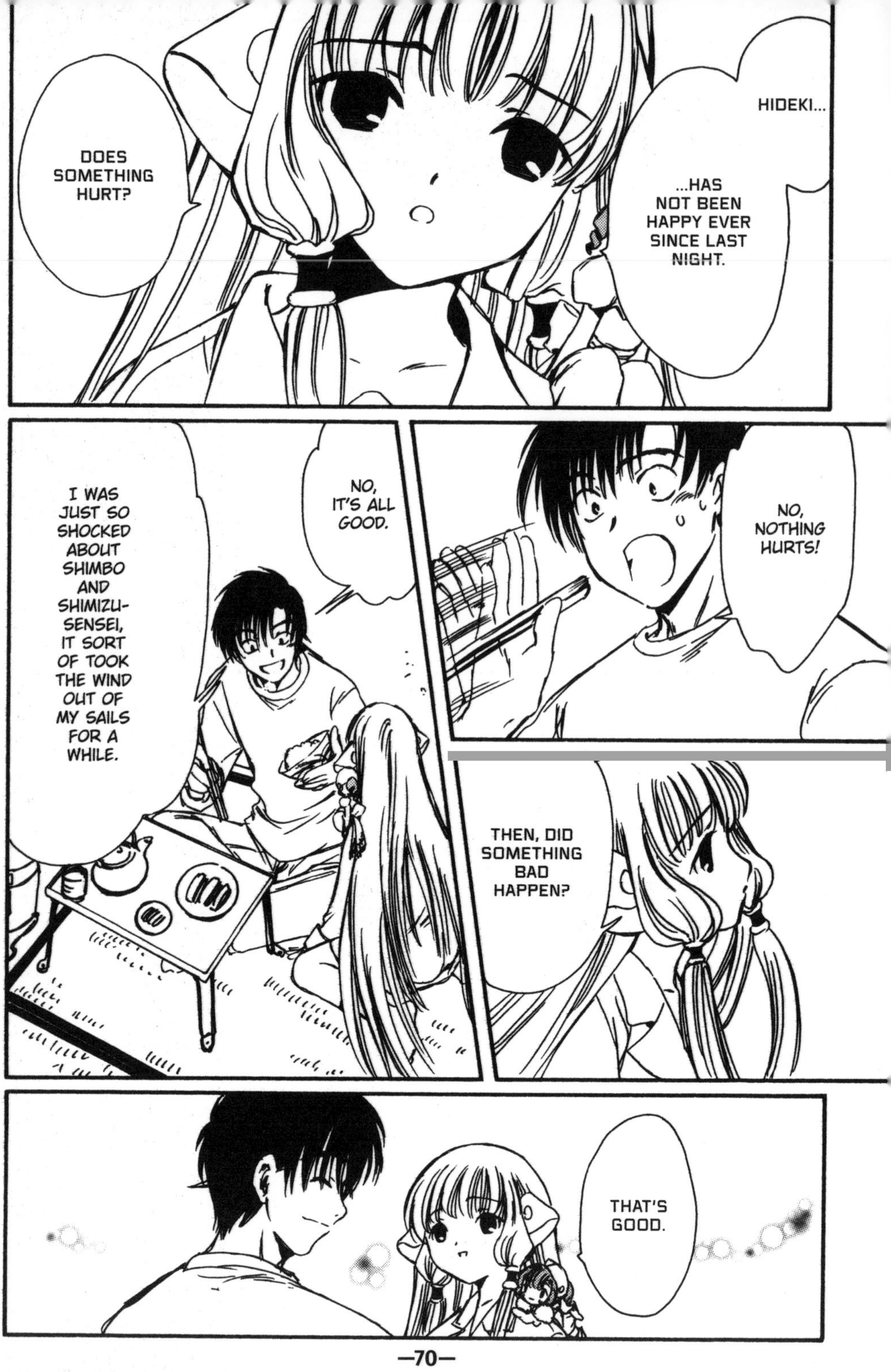
HIDEKI...
...HAS NOT BEEN HAPPY EVER SINCE LAST NIGHT.
DOES SOMETHING HURT?
NO, NOTHING HURTS!
THEN, DID SOMETHING BAD HAPPEN?
NO, IT'S ALL GOOD.
I WAS JUST SO SHOCKED ABOUT SHIMBO AND SHIMIZU-SENSEI, IT SORT OF TOOK THE WIND OUT OF MY SAILS FOR A WHILE.
THAT'S GOOD.

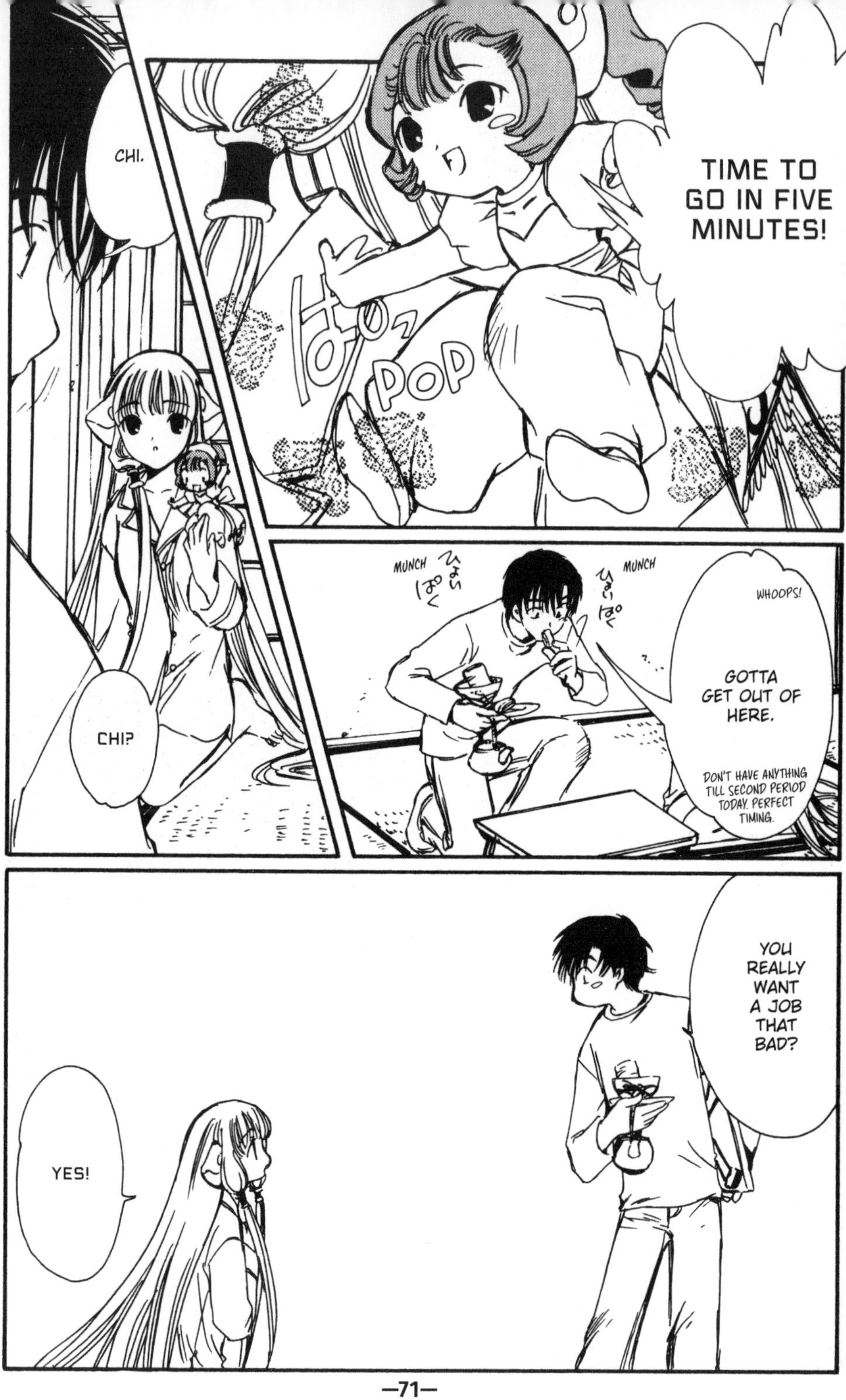
TIME TO GO IN FIVE MINUTES!
POP
MUNCH
MUNCH
WHOOPS!
GOTTA GET OUT OF HERE.
DON'T HAVE ANYTHING TILL SECOND PERIOD TODAY. PERFECT TIMING.
CHI.
CHI?
YOU REALLY WANT A JOB THAT BAD?
YES!

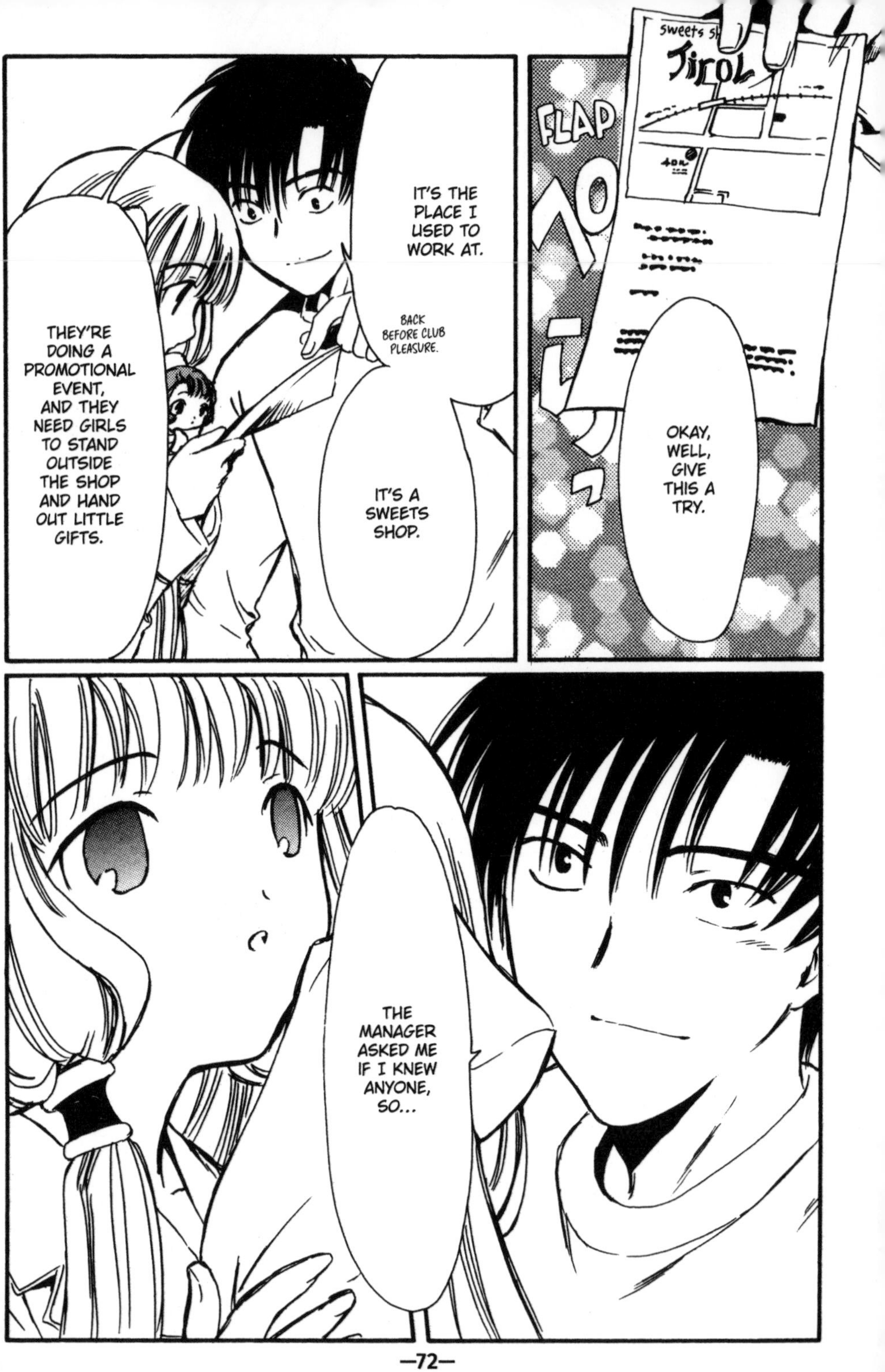
FLAP
OKAY, WELL, GIVE THIS A TRY.
IT'S THE PLACE I USED TO WORK AT.
BACK BEFORE CLUB PLEASURE.
IT'S A SWEETS SHOP.
THEY'RE DOING A PROMOTIONAL EVENT, AND THEY NEED GIRLS TO STAND OUTSIDE THE SHOP AND HAND OUT LITTLE GIFTS.
THE MANAGER ASKED ME IF I KNEW ANYONE, SO...

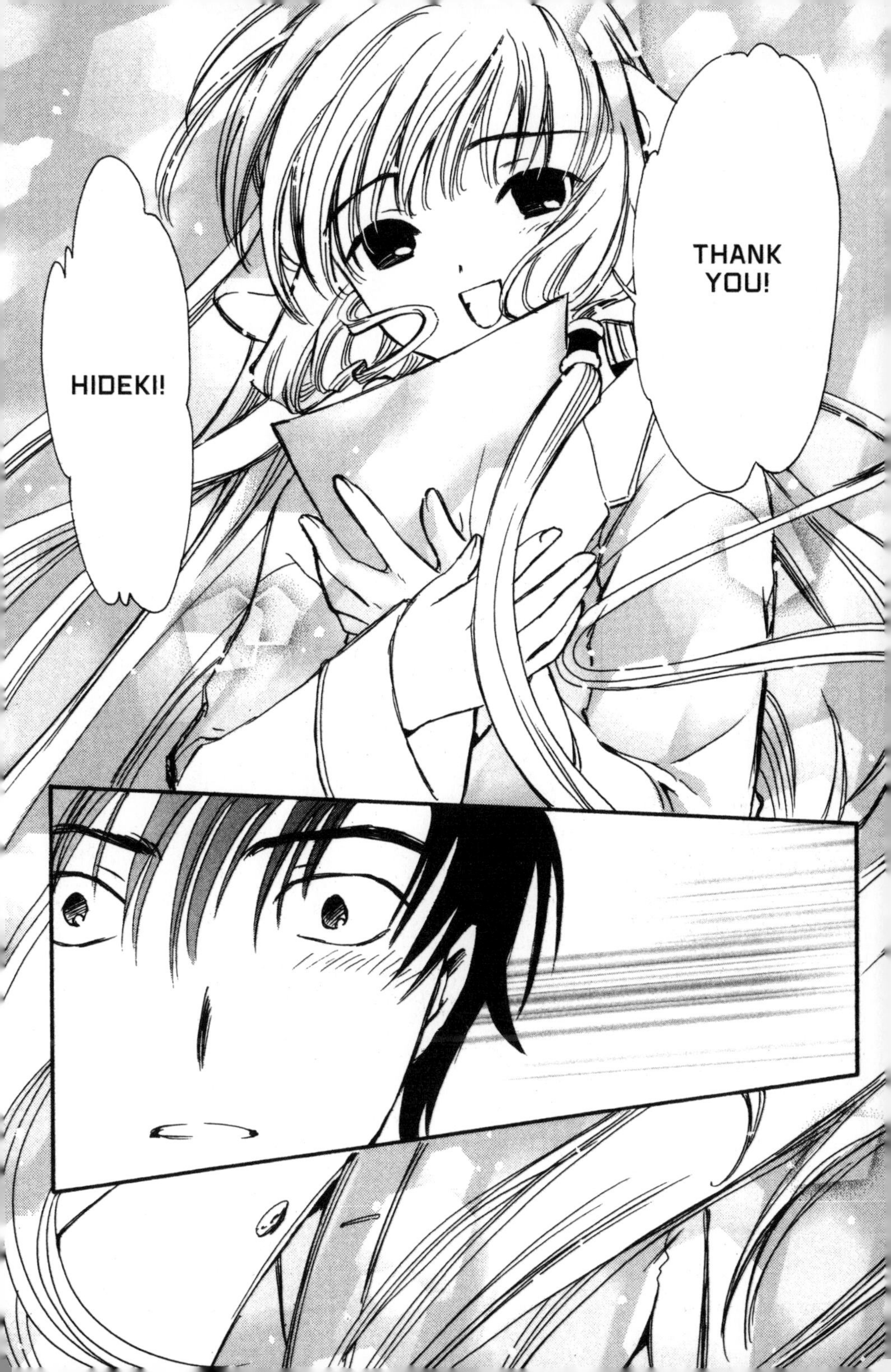
THANK YOU!
HIDEKI!

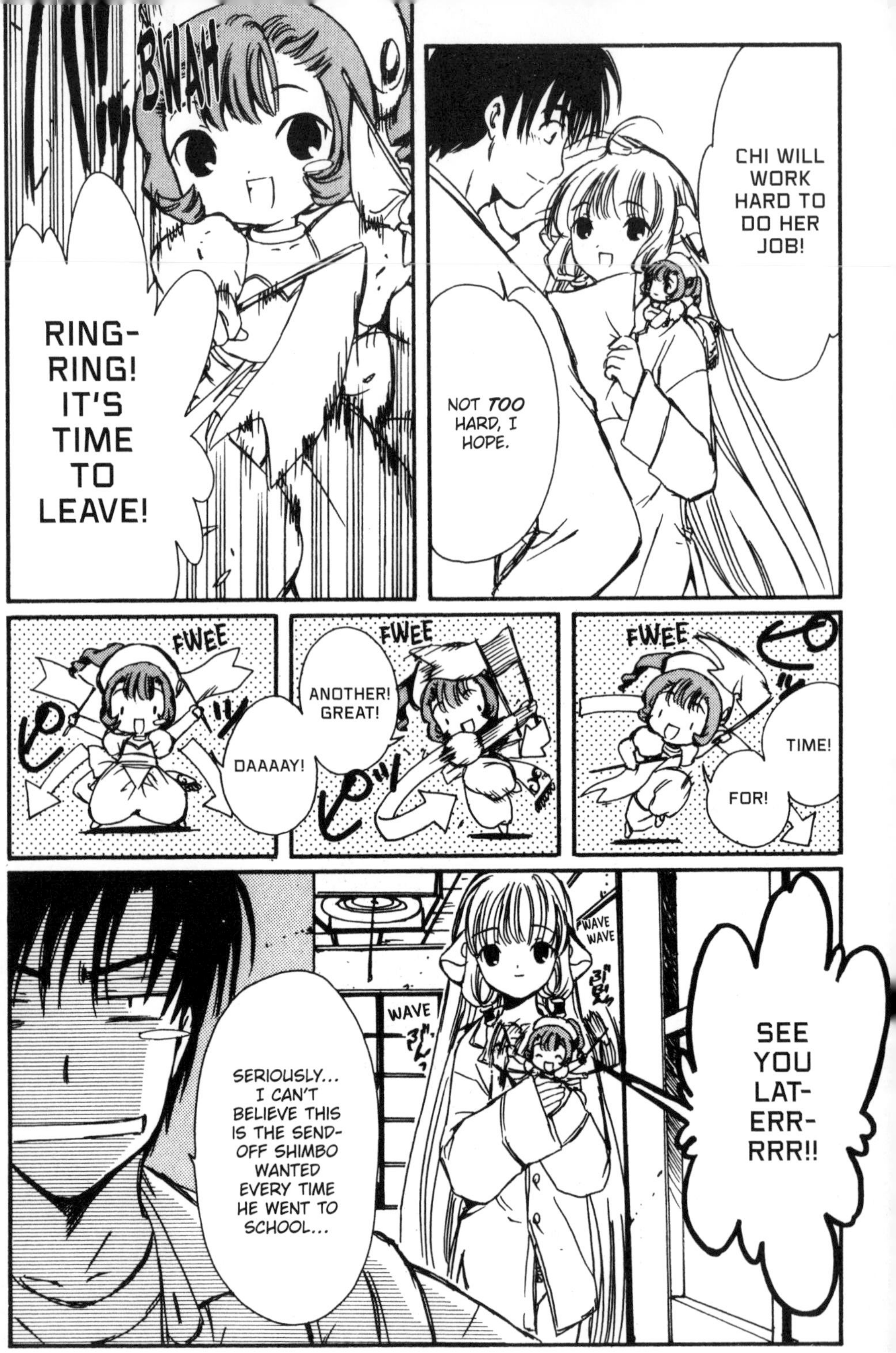
CHI WILL WORK HARD TO DO HER JOB!
NOT *TOO* HARD, I HOPE.
BWAH
RING-RING! IT'S TIME TO LEAVE!
FWEE
TIME!
FOR!
FWEE
ANOTHER! GREAT!
FWEE
DAAAAY!
SEE YOU LAT-ERR-RRR!!
WAVE WAVE
WAVE
SERIOUSLY... I CAN'T BELIEVE THIS IS THE SEND-OFF SHIMBO WANTED EVERY TIME HE WENT TO SCHOOL...

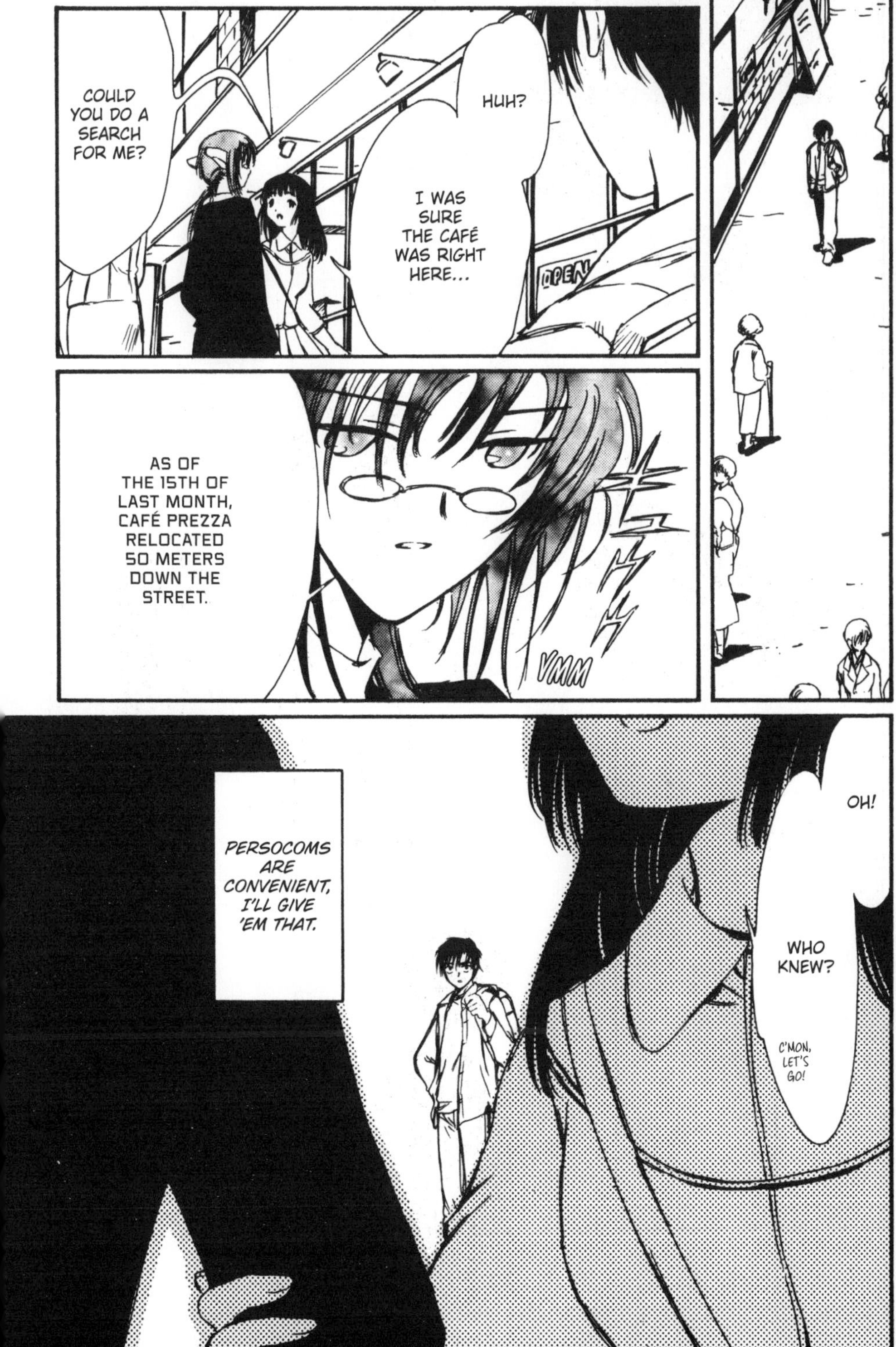
HUH?
I WAS SURE THE CAFÉ WAS RIGHT HERE...
COULD YOU DO A SEARCH FOR ME?
VMM
AS OF THE 15TH OF LAST MONTH, CAFÉ PREZZA RELOCATED 50 METERS DOWN THE STREET.
OH!
WHO KNEW?
C'MON, LET'S GO!
PERSOCOMS ARE CONVENIENT, I'LL GIVE 'EM THAT.

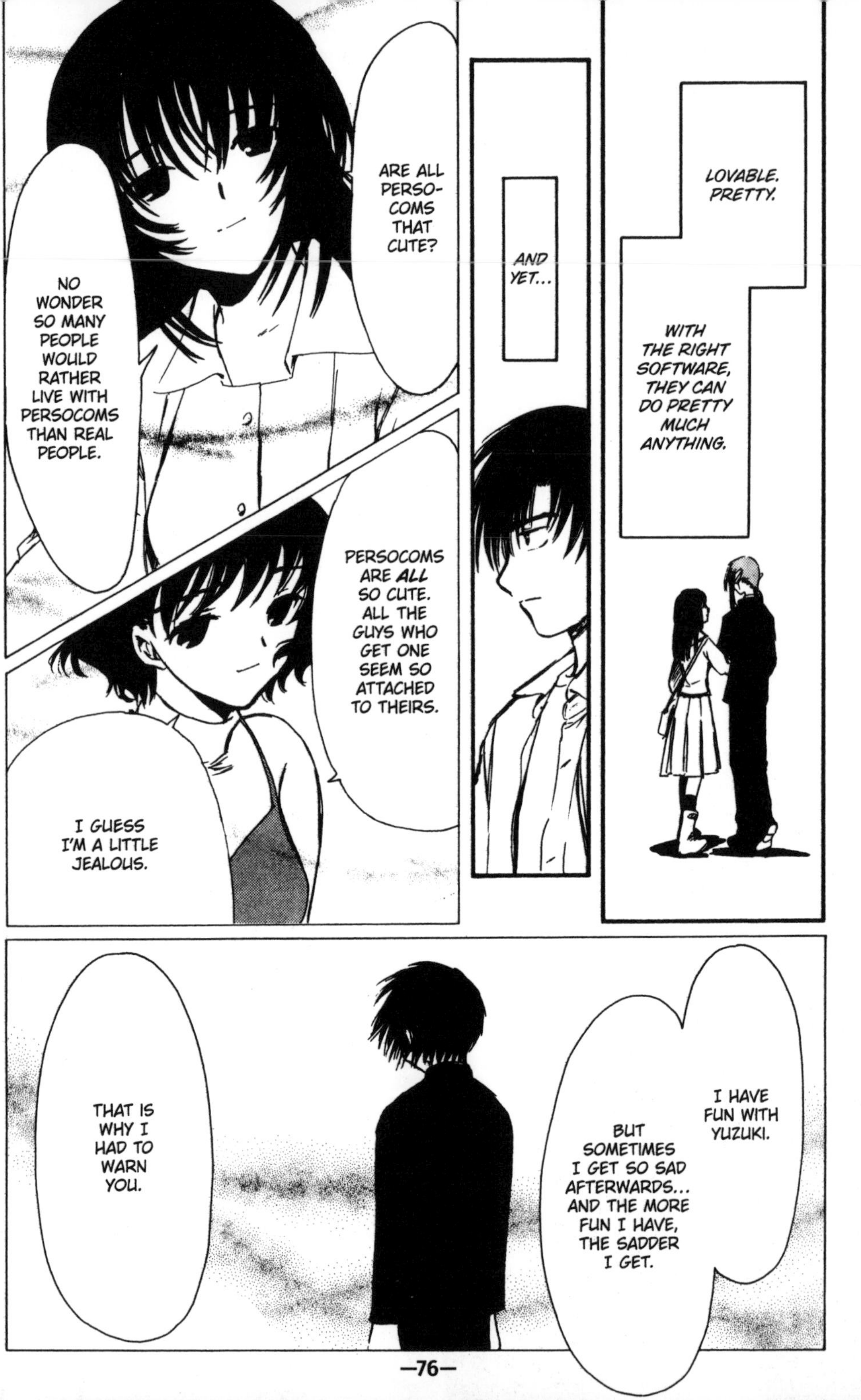
LOVABLE. PRETTY.
WITH THE RIGHT SOFTWARE, THEY CAN DO PRETTY MUCH ANYTHING.
AND YET...
ARE ALL PERSO-COMS THAT CUTE?
NO WONDER SO MANY PEOPLE WOULD RATHER LIVE WITH PERSOCOMS THAN REAL PEOPLE.
PERSOCOMS ARE *ALL* SO CUTE. ALL THE GUYS WHO GET ONE SEEM SO ATTACHED TO THEIRS.
I GUESS I'M A LITTLE JEALOUS.
I HAVE FUN WITH YUZUKI.
BUT SOMETIMES I GET SO SAD AFTERWARDS... AND THE MORE FUN I HAVE, THE SADDER I GET.
THAT IS WHY I HAD TO WARN YOU.

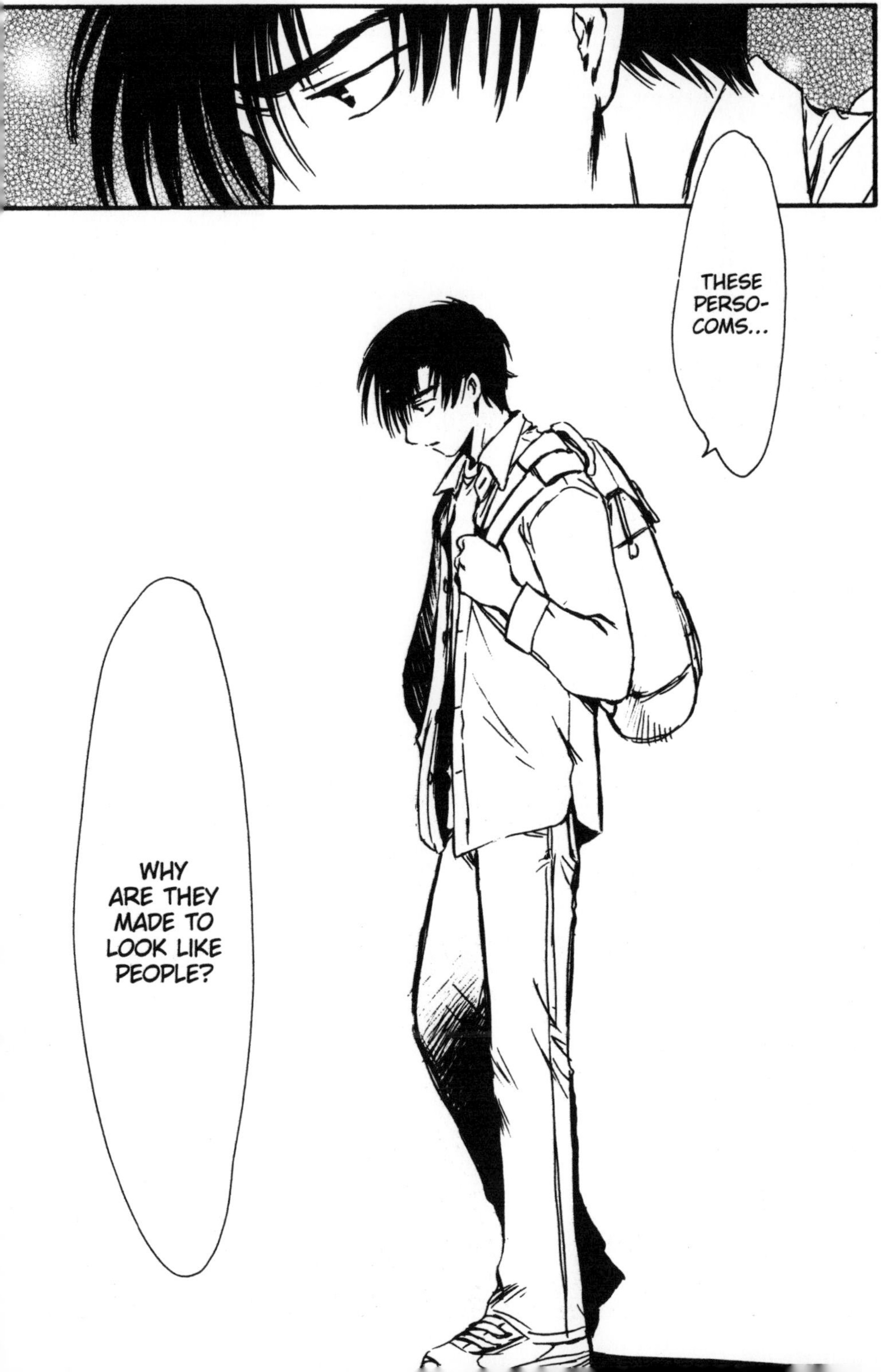
THESE PERSO-COMS...
WHY ARE THEY MADE TO LOOK LIKE PEOPLE?

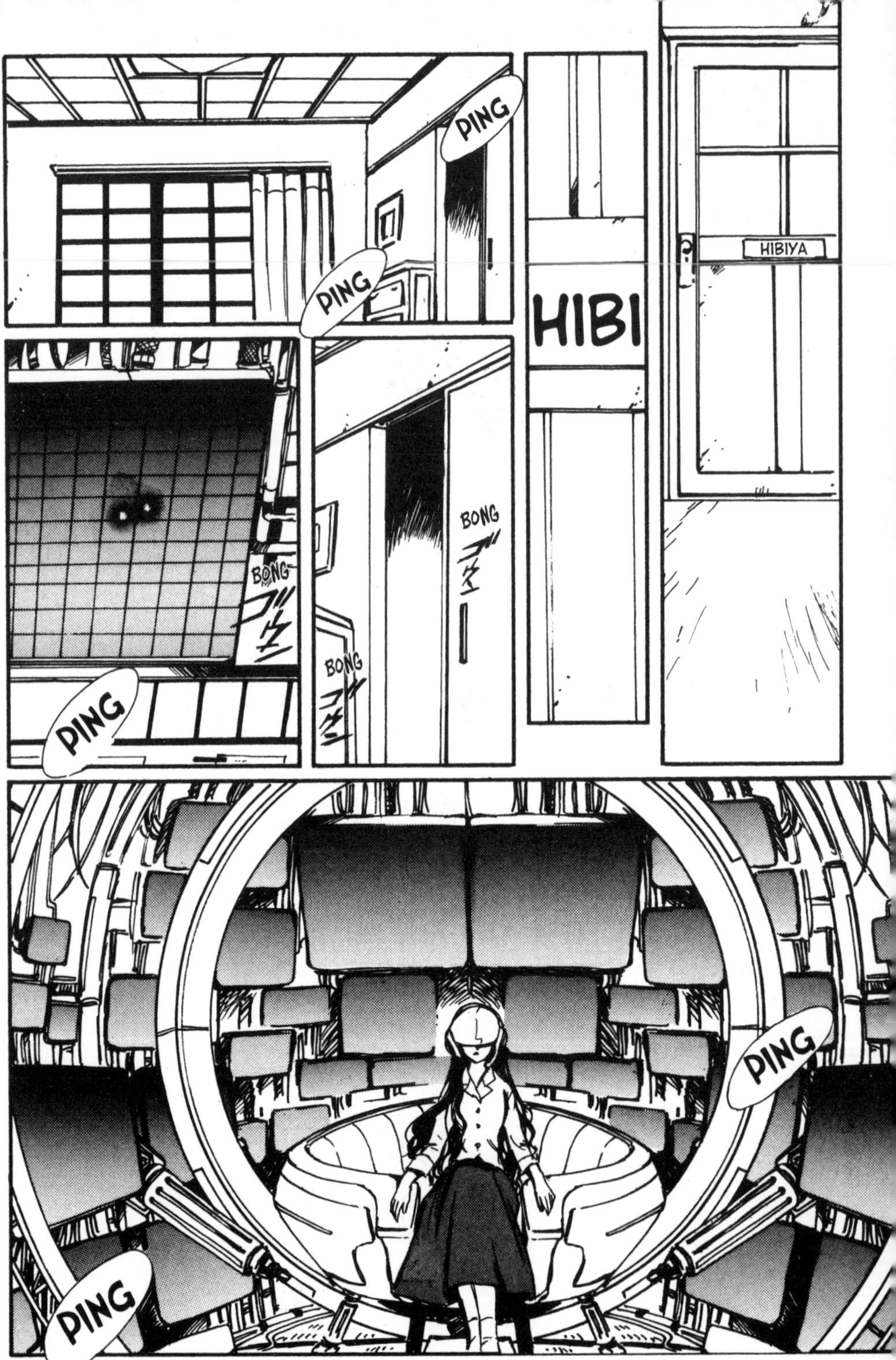

HIBIYA
HIBI
PING
PING
BONG
BONG
BONG
PING
PING
PING

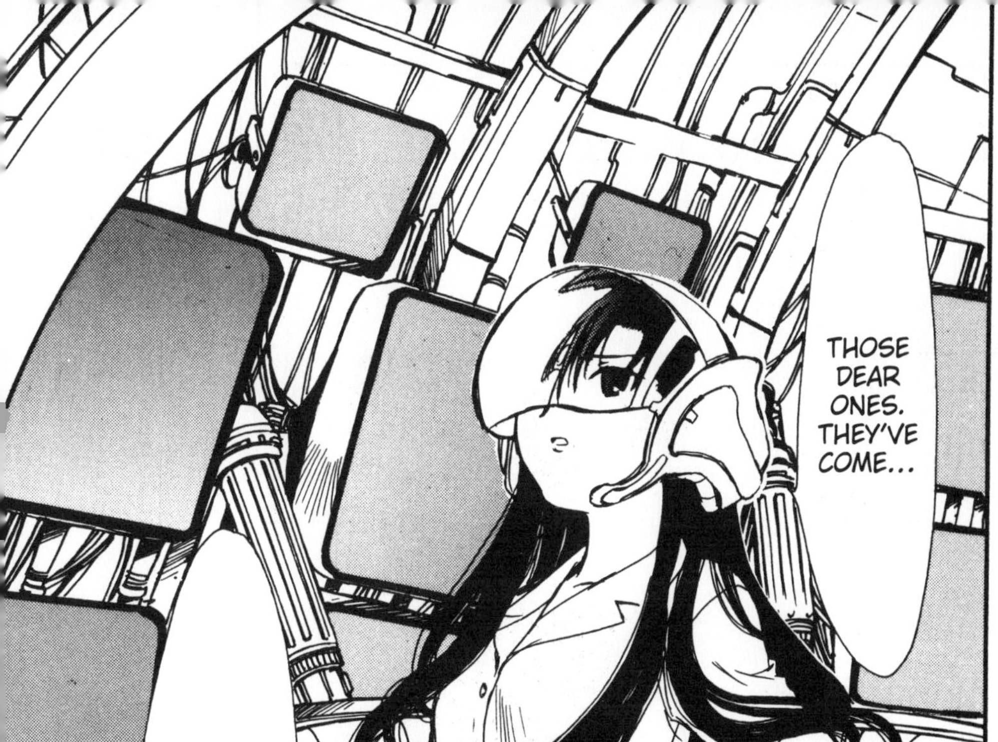
THOSE DEAR ONES. THEY'VE COME...
AS I KNEW THEY WOULD.

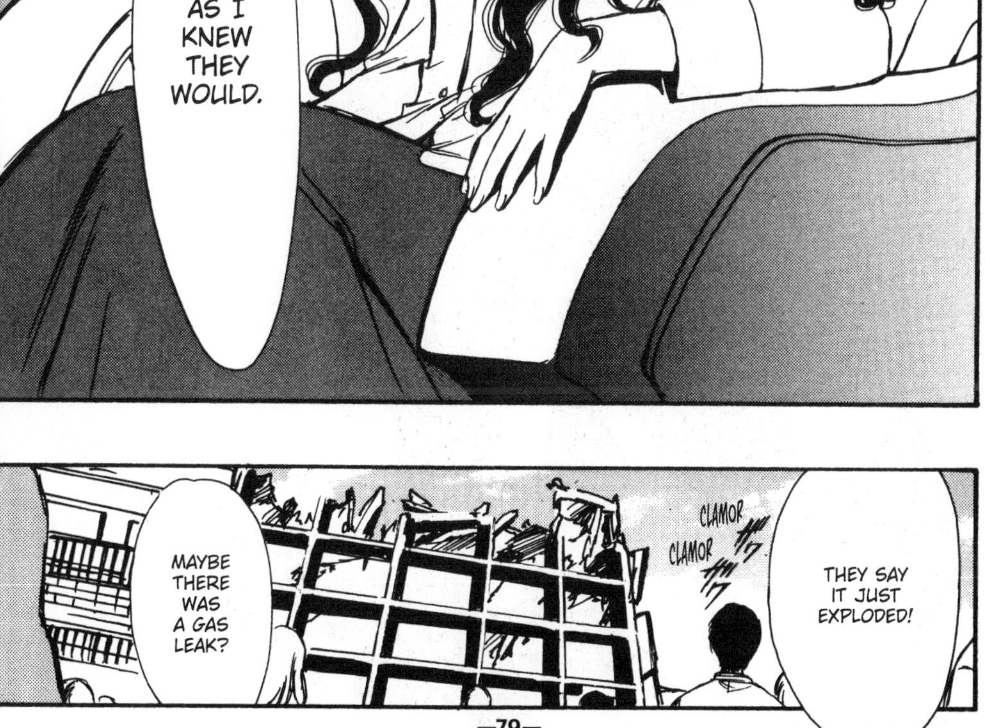
THEY SAY IT JUST EXPLODED!
CLAMOR
CLAMOR
MAYBE THERE WAS A GAS LEAK?

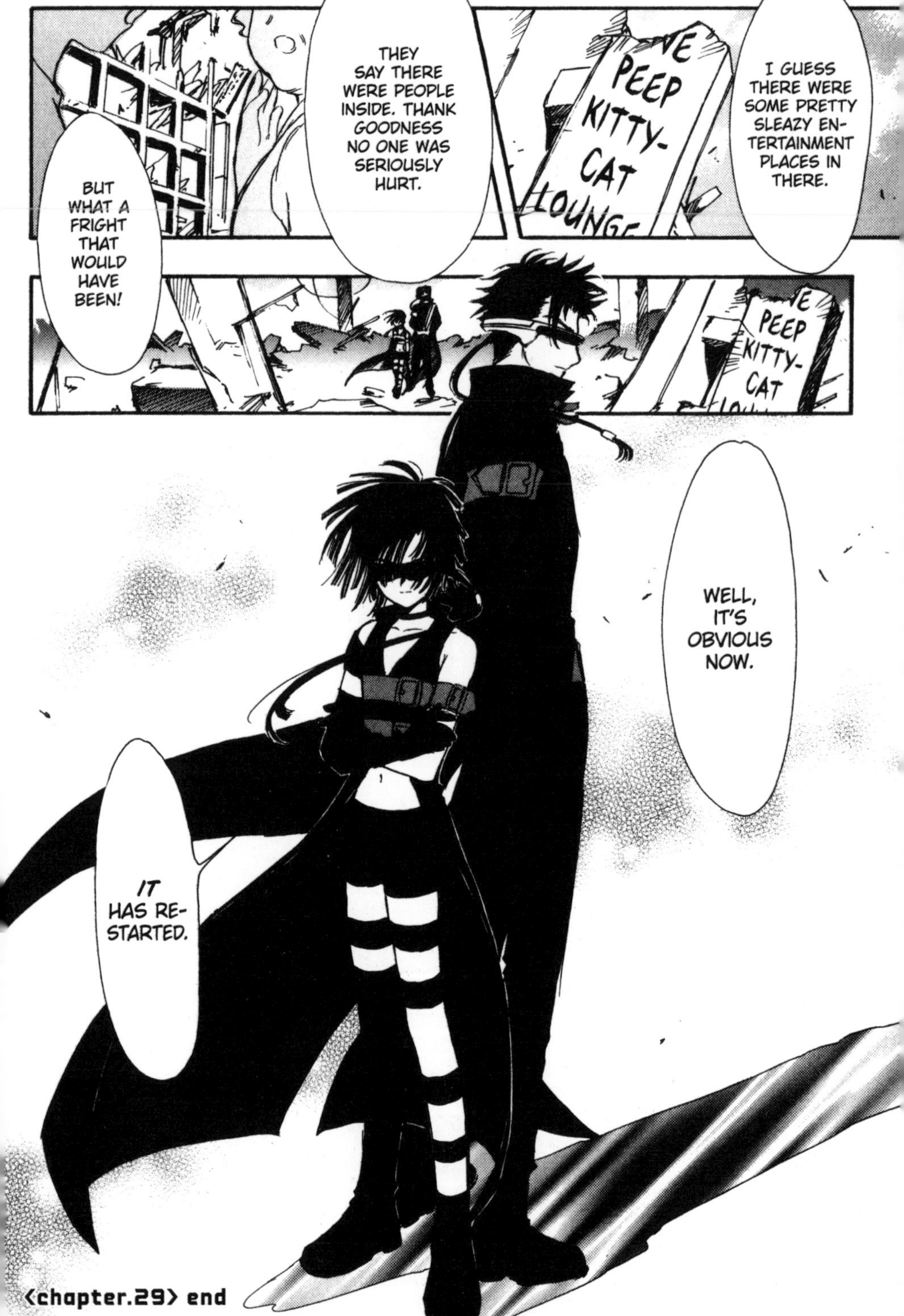
PEEP KITTY-CAT LOUNGE
I GUESS THERE WERE SOME PRETTY SLEAZY EN-TERTAINMENT PLACES IN THERE.
THEY SAY THERE WERE PEOPLE INSIDE. THANK GOODNESS NO ONE WAS SERIOUSLY HURT.
BUT WHAT A FRIGHT THAT WOULD HAVE BEEN!
WELL, IT'S OBVIOUS NOW.
IT HAS RE-STARTED.

<chapter.29> end

⟨chapter.30⟩

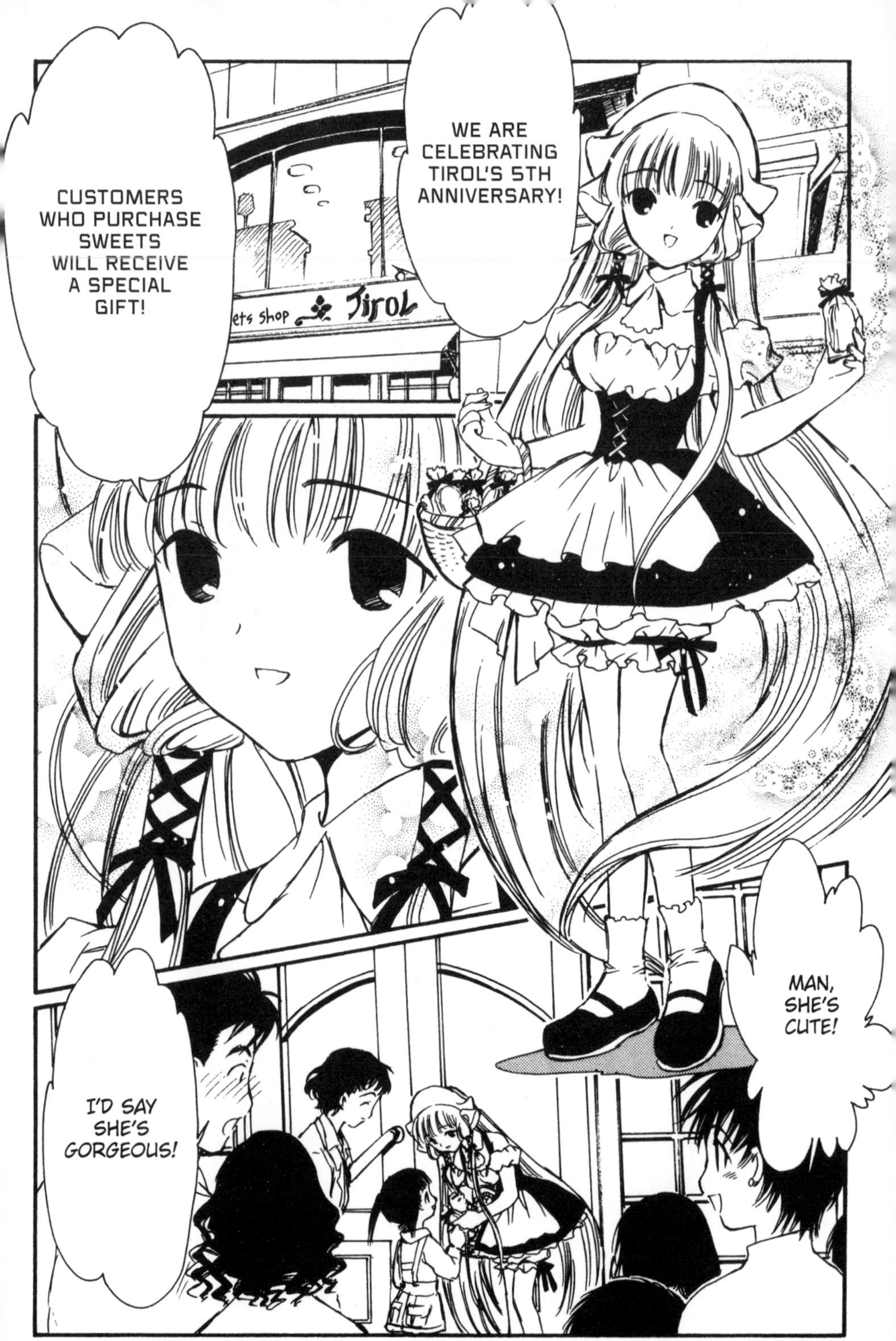
WE ARE CELEBRATING TIROL'S 5TH ANNIVERSARY!
CUSTOMERS WHO PURCHASE SWEETS WILL RECEIVE A SPECIAL GIFT!
Tirol
MAN, SHE'S CUTE!
I'D SAY SHE'S GORGEOUS!

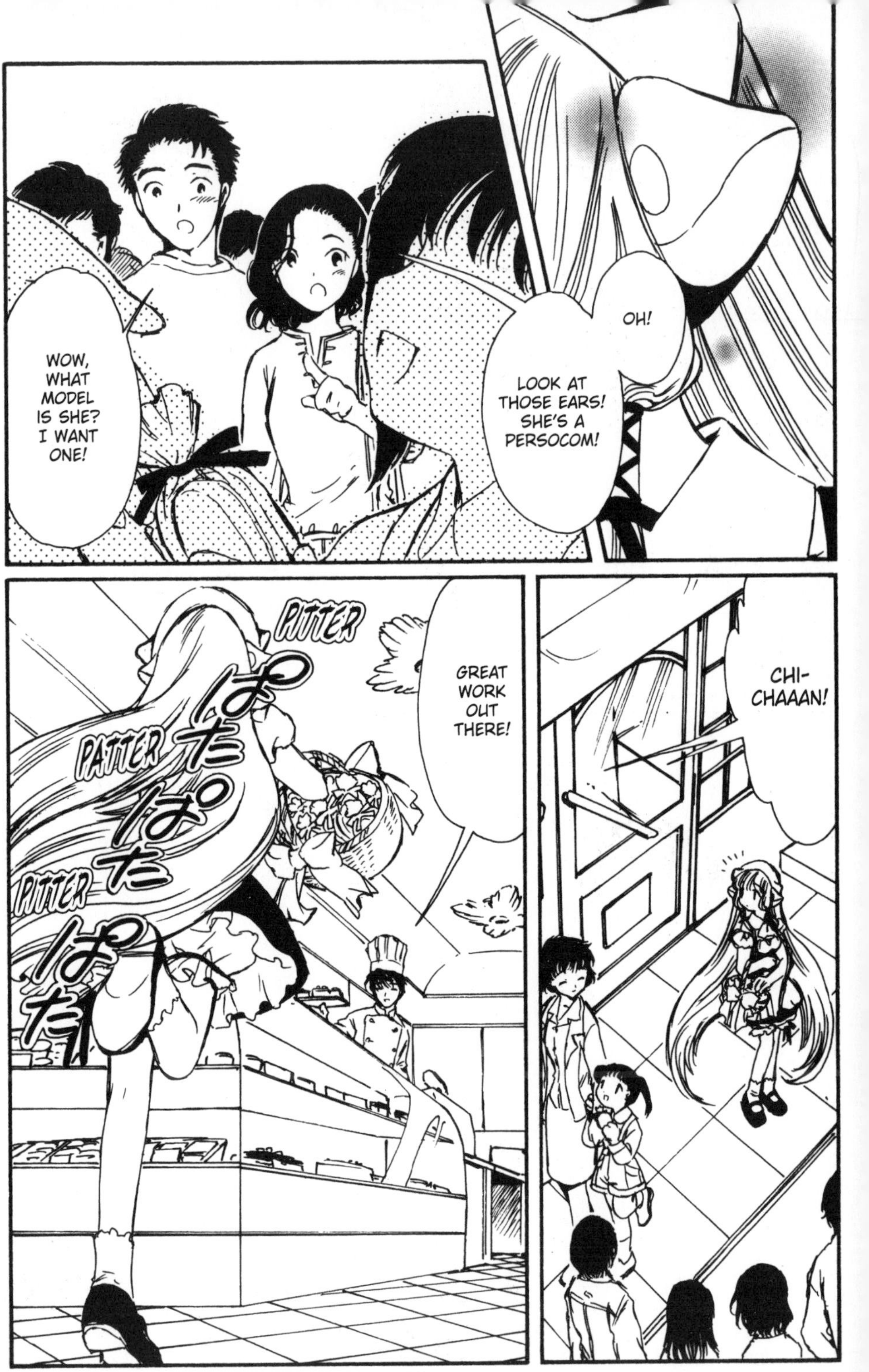
OH!
LOOK AT THOSE EARS! SHE'S A PERSOCOM!
WOW, WHAT MODEL IS SHE? I WANT ONE!
CHI-CHAAAN!
GREAT WORK OUT THERE!
PITTER
ぱたぱたぱた
PATTER
PITTER

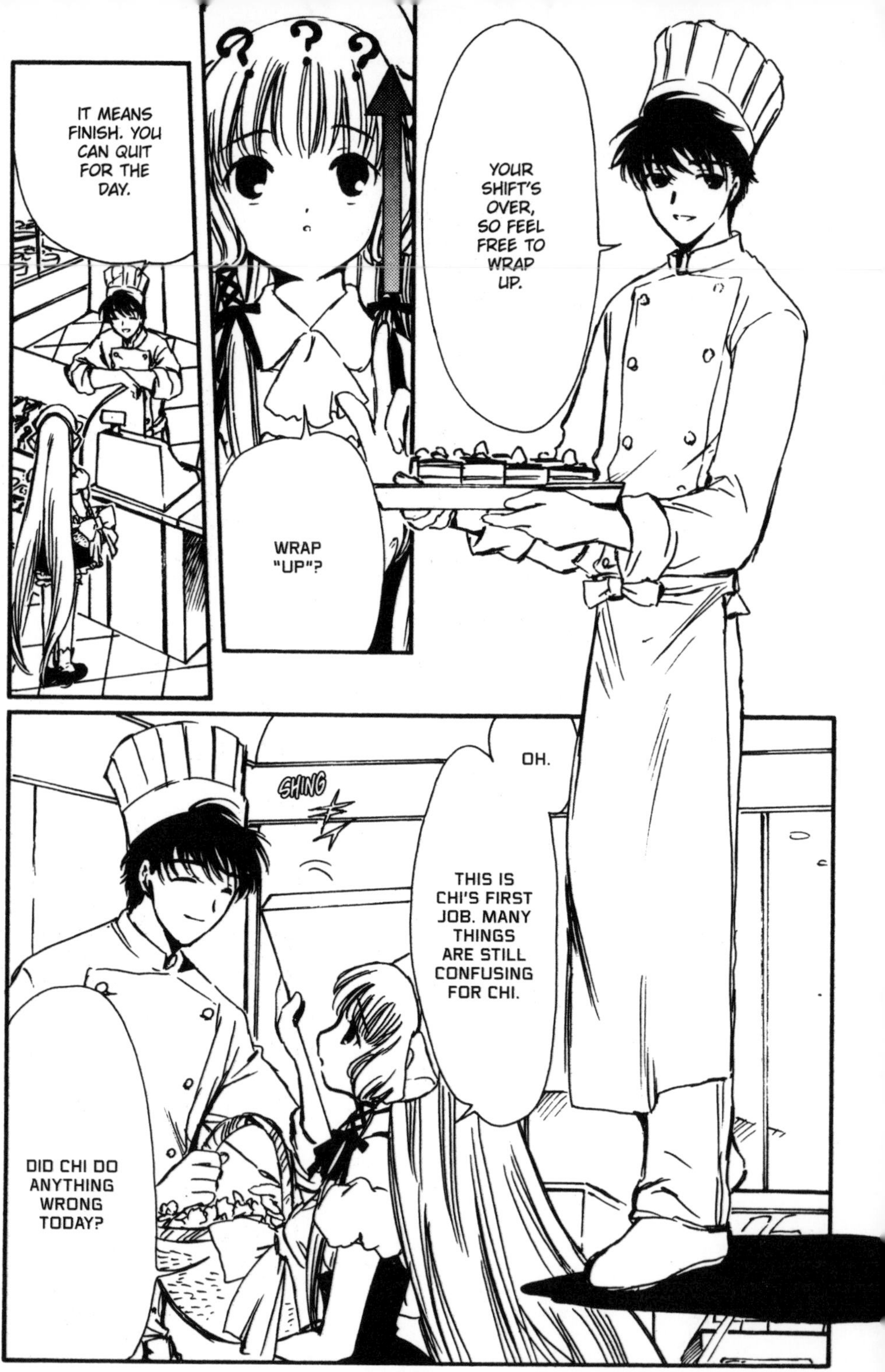
YOUR SHIFT'S OVER, SO FEEL FREE TO WRAP UP.
WRAP "UP"?
IT MEANS FINISH. YOU CAN QUIT FOR THE DAY.
OH.
THIS IS CHI'S FIRST JOB. MANY THINGS ARE STILL CONFUSING FOR CHI.
SHING
DID CHI DO ANYTHING WRONG TODAY?

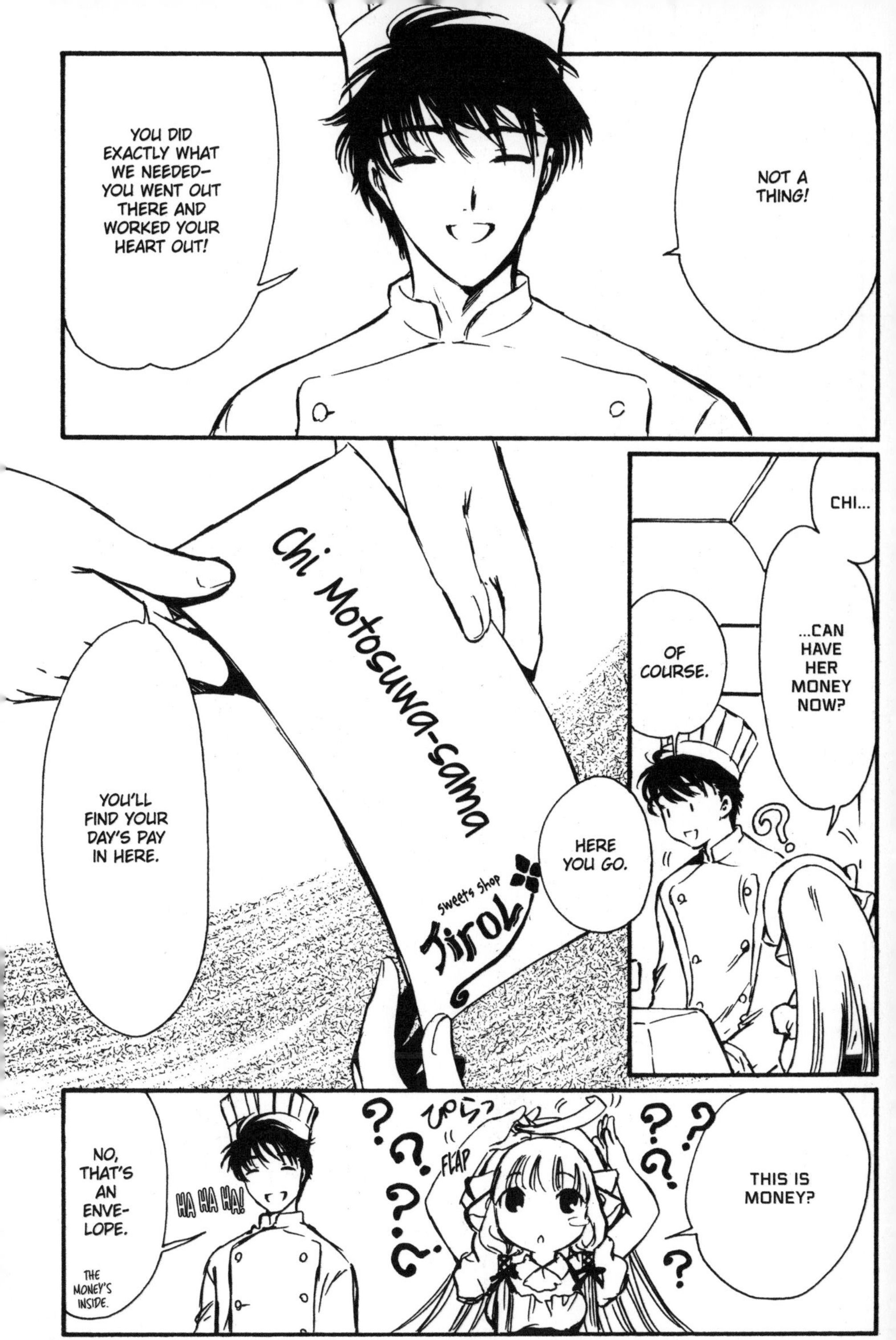
NOT A THING!
YOU DID EXACTLY WHAT WE NEEDED— YOU WENT OUT THERE AND WORKED YOUR HEART OUT!
CHI...
...CAN HAVE HER MONEY NOW?
OF COURSE.
HERE YOU GO.
Chi Motosuwa-sama
sweets shop Jirol
YOU'LL FIND YOUR DAY'S PAY IN HERE.
THIS IS MONEY?
ぴらっ
FLAP
HA HA HA!
NO, THAT'S AN ENVE-LOPE.
THE MONEY'S INSIDE.

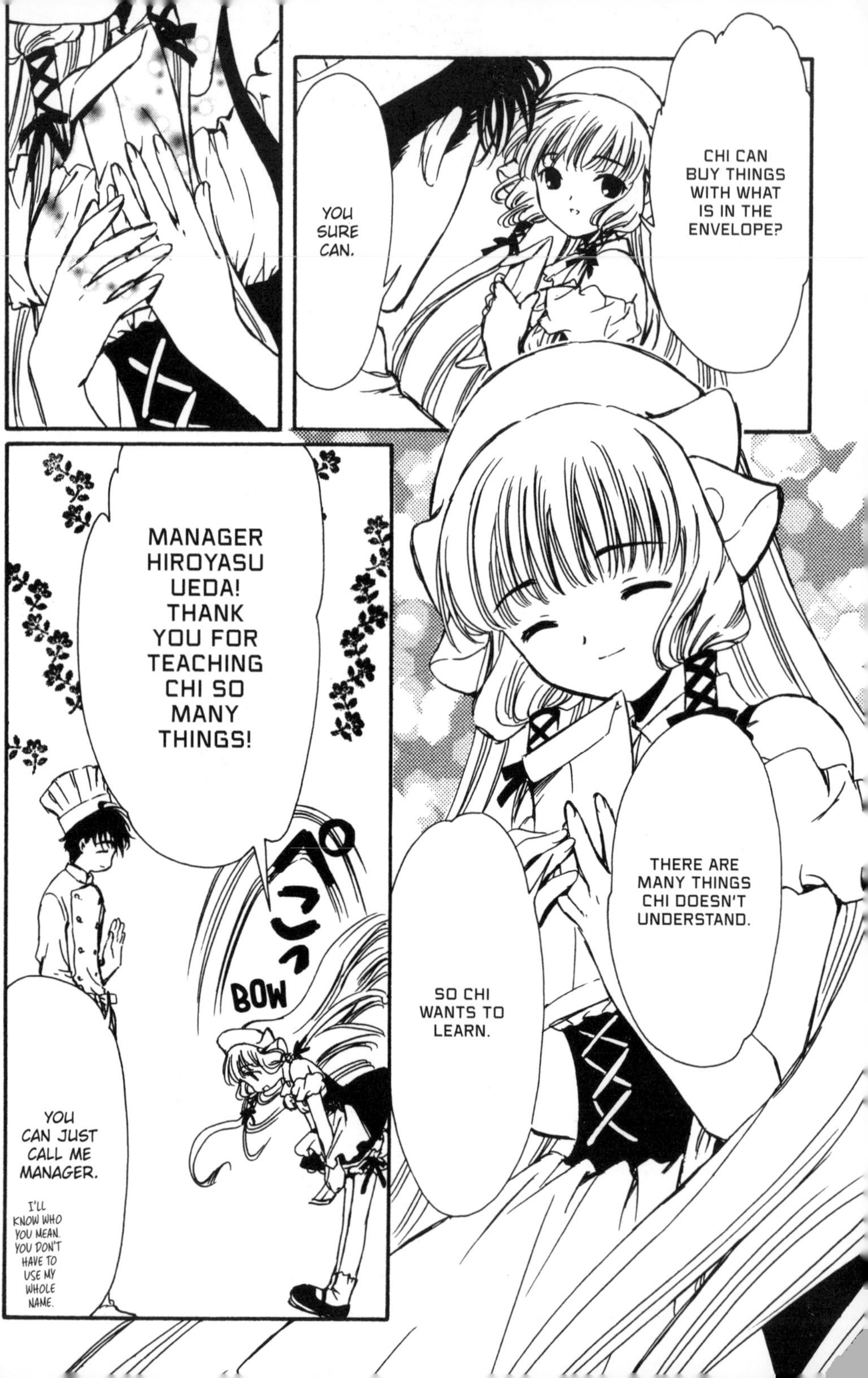
CHI CAN BUY THINGS WITH WHAT IS IN THE ENVELOPE?
YOU SURE CAN.
THERE ARE MANY THINGS CHI DOESN'T UNDERSTAND.
SO CHI WANTS TO LEARN.
MANAGER HIROYASU UEDA! THANK YOU FOR TEACHING CHI SO MANY THINGS!
BOW
YOU CAN JUST CALL ME MANAGER.
I'LL KNOW WHO YOU MEAN. YOU DON'T HAVE TO USE MY WHOLE NAME.

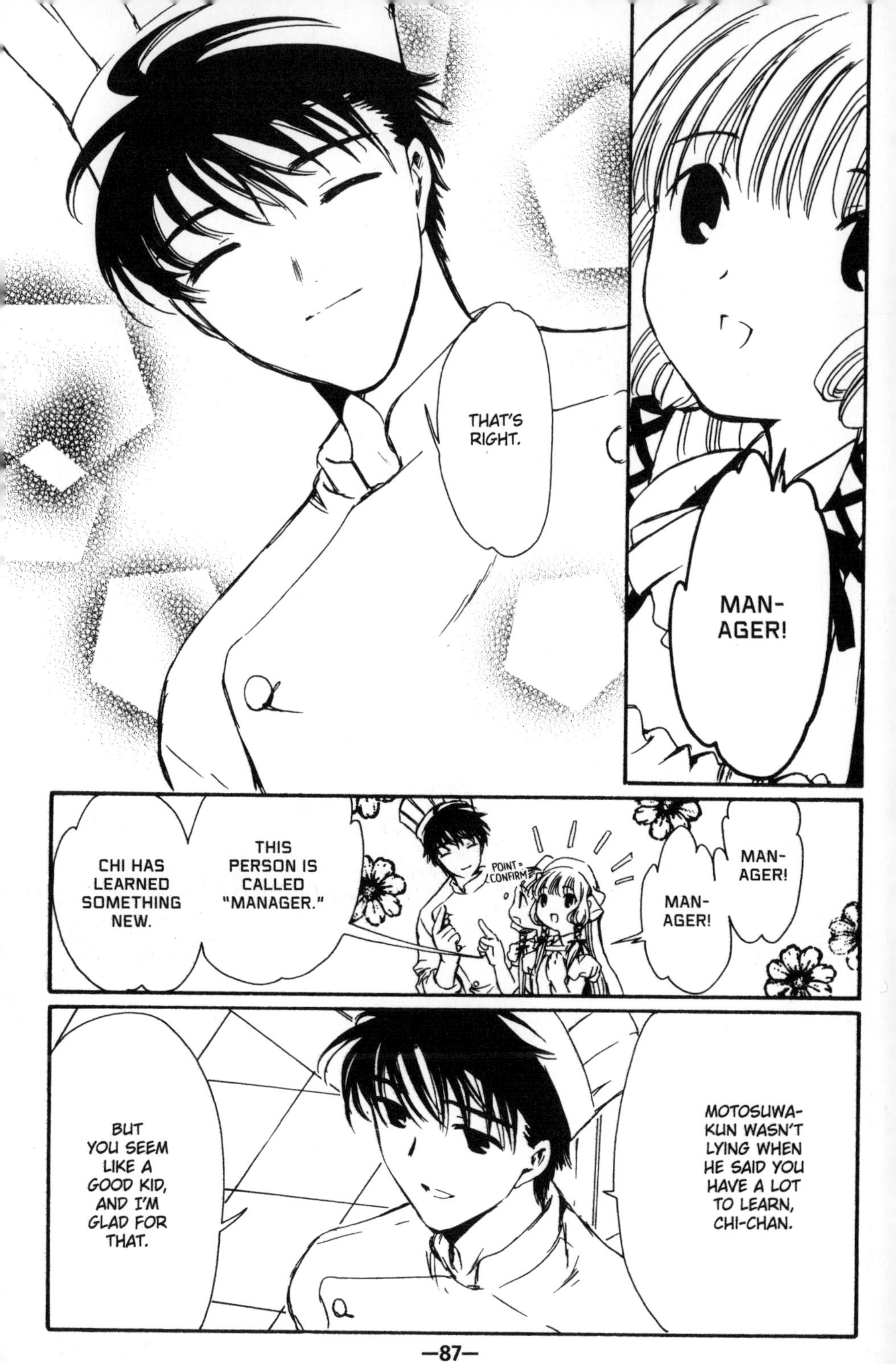
MAN-AGER!
THAT'S RIGHT.
MAN-AGER!
MAN-AGER!
POINT = CONFIRM
THIS PERSON IS CALLED "MANAGER."
CHI HAS LEARNED SOMETHING NEW.
MOTOSUWA-KUN WASN'T LYING WHEN HE SAID YOU HAVE A LOT TO LEARN, CHI-CHAN.
BUT YOU SEEM LIKE A GOOD KID, AND I'M GLAD FOR THAT.

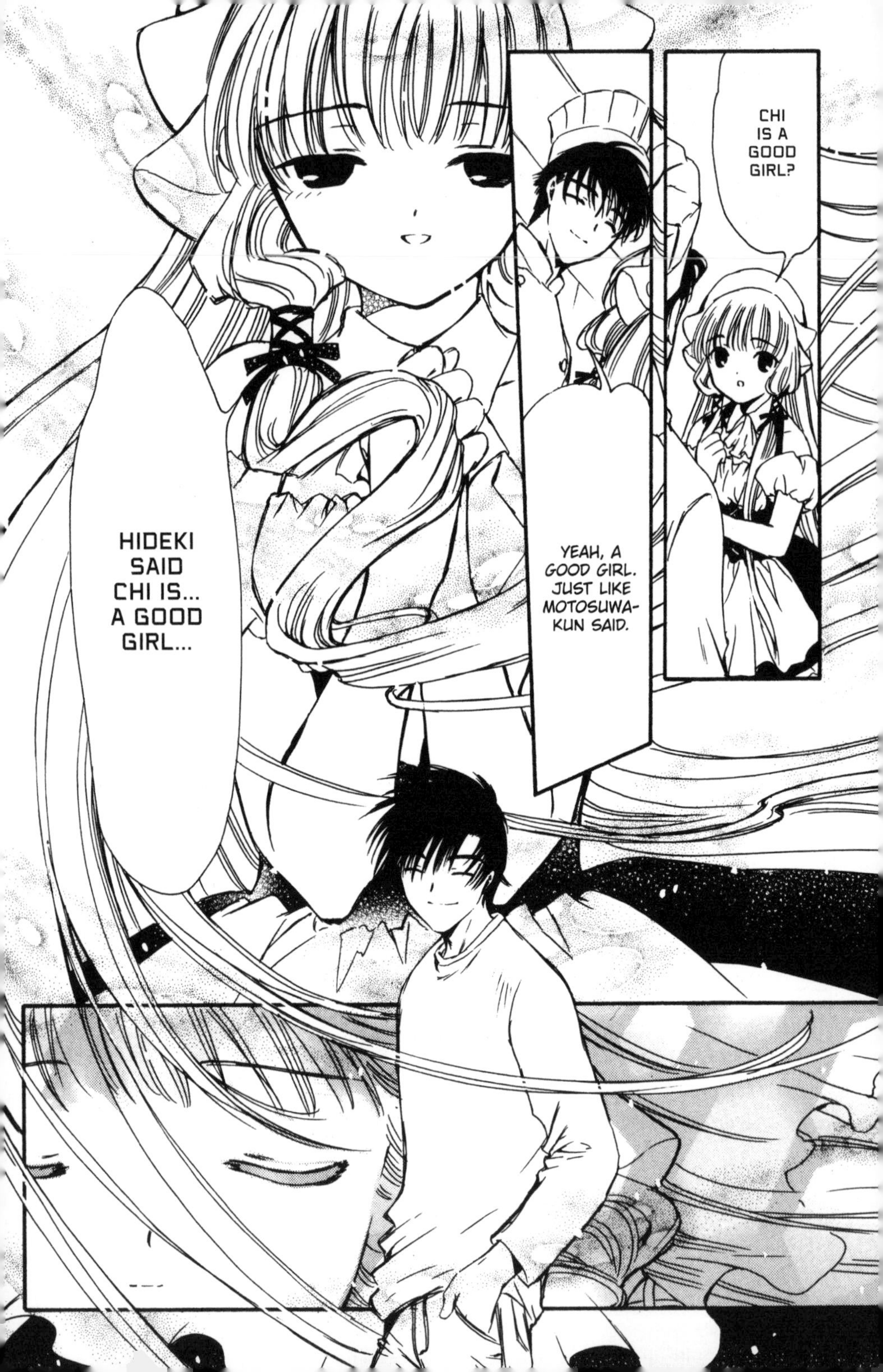
CHI IS A GOOD GIRL?
YEAH, A GOOD GIRL. JUST LIKE MOTOSUWA-KUN SAID.
HIDEKI SAID CHI IS... A GOOD GIRL...

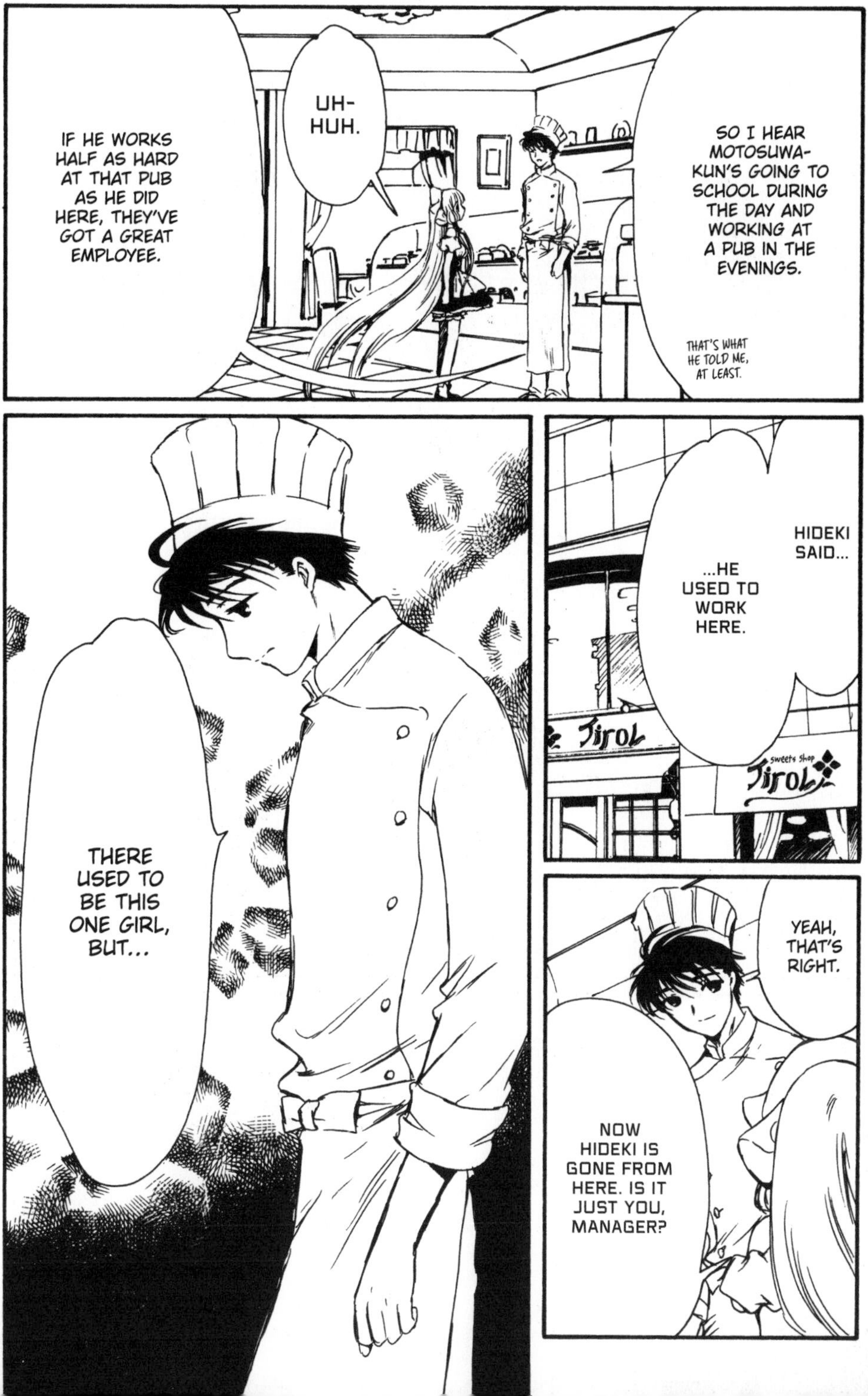
SO I HEAR MOTOSUWA-KUN'S GOING TO SCHOOL DURING THE DAY AND WORKING AT A PUB IN THE EVENINGS.
THAT'S WHAT HE TOLD ME, AT LEAST.
UH-HUH.
IF HE WORKS HALF AS HARD AT THAT PUB AS HE DID HERE, THEY'VE GOT A GREAT EMPLOYEE.
HIDEKI SAID...
...HE USED TO WORK HERE.
Jirol
sweets shop
Jirol
YEAH, THAT'S RIGHT.
NOW HIDEKI IS GONE FROM HERE. IS IT JUST YOU, MANAGER?
THERE USED TO BE THIS ONE GIRL, BUT...

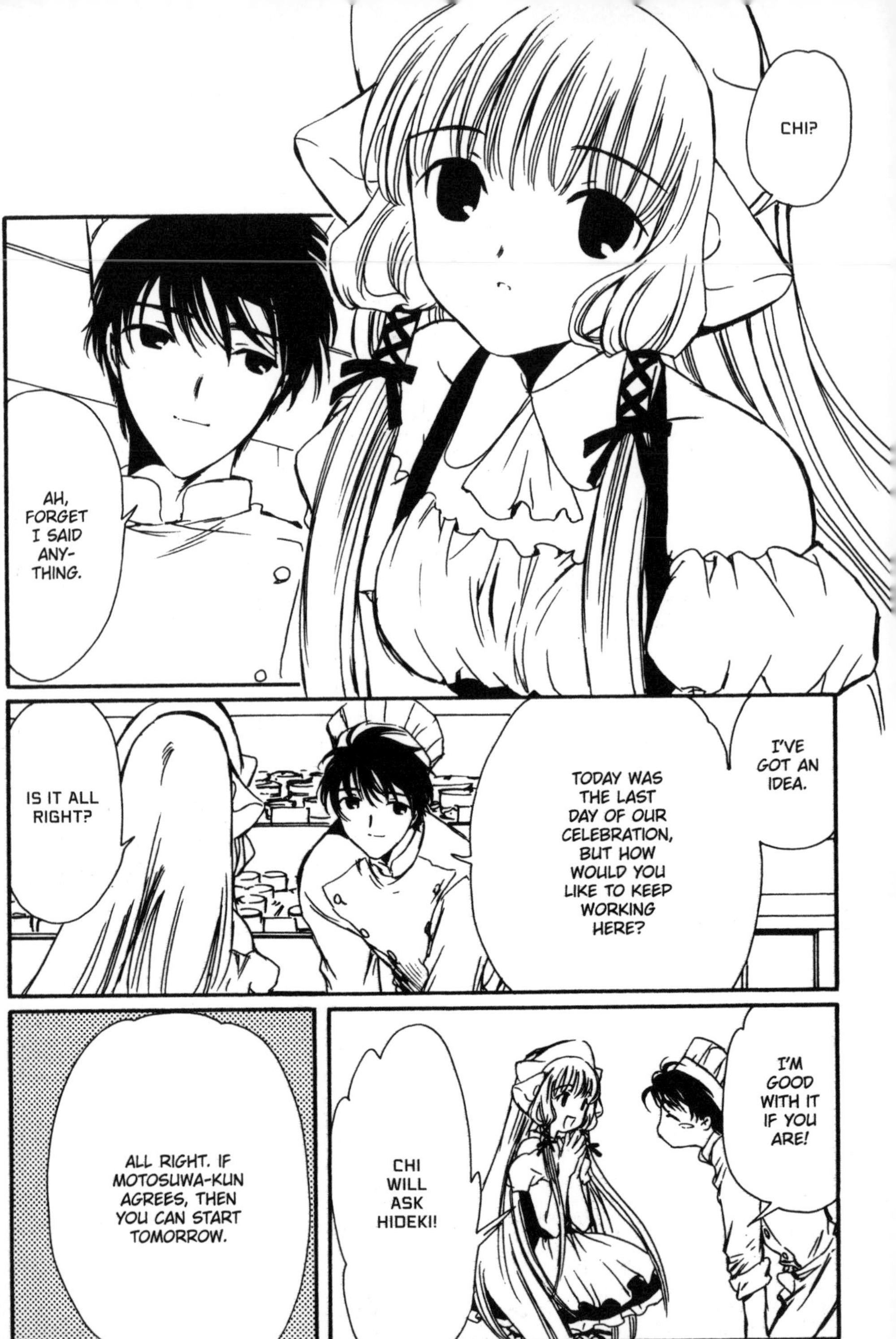
CHI?
AH, FORGET I SAID ANY-THING.
I'VE GOT AN IDEA.
TODAY WAS THE LAST DAY OF OUR CELEBRATION, BUT HOW WOULD YOU LIKE TO KEEP WORKING HERE?
IS IT ALL RIGHT?
I'M GOOD WITH IT IF YOU ARE!
CHI WILL ASK HIDEKI!
ALL RIGHT. IF MOTOSUWA-KUN AGREES, THEN YOU CAN START TOMORROW.

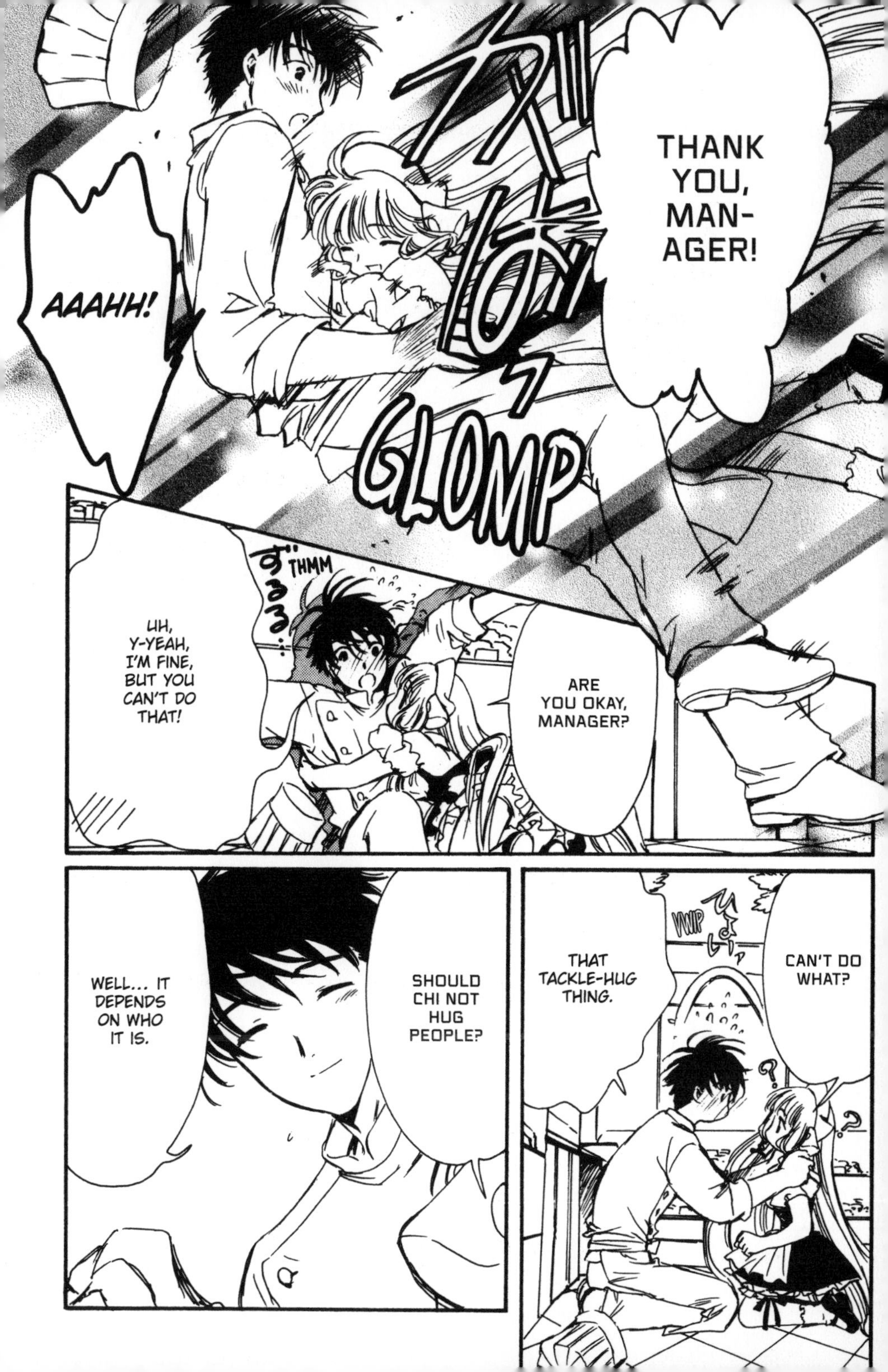
THANK YOU, MANAGER!
GLOMP
AAAHH!
ARE YOU OKAY, MANAGER?
THMM
UH, Y-YEAH, I'M FINE, BUT YOU CAN'T DO THAT!
CAN'T DO WHAT?
VWIP
THAT TACKLE-HUG THING.
SHOULD CHI NOT HUG PEOPLE?
WELL... IT DEPENDS ON WHO IT IS.

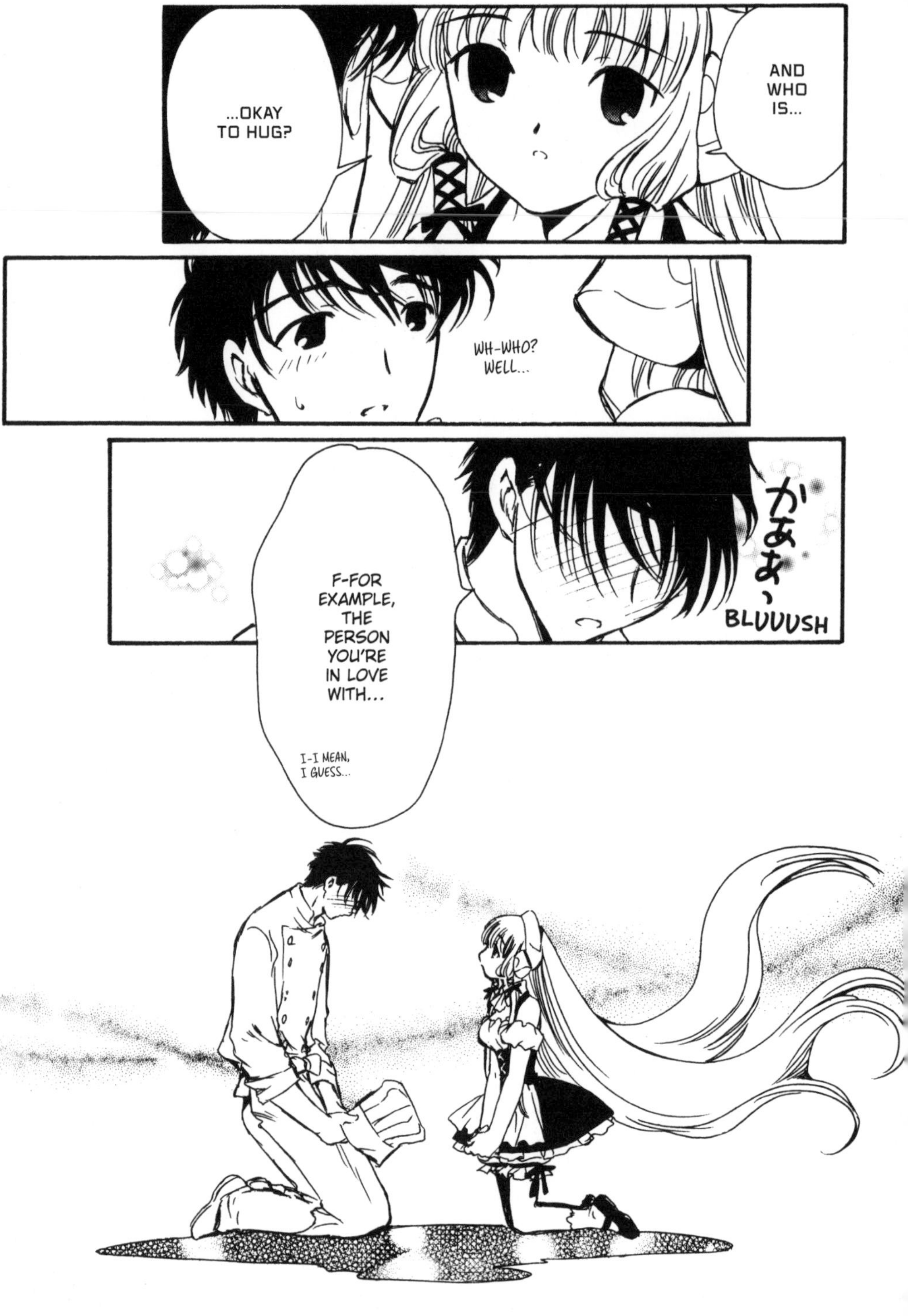
AND WHO IS...
...OKAY TO HUG?
WH-WHO? WELL...
かあぁ
BLUUUSH
F-FOR EXAMPLE, THE PERSON YOU'RE IN LOVE WITH...
I-I MEAN, I GUESS...

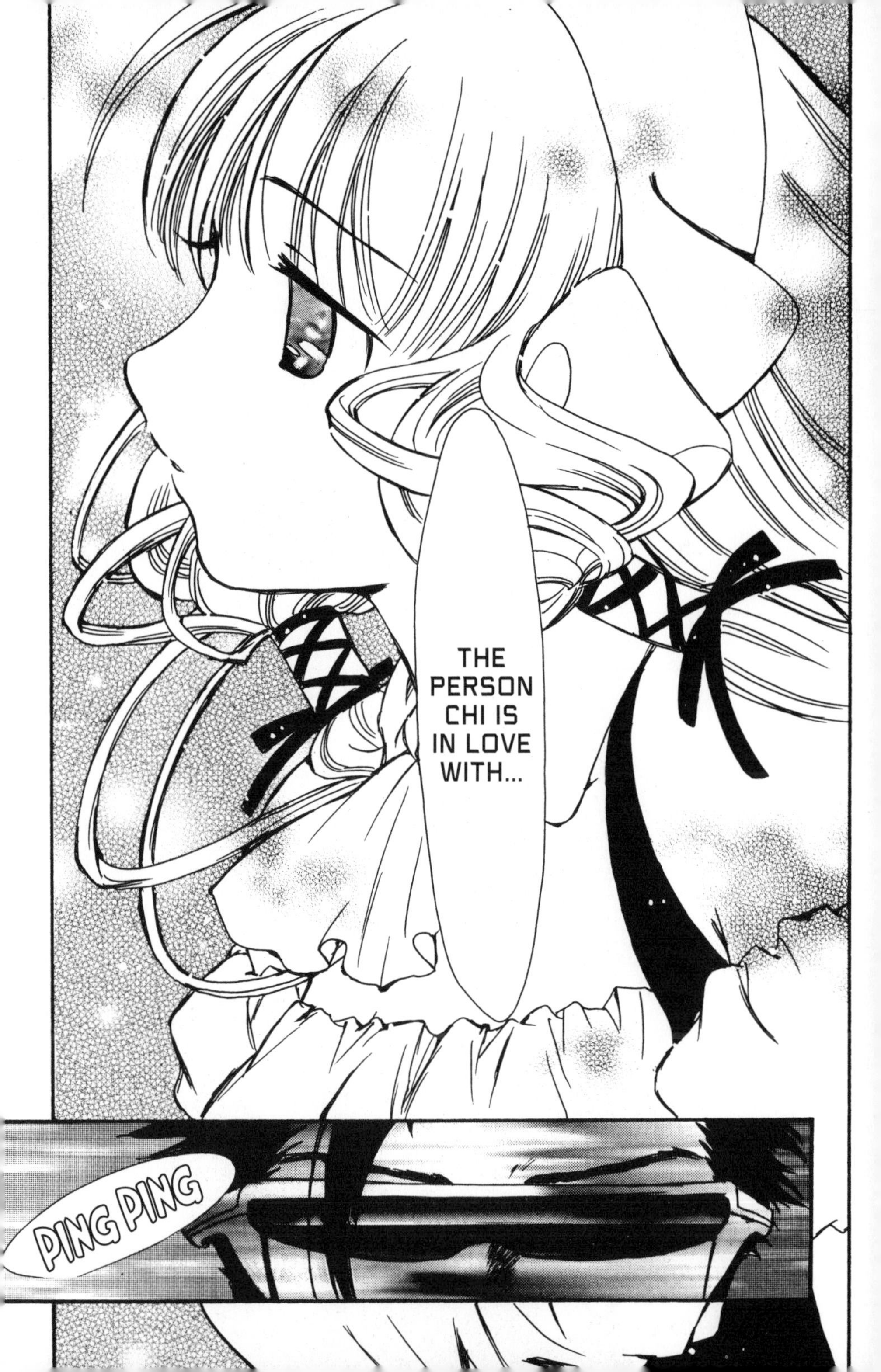
THE PERSON CHI IS IN LOVE WITH...
PING PING

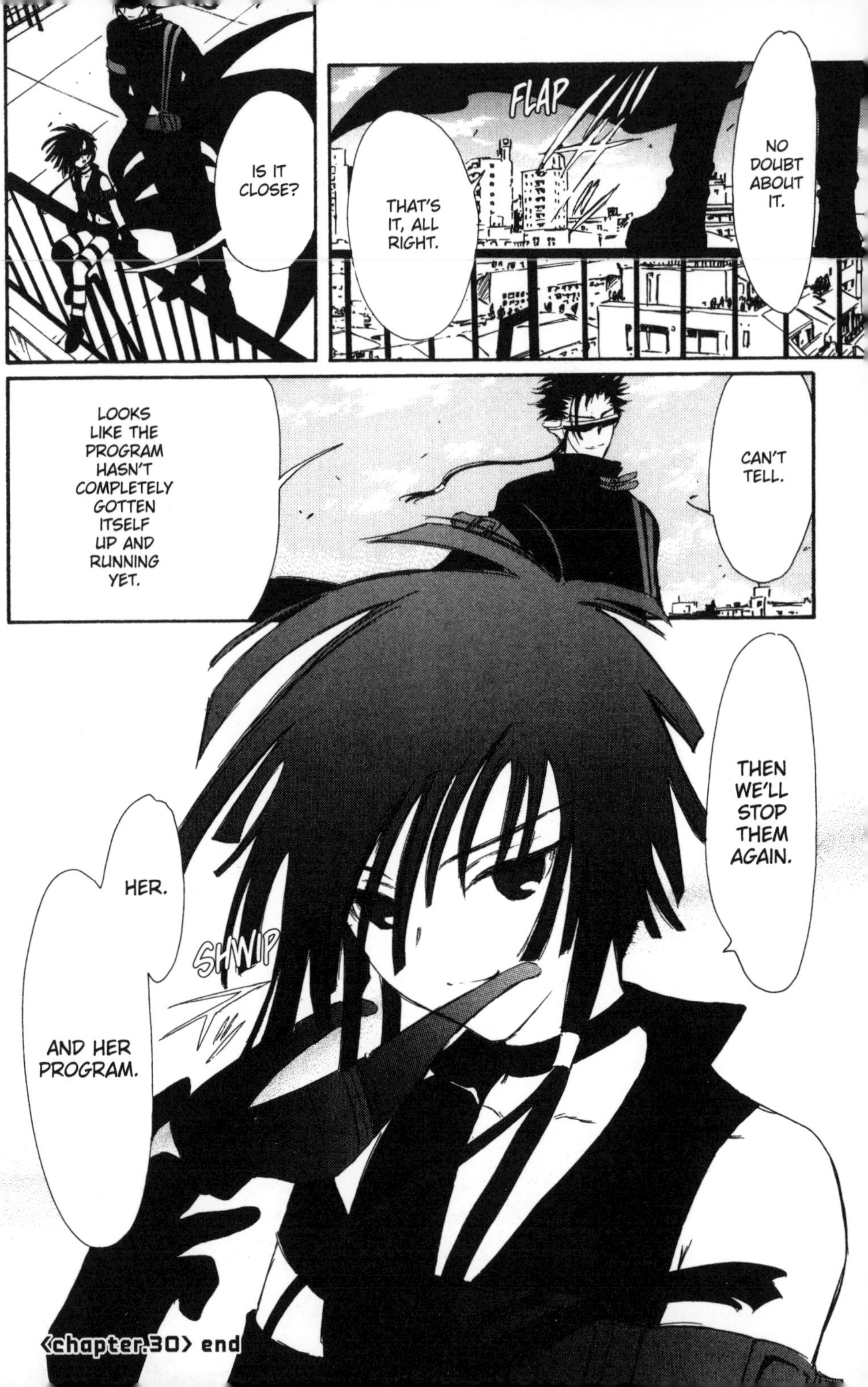
NO DOUBT ABOUT IT.
FLAP
THAT'S IT, ALL RIGHT.
IS IT CLOSE?
CAN'T TELL.
LOOKS LIKE THE PROGRAM HASN'T COMPLETELY GOTTEN ITSELF UP AND RUNNING YET.
THEN WE'LL STOP THEM AGAIN.
HER.
SHWIP
AND HER PROGRAM.
<chapter.30> end

⟨chapter.31⟩

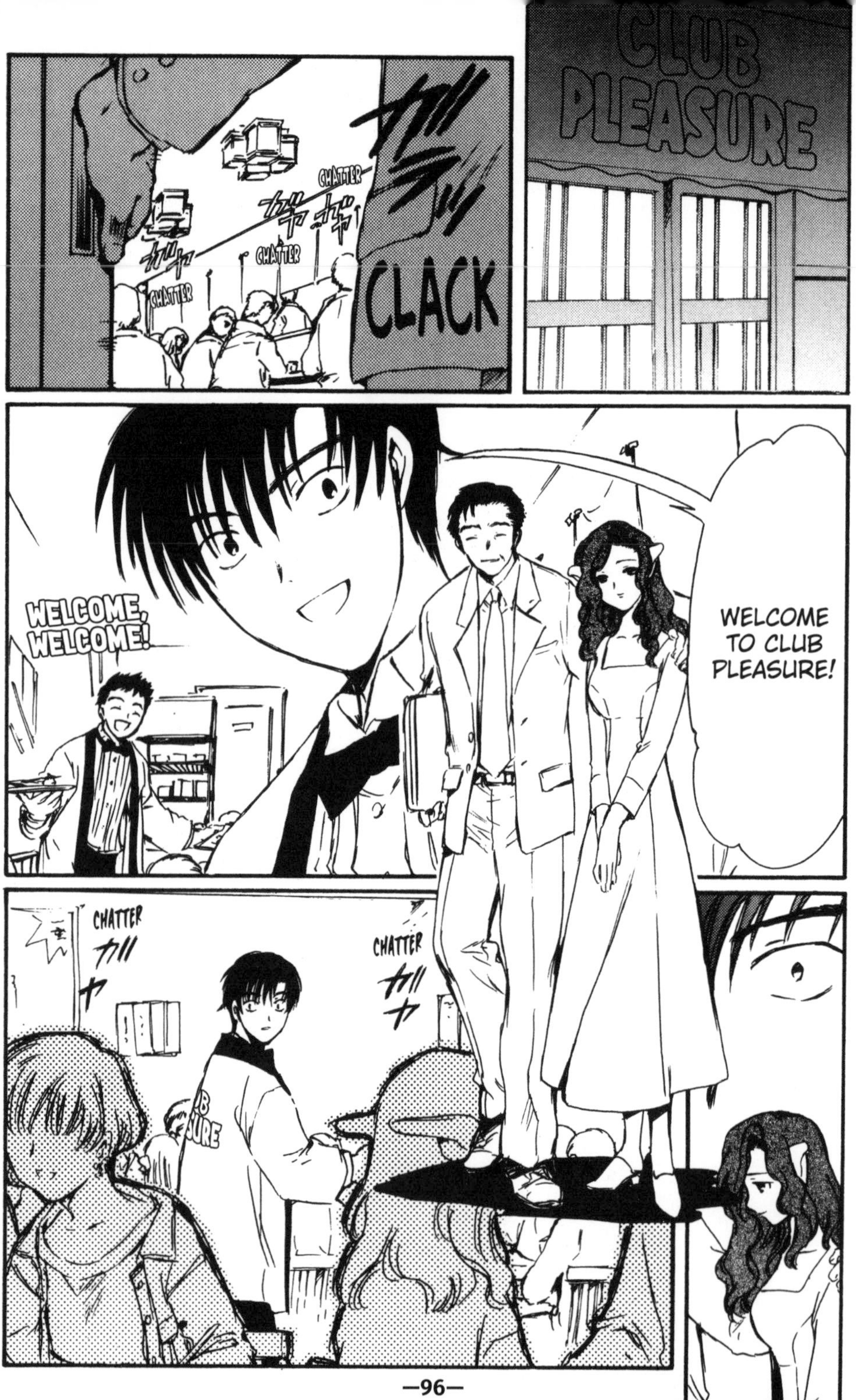
CLUB
PLEASURE
CLACK
CHATTER
CHATTER
CHATTER
WELCOME TO CLUB PLEASURE!
WELCOME, WELCOME!
CHATTER
CHATTER

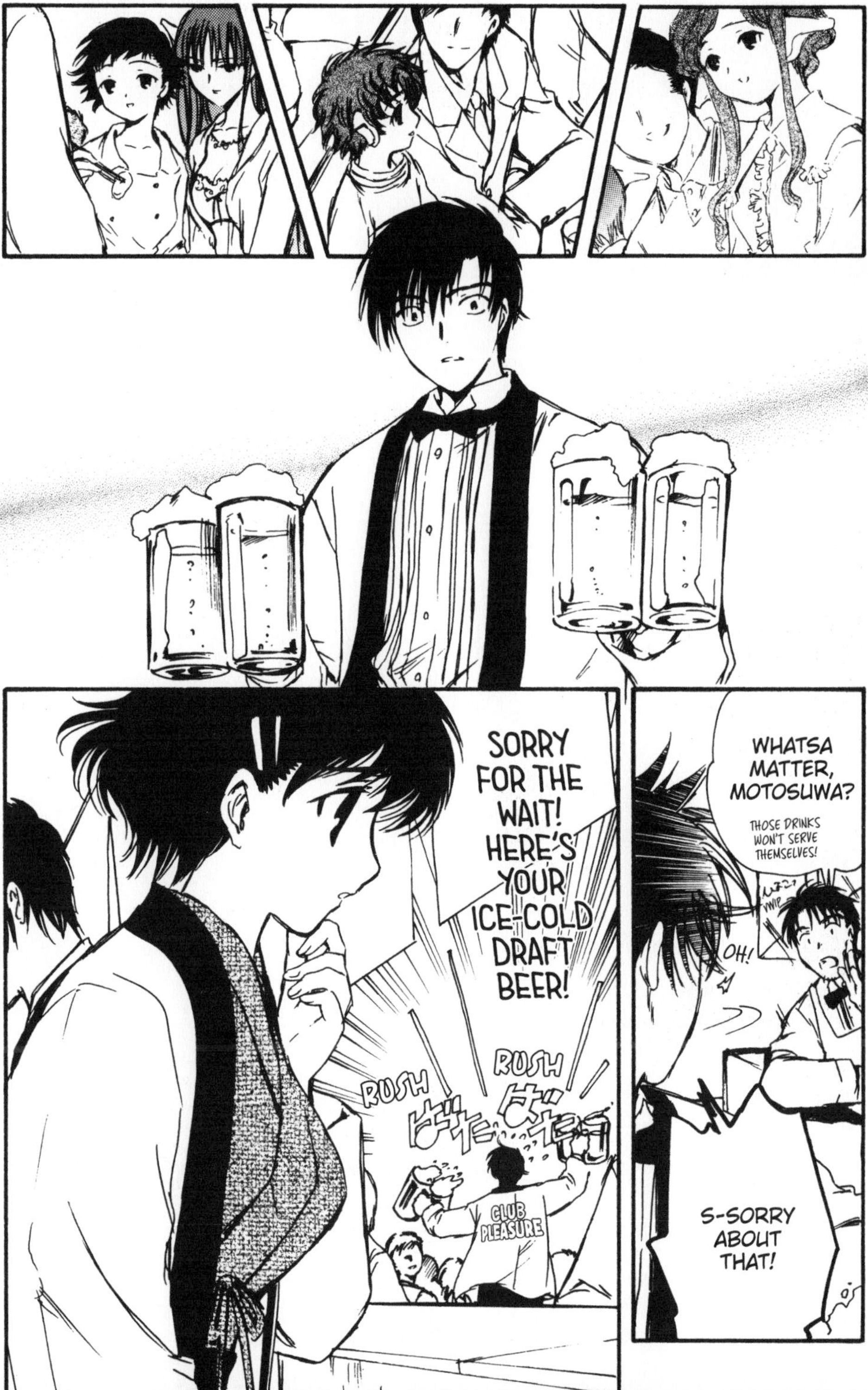

WHATSA MATTER, MOTOSUWA?
THOSE DRINKS WON'T SERVE THEMSELVES!
WHIP
OH!
S-SORRY ABOUT THAT!
SORRY FOR THE WAIT! HERE'S YOUR ICE-COLD DRAFT BEER!
RUSH
RUSH
CLUB PLEASURE

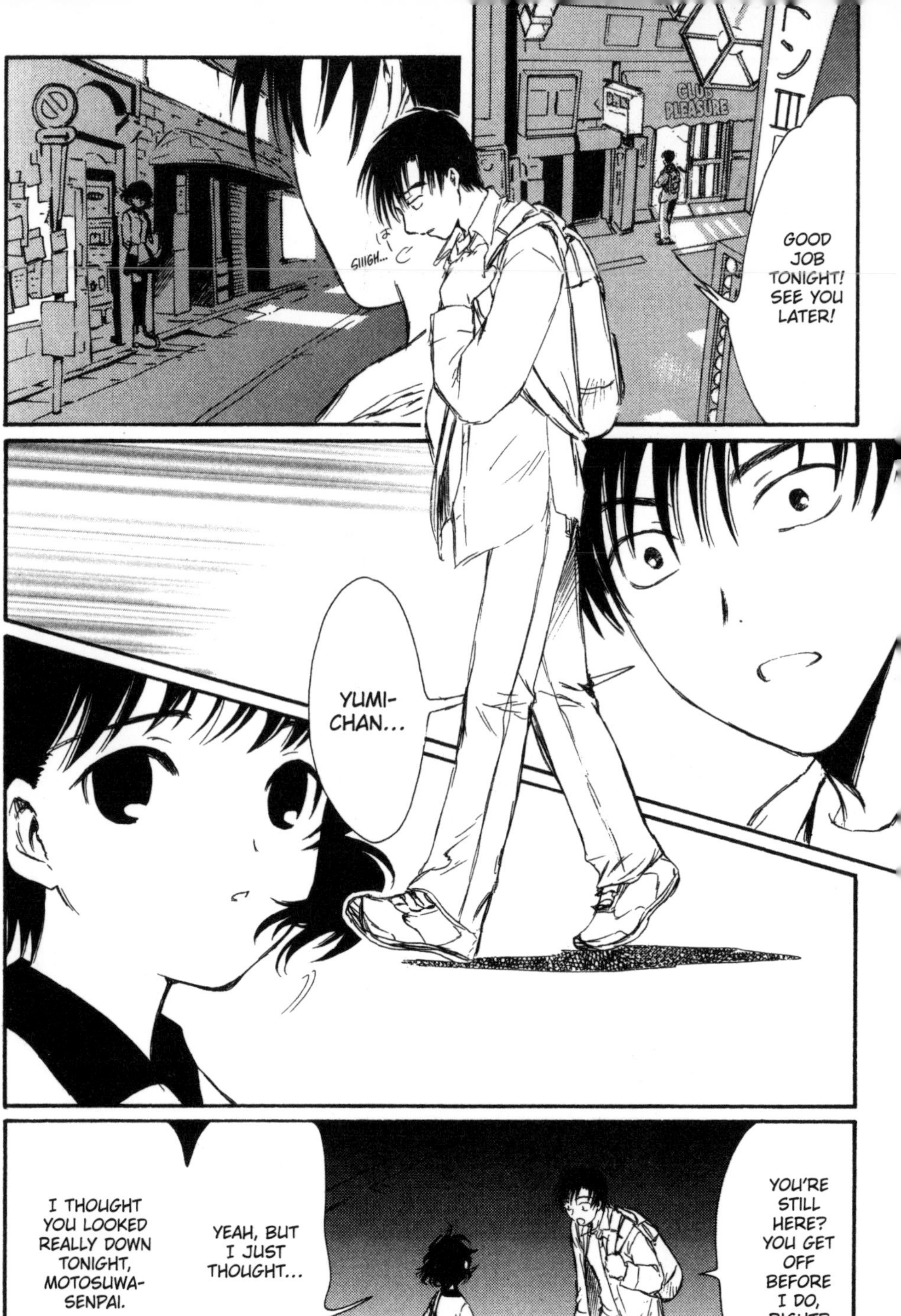
GOOD JOB TONIGHT! SEE YOU LATER!
SIIIGH...
YUMI-CHAN...
YOU'RE STILL HERE? YOU GET OFF BEFORE I DO, RIGHT?
YEAH, BUT I JUST THOUGHT...
I THOUGHT YOU LOOKED REALLY DOWN TONIGHT, MOTOSUWA-SENPAI.

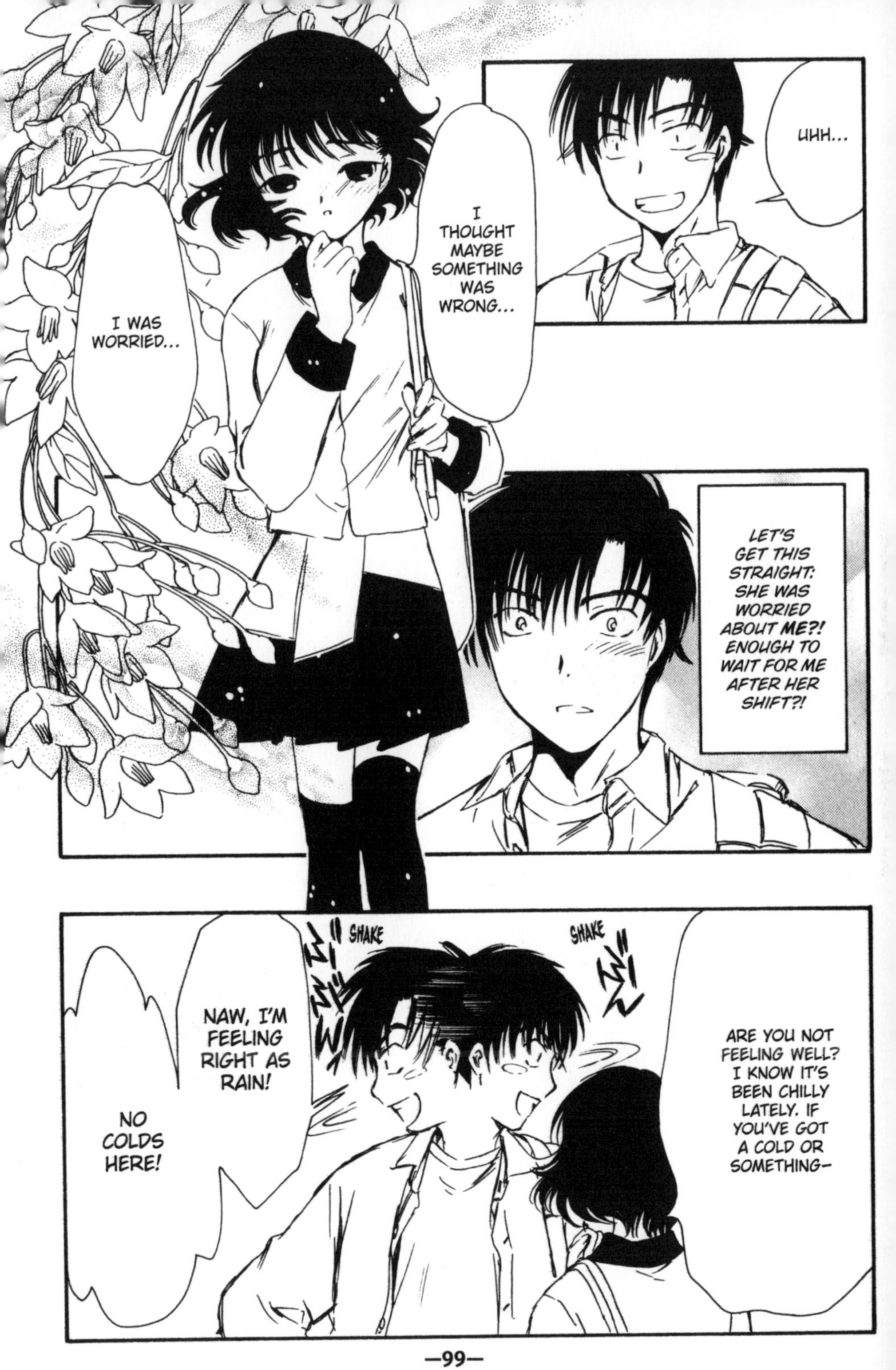
UHH...
I THOUGHT MAYBE SOMETHING WAS WRONG...
I WAS WORRIED...
LET'S GET THIS STRAIGHT: SHE WAS WORRIED ABOUT **ME?!** ENOUGH TO WAIT FOR ME AFTER HER SHIFT?!
ARE YOU NOT FEELING WELL? I KNOW IT'S BEEN CHILLY LATELY. IF YOU'VE GOT A COLD OR SOMETHING–
SHAKE
SHAKE
NAW, I'M FEELING RIGHT AS RAIN!
NO COLDS HERE!

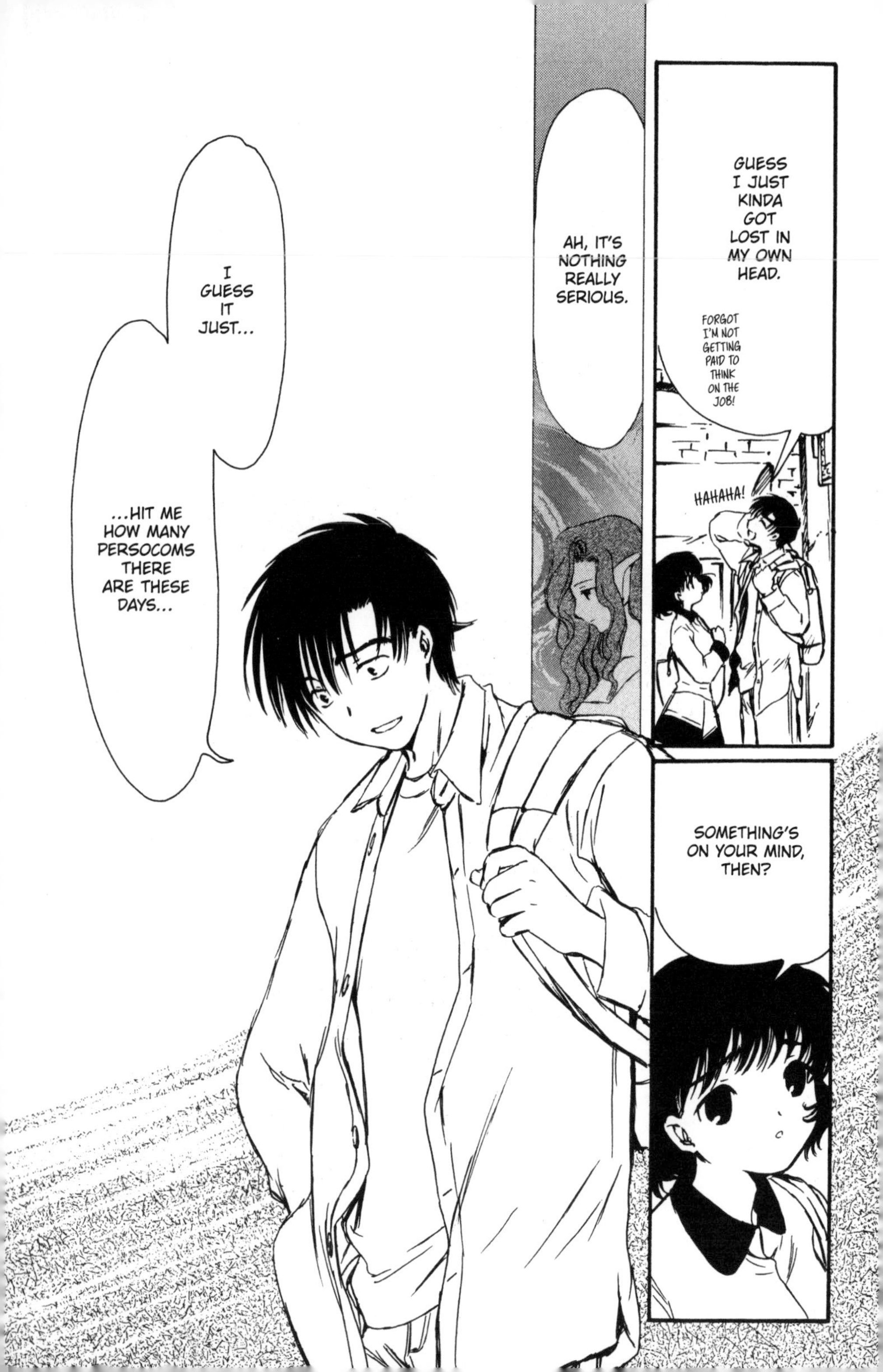
GUESS I JUST KINDA GOT LOST IN MY OWN HEAD.
FORGOT I'M NOT GETTING PAID TO THINK ON THE JOB!
HAHAHA!
SOMETHING'S ON YOUR MIND, THEN?
AH, IT'S NOTHING REALLY SERIOUS.
I GUESS IT JUST...
...HIT ME HOW MANY PERSOCOMS THERE ARE THESE DAYS...

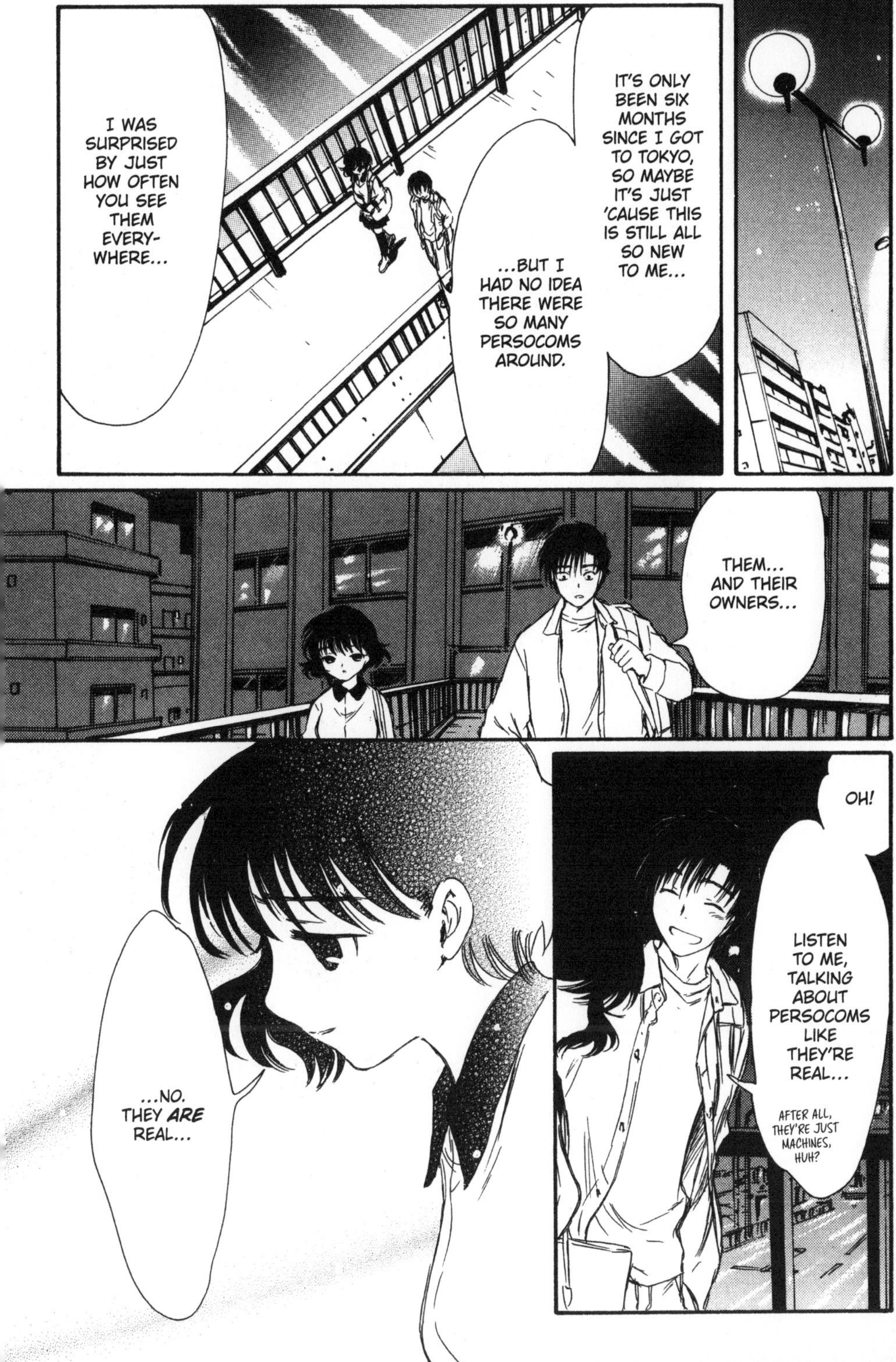
IT'S ONLY BEEN SIX MONTHS SINCE I GOT TO TOKYO, SO MAYBE IT'S JUST 'CAUSE THIS IS STILL ALL SO NEW TO ME...
...BUT I HAD NO IDEA THERE WERE SO MANY PERSOCOMS AROUND.
I WAS SURPRISED BY JUST HOW OFTEN YOU SEE THEM EVERY-WHERE...
THEM... AND THEIR OWNERS...
OH!
LISTEN TO ME, TALKING ABOUT PERSOCOMS LIKE THEY'RE REAL...
AFTER ALL, THEY'RE JUST MACHINES, HUH?
...NO. THEY *ARE* REAL...

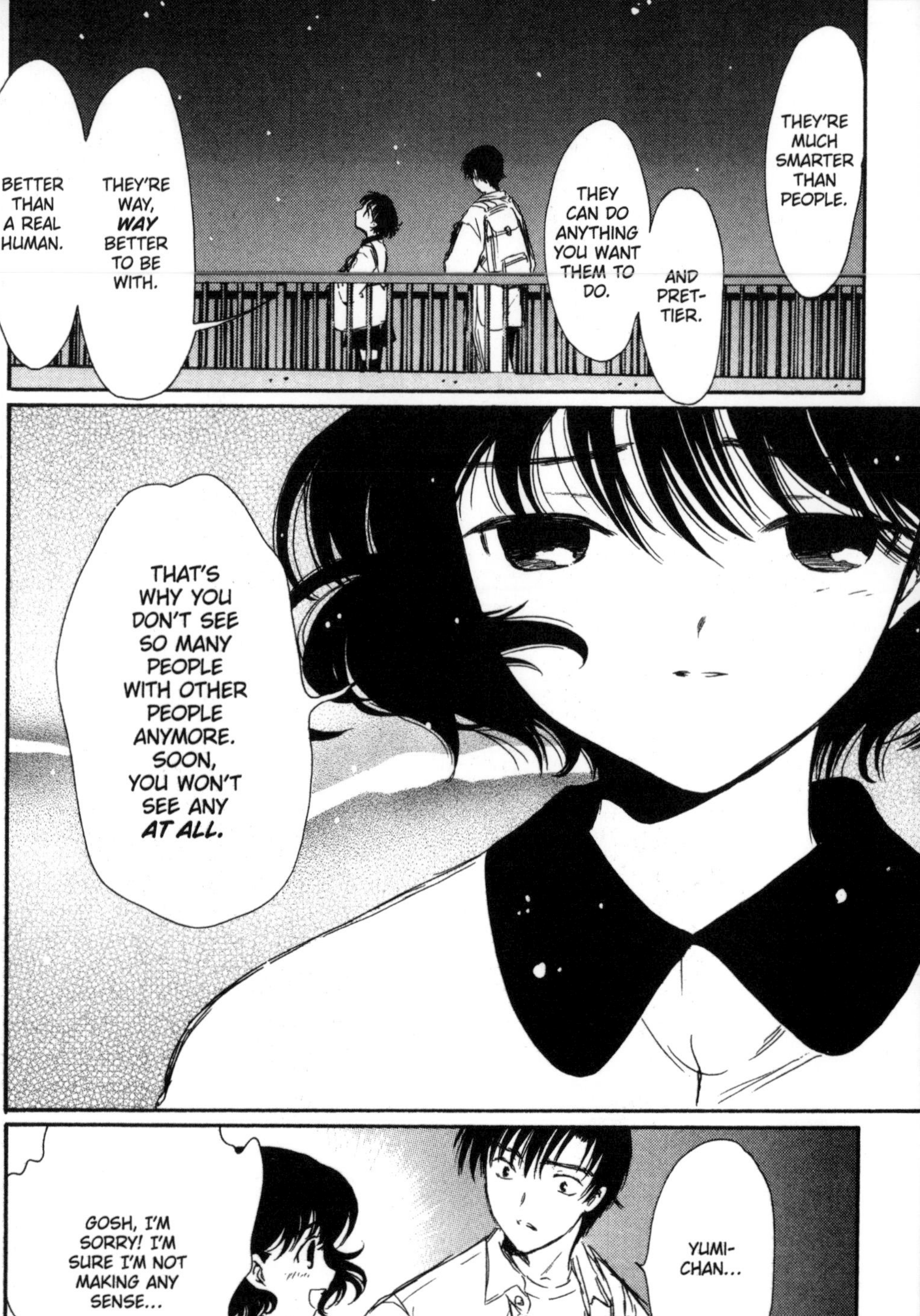
THEY'RE MUCH SMARTER THAN PEOPLE.
AND PRET-TIER.
THEY CAN DO ANYTHING YOU WANT THEM TO DO.
THEY'RE WAY, ***WAY*** BETTER TO BE WITH.
BETTER THAN A REAL HUMAN.
THAT'S WHY YOU DON'T SEE SO MANY PEOPLE WITH OTHER PEOPLE ANYMORE. SOON, YOU WON'T SEE ANY ***AT ALL.***
YUMI-CHAN...
GOSH, I'M SORRY! I'M SURE I'M NOT MAKING ANY SENSE...

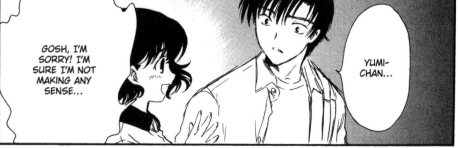

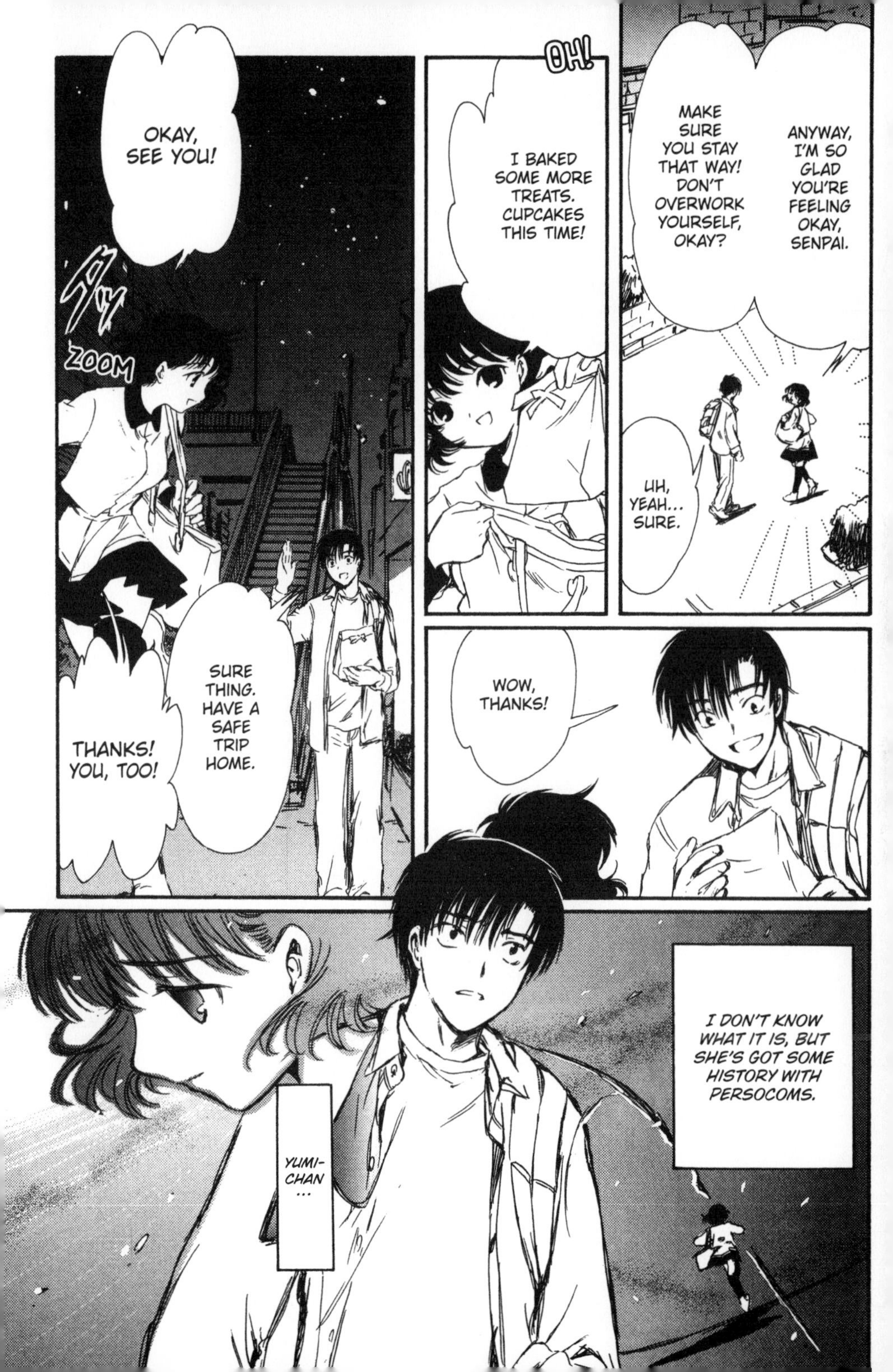
ANYWAY, I'M SO GLAD YOU'RE FEELING OKAY, SENPAI.
MAKE SURE YOU STAY THAT WAY! DON'T OVERWORK YOURSELF, OKAY?
UH, YEAH... SURE.
OH!
I BAKED SOME MORE TREATS. CUPCAKES THIS TIME!
WOW, THANKS!
SURE THING. HAVE A SAFE TRIP HOME.
THANKS! YOU, TOO!
OKAY, SEE YOU!
ZOOM
I DON'T KNOW WHAT IT IS, BUT SHE'S GOT SOME HISTORY WITH PERSOCOMS.
YUMI-CHAN...

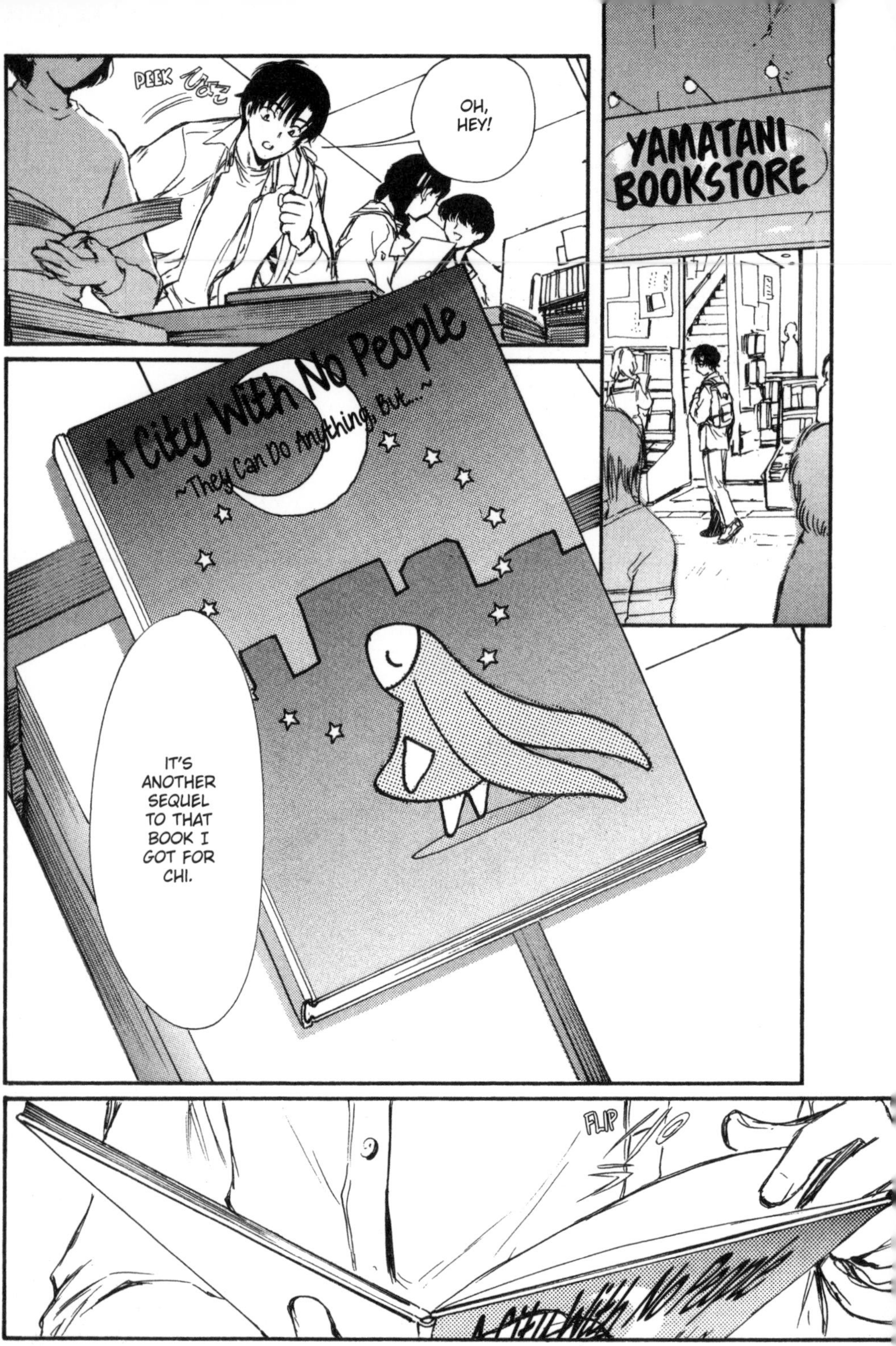
YAMATANI BOOKSTORE
PEEK
OH, HEY!
A City With No People
~They Can Do Anything, But...~
IT'S ANOTHER SEQUEL TO THAT BOOK I GOT FOR CHI.
FLIP

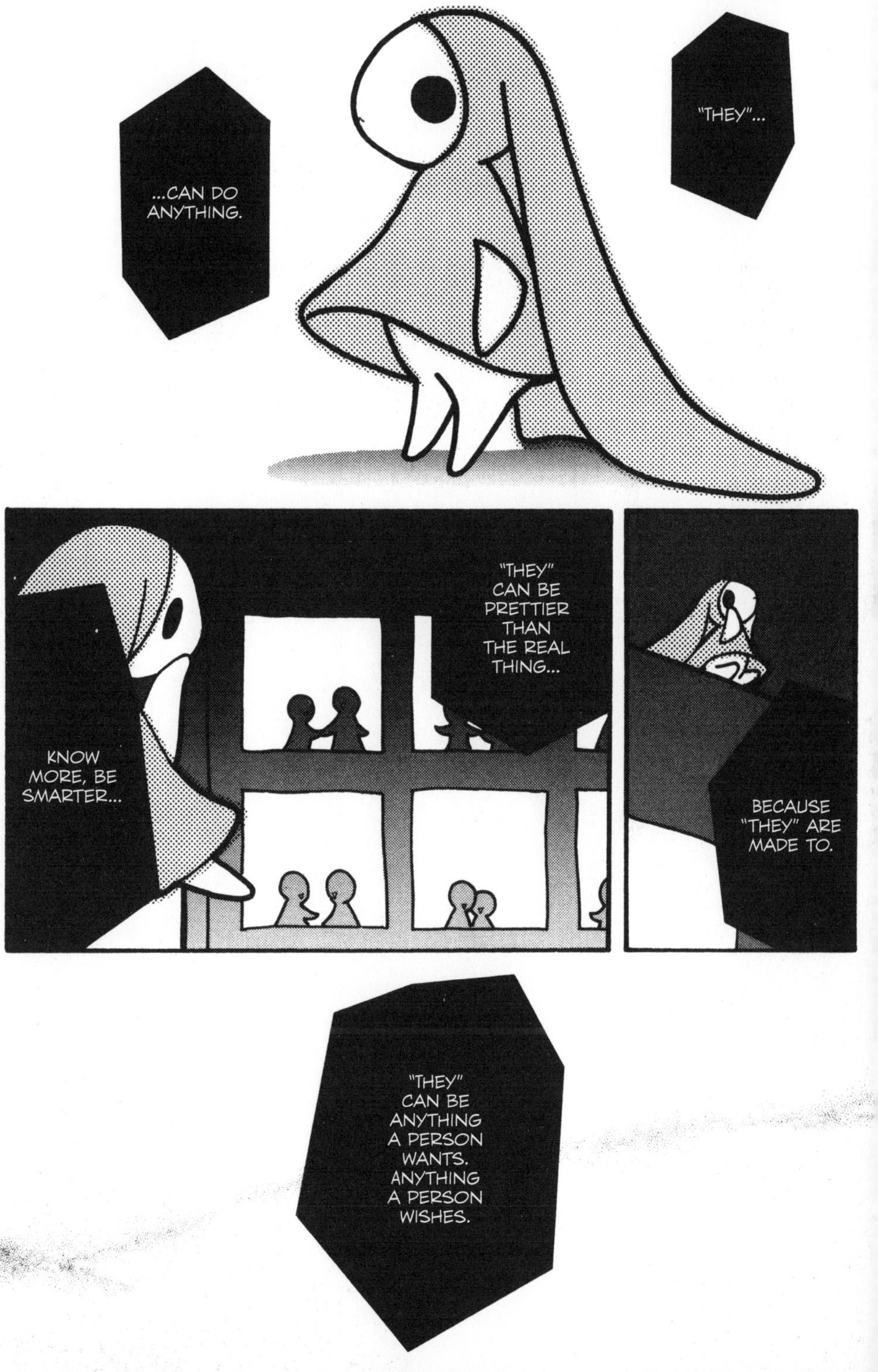
"THEY"...
...CAN DO ANYTHING.
BECAUSE "THEY" ARE MADE TO.
"THEY" CAN BE PRETTIER THAN THE REAL THING...
KNOW MORE, BE SMARTER...
"THEY" CAN BE ANYTHING A PERSON WANTS. ANYTHING A PERSON WISHES.

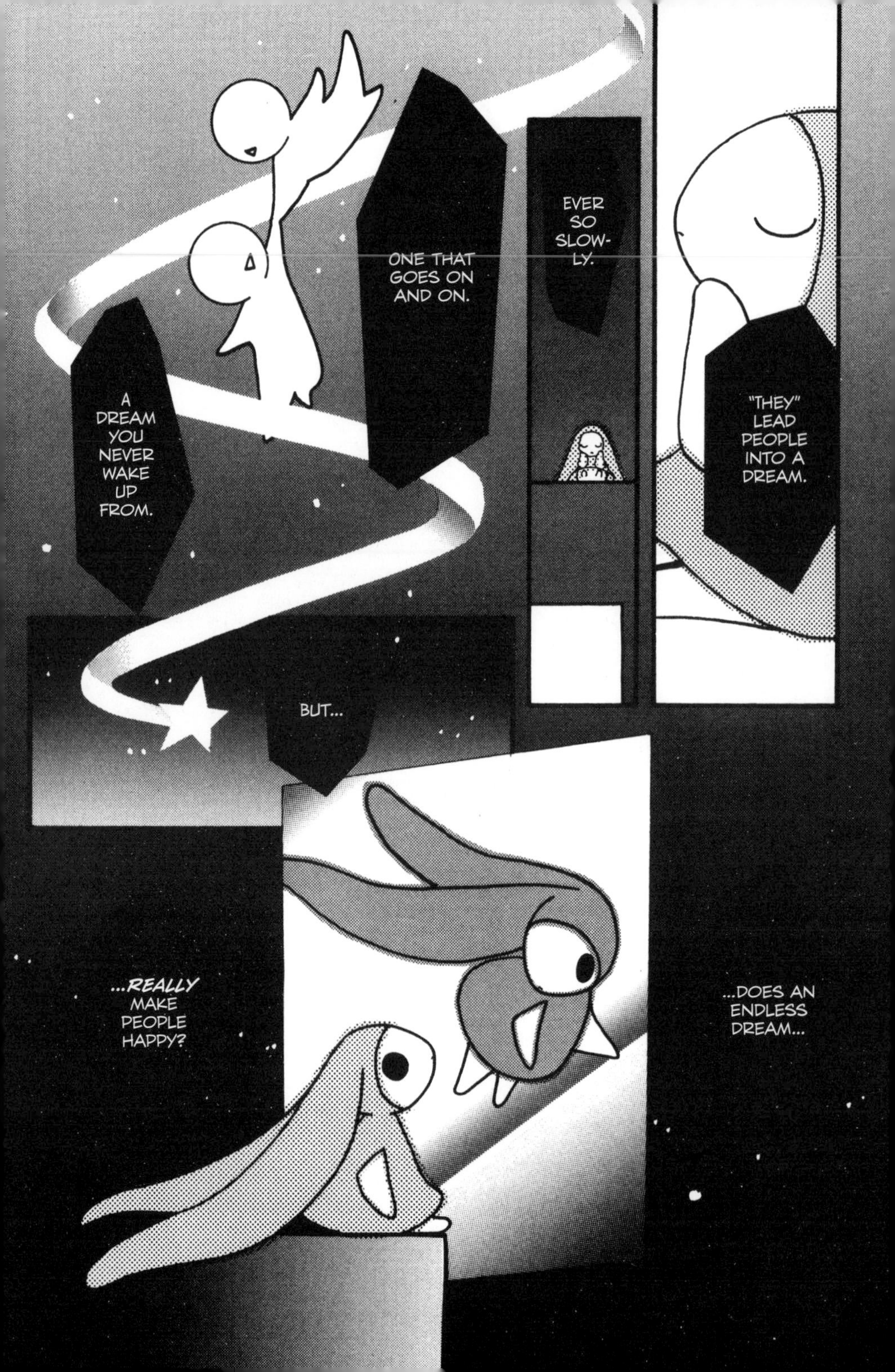
"THEY" LEAD PEOPLE INTO A DREAM.
EVER SO SLOW-LY.
A DREAM YOU NEVER WAKE UP FROM.
ONE THAT GOES ON AND ON.
BUT...
...DOES AN ENDLESS DREAM...
...*REALLY* MAKE PEOPLE HAPPY?

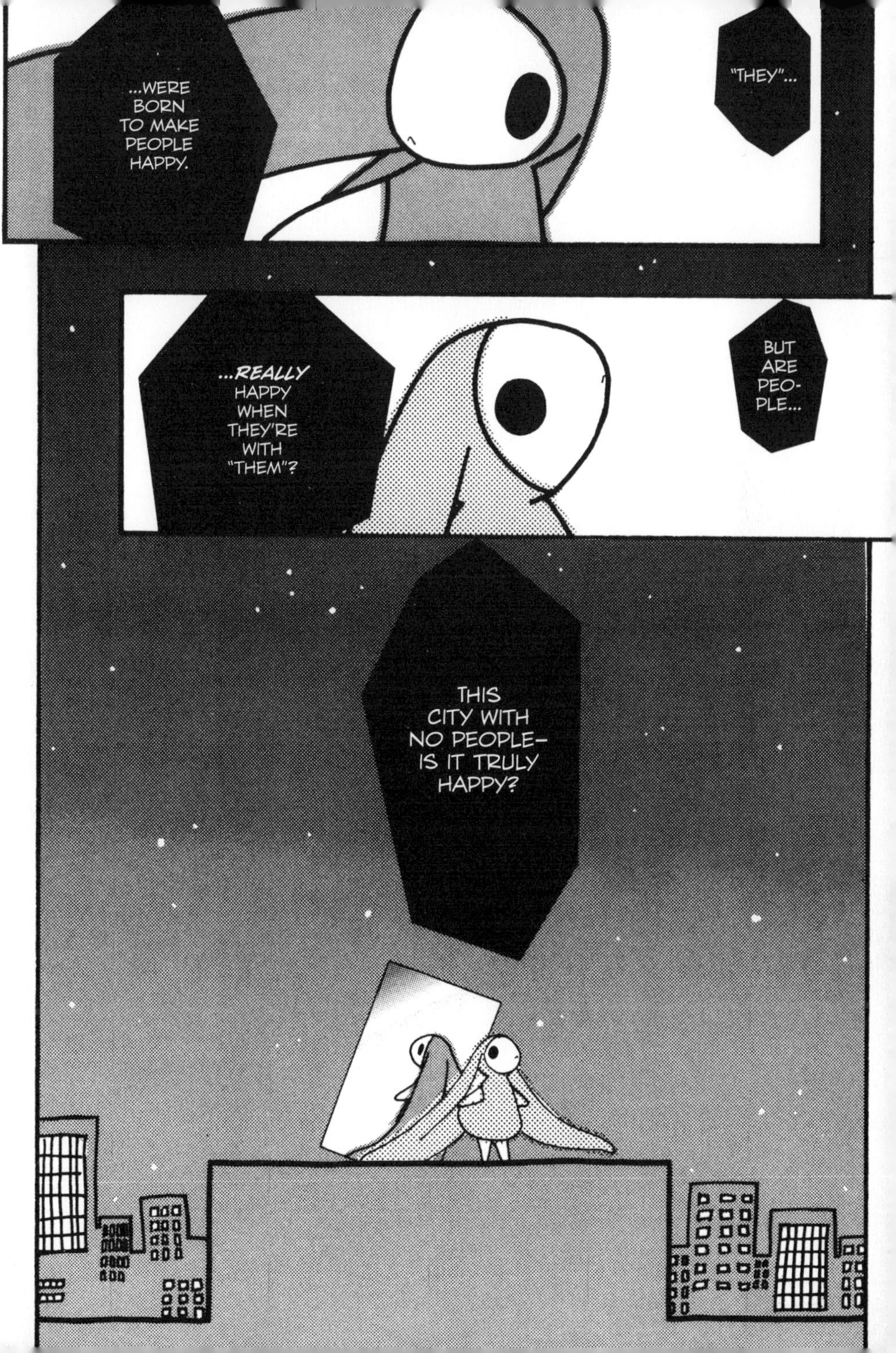
"THEY"...
...WERE BORN TO MAKE PEOPLE HAPPY.
BUT ARE PEO-PLE...
...*REALLY* HAPPY WHEN THEY'RE WITH "THEM"?
THIS CITY WITH NO PEOPLE– IS IT TRULY HAPPY?

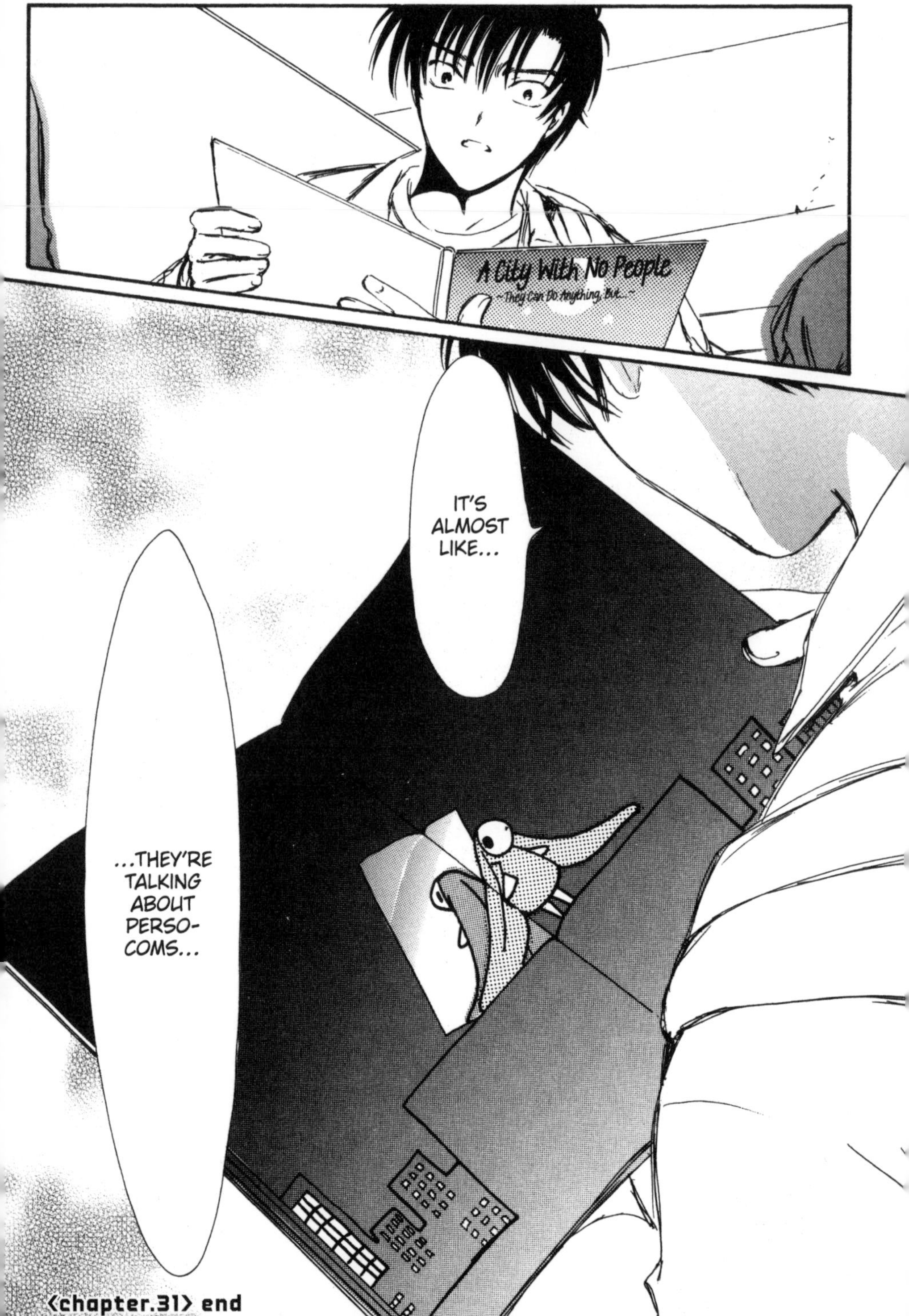
A City With No People
~They Can Do Anything, But...~
IT'S ALMOST LIKE...
...THEY'RE TALKING ABOUT PERSO-COMS...

〈chapter.31〉 end

Chobits

〈chapter.32〉

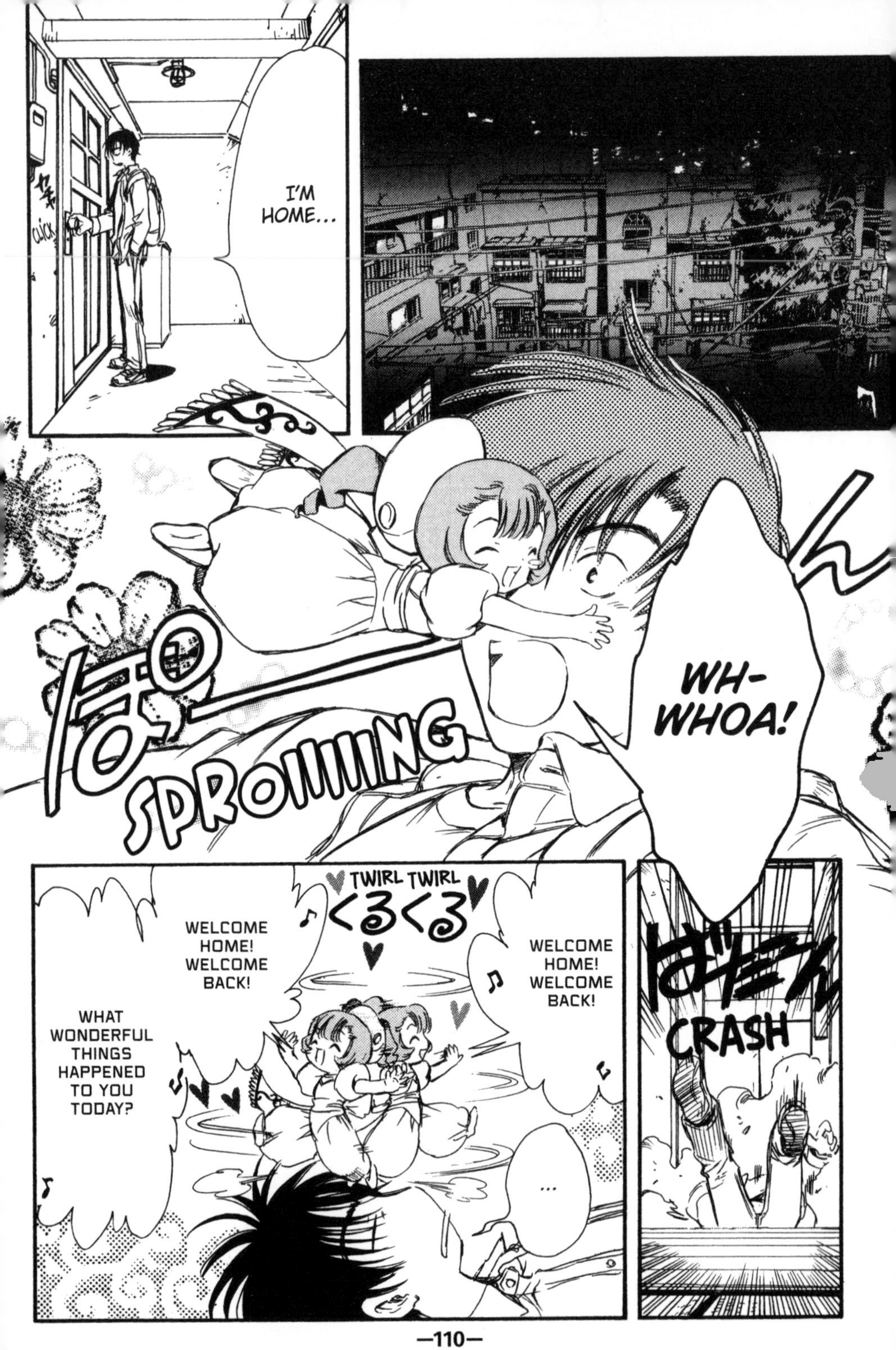

I'M HOME...
CLICK
WH- WHOA!
ぽー
SPROIIIIING
ばたん
CRASH
WELCOME HOME! WELCOME BACK!
TWIRL TWIRL
くるくる
WELCOME HOME! WELCOME BACK!
WHAT WONDERFUL THINGS HAPPENED TO YOU TODAY?
...

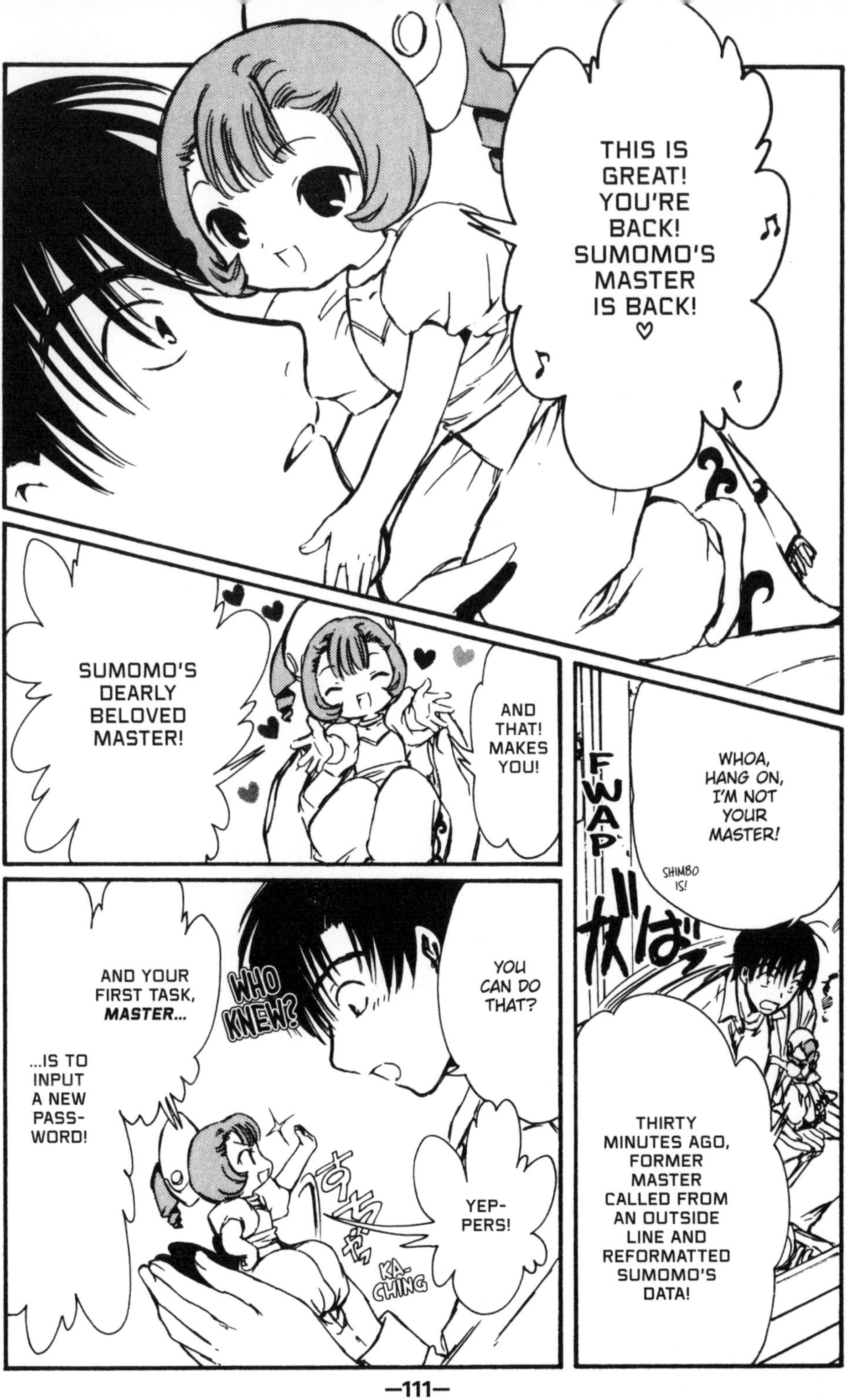
THIS IS GREAT! YOU'RE BACK! SUMOMO'S MASTER IS BACK! ♡
WHOA, HANG ON, I'M NOT YOUR MASTER!
SHIMBO IS!
FWAP
THIRTY MINUTES AGO, FORMER MASTER CALLED FROM AN OUTSIDE LINE AND REFORMATTED SUMOMO'S DATA!
AND THAT! MAKES YOU!
SUMOMO'S DEARLY BELOVED MASTER!
YOU CAN DO THAT?
WHO KNEW?
AND YOUR FIRST TASK, ***MASTER...***
YEP-PERS!
...IS TO INPUT A NEW PASS-WORD!
KA-CHING

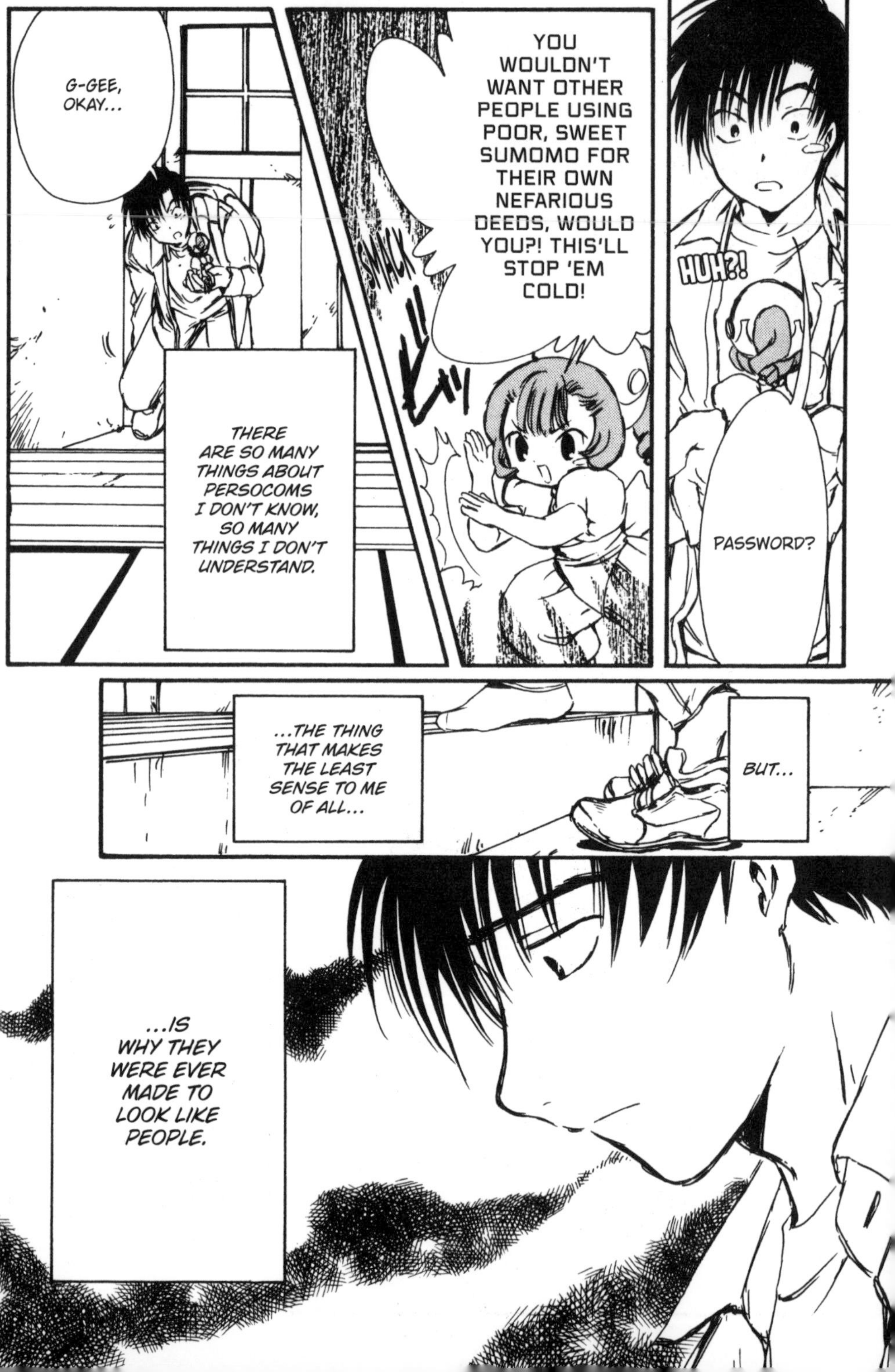

HUH?!
PASSWORD?
SMACK
YOU WOULDN'T WANT OTHER PEOPLE USING POOR, SWEET SUMOMO FOR THEIR OWN NEFARIOUS DEEDS, WOULD YOU?! THIS'LL STOP 'EM COLD!
G-GEE, OKAY...
THERE ARE SO MANY THINGS ABOUT PERSOCOMS I DON'T KNOW, SO MANY THINGS I DON'T UNDERSTAND.
BUT...
...THE THING THAT MAKES THE LEAST SENSE TO ME OF ALL...
...IS WHY THEY WERE EVER MADE TO LOOK LIKE PEOPLE.

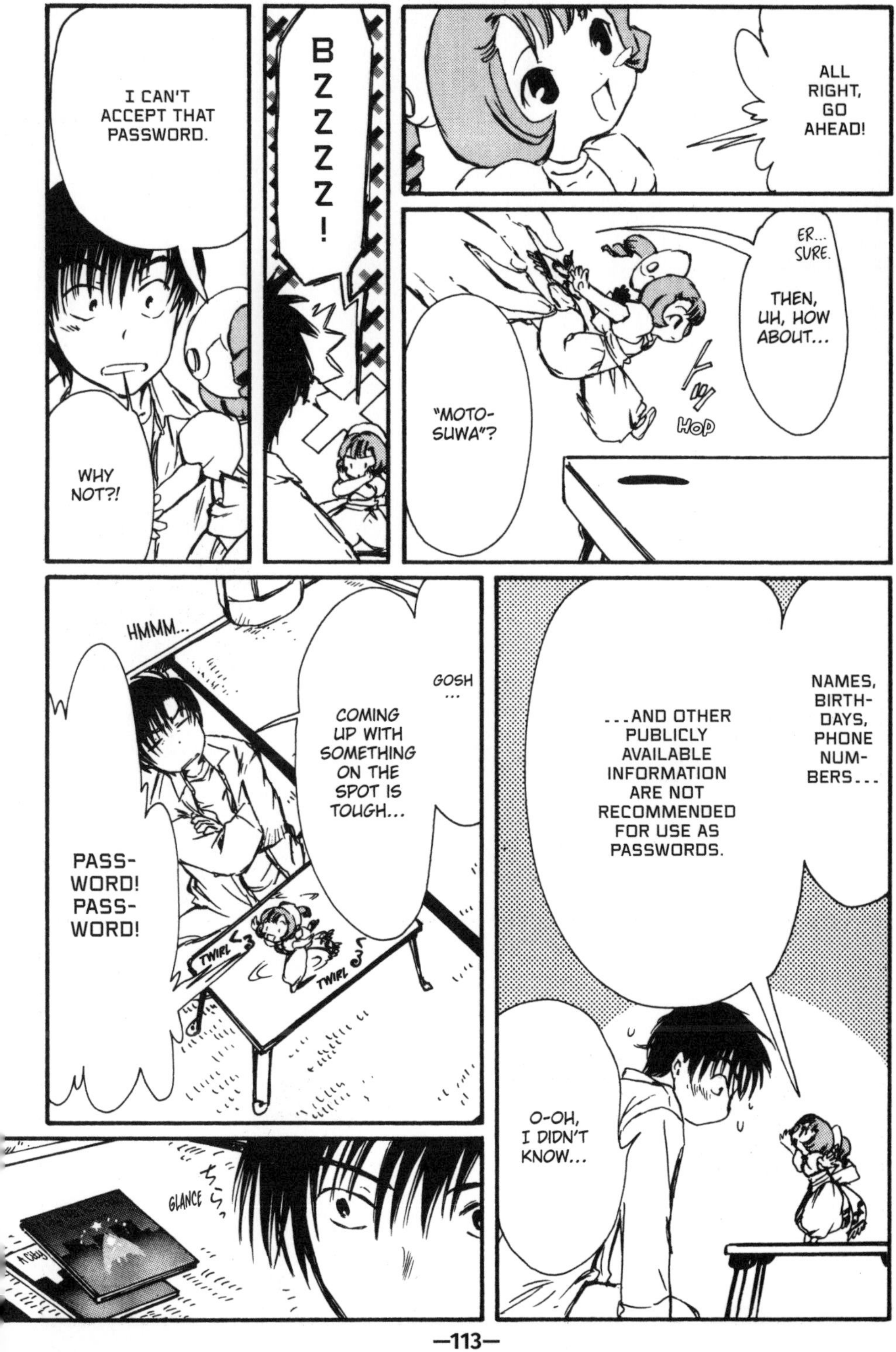
ALL RIGHT, GO AHEAD!
ER... SURE.
THEN, UH, HOW ABOUT...
HOP
"MOTO-SUWA"?
BZZZZ!
I CAN'T ACCEPT THAT PASSWORD.
WHY NOT?!
NAMES, BIRTH-DAYS, PHONE NUM-BERS...
...AND OTHER PUBLICLY AVAILABLE INFORMATION ARE NOT RECOMMENDED FOR USE AS PASSWORDS.
O-OH, I DIDN'T KNOW...
GOSH...
COMING UP WITH SOMETHING ON THE SPOT IS TOUGH...
HMMM...
PASS-WORD! PASS-WORD!
TWIRL
TWIRL
GLANCE

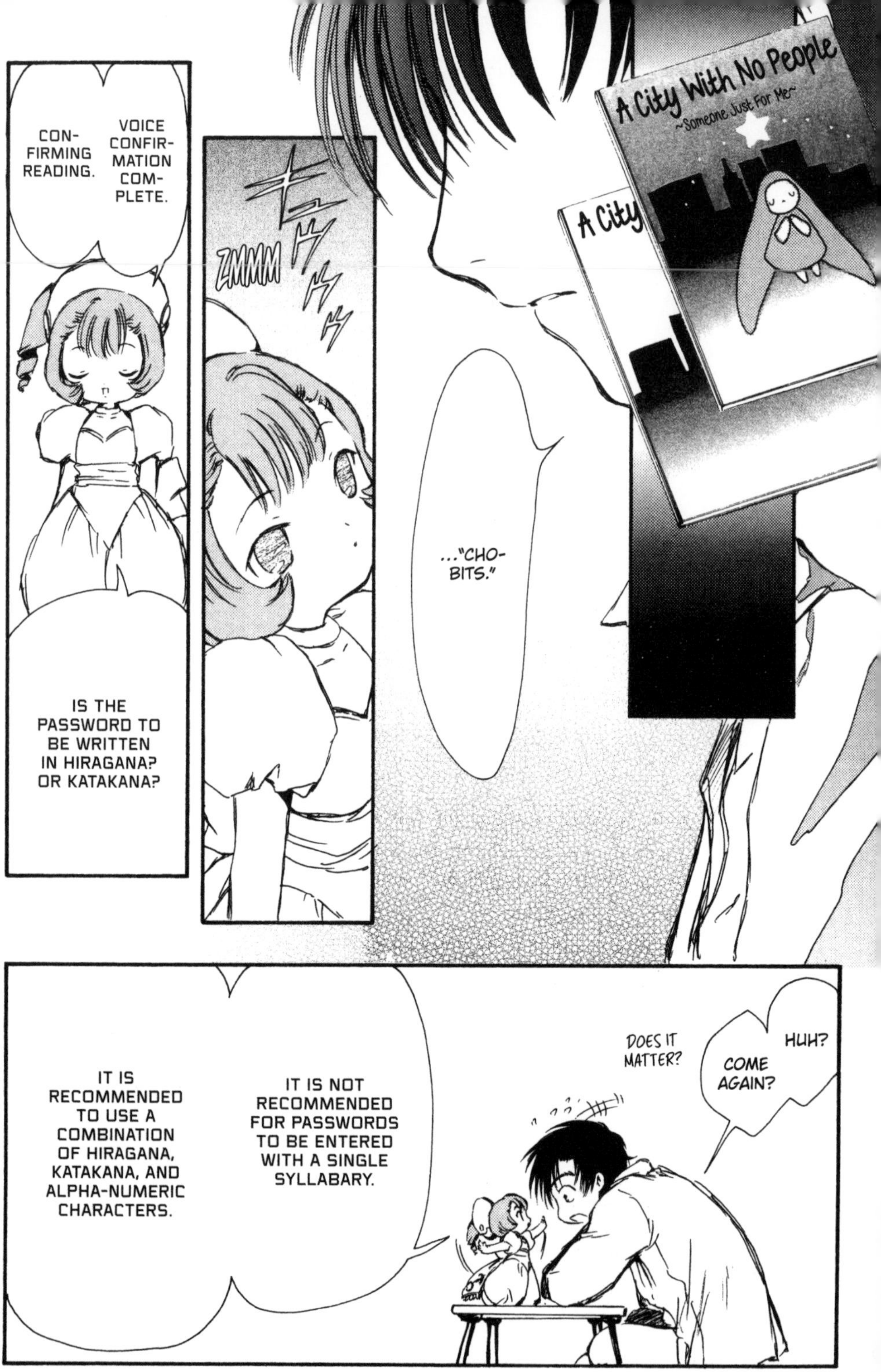
A City With No People
~Someone Just For Me~
A City
..."CHO-BITS."
ZMMM
VOICE CONFIRMATION COMPLETE.
CON-FIRMING READING.
IS THE PASSWORD TO BE WRITTEN IN HIRAGANA? OR KATAKANA?
HUH?
COME AGAIN?
DOES IT MATTER?
IT IS NOT RECOMMENDED FOR PASSWORDS TO BE ENTERED WITH A SINGLE SYLLABARY.
IT IS RECOMMENDED TO USE A COMBINATION OF HIRAGANA, KATAKANA, AND ALPHA-NUMERIC CHARACTERS.

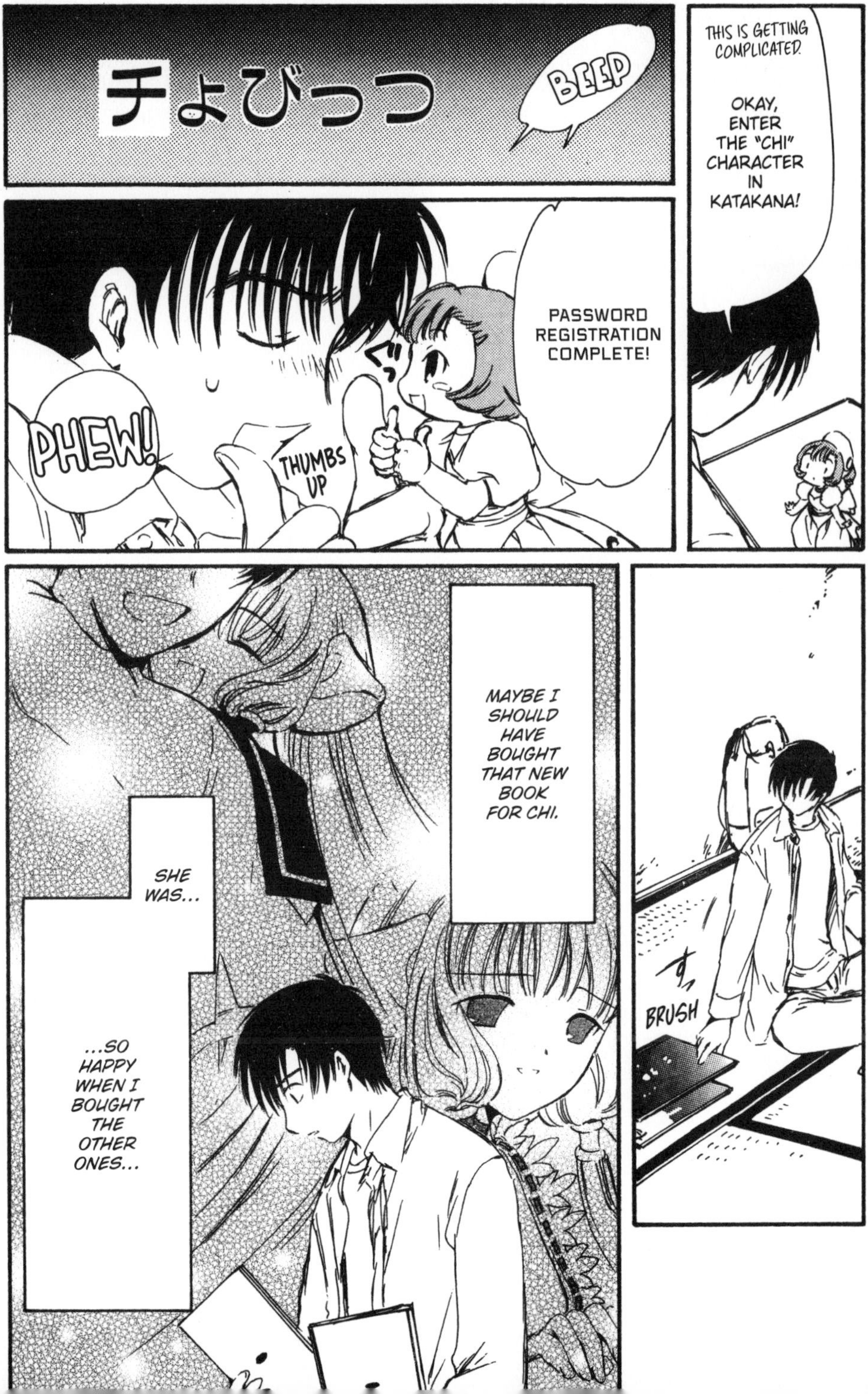
THIS IS GETTING COMPLICATED.
OKAY, ENTER THE "CHI" CHARACTER IN KATAKANA!
チょびっつ
BEEP
PASSWORD REGISTRATION COMPLETE!
THUMBS UP
PHEW!
BRUSH
MAYBE I SHOULD HAVE BOUGHT THAT NEW BOOK FOR CHI.
SHE WAS...
...SO HAPPY WHEN I BOUGHT THE OTHER ONES...

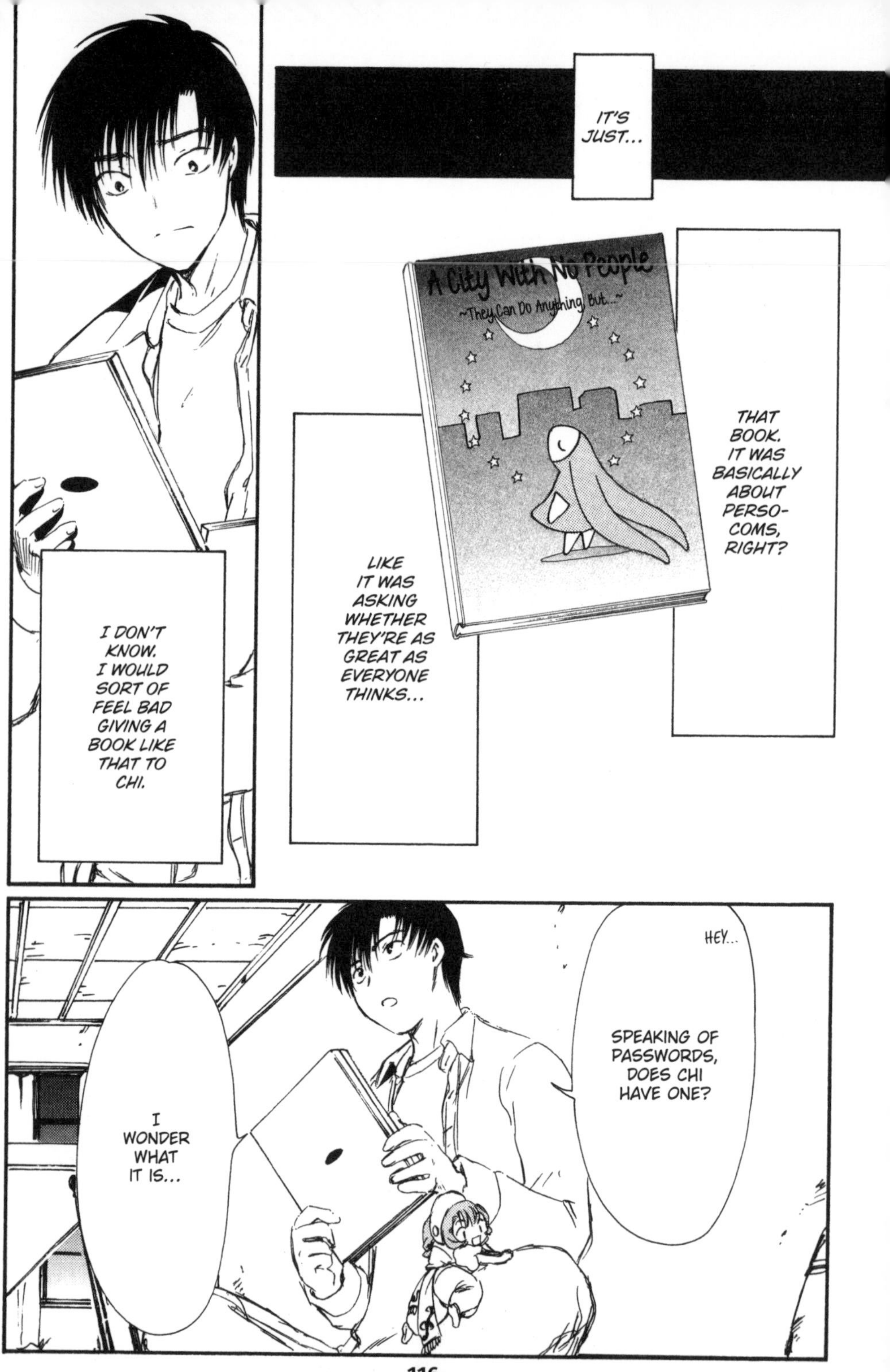
IT'S JUST...
A City With No People
~They Can Do Anything, But...~
THAT BOOK. IT WAS BASICALLY ABOUT PERSO-COMS, RIGHT?
LIKE IT WAS ASKING WHETHER THEY'RE AS GREAT AS EVERYONE THINKS...
I DON'T KNOW. I WOULD SORT OF FEEL BAD GIVING A BOOK LIKE THAT TO CHI.
HEY...
SPEAKING OF PASSWORDS, DOES CHI HAVE ONE?
I WONDER WHAT IT IS...

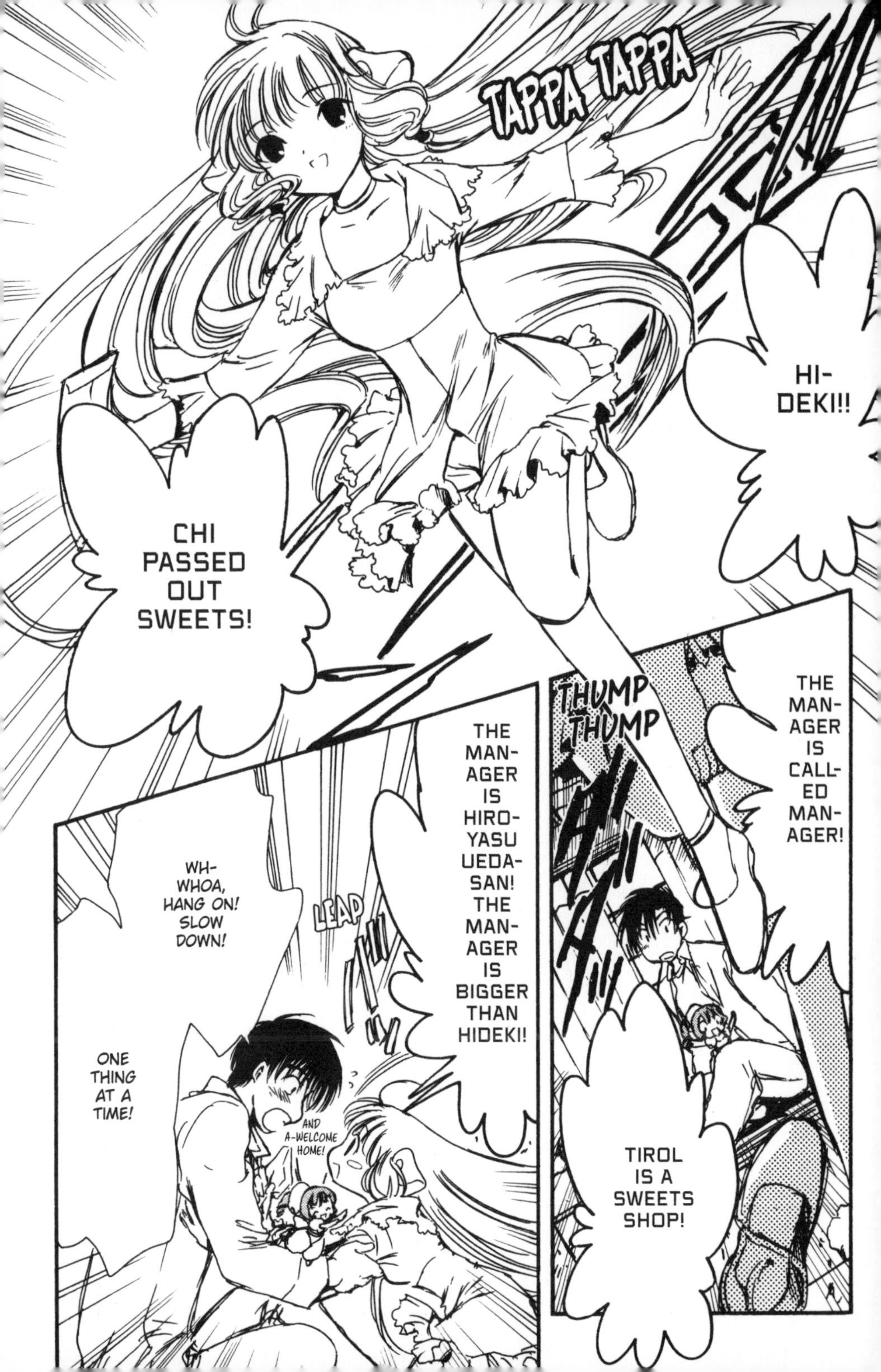
TAPPA TAPPA
HIDEKI!!
CHI PASSED OUT SWEETS!
THUMP THUMP
THE MANAGER IS CALLED MANAGER!
TIROL IS A SWEETS SHOP!
THE MANAGER IS HIROYASU UEDA-SAN! THE MANAGER IS BIGGER THAN HIDEKI!
LEAP
WH-WHOA, HANG ON! SLOW DOWN!
ONE THING AT A TIME!
AND A-WELCOME HOME!

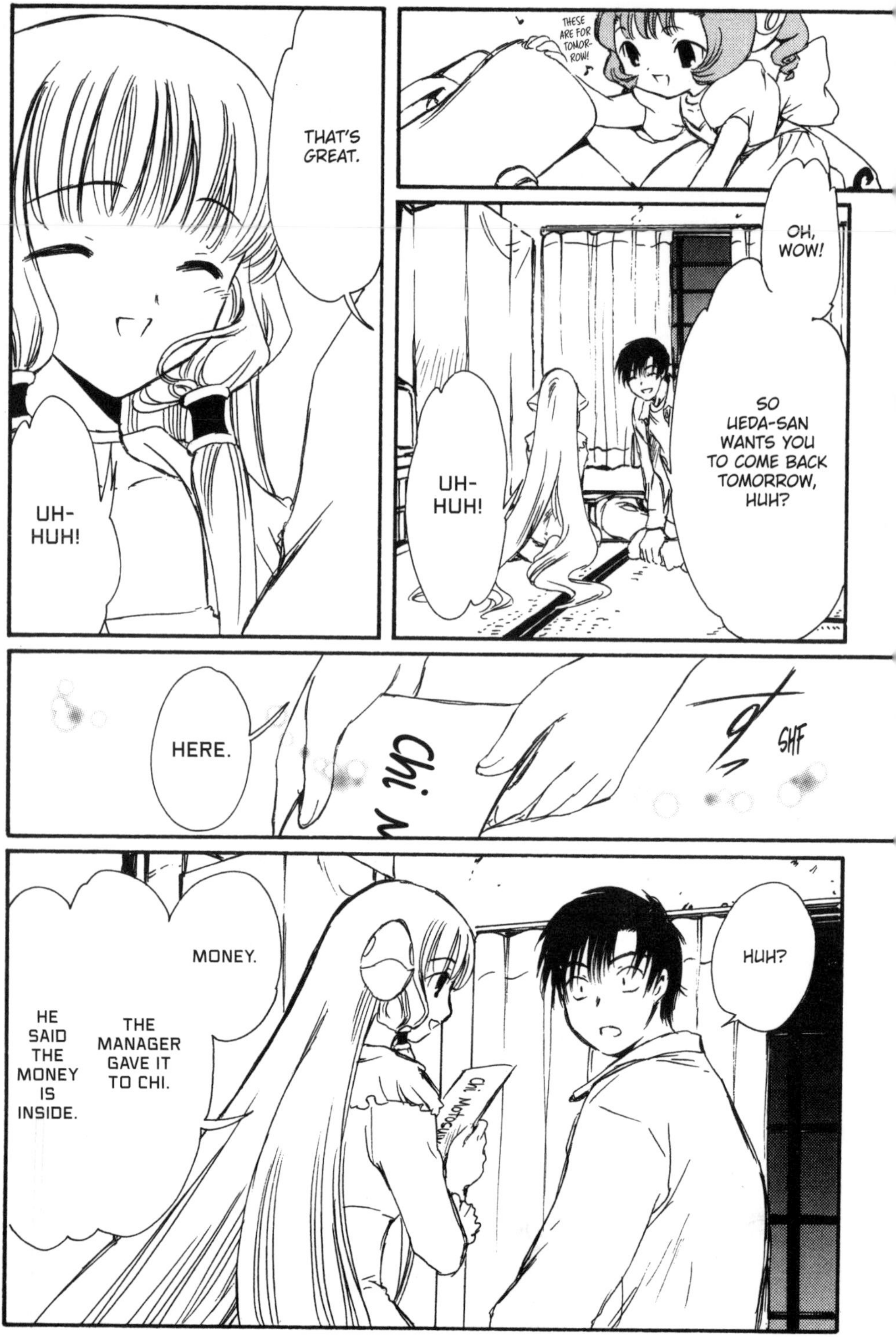
THESE ARE FOR TOMORROW!
OH, WOW!
SO UEDA-SAN WANTS YOU TO COME BACK TOMORROW, HUH?
UH-HUH!
THAT'S GREAT.
UH-HUH!
SHF
HERE.
HUH?
MONEY.
THE MANAGER GAVE IT TO CHI.
HE SAID THE MONEY IS INSIDE.

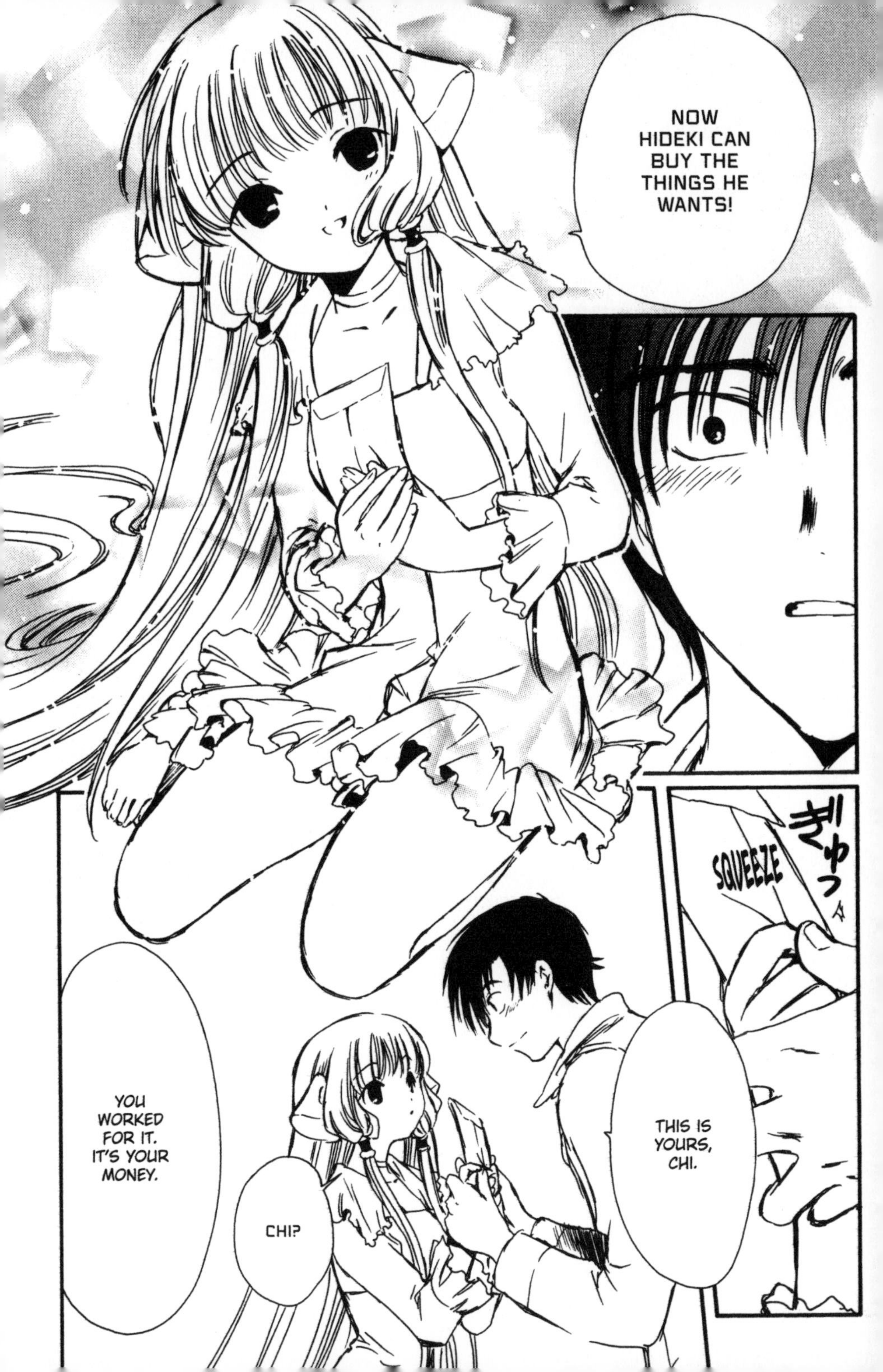
NOW HIDEKI CAN BUY THE THINGS HE WANTS!
ぎゅっ
SQUEEZE
THIS IS YOURS, CHI.
CHI?
YOU WORKED FOR IT. IT'S YOUR MONEY.

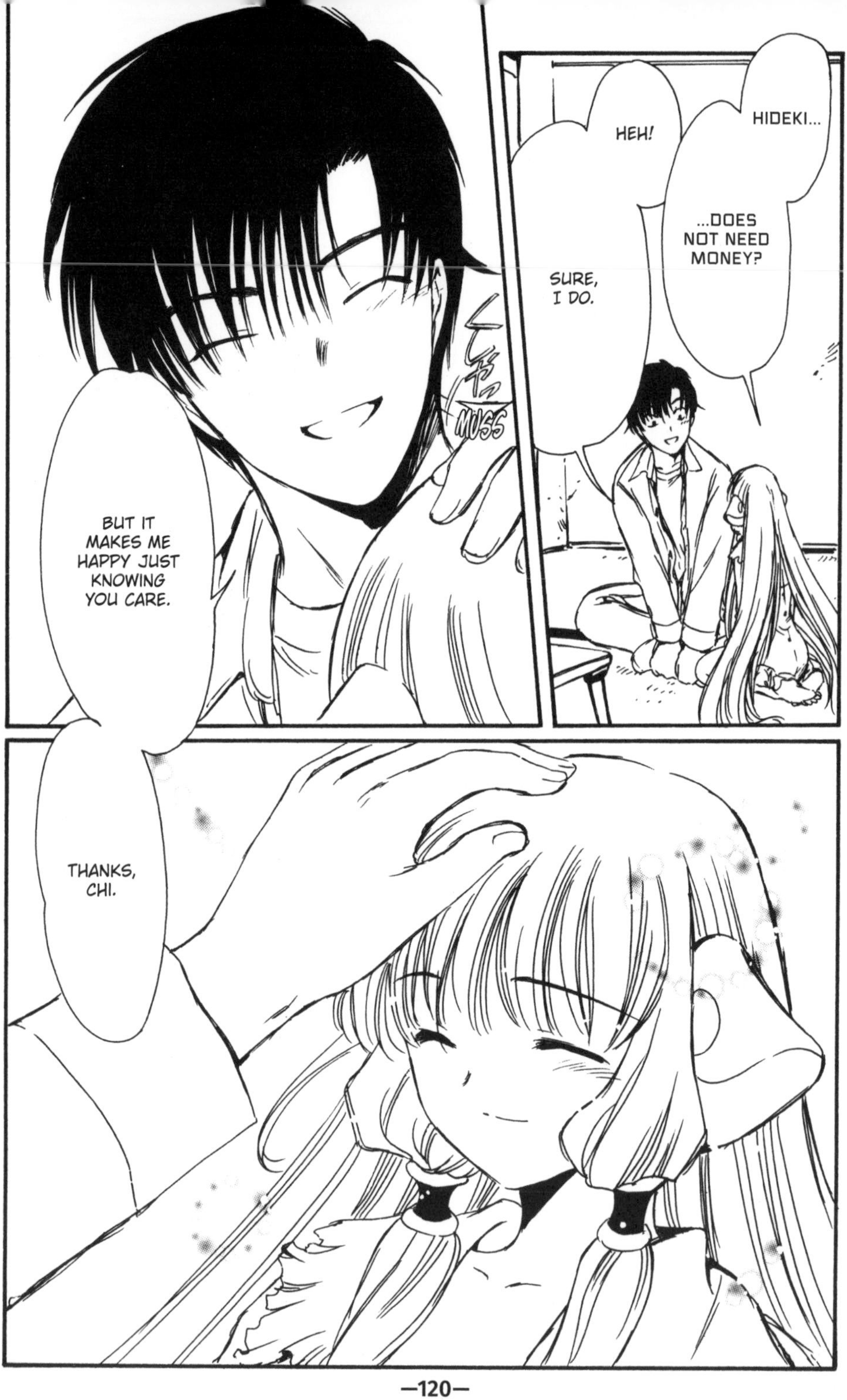
HIDEKI...
...DOES NOT NEED MONEY?
HEH!
SURE, I DO.
MUSS
BUT IT MAKES ME HAPPY JUST KNOWING YOU CARE.
THANKS, CHI.

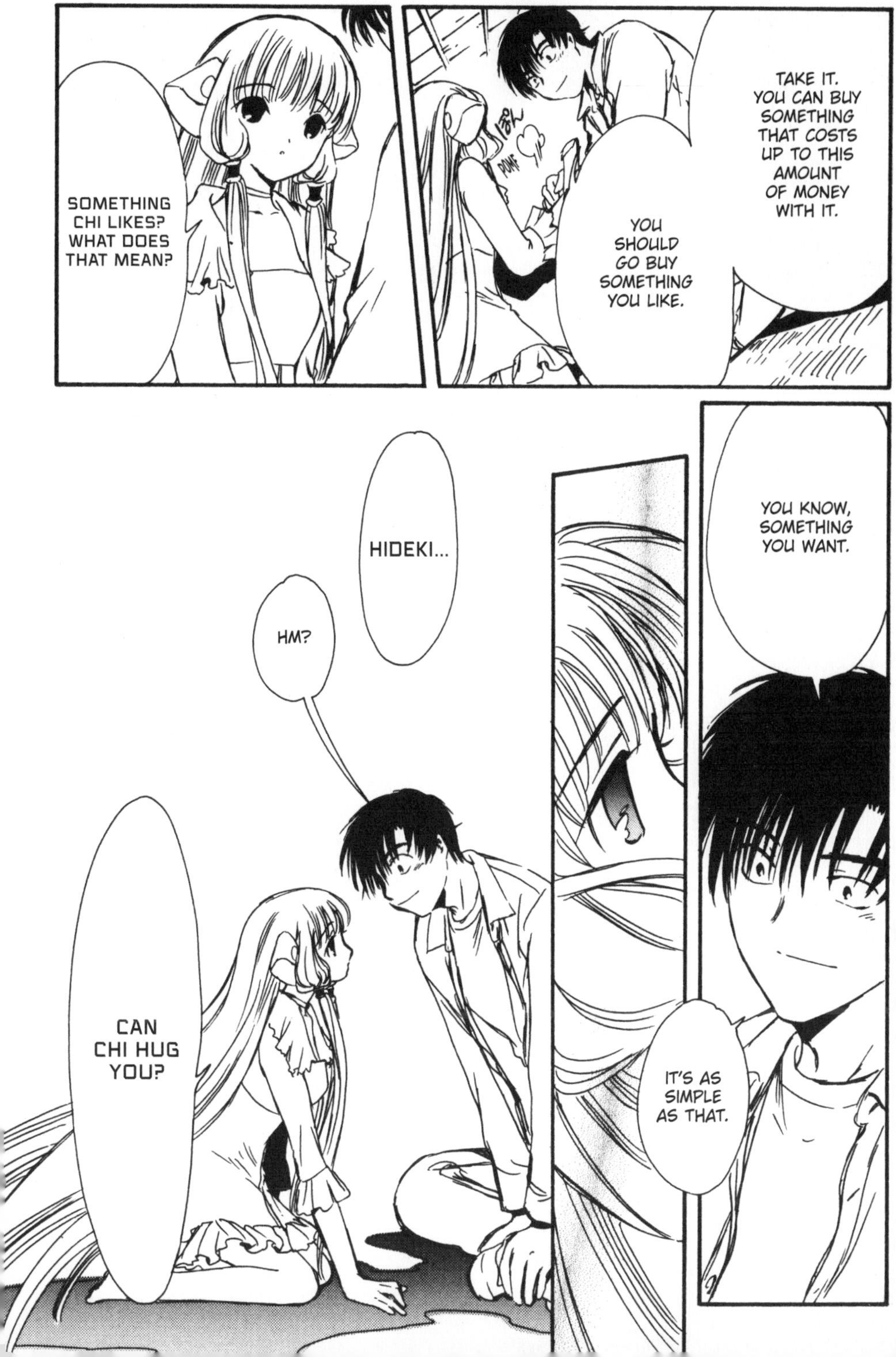
TAKE IT. YOU CAN BUY SOMETHING THAT COSTS UP TO THIS AMOUNT OF MONEY WITH IT.
YOU SHOULD GO BUY SOMETHING YOU LIKE.
POMF
SOMETHING CHI LIKES? WHAT DOES THAT MEAN?
YOU KNOW, SOMETHING YOU WANT.
IT'S AS SIMPLE AS THAT.
HIDEKI...
HM?
CAN CHI HUG YOU?

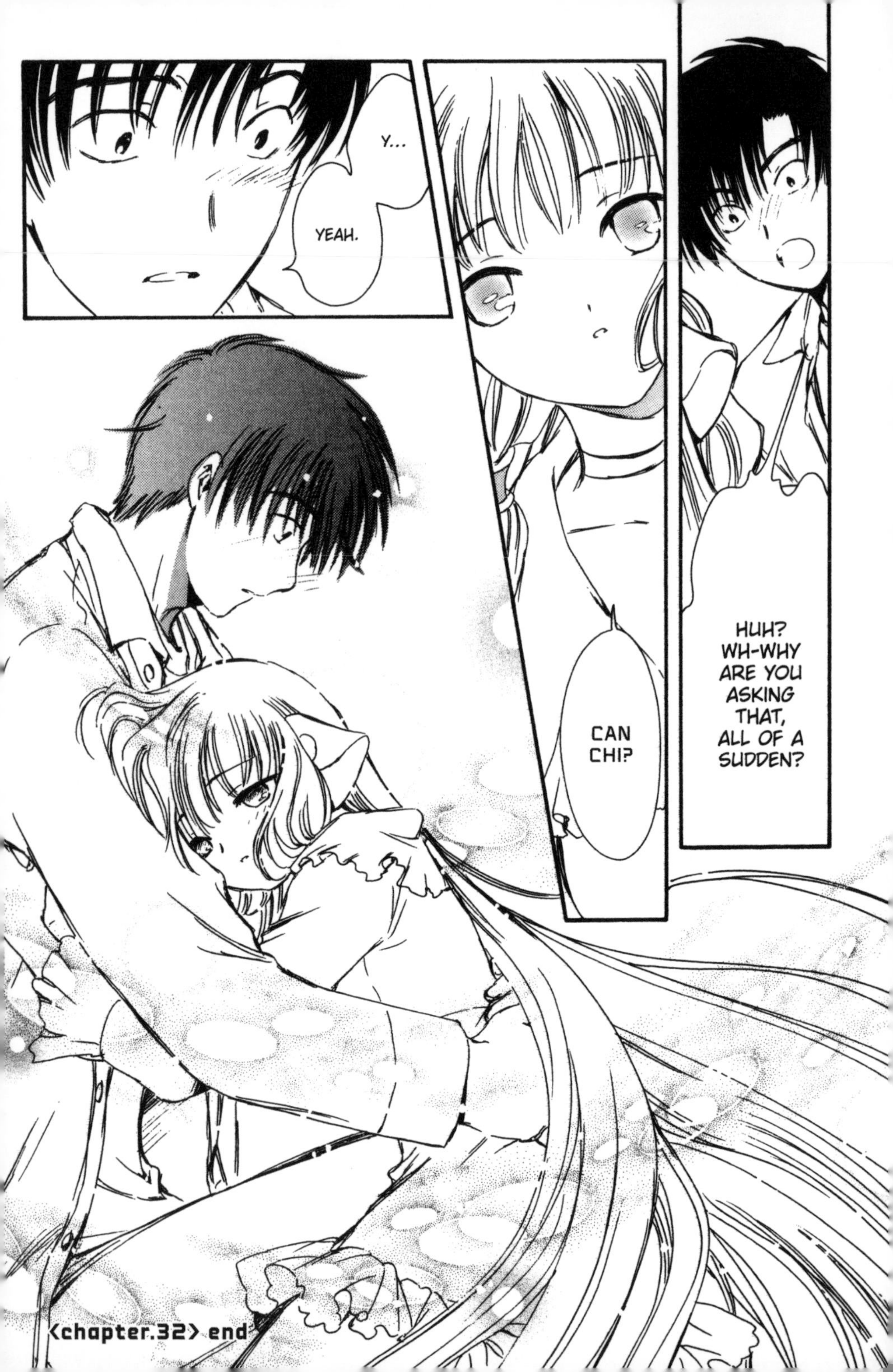

HUH? WH-WHY ARE YOU ASKING THAT, ALL OF A SUDDEN?
CAN CHI?
Y...
YEAH.
<chapter.32> end

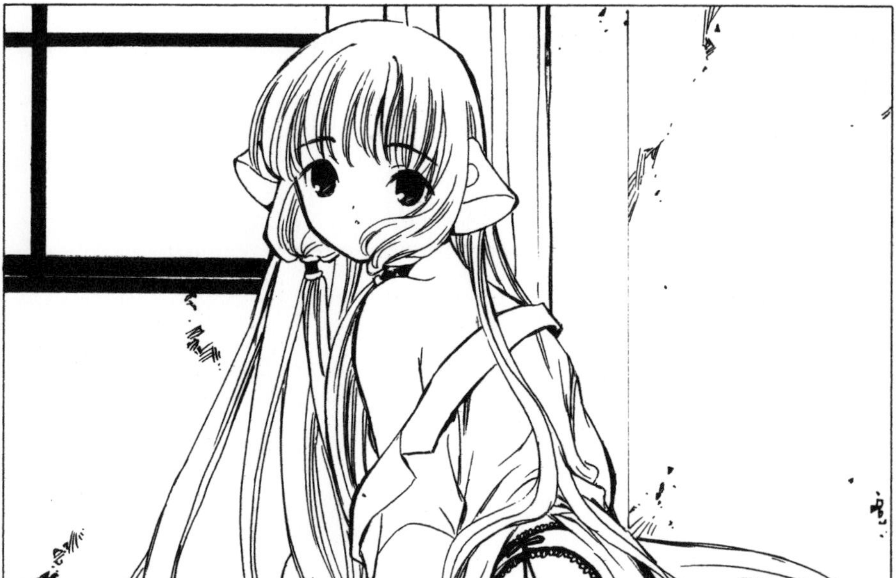

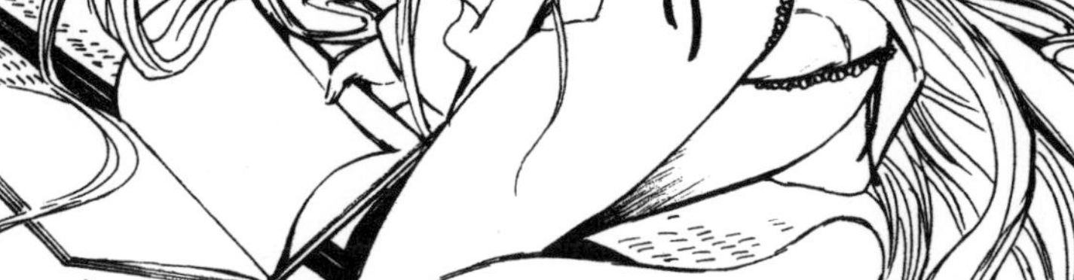
Chobits

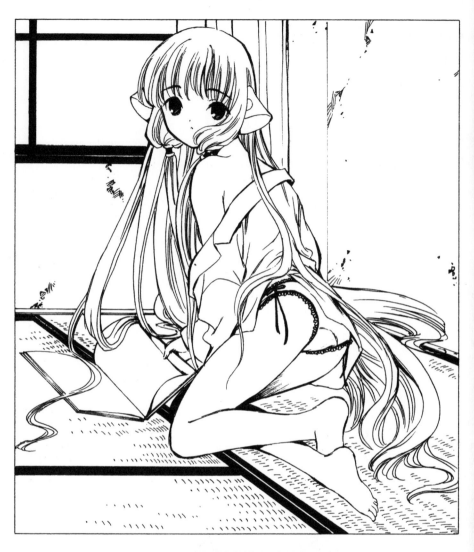

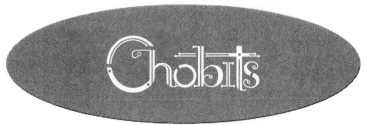

‹chapter.33›

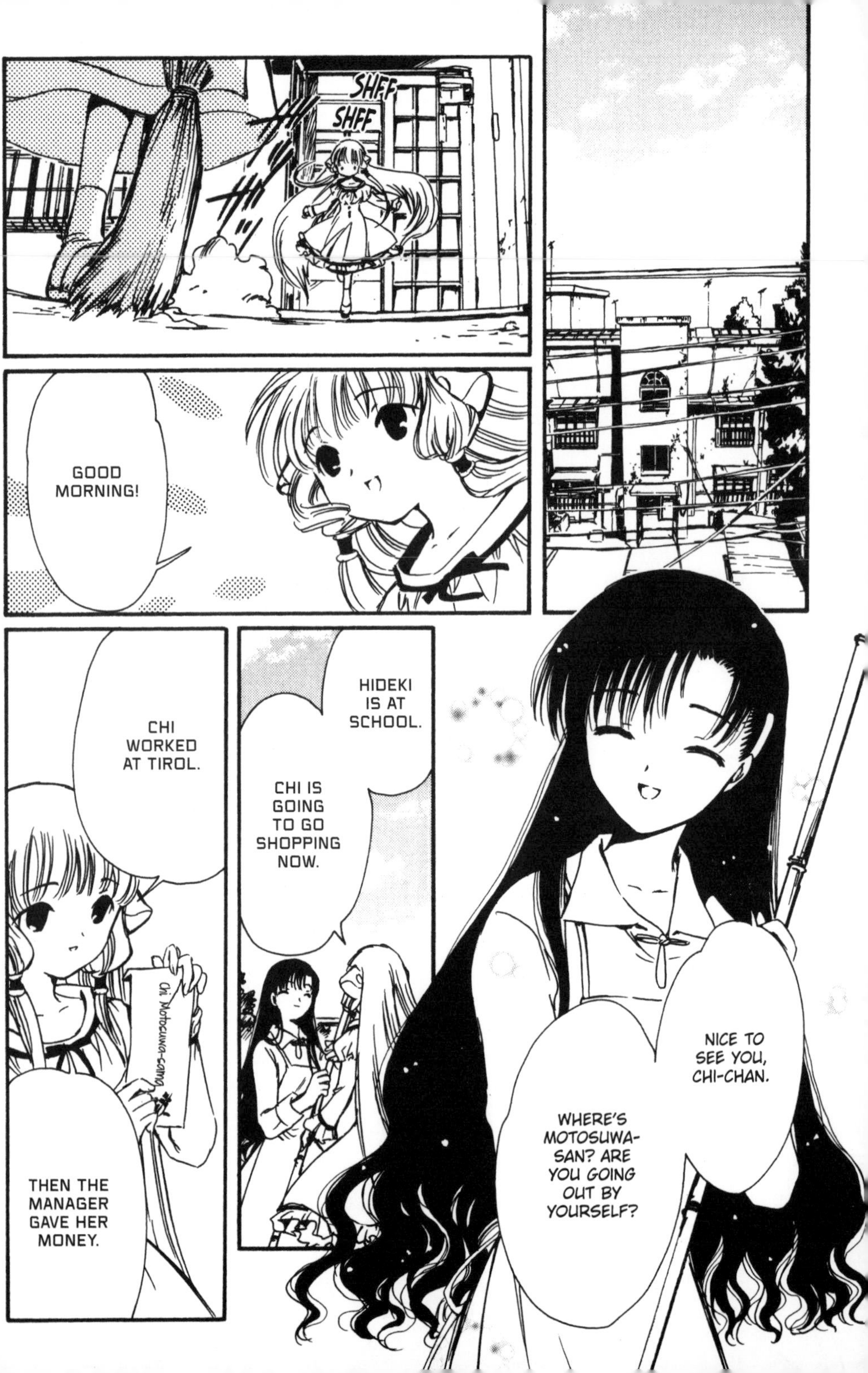
SHFF
SHFF
GOOD MORNING!
NICE TO SEE YOU, CHI-CHAN.
WHERE'S MOTOSUWA-SAN? ARE YOU GOING OUT BY YOURSELF?
HIDEKI IS AT SCHOOL.
CHI IS GOING TO GO SHOPPING NOW.
CHI WORKED AT TIROL.
Chi Motosuwa-sama
THEN THE MANAGER GAVE HER MONEY.

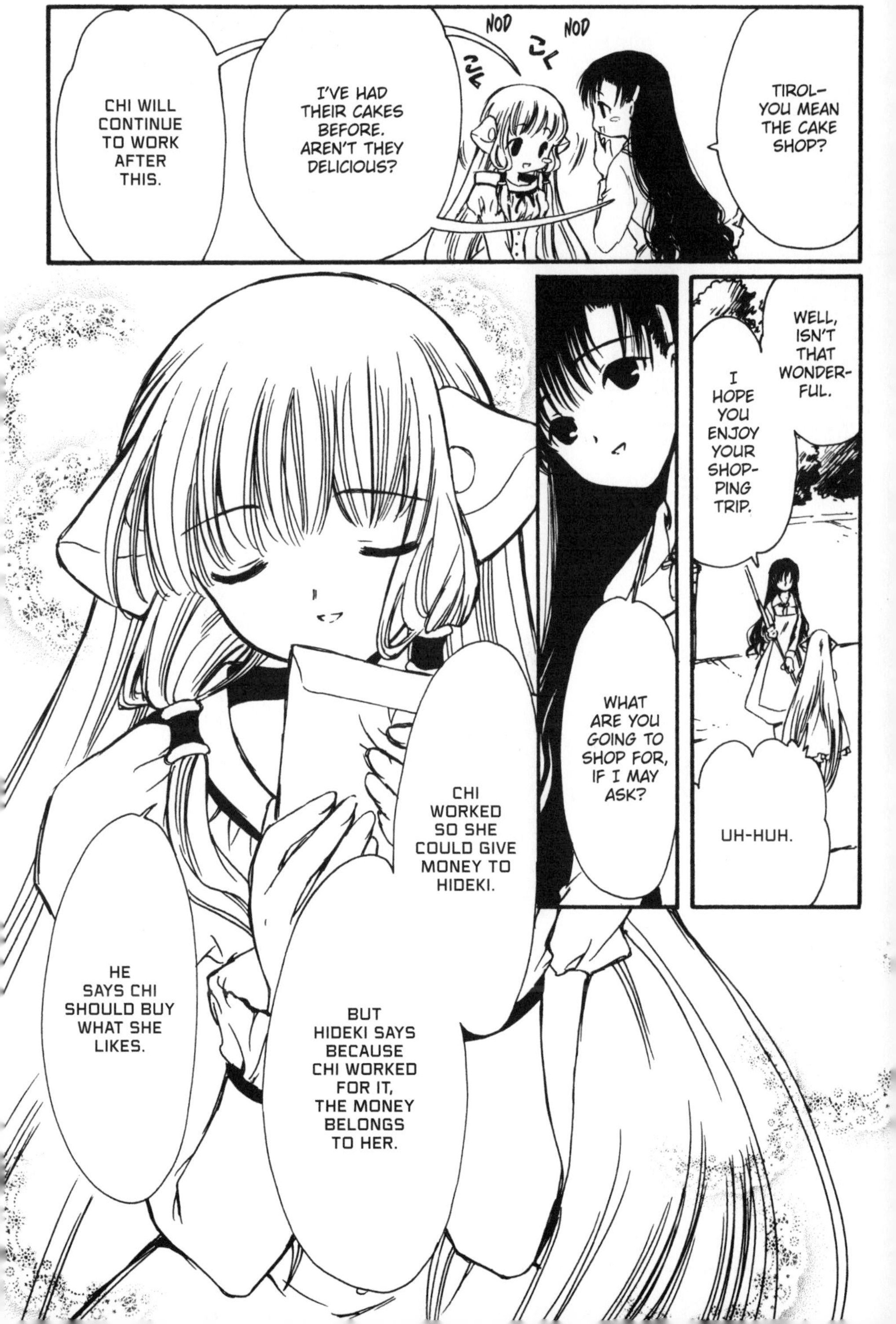
TIROL- YOU MEAN THE CAKE SHOP?
NOD
NOD
I'VE HAD THEIR CAKES BEFORE. AREN'T THEY DELICIOUS?
CHI WILL CONTINUE TO WORK AFTER THIS.
WELL, ISN'T THAT WONDERFUL.
I HOPE YOU ENJOY YOUR SHOPPING TRIP.
UH-HUH.
WHAT ARE YOU GOING TO SHOP FOR, IF I MAY ASK?
CHI WORKED SO SHE COULD GIVE MONEY TO HIDEKI.
BUT HIDEKI SAYS BECAUSE CHI WORKED FOR IT, THE MONEY BELONGS TO HER.
HE SAYS CHI SHOULD BUY WHAT SHE LIKES.

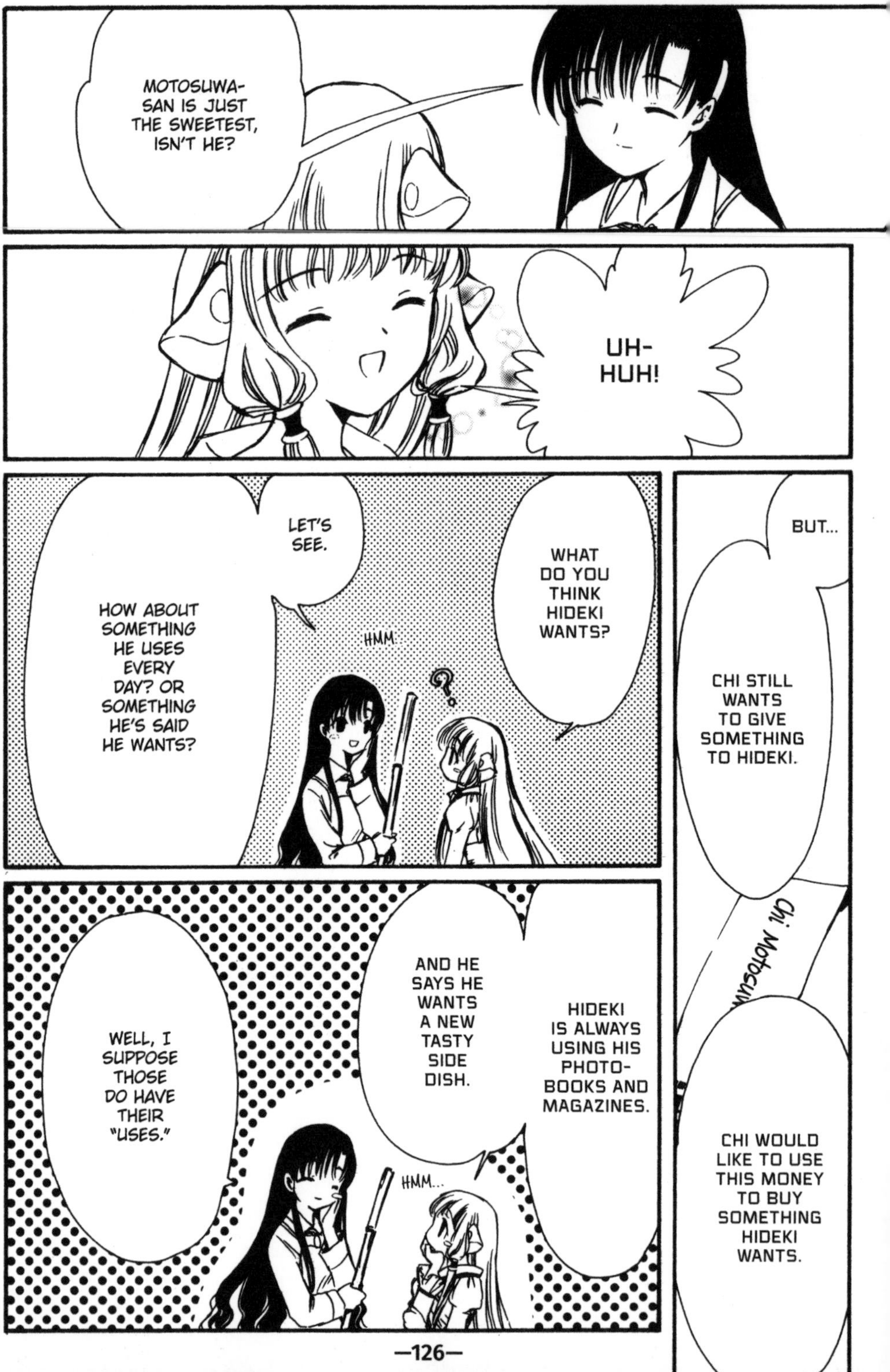
MOTOSUWA-SAN IS JUST THE SWEETEST, ISN'T HE?
UH-HUH!
BUT...
CHI STILL WANTS TO GIVE SOMETHING TO HIDEKI.
CHI WOULD LIKE TO USE THIS MONEY TO BUY SOMETHING HIDEKI WANTS.
WHAT DO YOU THINK HIDEKI WANTS?
LET'S SEE.
HMM.
HOW ABOUT SOMETHING HE USES EVERY DAY? OR SOMETHING HE'S SAID HE WANTS?
HIDEKI IS ALWAYS USING HIS PHOTO-BOOKS AND MAGAZINES.
AND HE SAYS HE WANTS A NEW TASTY SIDE DISH.
HMM...
WELL, I SUPPOSE THOSE DO HAVE THEIR "USES."

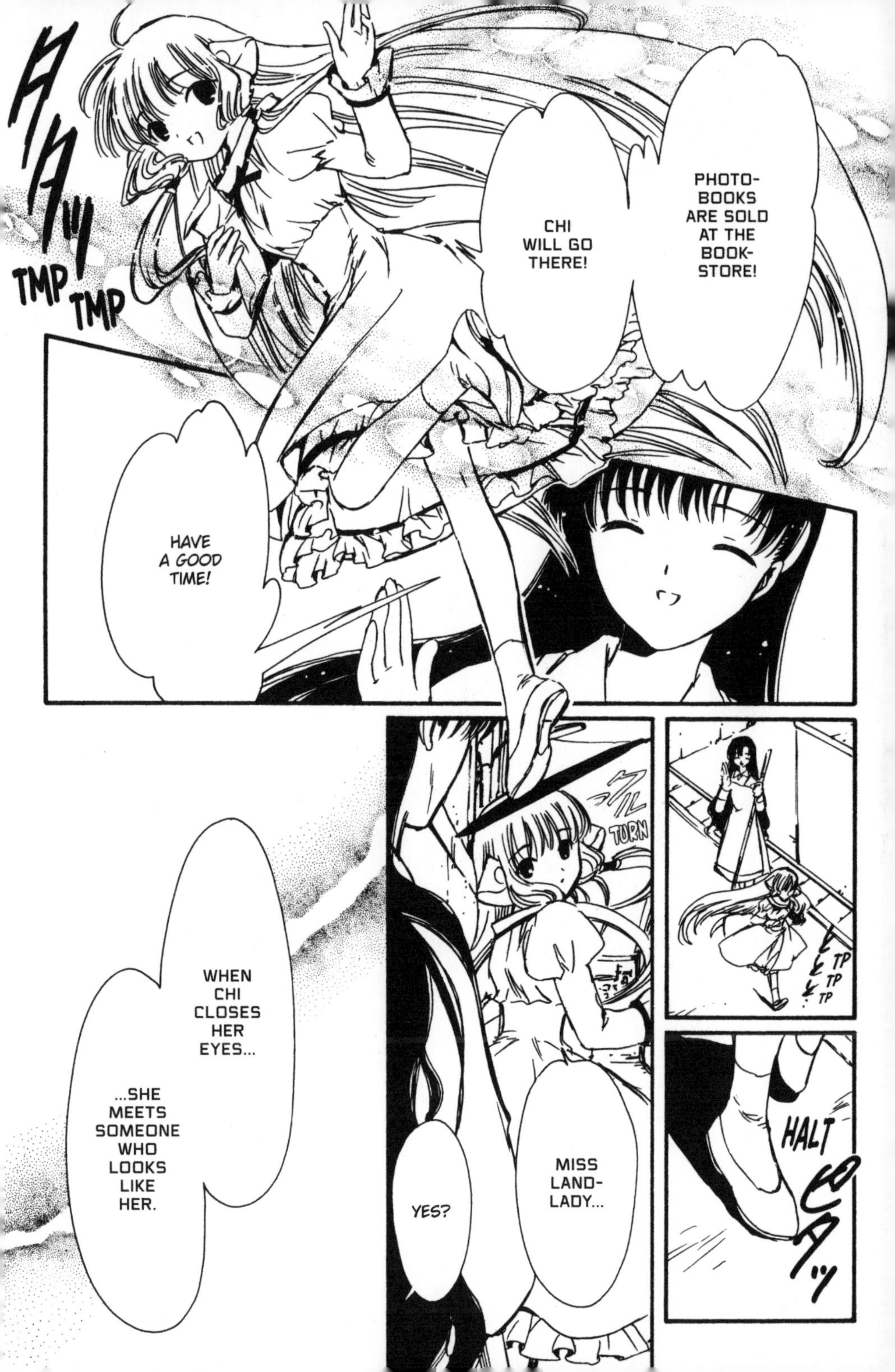
PHOTO-BOOKS ARE SOLD AT THE BOOK-STORE!
CHI WILL GO THERE!
TMP TMP
HAVE A GOOD TIME!
TP TP TP
HALT
TURN
MISS LAND-LADY...
YES?
WHEN CHI CLOSES HER EYES...
...SHE MEETS SOMEONE WHO LOOKS LIKE HER.

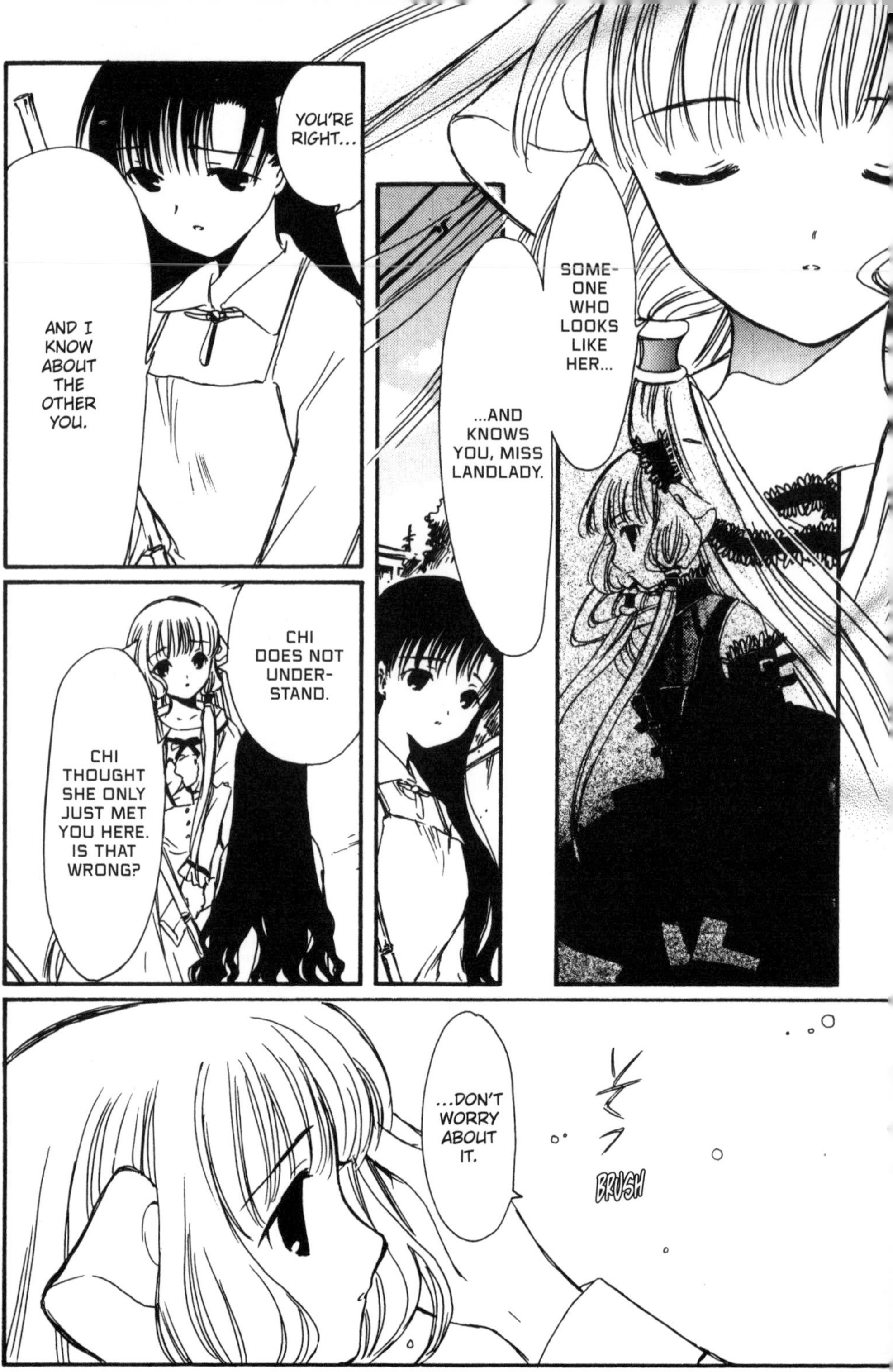
SOME-ONE WHO LOOKS LIKE HER...
...AND KNOWS YOU, MISS LANDLADY.
YOU'RE RIGHT...
AND I KNOW ABOUT THE OTHER YOU.
CHI DOES NOT UNDER-STAND.
CHI THOUGHT SHE ONLY JUST MET YOU HERE. IS THAT WRONG?
...DON'T WORRY ABOUT IT.
BRUSH

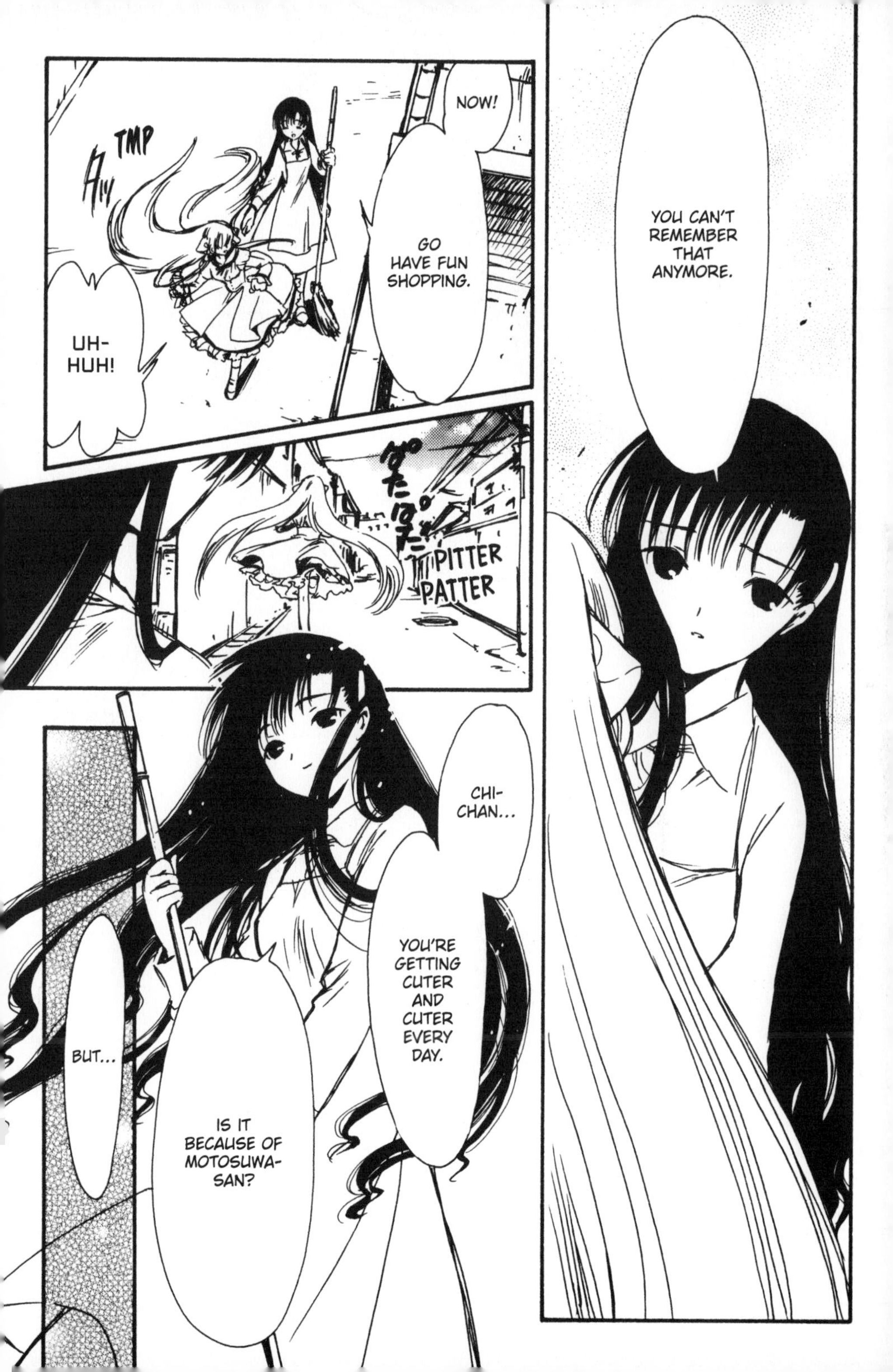
YOU CAN'T REMEMBER THAT ANYMORE.
NOW!
GO HAVE FUN SHOPPING.
TMP
UH-HUH!
PITTER PATTER
CHI-CHAN...
YOU'RE GETTING CUTER AND CUTER EVERY DAY.
BUT...
IS IT BECAUSE OF MOTOSUWA-SAN?

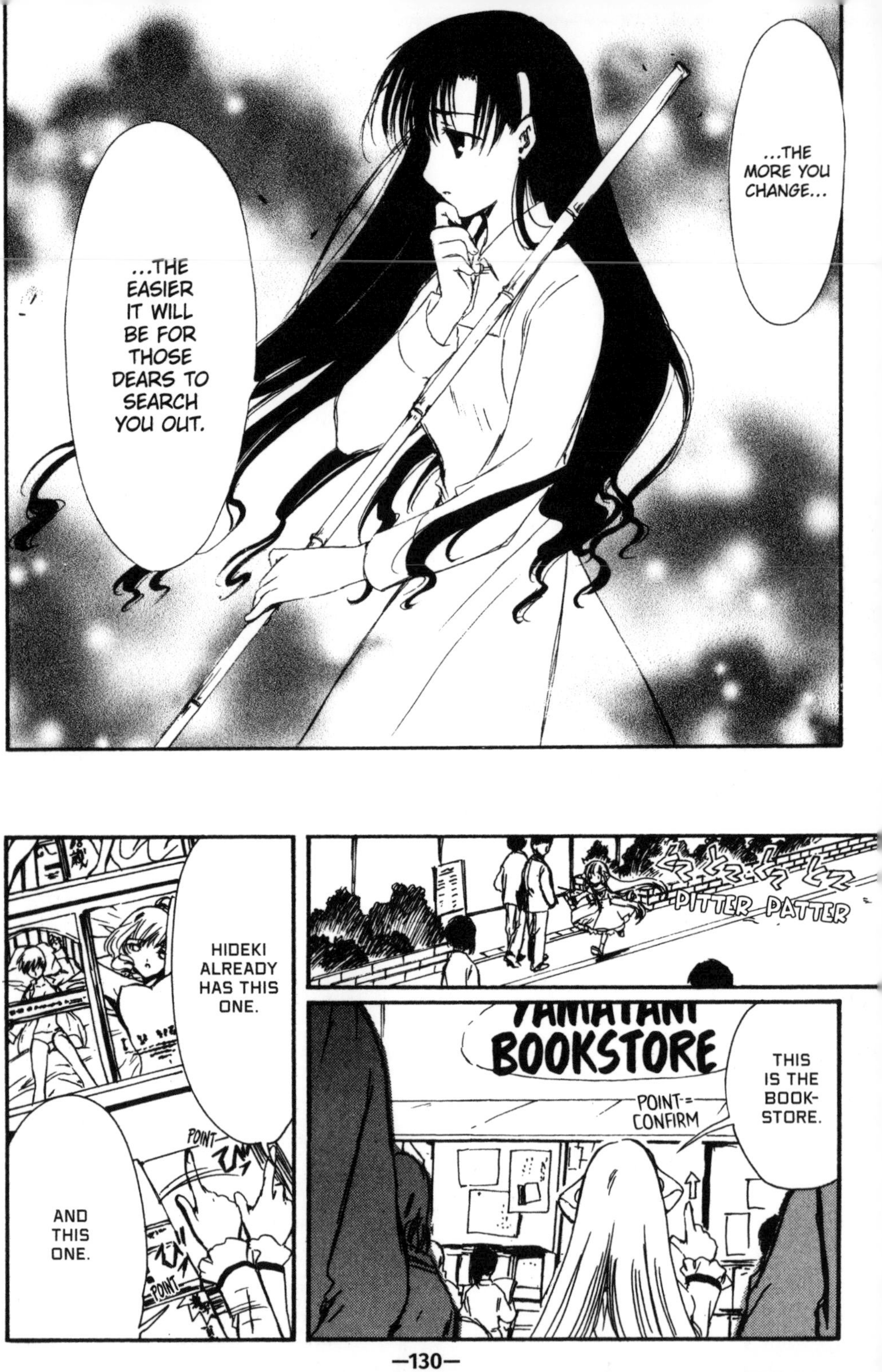
...THE MORE YOU CHANGE...
...THE EASIER IT WILL BE FOR THOSE DEARS TO SEARCH YOU OUT.
PITTER PATTER
THIS IS THE BOOK-STORE.
BOOKSTORE
POINT-= CONFIRM
HIDEKI ALREADY HAS THIS ONE.
POINT
AND THIS ONE.
POINT

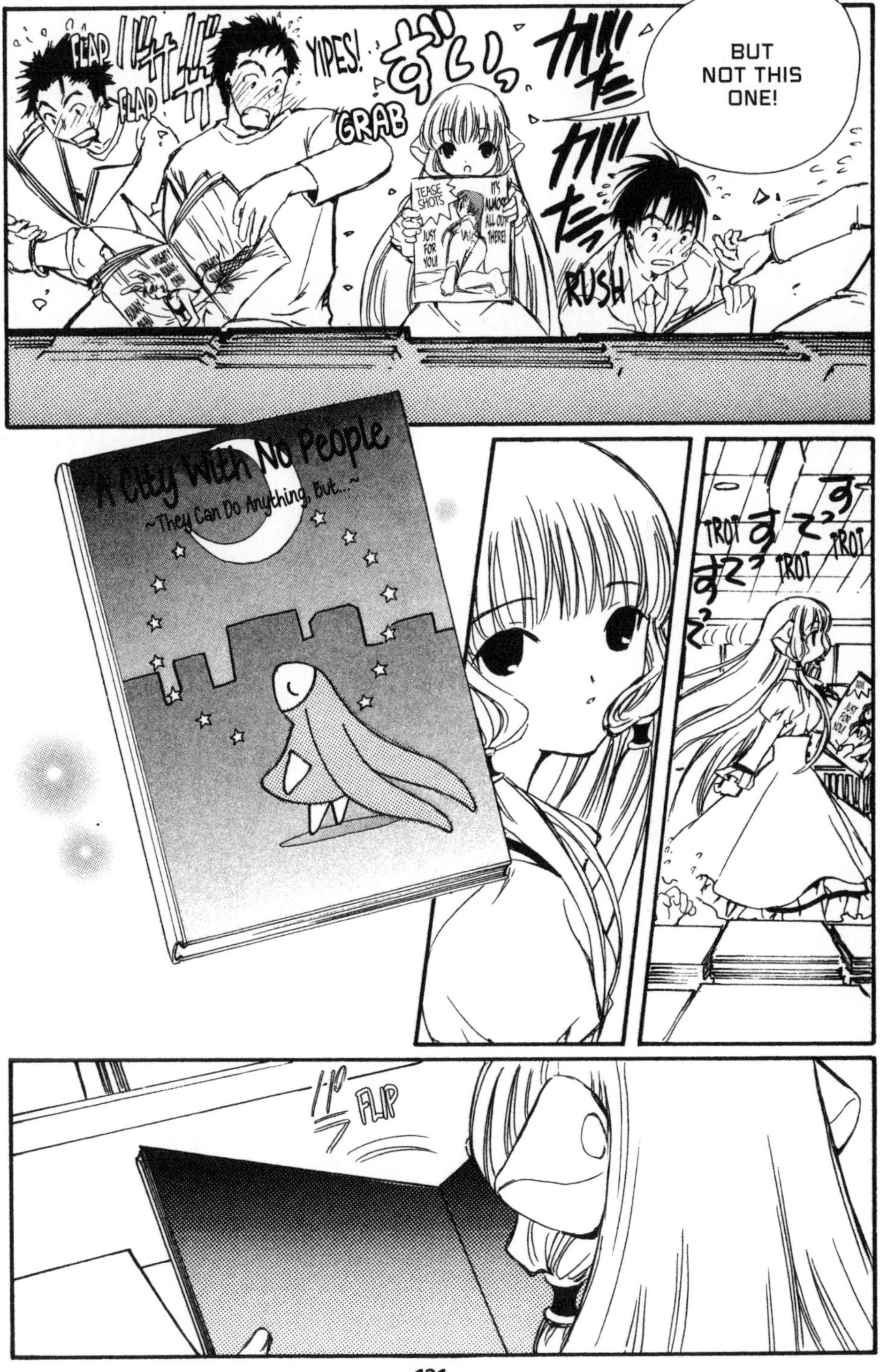
BUT NOT THIS ONE!
RUSH
TEASE SHOTS
IT'S ALMOST ALL OUT THERE!
JUST FOR YOU!
GRAB
YIPES!
FLAP
FLAP
TROT
TROT
TROT
A City With No People
~They Can Do Anything, But...~
FLIP

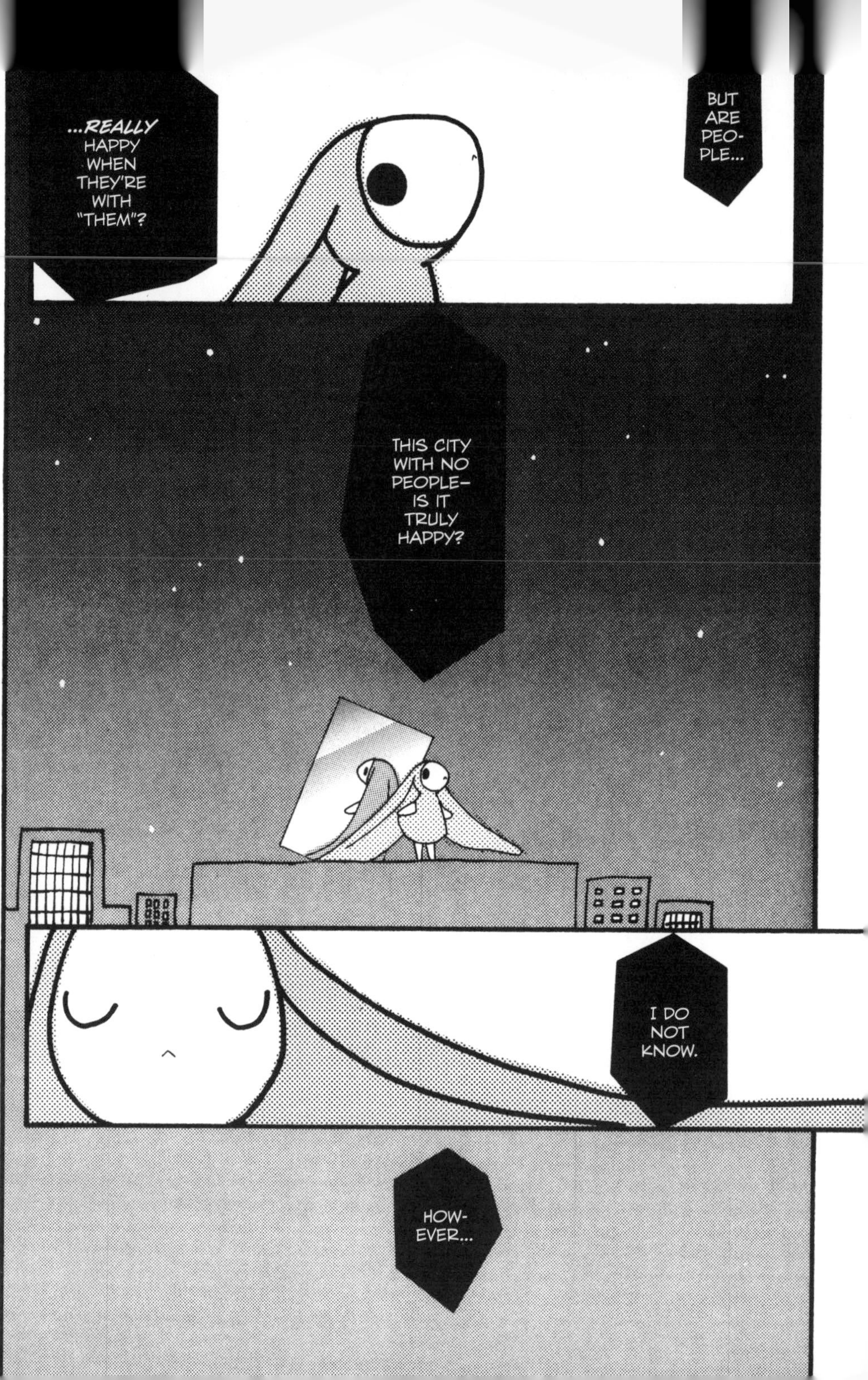
BUT ARE PEO-PLE...
...*REALLY* HAPPY WHEN THEY'RE WITH "THEM"?
THIS CITY WITH NO PEOPLE— IS IT TRULY HAPPY?
I DO NOT KNOW.
HOW-EVER...

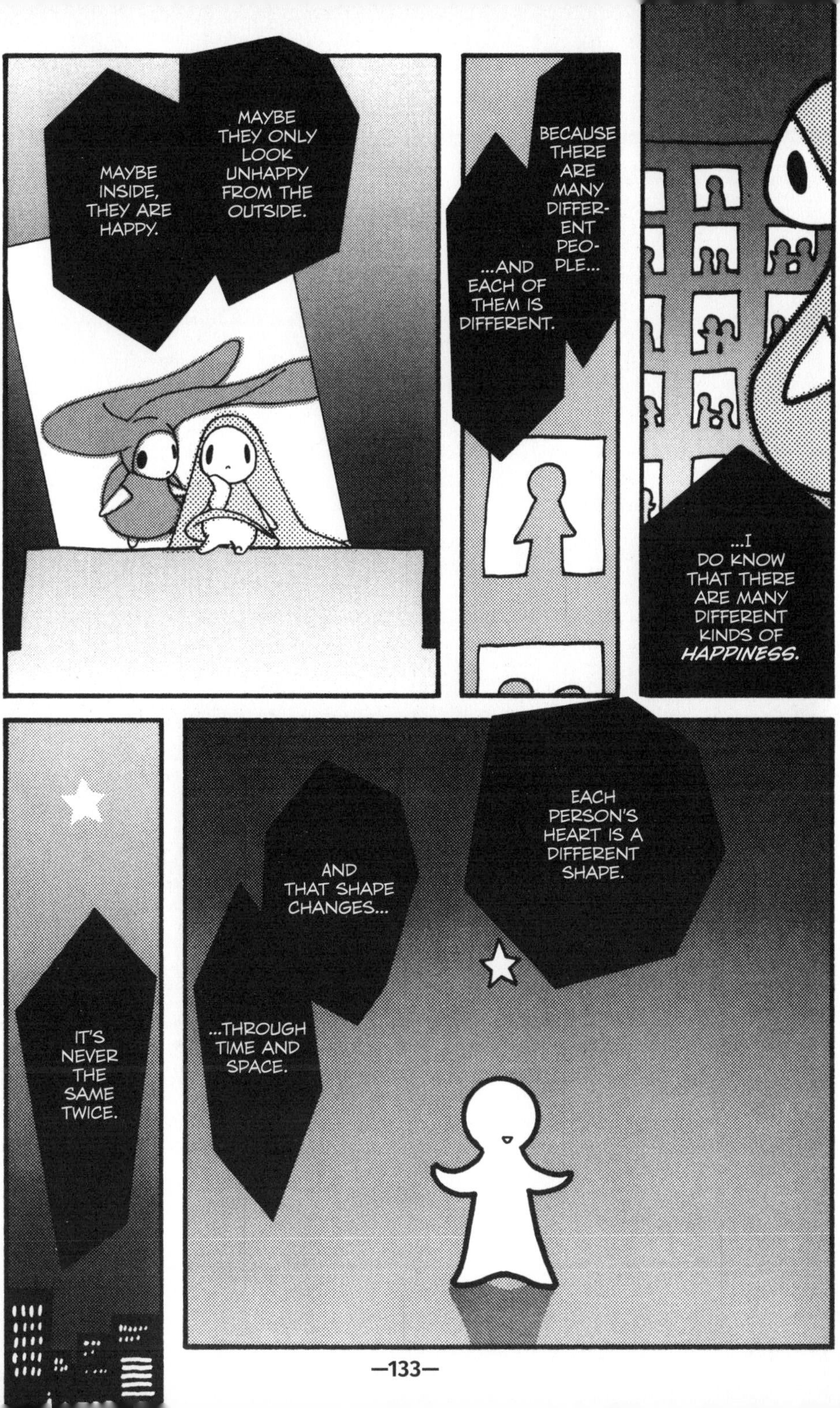
...I DO KNOW THAT THERE ARE MANY DIFFERENT KINDS OF *HAPPINESS.*
BECAUSE THERE ARE MANY DIFFER-ENT PEO-PLE...
...AND EACH OF THEM IS DIFFERENT.
MAYBE THEY ONLY LOOK UNHAPPY FROM THE OUTSIDE.
MAYBE INSIDE, THEY ARE HAPPY.
EACH PERSON'S HEART IS A DIFFERENT SHAPE.
AND THAT SHAPE CHANGES...
...THROUGH TIME AND SPACE.
IT'S NEVER THE SAME TWICE.

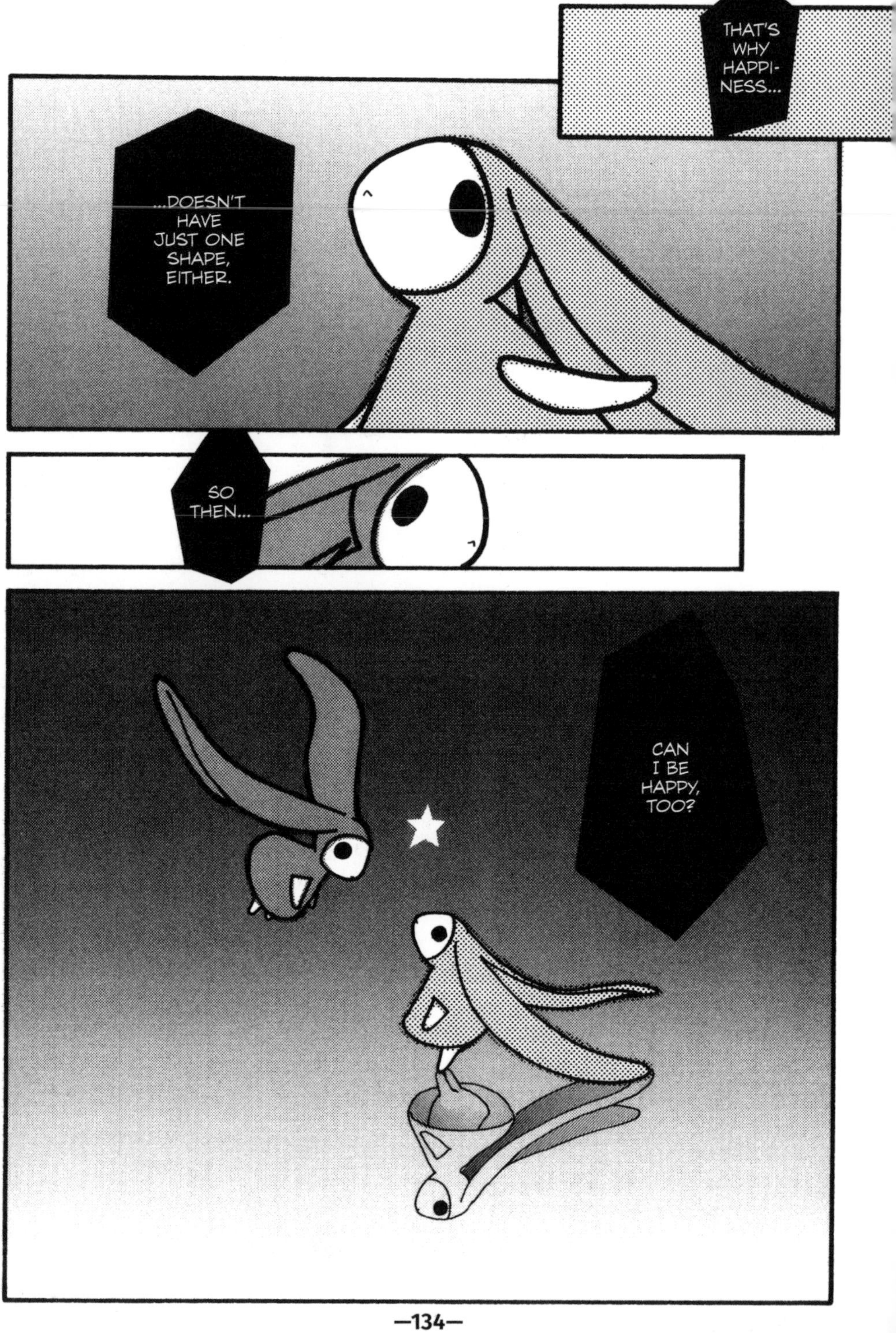
THAT'S WHY HAPPI-NESS...
...DOESN'T HAVE JUST ONE SHAPE, EITHER.
SO THEN...
CAN I BE HAPPY, TOO?

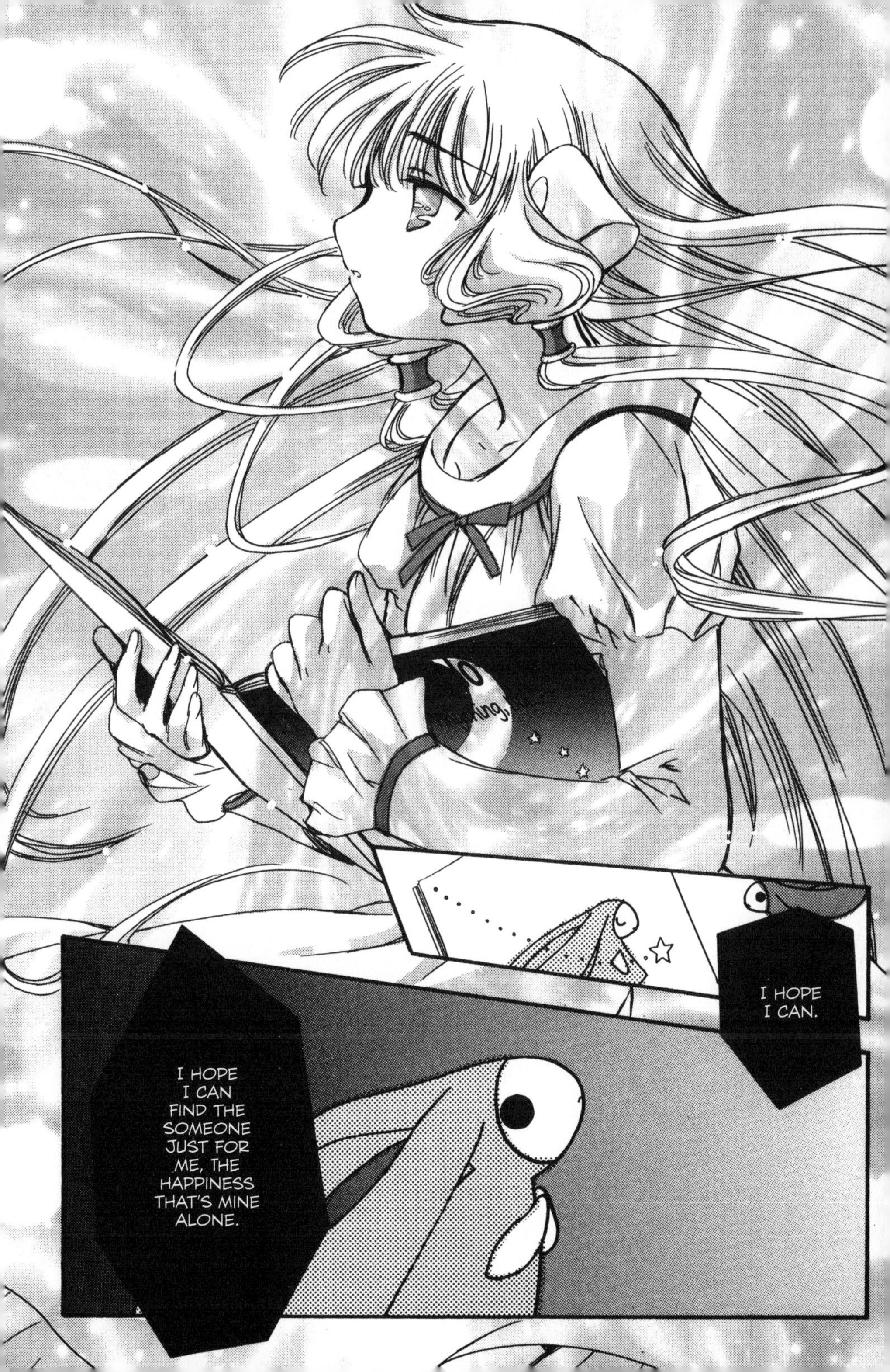
I HOPE I CAN.
I HOPE I CAN FIND THE SOMEONE JUST FOR ME, THE HAPPINESS THAT'S MINE ALONE.

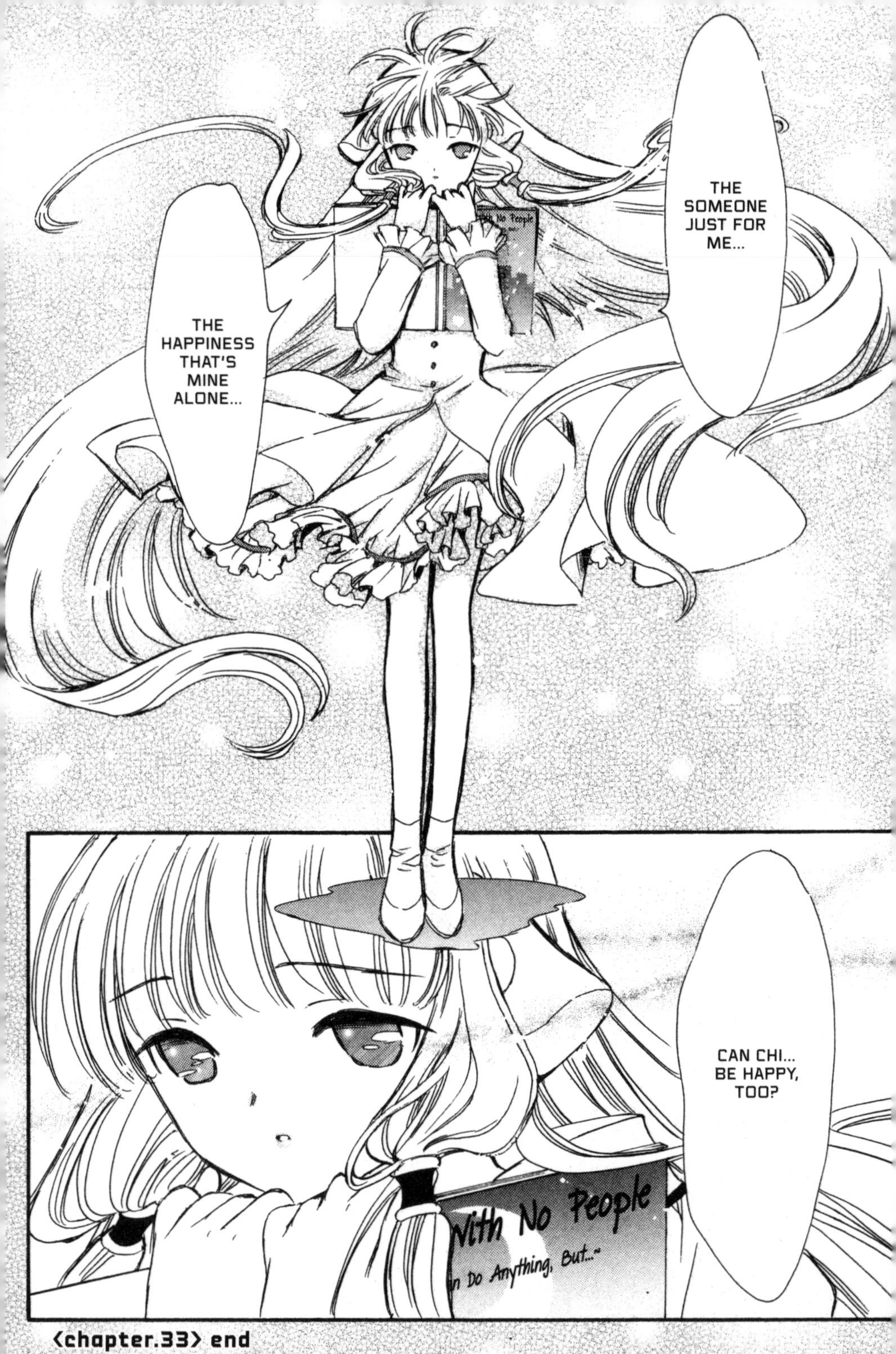
THE SOMEONE JUST FOR ME...
THE HAPPINESS THAT'S MINE ALONE...
CAN CHI... BE HAPPY, TOO?
With No People

<chapter.33> end

〈chapter.34〉

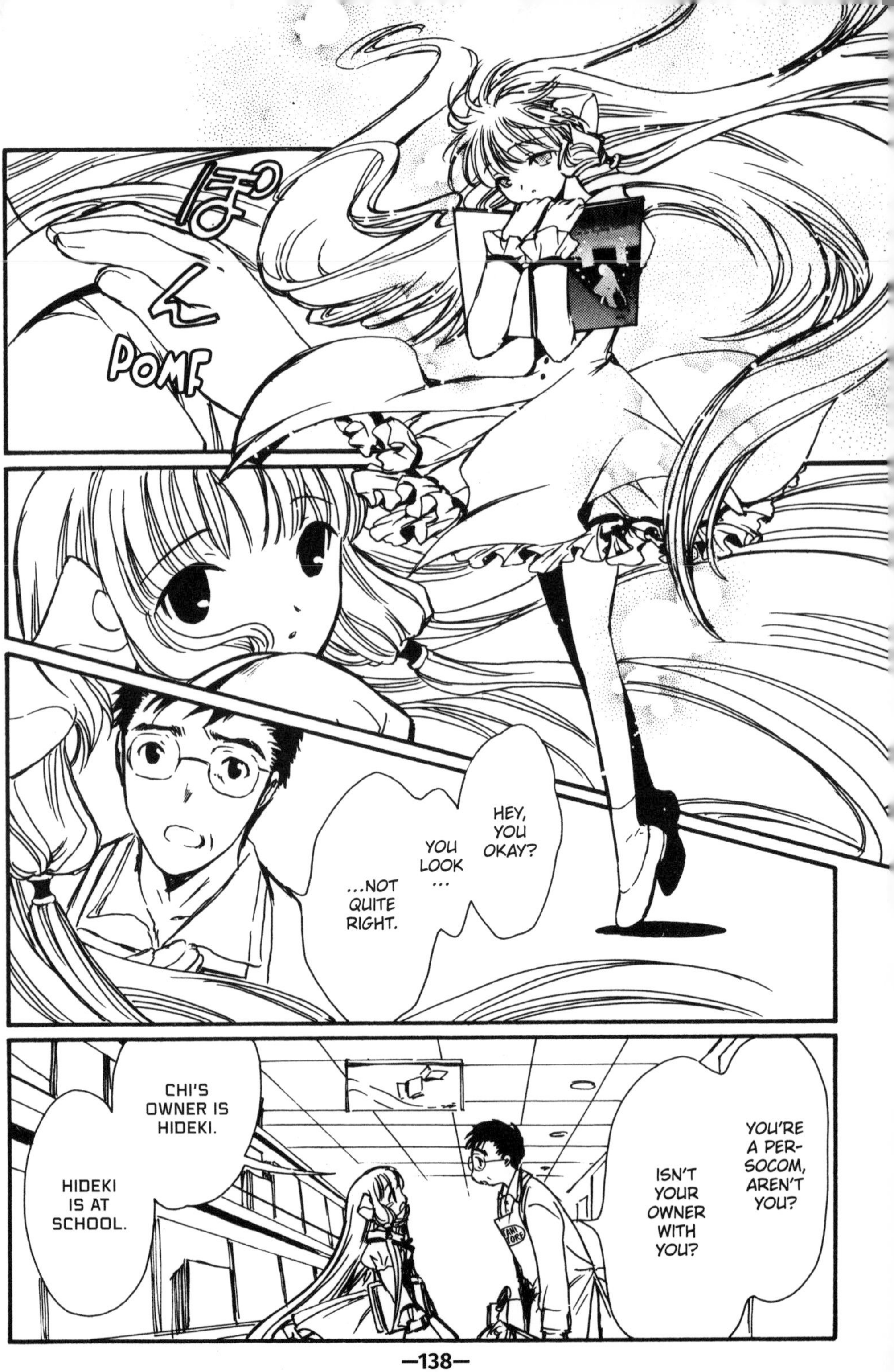
ぽん
POMF
HEY, YOU OKAY?
YOU LOOK ...
...NOT QUITE RIGHT.
YOU'RE A PER-SOCOM, AREN'T YOU?
ISN'T YOUR OWNER WITH YOU?
CHI'S OWNER IS HIDEKI.
HIDEKI IS AT SCHOOL.

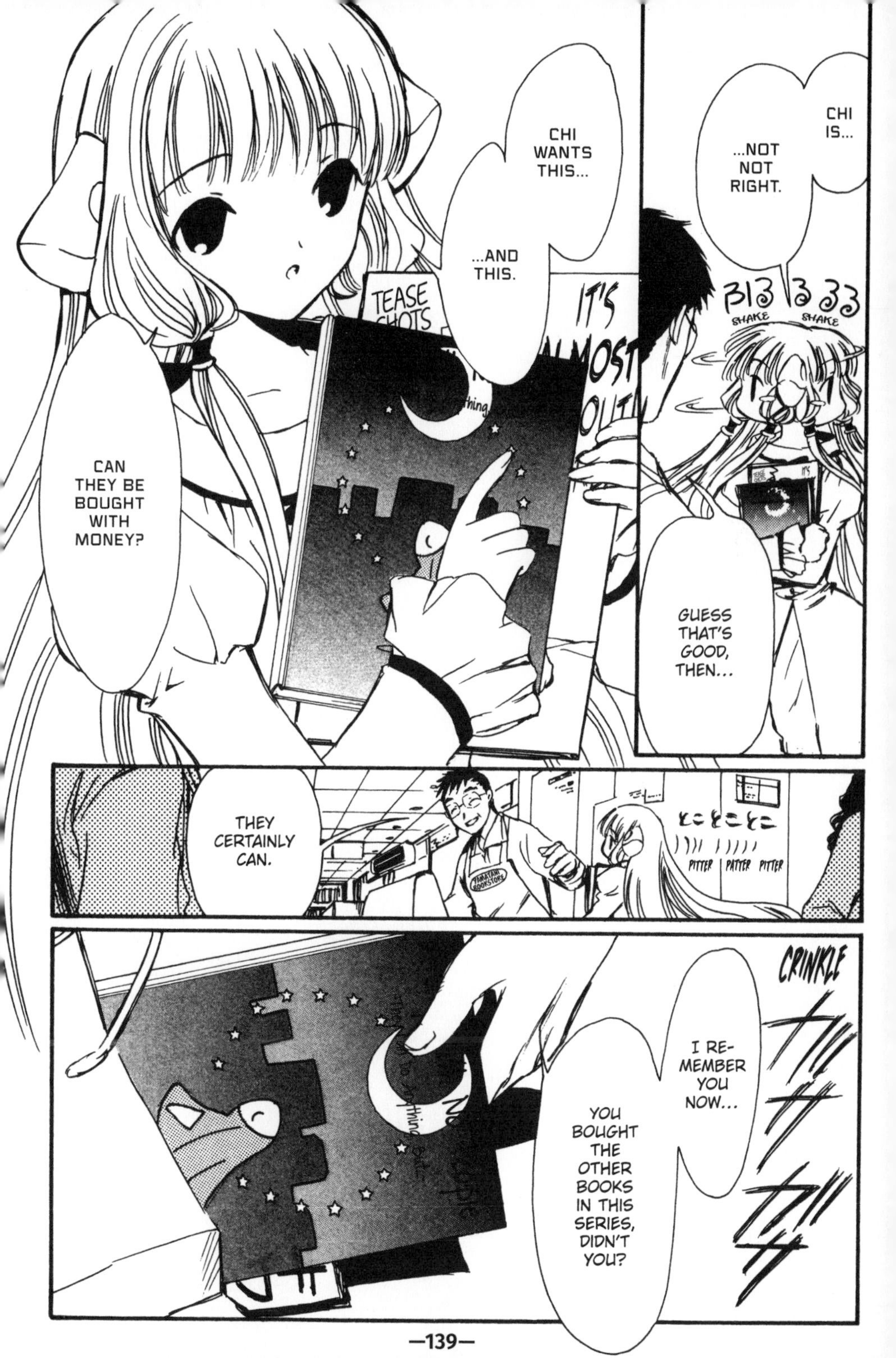
CHI IS...
...NOT NOT RIGHT.
SHAKE SHAKE
GUESS THAT'S GOOD, THEN...
CHI WANTS THIS...
...AND THIS.
TEASE SHOTS
IT'S
CAN THEY BE BOUGHT WITH MONEY?
THEY CERTAINLY CAN.
YAMATANI BOOKSTORE
PITTER PATTER PITTER
CRINKLE
I RE-MEMBER YOU NOW...
YOU BOUGHT THE OTHER BOOKS IN THIS SERIES, DIDN'T YOU?

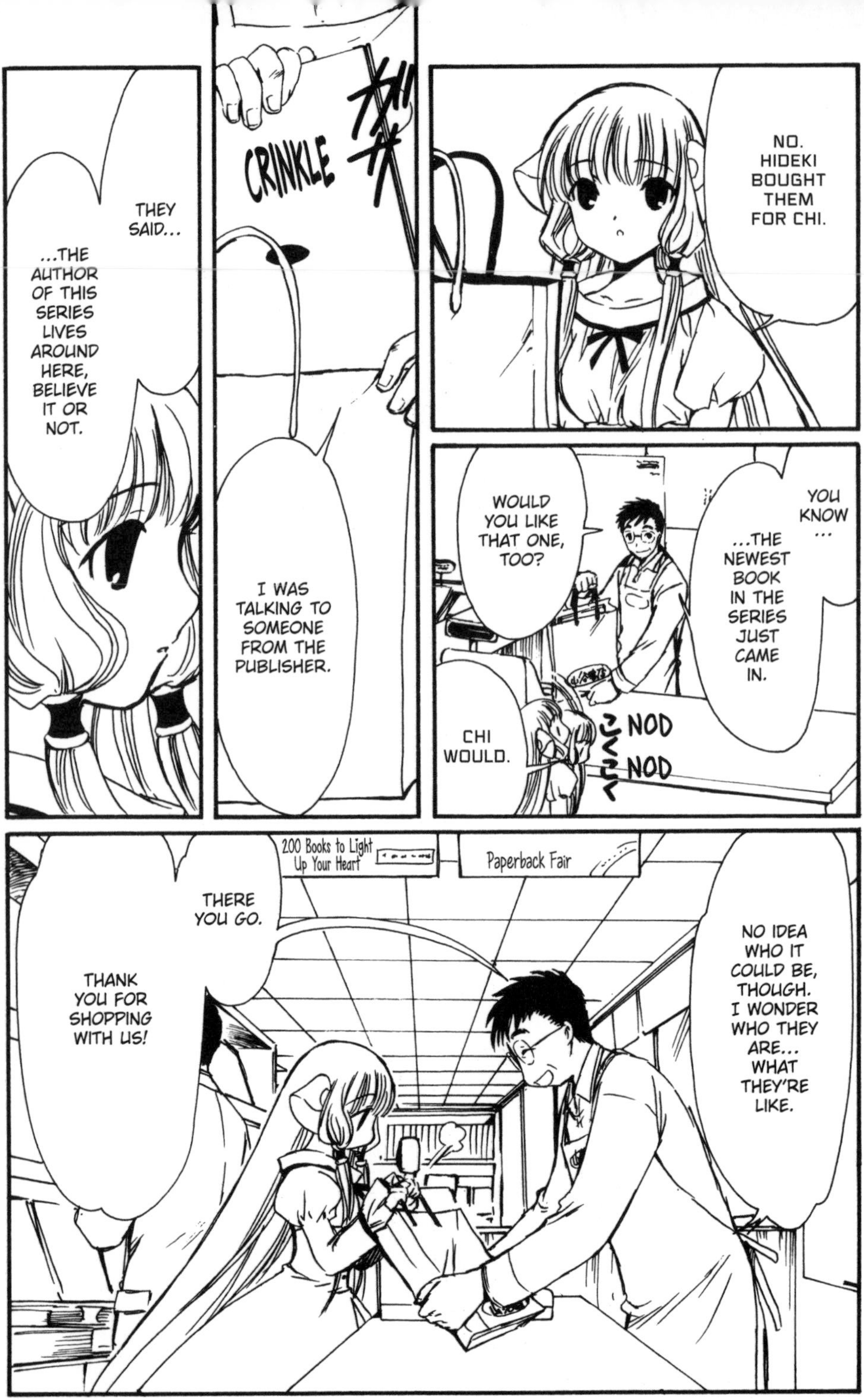
NO. HIDEKI BOUGHT THEM FOR CHI.
YOU KNOW...
...THE NEWEST BOOK IN THE SERIES JUST CAME IN.
WOULD YOU LIKE THAT ONE, TOO?
NOD
NOD
CHI WOULD.
CRINKLE
I WAS TALKING TO SOMEONE FROM THE PUBLISHER.
THEY SAID...
...THE AUTHOR OF THIS SERIES LIVES AROUND HERE, BELIEVE IT OR NOT.
Paperback Fair
200 Books to Light Up Your Heart
NO IDEA WHO IT COULD BE, THOUGH. I WONDER WHO THEY ARE... WHAT THEY'RE LIKE.
THERE YOU GO.
THANK YOU FOR SHOPPING WITH US!

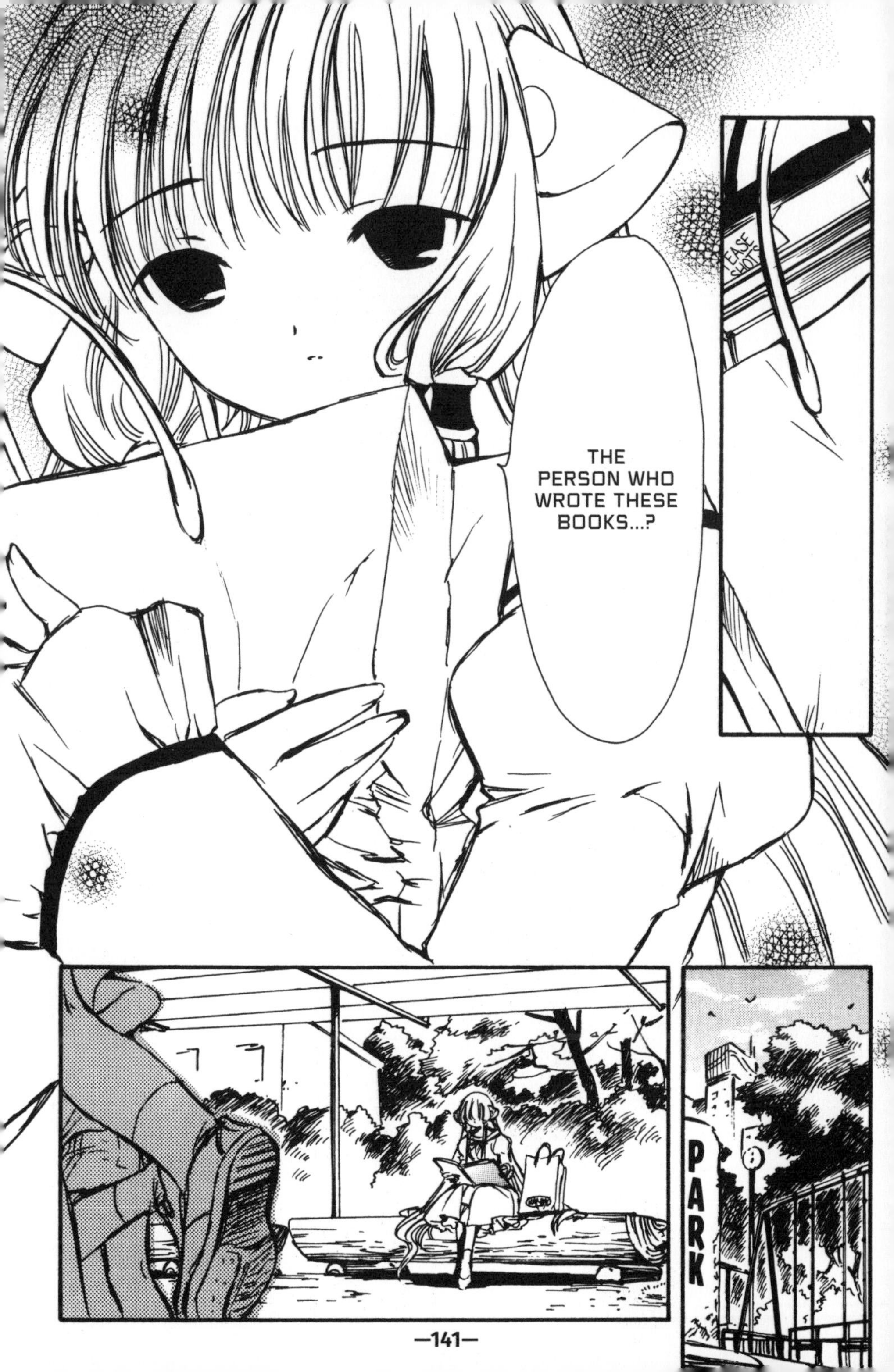
THE PERSON WHO WROTE THESE BOOKS...?
PARK

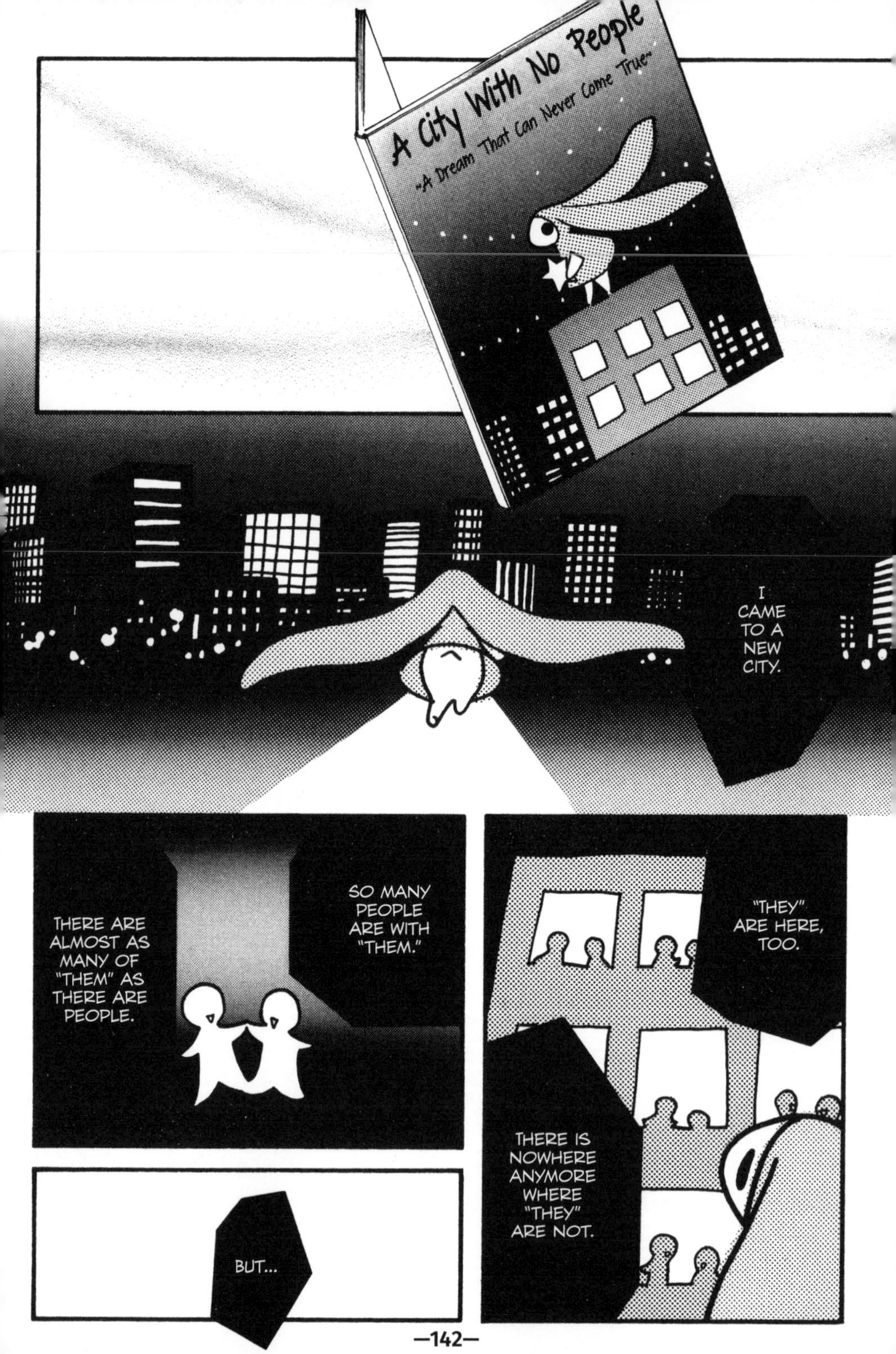
A City With No People
"A Dream That Can Never Come True"
I CAME TO A NEW CITY.
"THEY" ARE HERE, TOO.
THERE IS NOWHERE ANYMORE WHERE "THEY" ARE NOT.
SO MANY PEOPLE ARE WITH "THEM."
THERE ARE ALMOST AS MANY OF "THEM" AS THERE ARE PEOPLE.
BUT...

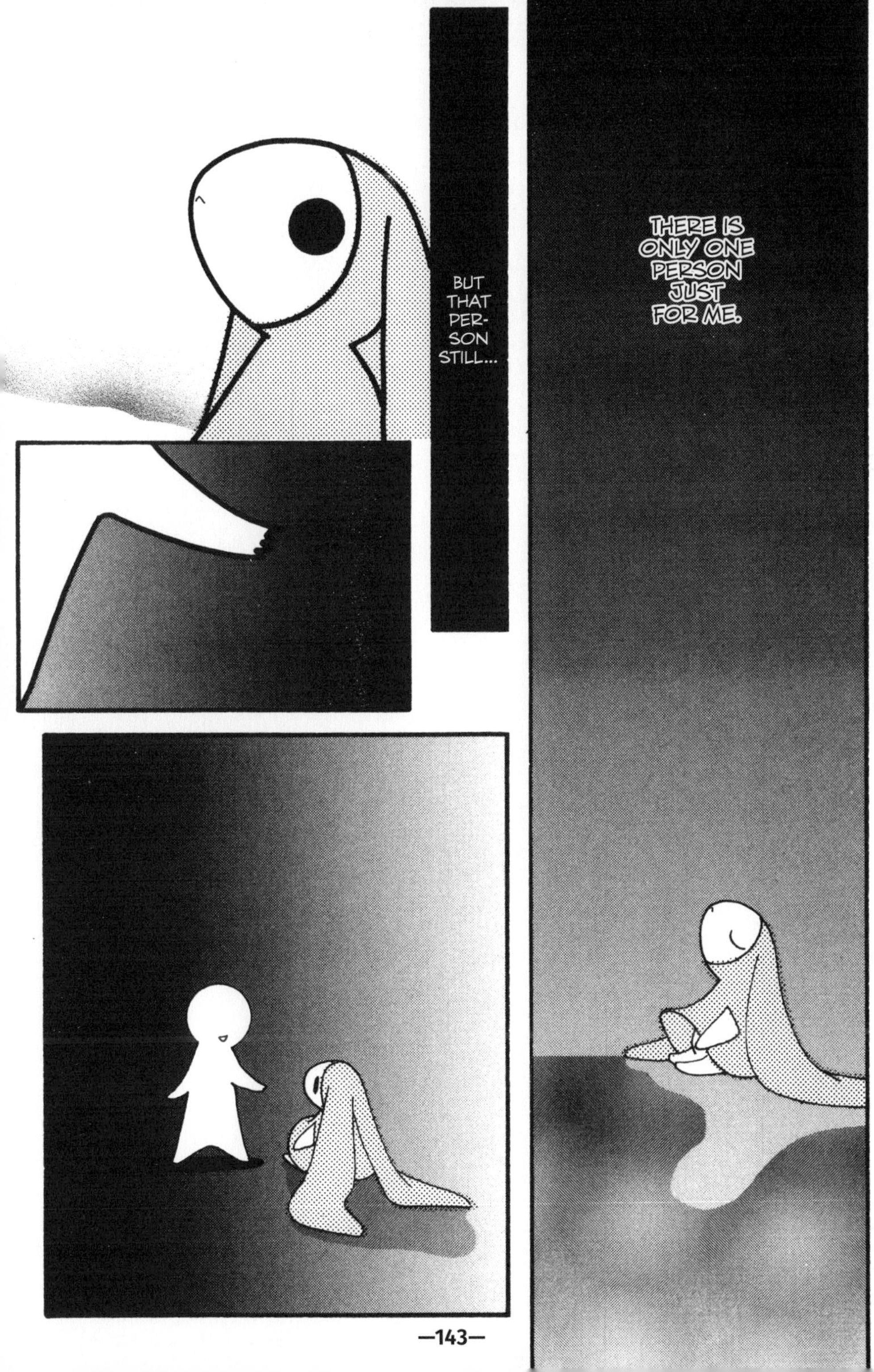
THERE IS ONLY ONE PERSON JUST FOR ME.
BUT THAT PER-SON STILL...

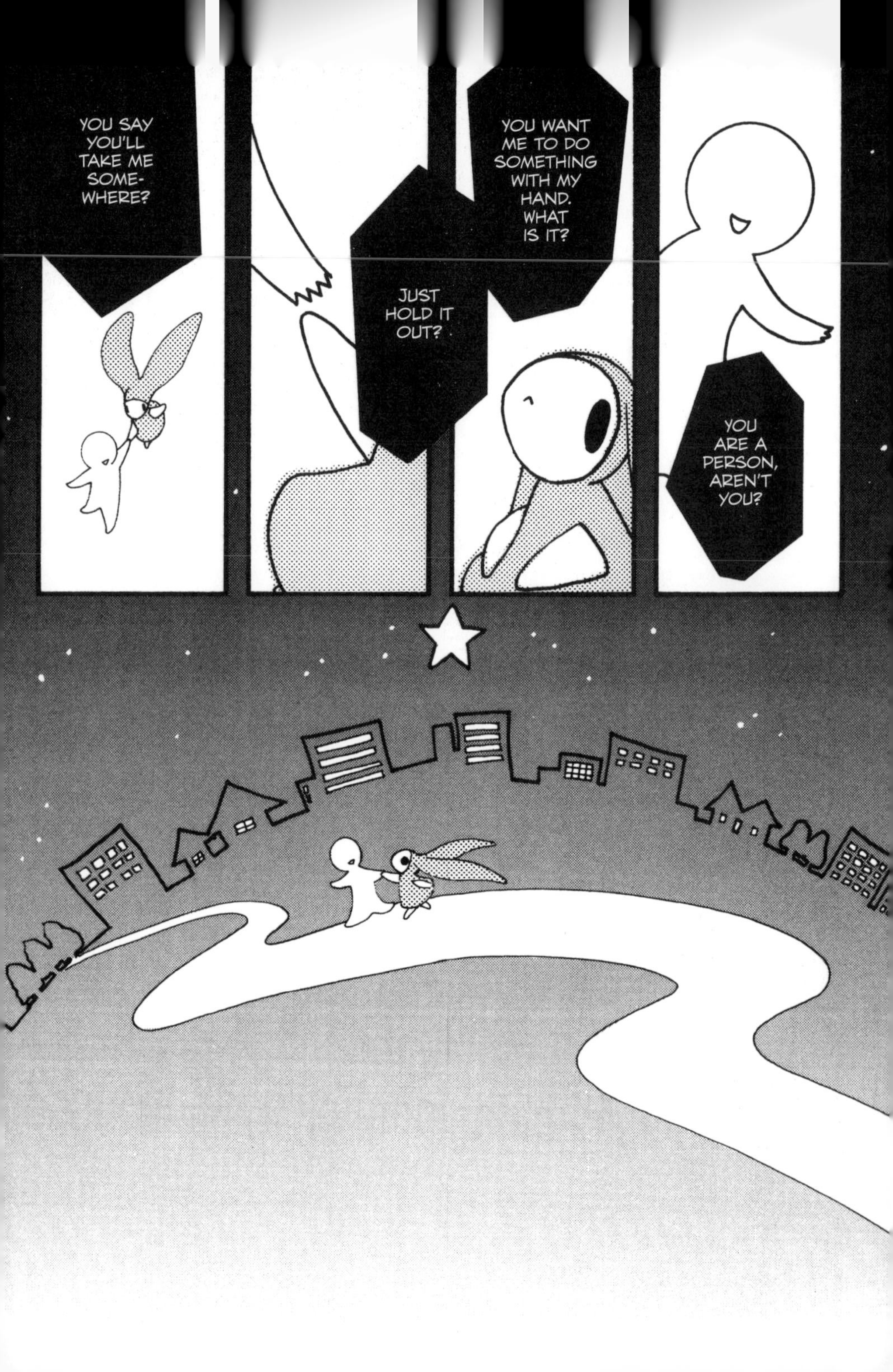
YOU SAY YOU'LL TAKE ME SOME-WHERE?
YOU WANT ME TO DO SOMETHING WITH MY HAND. WHAT IS IT?
JUST HOLD IT OUT?
YOU ARE A PERSON, AREN'T YOU?

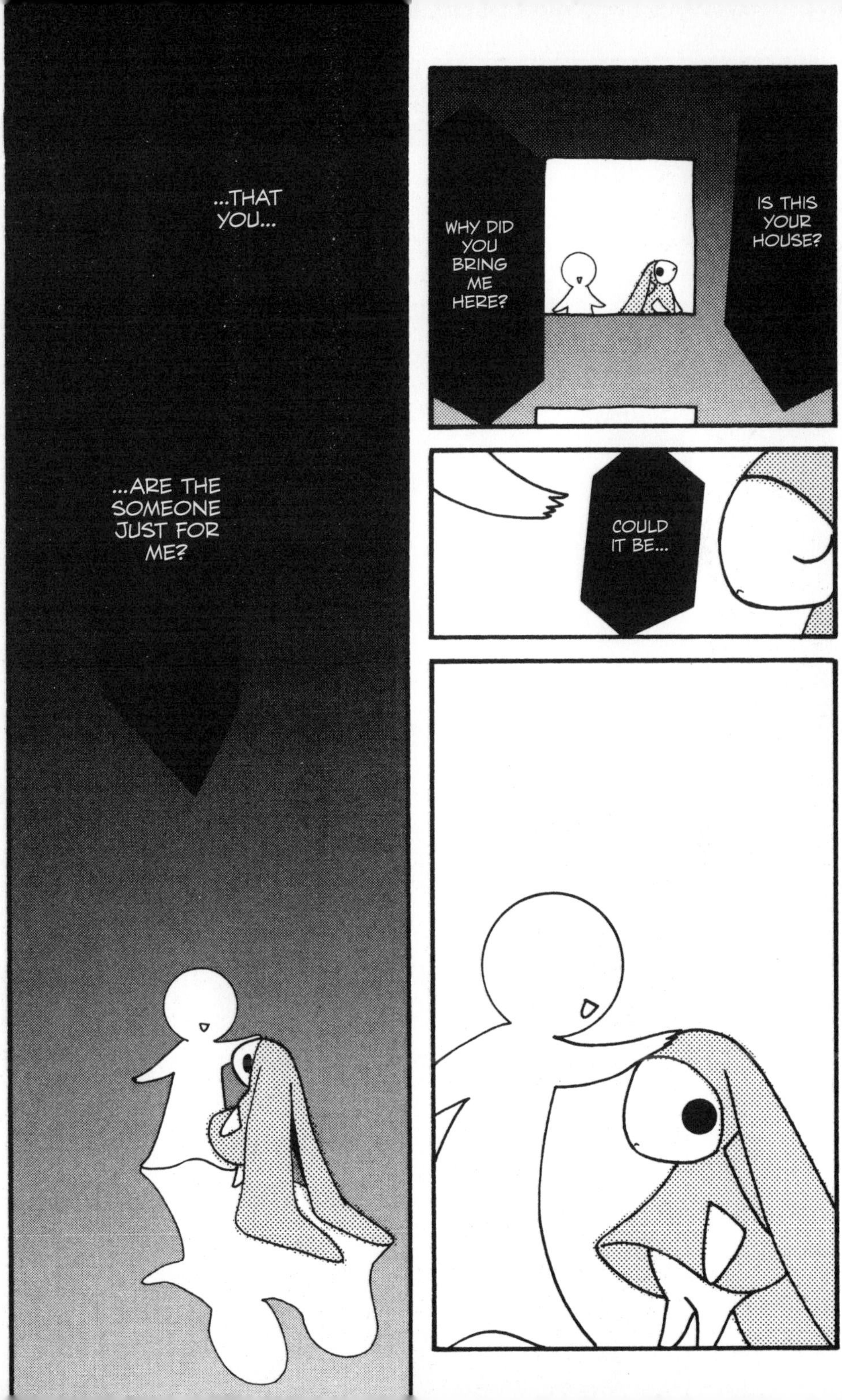
IS THIS YOUR HOUSE?
WHY DID YOU BRING ME HERE?
COULD IT BE...
...THAT YOU...
...ARE THE SOMEONE JUST FOR ME?

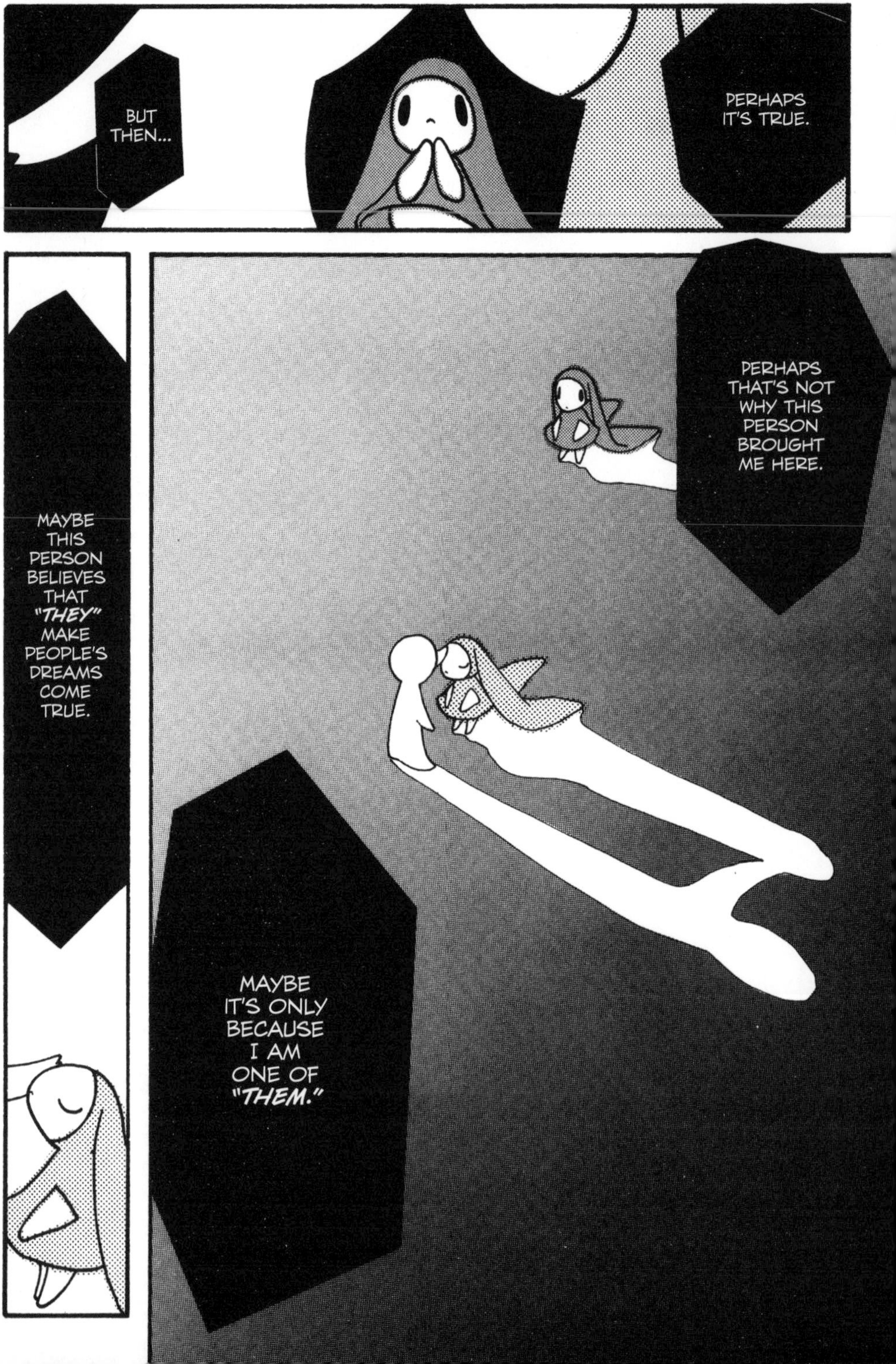
PERHAPS IT'S TRUE.
BUT THEN...
PERHAPS THAT'S NOT WHY THIS PERSON BROUGHT ME HERE.
MAYBE IT'S ONLY BECAUSE I AM ONE OF "THEM."
MAYBE THIS PERSON BELIEVES THAT "THEY" MAKE PEOPLE'S DREAMS COME TRUE.

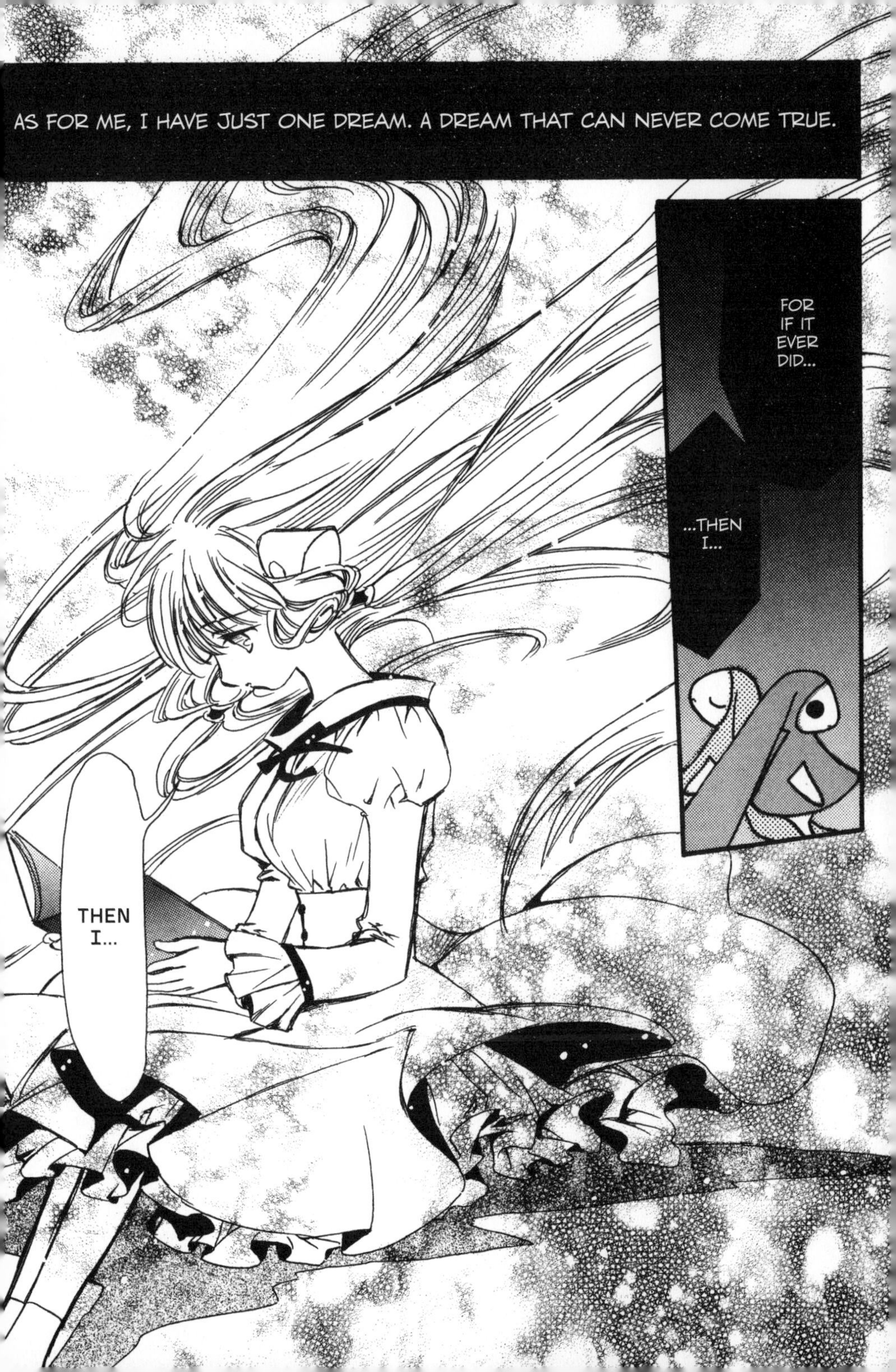
AS FOR ME, I HAVE JUST ONE DREAM. A DREAM THAT CAN NEVER COME TRUE.
FOR IF IT EVER DID...
...THEN I...
THEN I...

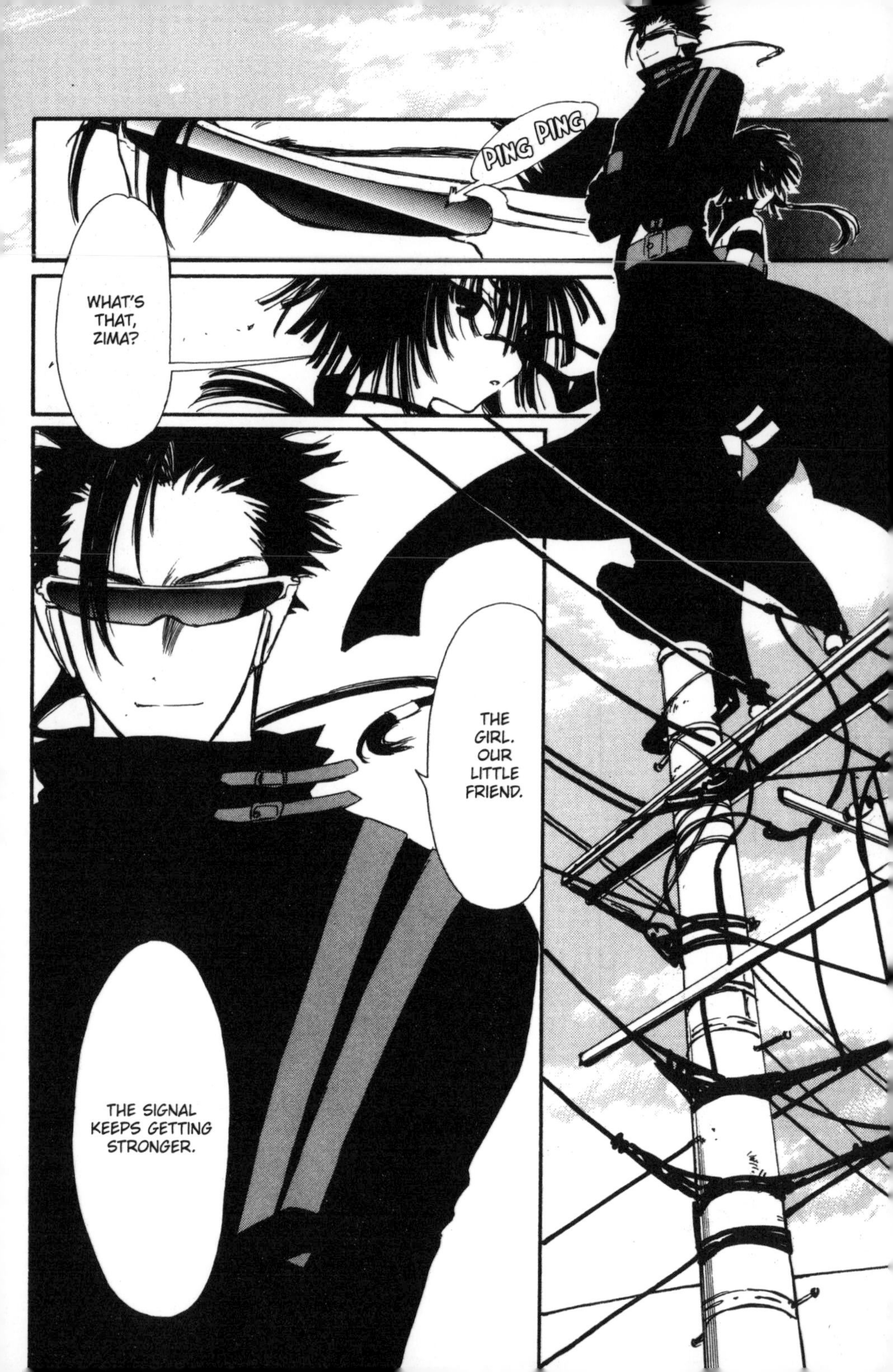
PING PING
WHAT'S THAT, ZIMA?
THE GIRL. OUR LITTLE FRIEND.
THE SIGNAL KEEPS GETTING STRONGER.

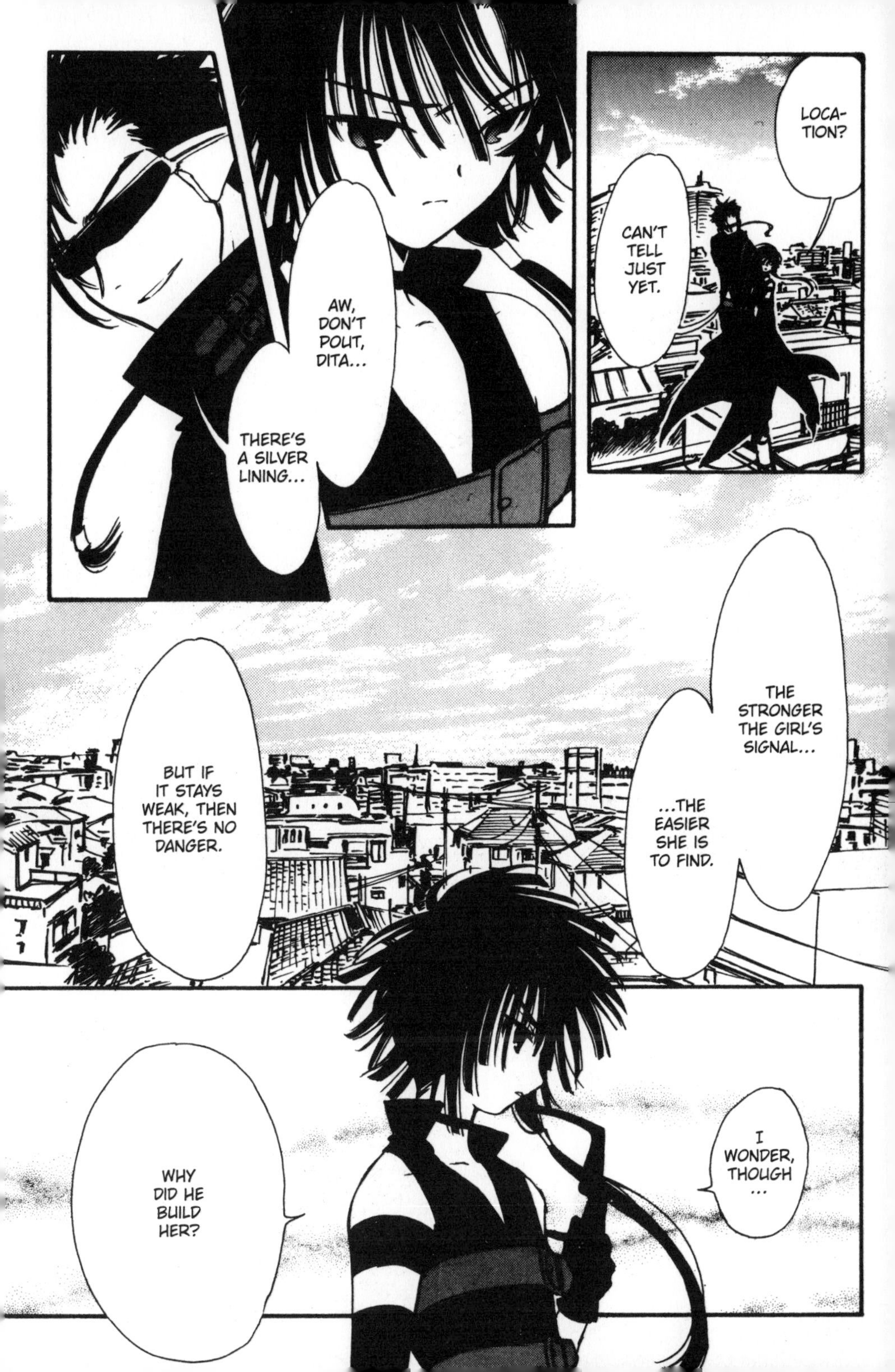
LOCA-TION?
CAN'T TELL JUST YET.
AW, DON'T POUT, DITA...
THERE'S A SILVER LINING...
THE STRONGER THE GIRL'S SIGNAL...
...THE EASIER SHE IS TO FIND.
BUT IF IT STAYS WEAK, THEN THERE'S NO DANGER.
I WONDER, THOUGH...
WHY DID HE BUILD HER?

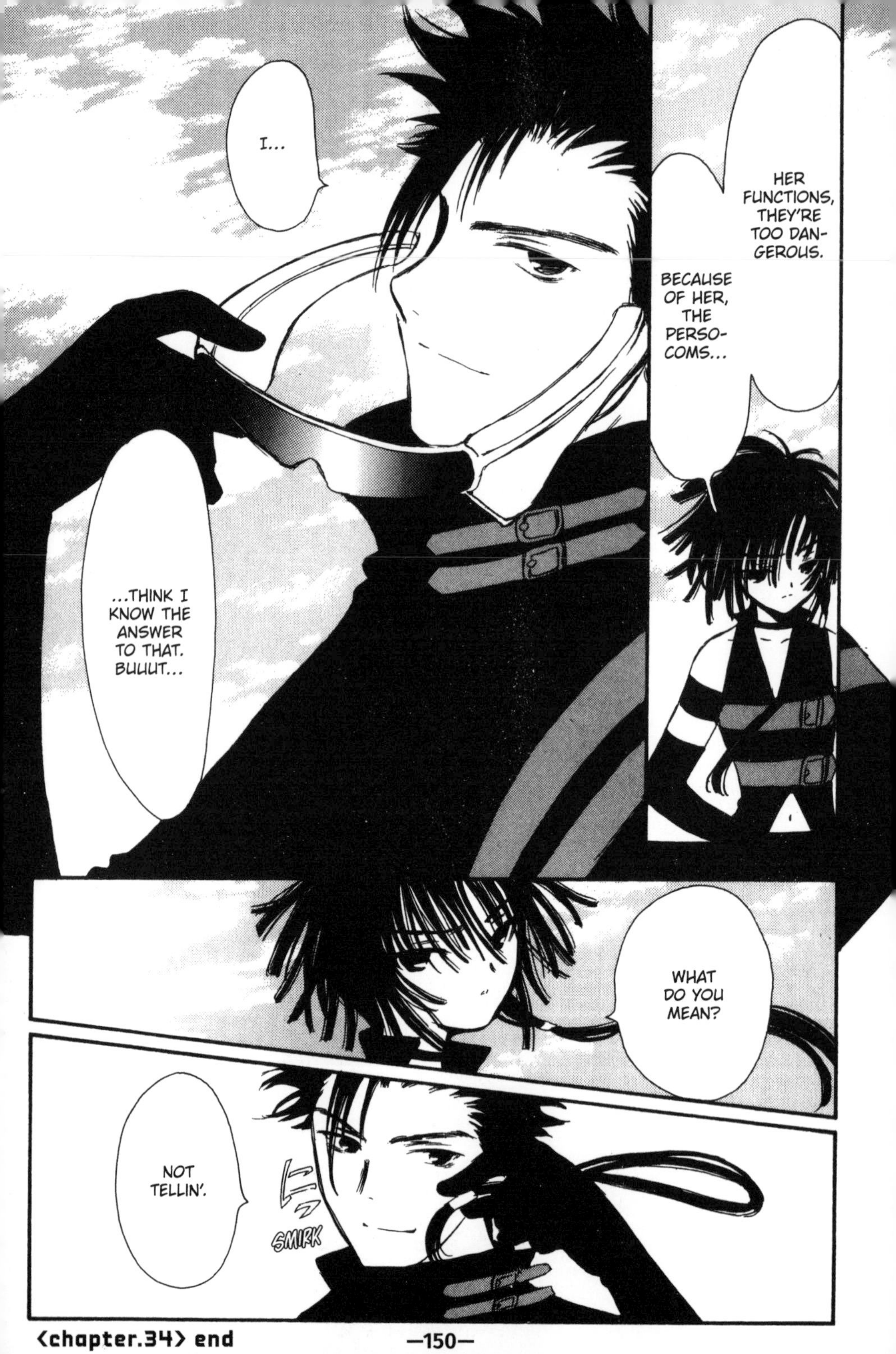
HER FUNCTIONS, THEY'RE TOO DAN-GEROUS.
BECAUSE OF HER, THE PERSO-COMS...
I...
...THINK I KNOW THE ANSWER TO THAT. BUUUT...
WHAT DO YOU MEAN?
NOT TELLIN'.
SMIRK

<chapter.34> end

⟨chapter.35⟩

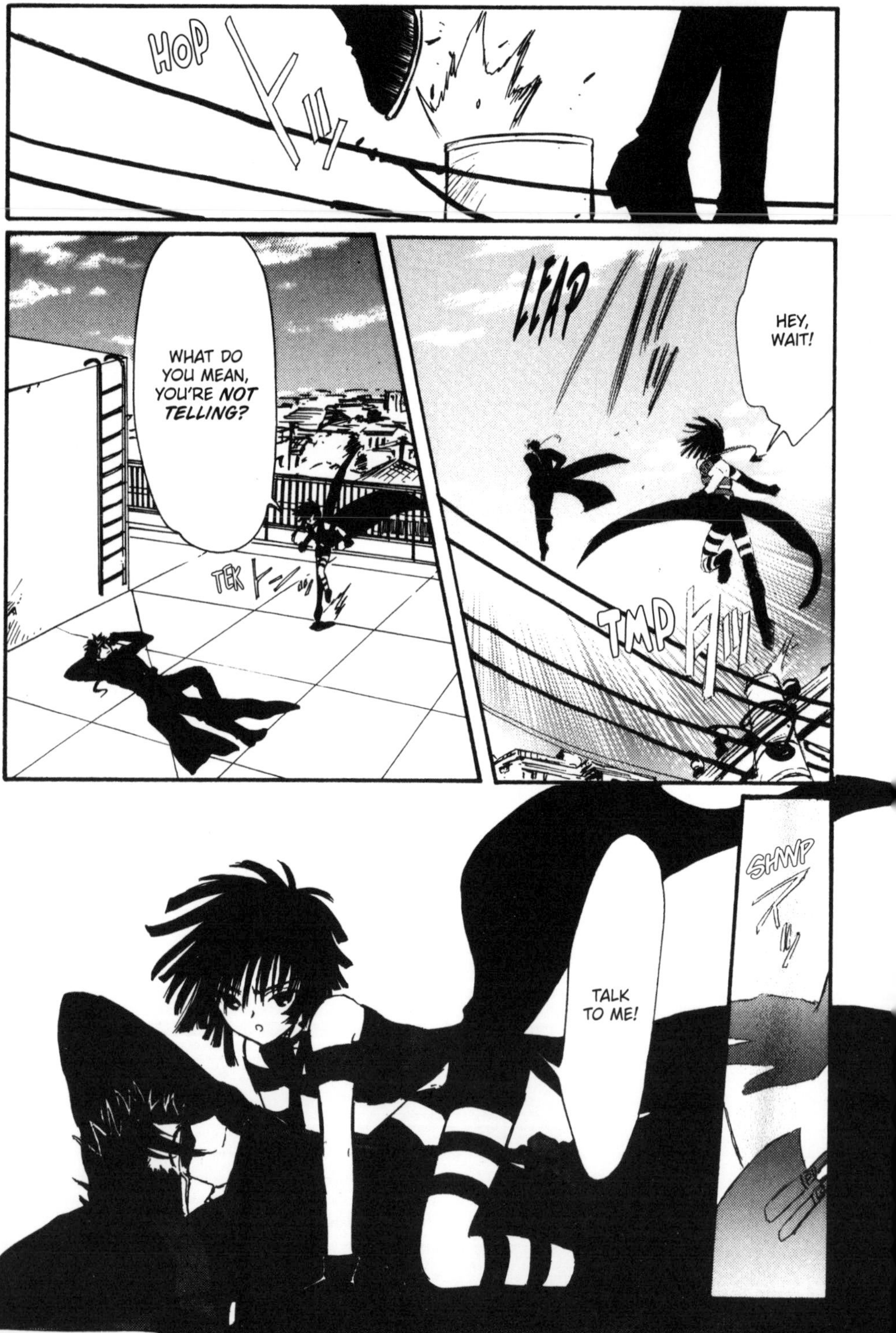
HOP
LEAP
HEY, WAIT!
TMP
WHAT DO YOU MEAN, YOU'RE *NOT TELLING?*
TEK
SHNP
TALK TO ME!

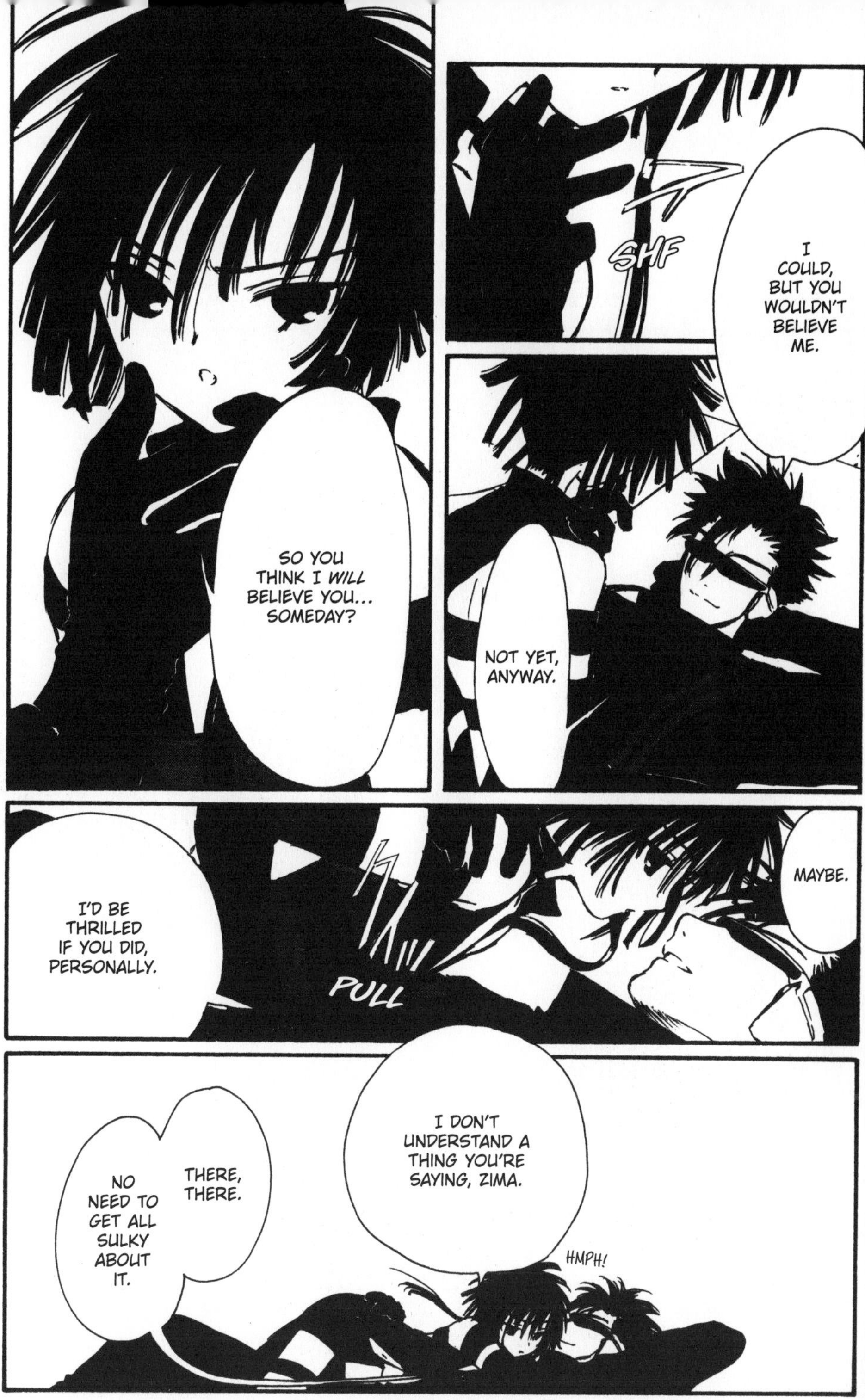
SHF
I COULD, BUT YOU WOULDN'T BELIEVE ME.
NOT YET, ANYWAY.
SO YOU THINK I *WILL* BELIEVE YOU... SOMEDAY?
MAYBE.
PULL
I'D BE THRILLED IF YOU DID, PERSONALLY.
I DON'T UNDERSTAND A THING YOU'RE SAYING, ZIMA.
HMPH!
THERE, THERE.
NO NEED TO GET ALL SULKY ABOUT IT.

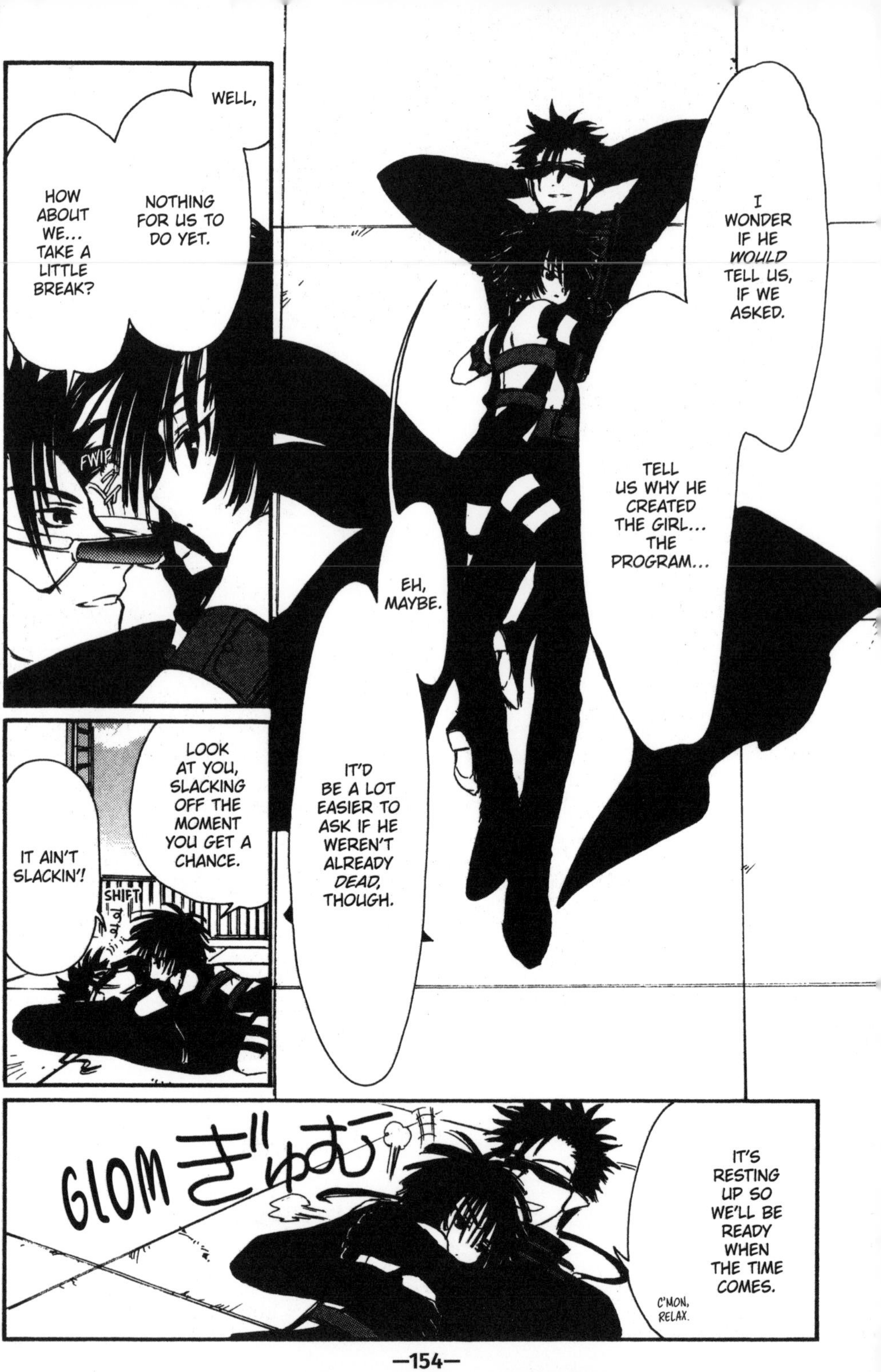
I WONDER IF HE *WOULD* TELL US, IF WE ASKED.
TELL US WHY HE CREATED THE GIRL... THE PROGRAM...
EH, MAYBE.
IT'D BE A LOT EASIER TO ASK IF HE WEREN'T ALREADY *DEAD*, THOUGH.
WELL,
NOTHING FOR US TO DO YET.
HOW ABOUT WE... TAKE A LITTLE BREAK?
FWIP
LOOK AT YOU, SLACKING OFF THE MOMENT YOU GET A CHANCE.
IT AIN'T SLACKIN'!
SHIFT
IT'S RESTING UP SO WE'LL BE READY WHEN THE TIME COMES.
C'MON, RELAX.
GLOM ぎゅむ

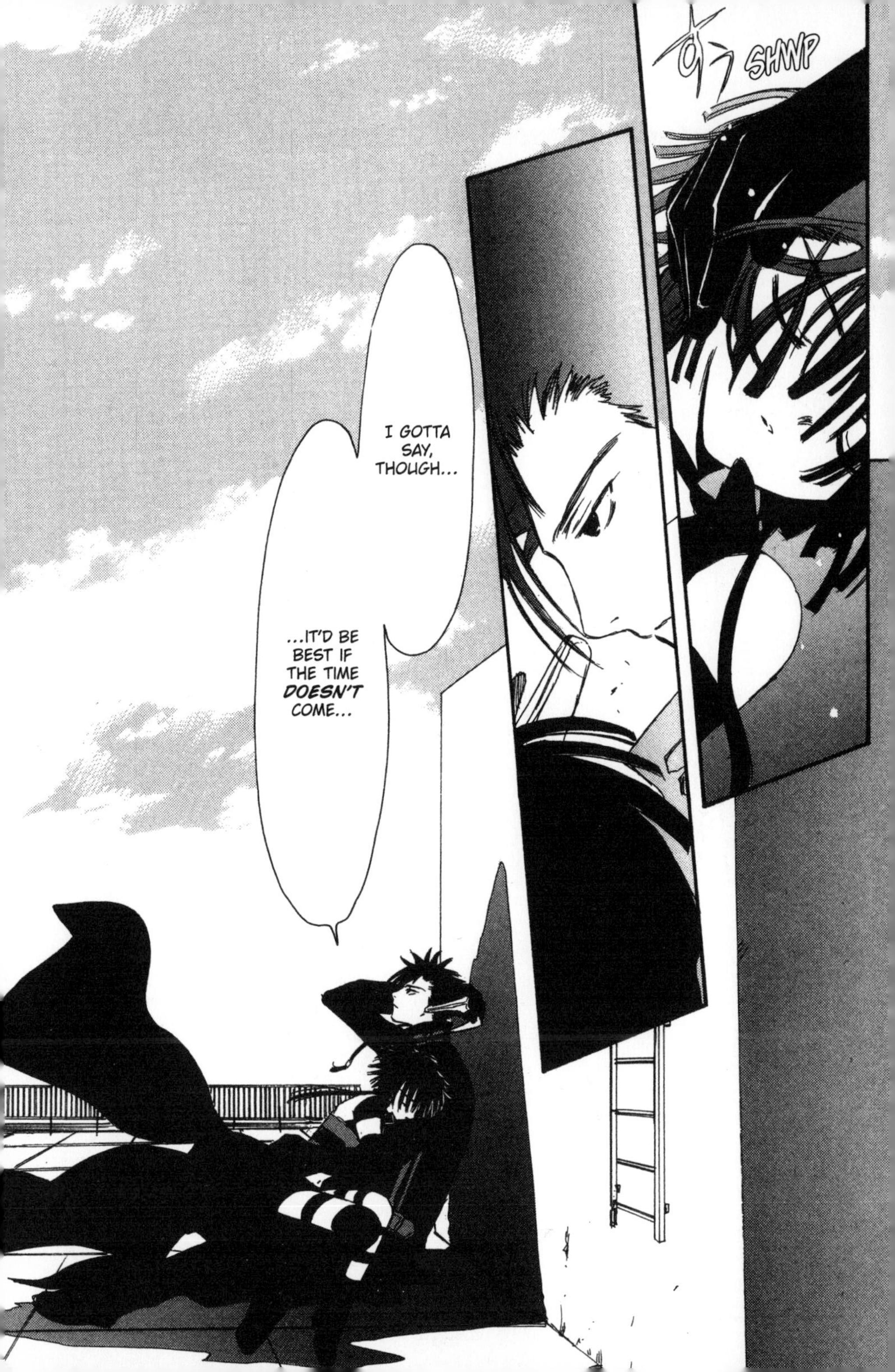
SHWP
I GOTTA SAY, THOUGH...
...IT'D BE BEST IF THE TIME ***DOESN'T*** COME...

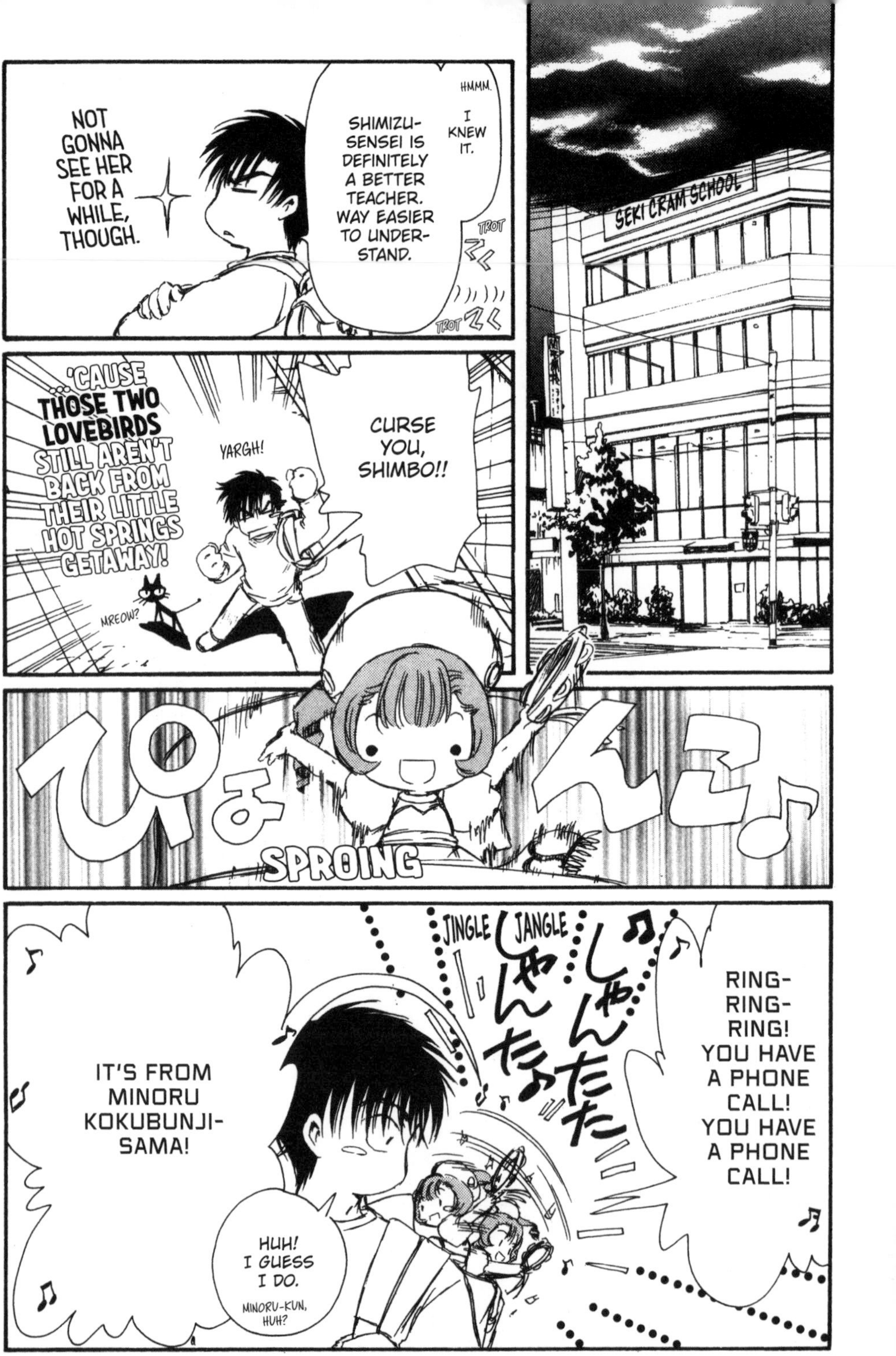
SEKI CRAM SCHOOL
HMMM.
I KNEW IT.
SHIMIZU-SENSEI IS DEFINITELY A BETTER TEACHER. WAY EASIER TO UNDERSTAND.
TROT
TROT
NOT GONNA SEE HER FOR A WHILE, THOUGH.
CURSE YOU, SHIMBO!!
YARGH!
...'CAUSE THOSE TWO LOVEBIRDS STILL AREN'T BACK FROM THEIR LITTLE HOT SPRINGS GETAWAY!
MREOW?
ぴょんっ♪
SPROING
しゃんたた♪しゃんたた!!
JINGLE JANGLE
RING-RING-RING! YOU HAVE A PHONE CALL! YOU HAVE A PHONE CALL!
IT'S FROM MINORU KOKUBUNJI-SAMA!
HUH! I GUESS I DO.
MINORU-KUN, HUH?

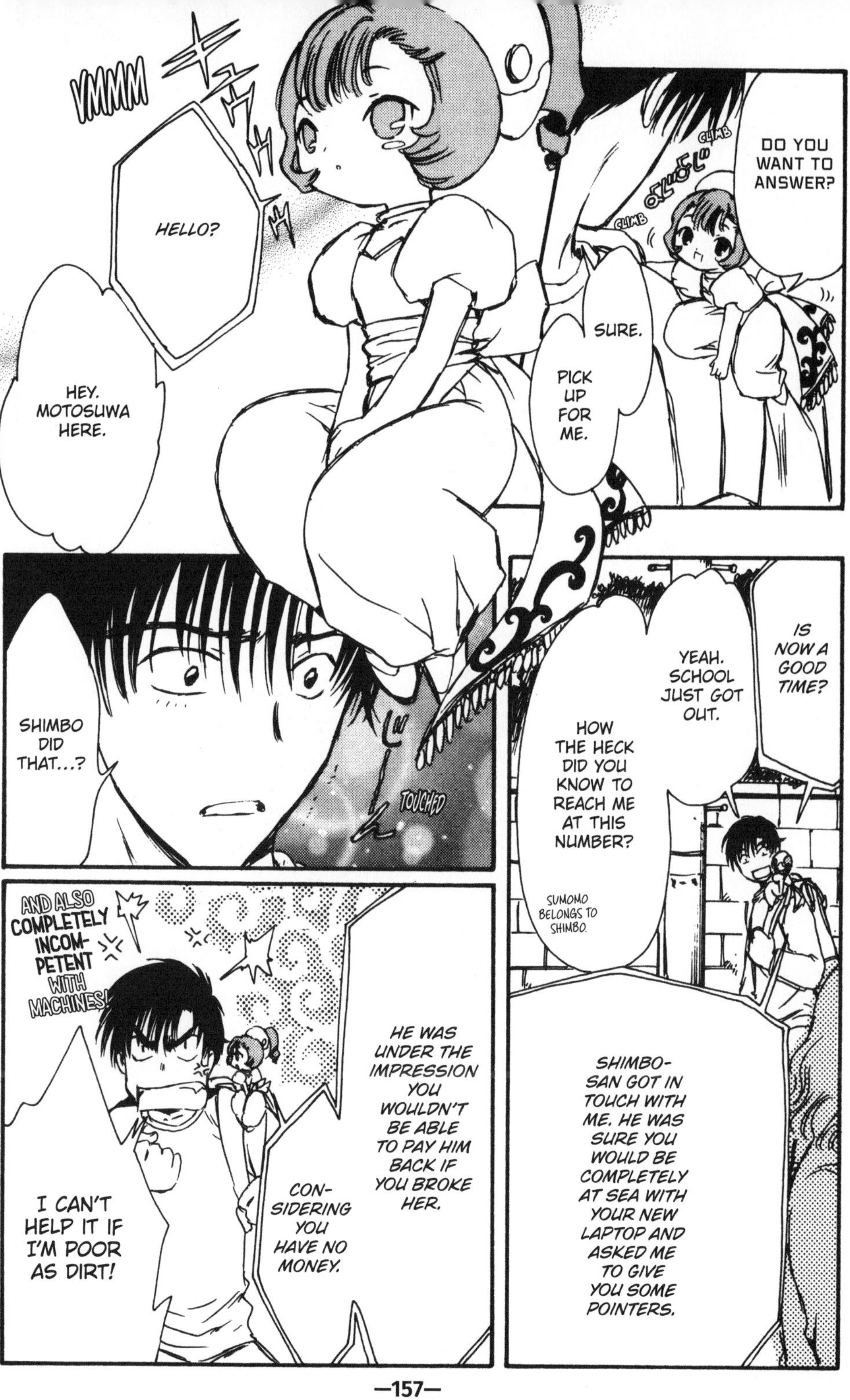
DO YOU WANT TO ANSWER?
CLIMB
CLIMB
SURE.
PICK UP FOR ME.
VMMM
HELLO?
HEY. MOTOSUWA HERE.
IS NOW A GOOD TIME?
YEAH. SCHOOL JUST GOT OUT.
HOW THE HECK DID YOU KNOW TO REACH ME AT THIS NUMBER?
SUMOMO BELONGS TO SHIMBO.
SHIMBO DID THAT...?
TOUCHED
SHIMBO-SAN GOT IN TOUCH WITH ME. HE WAS SURE YOU WOULD BE COMPLETELY AT SEA WITH YOUR NEW LAPTOP AND ASKED ME TO GIVE YOU SOME POINTERS.
HE WAS UNDER THE IMPRESSION YOU WOULDN'T BE ABLE TO PAY HIM BACK IF YOU BROKE HER.
CON-SIDERING YOU HAVE NO MONEY.
AND ALSO COMPLETELY INCOM-PETENT WITH MACHINES!
I CAN'T HELP IT IF I'M POOR AS DIRT!

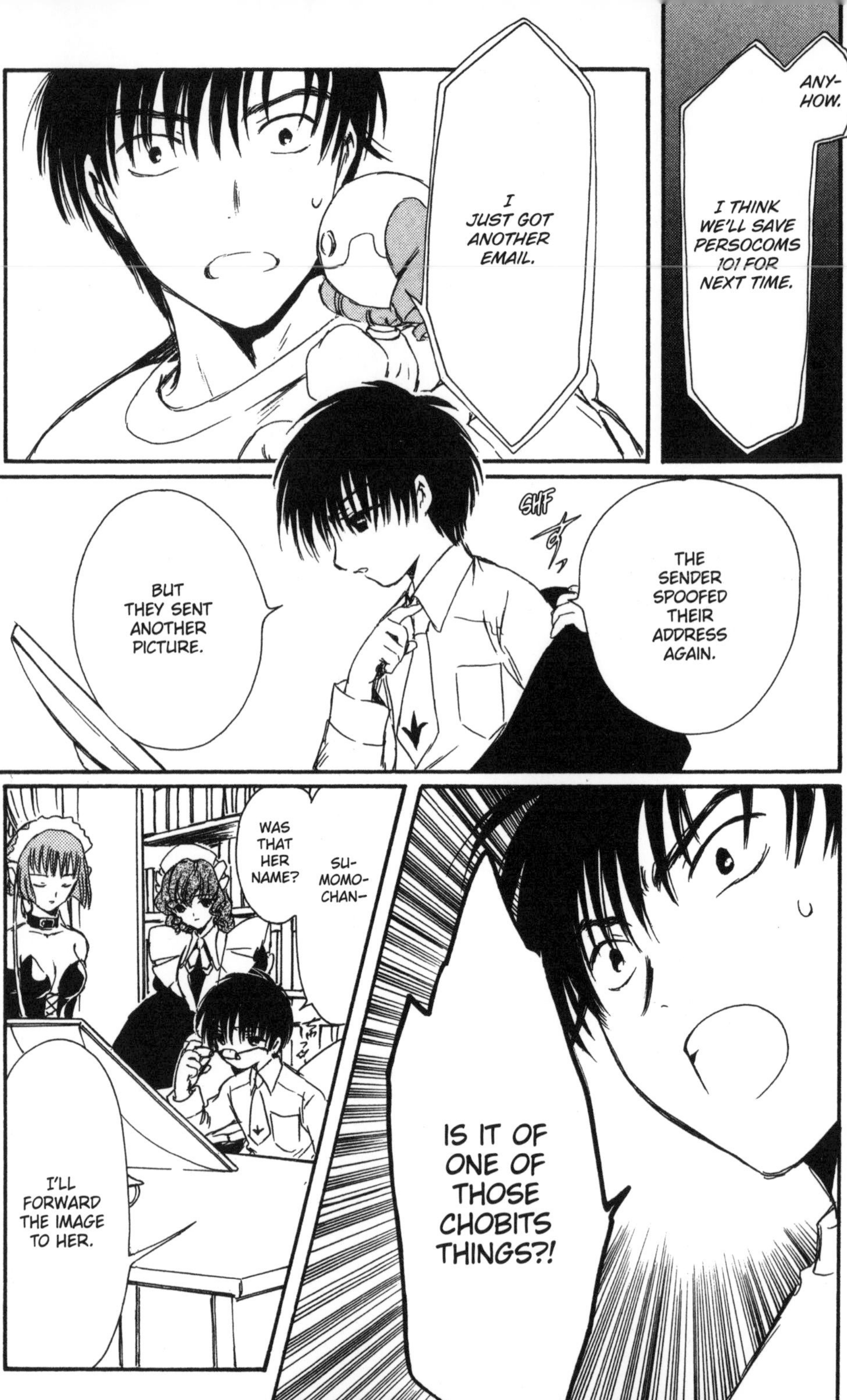
ANY-HOW.
I THINK WE'LL SAVE PERSOCOMS 101 FOR NEXT TIME.
I JUST GOT ANOTHER EMAIL.
SHF
THE SENDER SPOOFED THEIR ADDRESS AGAIN.
BUT THEY SENT ANOTHER PICTURE.
IS IT OF ONE OF THOSE CHOBITS THINGS?!
SU-MOMO-CHAN-
WAS THAT HER NAME?
I'LL FORWARD THE IMAGE TO HER.

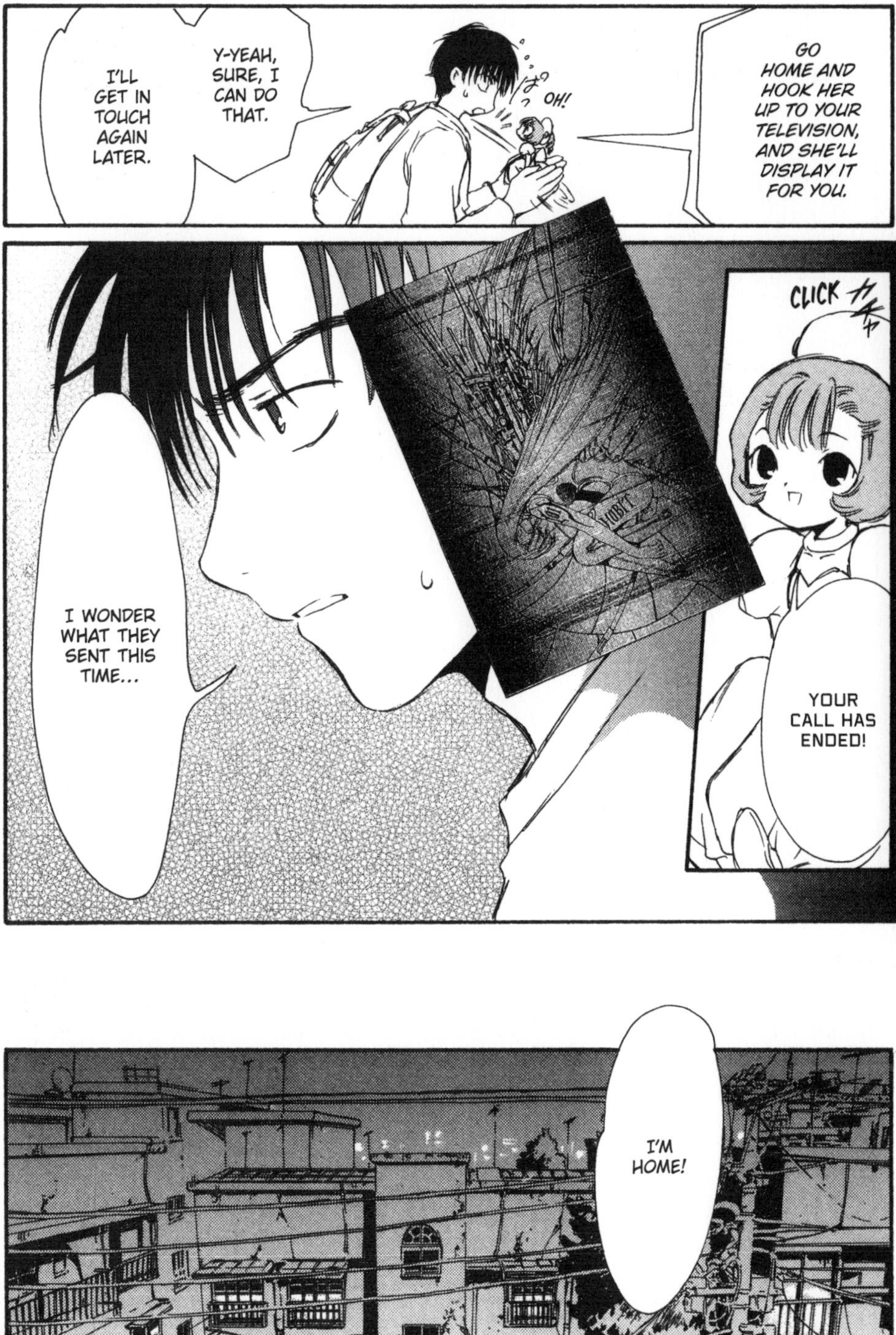
GO HOME AND HOOK HER UP TO YOUR TELEVISION, AND SHE'LL DISPLAY IT FOR YOU.
OH!
Y-YEAH, SURE, I CAN DO THAT.
I'LL GET IN TOUCH AGAIN LATER.
CLICK
YOUR CALL HAS ENDED!
I WONDER WHAT THEY SENT THIS TIME...
I'M HOME!

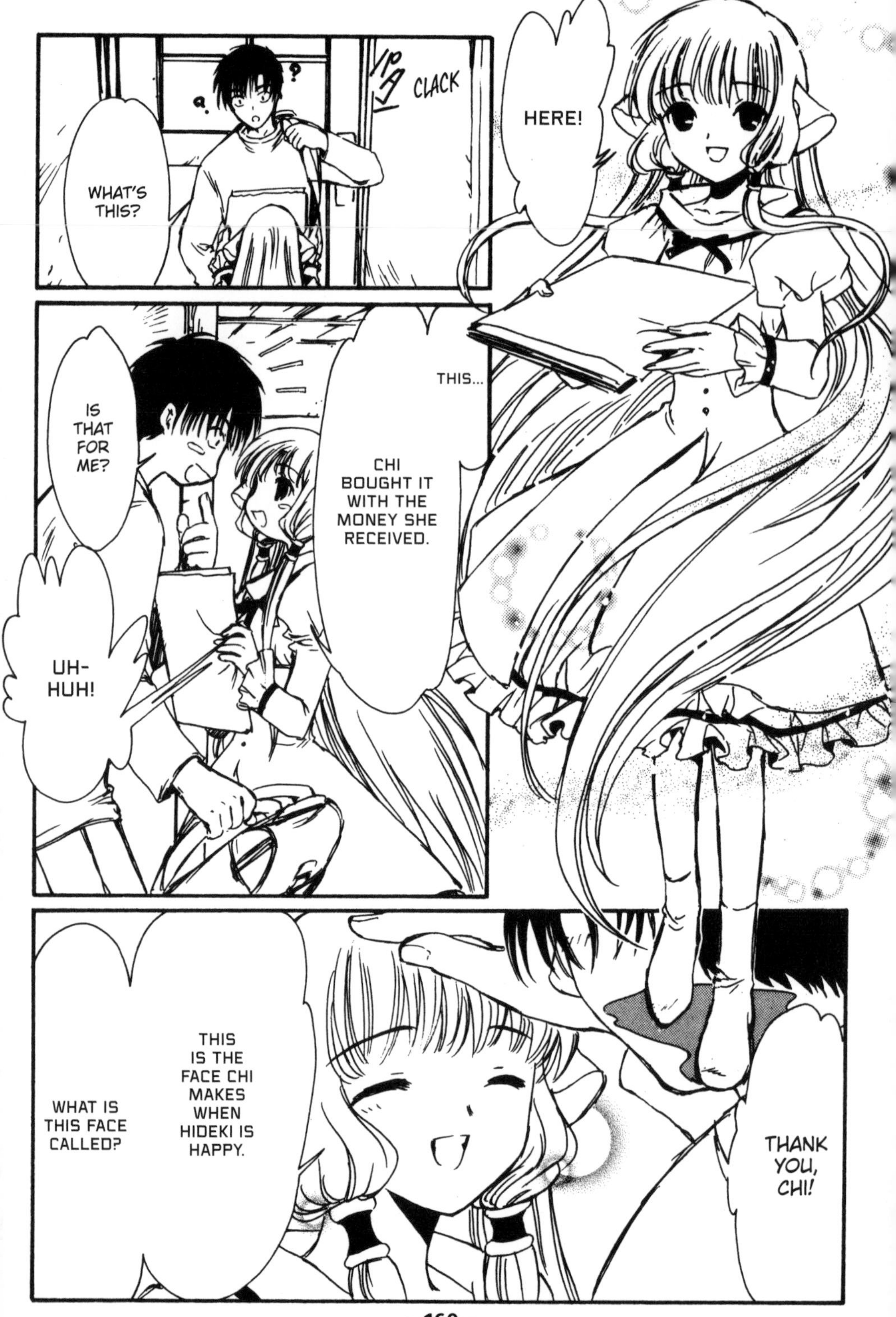
HERE!
CLACK
WHAT'S THIS?
THIS...
CHI BOUGHT IT WITH THE MONEY SHE RECEIVED.
IS THAT FOR ME?
UH-HUH!
THANK YOU, CHI!
THIS IS THE FACE CHI MAKES WHEN HIDEKI IS HAPPY.
WHAT IS THIS FACE CALLED?

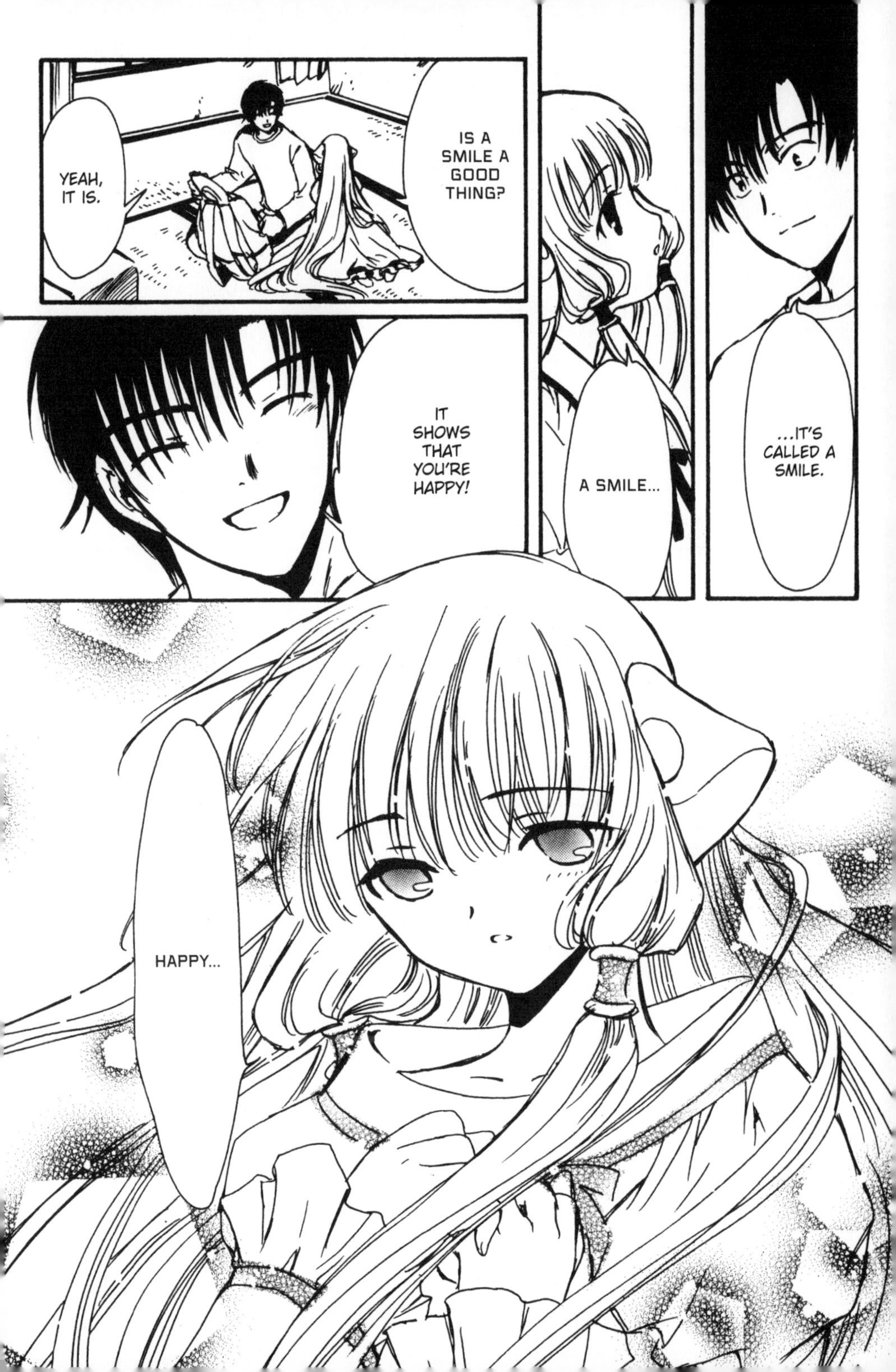
...IT'S CALLED A SMILE.
A SMILE...
IS A SMILE A GOOD THING?
YEAH, IT IS.
IT SHOWS THAT YOU'RE HAPPY!
HAPPY...

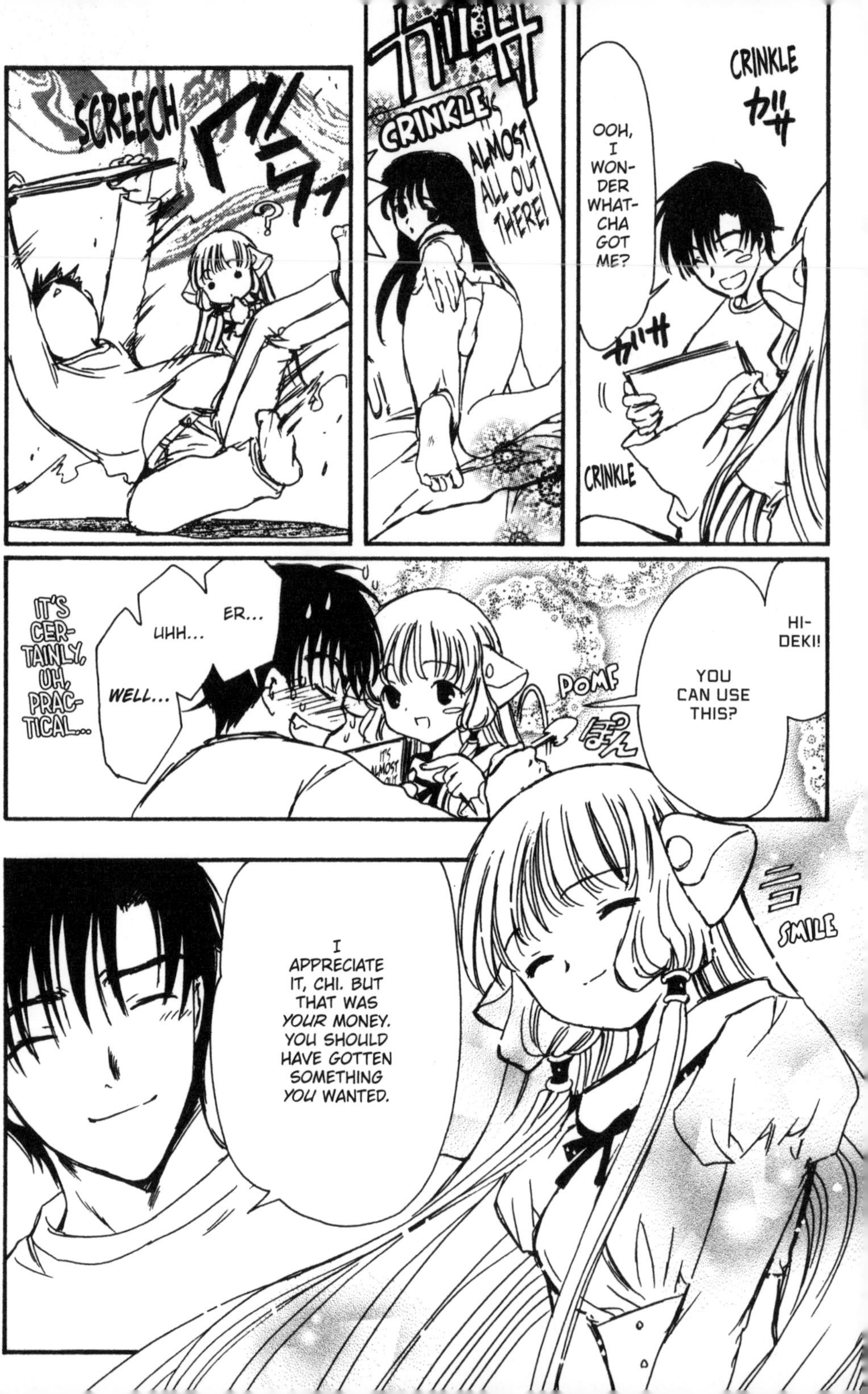
CRINKLE
OOH, I WONDER WHAT-CHA GOT ME?
CRINKLE
CRINKLE
IT'S ALMOST ALL OUT THERE!
SCREECH
HI-DEKI!
YOU CAN USE THIS?
POMF
ER...
UHH...
WELL...
IT'S CER-TAINLY, UH, PRAC-TICAL...
IT'S ALMOST OUT
SMILE
I APPRECIATE IT, CHI. BUT THAT WAS *YOUR* MONEY. YOU SHOULD HAVE GOTTEN SOMETHING *YOU* WANTED.

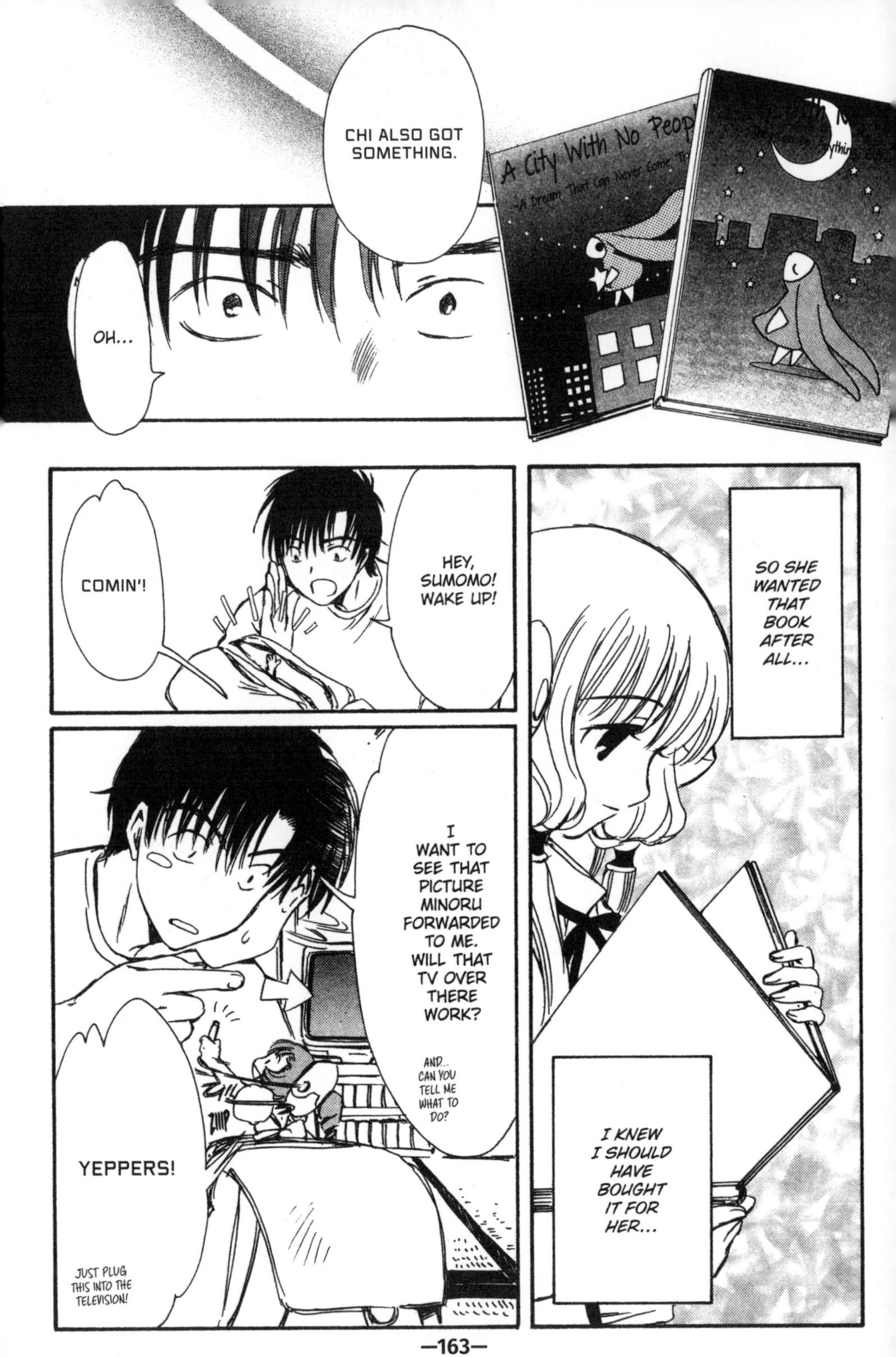
CHI ALSO GOT SOMETHING.
OH...
SO SHE WANTED THAT BOOK AFTER ALL...
I KNEW I SHOULD HAVE BOUGHT IT FOR HER...
HEY, SUMOMO! WAKE UP!
COMIN'!
I WANT TO SEE THAT PICTURE MINORU FORWARDED TO ME. WILL THAT TV OVER THERE WORK?
AND.. CAN YOU TELL ME WHAT TO DO?
YEPPERS!
JUST PLUG THIS INTO THE TELEVISION!

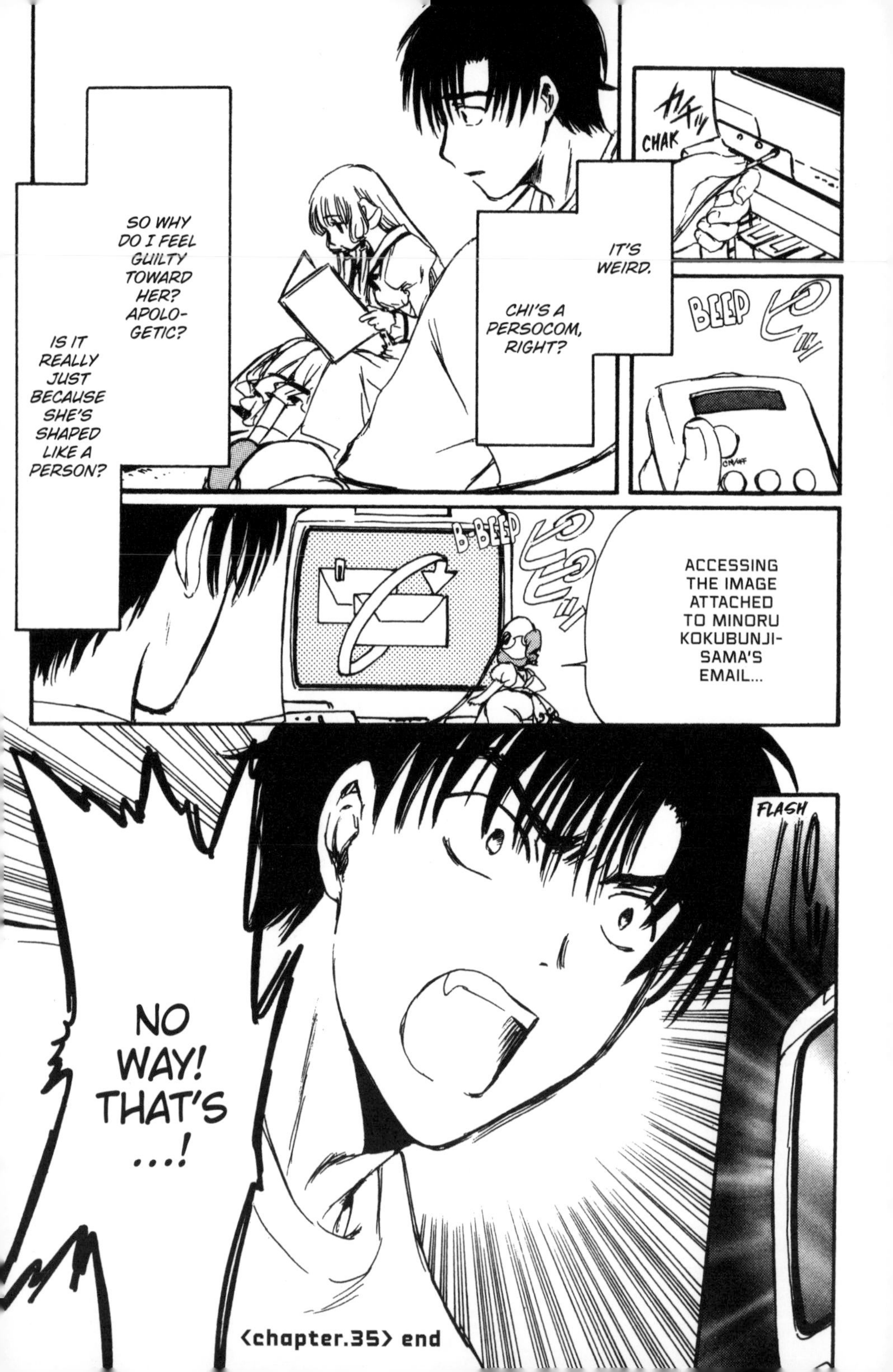
CHAK
BEEP
IT'S WEIRD.
CHI'S A PERSOCOM, RIGHT?
SO WHY DO I FEEL GUILTY TOWARD HER? APOLOGETIC?
IS IT REALLY JUST BECAUSE SHE'S SHAPED LIKE A PERSON?
B-BEEP
ACCESSING THE IMAGE ATTACHED TO MINORU KOKUBUNJI-SAMA'S EMAIL...
FLASH
NO WAY! THAT'S ...!
<chapter.35> end

⟨chapter.36⟩

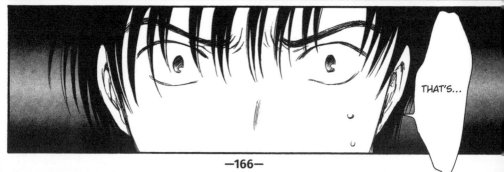

THAT'S...

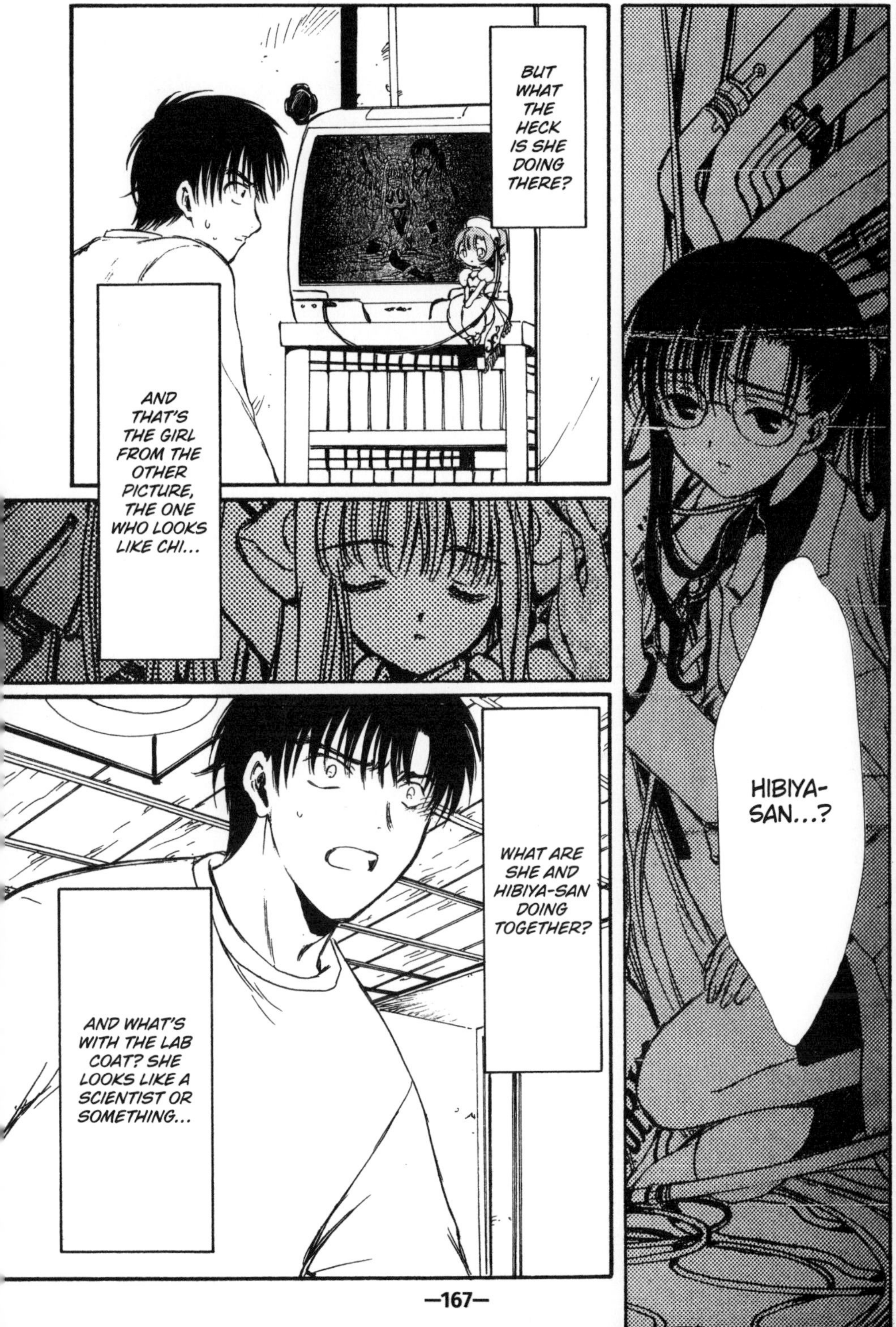
HIBIYA-SAN...?
BUT WHAT THE HECK IS SHE DOING THERE?
AND THAT'S THE GIRL FROM THE OTHER PICTURE, THE ONE WHO LOOKS LIKE CHI...
WHAT ARE SHE AND HIBIYA-SAN DOING TOGETHER?
AND WHAT'S WITH THE LAB COAT? SHE LOOKS LIKE A SCIENTIST OR SOMETHING...

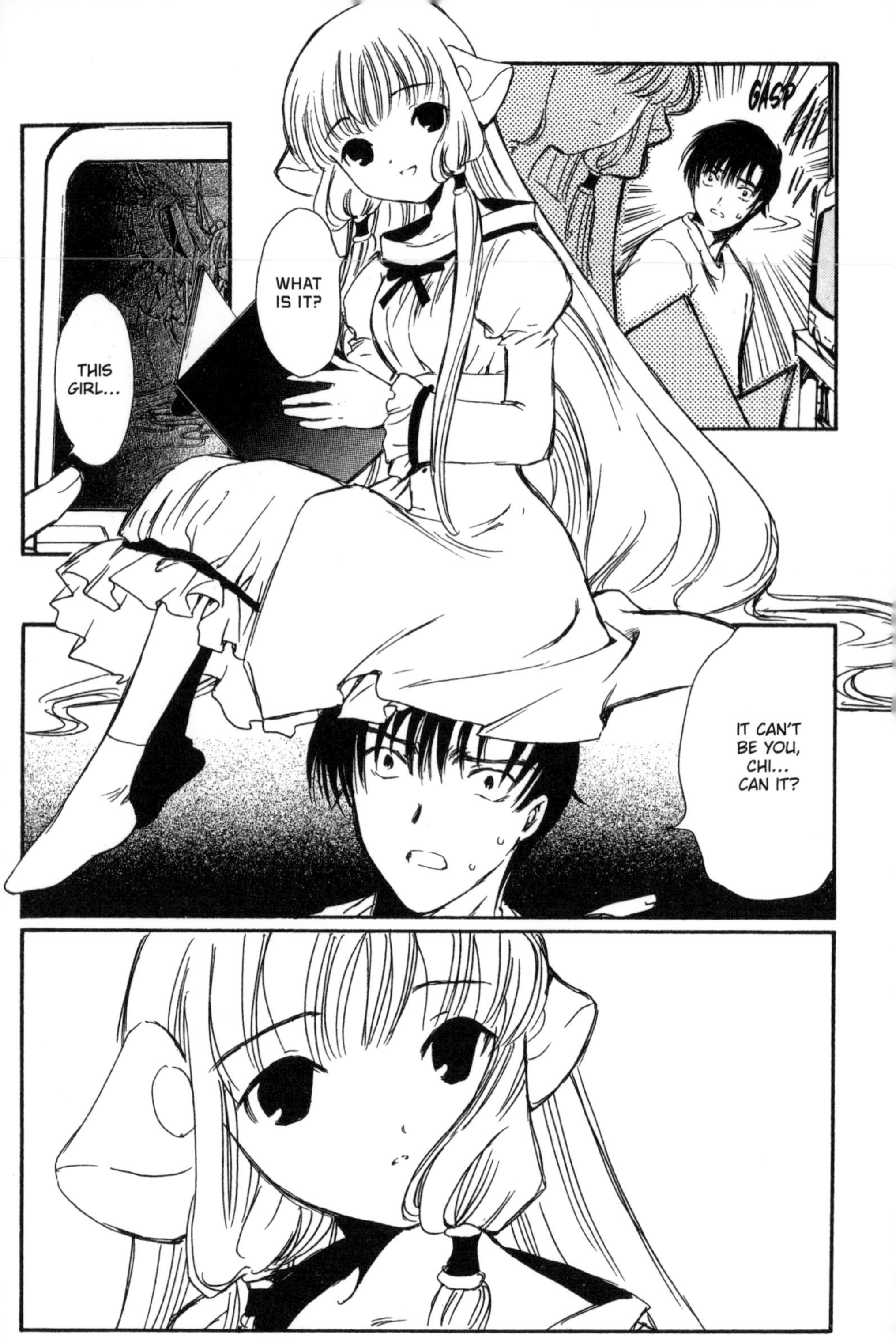
GASP
THIS GIRL...
WHAT IS IT?
IT CAN'T BE YOU, CHI... CAN IT?

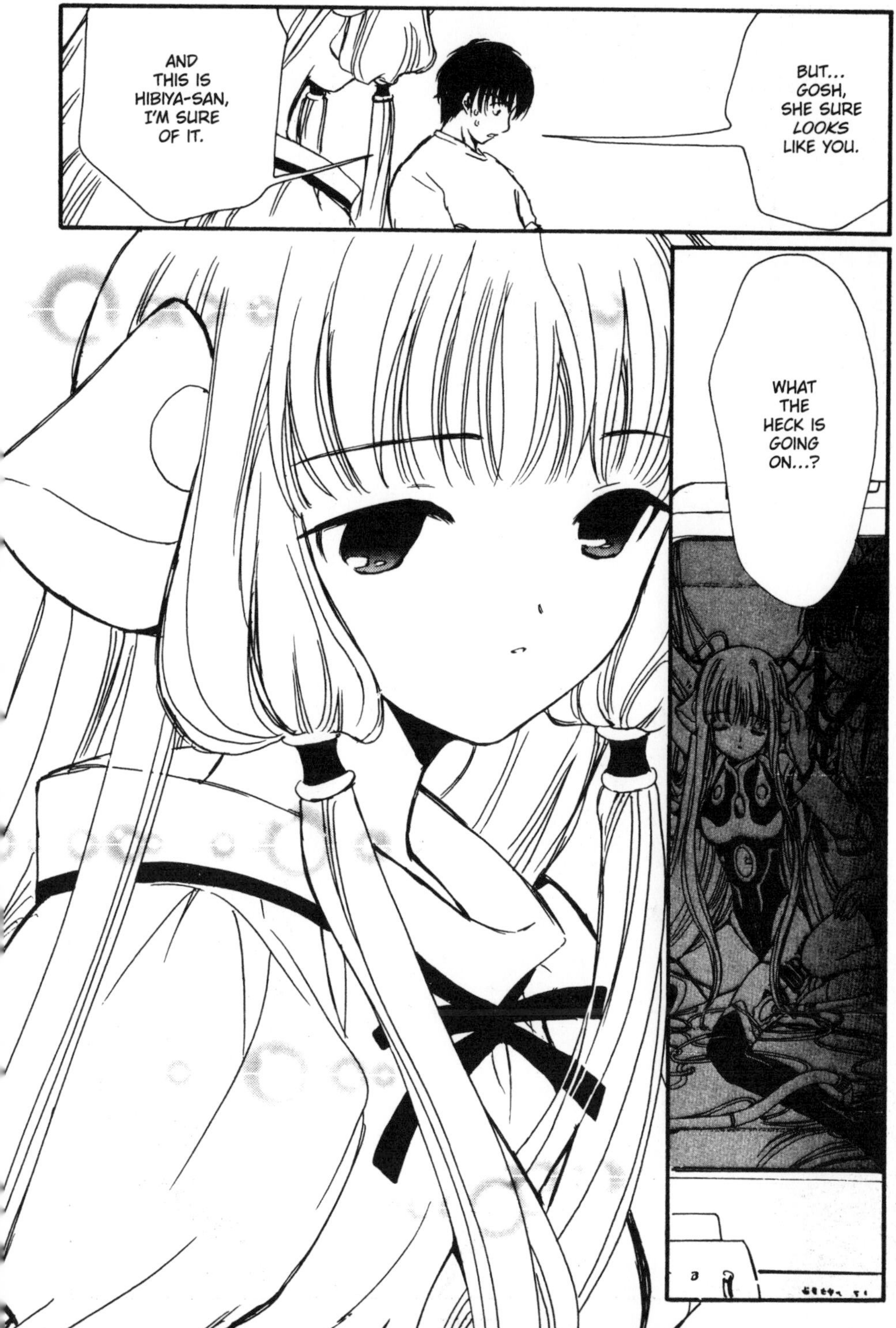
BUT... GOSH, SHE SURE *LOOKS* LIKE YOU.
AND THIS IS HIBIYA-SAN, I'M SURE OF IT.
WHAT THE HECK IS GOING ON...?

NAH, JUST A FEW MINUTES.

I'M SORRY. I HOPE YOU DIDN'T WAIT LONG.

DUKLYON

IT'S FINE.

I DON'T GO TO EXTRA CLASSES OR ANYTHING.

I'M SORRY, TOO, RUSHING YOU TO MEET ME RIGHT AFTER SCHOOL.

YOU SAY YOU KNOW HER?

SO THE SECOND PERSON IN THIS PICTURE CAUGHT YOUR ATTENTION.

FWIP

YEAH... I THINK SO.

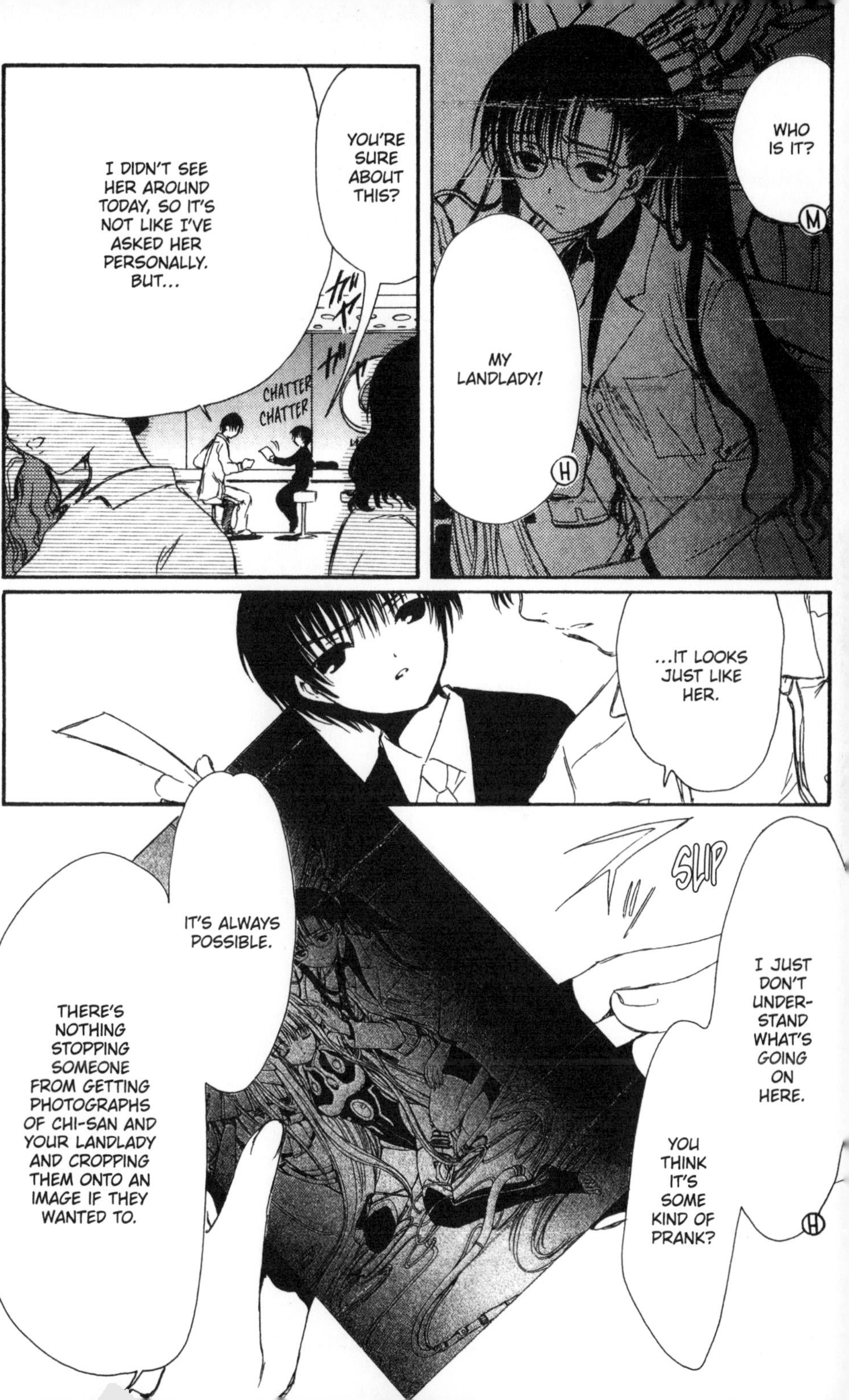
WHO IS IT?
MY LANDLADY!
YOU'RE SURE ABOUT THIS?
I DIDN'T SEE HER AROUND TODAY, SO IT'S NOT LIKE I'VE ASKED HER PERSONALLY. BUT...
CHATTER CHATTER
...IT LOOKS JUST LIKE HER.
SLIP
I JUST DON'T UNDER-STAND WHAT'S GOING ON HERE.
YOU THINK IT'S SOME KIND OF PRANK?
IT'S ALWAYS POSSIBLE.
THERE'S NOTHING STOPPING SOMEONE FROM GETTING PHOTOGRAPHS OF CHI-SAN AND YOUR LANDLADY AND CROPPING THEM ONTO AN IMAGE IF THEY WANTED TO.

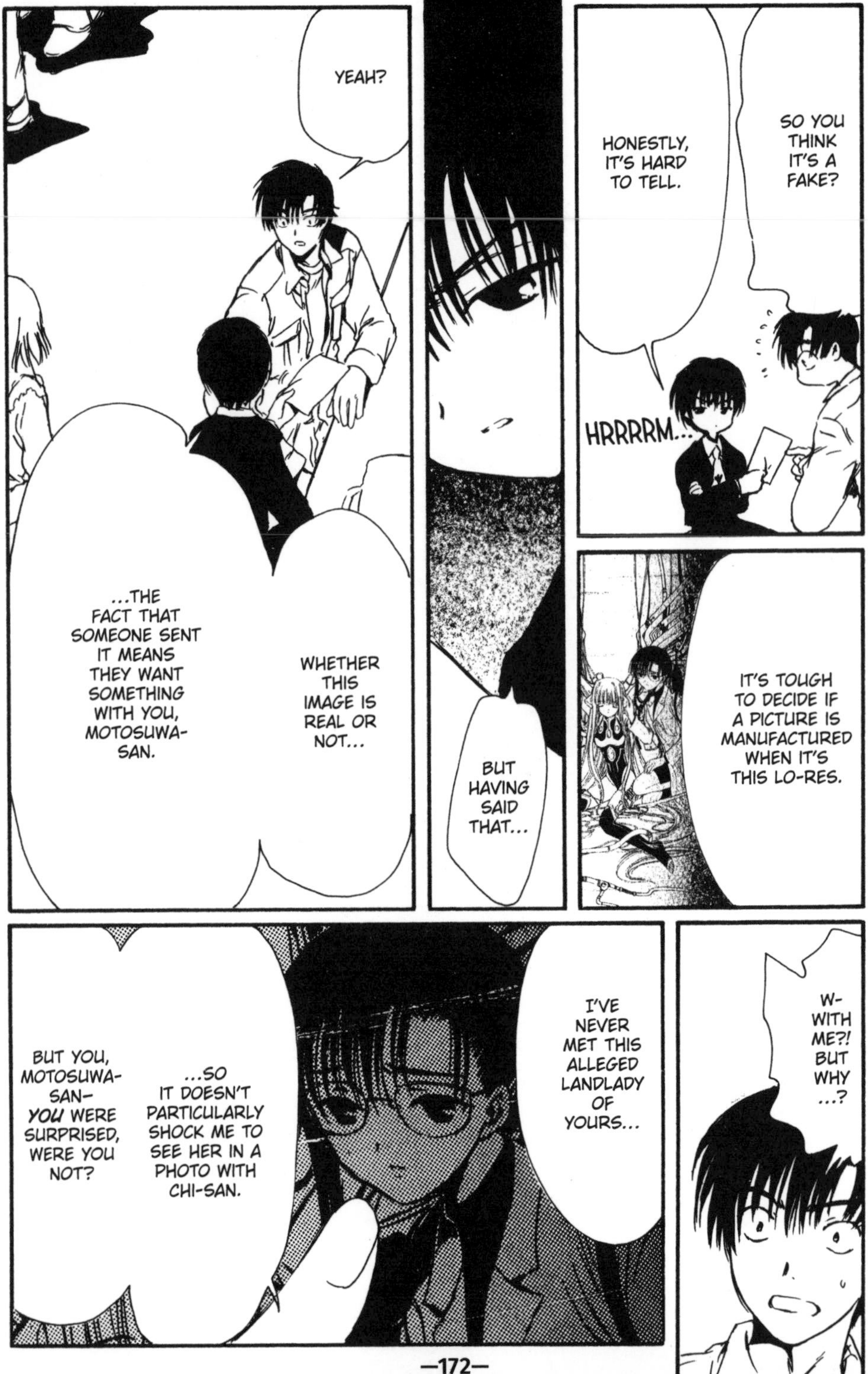
SO YOU THINK IT'S A FAKE?
HONESTLY, IT'S HARD TO TELL.
HRRRRM...
IT'S TOUGH TO DECIDE IF A PICTURE IS MANUFACTURED WHEN IT'S THIS LO-RES.
BUT HAVING SAID THAT...
YEAH?
WHETHER THIS IMAGE IS REAL OR NOT...
...THE FACT THAT SOMEONE SENT IT MEANS THEY WANT SOMETHING WITH YOU, MOTOSUWA-SAN.
W-WITH ME?! BUT WHY...?
I'VE NEVER MET THIS ALLEGED LANDLADY OF YOURS...
...SO IT DOESN'T PARTICULARLY SHOCK ME TO SEE HER IN A PHOTO WITH CHI-SAN.
BUT YOU, MOTOSUWA-SAN– *YOU* WERE SURPRISED, WERE YOU NOT?

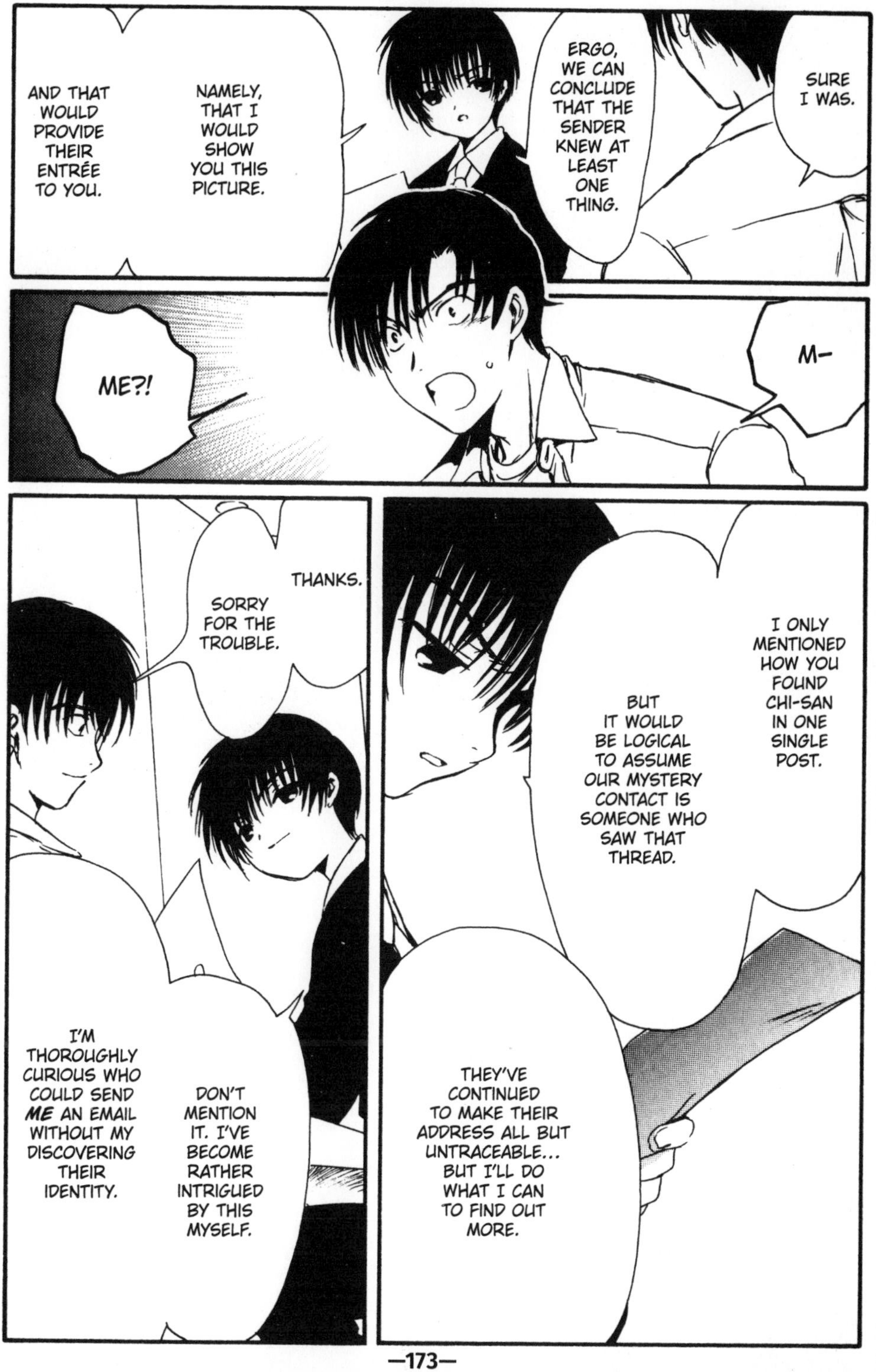
SURE I WAS.
ERGO, WE CAN CONCLUDE THAT THE SENDER KNEW AT LEAST ONE THING.
NAMELY, THAT I WOULD SHOW YOU THIS PICTURE.
AND THAT WOULD PROVIDE THEIR ENTRÉE TO YOU.
M–
ME?!
I ONLY MENTIONED HOW YOU FOUND CHI-SAN IN ONE SINGLE POST.
BUT IT WOULD BE LOGICAL TO ASSUME OUR MYSTERY CONTACT IS SOMEONE WHO SAW THAT THREAD.
THEY'VE CONTINUED TO MAKE THEIR ADDRESS ALL BUT UNTRACEABLE... BUT I'LL DO WHAT I CAN TO FIND OUT MORE.
THANKS.
SORRY FOR THE TROUBLE.
DON'T MENTION IT. I'VE BECOME RATHER INTRIGUED BY THIS MYSELF.
I'M THOROUGHLY CURIOUS WHO COULD SEND ***ME*** AN EMAIL WITHOUT MY DISCOVERING THEIR IDENTITY.

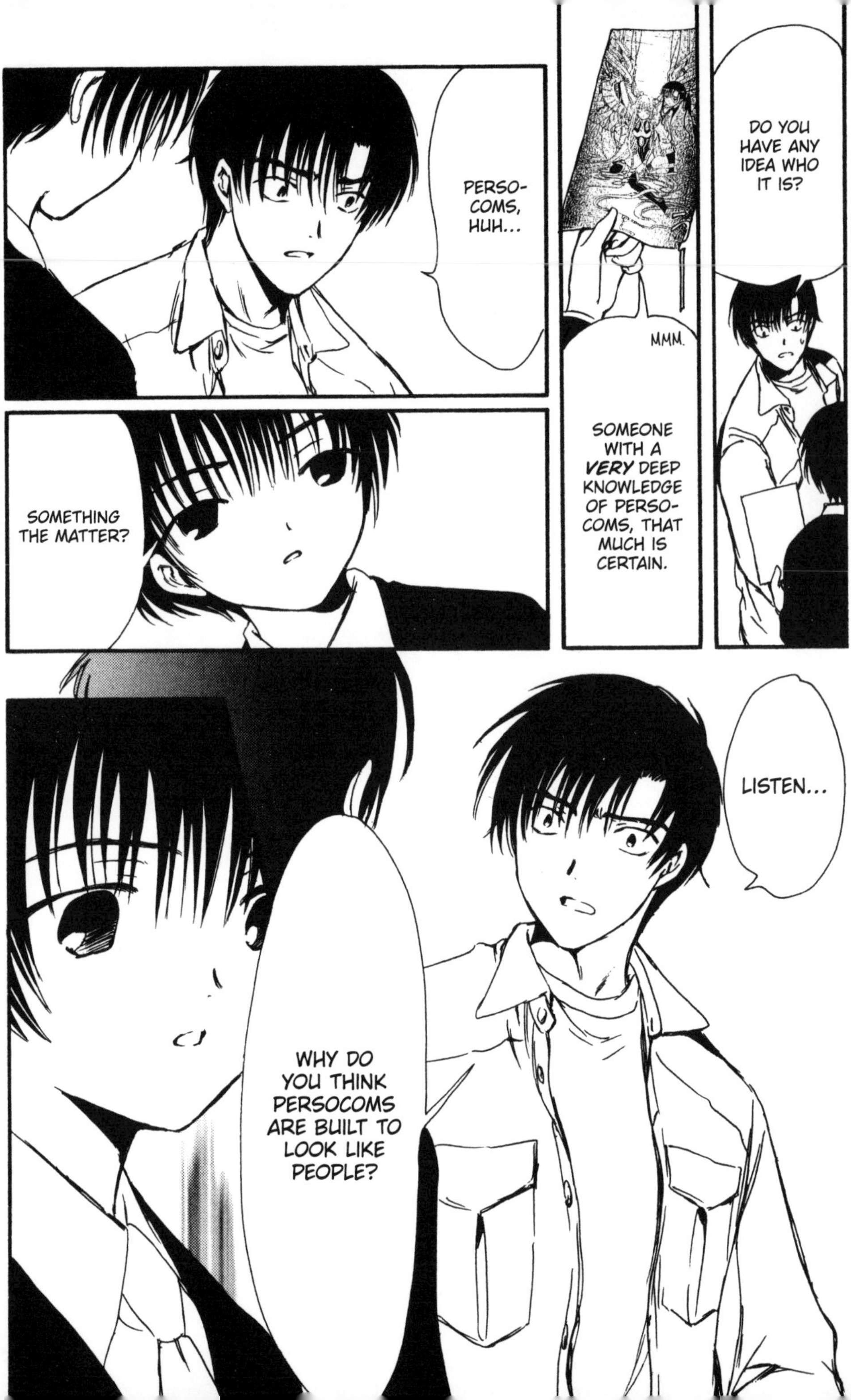
DO YOU HAVE ANY IDEA WHO IT IS?
MMM.
SOMEONE WITH A VERY DEEP KNOWLEDGE OF PERSO-COMS, THAT MUCH IS CERTAIN.
PERSO-COMS, HUH...
SOMETHING THE MATTER?
LISTEN...
WHY DO YOU THINK PERSOCOMS ARE BUILT TO LOOK LIKE PEOPLE?

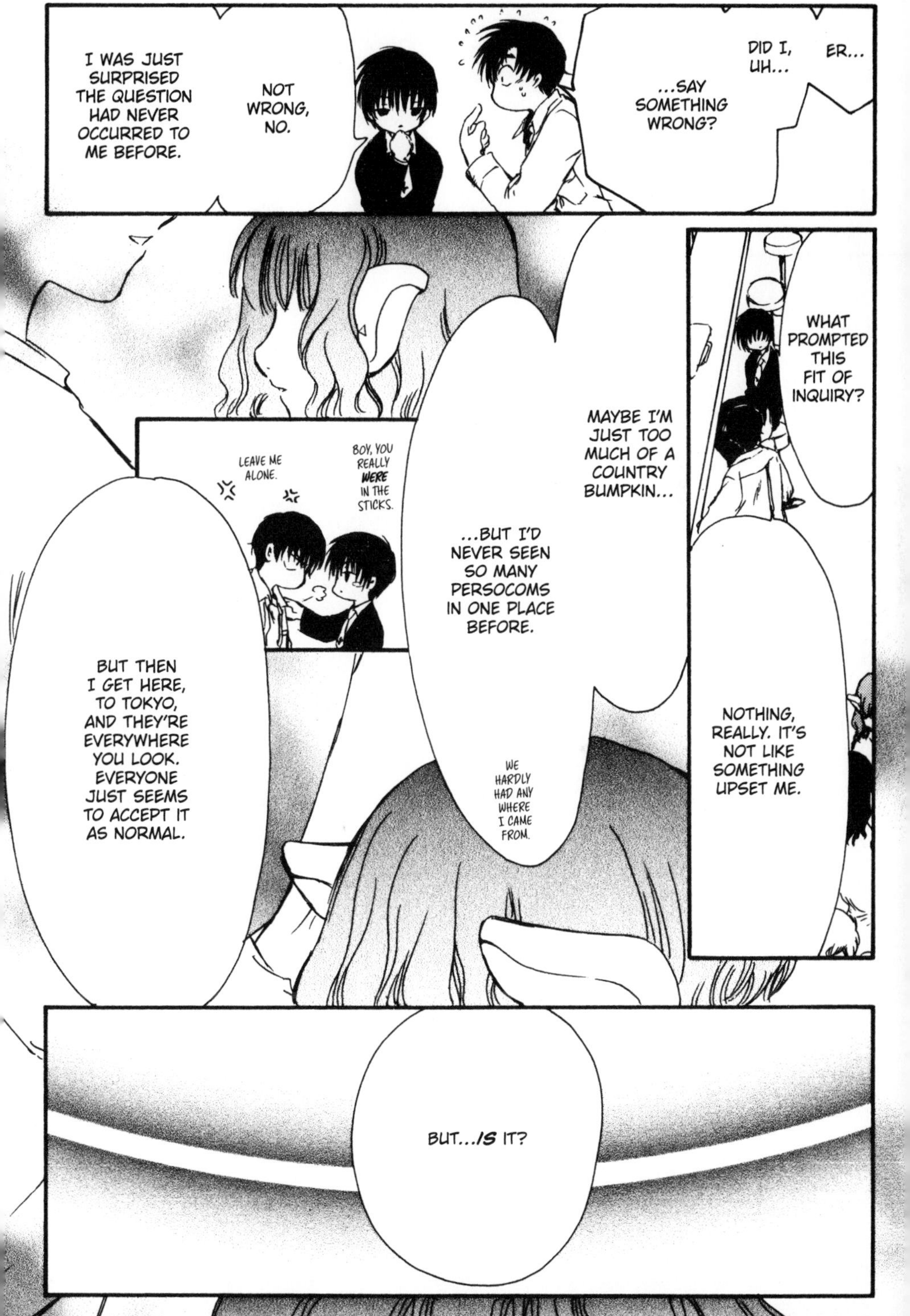
ER…
DID I, UH…
…SAY SOMETHING WRONG?
NOT WRONG, NO.
I WAS JUST SURPRISED THE QUESTION HAD NEVER OCCURRED TO ME BEFORE.
WHAT PROMPTED THIS FIT OF INQUIRY?
NOTHING, REALLY. IT'S NOT LIKE SOMETHING UPSET ME.
MAYBE I'M JUST TOO MUCH OF A COUNTRY BUMPKIN…
…BUT I'D NEVER SEEN SO MANY PERSOCOMS IN ONE PLACE BEFORE.
WE HARDLY HAD ANY WHERE I CAME FROM.
BOY, YOU REALLY *WERE* IN THE STICKS.
LEAVE ME ALONE.
BUT THEN I GET HERE, TO TOKYO, AND THEY'RE EVERYWHERE YOU LOOK. EVERYONE JUST SEEMS TO ACCEPT IT AS NORMAL.
BUT…*IS* IT?

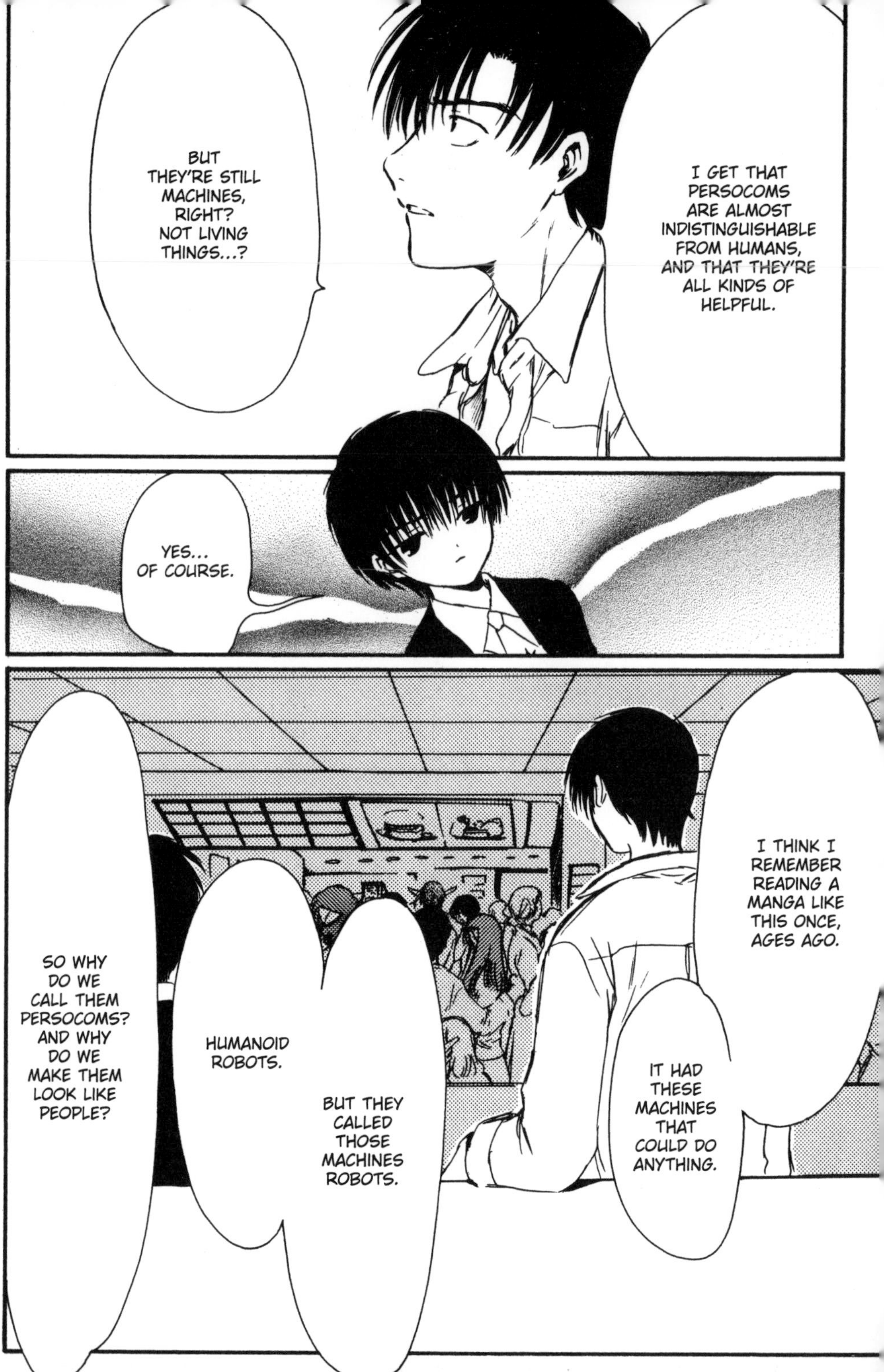
I GET THAT PERSOCOMS ARE ALMOST INDISTINGUISHABLE FROM HUMANS, AND THAT THEY'RE ALL KINDS OF HELPFUL.
BUT THEY'RE STILL MACHINES, RIGHT? NOT LIVING THINGS...?
YES... OF COURSE.
I THINK I REMEMBER READING A MANGA LIKE THIS ONCE, AGES AGO.
IT HAD THESE MACHINES THAT COULD DO ANYTHING.
BUT THEY CALLED THOSE MACHINES ROBOTS.
HUMANOID ROBOTS.
SO WHY DO WE CALL THEM PERSOCOMS? AND WHY DO WE MAKE THEM LOOK LIKE PEOPLE?

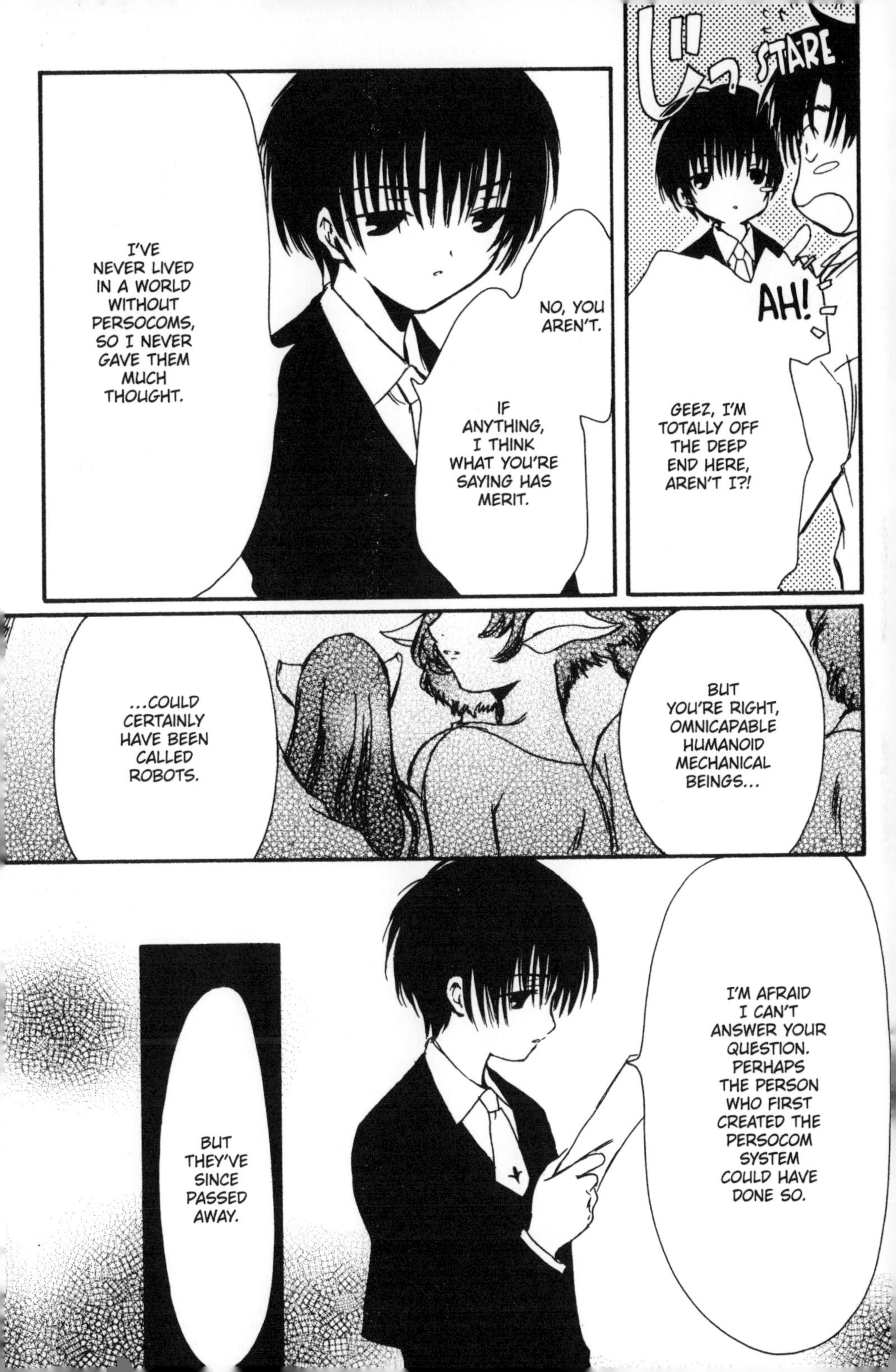
じっ
STARE
AH!
GEEZ, I'M TOTALLY OFF THE DEEP END HERE, AREN'T I?!
NO, YOU AREN'T.
IF ANYTHING, I THINK WHAT YOU'RE SAYING HAS MERIT.
I'VE NEVER LIVED IN A WORLD WITHOUT PERSOCOMS, SO I NEVER GAVE THEM MUCH THOUGHT.
BUT YOU'RE RIGHT, OMNICAPABLE HUMANOID MECHANICAL BEINGS...
...COULD CERTAINLY HAVE BEEN CALLED ROBOTS.
I'M AFRAID I CAN'T ANSWER YOUR QUESTION. PERHAPS THE PERSON WHO FIRST CREATED THE PERSOCOM SYSTEM COULD HAVE DONE SO.
BUT THEY'VE SINCE PASSED AWAY.

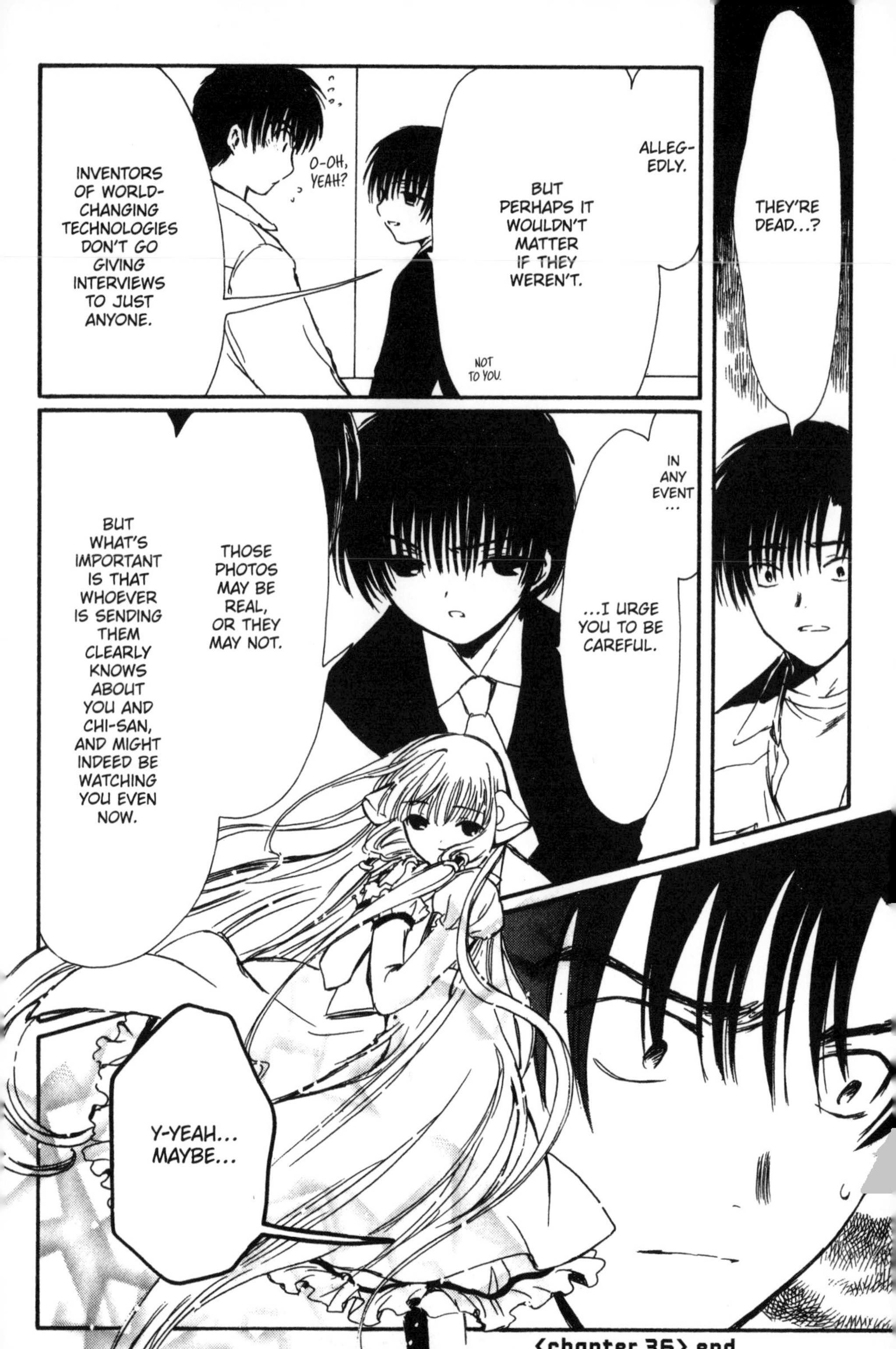
THEY'RE DEAD...?
ALLEGEDLY.
BUT PERHAPS IT WOULDN'T MATTER IF THEY WEREN'T.
NOT TO YOU.
INVENTORS OF WORLD-CHANGING TECHNOLOGIES DON'T GO GIVING INTERVIEWS TO JUST ANYONE.
O-OH, YEAH?
IN ANY EVENT...
...I URGE YOU TO BE CAREFUL.
THOSE PHOTOS MAY BE REAL, OR THEY MAY NOT.
BUT WHAT'S IMPORTANT IS THAT WHOEVER IS SENDING THEM CLEARLY KNOWS ABOUT YOU AND CHI-SAN, AND MIGHT INDEED BE WATCHING YOU EVEN NOW.
Y-YEAH... MAYBE...
‹chapter.36› end

Chobits

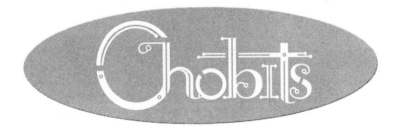

Translation Notes

Morning exercises, page 18

Every morning in Japan, public broadcaster NHK presents a segment on their radio station known as *rajio taisou* ("radio calisthenics"). It's a short program of basic stretches and exercises, and although participation is no longer as universal as it once was, you can still see everyone from office workers to the elderly taking a few minutes out of their day to warm up with some exercise. *Rajio taisou* is a more sedate routine than what Sumomo imposes on Hideki here, but it wouldn't be so surprising if in a future with humanoid machines, people trusted their persocoms to guide them through a similar regimen in the mornings.

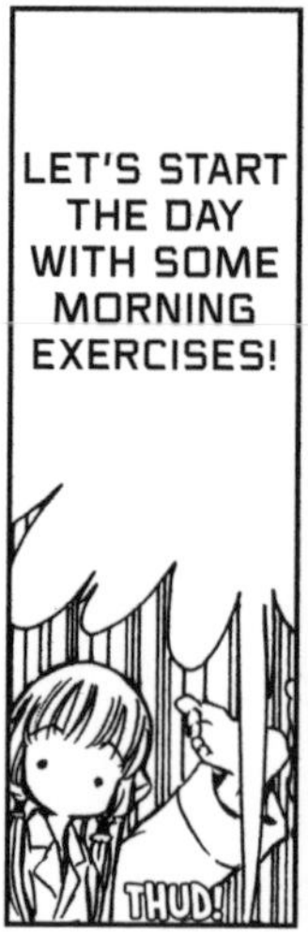
LET'S START THE DAY WITH SOME MORNING EXERCISES!
THUD!

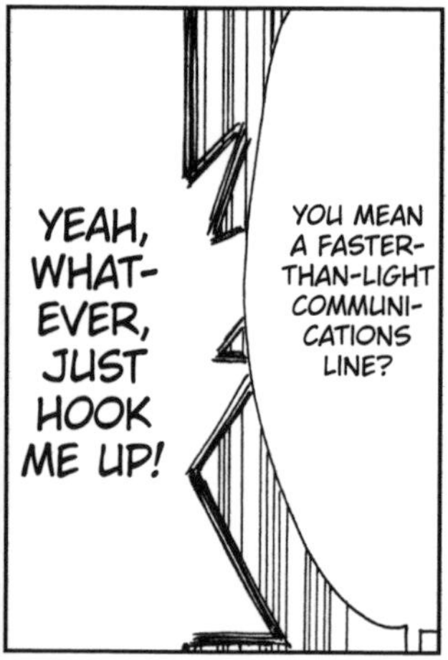
YOU MEAN A FASTER-THAN-LIGHT COMMUNI-CATIONS LINE?
YEAH, WHAT-EVER, JUST HOOK ME UP!

A faster-than-light communications line, page 31

The Japanese (*chou-kousoku tsuushin kaisen*) has been rendered literally here. Faster-than-light communication isn't currently possible, and it's not completely clear whether it has become possible in the world of *Chobits*, or if Minoru is having a bit of fun at Hideki's expense. Hideki's blunt response in the original Japanese, "*Nanka sonna no!*" ("Something more or less like that!") suggests he either isn't quite listening, or doesn't quite get it.

Chi Motosuwa-sama, page 85

The addressee of an envelope in Japan (whether for a letter sent through the postal service or handed over personally, like here) is always given the very polite honorific *-sama*. Notice, by the way, that the envelope is narrower and taller than most envelopes in, for example, the United States. Since Japanese is written vertically, letters are folded along the length rather than the width, so a taller envelope is called for.

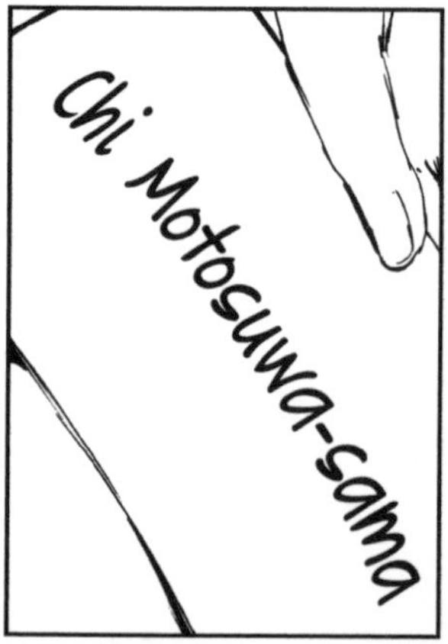
Chi Motosuwa-sama

"No, they *are* real," page 101

In the Japanese, Hideki realizes he's been talking about persocoms using the verb *iru*, which means "to be," but is used only of living things, chiefly people and animals. In the aside, he says "Guess I should use *aru*" ("to be" for inanimate objects, including computers). The dialogue had to be massaged a little for the English, which of course doesn't make such a distinction in the use of the verb "to be."

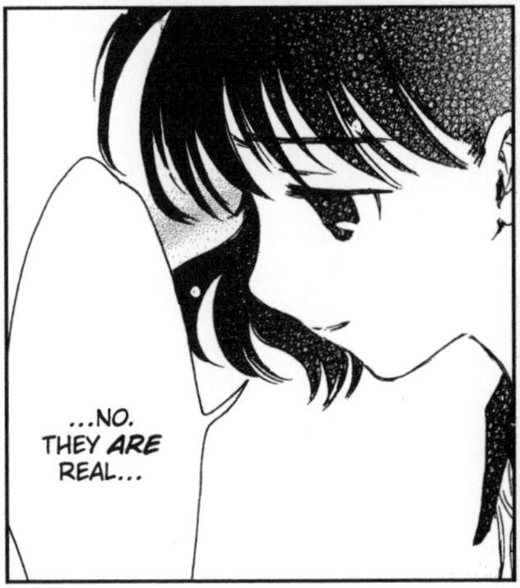
...NO. THEY *ARE* REAL...

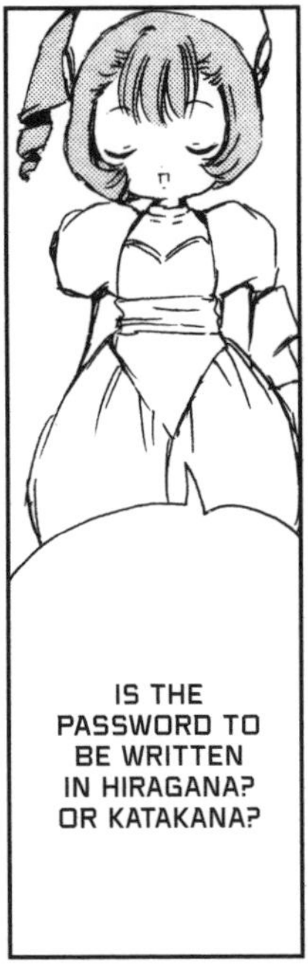
IS THE PASSWORD TO BE WRITTEN IN HIRAGANA? OR KATAKANA?

Hiragana or katakana, page 114

These are the two syllabaries of the written Japanese language; that is, systems in which the characters stand for individual sounds, unlike kanji, where each character represents an entire word. Hiragana and katakana contain the same set of sounds and differ only in their appearance—hiragana is rounder, while katana is more angular. In practice, they're used for different purposes—hiragana is the most common syllabary, but katakana may be used to write sound effects, foreign words, or other things that are seen to need emphasis or distinction. Interestingly, the way Hideki enters his password is the opposite of how the word *Chobits* is styled in the title of the series. Hideki enters the character *chi* (in Japanese, *chi* + *yo* = *cho*) in katakana, whereas in the title of the series it is the *ts* (*tsu* in Japanese) that gets this treatment.

200 Books to Light Up Your Heart, page 140

Japanese publishers commonly put out lists (of their titles, naturally), sometimes quite extensive, on various themes. In particular, the summer season tends to produce a lot of "100 books you should read this summer"-type lists. This particular list (*kokoro no tomoshibi ni-hyaku-satsu*) doesn't appear to have a real-world antecedent and is just a bit of set dressing.

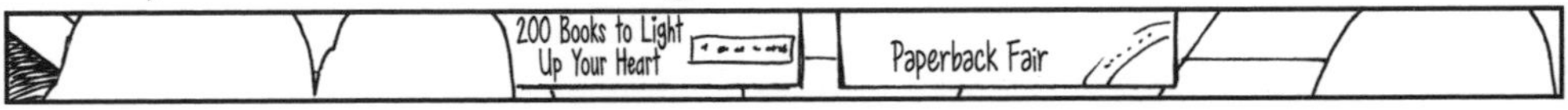
200 Books to Light Up Your Heart
Paperback Fair

Chobits

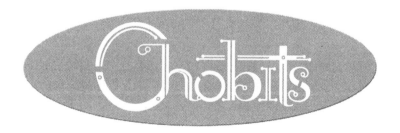

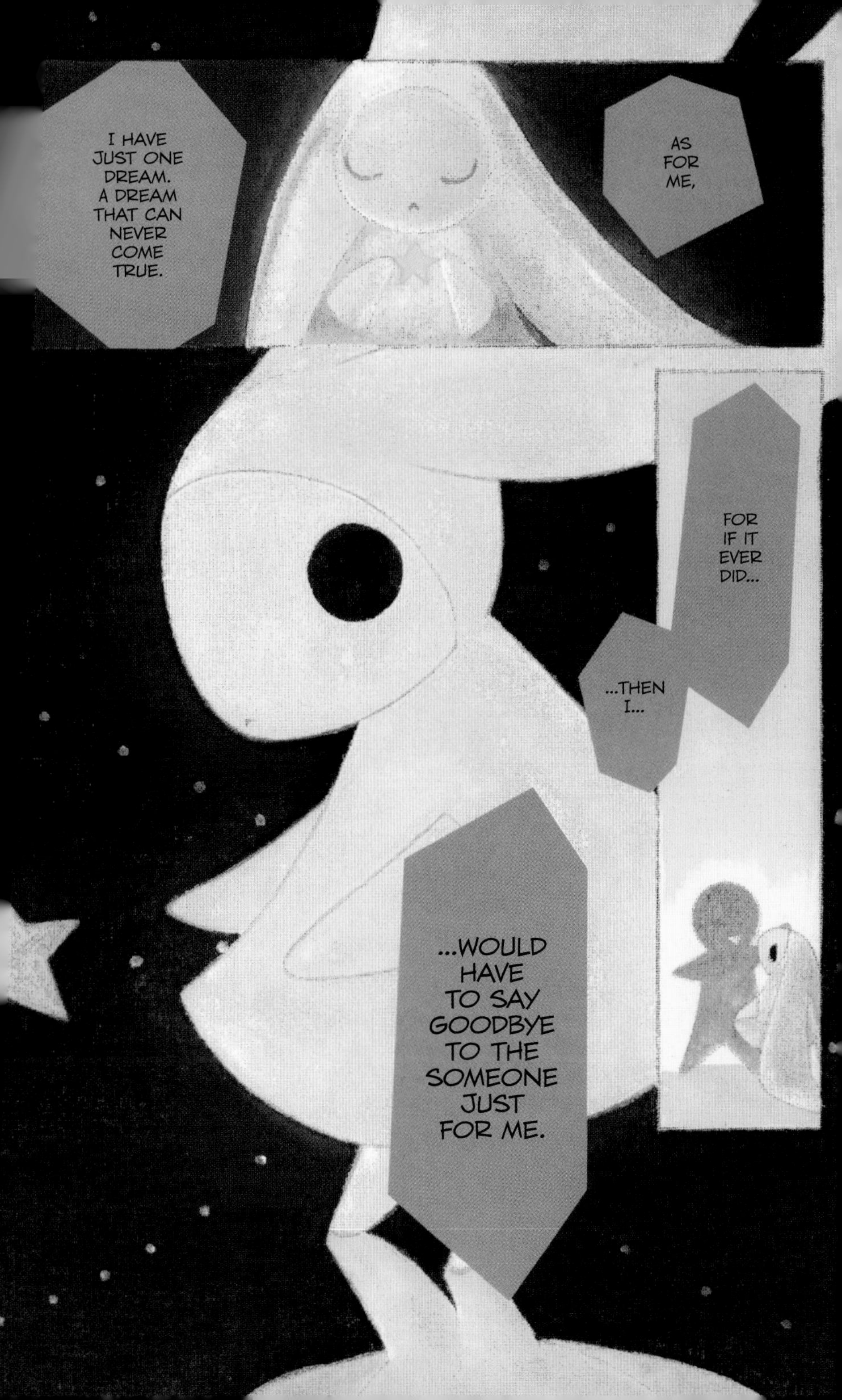
AS FOR ME,
I HAVE JUST ONE DREAM. A DREAM THAT CAN NEVER COME TRUE.
FOR IF IT EVER DID...
...THEN I...
...WOULD HAVE TO SAY GOODBYE TO THE SOMEONE JUST FOR ME.

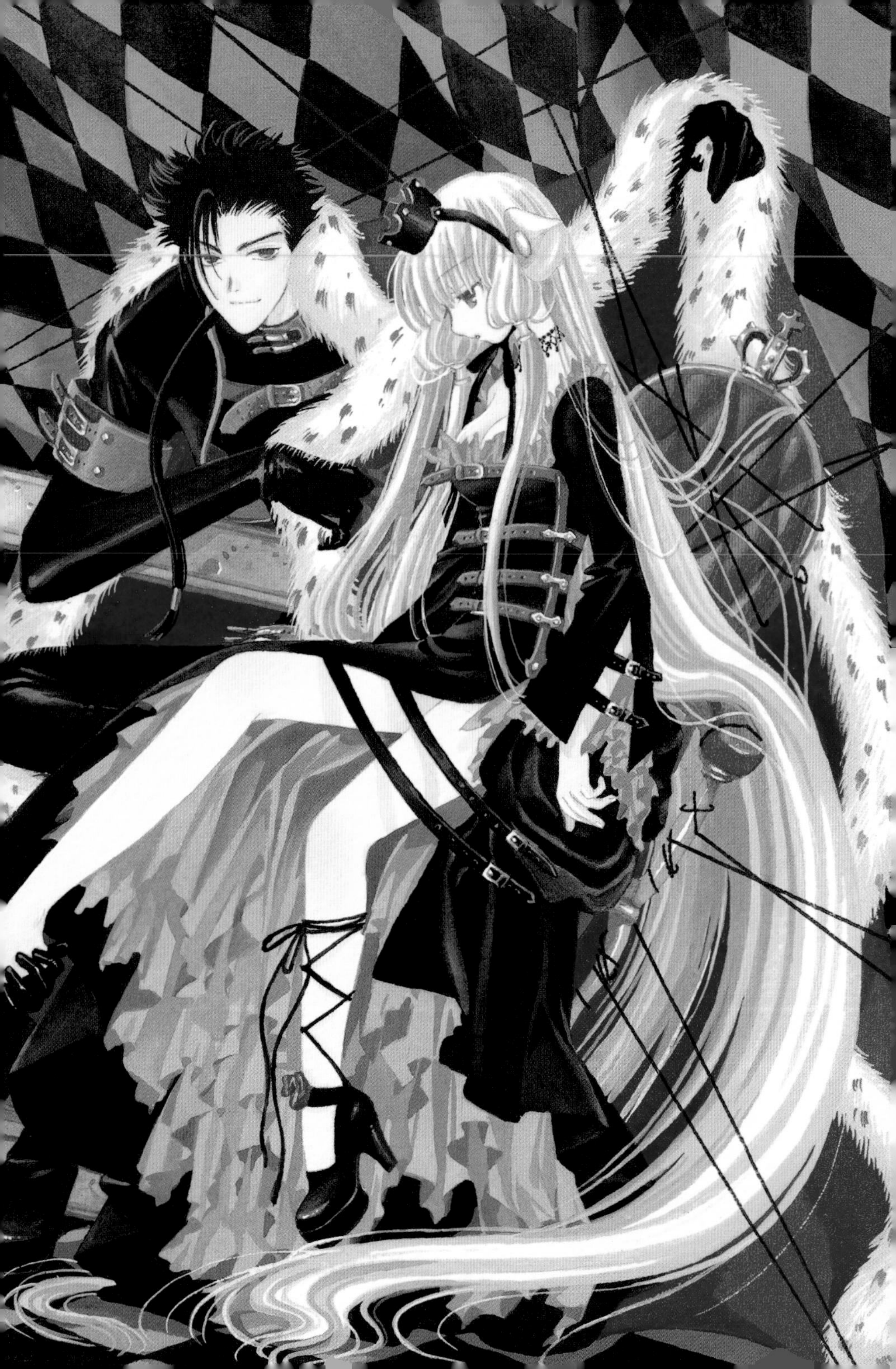

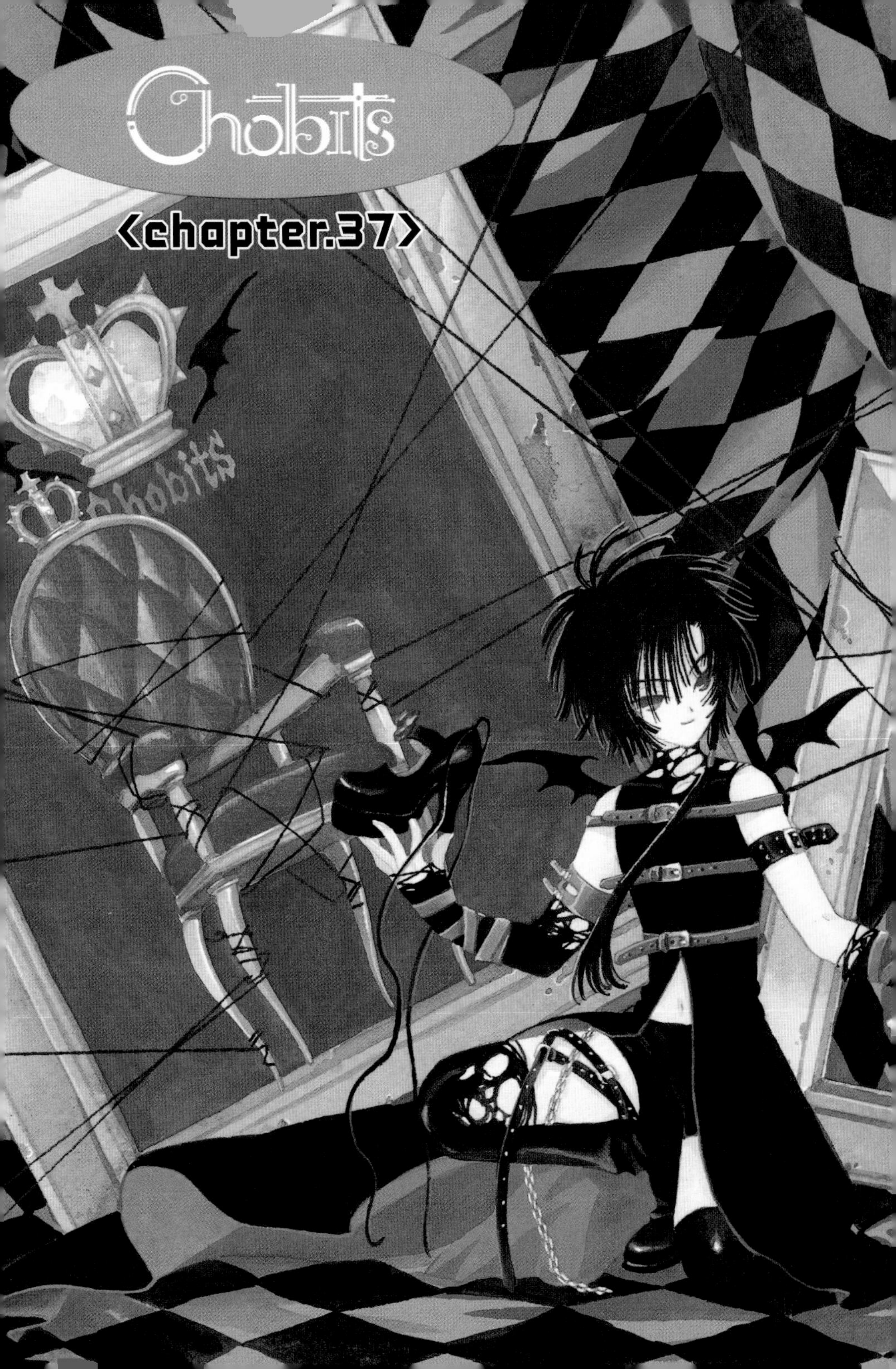
Chobits
<chapter.37>
Chobits

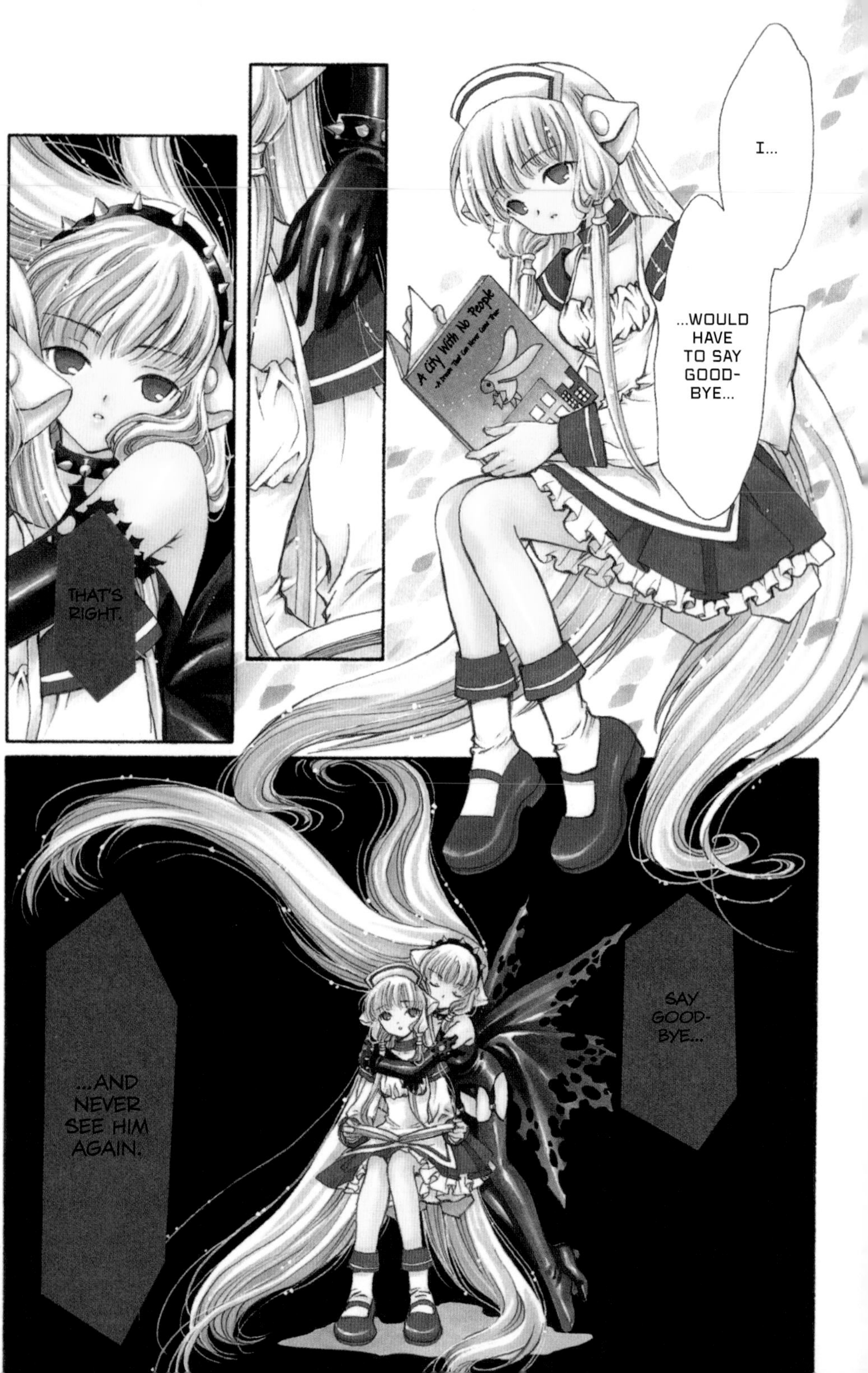
I...
...WOULD HAVE TO SAY GOOD-BYE...
A City With No People
THAT'S RIGHT.
SAY GOOD-BYE...
...AND NEVER SEE HIM AGAIN.

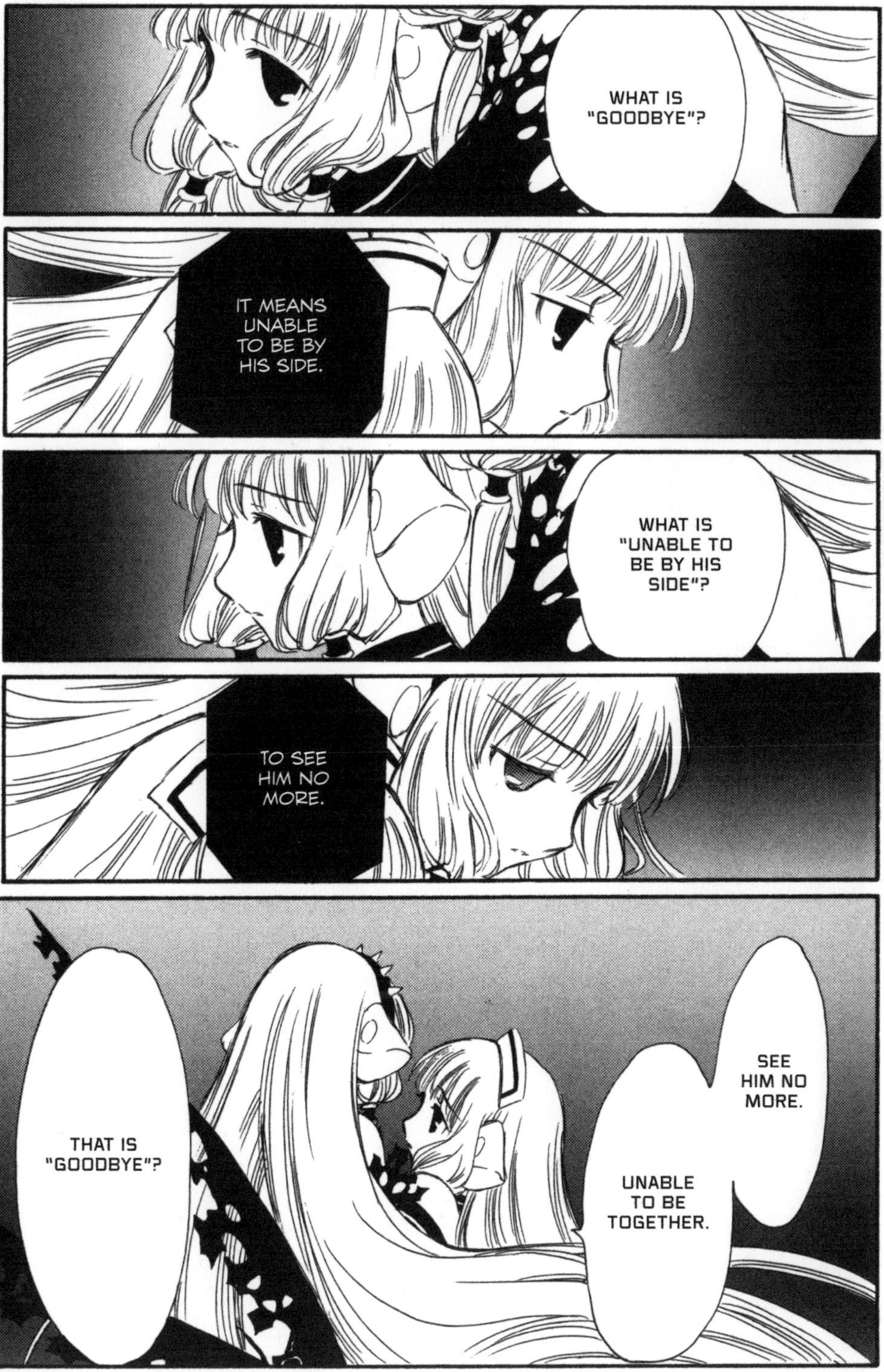
WHAT IS "GOODBYE"?
IT MEANS UNABLE TO BE BY HIS SIDE.
WHAT IS "UNABLE TO BE BY HIS SIDE"?
TO SEE HIM NO MORE.
SEE HIM NO MORE.
UNABLE TO BE TOGETHER.
THAT IS "GOODBYE"?

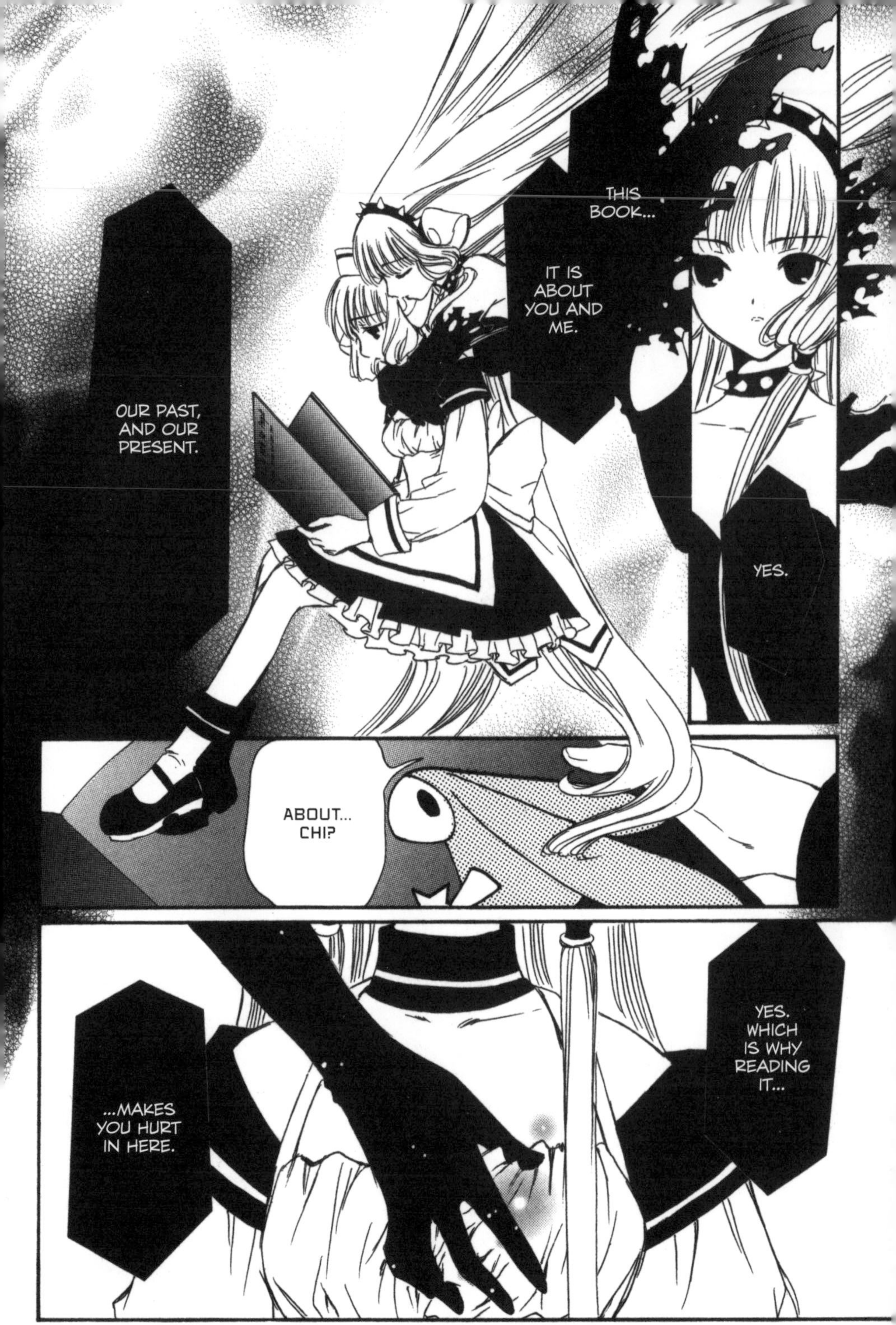

THIS BOOK...
IT IS ABOUT YOU AND ME.
OUR PAST, AND OUR PRESENT.
YES.
ABOUT... CHI?
YES. WHICH IS WHY READING IT...
...MAKES YOU HURT IN HERE.

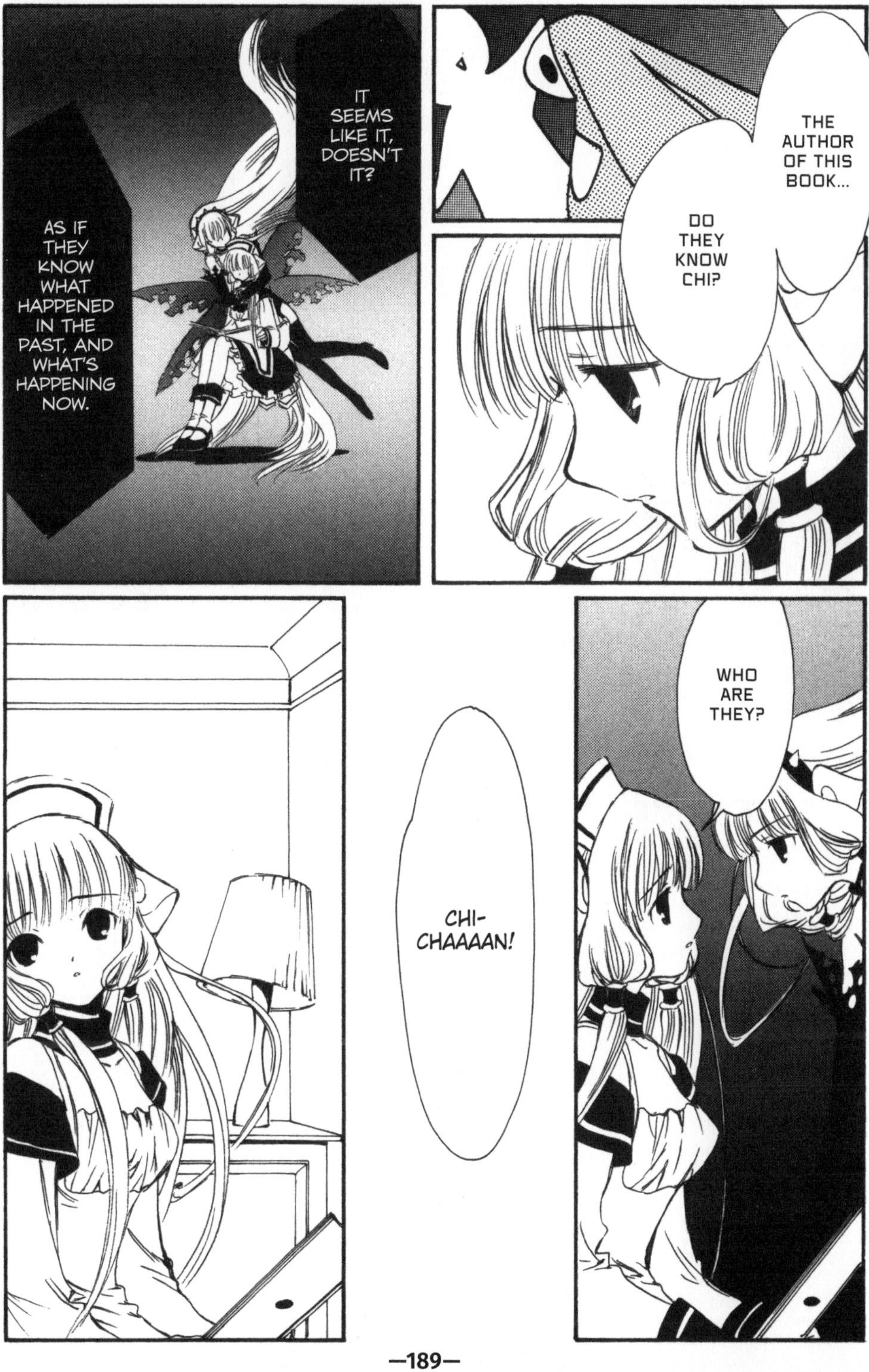

THE AUTHOR OF THIS BOOK...
DO THEY KNOW CHI?
IT SEEMS LIKE IT, DOESN'T IT?
AS IF THEY KNOW WHAT HAPPENED IN THE PAST, AND WHAT'S HAPPENING NOW.
WHO ARE THEY?
CHI-CHAAAAN!

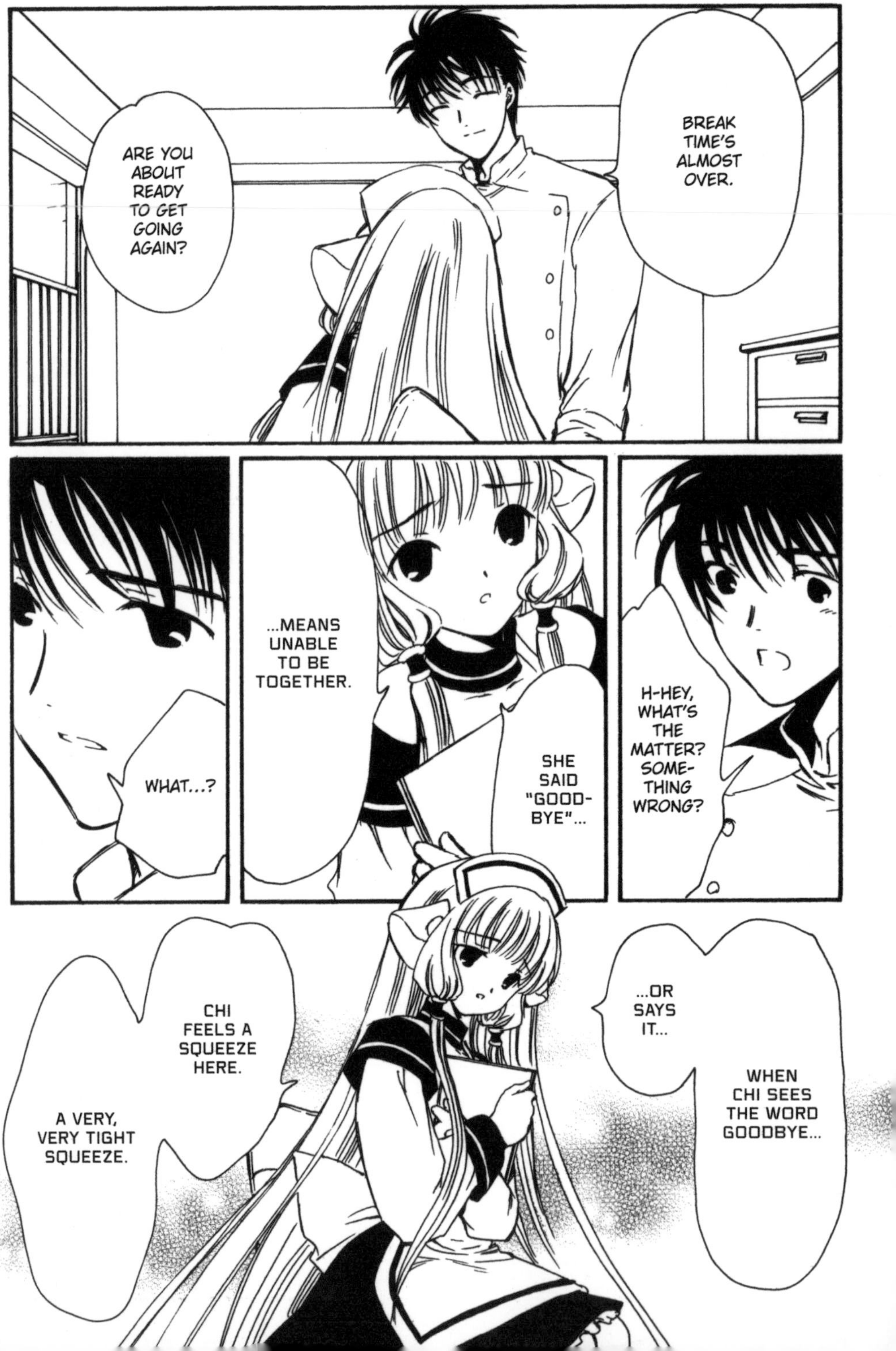
BREAK TIME'S ALMOST OVER.
ARE YOU ABOUT READY TO GET GOING AGAIN?
H-HEY, WHAT'S THE MATTER? SOME-THING WRONG?
SHE SAID "GOOD-BYE"...
...MEANS UNABLE TO BE TOGETHER.
WHAT...?
WHEN CHI SEES THE WORD GOODBYE...
...OR SAYS IT...
CHI FEELS A SQUEEZE HERE.
A VERY, VERY TIGHT SQUEEZE.

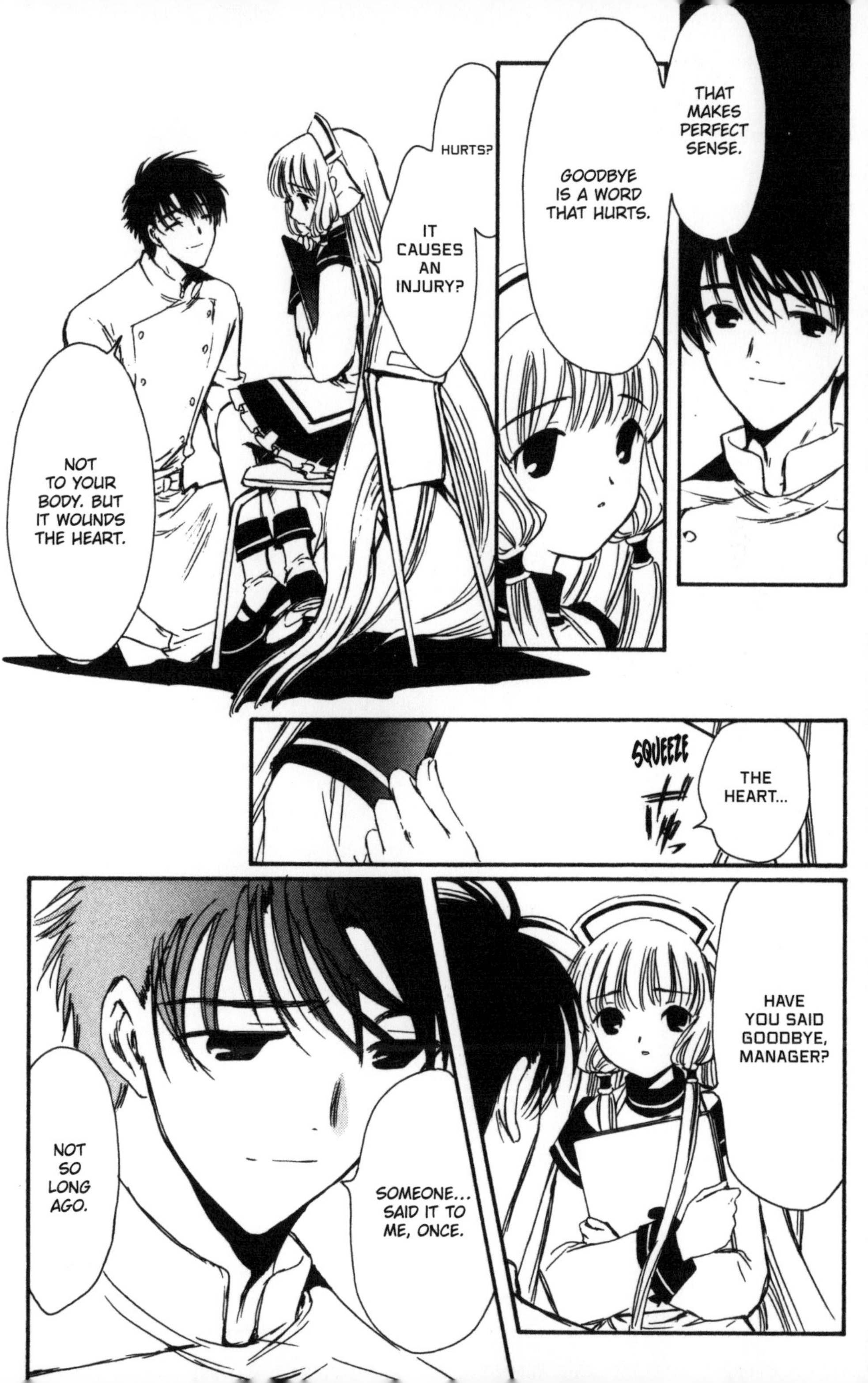
THAT MAKES PERFECT SENSE.
GOODBYE IS A WORD THAT HURTS.
HURTS?
IT CAUSES AN INJURY?
NOT TO YOUR BODY. BUT IT WOUNDS THE HEART.
THE HEART...
SQUEEZE
HAVE YOU SAID GOODBYE, MANAGER?
SOMEONE... SAID IT TO ME, ONCE.
NOT SO LONG AGO.

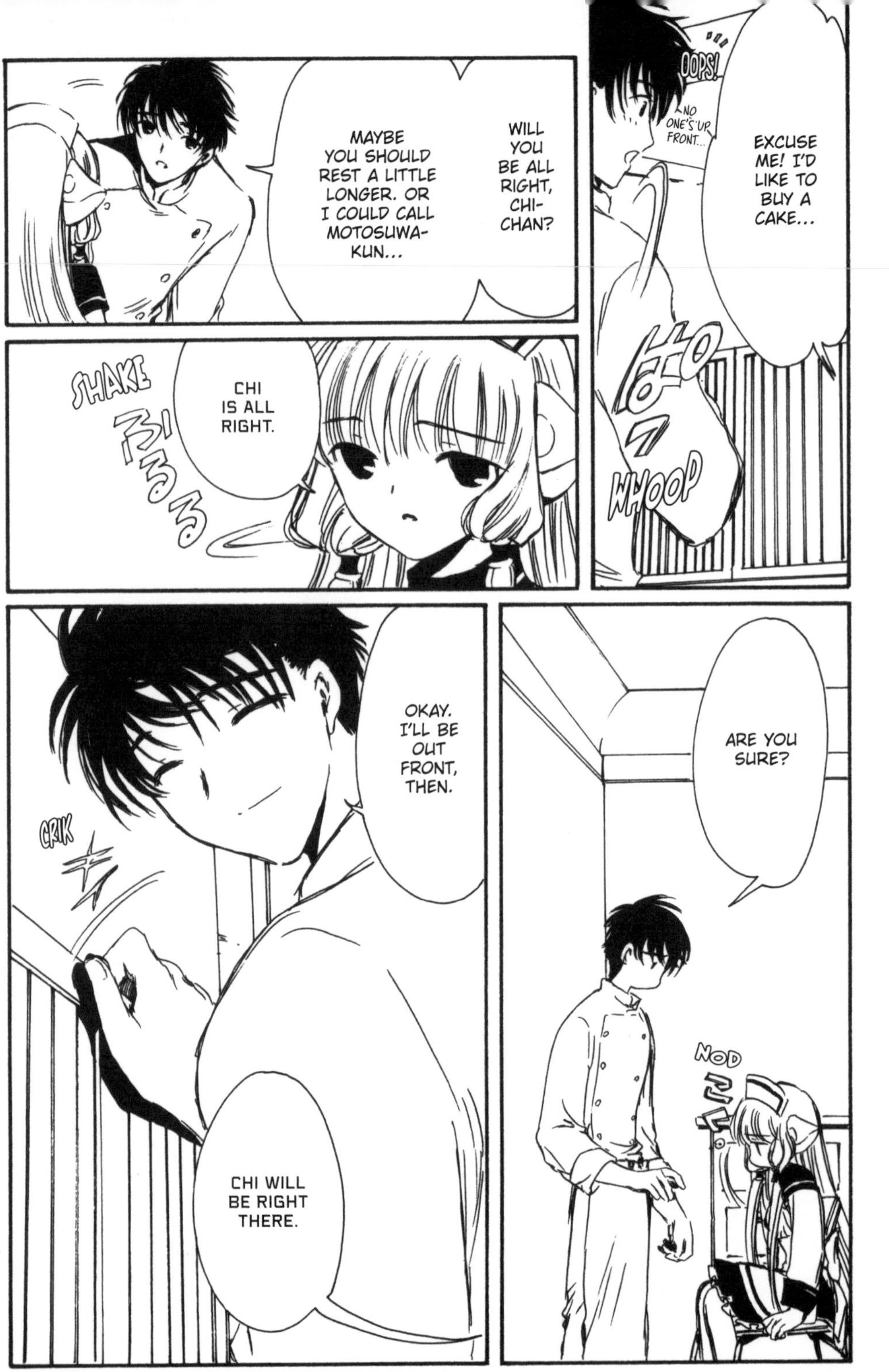
OOPS!
NO ONE'S UP FRONT...
EXCUSE ME! I'D LIKE TO BUY A CAKE...
WHOOP
WILL YOU BE ALL RIGHT, CHI-CHAN?
MAYBE YOU SHOULD REST A LITTLE LONGER. OR I COULD CALL MOTOSUWA-KUN...
SHAKE
CHI IS ALL RIGHT.
ARE YOU SURE?
NOD
OKAY. I'LL BE OUT FRONT, THEN.
CRIK
CHI WILL BE RIGHT THERE.

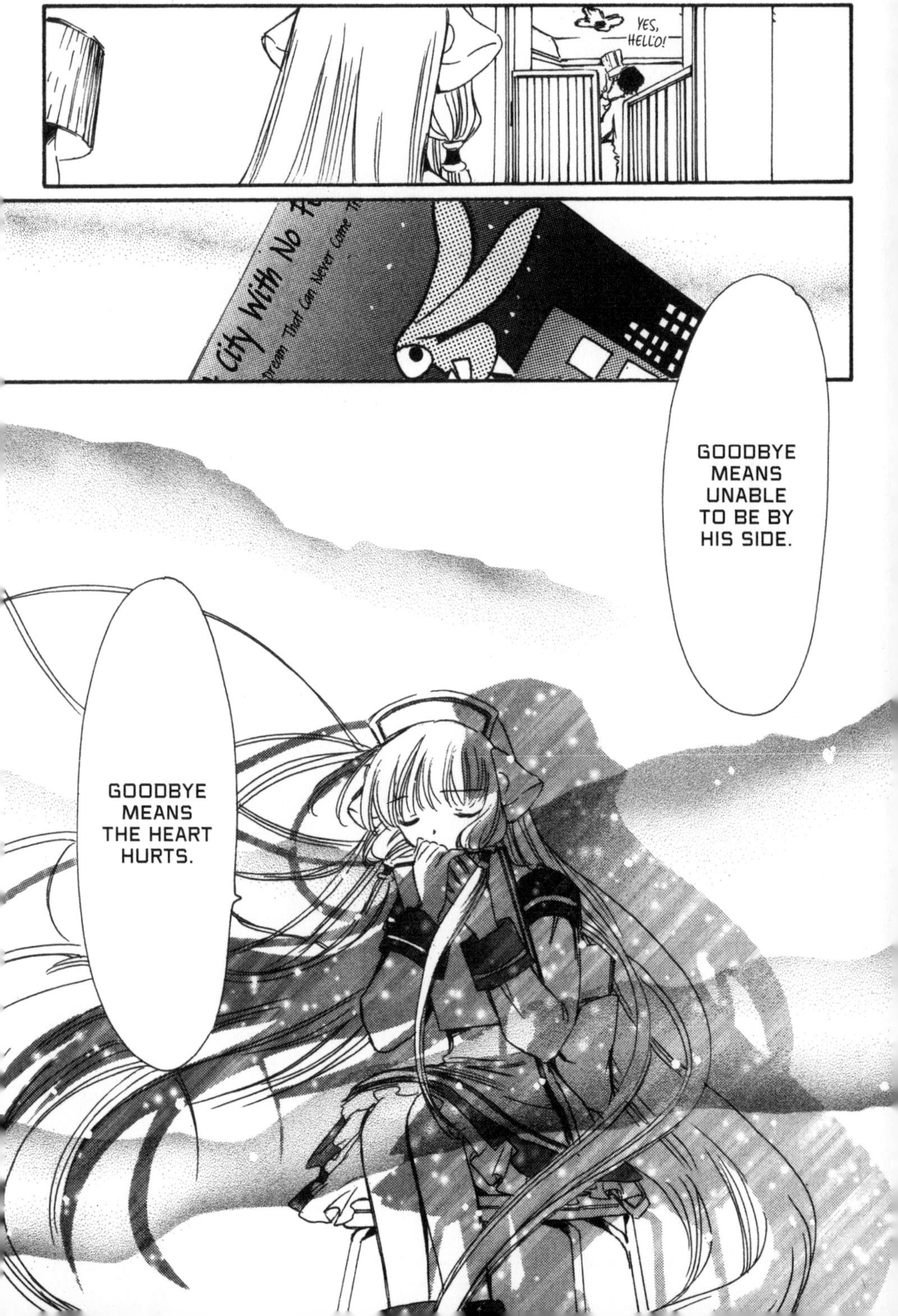
YES, HELLO!
City With No
GOODBYE MEANS UNABLE TO BE BY HIS SIDE.
GOODBYE MEANS THE HEART HURTS.

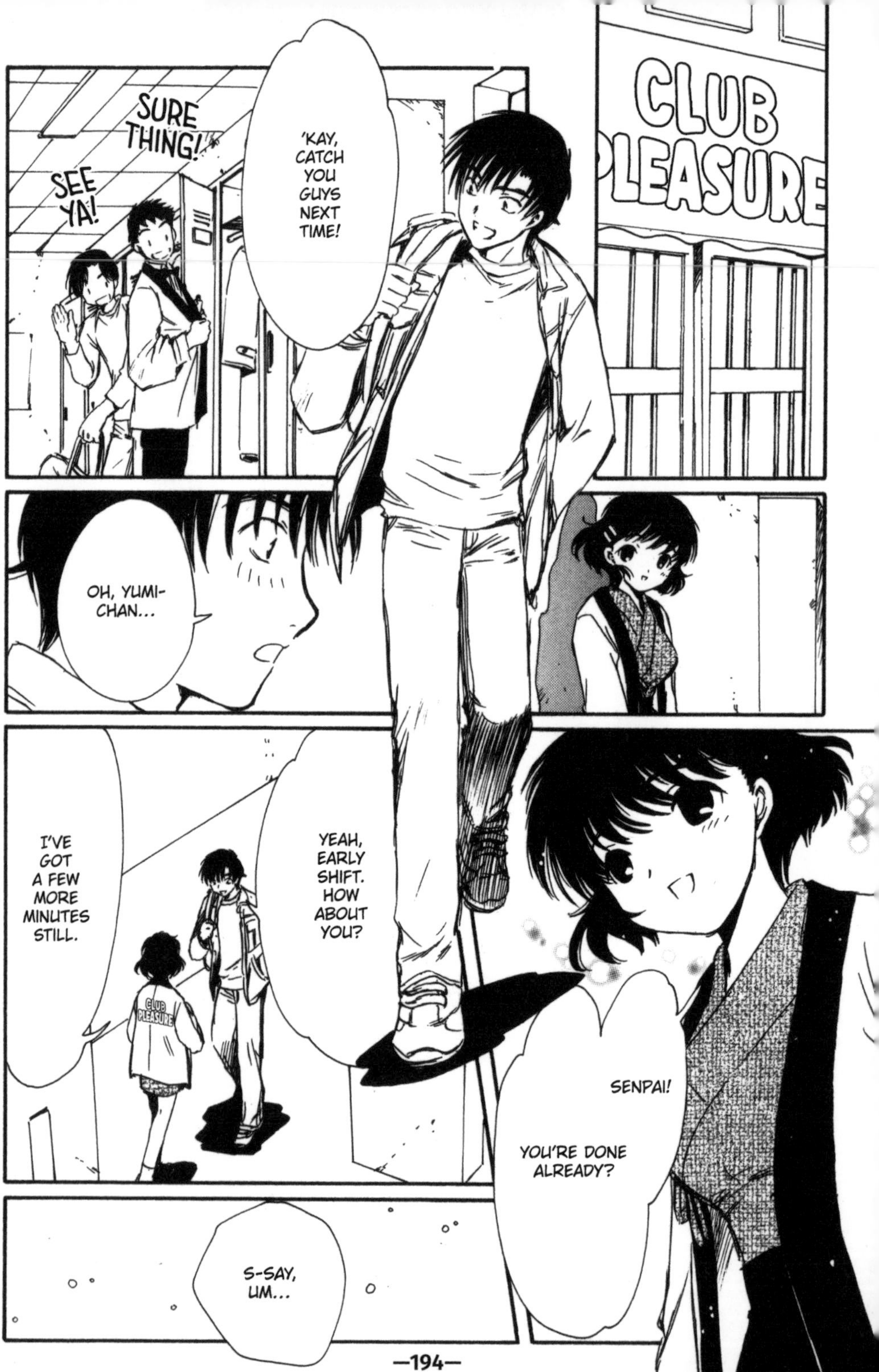
CLUB PLEASURE
'KAY, CATCH YOU GUYS NEXT TIME!
SURE THING!
SEE YA!
OH, YUMI-CHAN...
SENPAI!
YOU'RE DONE ALREADY?
YEAH, EARLY SHIFT. HOW ABOUT YOU?
I'VE GOT A FEW MORE MINUTES STILL.
CLUB PLEASURE
S-SAY, UM...

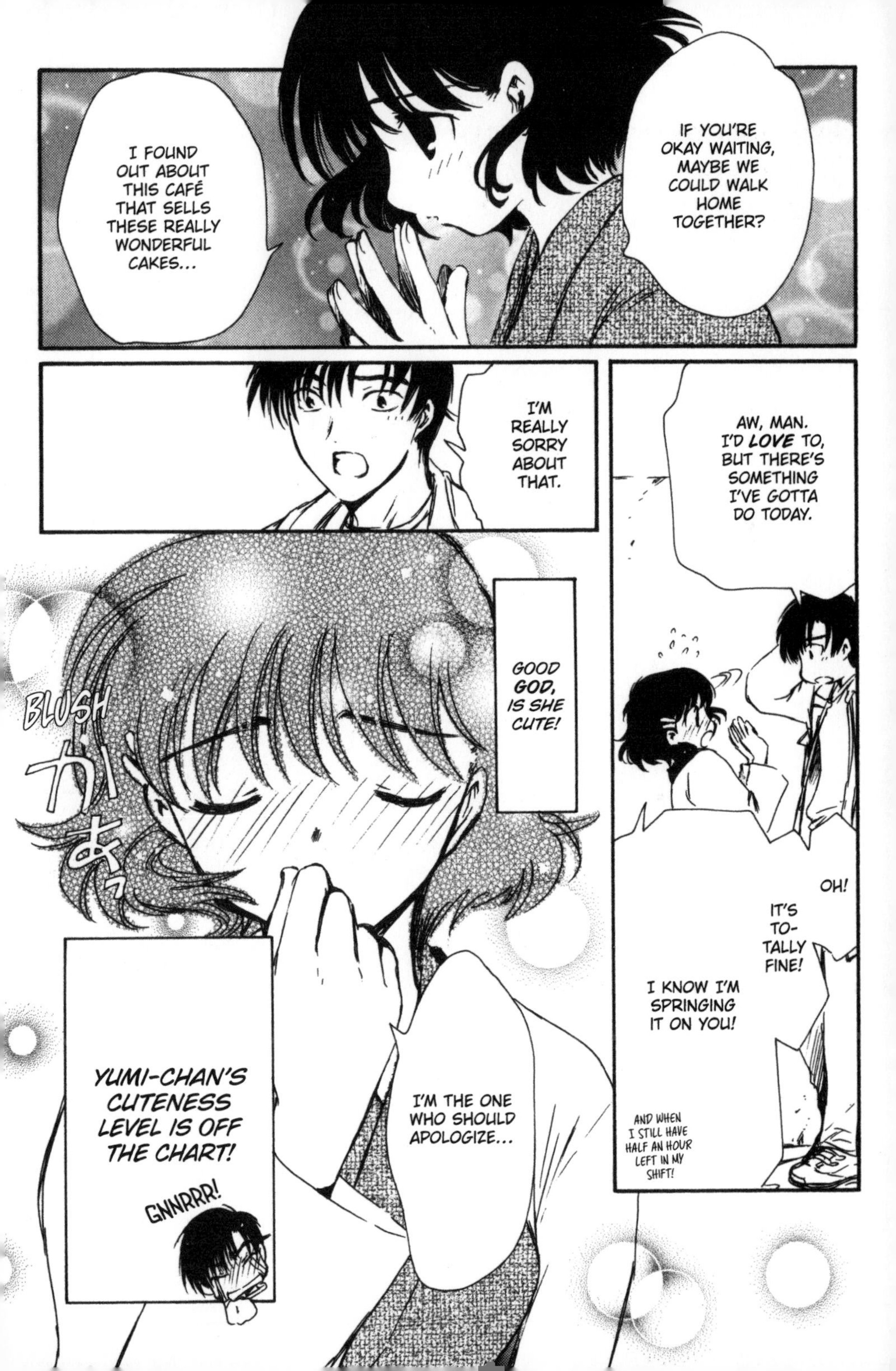
IF YOU'RE OKAY WAITING, MAYBE WE COULD WALK HOME TOGETHER?
I FOUND OUT ABOUT THIS CAFÉ THAT SELLS THESE REALLY WONDERFUL CAKES...
AW, MAN. I'D *LOVE* TO, BUT THERE'S SOMETHING I'VE GOTTA DO TODAY.
OH!
IT'S TO-TALLY FINE!
I KNOW I'M SPRINGING IT ON YOU!
AND WHEN I STILL HAVE HALF AN HOUR LEFT IN MY SHIFT!
I'M REALLY SORRY ABOUT THAT.
GOOD *GOD*, IS SHE CUTE!
BLUSH
I'M THE ONE WHO SHOULD APOLOGIZE...
YUMI-CHAN'S CUTENESS LEVEL IS OFF THE CHART!
GNNRRR!

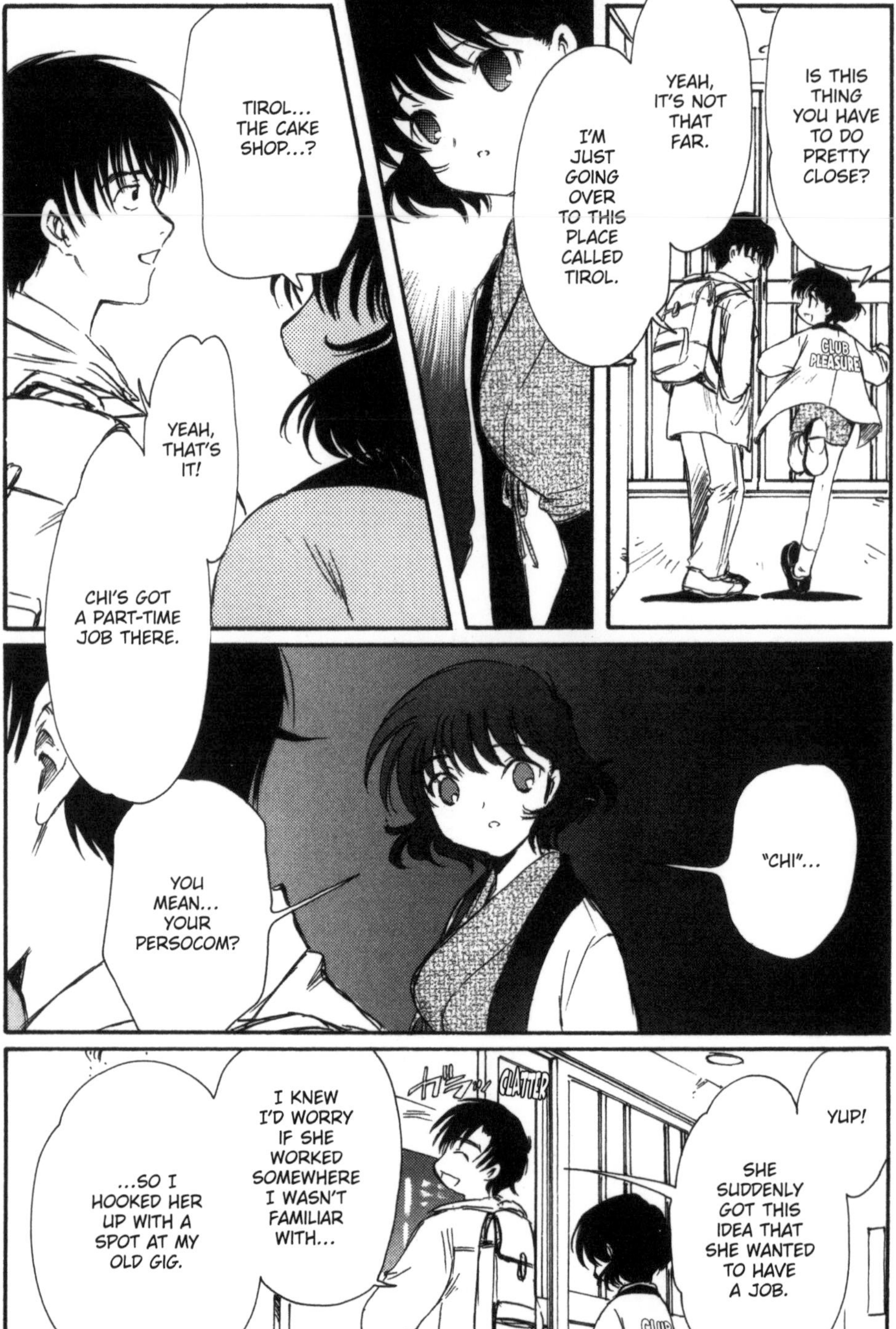
IS THIS THING YOU HAVE TO DO PRETTY CLOSE?
YEAH, IT'S NOT THAT FAR.
I'M JUST GOING OVER TO THIS PLACE CALLED TIROL.
CLUB PLEASURE
TIROL... THE CAKE SHOP...?
YEAH, THAT'S IT!
CHI'S GOT A PART-TIME JOB THERE.
"CHI"...
YOU MEAN... YOUR PERSOCOM?
YUP!
SHE SUDDENLY GOT THIS IDEA THAT SHE WANTED TO HAVE A JOB.
CLUB PLEASU
CLATTER
I KNEW I'D WORRY IF SHE WORKED SOMEWHERE I WASN'T FAMILIAR WITH...
...SO I HOOKED HER UP WITH A SPOT AT MY OLD GIG.

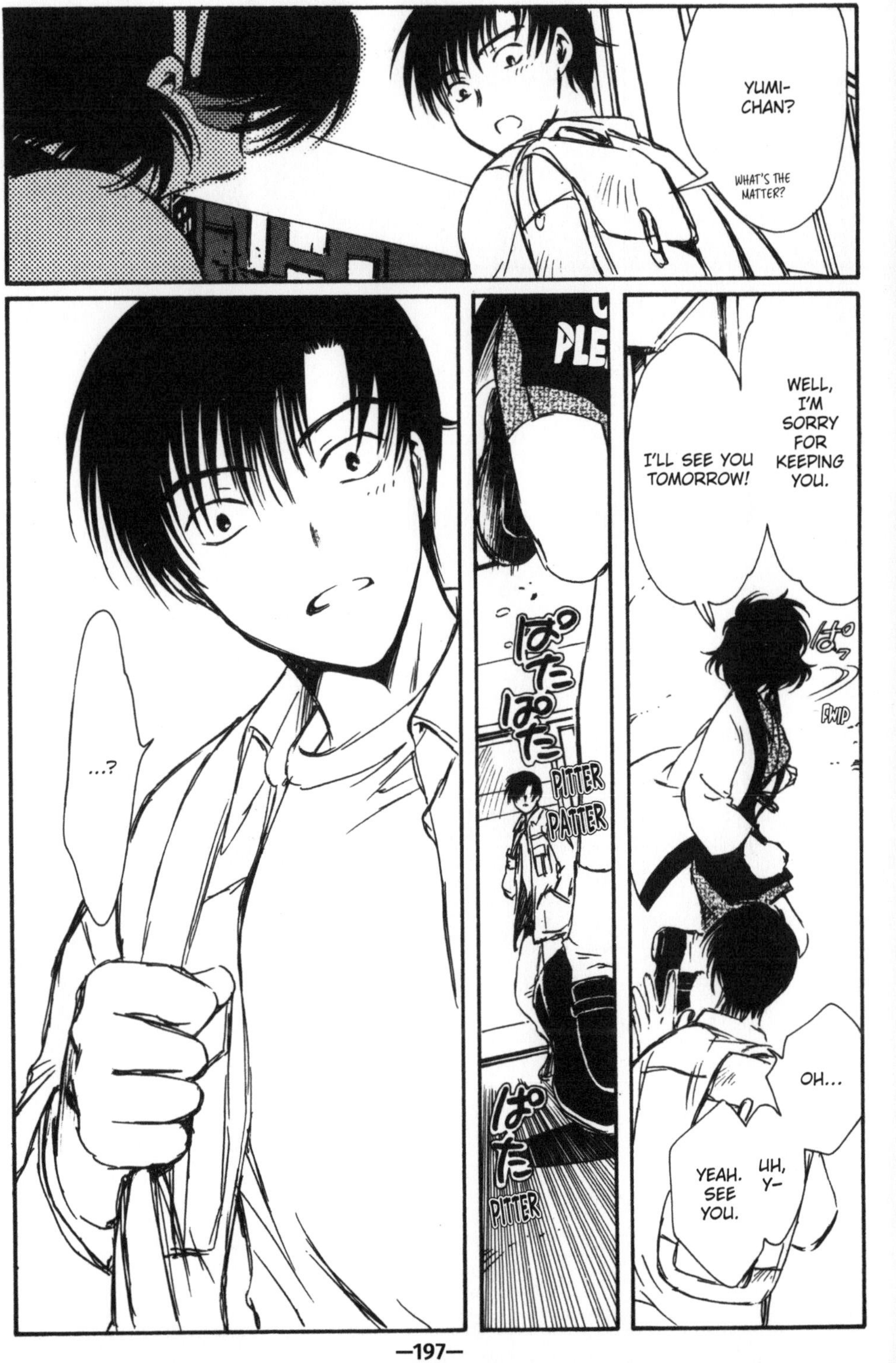
YUMI-CHAN?
WHAT'S THE MATTER?
WELL, I'M SORRY FOR KEEPING YOU.
I'LL SEE YOU TOMORROW!
ぱっ
FWIP
OH...
UH, Y—
YEAH. SEE YOU.
ぱたぱた
PITTER PATTER
ぱた
PITTER
...?

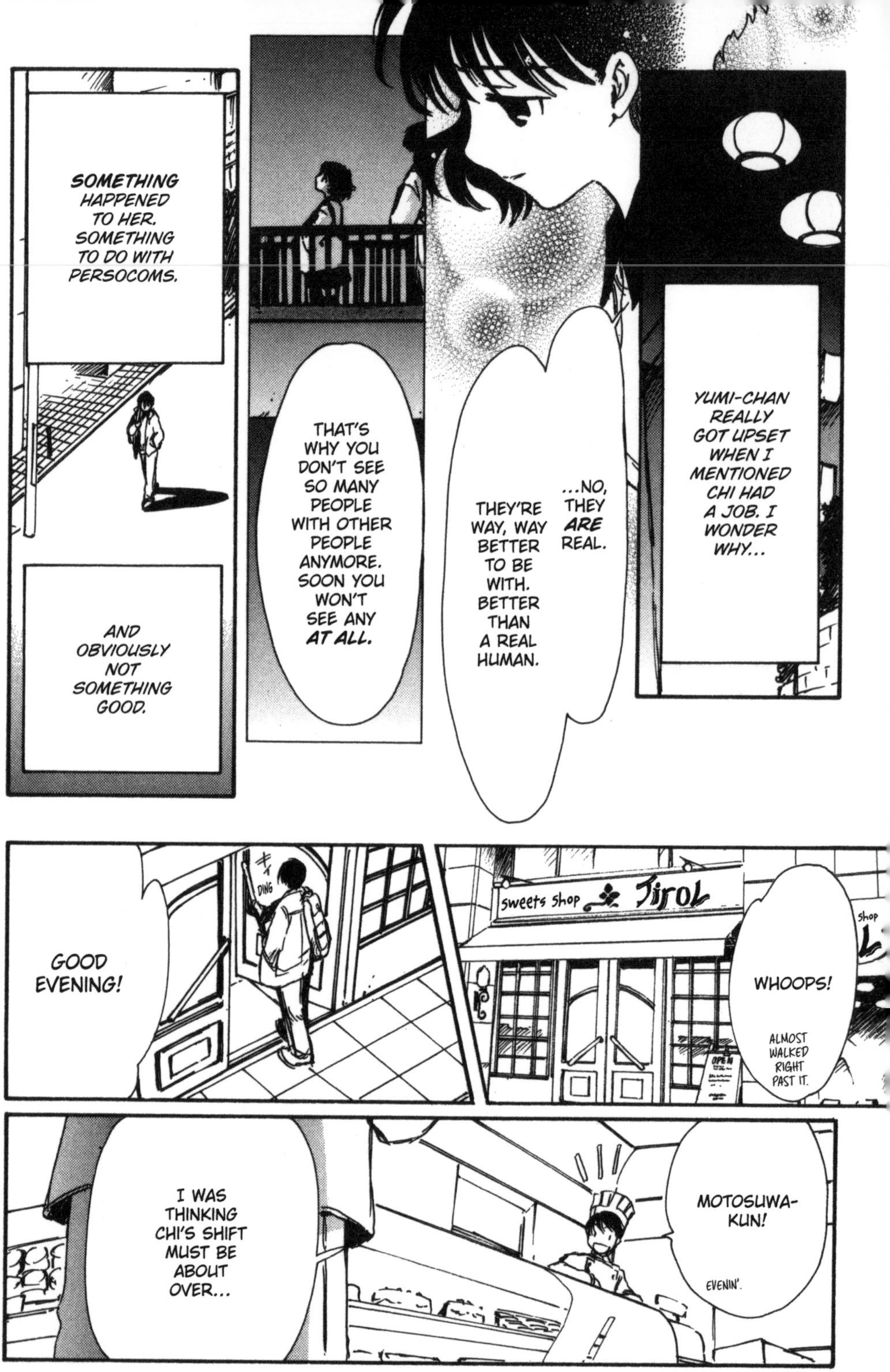

YUMI-CHAN REALLY GOT UPSET WHEN I MENTIONED CHI HAD A JOB. I WONDER WHY...
...NO, THEY *ARE* REAL.
THEY'RE WAY, WAY BETTER TO BE WITH. BETTER THAN A REAL HUMAN.
THAT'S WHY YOU DON'T SEE SO MANY PEOPLE WITH OTHER PEOPLE ANYMORE. SOON YOU WON'T SEE ANY *AT ALL.*
SOMETHING HAPPENED TO HER. SOMETHING TO DO WITH PERSOCOMS.
AND OBVIOUSLY NOT SOMETHING GOOD.
sweets shop Tirol
WHOOPS!
ALMOST WALKED RIGHT PAST IT.
OPEN
DING
GOOD EVENING!
MOTOSUWA-KUN!
EVENIN'.
I WAS THINKING CHI'S SHIFT MUST BE ABOUT OVER...

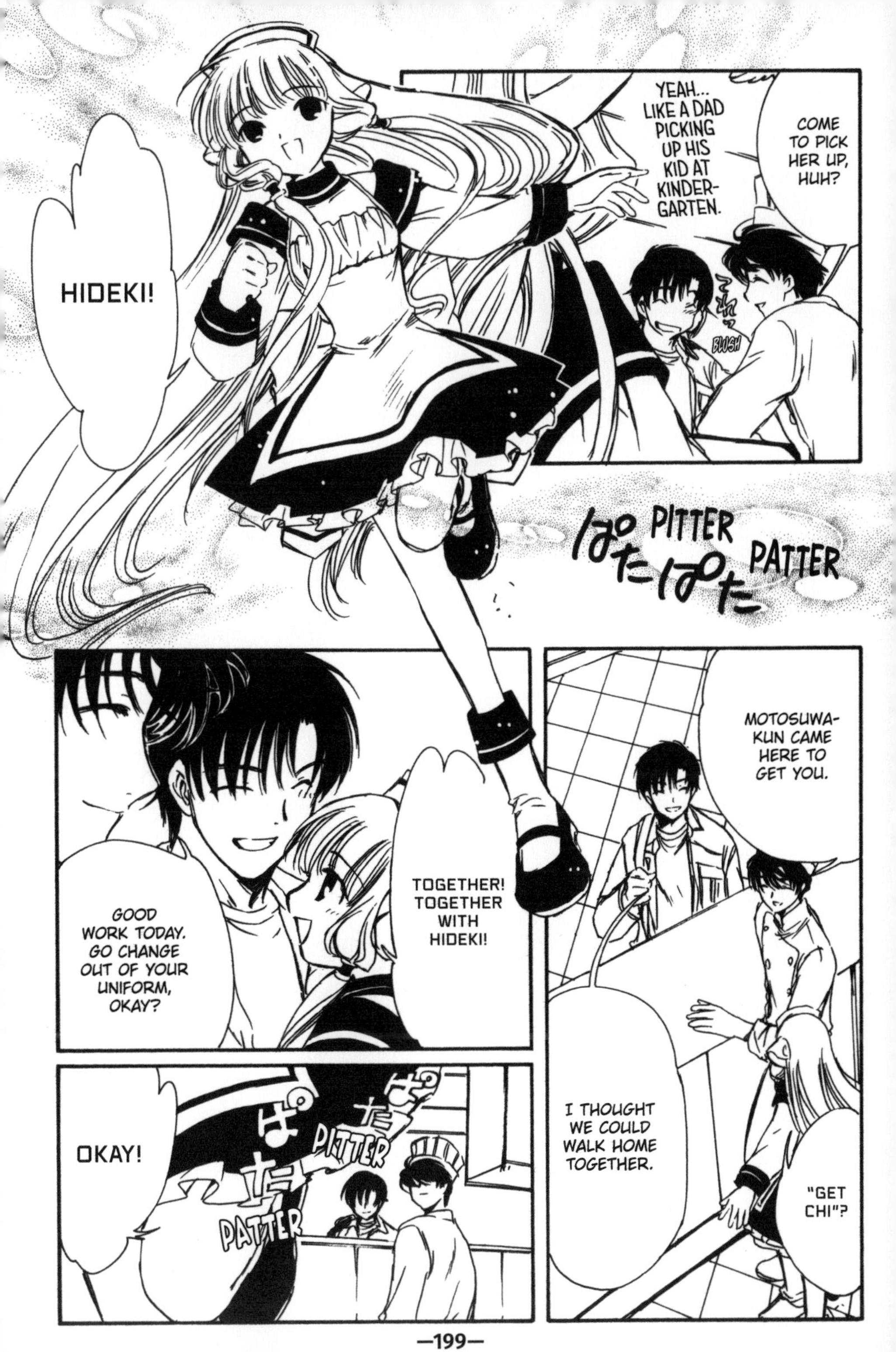

COME TO PICK HER UP, HUH?
YEAH... LIKE A DAD PICKING UP HIS KID AT KINDER-GARTEN.
BLUSH
HIDEKI!
ぱたぱた PITTER PATTER
MOTOSUWA-KUN CAME HERE TO GET YOU.
"GET CHI"?
I THOUGHT WE COULD WALK HOME TOGETHER.
TOGETHER! TOGETHER WITH HIDEKI!
GOOD WORK TODAY. GO CHANGE OUT OF YOUR UNIFORM, OKAY?
ぱたぱた PITTER PATTER
OKAY!

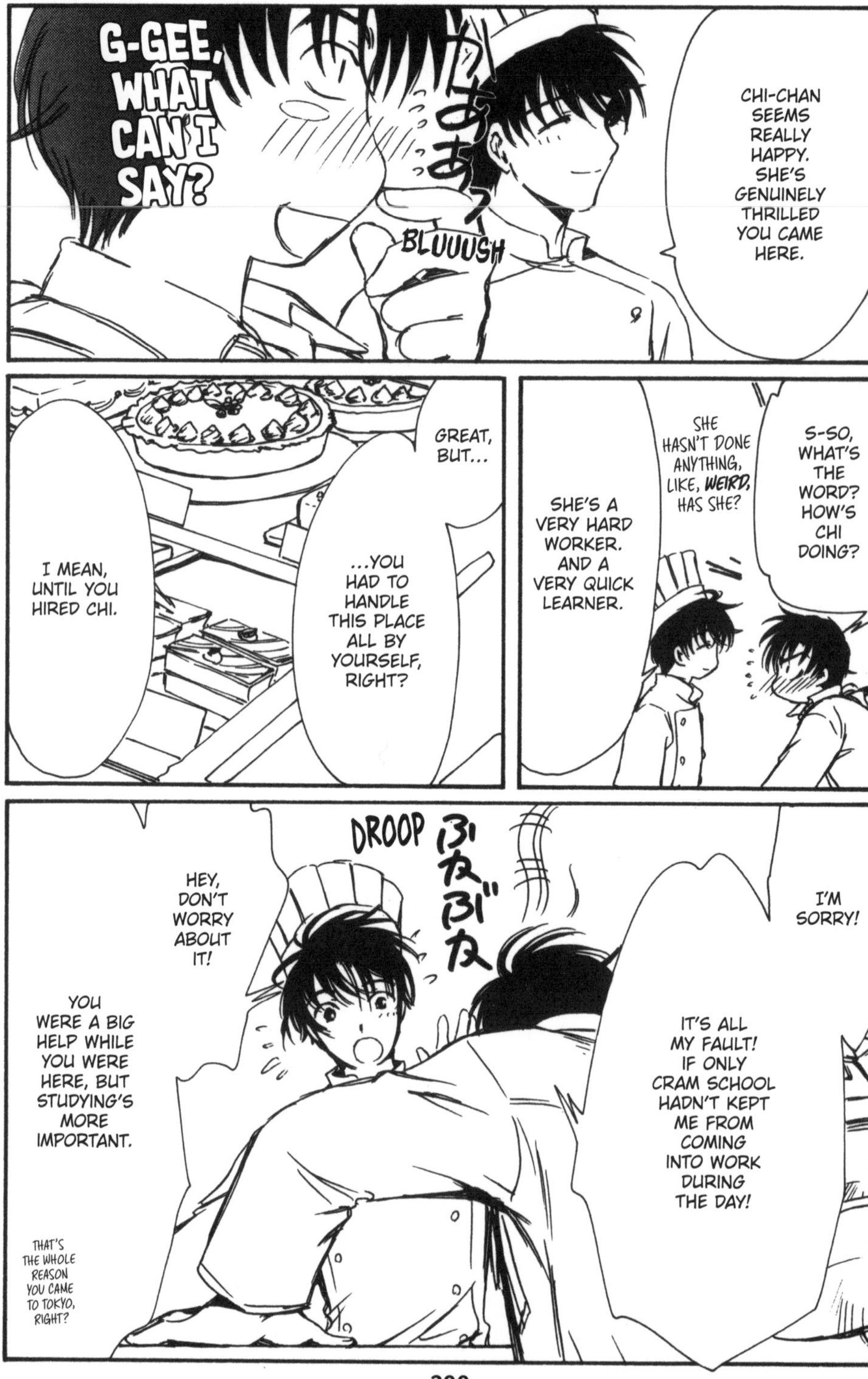
CHI-CHAN SEEMS REALLY HAPPY. SHE'S GENUINELY THRILLED YOU CAME HERE.
BLUUUSH
G-GEE, WHAT CAN I SAY?
S-SO, WHAT'S THE WORD? HOW'S CHI DOING?
SHE HASN'T DONE ANYTHING, LIKE, WEIRD, HAS SHE?
SHE'S A VERY HARD WORKER. AND A VERY QUICK LEARNER.
GREAT, BUT...
...YOU HAD TO HANDLE THIS PLACE ALL BY YOURSELF, RIGHT?
I MEAN, UNTIL YOU HIRED CHI.
I'M SORRY!
IT'S ALL MY FAULT! IF ONLY CRAM SCHOOL HADN'T KEPT ME FROM COMING INTO WORK DURING THE DAY!
DROOP
HEY, DON'T WORRY ABOUT IT!
YOU WERE A BIG HELP WHILE YOU WERE HERE, BUT STUDYING'S MORE IMPORTANT.
THAT'S THE WHOLE REASON YOU CAME TO TOKYO, RIGHT?

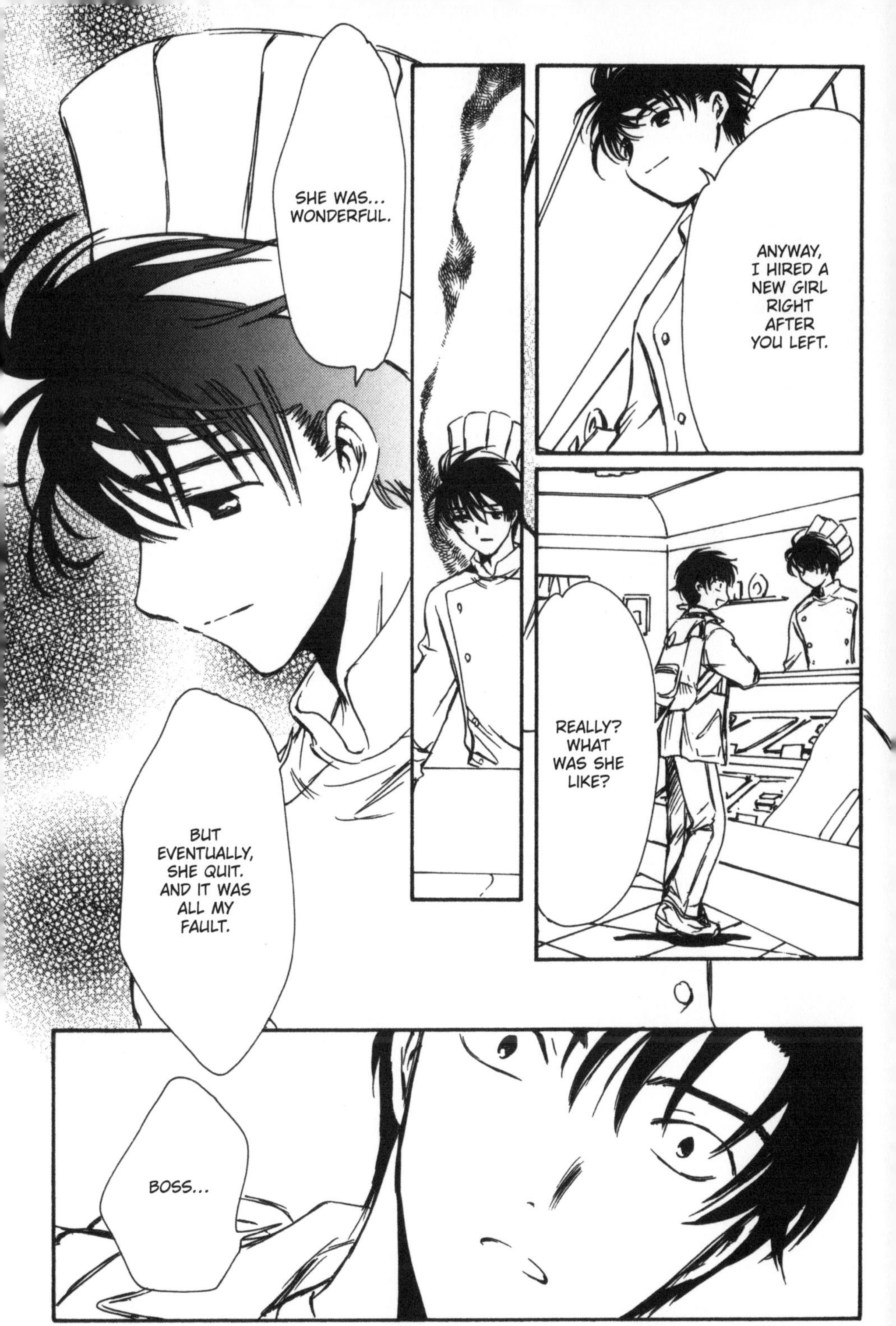
ANYWAY, I HIRED A NEW GIRL RIGHT AFTER YOU LEFT.
REALLY? WHAT WAS SHE LIKE?
SHE WAS... WONDERFUL.
BUT EVENTUALLY, SHE QUIT. AND IT WAS ALL MY FAULT.
BOSS...

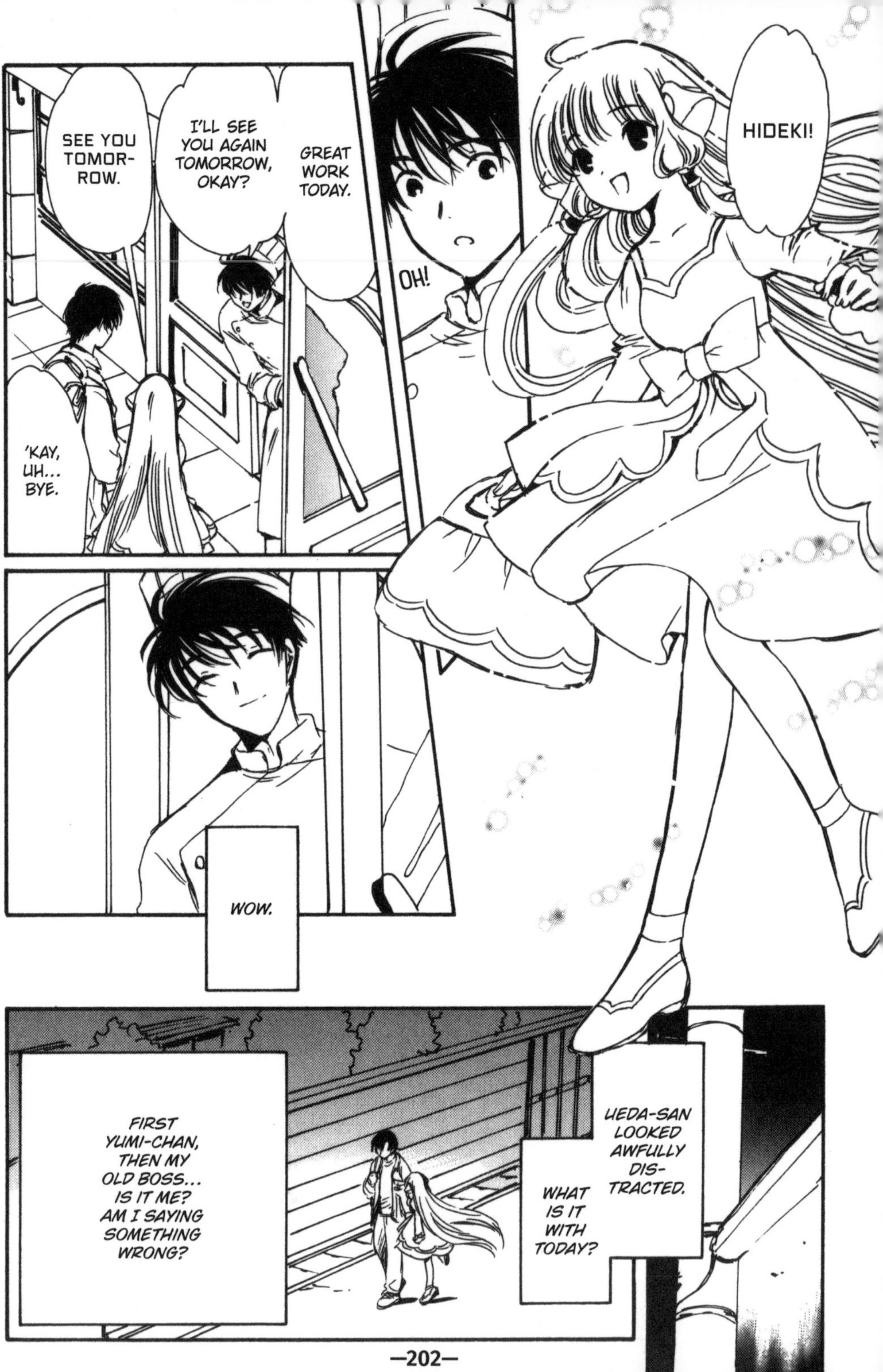
HIDEKI!
OH!
GREAT WORK TODAY.
I'LL SEE YOU AGAIN TOMORROW, OKAY?
SEE YOU TOMORROW.
'KAY, UH... BYE.
WOW.
UEDA-SAN LOOKED AWFULLY DIS-TRACTED.
WHAT IS IT WITH TODAY?
FIRST YUMI-CHAN, THEN MY OLD BOSS... IS IT ME? AM I SAYING SOMETHING WRONG?

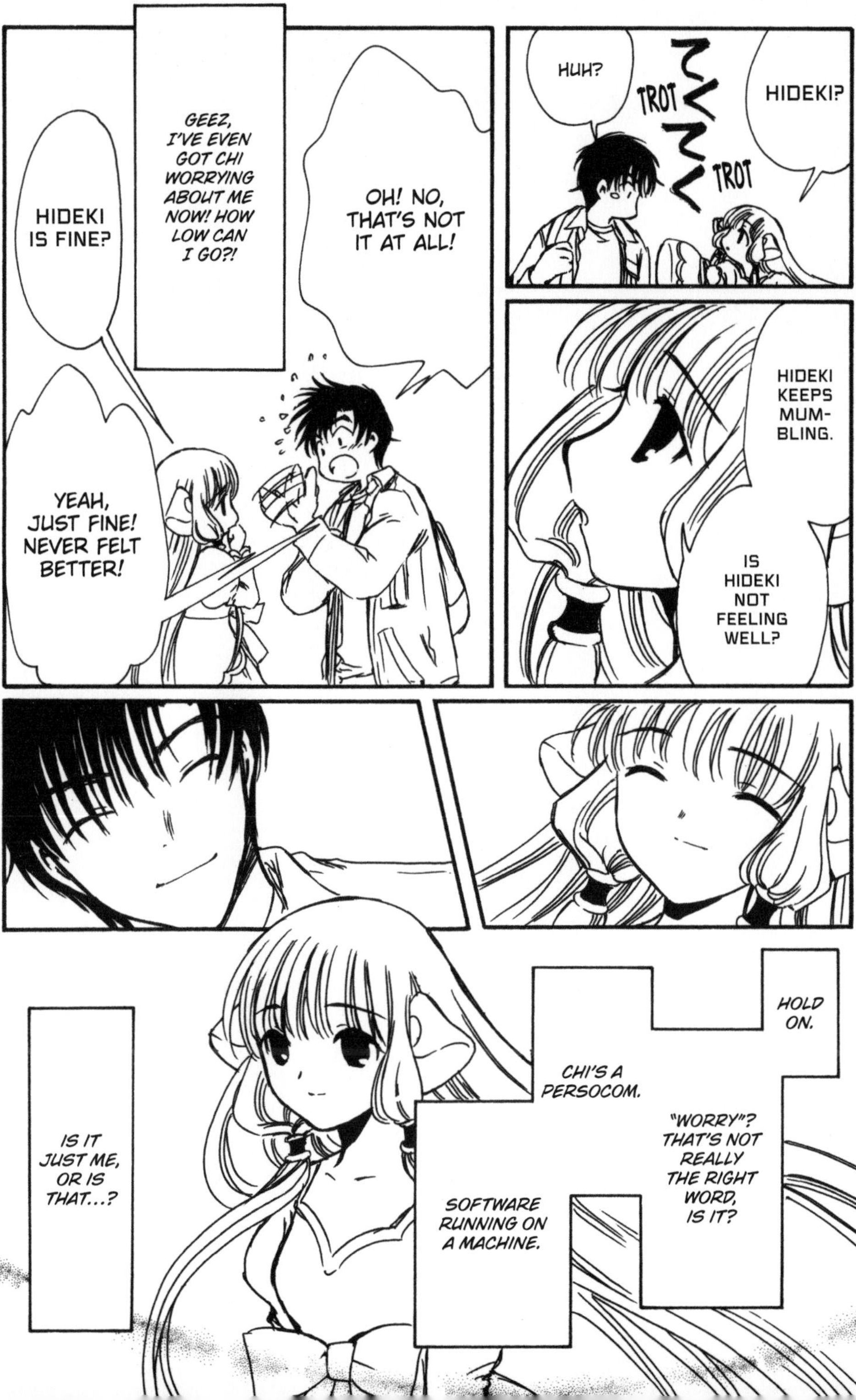
HIDEKI!?
TROT
TROT
HUH?
HIDEKI KEEPS MUM-BLING.
IS HIDEKI NOT FEELING WELL?
OH! NO, THAT'S NOT IT AT ALL!
GEEZ, I'VE EVEN GOT CHI WORRYING ABOUT ME NOW! HOW LOW CAN I GO?!
HIDEKI IS FINE?
YEAH, JUST FINE! NEVER FELT BETTER!
HOLD ON.
CHI'S A PERSOCOM.
"WORRY"? THAT'S NOT REALLY THE RIGHT WORD, IS IT?
SOFTWARE RUNNING ON A MACHINE.
IS IT JUST ME, OR IS THAT...?

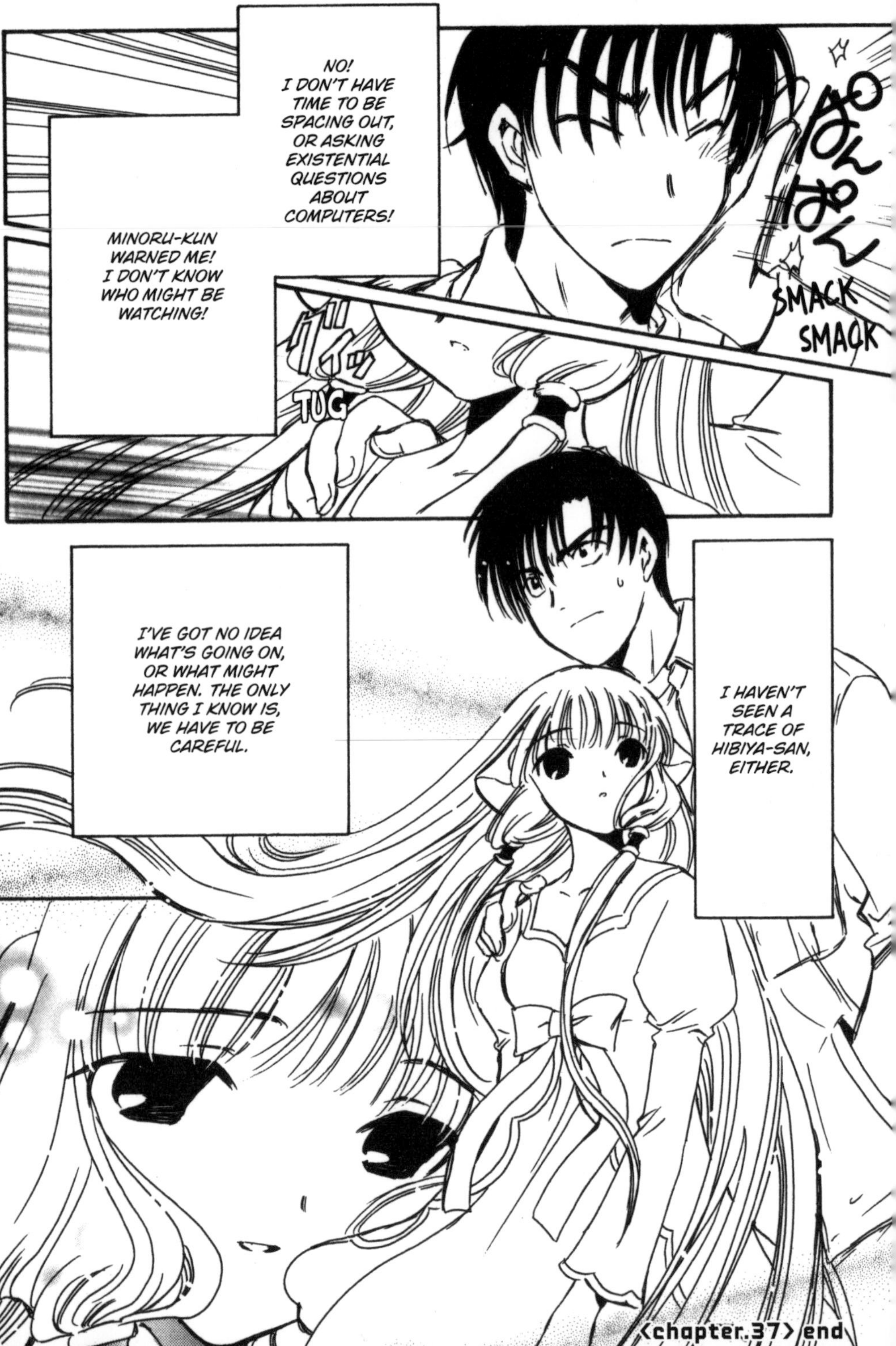
ぱんぱん
SMACK SMACK
NO! I DON'T HAVE TIME TO BE SPACING OUT, OR ASKING EXISTENTIAL QUESTIONS ABOUT COMPUTERS!
MINORU-KUN WARNED ME! I DON'T KNOW WHO MIGHT BE WATCHING!
グイッ
TUG
I'VE GOT NO IDEA WHAT'S GOING ON, OR WHAT MIGHT HAPPEN. THE ONLY THING I KNOW IS, WE HAVE TO BE CAREFUL.
I HAVEN'T SEEN A TRACE OF HIBIYA-SAN, EITHER.
<chapter.37> end

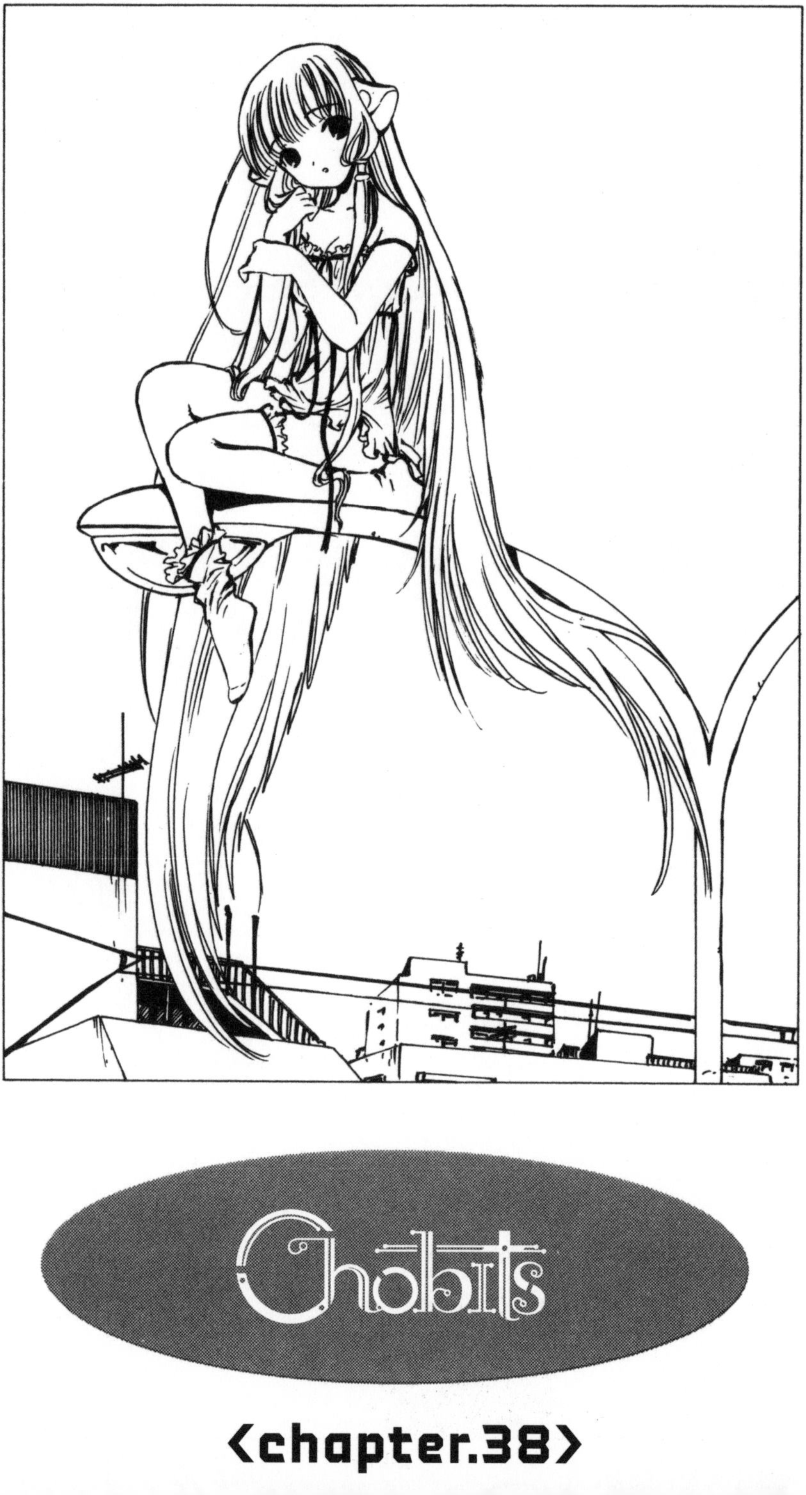

Chobits

<chapter.38>

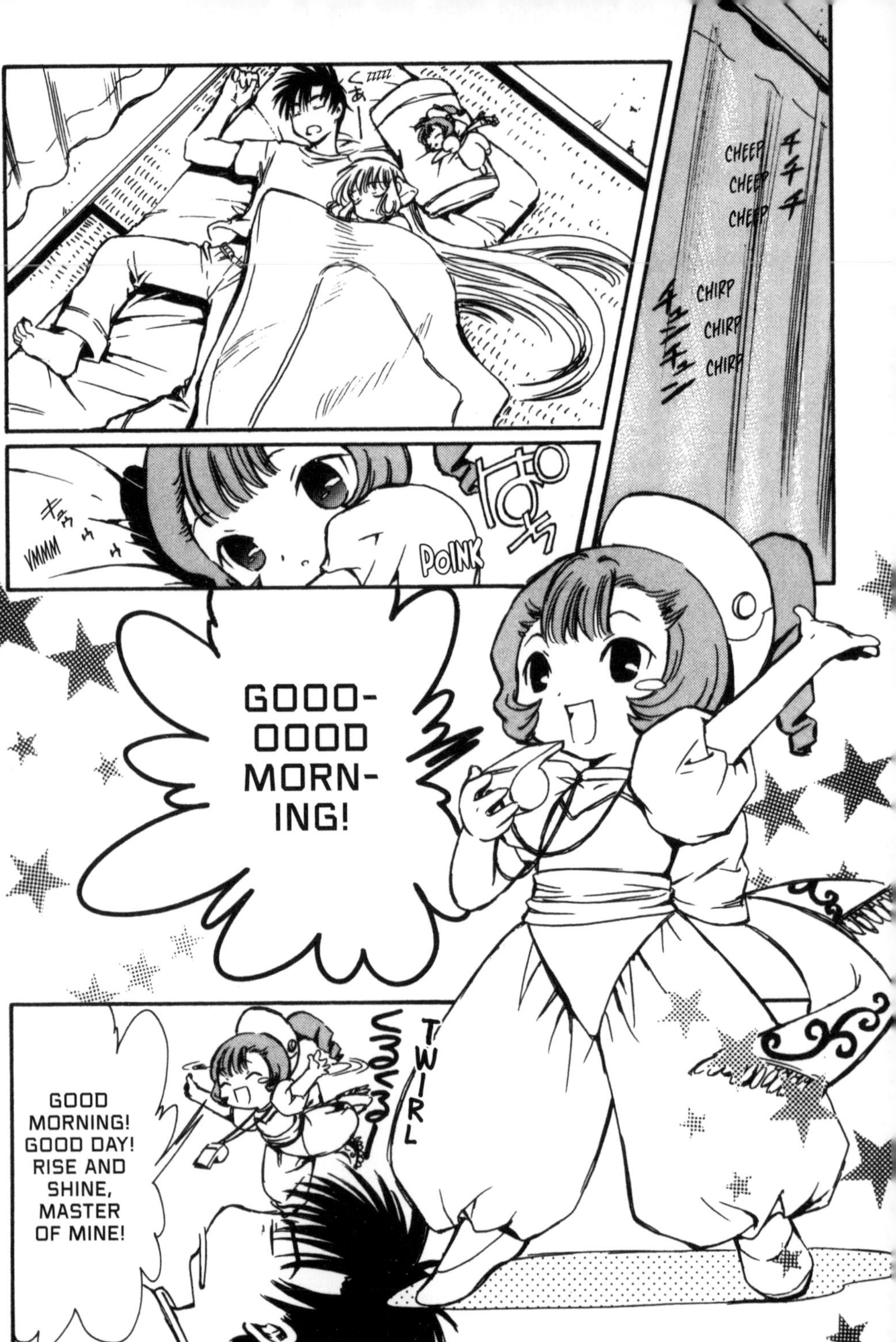
チチチ
CHEEP
CHEEP
CHEEP
チュンチュン
CHIRP
CHIRP
CHIRP
ZZZZZ
ぱちっ
POINK
VMMM
GOOO-OOOD MORNING!
TWIRL
GOOD MORNING! GOOD DAY! RISE AND SHINE, MASTER OF MINE!

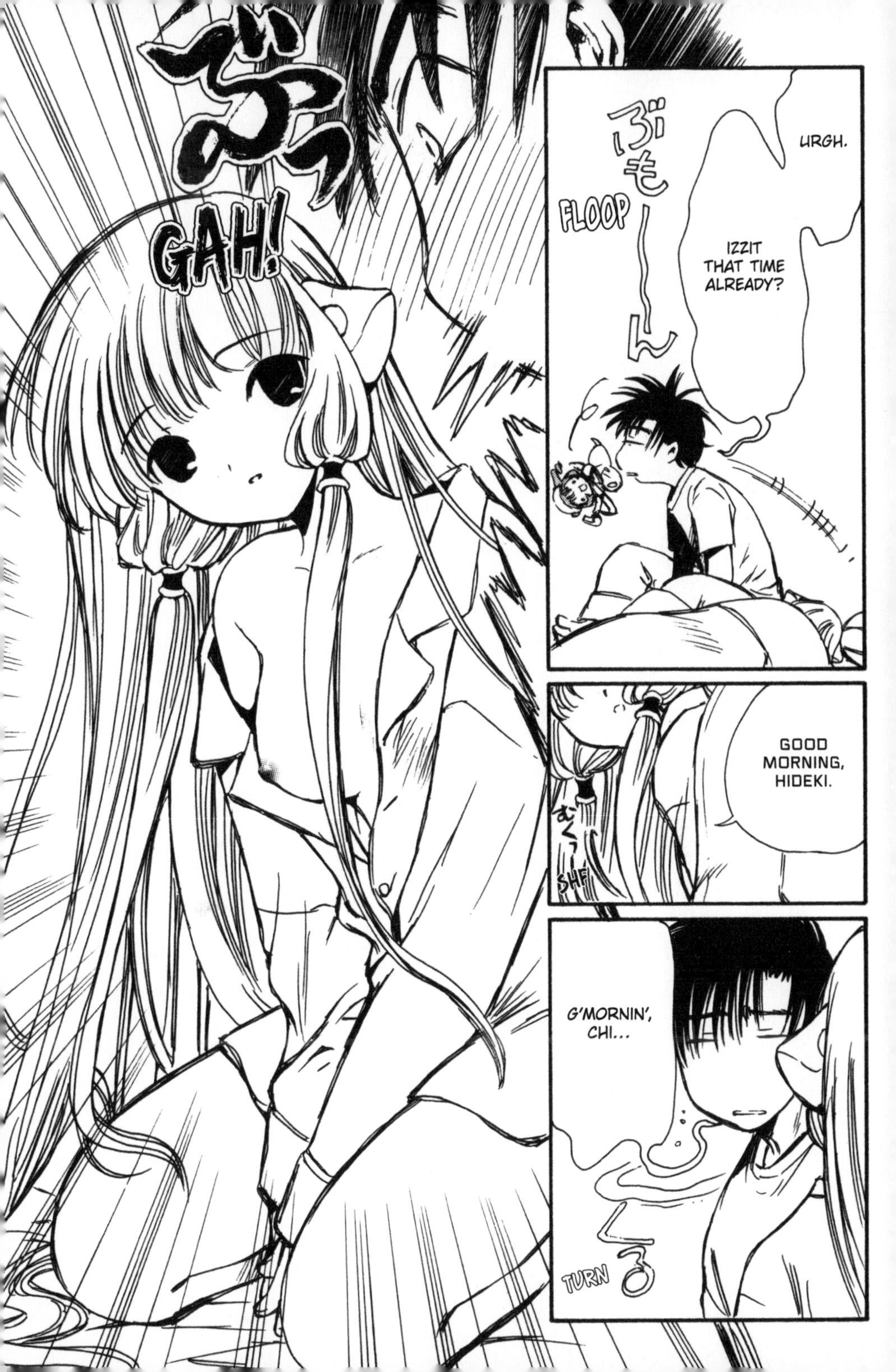
URGH.
IZZIT THAT TIME ALREADY?
ぶもーーん
FLOOP
GOOD MORNING, HIDEKI.
むくっ
SHF
G'MORNIN', CHI...
くるっ
TURN
ぶっ
GAH!

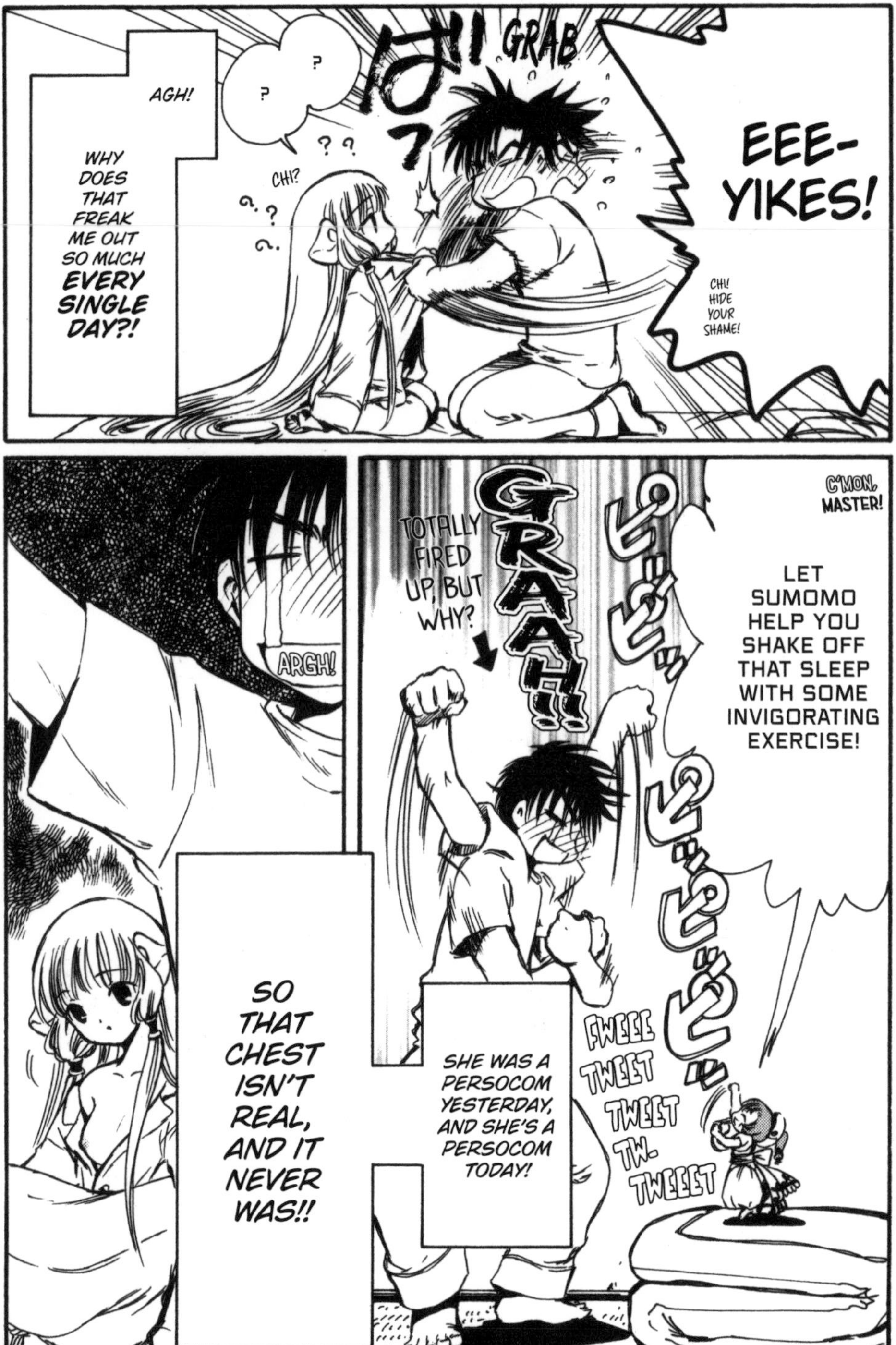
EEE-YIKES!
CHI! HIDE YOUR SHAME!
GRAB
? ?
AGH!
? ?
CHI?
WHY DOES THAT FREAK ME OUT SO MUCH EVERY SINGLE DAY?!
C'MON, MASTER!
LET SUMOMO HELP YOU SHAKE OFF THAT SLEEP WITH SOME INVIGORATING EXERCISE!
GRAAH!!
TOTALLY FIRED UP, BUT WHY?
FWEEE TWEET TWEET TW. TWEEET
SHE WAS A PERSOCOM YESTERDAY, AND SHE'S A PERSOCOM TODAY!
ARGH!
SO THAT CHEST ISN'T REAL, AND IT NEVER WAS!!

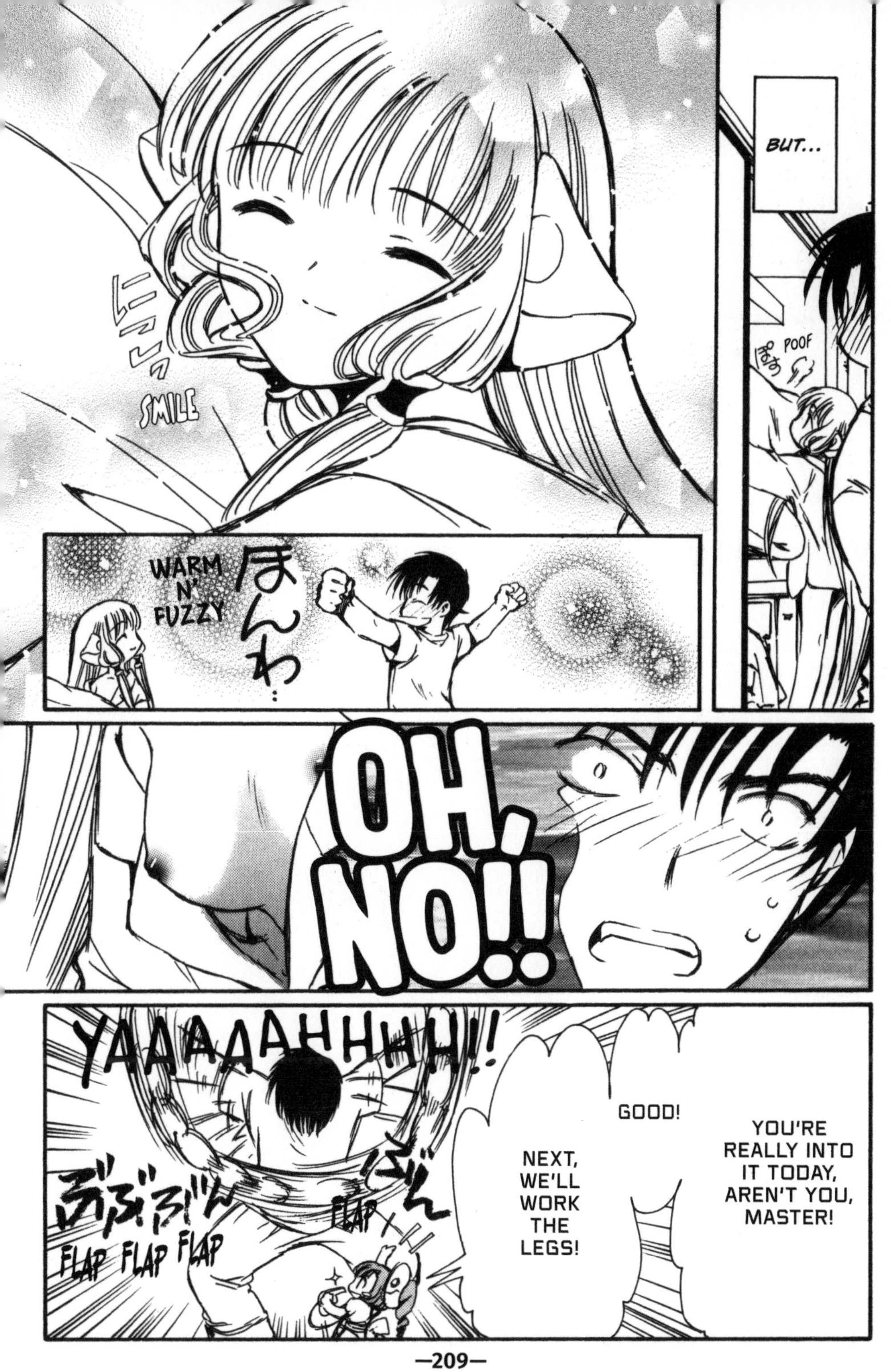
BUT...
ぽす
POOF
SMILE
ほんわ…
WARM N' FUZZY
OH, NO!!
YOU'RE REALLY INTO IT TODAY, AREN'T YOU, MASTER!
GOOD!
NEXT, WE'LL WORK THE LEGS!
YAAAAAHHHH!!
ぶん
FLAP
ぶぶぶん
FLAP FLAP FLAP

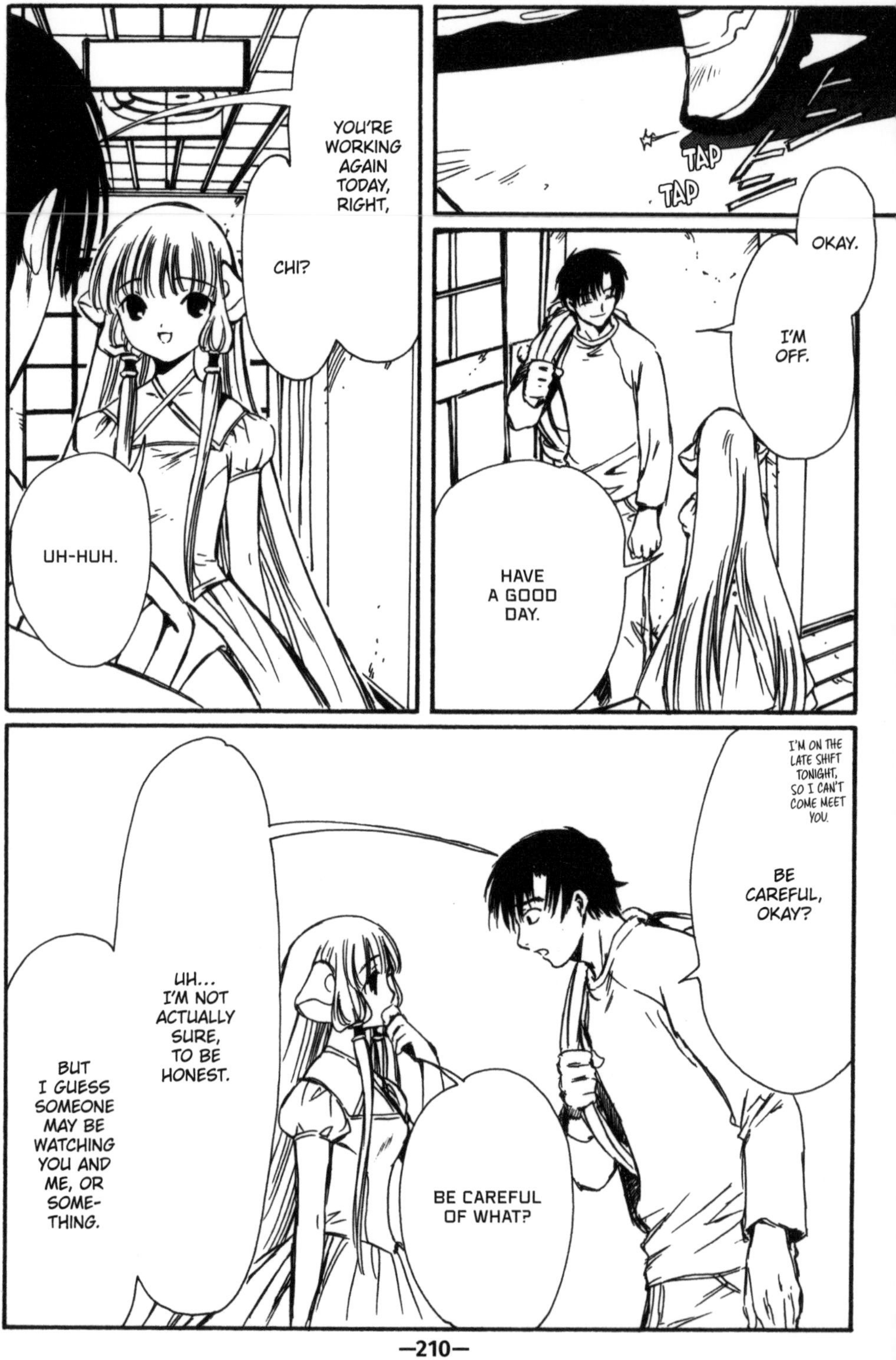
TAP
TAP
OKAY.
I'M OFF.
HAVE A GOOD DAY.
YOU'RE WORKING AGAIN TODAY, RIGHT,
CHI?
UH-HUH.
I'M ON THE LATE SHIFT TONIGHT, SO I CAN'T COME MEET YOU.
BE CAREFUL, OKAY?
BE CAREFUL OF WHAT?
UH... I'M NOT ACTUALLY SURE, TO BE HONEST.
BUT I GUESS SOMEONE MAY BE WATCHING YOU AND ME, OR SOME-THING.

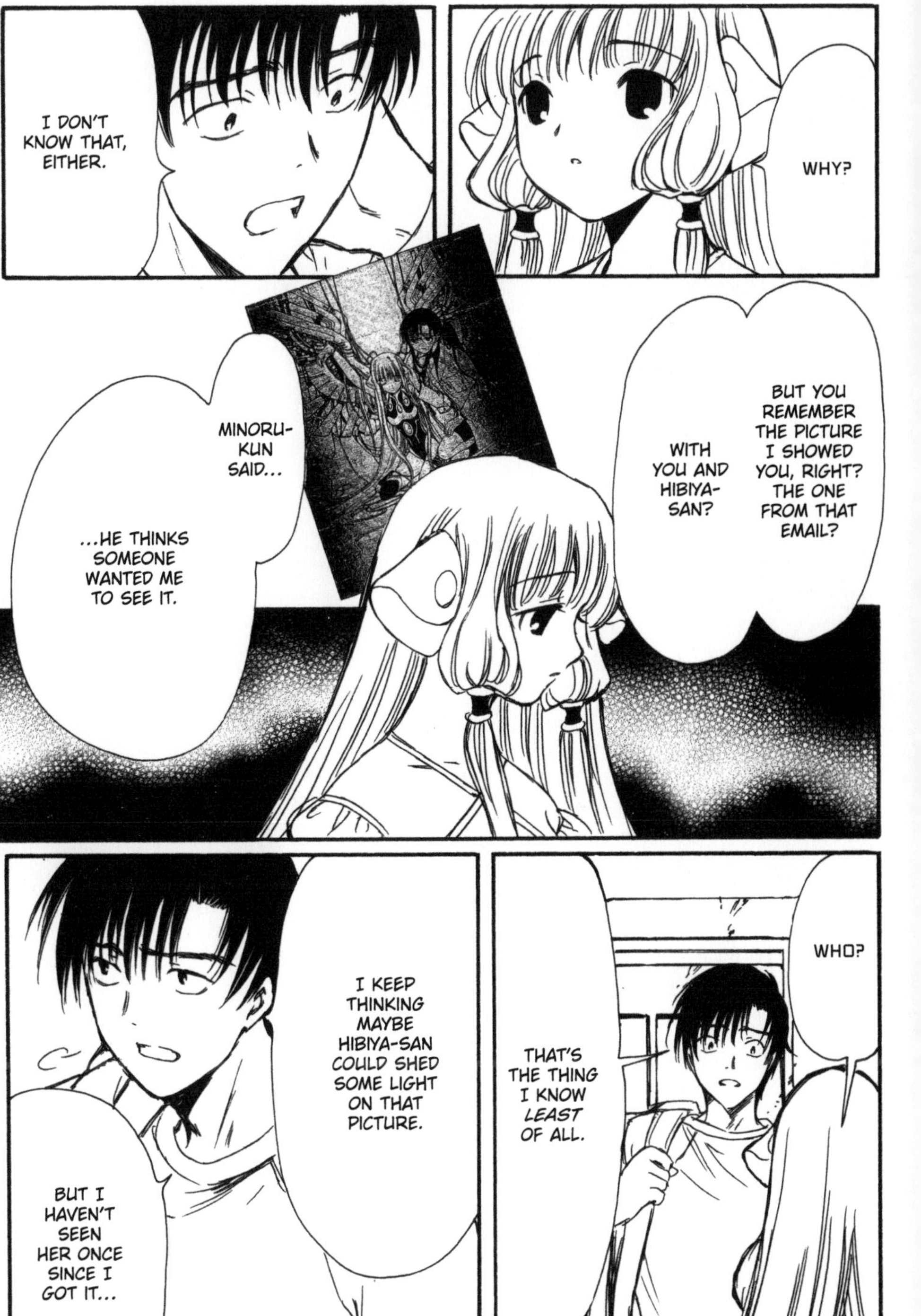
WHY?
I DON'T KNOW THAT, EITHER.
BUT YOU REMEMBER THE PICTURE I SHOWED YOU, RIGHT? THE ONE FROM THAT EMAIL?
WITH YOU AND HIBIYA-SAN?
MINORU-KUN SAID...
...HE THINKS SOMEONE WANTED ME TO SEE IT.
WHO?
THAT'S THE THING I KNOW *LEAST* OF ALL.
I KEEP THINKING MAYBE HIBIYA-SAN COULD SHED SOME LIGHT ON THAT PICTURE.
BUT I HAVEN'T SEEN HER ONCE SINCE I GOT IT...

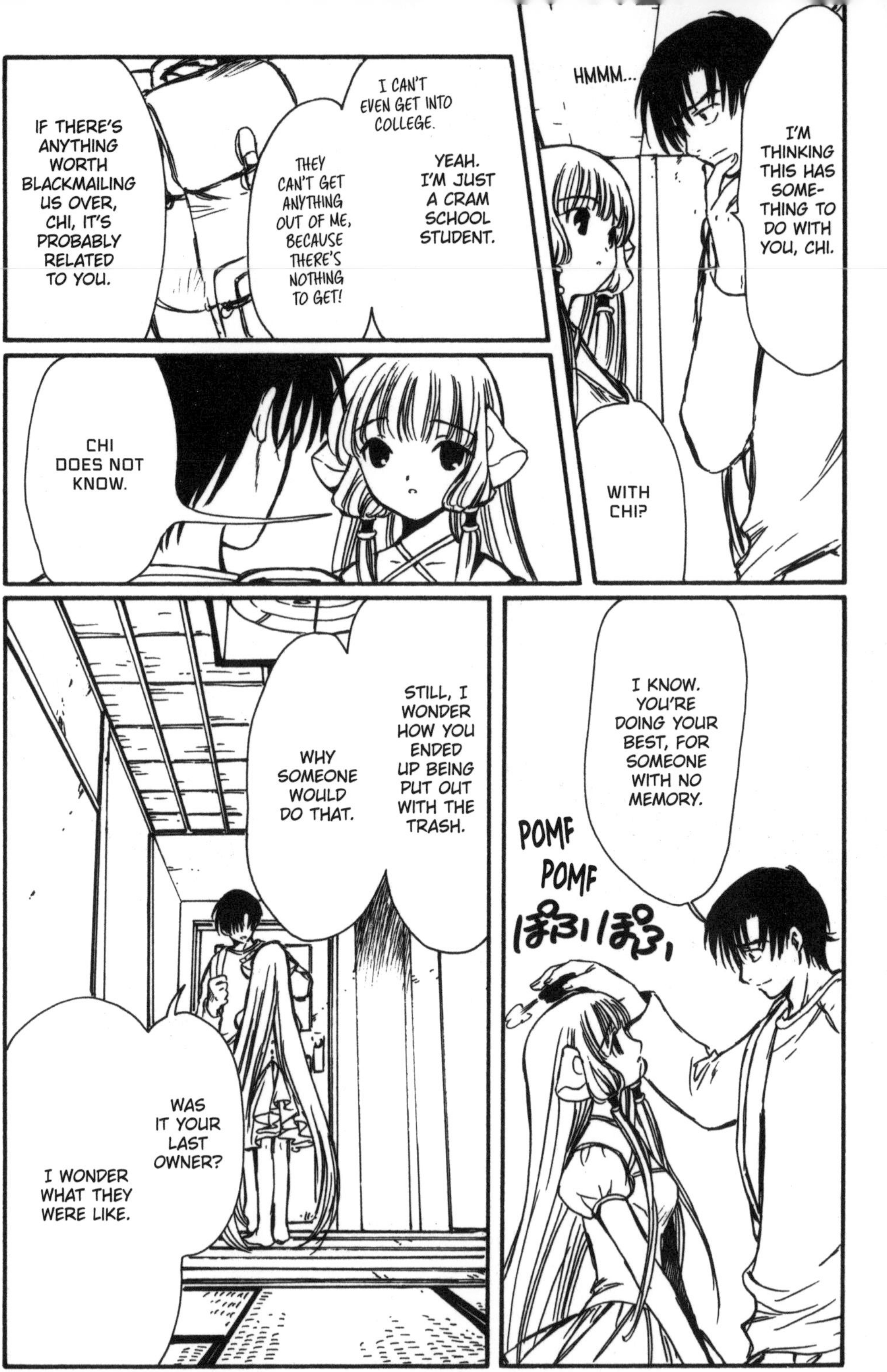
HMMM...
I'M THINKING THIS HAS SOME-THING TO DO WITH YOU, CHI.
WITH CHI?
YEAH. I'M JUST A CRAM SCHOOL STUDENT.
I CAN'T EVEN GET INTO COLLEGE.
THEY CAN'T GET ANYTHING OUT OF ME, BECAUSE THERE'S NOTHING TO GET!
IF THERE'S ANYTHING WORTH BLACKMAILING US OVER, CHI, IT'S PROBABLY RELATED TO YOU.
CHI DOES NOT KNOW.
I KNOW. YOU'RE DOING YOUR BEST, FOR SOMEONE WITH NO MEMORY.
POMF
POMF
ぽふぽふ
STILL, I WONDER HOW YOU ENDED UP BEING PUT OUT WITH THE TRASH.
WHY SOMEONE WOULD DO THAT.
WAS IT YOUR LAST OWNER?
I WONDER WHAT THEY WERE LIKE.

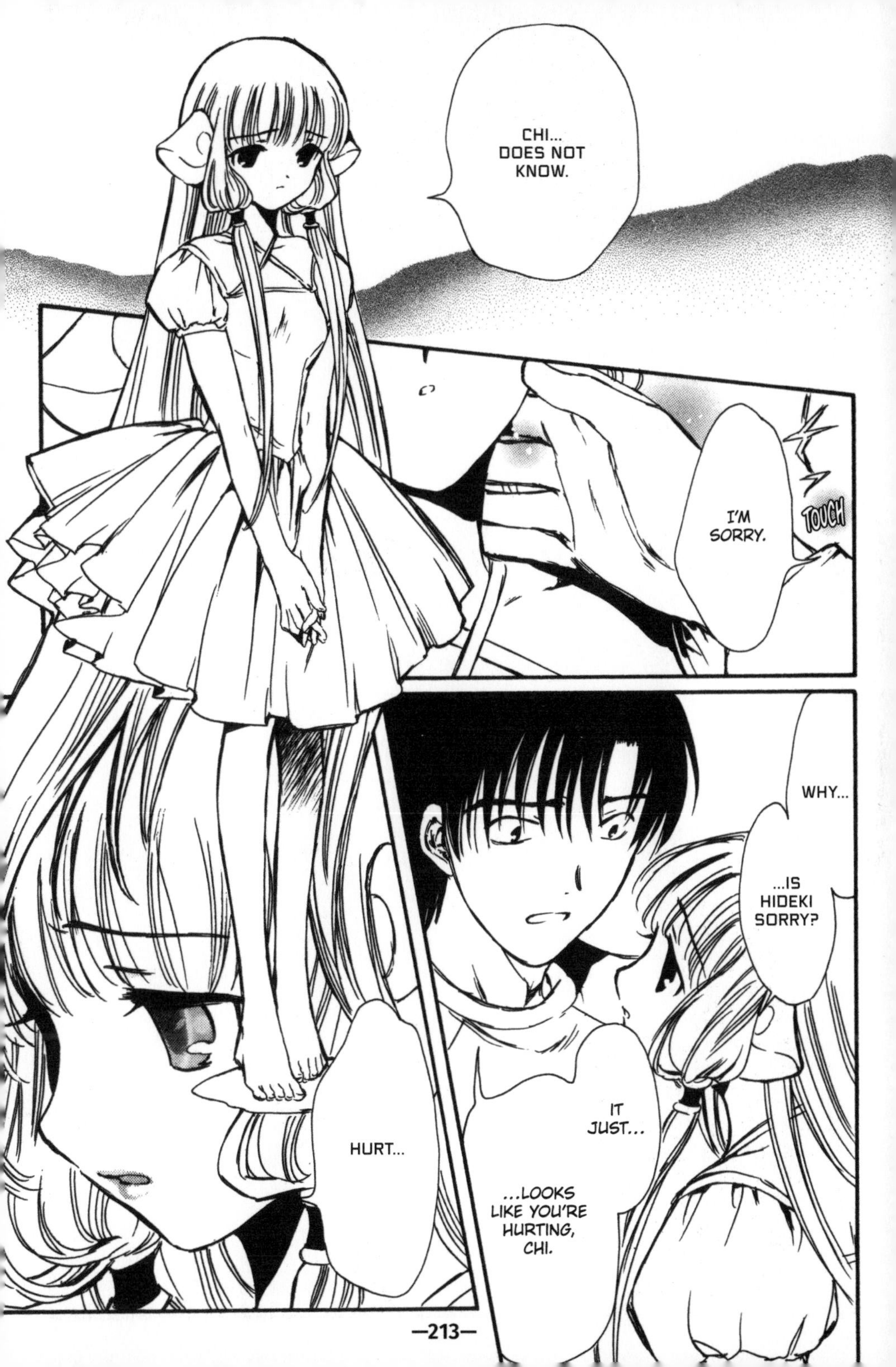
CHI... DOES NOT KNOW.
TOUCH
I'M SORRY.
WHY...
...IS HIDEKI SORRY?
IT JUST...
...LOOKS LIKE YOU'RE HURTING, CHI.
HURT...

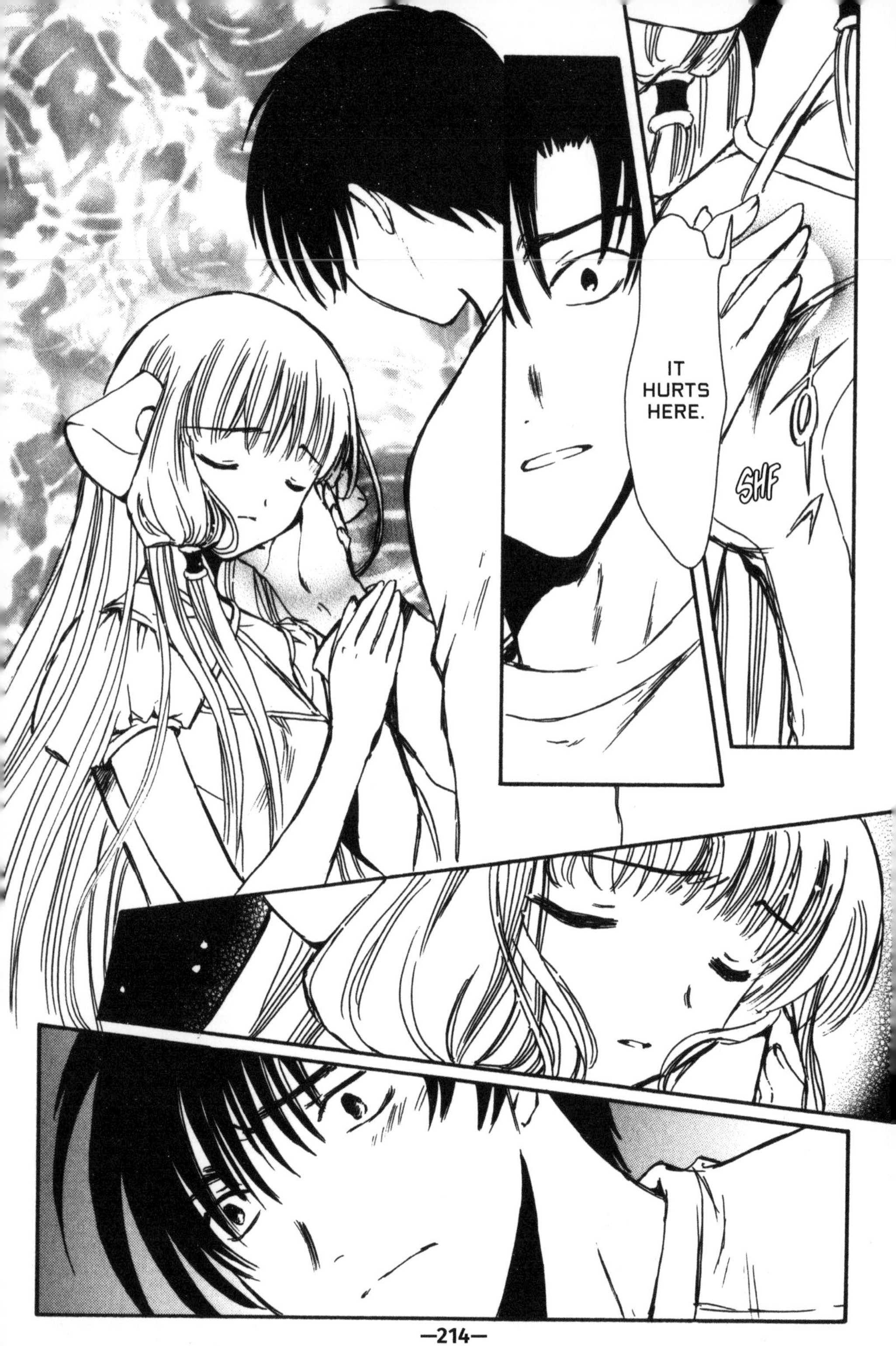
IT HURTS HERE.
SHF

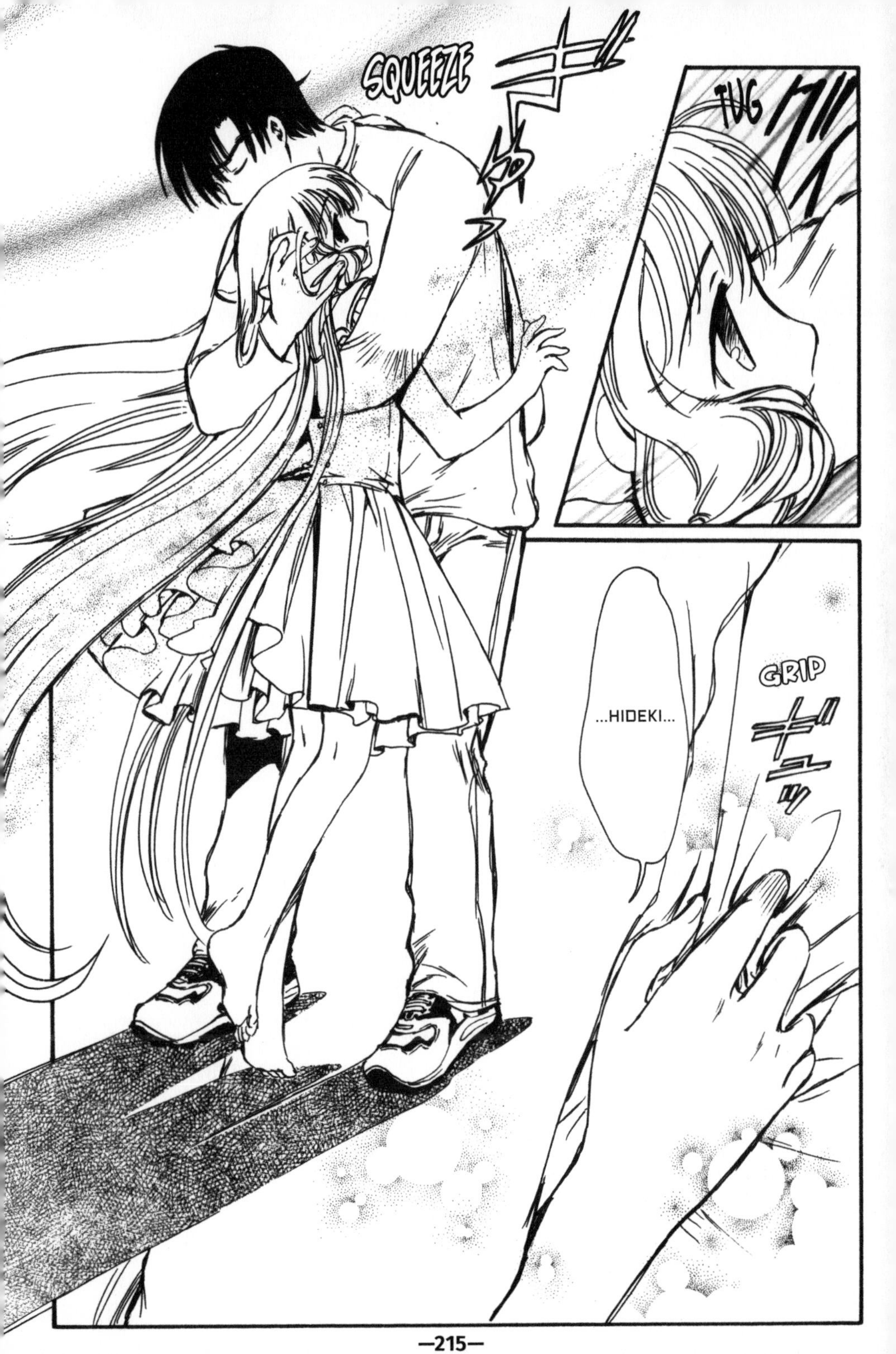
TUG
GRIP
...HIDEKI...
SQUEEZE

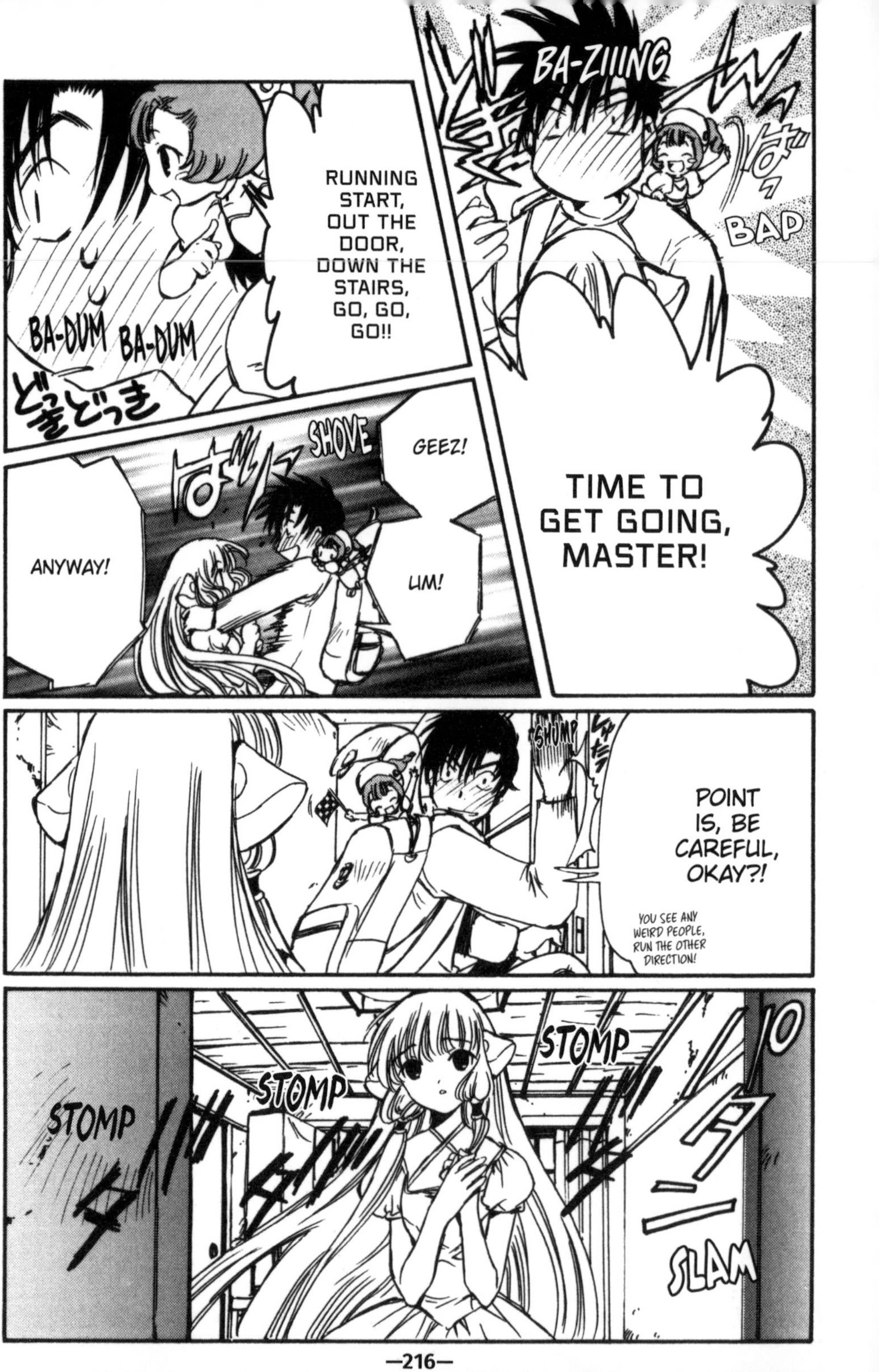
BA-ZIIING
BAP
TIME TO GET GOING, MASTER!
RUNNING START, OUT THE DOOR, DOWN THE STAIRS, GO, GO, GO!!
BA-DUM BA-DUM
どっきどっき
SHOVE
GEEZ!
UM!
ANYWAY!
SHOMP
POINT IS, BE CAREFUL, OKAY?!
YOU SEE ANY WEIRD PEOPLE, RUN THE OTHER DIRECTION!
SLAM
STOMP
STOMP
STOMP

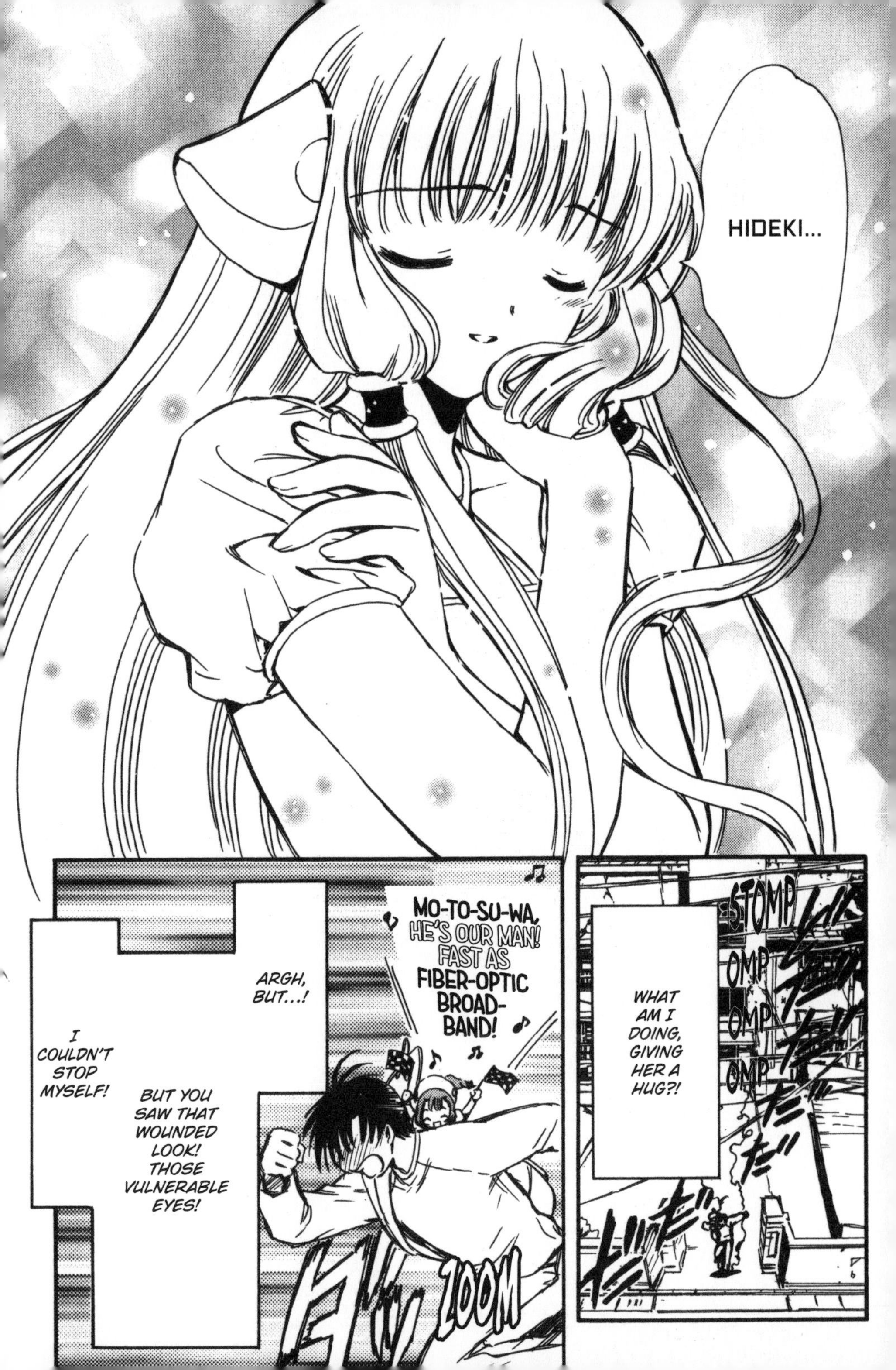

HIDEKI...
STOMP
OMP
OMP
OMP
WHAT AM I DOING, GIVING HER A HUG?!
MO-TO-SU-WA, HE'S OUR MAN! FAST AS FIBER-OPTIC BROAD-BAND!
ARGH, BUT...!
I COULDN'T STOP MYSELF!
BUT YOU SAW THAT WOUNDED LOOK! THOSE VULNERABLE EYES!
ZOOM

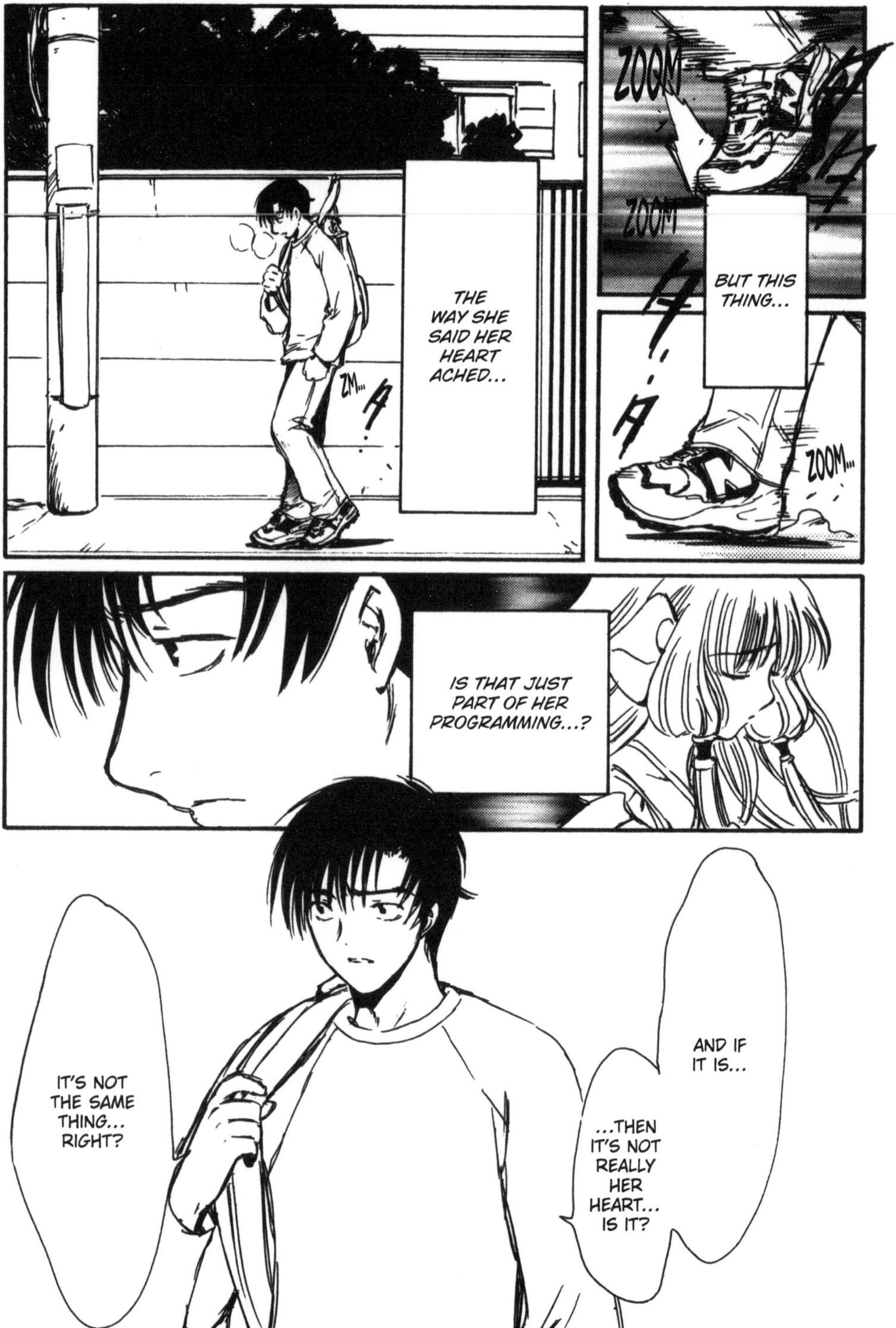
ZOOM
ZOOM
BUT THIS THING…
ZOOM…
THE WAY SHE SAID HER HEART ACHED…
ZM…
IS THAT JUST PART OF HER PROGRAMMING…?
AND IF IT IS…
…THEN IT'S NOT REALLY HER HEART… IS IT?
IT'S NOT THE SAME THING… RIGHT?

<chapter.38> end

Chobits

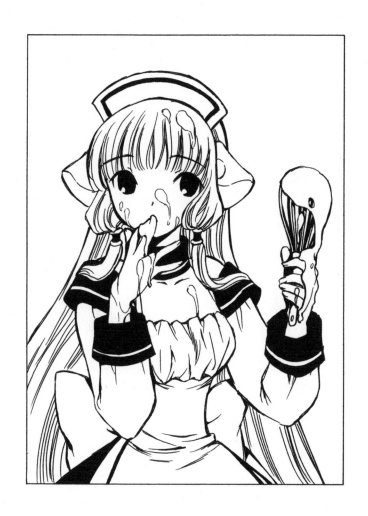

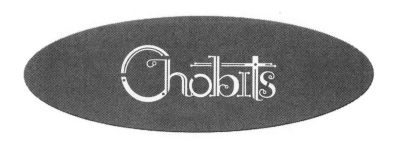

‹chapter.39›

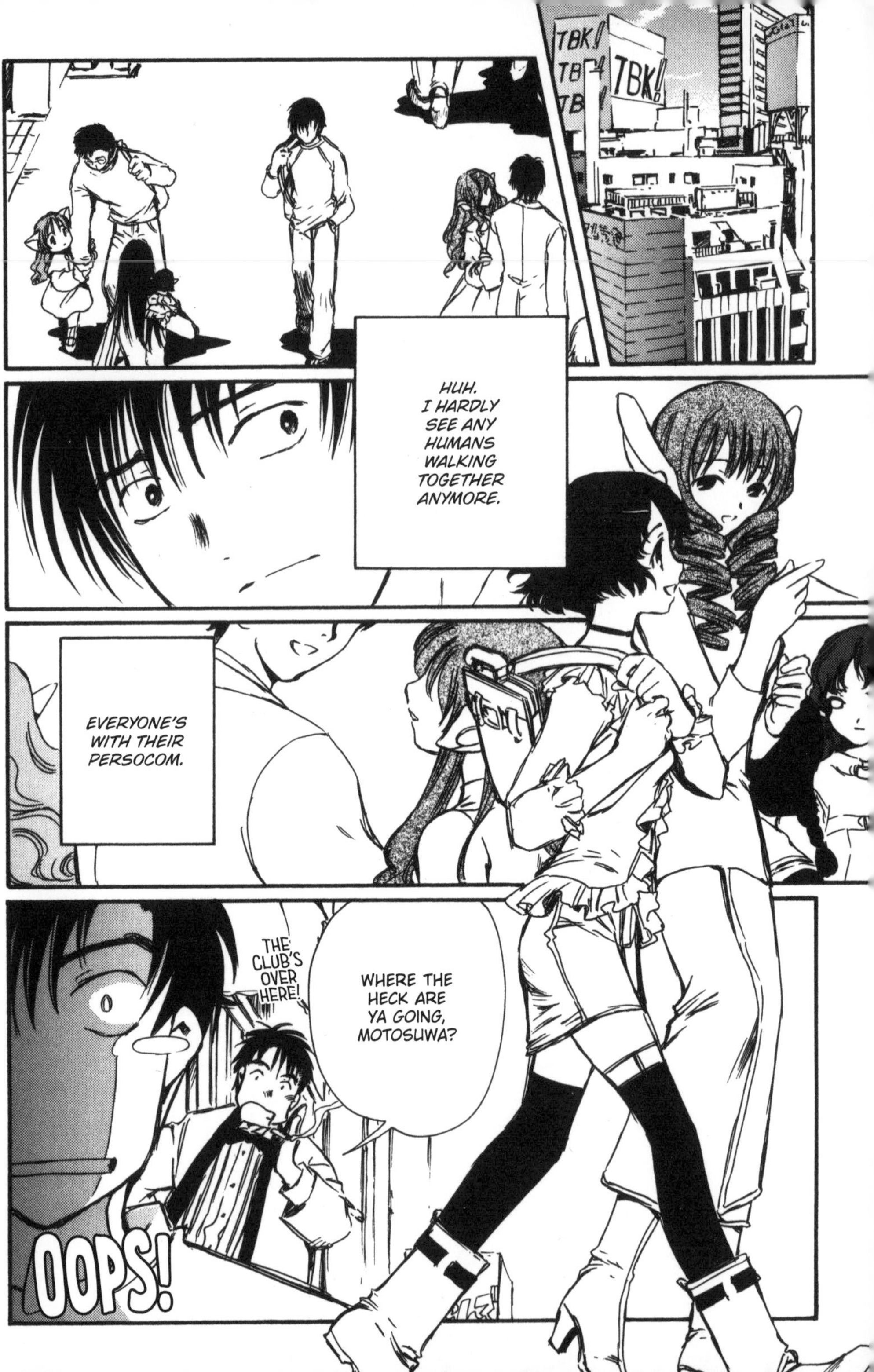
TBK!
TBK!
HUH. I HARDLY SEE ANY HUMANS WALKING TOGETHER ANYMORE.
EVERYONE'S WITH THEIR PERSOCOM.
WHERE THE HECK ARE YA GOING, MOTOSUWA?
THE CLUB'S OVER HERE!
OOPS!

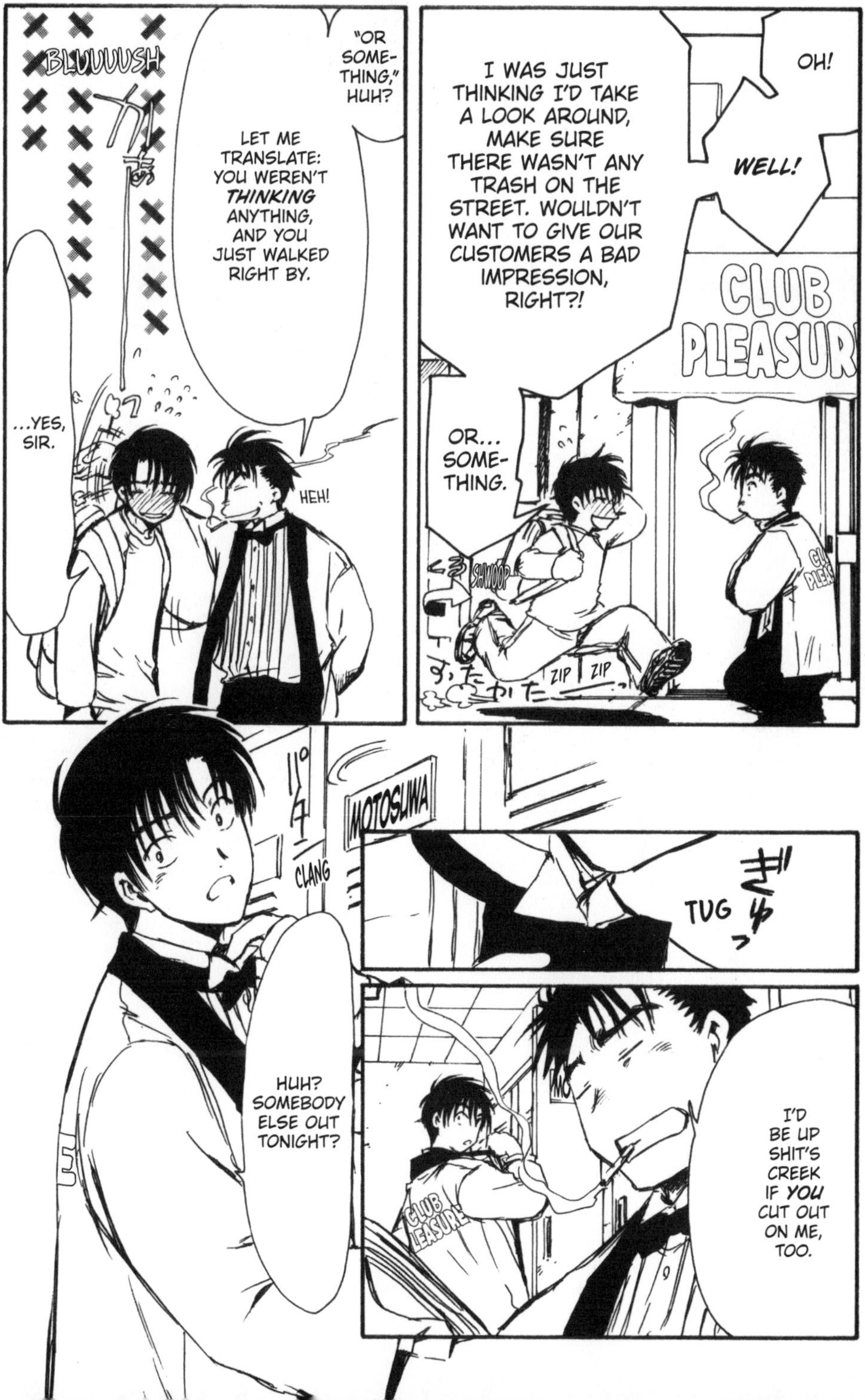
OH!
WELL!
I WAS JUST THINKING I'D TAKE A LOOK AROUND, MAKE SURE THERE WASN'T ANY TRASH ON THE STREET. WOULDN'T WANT TO GIVE OUR CUSTOMERS A BAD IMPRESSION, RIGHT?!
CLUB PLEASUR
OR... SOME-THING.
SHWOOP
ZIP ZIP
"OR SOME-THING," HUH?
LET ME TRANSLATE: YOU WEREN'T THINKING ANYTHING, AND YOU JUST WALKED RIGHT BY.
BLUUUUSH
HEH!
...YES, SIR.
MOTOSUWA
CLANG
HUH? SOMEBODY ELSE OUT TONIGHT?
TUG
I'D BE UP SHIT'S CREEK IF YOU CUT OUT ON ME, TOO.
CLUB LEASURE

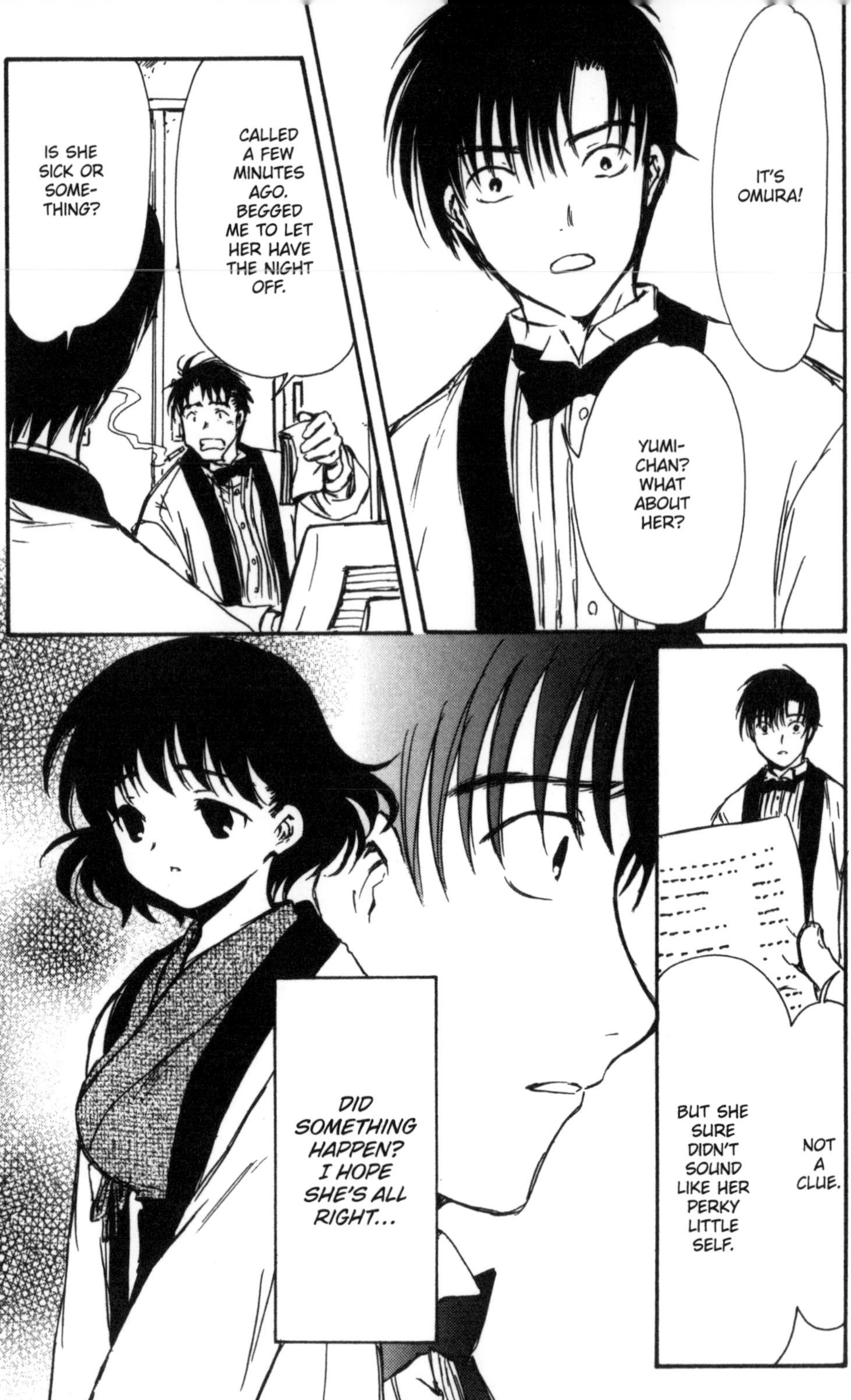
IT'S OMURA!
YUMI-CHAN? WHAT ABOUT HER?
CALLED A FEW MINUTES AGO. BEGGED ME TO LET HER HAVE THE NIGHT OFF.
IS SHE SICK OR SOME-THING?
NOT A CLUE.
BUT SHE SURE DIDN'T SOUND LIKE HER PERKY LITTLE SELF.
DID SOMETHING HAPPEN? I HOPE SHE'S ALL RIGHT...

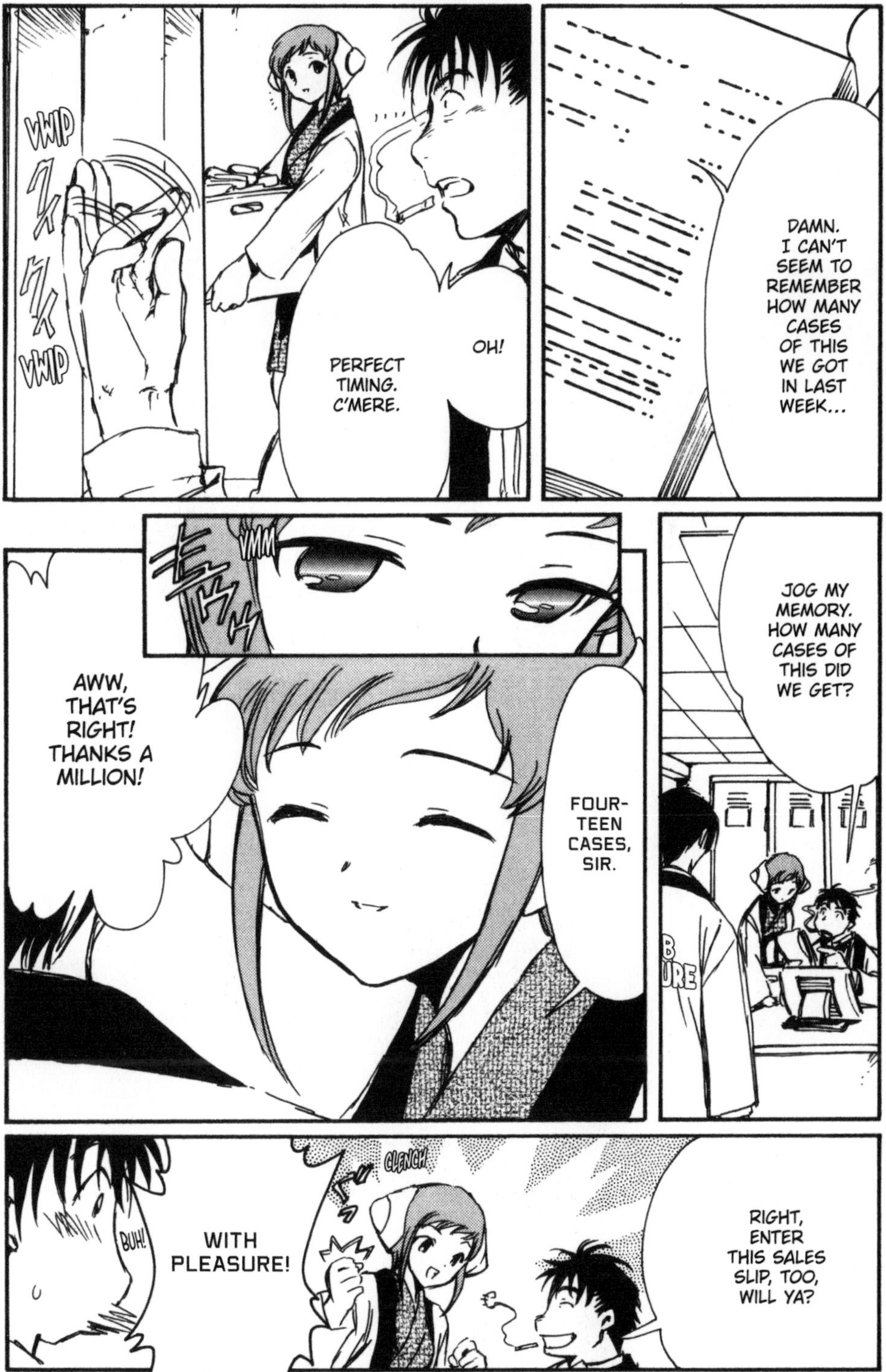
DAMN. I CAN'T SEEM TO REMEMBER HOW MANY CASES OF THIS WE GOT IN LAST WEEK...
OH!
PERFECT TIMING. C'MERE.
VWIP
VWIP
JOG MY MEMORY. HOW MANY CASES OF THIS DID WE GET?
VMM
FOUR-TEEN CASES, SIR.
AWW, THAT'S RIGHT! THANKS A MILLION!
RIGHT, ENTER THIS SALES SLIP, TOO, WILL YA?
CLENCH
WITH PLEASURE!
BUH!

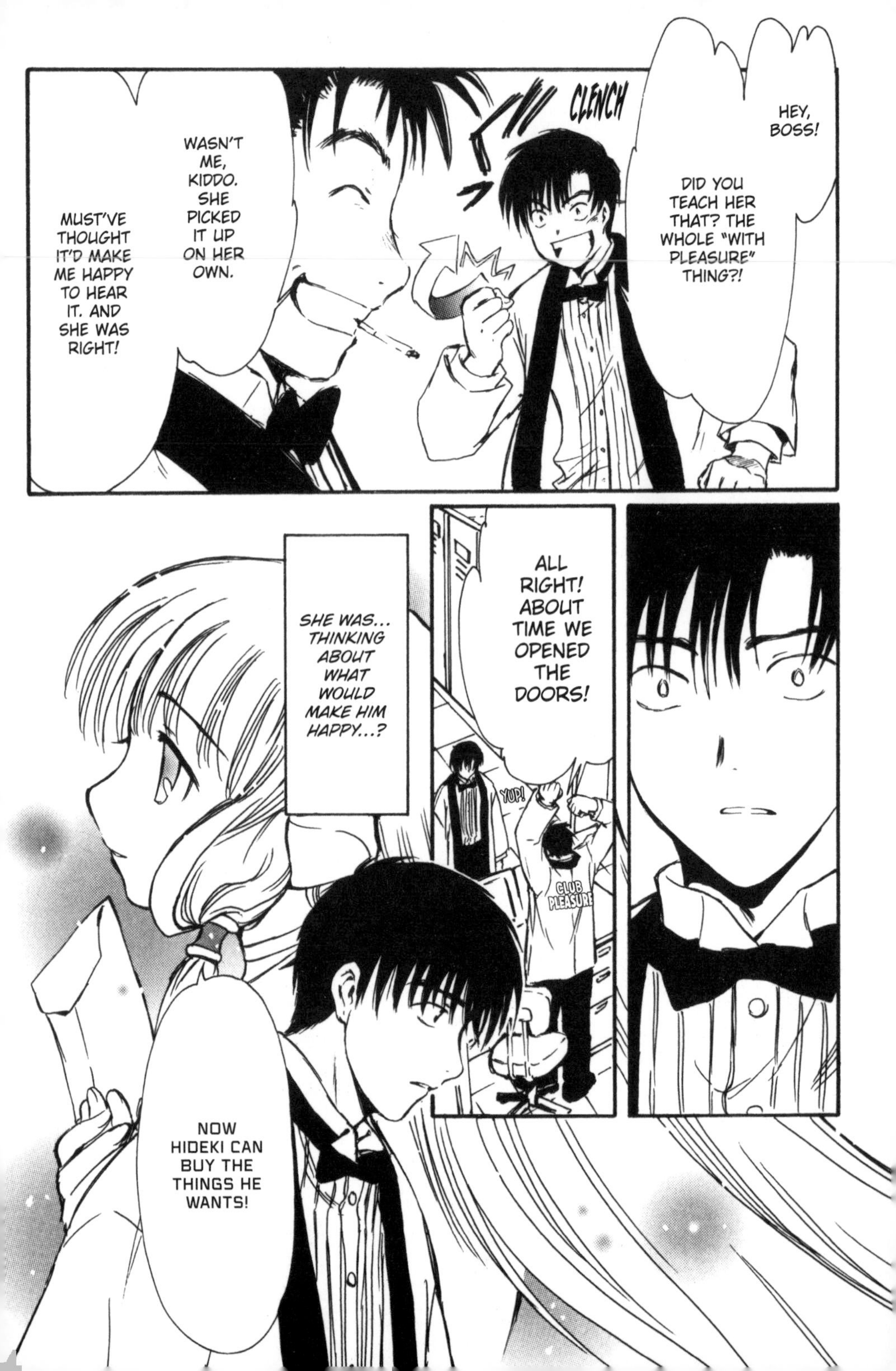

CLENCH
HEY, BOSS!
DID YOU TEACH HER THAT? THE WHOLE "WITH PLEASURE" THING?!
WASN'T ME, KIDDO. SHE PICKED IT UP ON HER OWN.
MUST'VE THOUGHT IT'D MAKE ME HAPPY TO HEAR IT. AND SHE WAS RIGHT!
ALL RIGHT! ABOUT TIME WE OPENED THE DOORS!
YUP!
CLUB PLEASURE
SHE WAS... THINKING ABOUT WHAT WOULD MAKE HIM HAPPY...?
NOW HIDEKI CAN BUY THE THINGS HE WANTS!

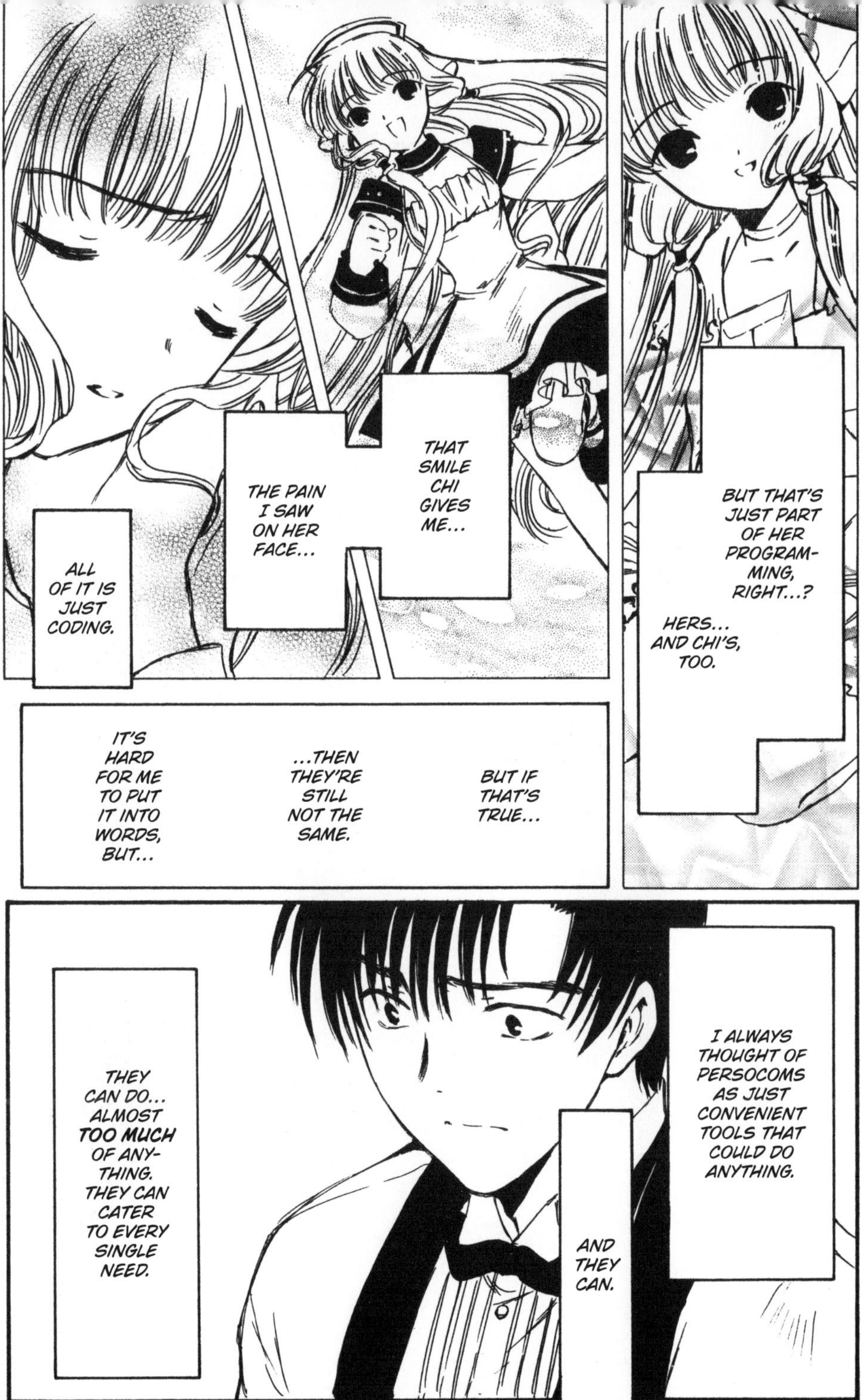
BUT THAT'S JUST PART OF HER PROGRAMMING, RIGHT...?
HERS... AND CHI'S, TOO.
THAT SMILE CHI GIVES ME...
THE PAIN I SAW ON HER FACE...
ALL OF IT IS JUST CODING.
BUT IF THAT'S TRUE...
...THEN THEY'RE STILL NOT THE SAME.
IT'S HARD FOR ME TO PUT IT INTO WORDS, BUT...
I ALWAYS THOUGHT OF PERSOCOMS AS JUST CONVENIENT TOOLS THAT COULD DO ANYTHING.
AND THEY CAN.
THEY CAN DO... ALMOST **TOO MUCH** OF ANYTHING. THEY CAN CATER TO EVERY SINGLE NEED.

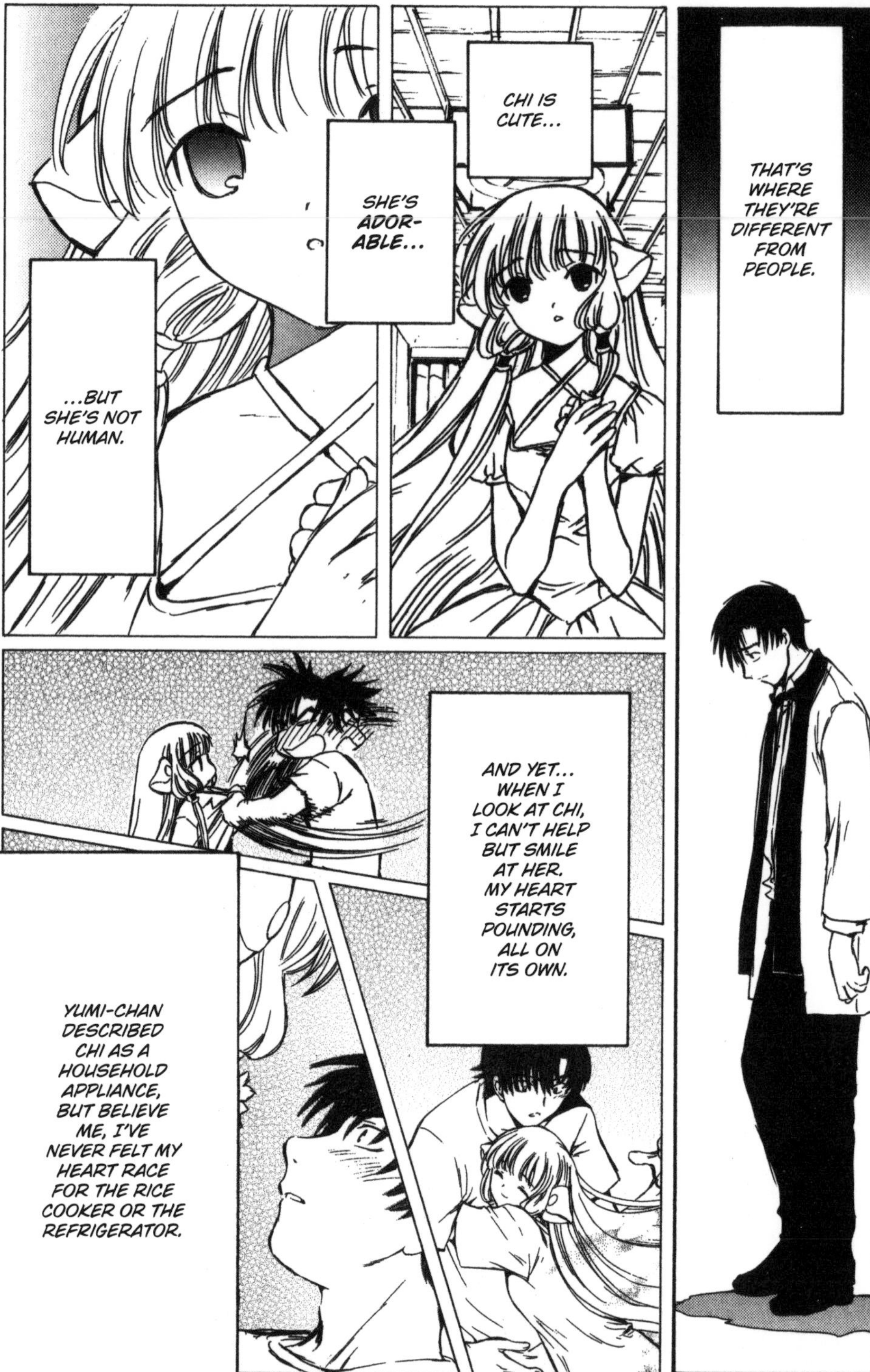
THAT'S WHERE THEY'RE DIFFERENT FROM PEOPLE.
CHI IS CUTE...
SHE'S ADOR-ABLE...
...BUT SHE'S NOT HUMAN.
AND YET... WHEN I LOOK AT CHI, I CAN'T HELP BUT SMILE AT HER. MY HEART STARTS POUNDING, ALL ON ITS OWN.
YUMI-CHAN DESCRIBED CHI AS A HOUSEHOLD APPLIANCE, BUT BELIEVE ME, I'VE NEVER FELT MY HEART RACE FOR THE RICE COOKER OR THE REFRIGERATOR.

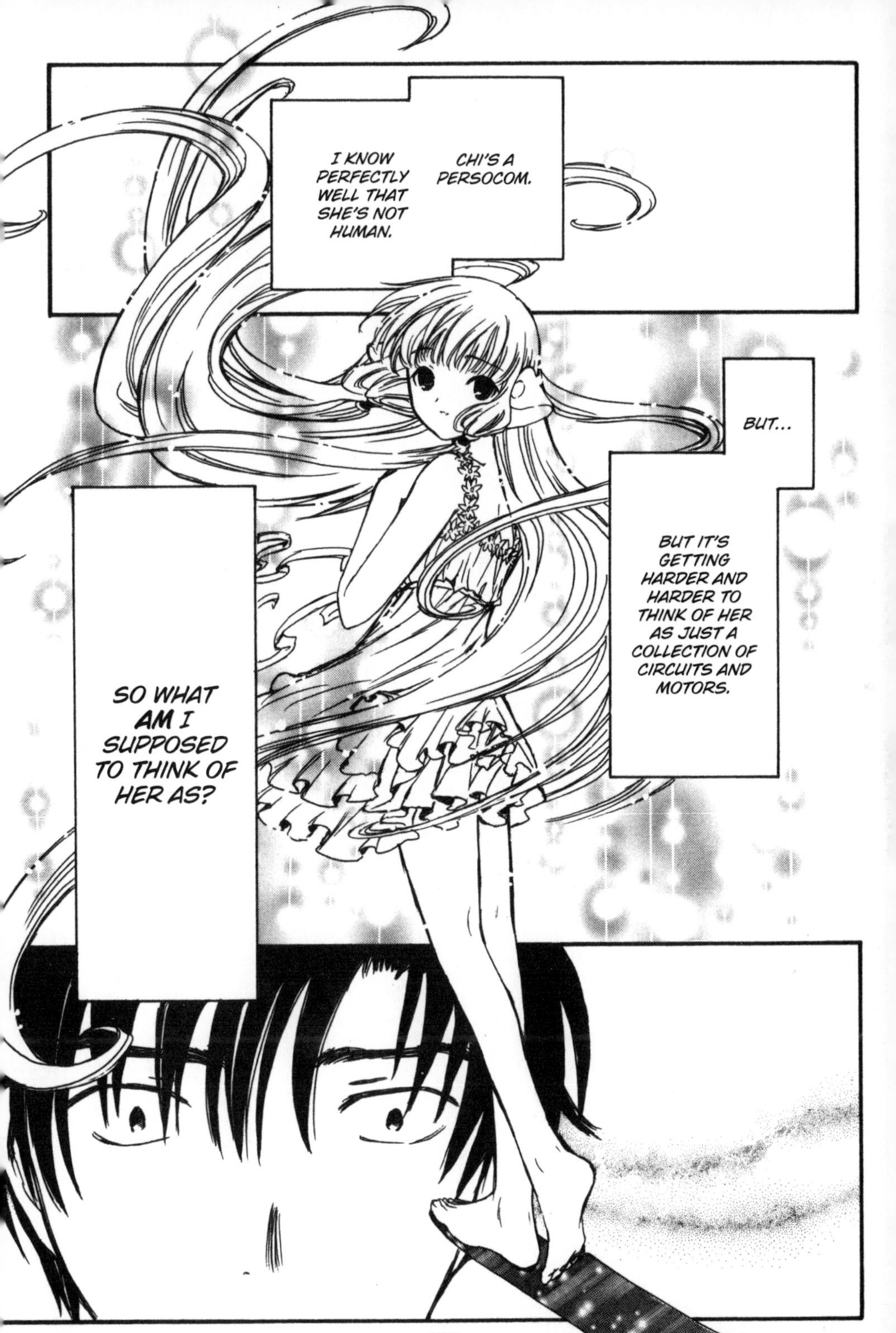
CHI'S A PERSOCOM.
I KNOW PERFECTLY WELL THAT SHE'S NOT HUMAN.
BUT...
BUT IT'S GETTING HARDER AND HARDER TO THINK OF HER AS JUST A COLLECTION OF CIRCUITS AND MOTORS.
SO WHAT **AM** I SUPPOSED TO THINK OF HER AS?

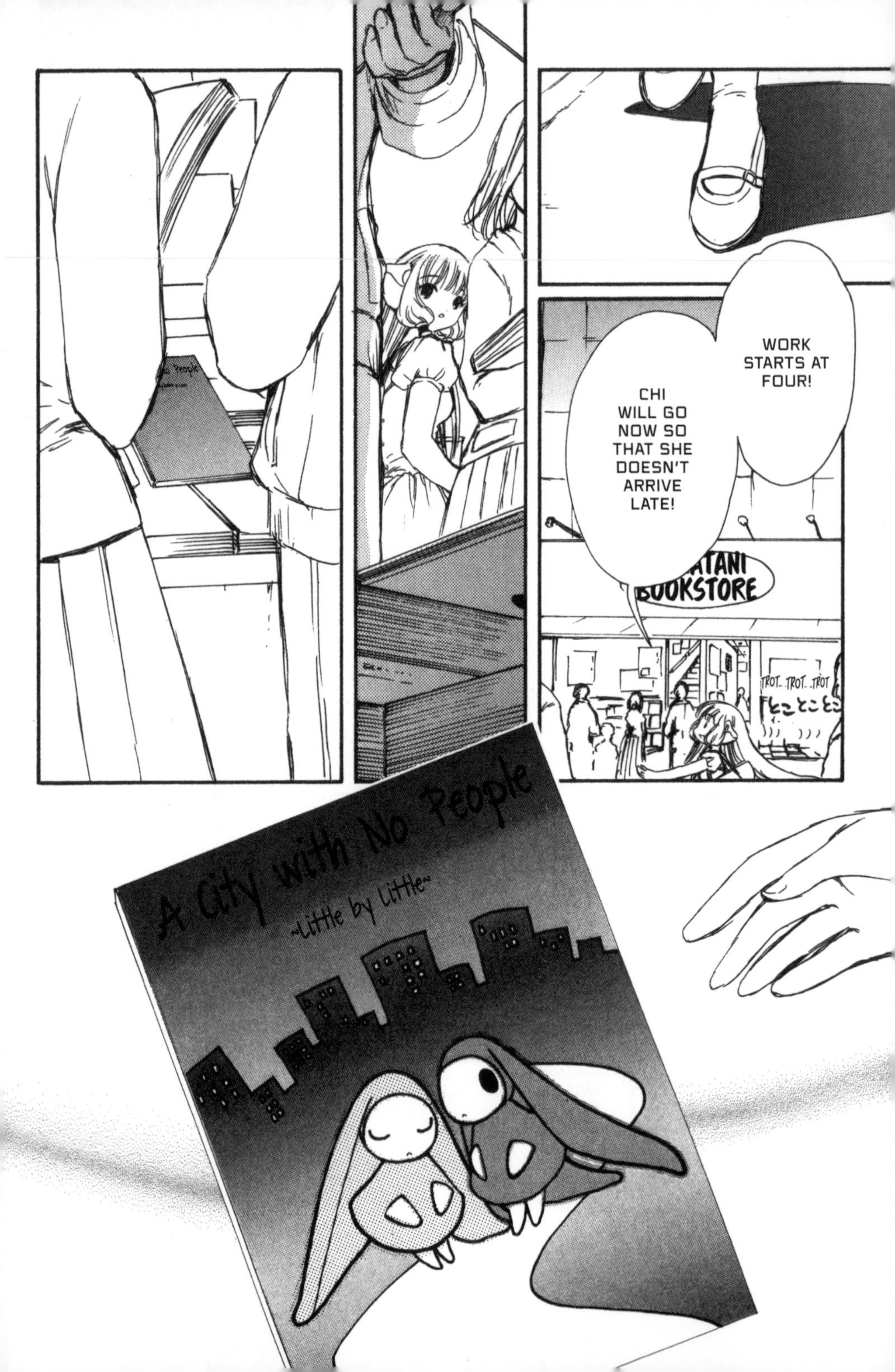
WORK STARTS AT FOUR!
CHI WILL GO NOW SO THAT SHE DOESN'T ARRIVE LATE!
BOOKSTORE
TROT TROT TROT
とことこと
A City with No People
~Little by Little~

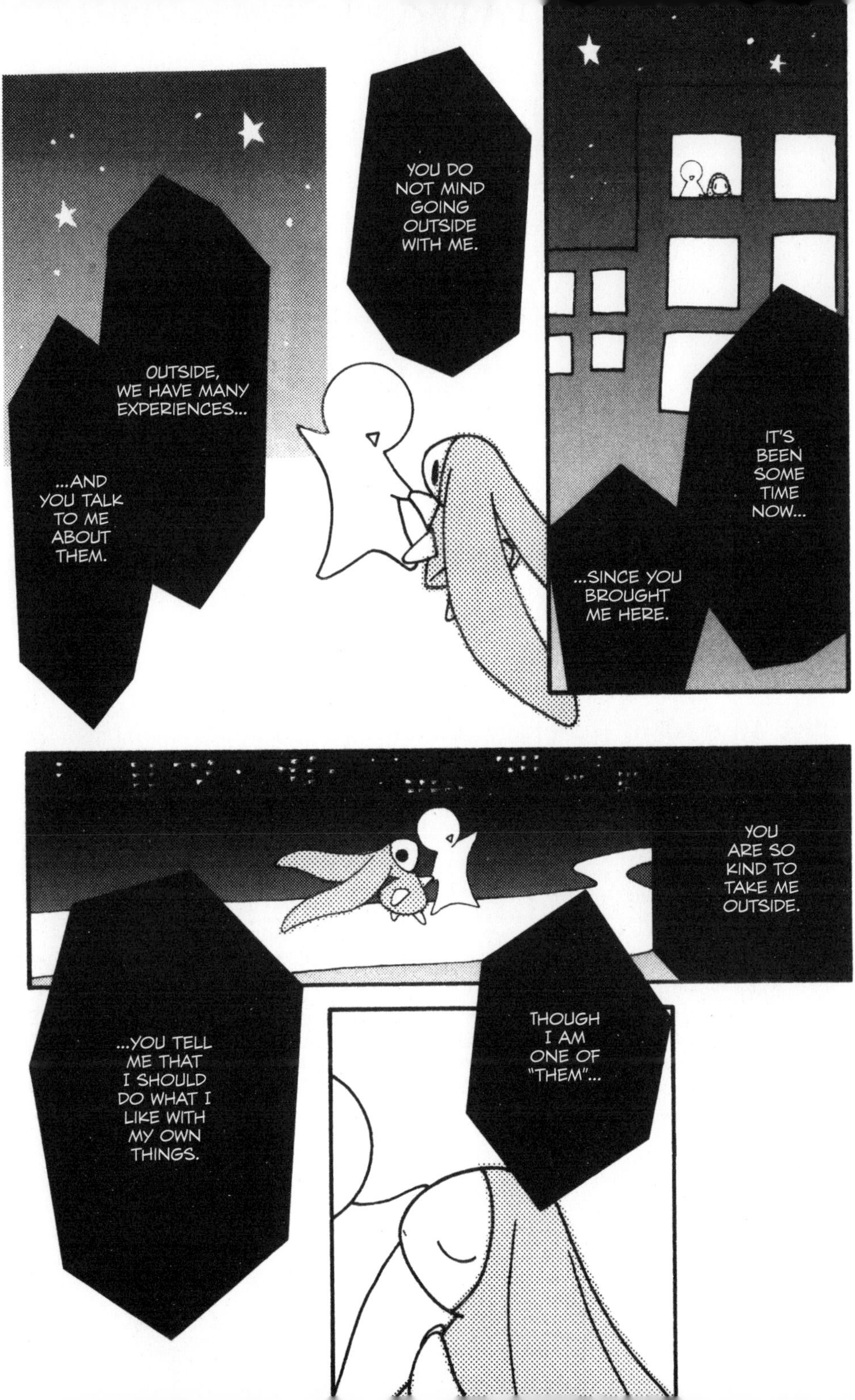
IT'S BEEN SOME TIME NOW...
...SINCE YOU BROUGHT ME HERE.
YOU DO NOT MIND GOING OUTSIDE WITH ME.
OUTSIDE, WE HAVE MANY EXPERIENCES...
...AND YOU TALK TO ME ABOUT THEM.
YOU ARE SO KIND TO TAKE ME OUTSIDE.
THOUGH I AM ONE OF "THEM"...
...YOU TELL ME THAT I SHOULD DO WHAT I LIKE WITH MY OWN THINGS.

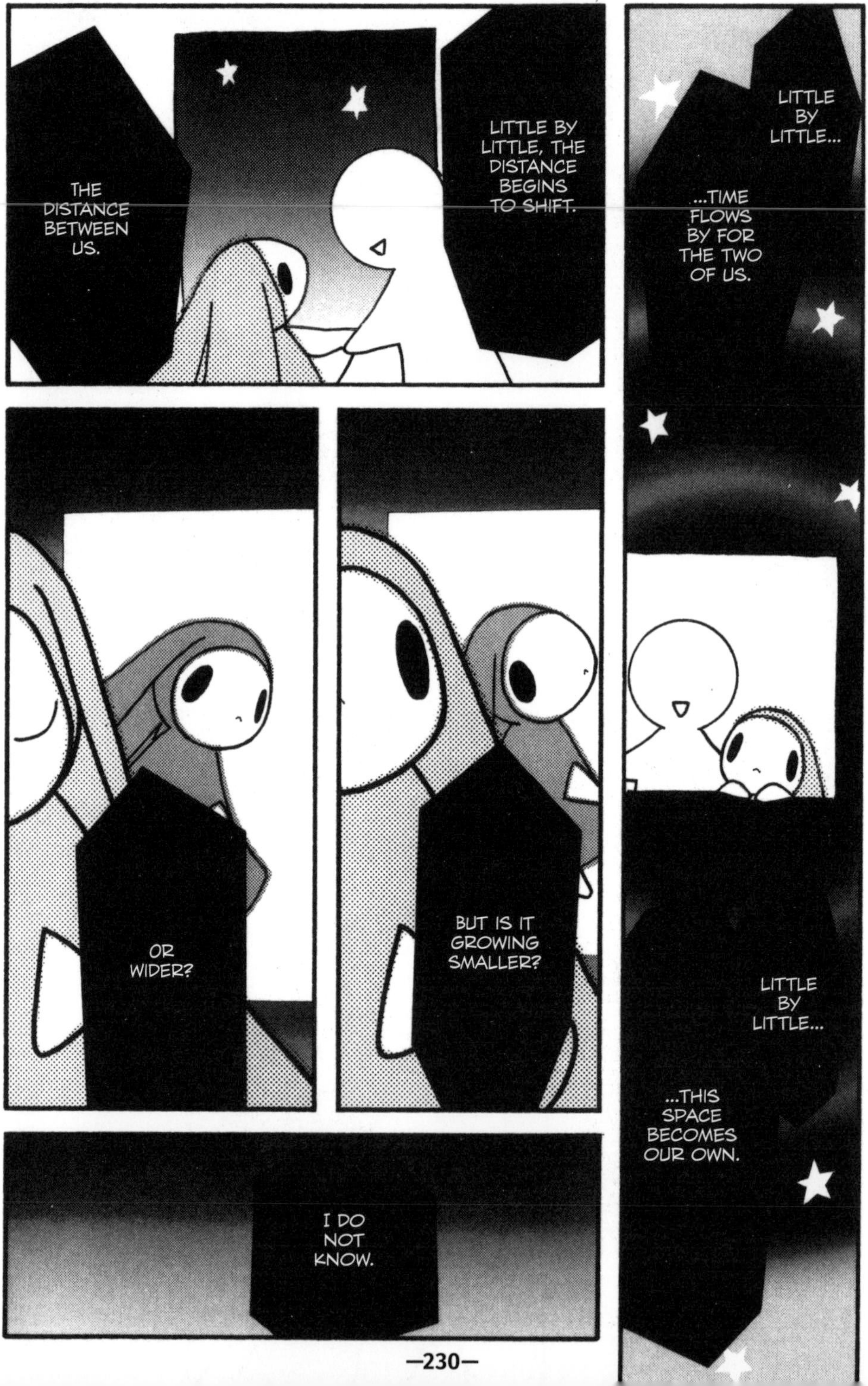
LITTLE BY LITTLE...
...TIME FLOWS BY FOR THE TWO OF US.
LITTLE BY LITTLE...
...THIS SPACE BECOMES OUR OWN.
LITTLE BY LITTLE, THE DISTANCE BEGINS TO SHIFT.
THE DISTANCE BETWEEN US.
BUT IS IT GROWING SMALLER?
OR WIDER?
I DO NOT KNOW.

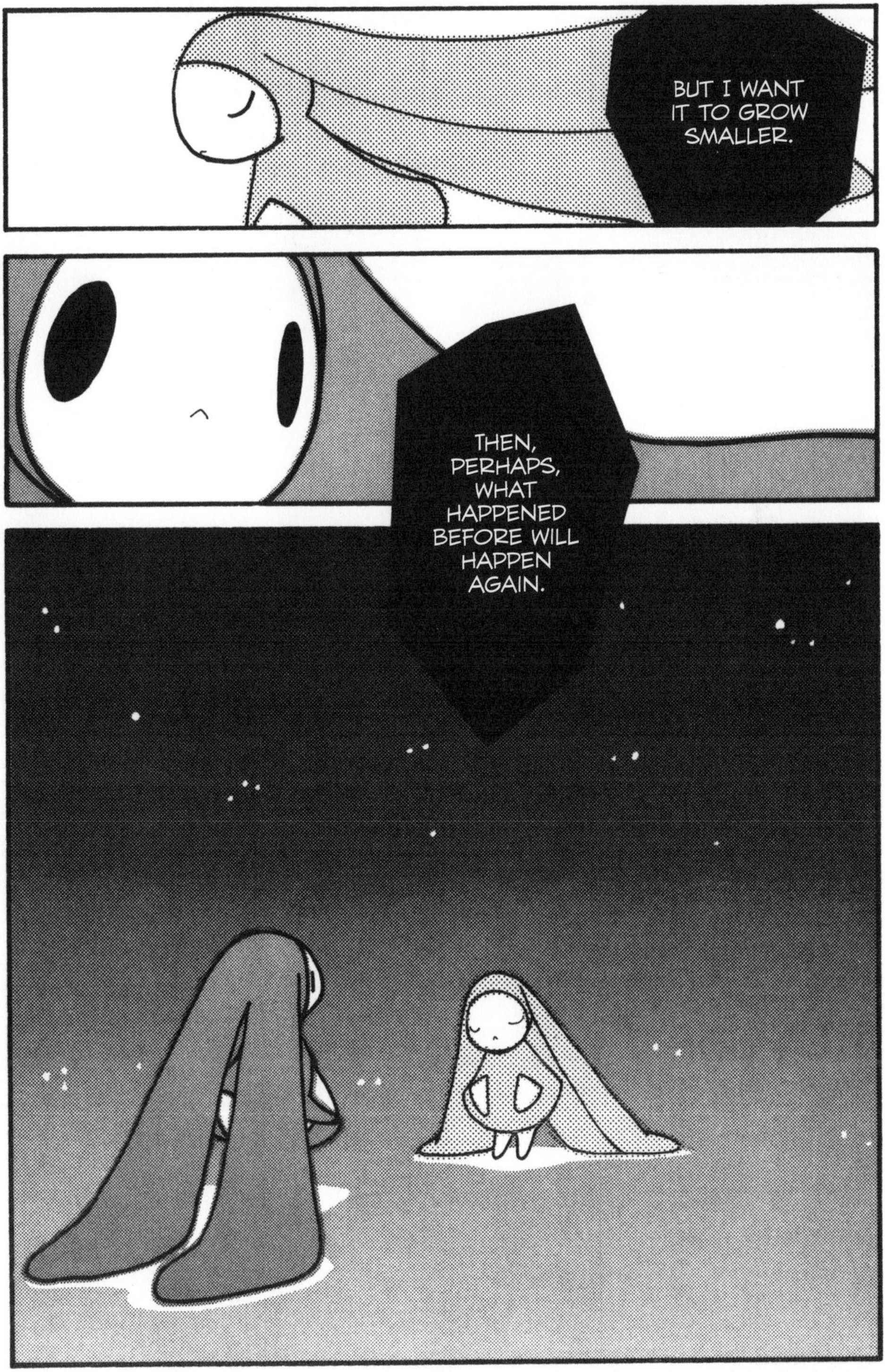
BUT I WANT IT TO GROW SMALLER.
THEN, PERHAPS, WHAT HAPPENED BEFORE WILL HAPPEN AGAIN.

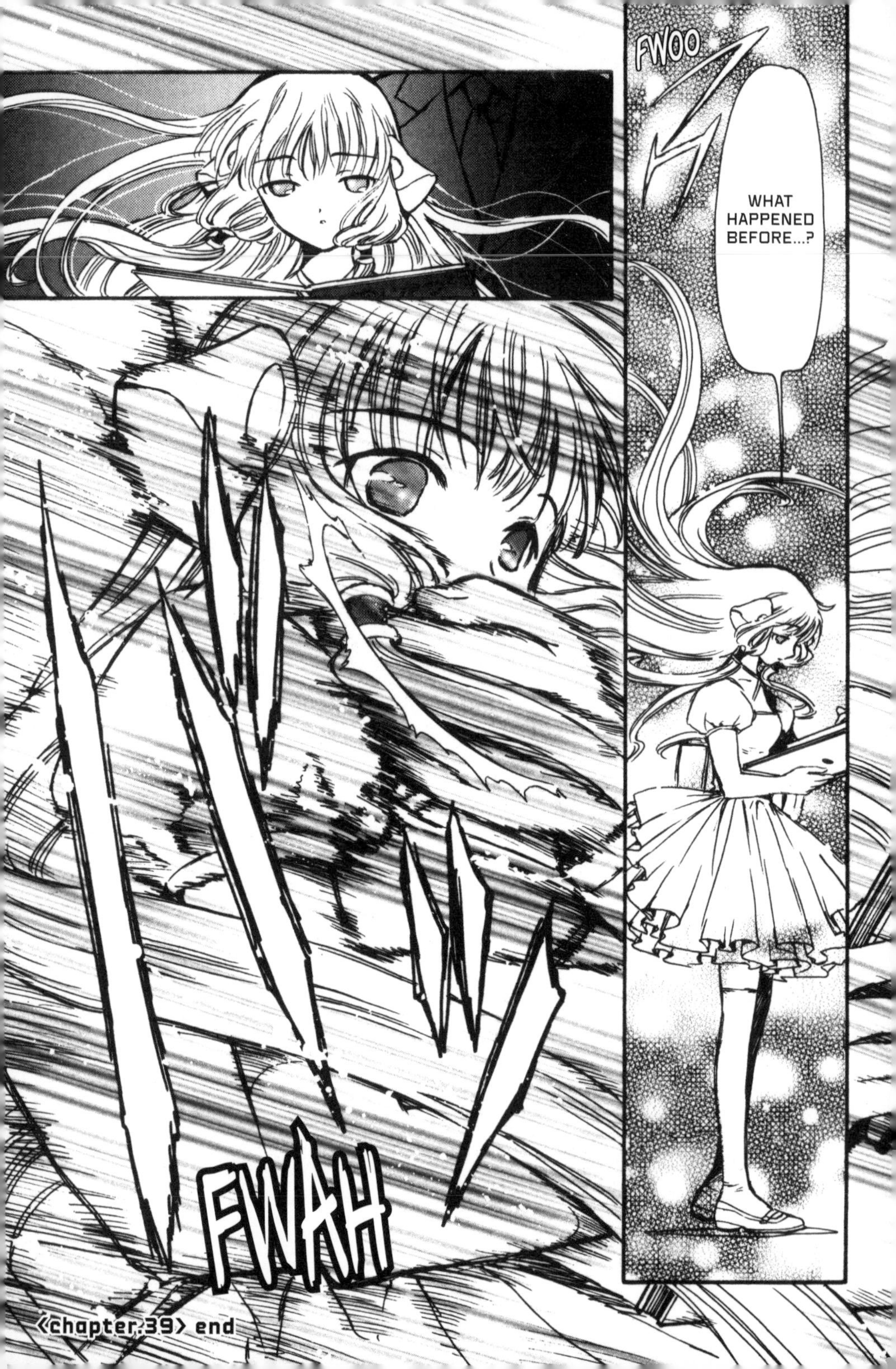
FWOO
WHAT HAPPENED BEFORE...?
FWAH
«chapter.39» end

Chobits

<chapter.40>

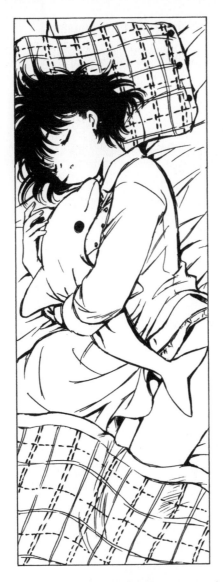

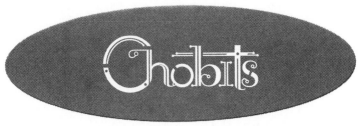

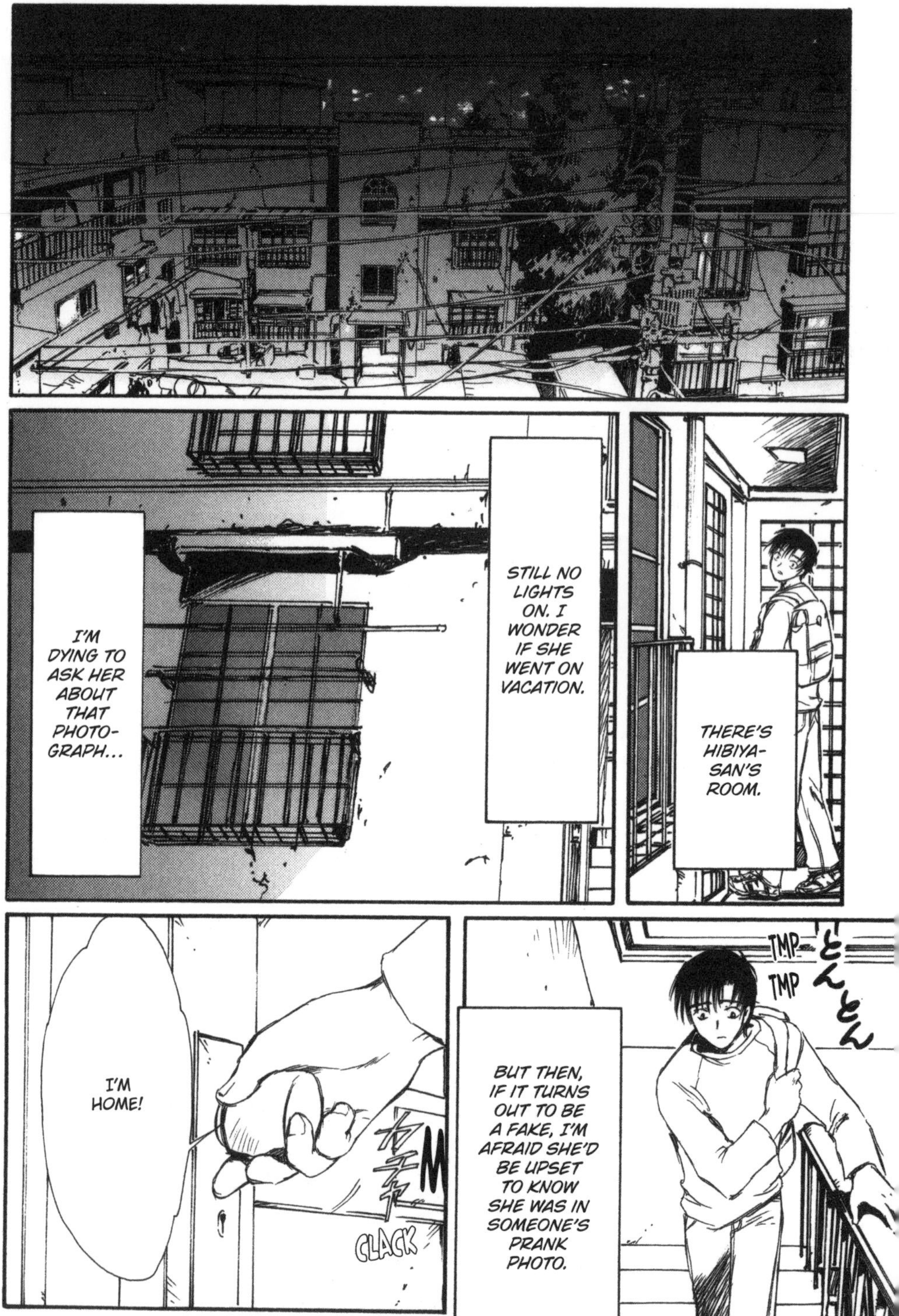
THERE'S HIBIYA-SAN'S ROOM.
STILL NO LIGHTS ON. I WONDER IF SHE WENT ON VACATION.
I'M DYING TO ASK HER ABOUT THAT PHOTOGRAPH...
TMP TMP
とんとん
BUT THEN, IF IT TURNS OUT TO BE A FAKE, I'M AFRAID SHE'D BE UPSET TO KNOW SHE WAS IN SOMEONE'S PRANK PHOTO.
カチャ
CLACK
I'M HOME!

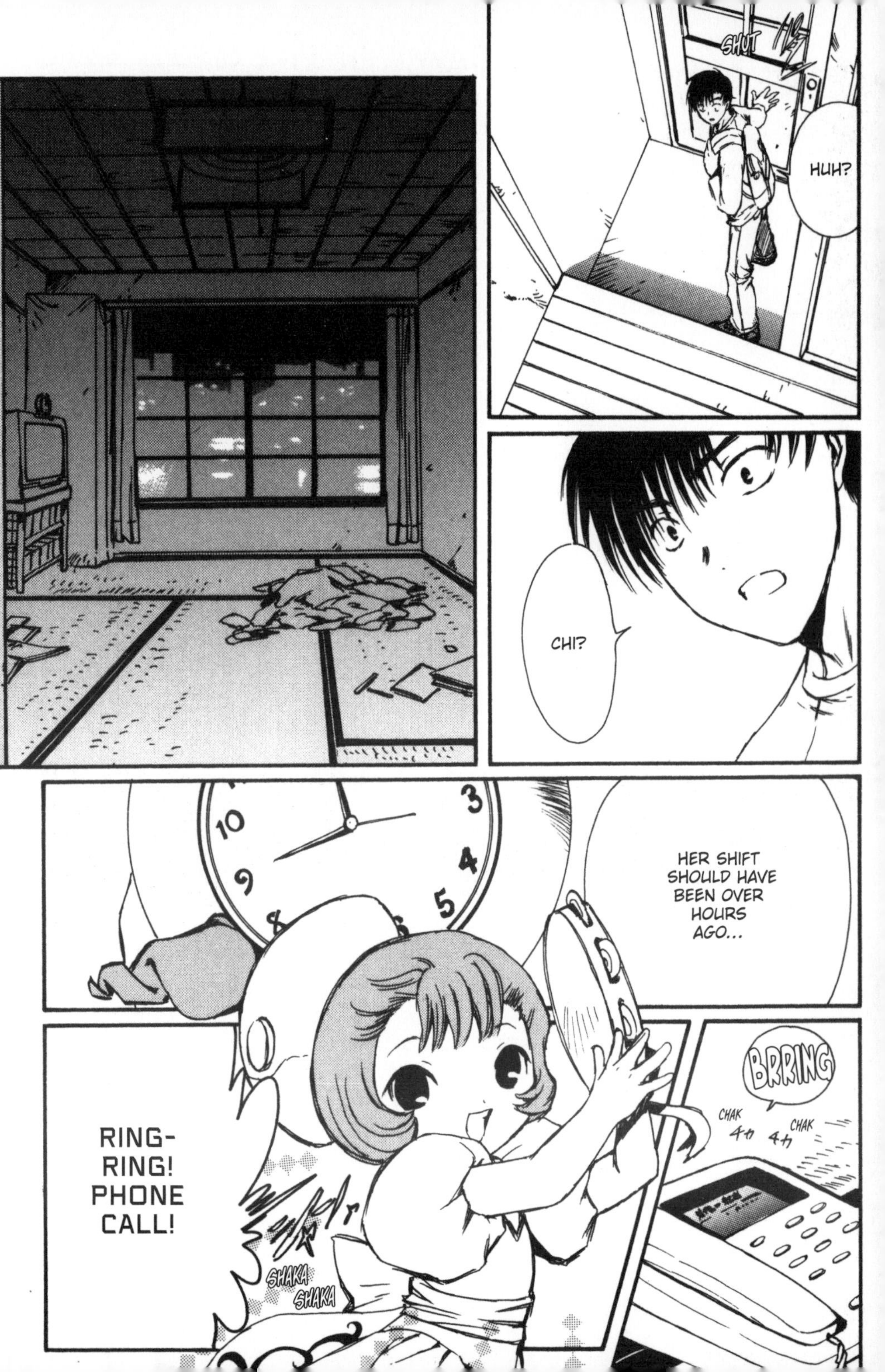
SHUT
HUH?
CHI?
HER SHIFT SHOULD HAVE BEEN OVER HOURS AGO...
BRRING
CHAK
CHAK
RING-RING! PHONE CALL!
SHAKA
SHAKA

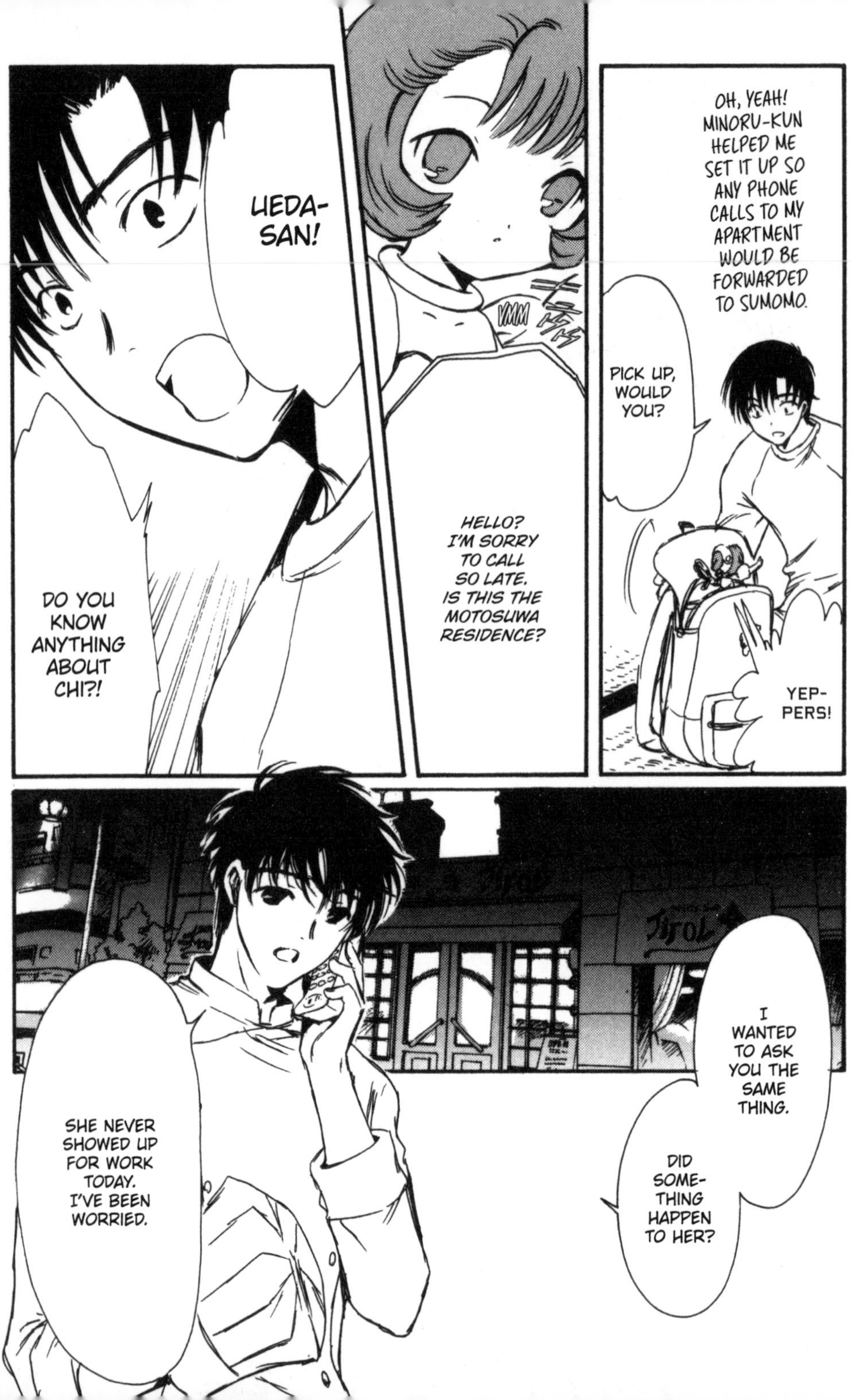
OH, YEAH! MINORU-KUN HELPED ME SET IT UP SO ANY PHONE CALLS TO MY APARTMENT WOULD BE FORWARDED TO SUMOMO.
PICK UP, WOULD YOU?
YEP-PERS!
YMM
HELLO? I'M SORRY TO CALL SO LATE. IS THIS THE MOTOSUWA RESIDENCE?
UEDA-SAN!
DO YOU KNOW ANYTHING ABOUT CHI?!
I WANTED TO ASK YOU THE SAME THING.
DID SOME-THING HAPPEN TO HER?
SHE NEVER SHOWED UP FOR WORK TODAY. I'VE BEEN WORRIED.

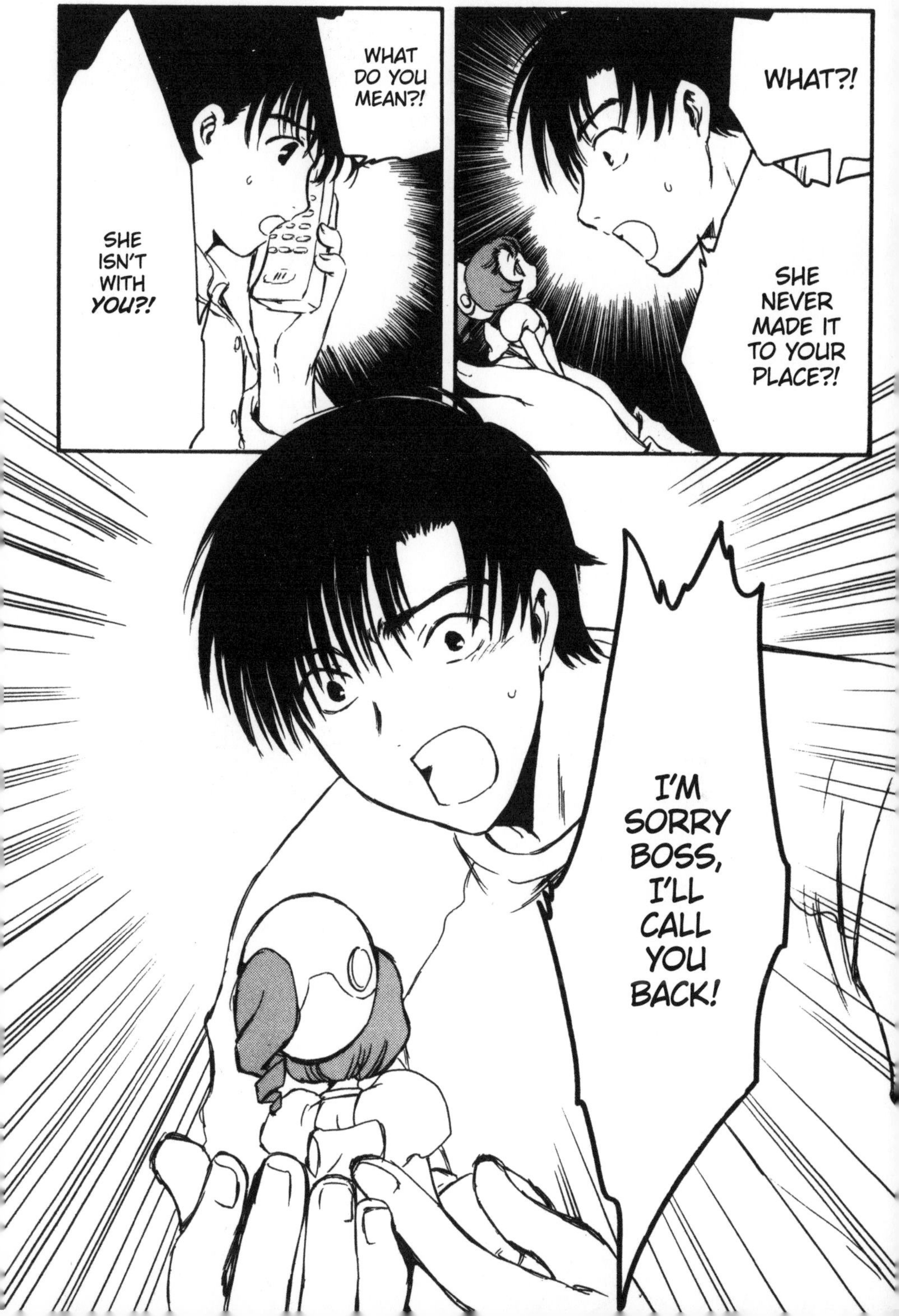
WHAT?!
SHE NEVER MADE IT TO YOUR PLACE?!
WHAT DO YOU MEAN?!
SHE ISN'T WITH *YOU?!*
I'M SORRY BOSS, I'LL CALL YOU BACK!

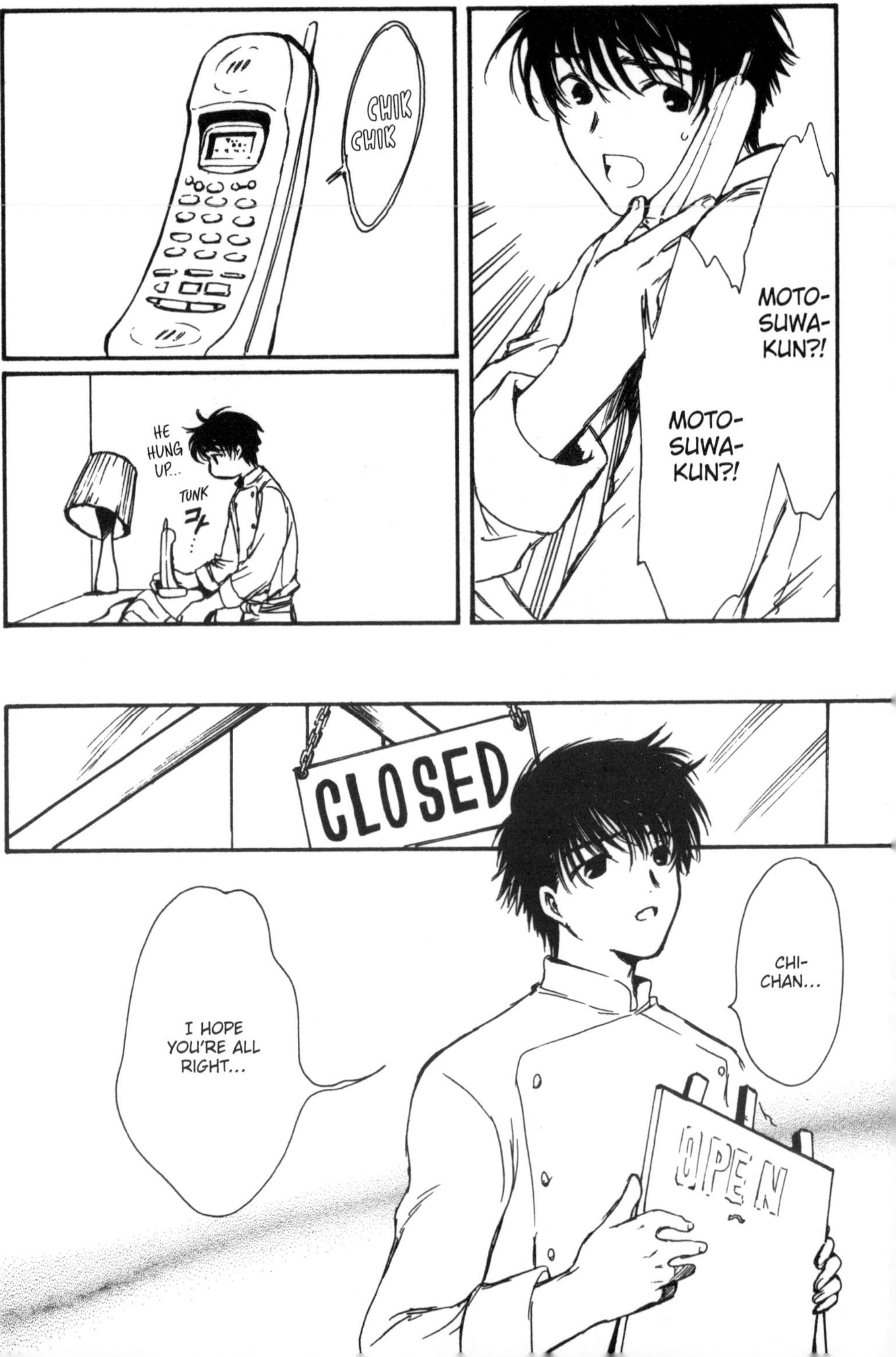
MOTO-SUWA-KUN?!
MOTO-SUWA-KUN?!
CHIK CHIK
HE HUNG UP...
TUNK
CLOSED
CHI-CHAN...
I HOPE YOU'RE ALL RIGHT...
OPEN

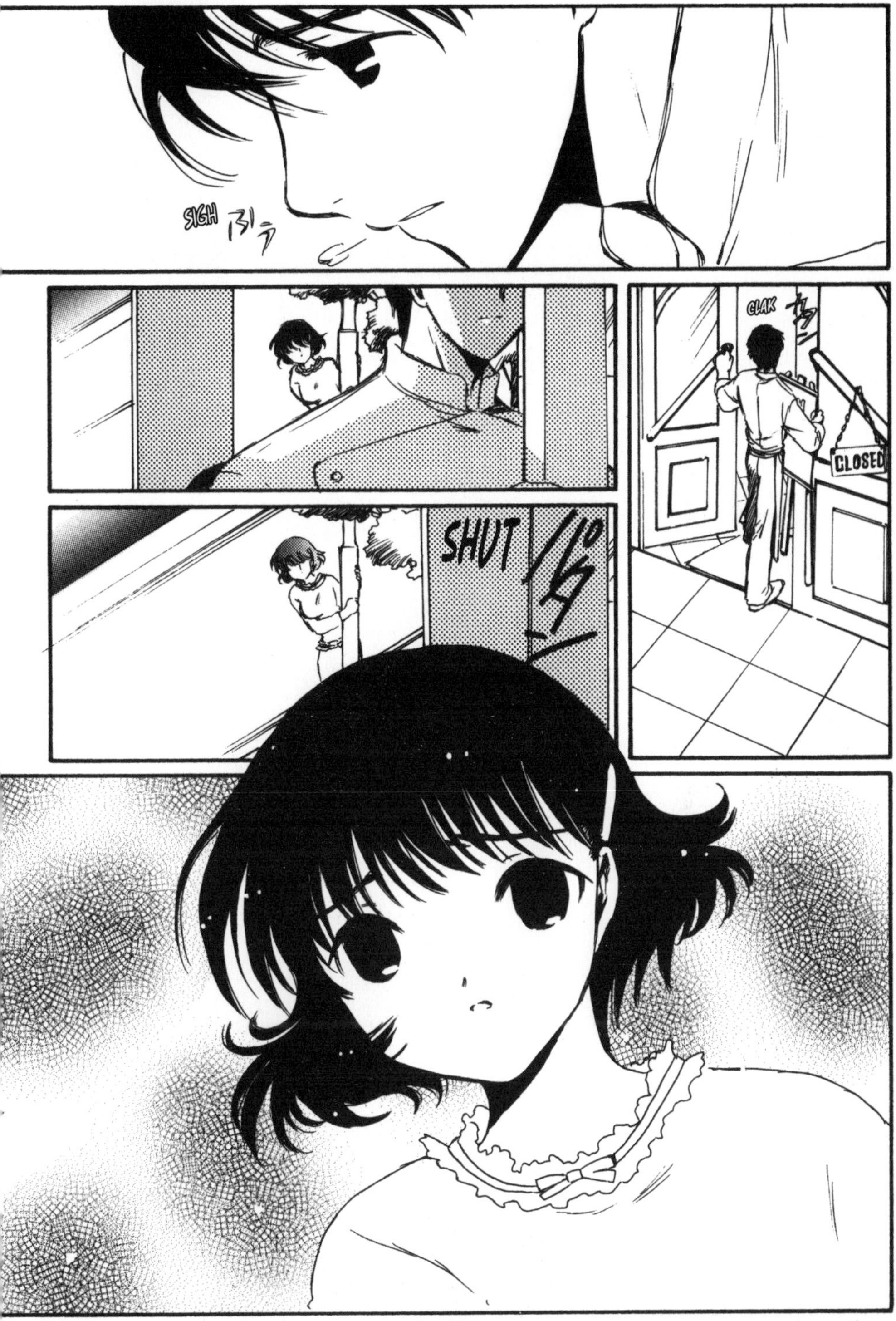
SIGH
CLAK
CLOSED
SHUT

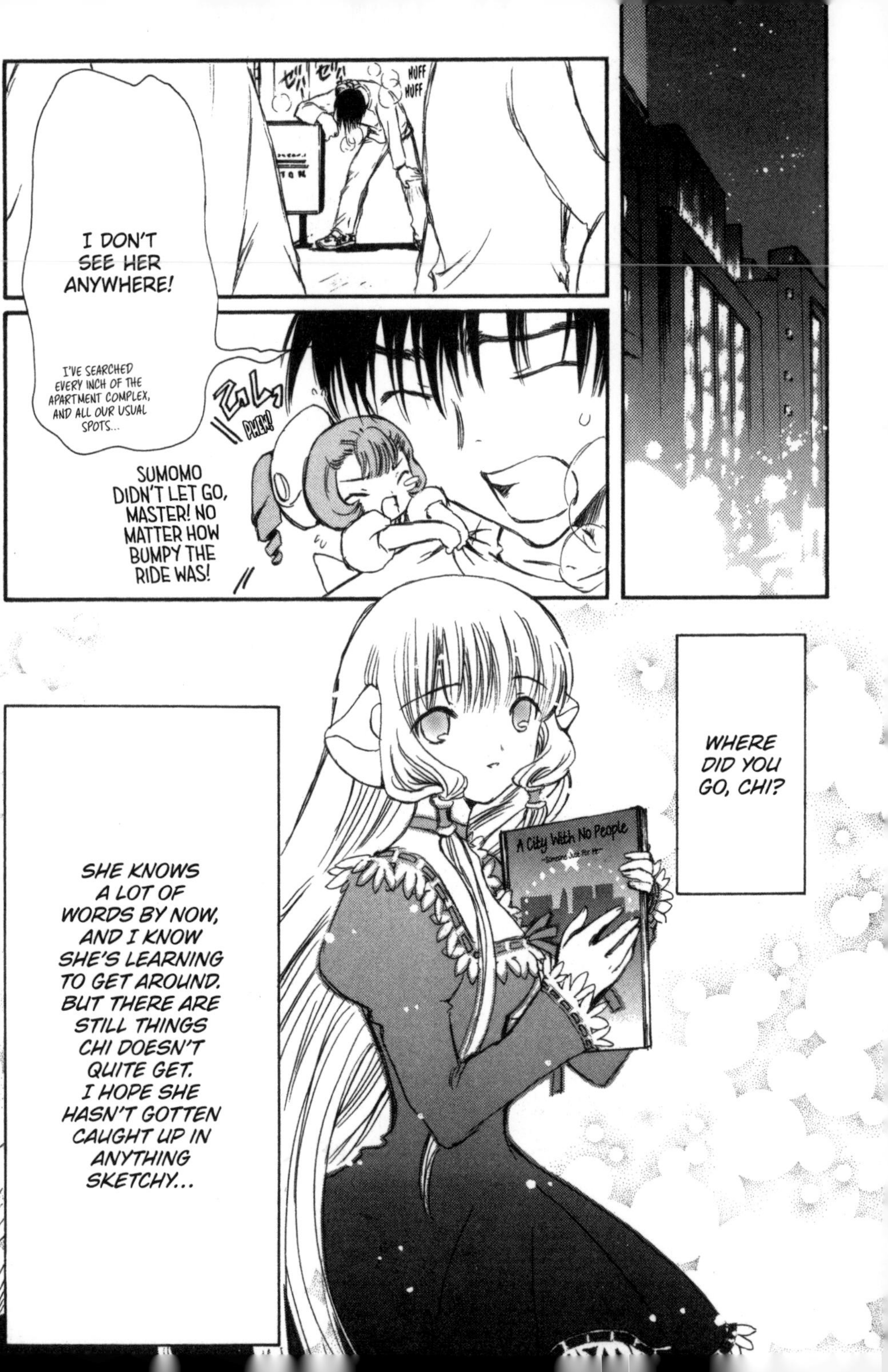
HUFF
HUFF
I DON'T SEE HER ANYWHERE!
I'VE SEARCHED EVERY INCH OF THE APARTMENT COMPLEX, AND ALL OUR USUAL SPOTS...
PHEW!
SUMOMO DIDN'T LET GO, MASTER! NO MATTER HOW BUMPY THE RIDE WAS!
WHERE DID YOU GO, CHI?
SHE KNOWS A LOT OF WORDS BY NOW, AND I KNOW SHE'S LEARNING TO GET AROUND. BUT THERE ARE STILL THINGS CHI DOESN'T QUITE GET. I HOPE SHE HASN'T GOTTEN CAUGHT UP IN ANYTHING SKETCHY...
A City With No People

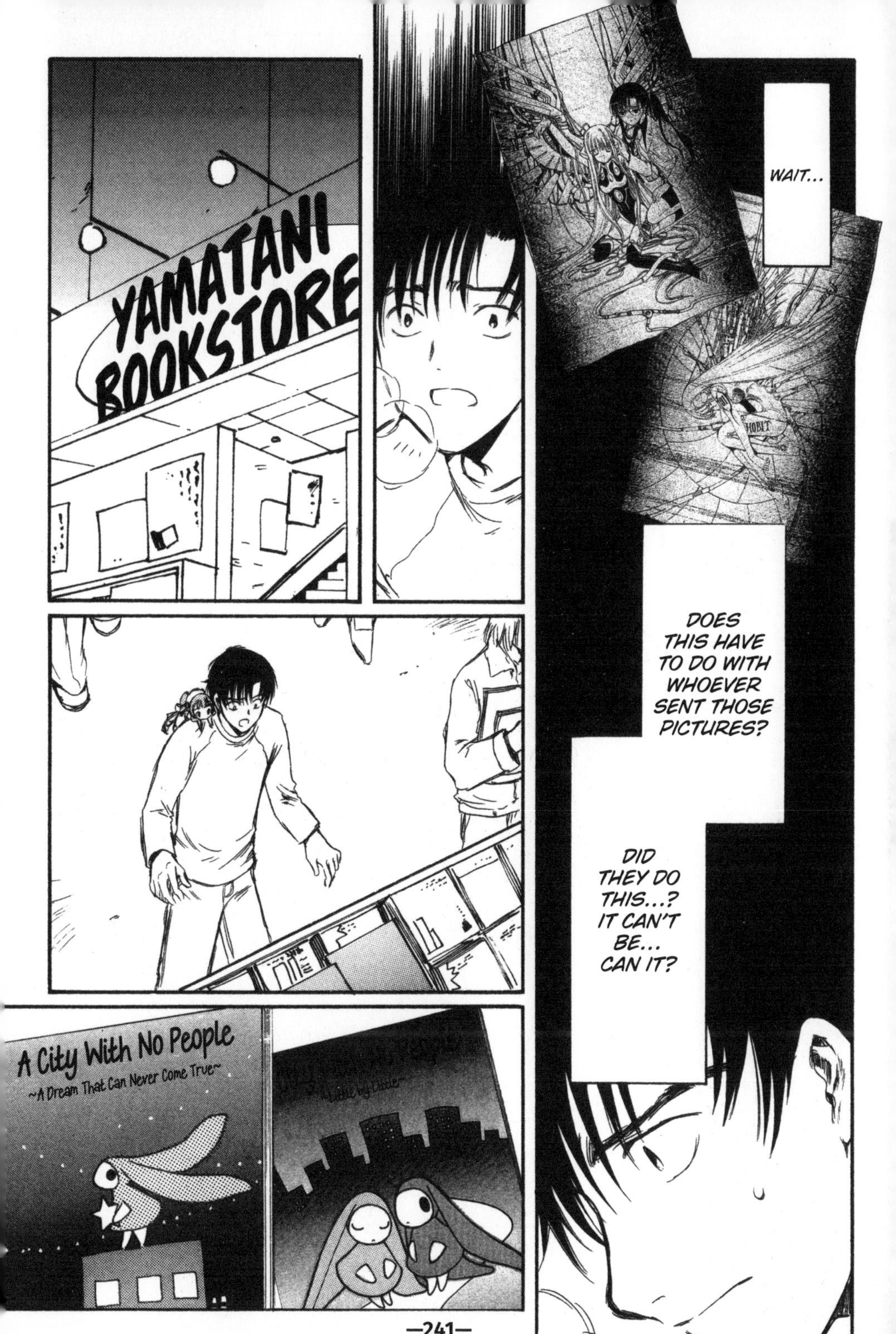
WAIT...
DOES THIS HAVE TO DO WITH WHOEVER SENT THOSE PICTURES?
DID THEY DO THIS...? IT CAN'T BE... CAN IT?
YAMATANI BOOKSTORE
~Little by Little~
A City With No People
~A Dream That Can Never Come True~

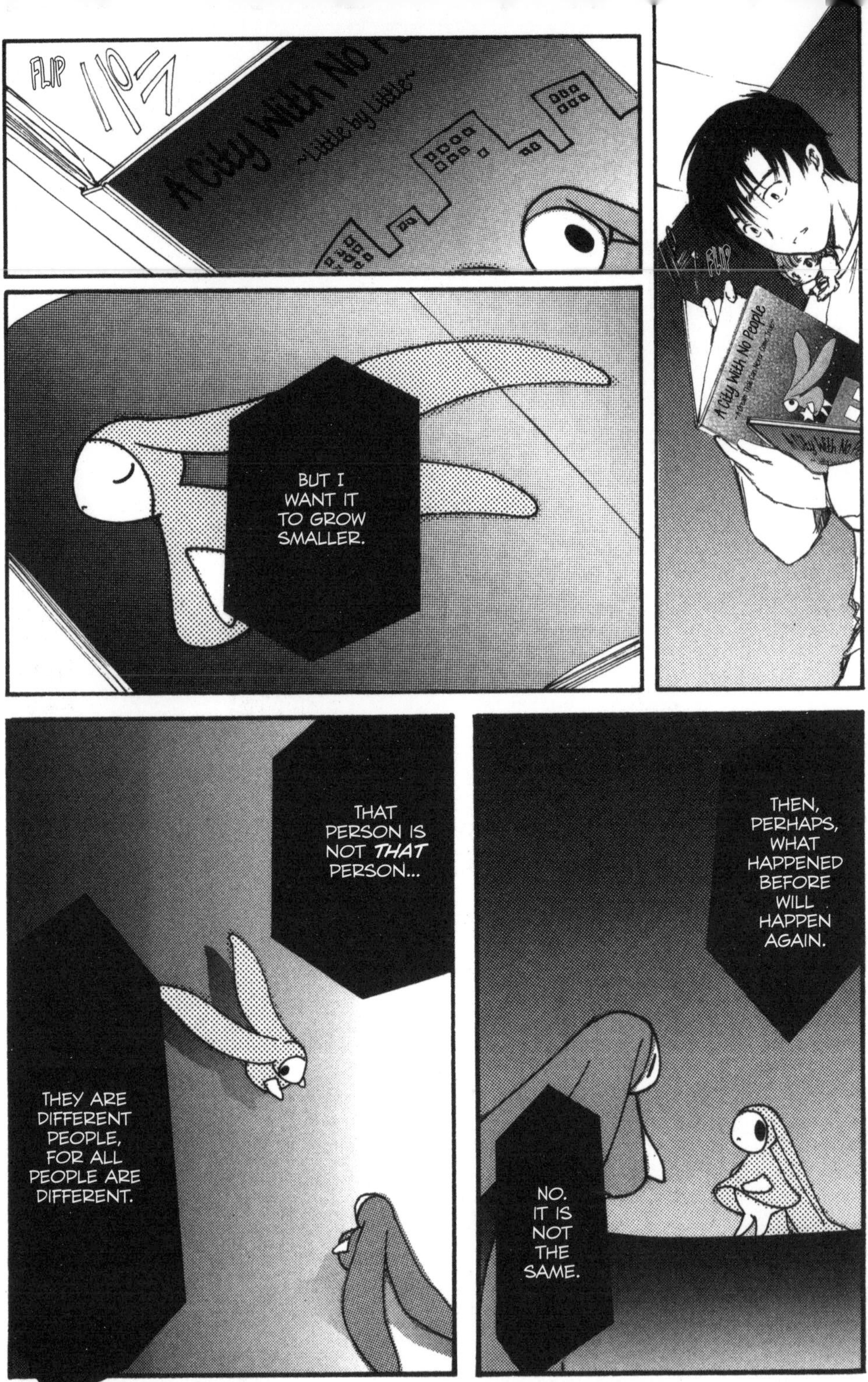
FLIP
A City With No People
FLIP
A City With No
~Little by Little~
BUT I WANT IT TO GROW SMALLER.
THEN, PERHAPS, WHAT HAPPENED BEFORE WILL HAPPEN AGAIN.
NO. IT IS NOT THE SAME.
THAT PERSON IS NOT *THAT* PERSON...
THEY ARE DIFFERENT PEOPLE, FOR ALL PEOPLE ARE DIFFERENT.

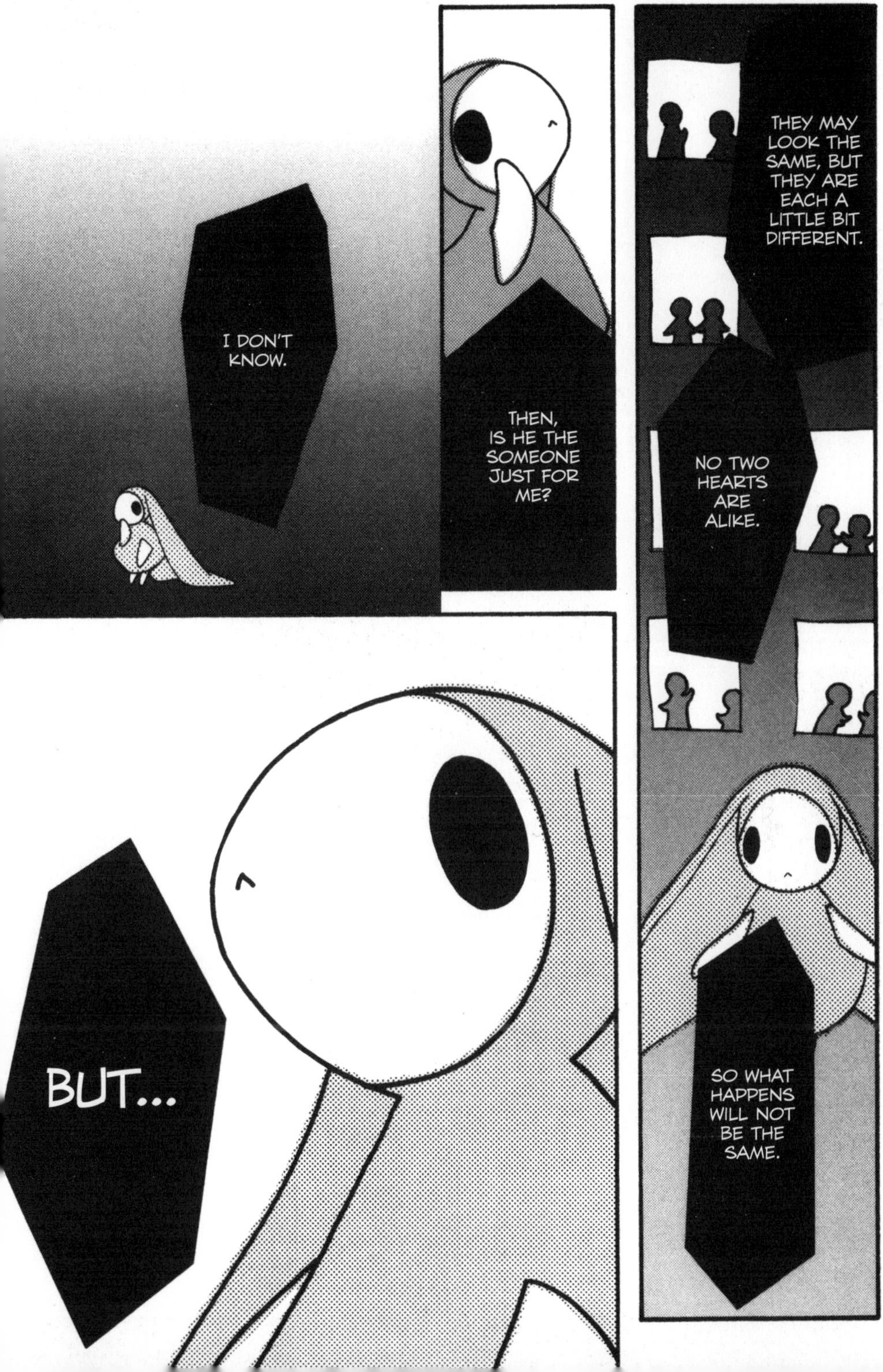
THEY MAY LOOK THE SAME, BUT THEY ARE EACH A LITTLE BIT DIFFERENT.
NO TWO HEARTS ARE ALIKE.
SO WHAT HAPPENS WILL NOT BE THE SAME.
THEN, IS HE THE SOMEONE JUST FOR ME?
I DON'T KNOW.
BUT...

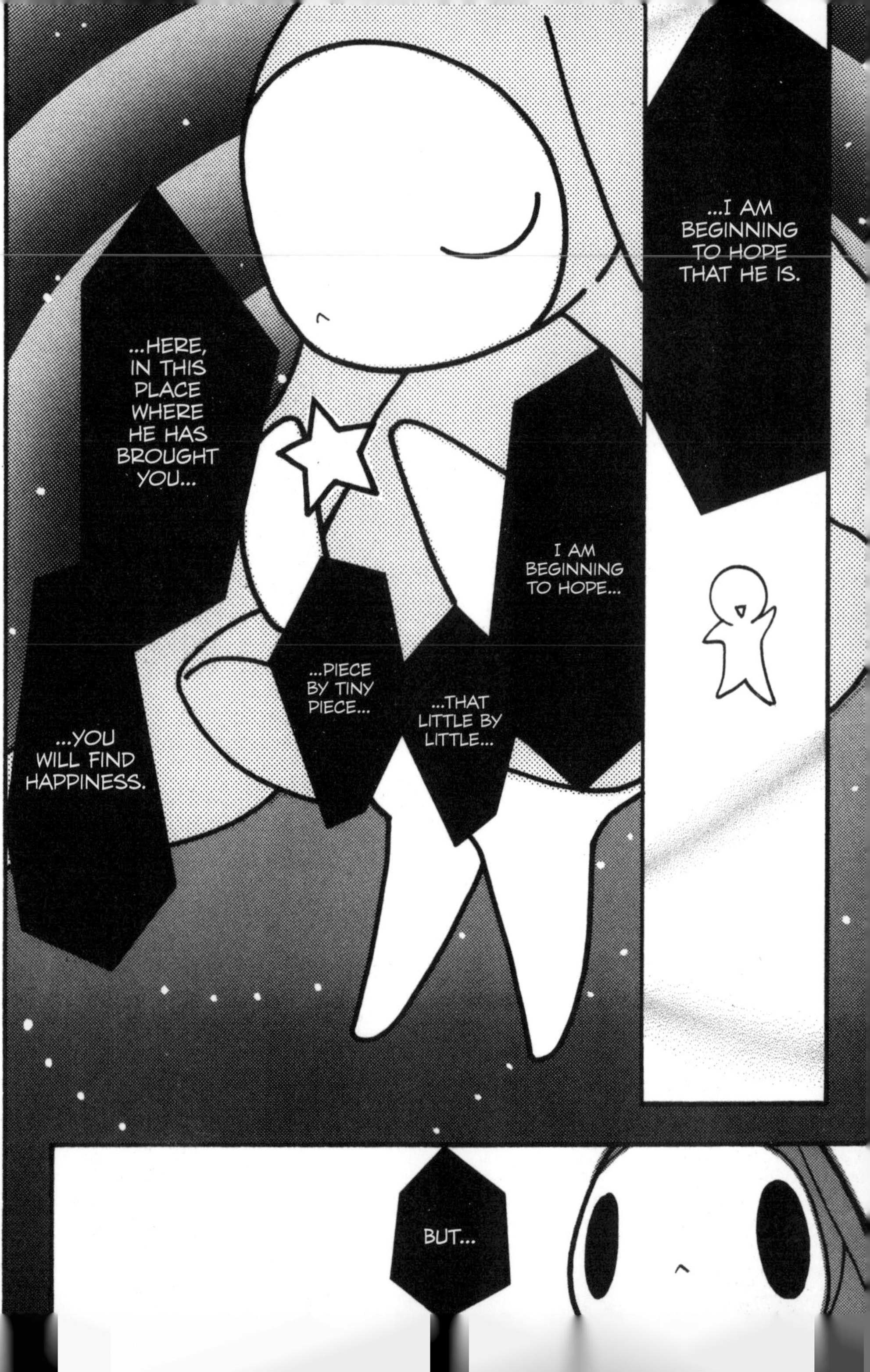
...I AM BEGINNING TO HOPE THAT HE IS.
I AM BEGINNING TO HOPE...
...THAT LITTLE BY LITTLE...
...PIECE BY TINY PIECE...
...HERE, IN THIS PLACE WHERE HE HAS BROUGHT YOU...
...YOU WILL FIND HAPPINESS.
BUT...

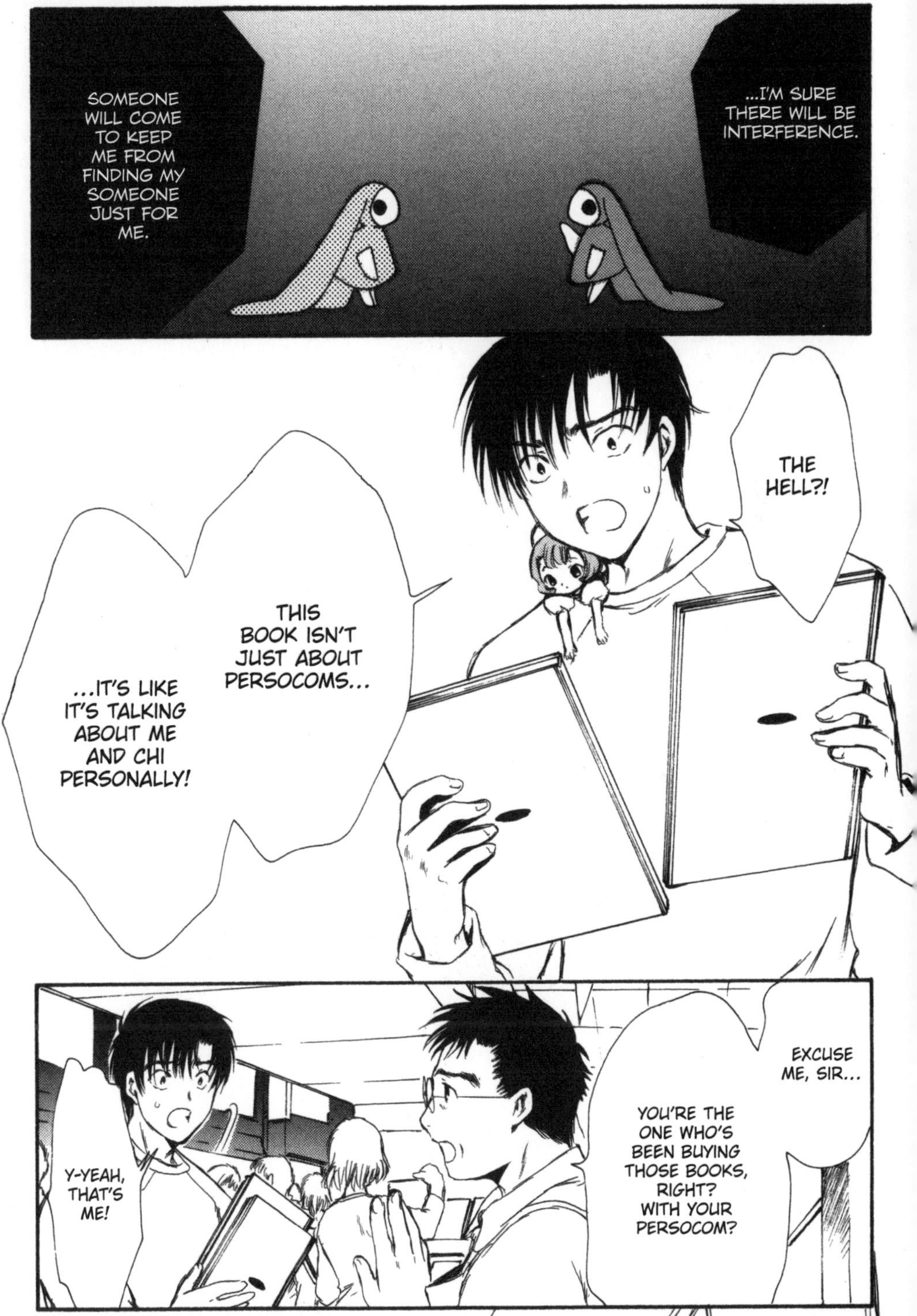
...I'M SURE THERE WILL BE INTERFERENCE.
SOMEONE WILL COME TO KEEP ME FROM FINDING MY SOMEONE JUST FOR ME.
THE HELL?!
THIS BOOK ISN'T JUST ABOUT PERSOCOMS...
...IT'S LIKE IT'S TALKING ABOUT ME AND CHI PERSONALLY!
EXCUSE ME, SIR...
YOU'RE THE ONE WHO'S BEEN BUYING THOSE BOOKS, RIGHT? WITH YOUR PERSOCOM?
Y-YEAH, THAT'S ME!

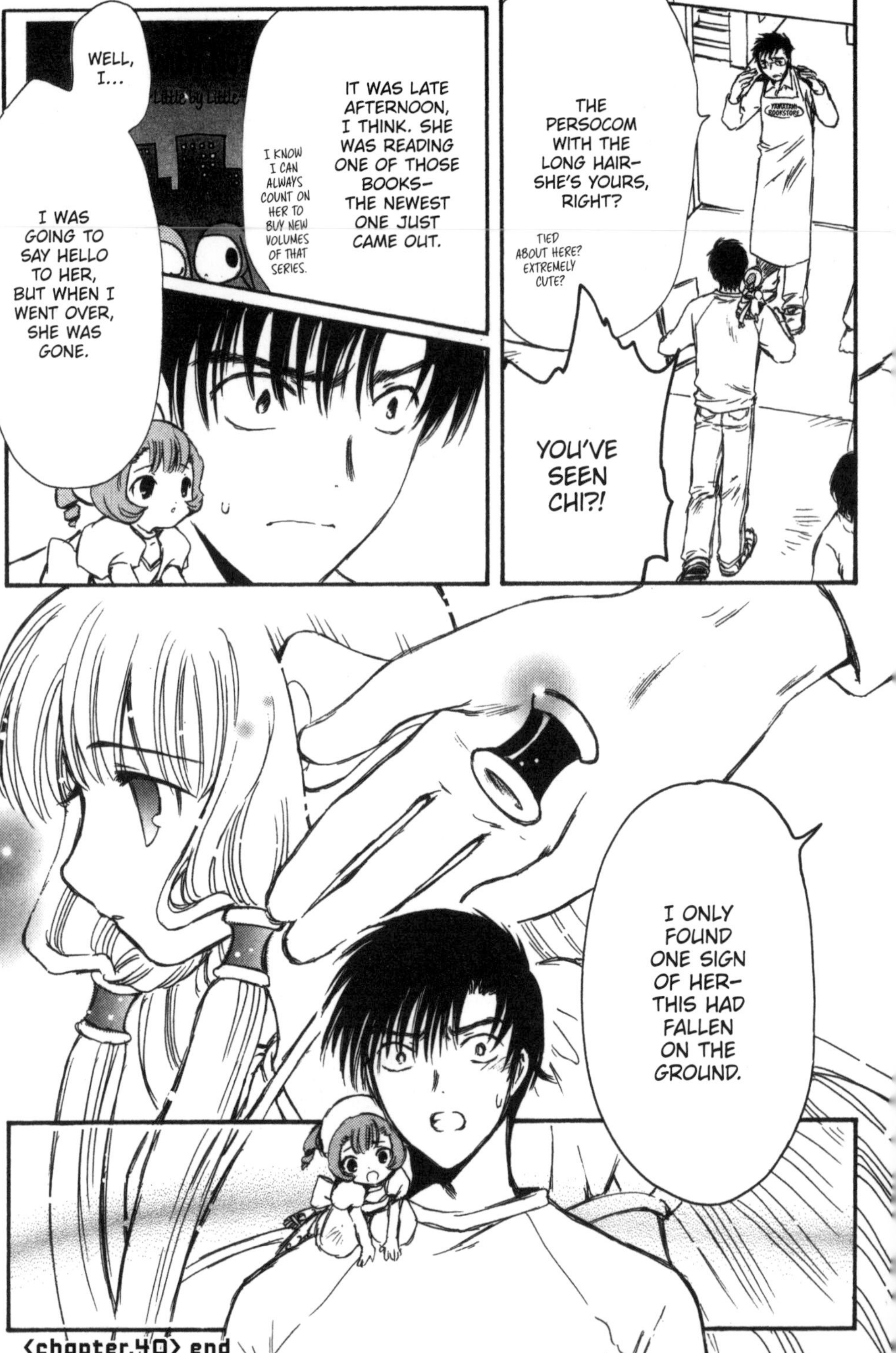

THE PERSOCOM WITH THE LONG HAIR-SHE'S YOURS, RIGHT?
TIED ABOUT HERE? EXTREMELY CUTE?
YAMATANI BOOKSTORE
YOU'VE SEEN CHI?!
IT WAS LATE AFTERNOON, I THINK. SHE WAS READING ONE OF THOSE BOOKS-THE NEWEST ONE JUST CAME OUT.
I KNOW I CAN ALWAYS COUNT ON HER TO BUY NEW VOLUMES OF THAT SERIES.
Little by Little
WELL, I...
I WAS GOING TO SAY HELLO TO HER, BUT WHEN I WENT OVER, SHE WAS GONE.
I ONLY FOUND ONE SIGN OF HER-THIS HAD FALLEN ON THE GROUND.

<chapter.40> end

〈chapter.41〉

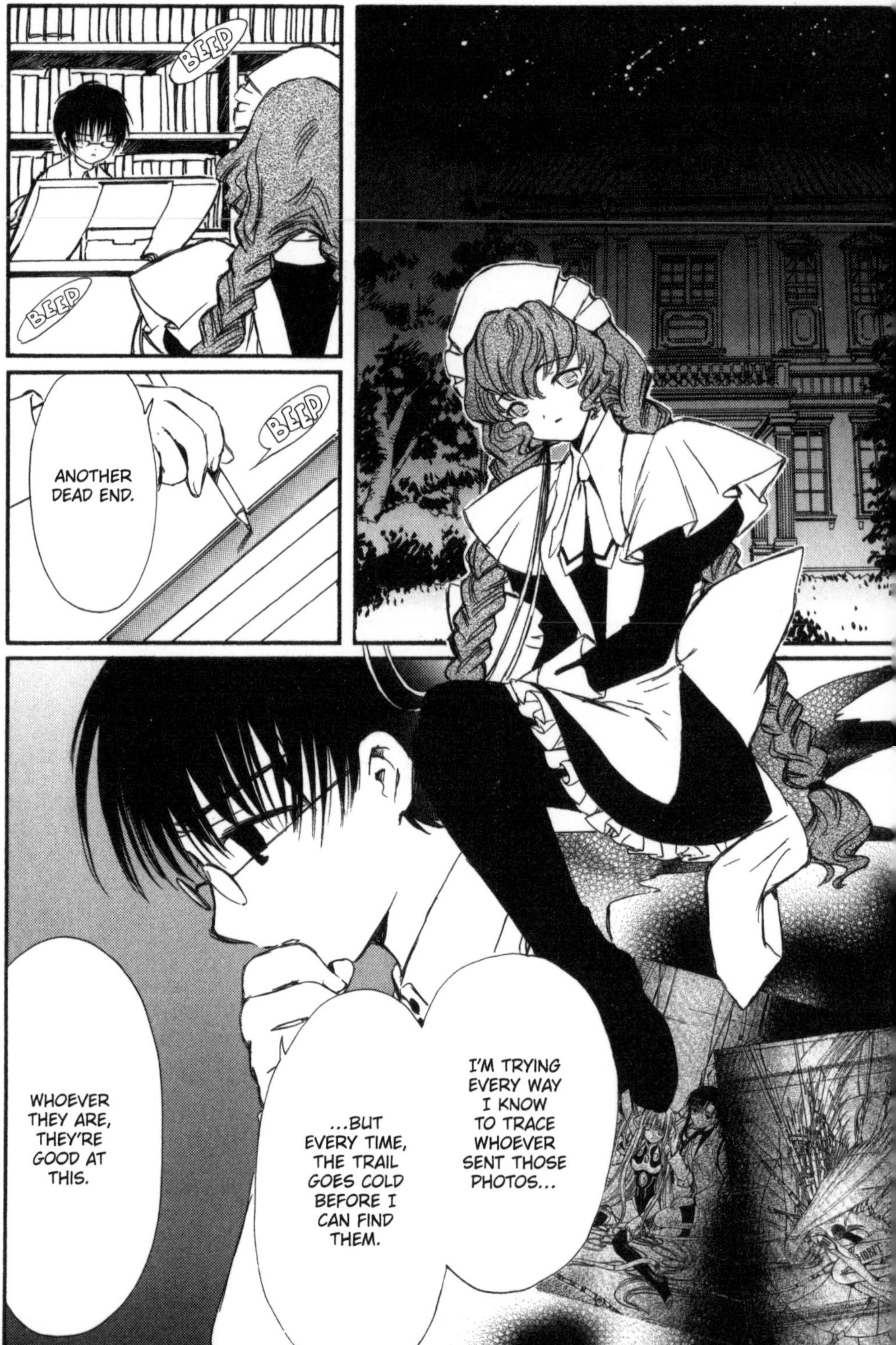
BEEP
BEEP
BEEP
ANOTHER DEAD END.
I'M TRYING EVERY WAY I KNOW TO TRACE WHOEVER SENT THOSE PHOTOS...
...BUT EVERY TIME, THE TRAIL GOES COLD BEFORE I CAN FIND THEM.
WHOEVER THEY ARE, THEY'RE GOOD AT THIS.

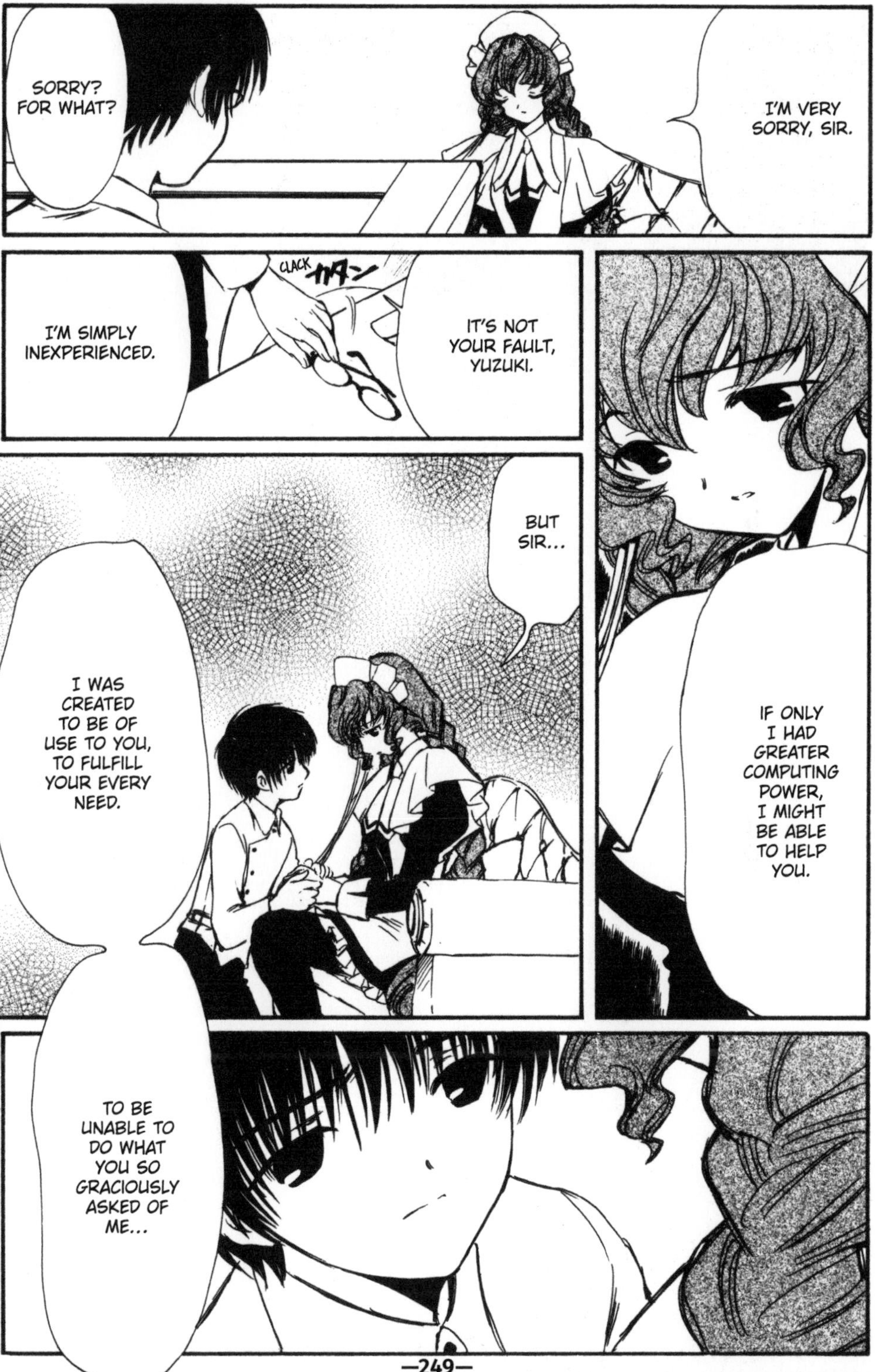

I'M VERY SORRY, SIR.
SORRY? FOR WHAT?
IF ONLY I HAD GREATER COMPUTING POWER, I MIGHT BE ABLE TO HELP YOU.
CLACK
IT'S NOT YOUR FAULT, YUZUKI.
I'M SIMPLY INEXPERIENCED.
BUT SIR...
I WAS CREATED TO BE OF USE TO YOU, TO FULFILL YOUR EVERY NEED.
TO BE UNABLE TO DO WHAT YOU SO GRACIOUSLY ASKED OF ME...

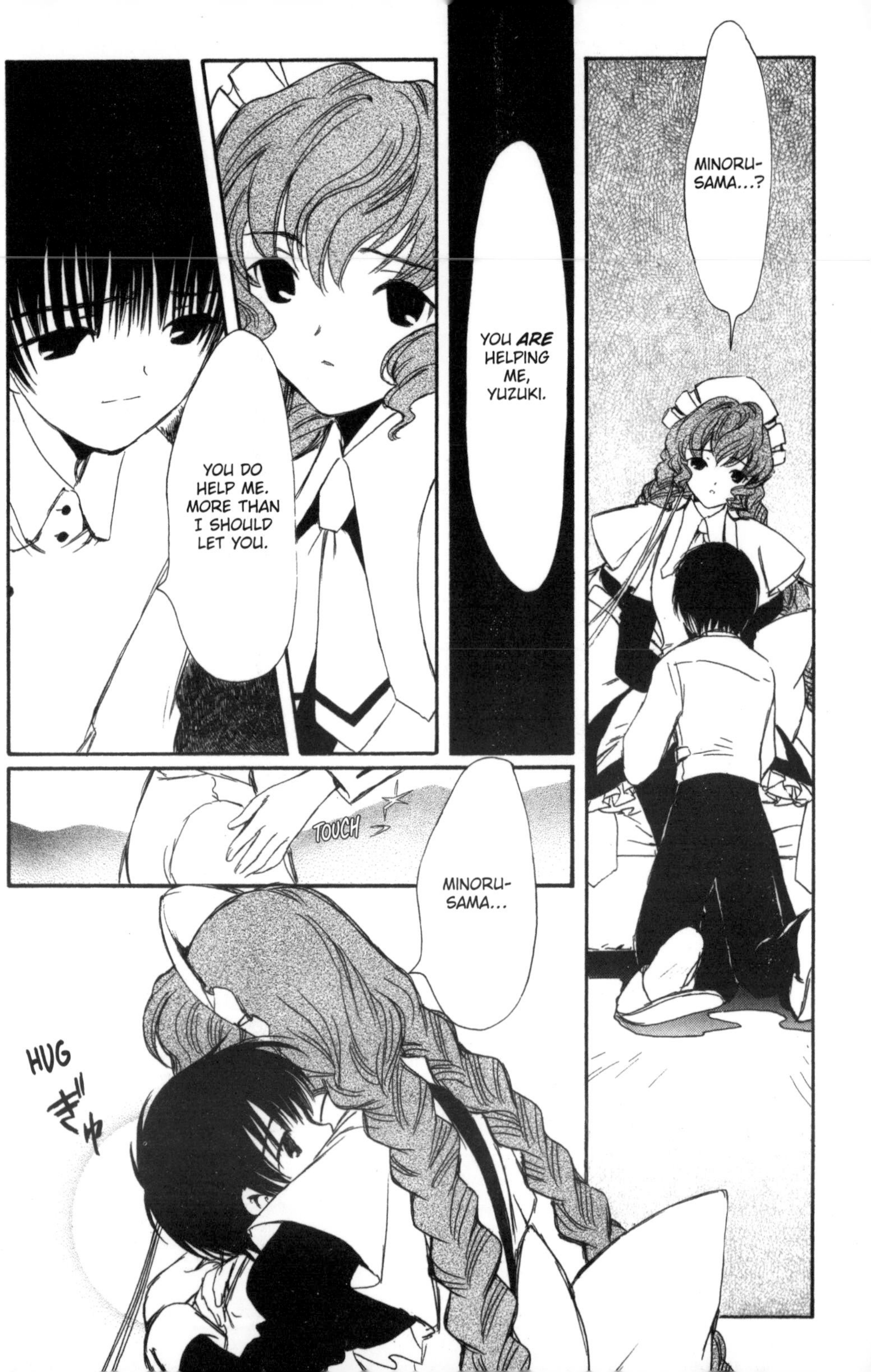
MINORU-SAMA...?
YOU **ARE** HELPING ME, YUZUKI.
YOU DO HELP ME. MORE THAN I SHOULD LET YOU.
TOUCH
MINORU-SAMA...
HUG
ぎゅ

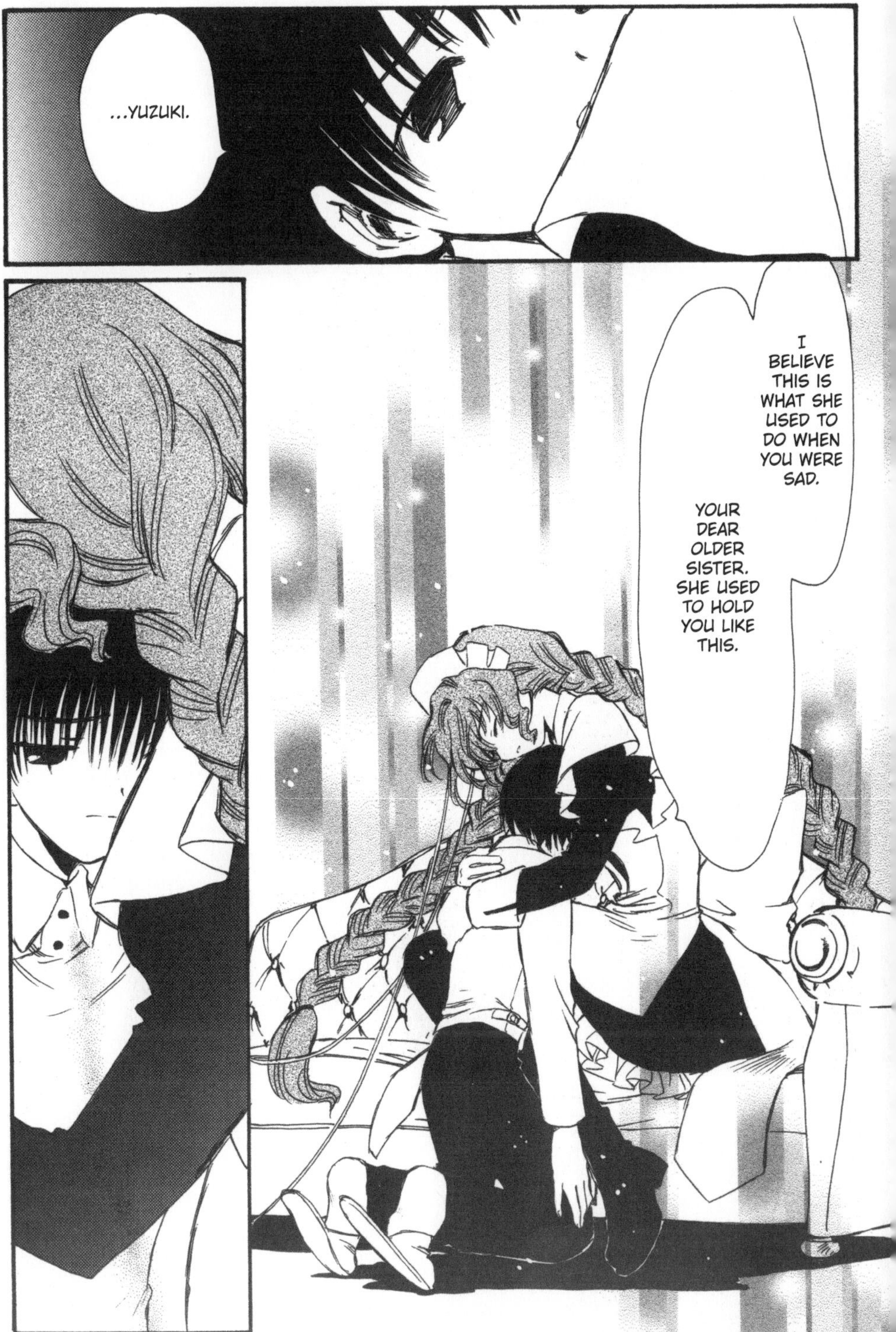
...YUZUKI.
I BELIEVE THIS IS WHAT SHE USED TO DO WHEN YOU WERE SAD.
YOUR DEAR OLDER SISTER. SHE USED TO HOLD YOU LIKE THIS.

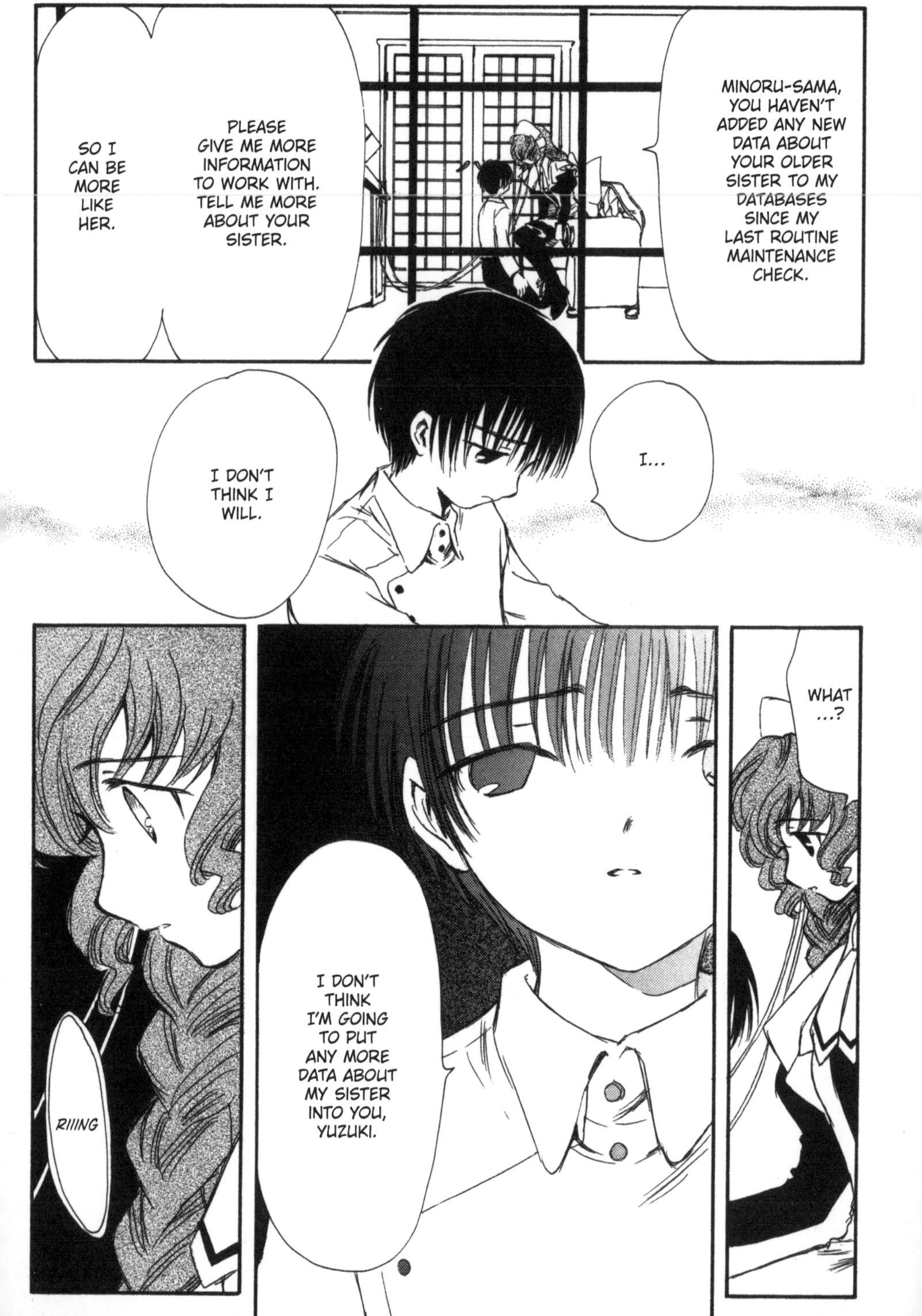
MINORU-SAMA, YOU HAVEN'T ADDED ANY NEW DATA ABOUT YOUR OLDER SISTER TO MY DATABASES SINCE MY LAST ROUTINE MAINTENANCE CHECK.
PLEASE GIVE ME MORE INFORMATION TO WORK WITH. TELL ME MORE ABOUT YOUR SISTER.
SO I CAN BE MORE LIKE HER.
I...
I DON'T THINK I WILL.
WHAT ...?
I DON'T THINK I'M GOING TO PUT ANY MORE DATA ABOUT MY SISTER INTO YOU, YUZUKI.
RIIING

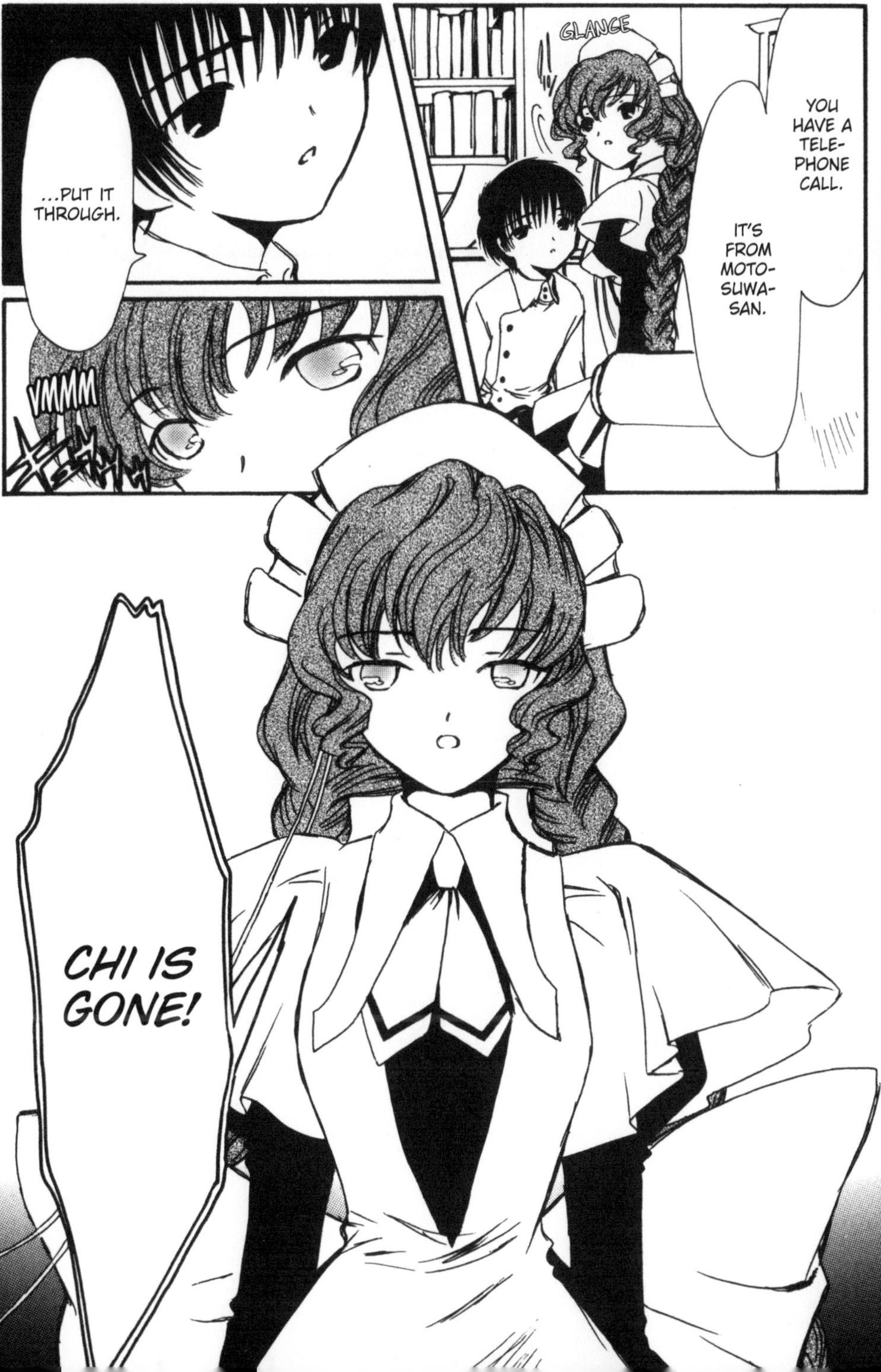
GLANCE
YOU HAVE A TELE-PHONE CALL.
IT'S FROM MOTO-SUWA-SAN.
...PUT IT THROUGH.
VMMM
CHI IS GONE!

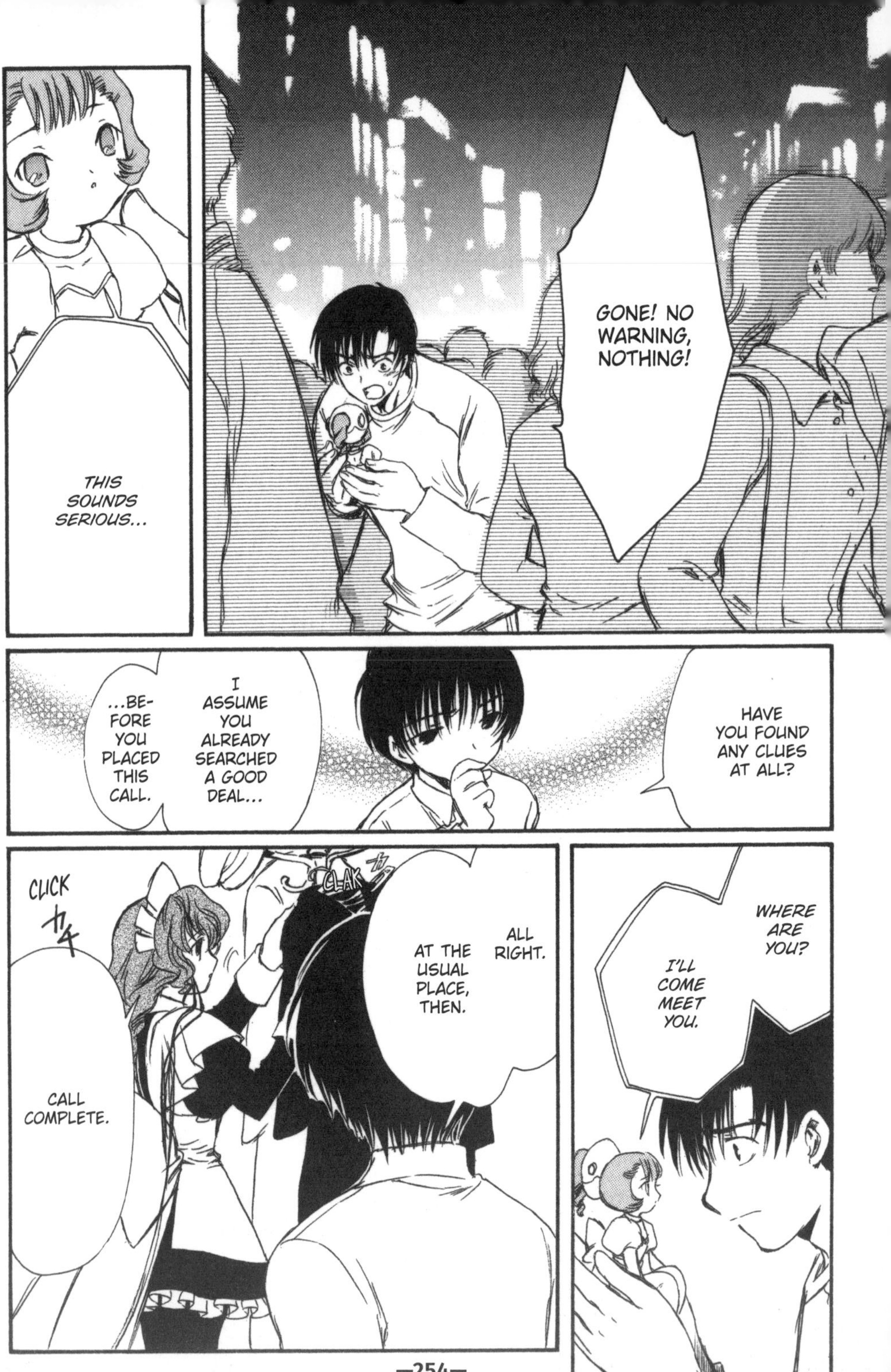
GONE! NO WARNING, NOTHING!
THIS SOUNDS SERIOUS...
HAVE YOU FOUND ANY CLUES AT ALL?
I ASSUME YOU ALREADY SEARCHED A GOOD DEAL...
...BE-FORE YOU PLACED THIS CALL.
WHERE ARE YOU?
I'LL COME MEET YOU.
CLAK
ALL RIGHT.
AT THE USUAL PLACE, THEN.
CLICK
カチ
CALL COMPLETE.

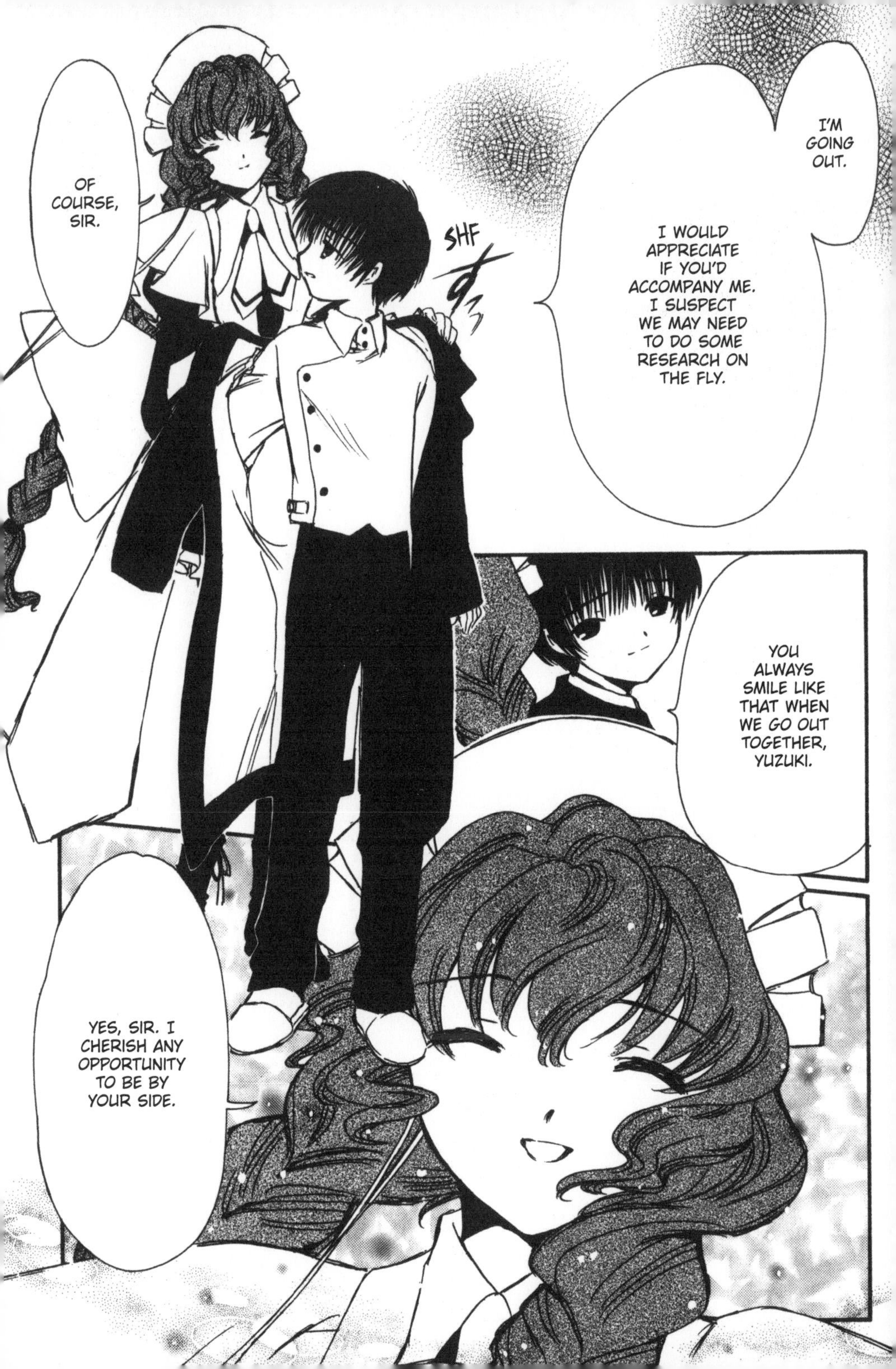
I'M GOING OUT.
I WOULD APPRECIATE IF YOU'D ACCOMPANY ME. I SUSPECT WE MAY NEED TO DO SOME RESEARCH ON THE FLY.
SHF
OF COURSE, SIR.
YOU ALWAYS SMILE LIKE THAT WHEN WE GO OUT TOGETHER, YUZUKI.
YES, SIR. I CHERISH ANY OPPORTUNITY TO BE BY YOUR SIDE.

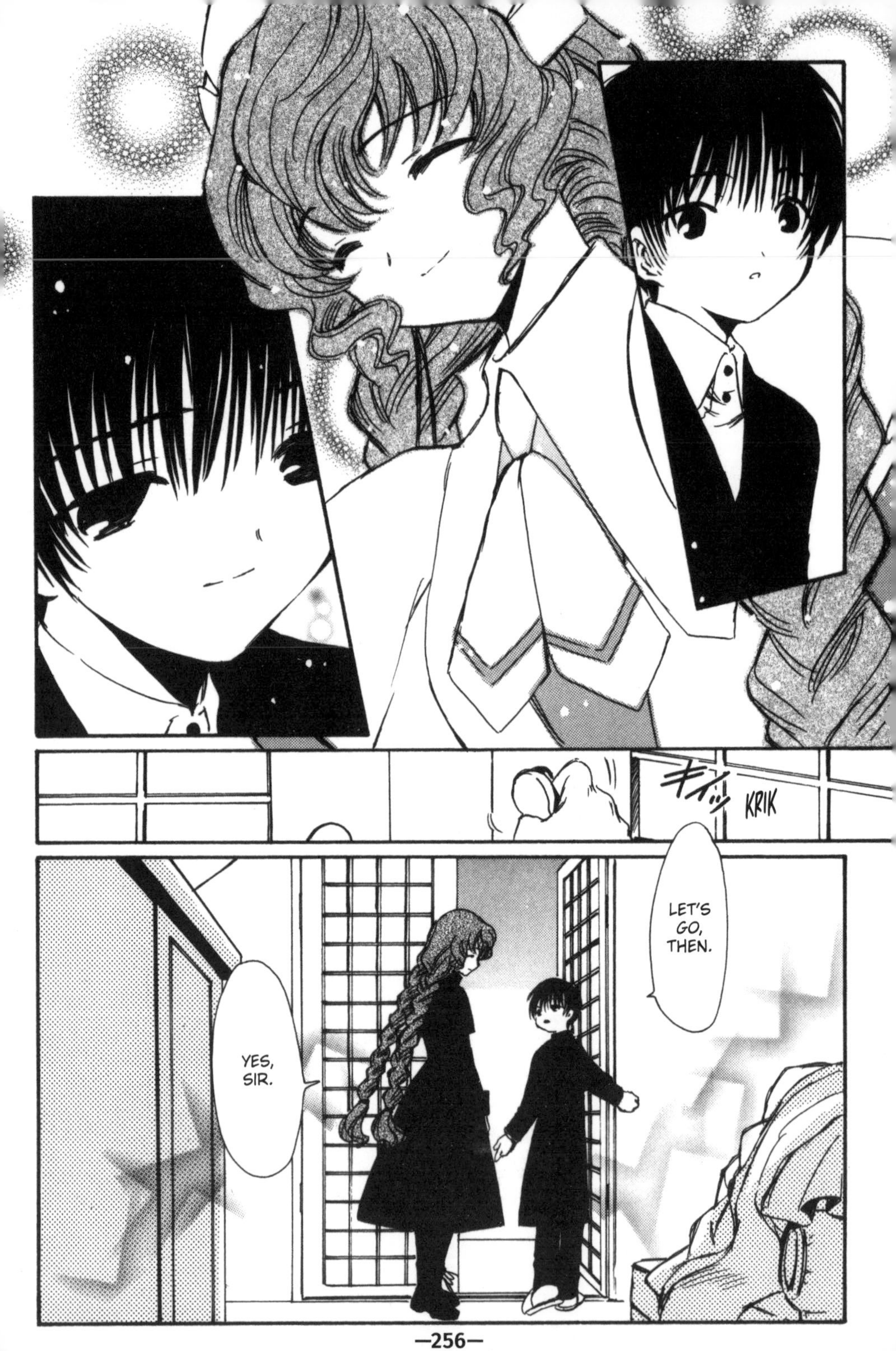
キィッ
KRIK
LET'S GO, THEN.
YES, SIR.

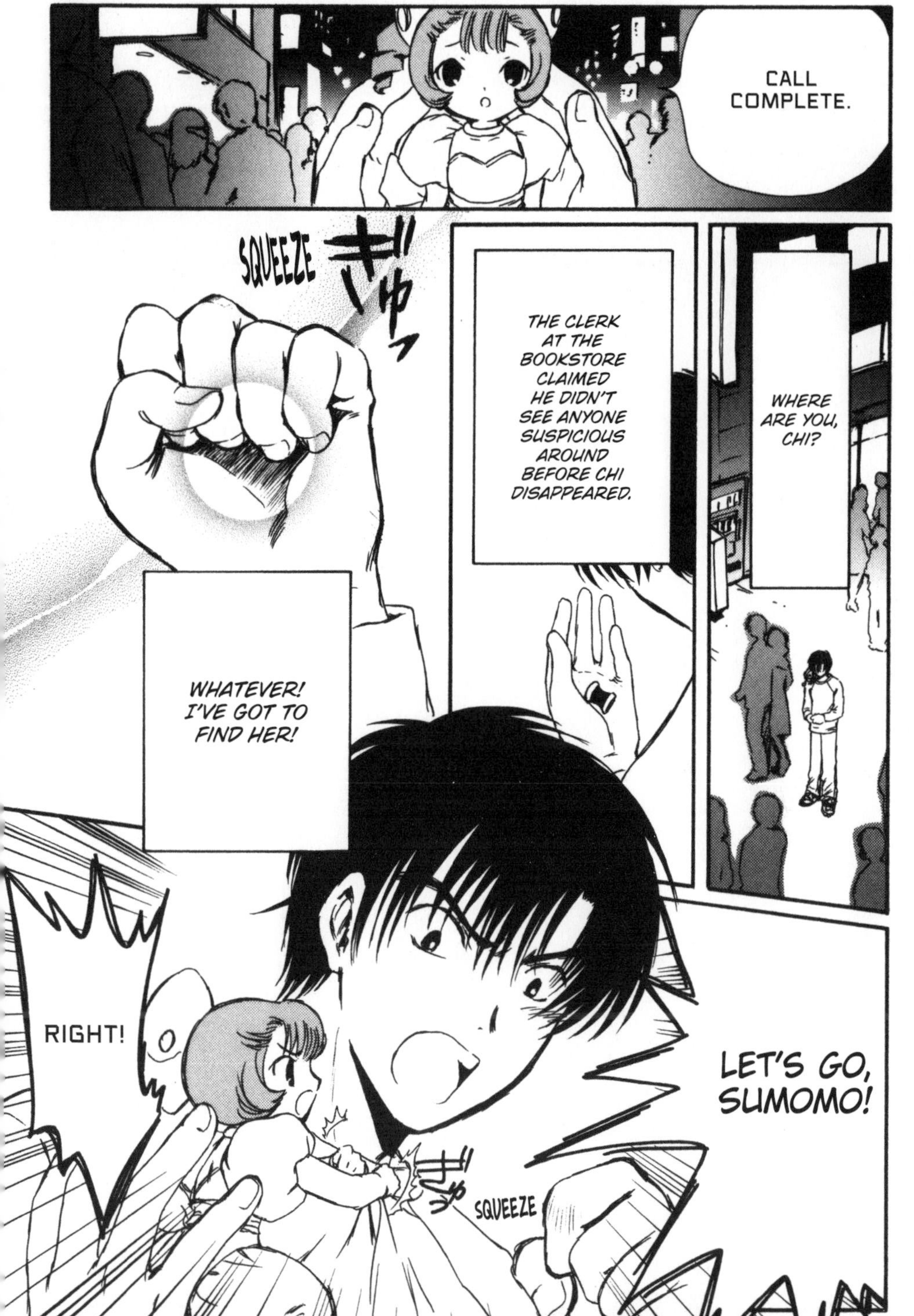
CALL COMPLETE.
WHERE ARE YOU, CHI?
THE CLERK AT THE BOOKSTORE CLAIMED HE DIDN'T SEE ANYONE SUSPICIOUS AROUND BEFORE CHI DISAPPEARED.
SQUEEZE
WHATEVER! I'VE GOT TO FIND HER!
LET'S GO, SUMOMO!
RIGHT!
SQUEEZE

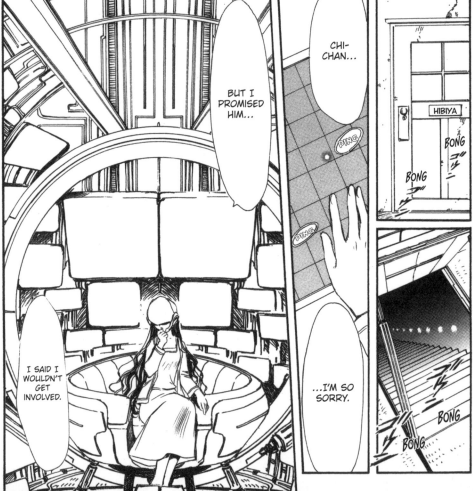

BUT I
PROMISED
HIM...

CHI-
CHAN...

PING

PING

HIBIYA

BONG

BONG

I SAID I
WOULDN'T
GET
INVOLVED.

...I'M SO
SORRY.

BONG

BONG

PULL

HUH.
DIDN'T
SEE THIS
COMING.

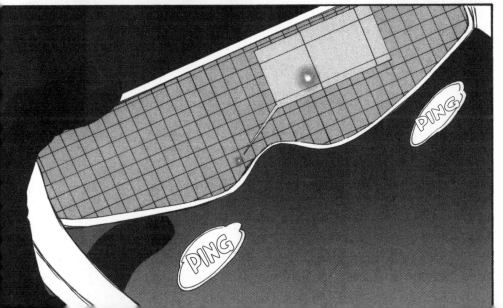

PING

PING

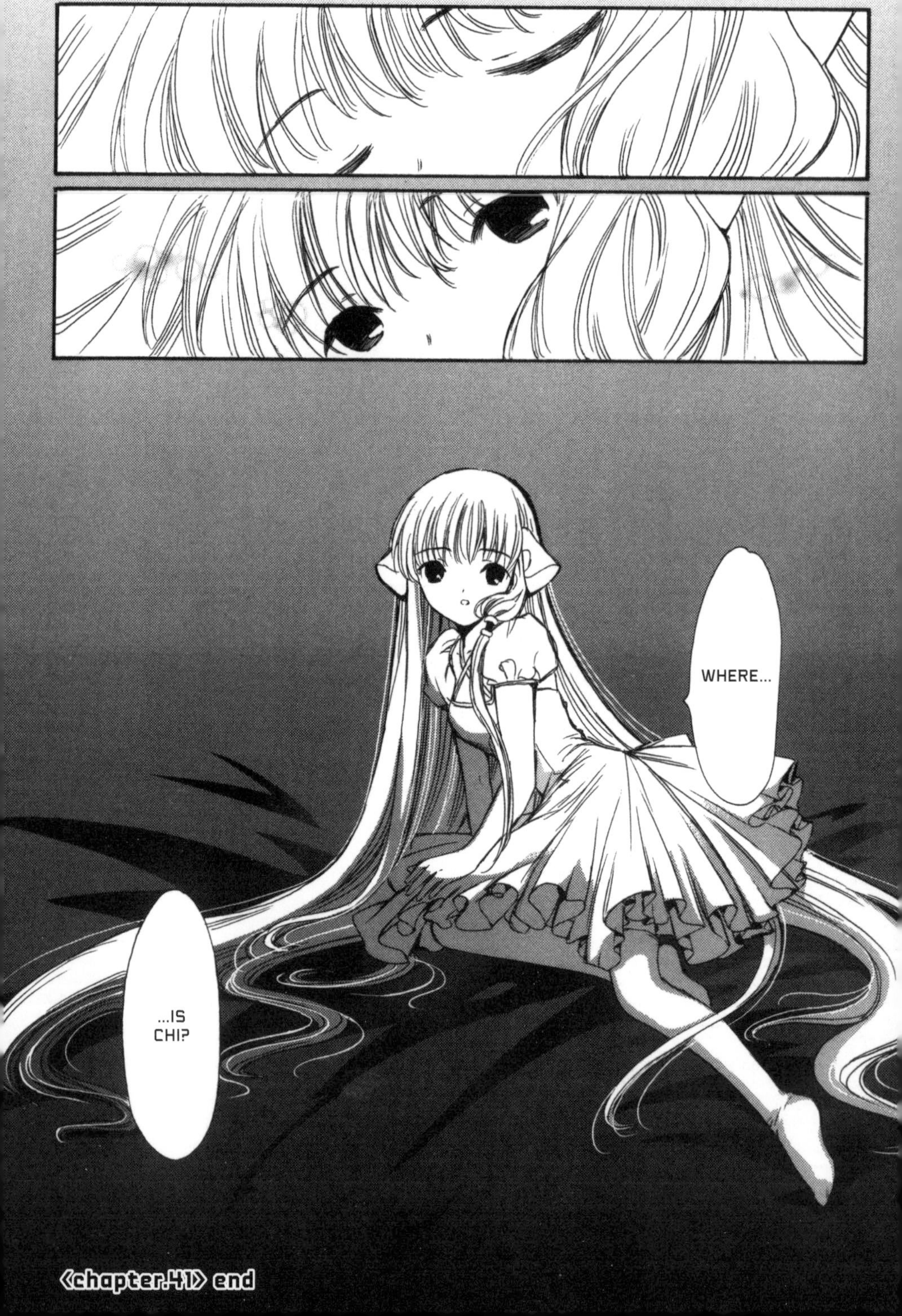
WHERE...
...IS CHI?
«chapter.41» end

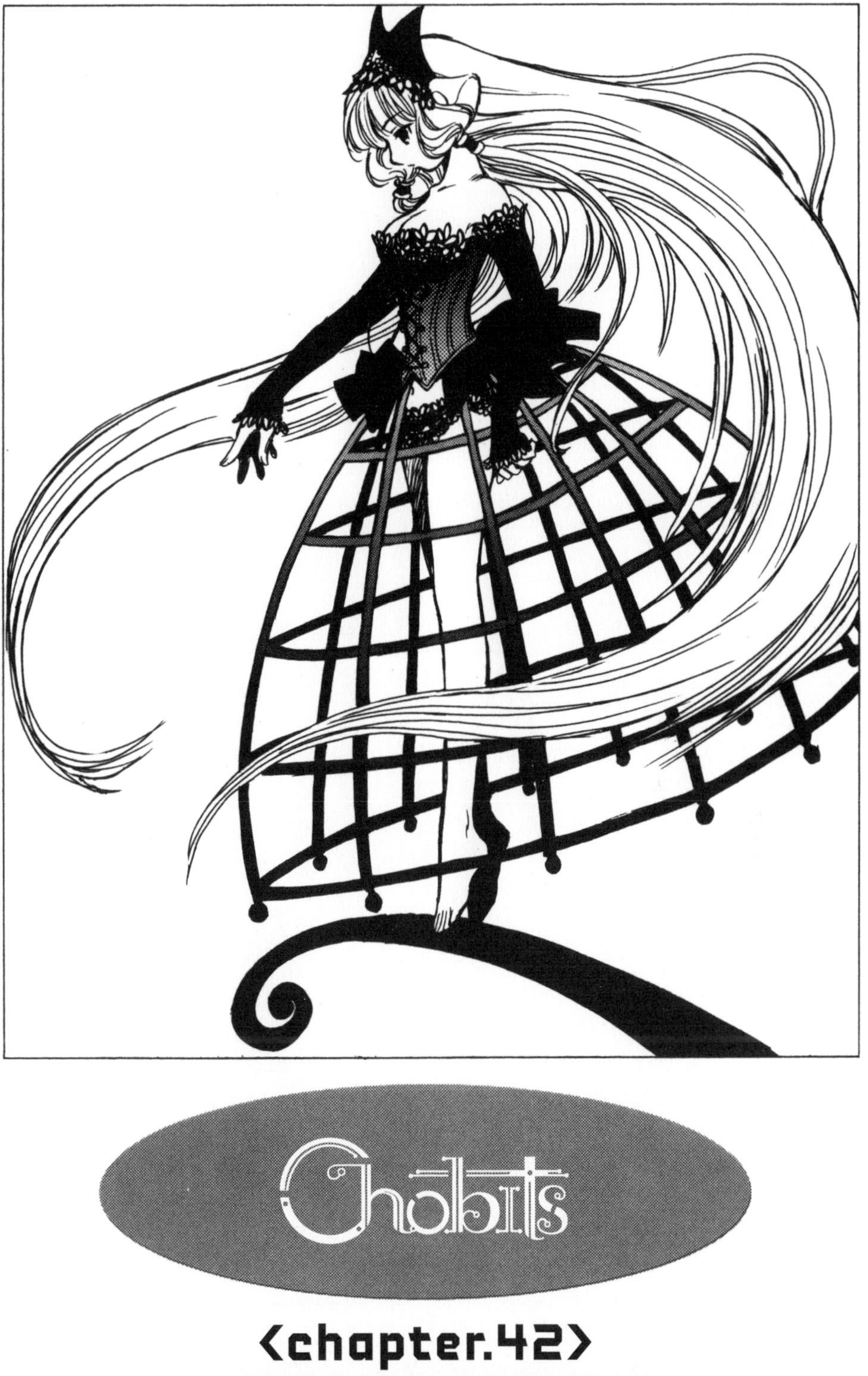

Chobits

<chapter.42>

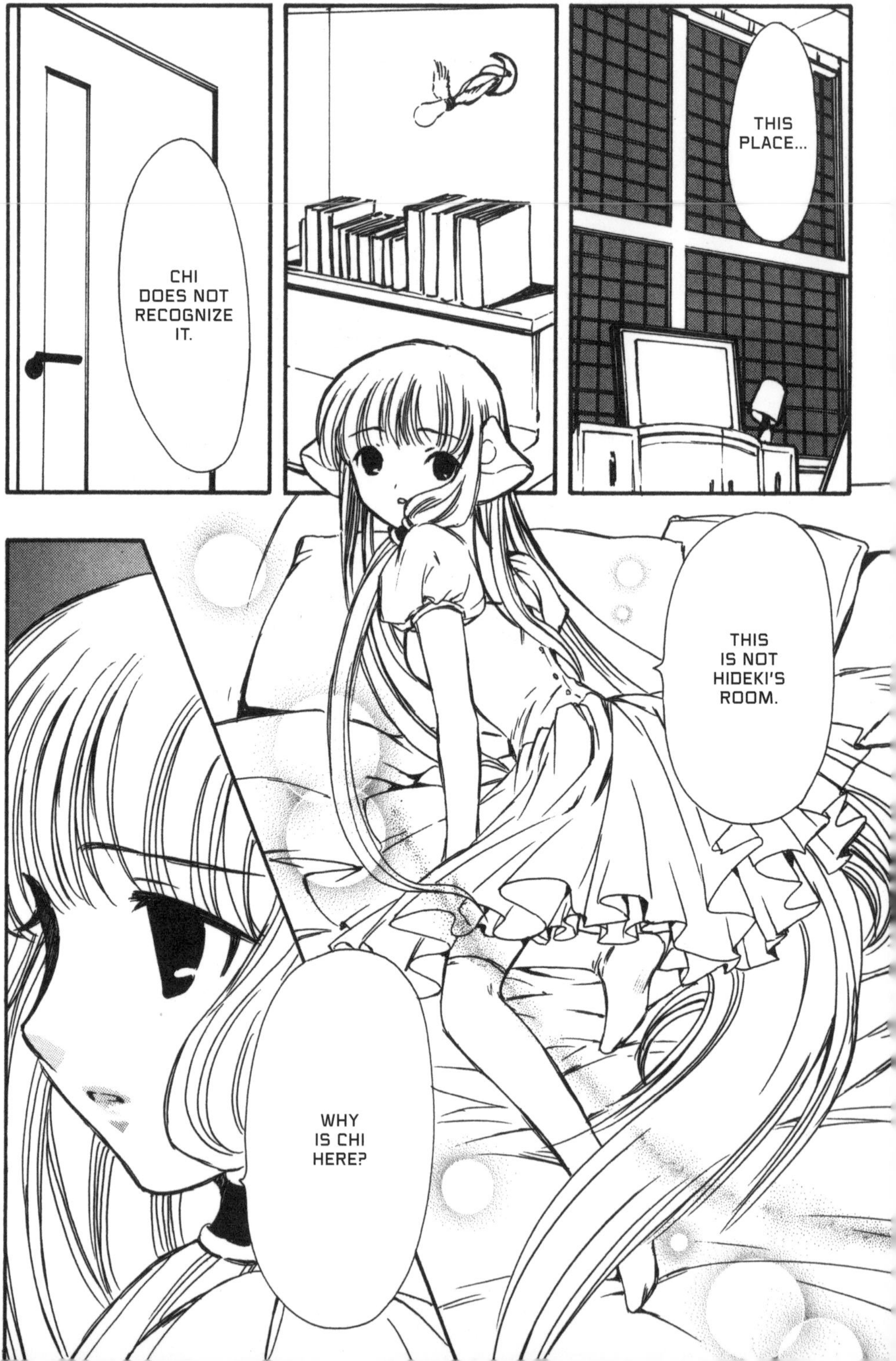
THIS PLACE...
CHI DOES NOT RECOGNIZE IT.
THIS IS NOT HIDEKI'S ROOM.
WHY IS CHI HERE?

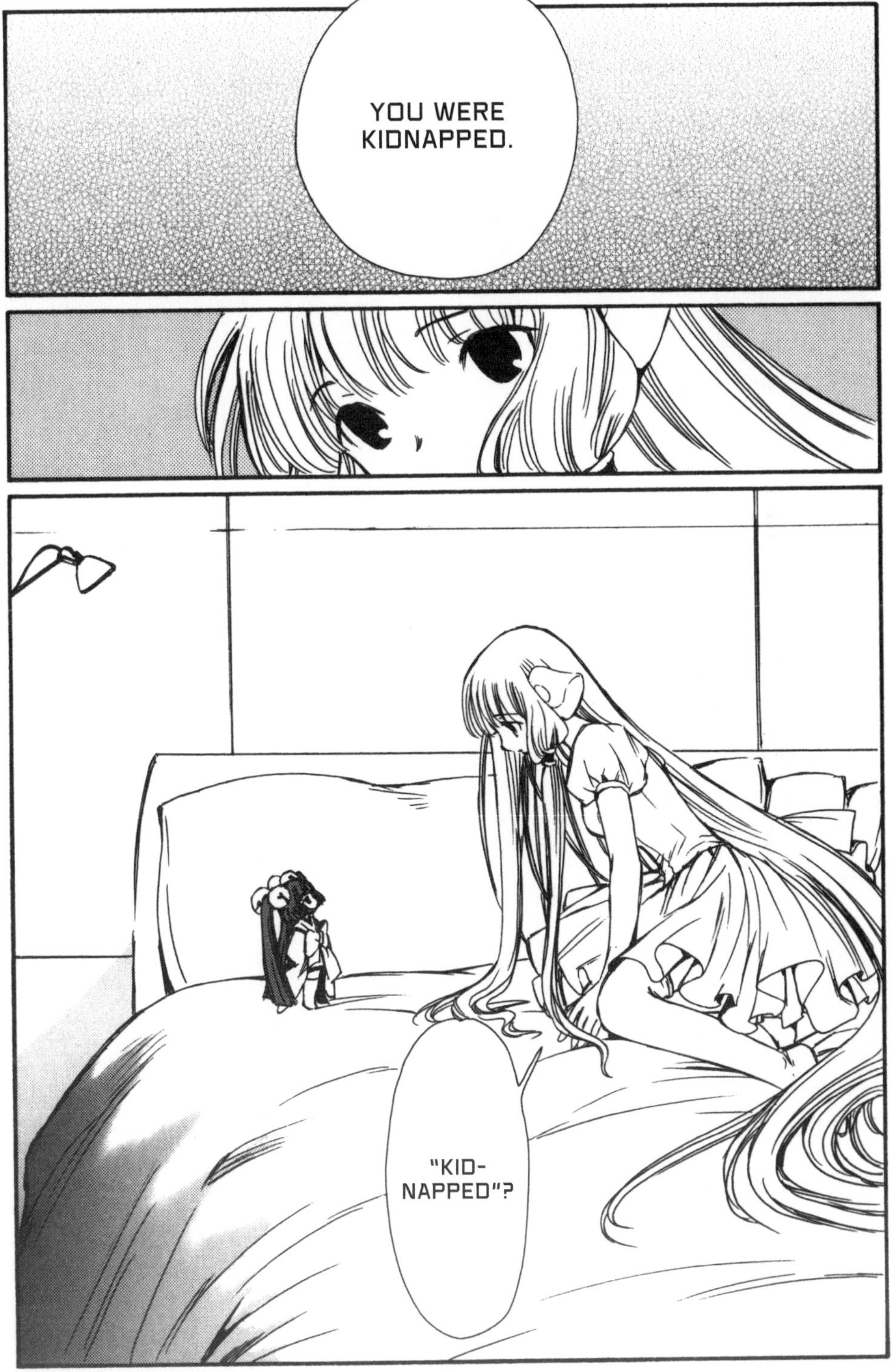
YOU WERE KIDNAPPED.
"KID-NAPPED"?

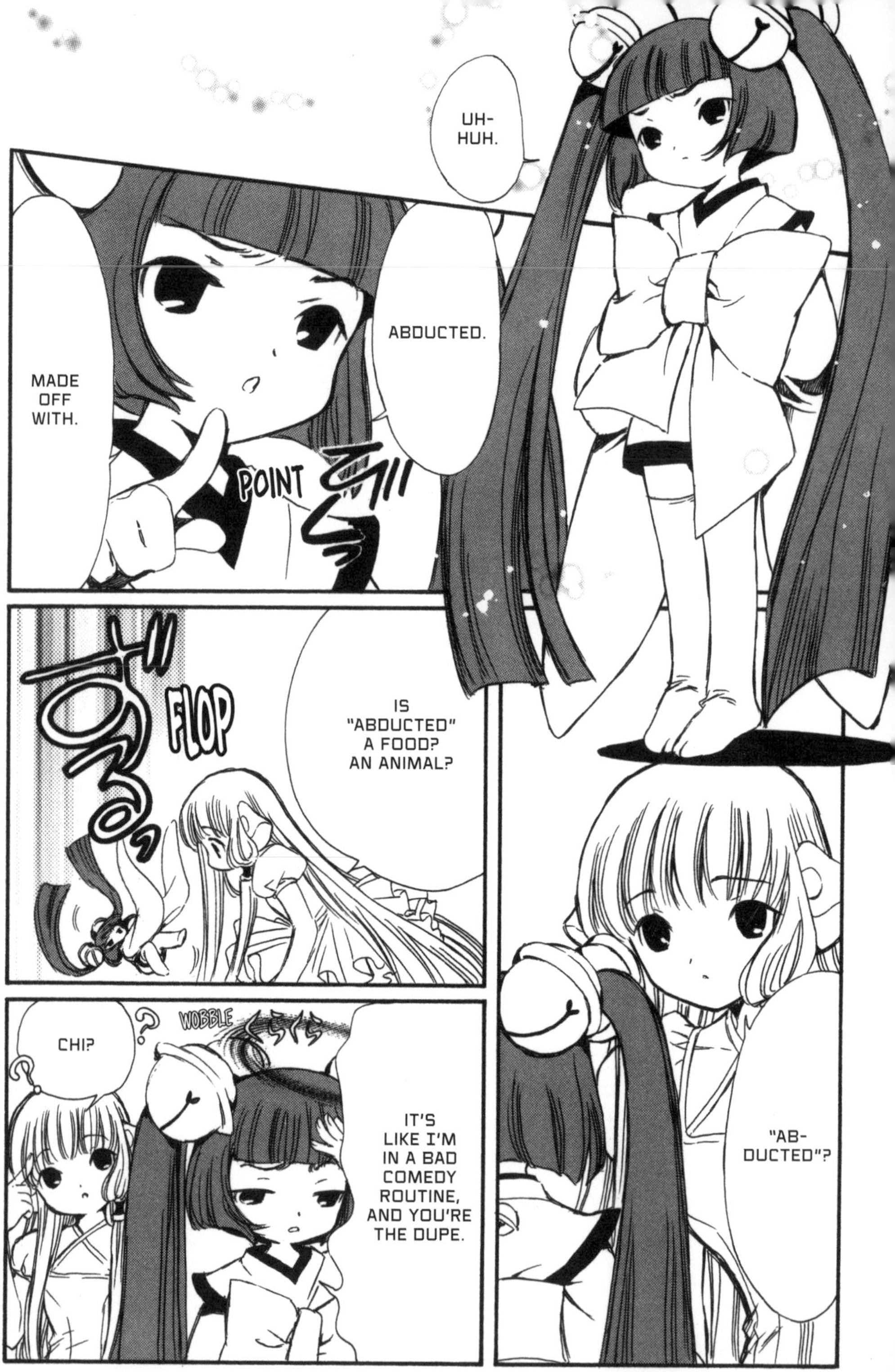
UH-
HUH.
ABDUCTED.
MADE OFF WITH.
POINT
"AB-
DUCTED"?
IS "ABDUCTED" A FOOD? AN ANIMAL?
FLOP
CHI?
WOBBLE
IT'S LIKE I'M IN A BAD COMEDY ROUTINE, AND YOU'RE THE DUPE.

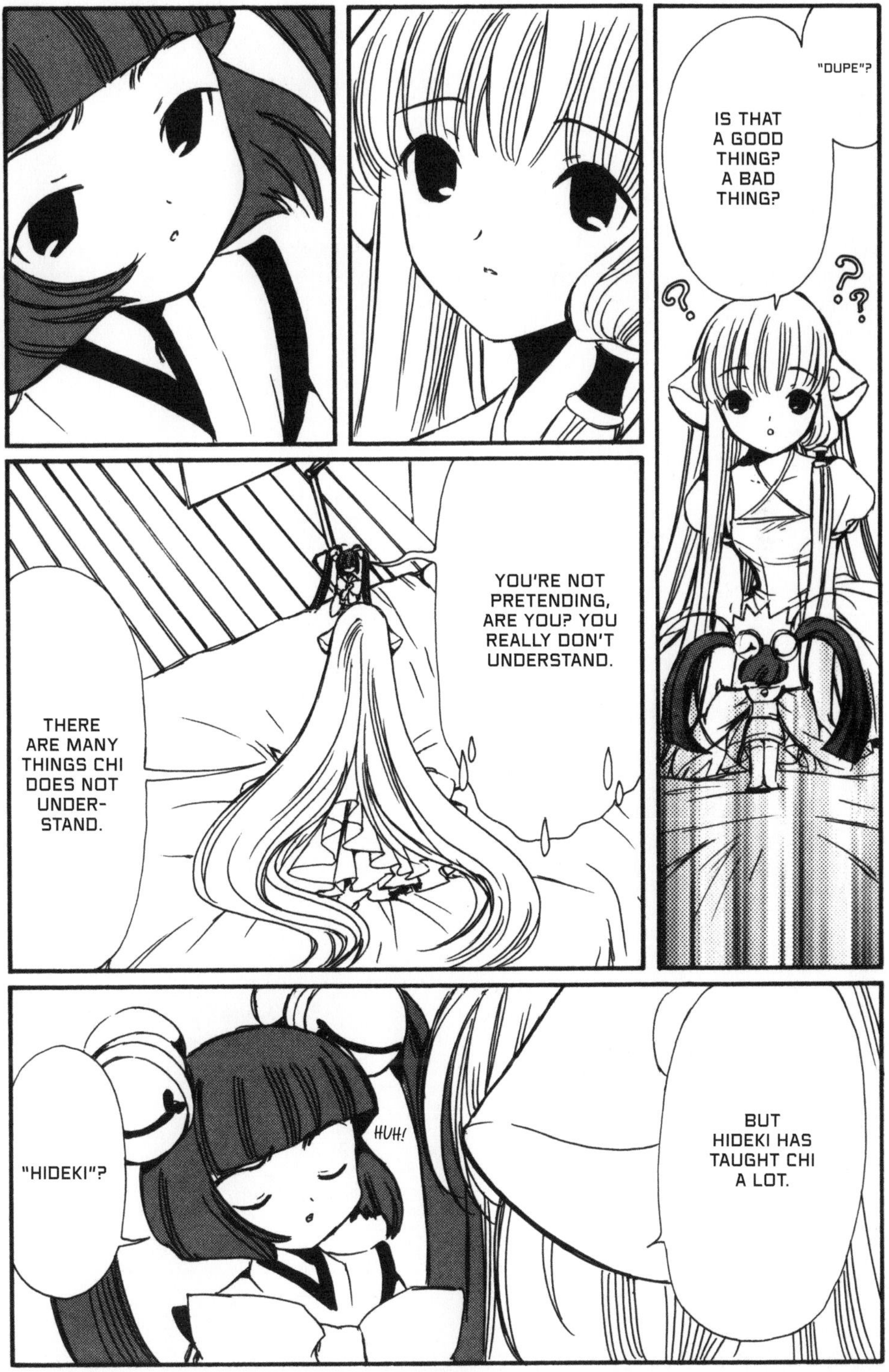
"DUPE"?
IS THAT A GOOD THING? A BAD THING?
YOU'RE NOT PRETENDING, ARE YOU? YOU REALLY DON'T UNDERSTAND.
THERE ARE MANY THINGS CHI DOES NOT UNDER-STAND.
BUT HIDEKI HAS TAUGHT CHI A LOT.
HUH!
"HIDEKI"?

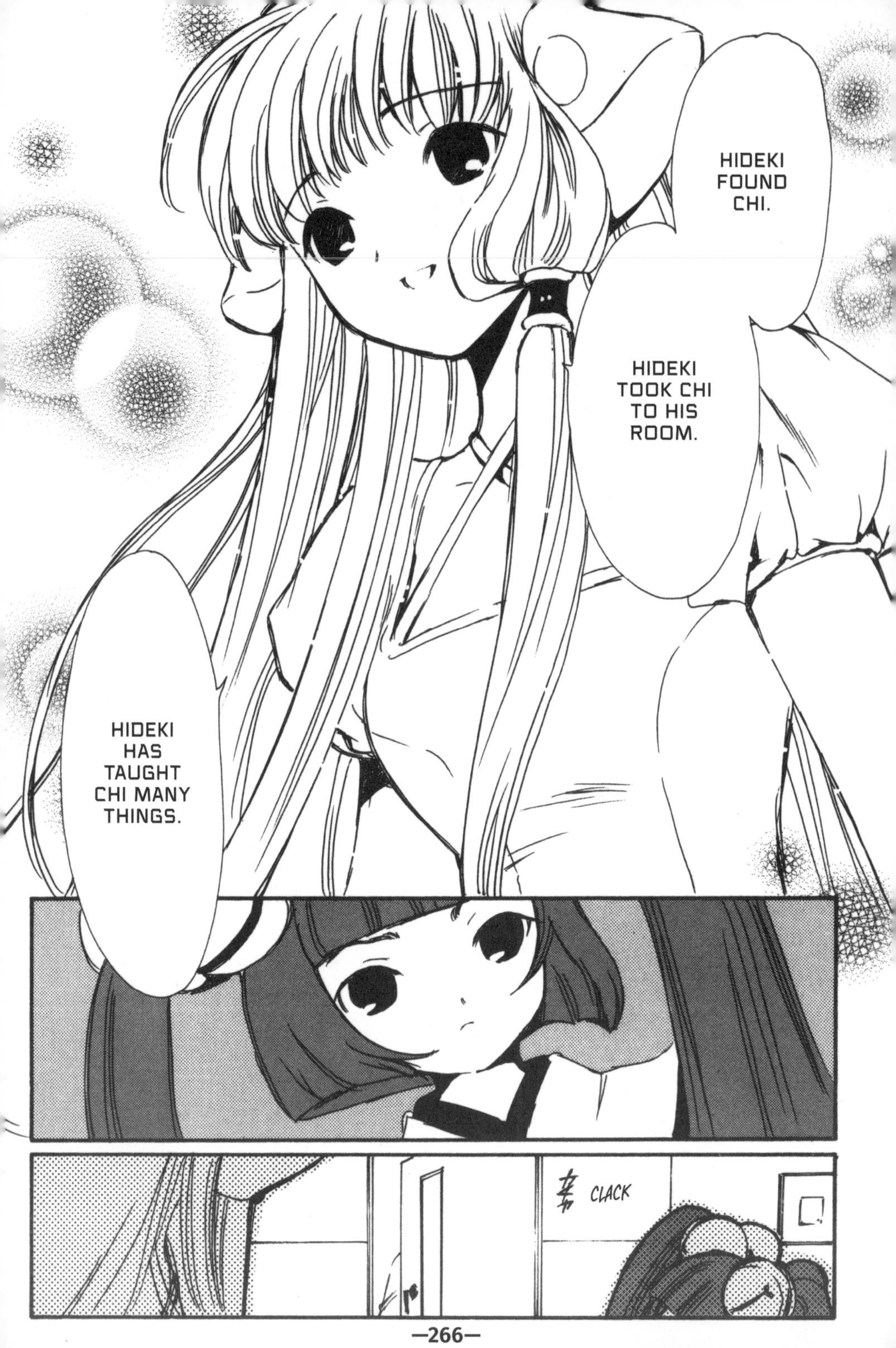
HIDEKI FOUND CHI.
HIDEKI TOOK CHI TO HIS ROOM.
HIDEKI HAS TAUGHT CHI MANY THINGS.
CLACK

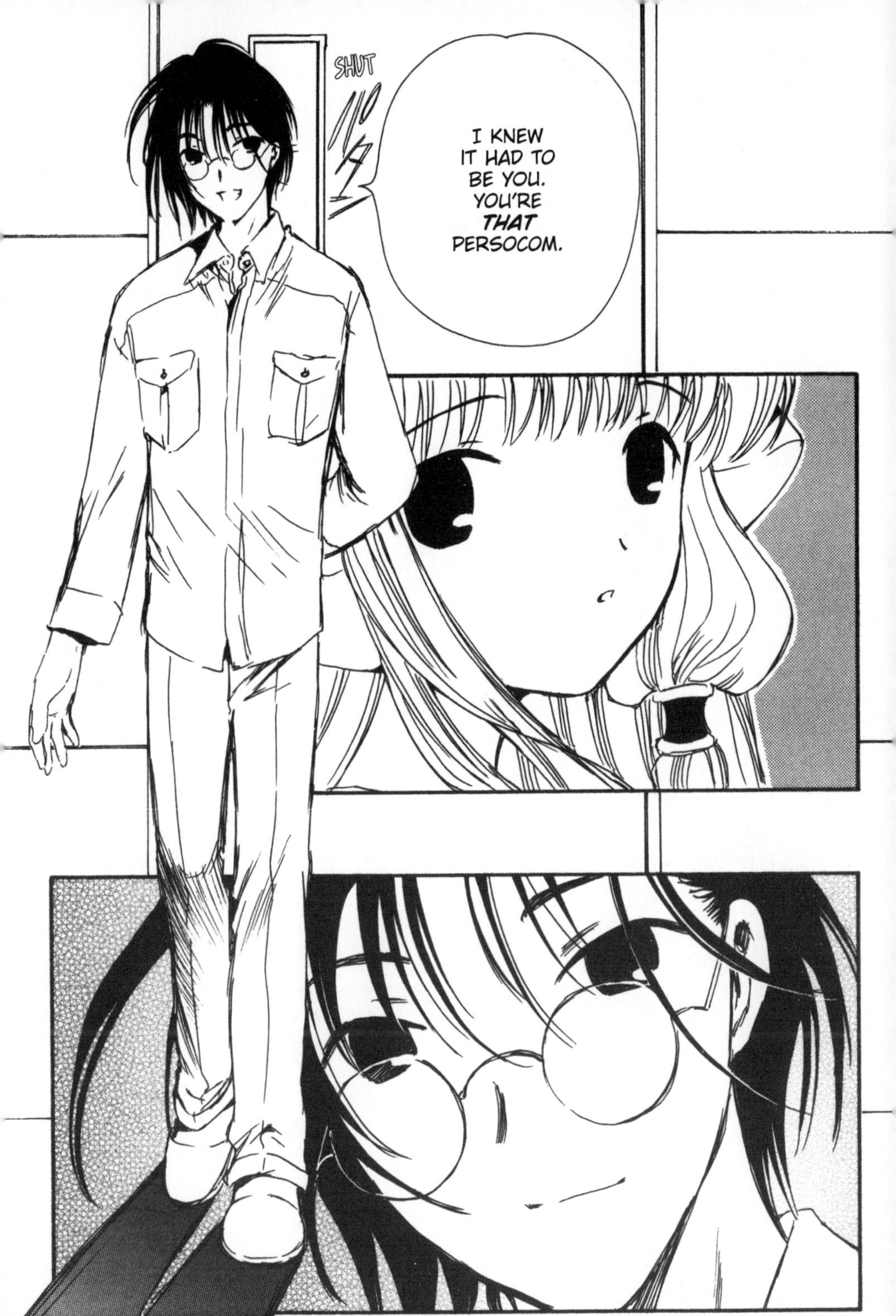
SHUT
I KNEW IT HAD TO BE YOU. YOU'RE THAT PERSOCOM.

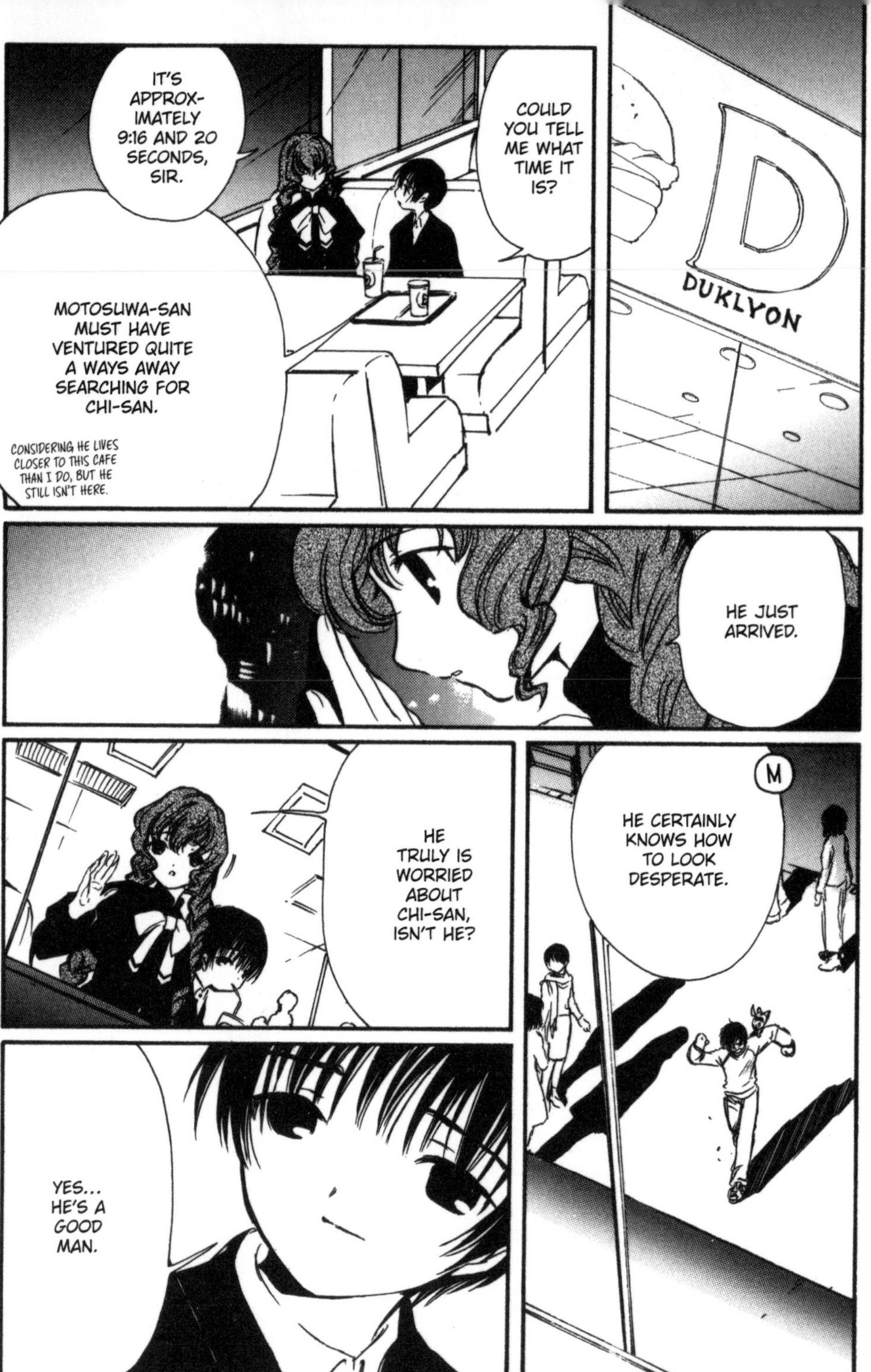
DUKLYON
COULD YOU TELL ME WHAT TIME IT IS?
IT'S APPROXIMATELY 9:16 AND 20 SECONDS, SIR.
MOTOSUWA-SAN MUST HAVE VENTURED QUITE A WAYS AWAY SEARCHING FOR CHI-SAN.
CONSIDERING HE LIVES CLOSER TO THIS CAFE THAN I DO, BUT HE STILL ISN'T HERE.
HE JUST ARRIVED.
M
HE CERTAINLY KNOWS HOW TO LOOK DESPERATE.
HE TRULY IS WORRIED ABOUT CHI-SAN, ISN'T HE?
YES... HE'S A GOOD MAN.

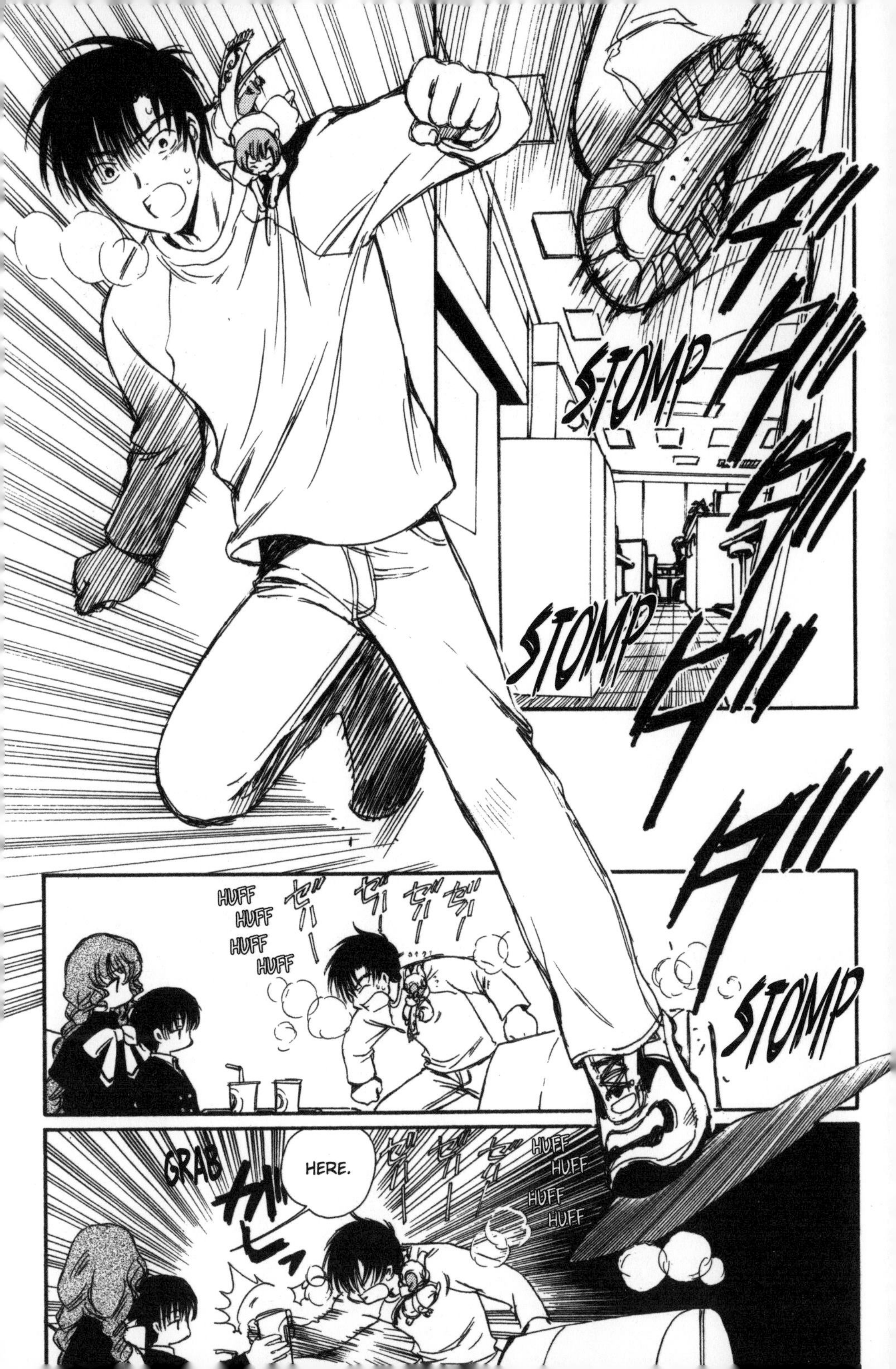
STOMP
STOMP
STOMP
HUFF
HUFF
HUFF
HUFF
HUFF
HUFF
HUFF
HUFF
HERE.
GRAB

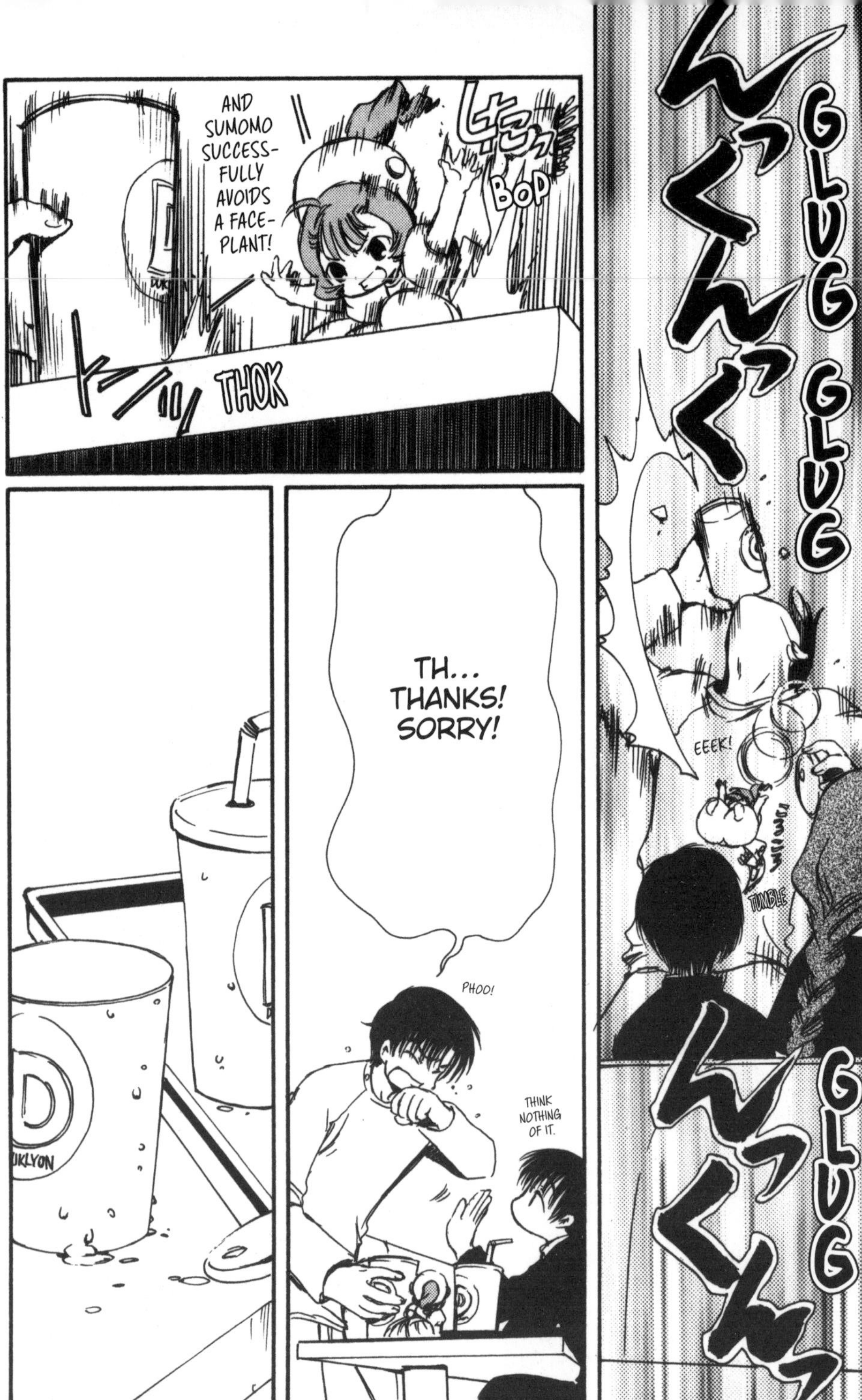
GLUG GLUG GLUG
EEEK!
TUMBLE
GLUG
AND SUMOMO SUCCESSFULLY AVOIDS A FACE-PLANT!
BOP
THOK
TH... THANKS! SORRY!
PHOO!
THINK NOTHING OF IT.

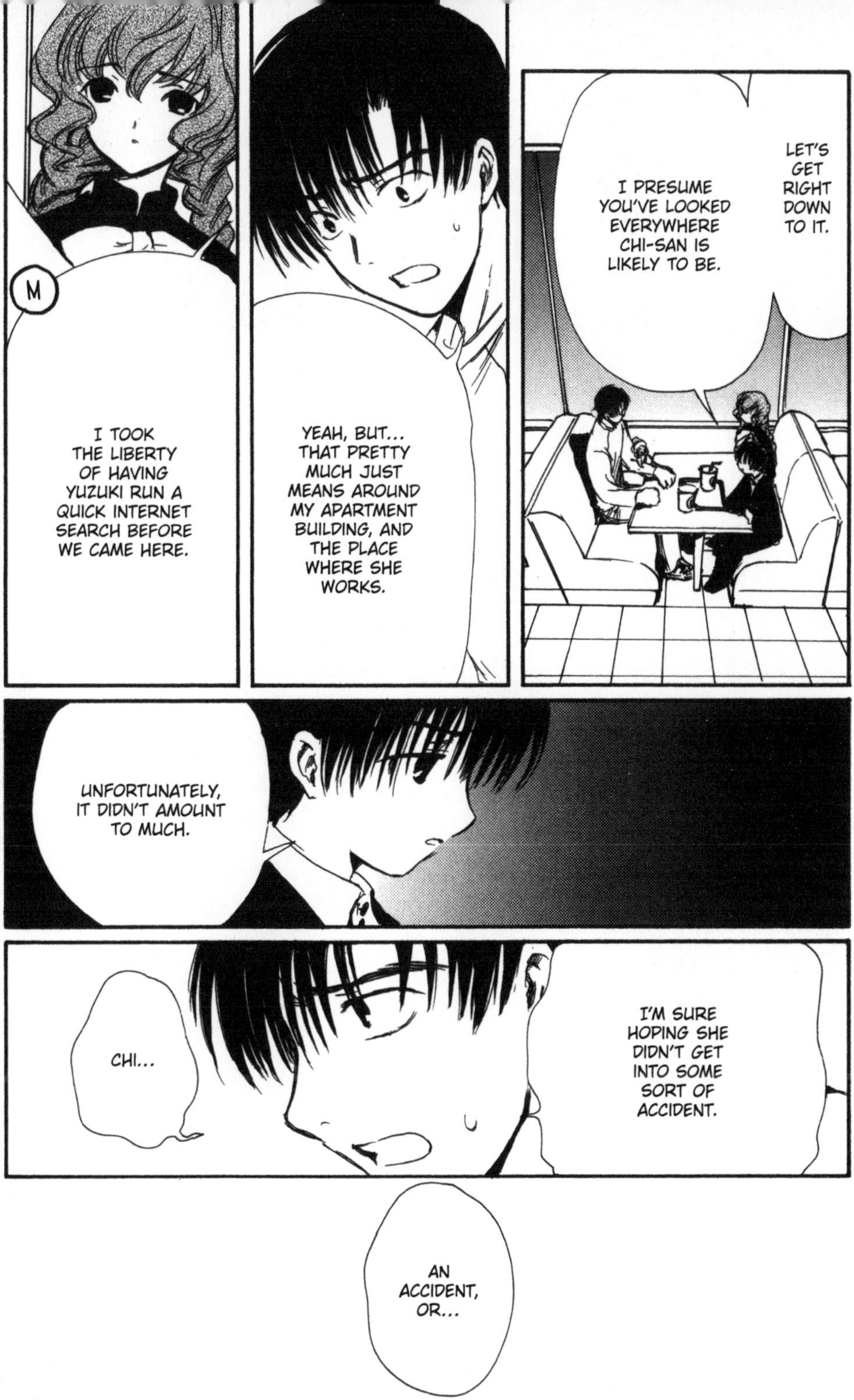
LET'S GET RIGHT DOWN TO IT.
I PRESUME YOU'VE LOOKED EVERYWHERE CHI-SAN IS LIKELY TO BE.
YEAH, BUT... THAT PRETTY MUCH JUST MEANS AROUND MY APARTMENT BUILDING, AND THE PLACE WHERE SHE WORKS.
M
I TOOK THE LIBERTY OF HAVING YUZUKI RUN A QUICK INTERNET SEARCH BEFORE WE CAME HERE.
UNFORTUNATELY, IT DIDN'T AMOUNT TO MUCH.
I'M SURE HOPING SHE DIDN'T GET INTO SOME SORT OF ACCIDENT.
CHI...
AN ACCIDENT, OR...

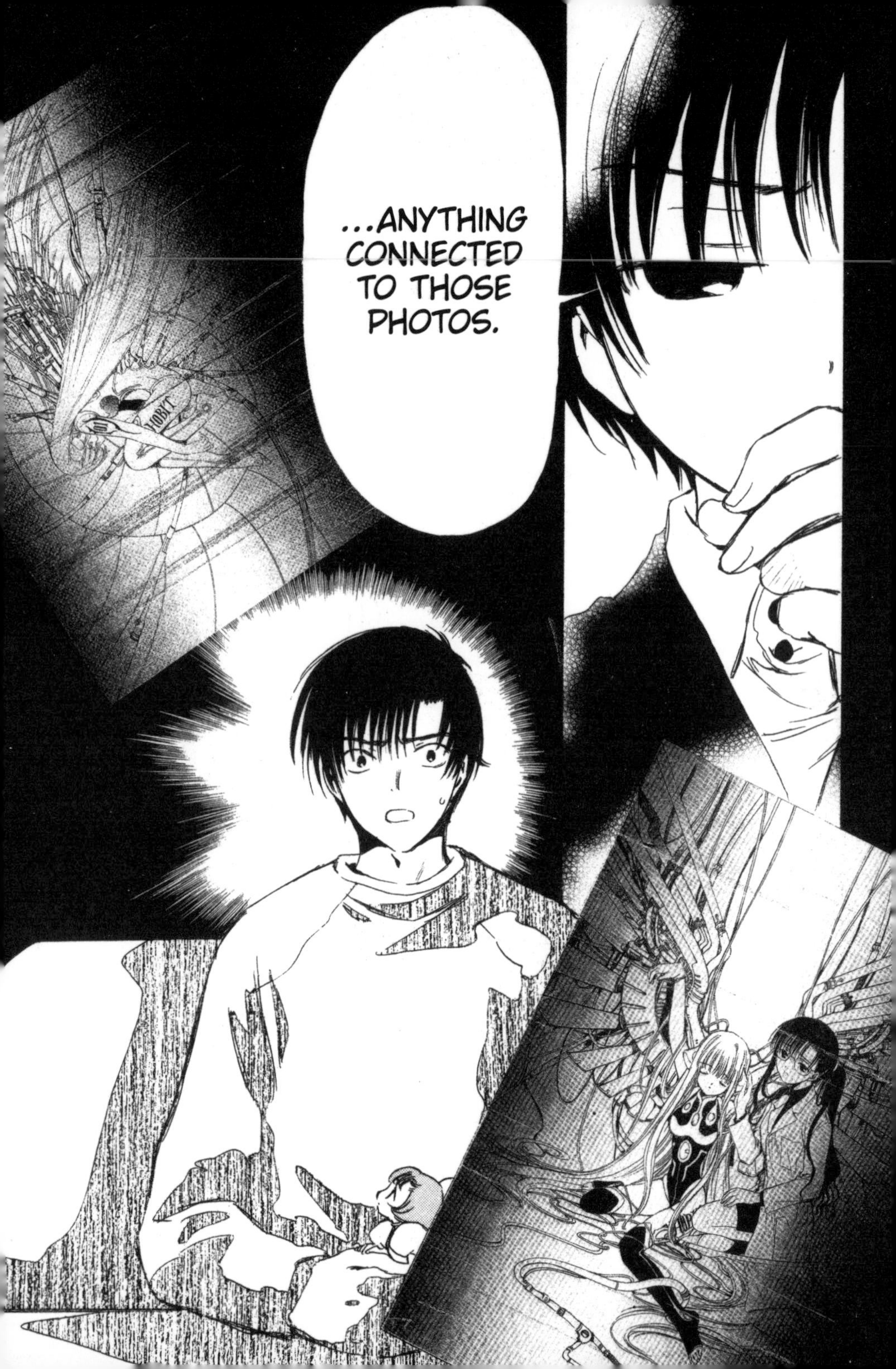
...ANYTHING CONNECTED TO THOSE PHOTOS.

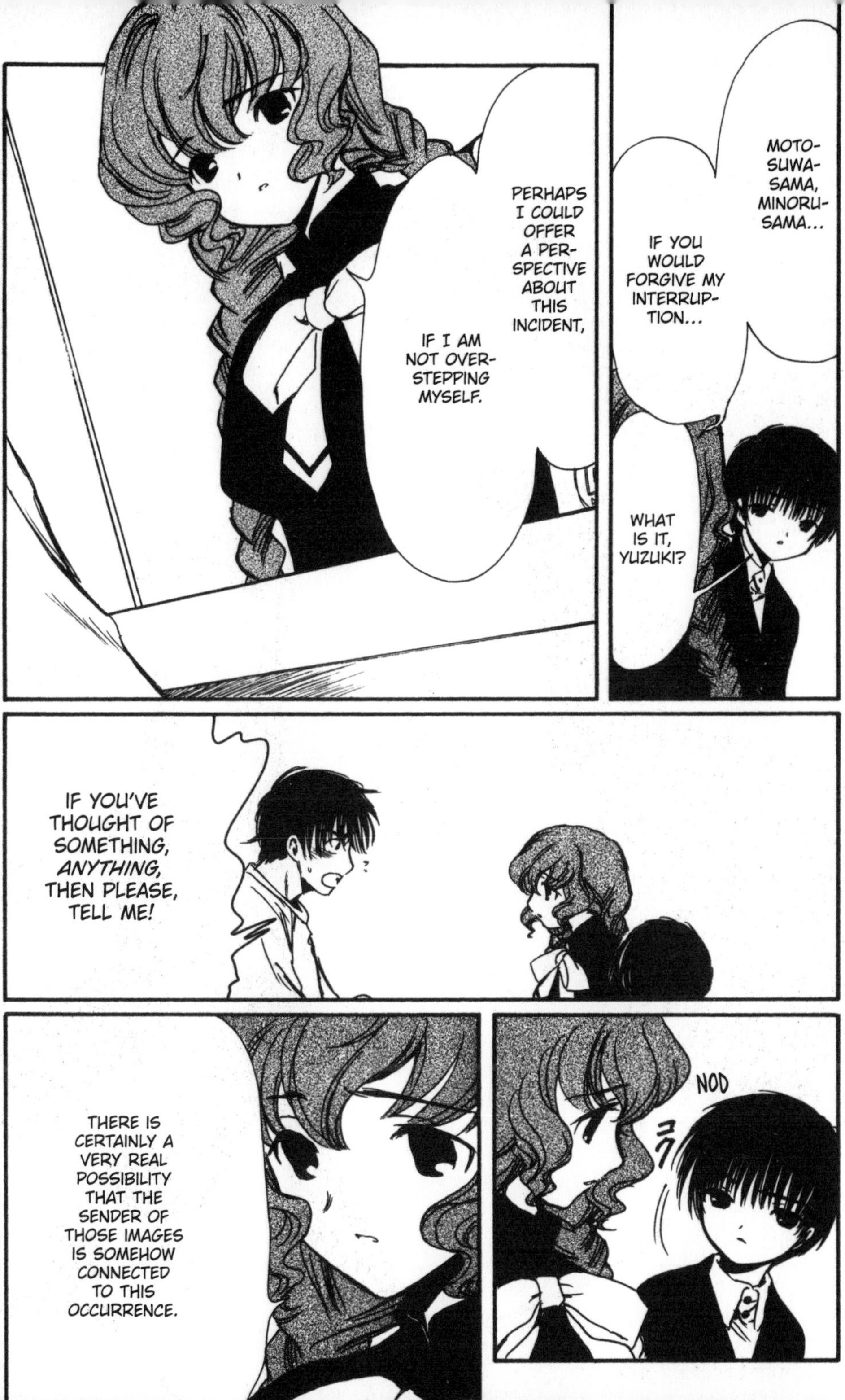
MOTO-SUWA-SAMA, MINORU-SAMA…
IF YOU WOULD FORGIVE MY INTERRUP-TION…
WHAT IS IT, YUZUKI?
PERHAPS I COULD OFFER A PER-SPECTIVE ABOUT THIS INCIDENT,
IF I AM NOT OVER-STEPPING MYSELF.
IF YOU'VE THOUGHT OF SOMETHING, *ANYTHING*, THEN PLEASE, TELL ME!
NOD
THERE IS CERTAINLY A VERY REAL POSSIBILITY THAT THE SENDER OF THOSE IMAGES IS SOMEHOW CONNECTED TO THIS OCCURRENCE.

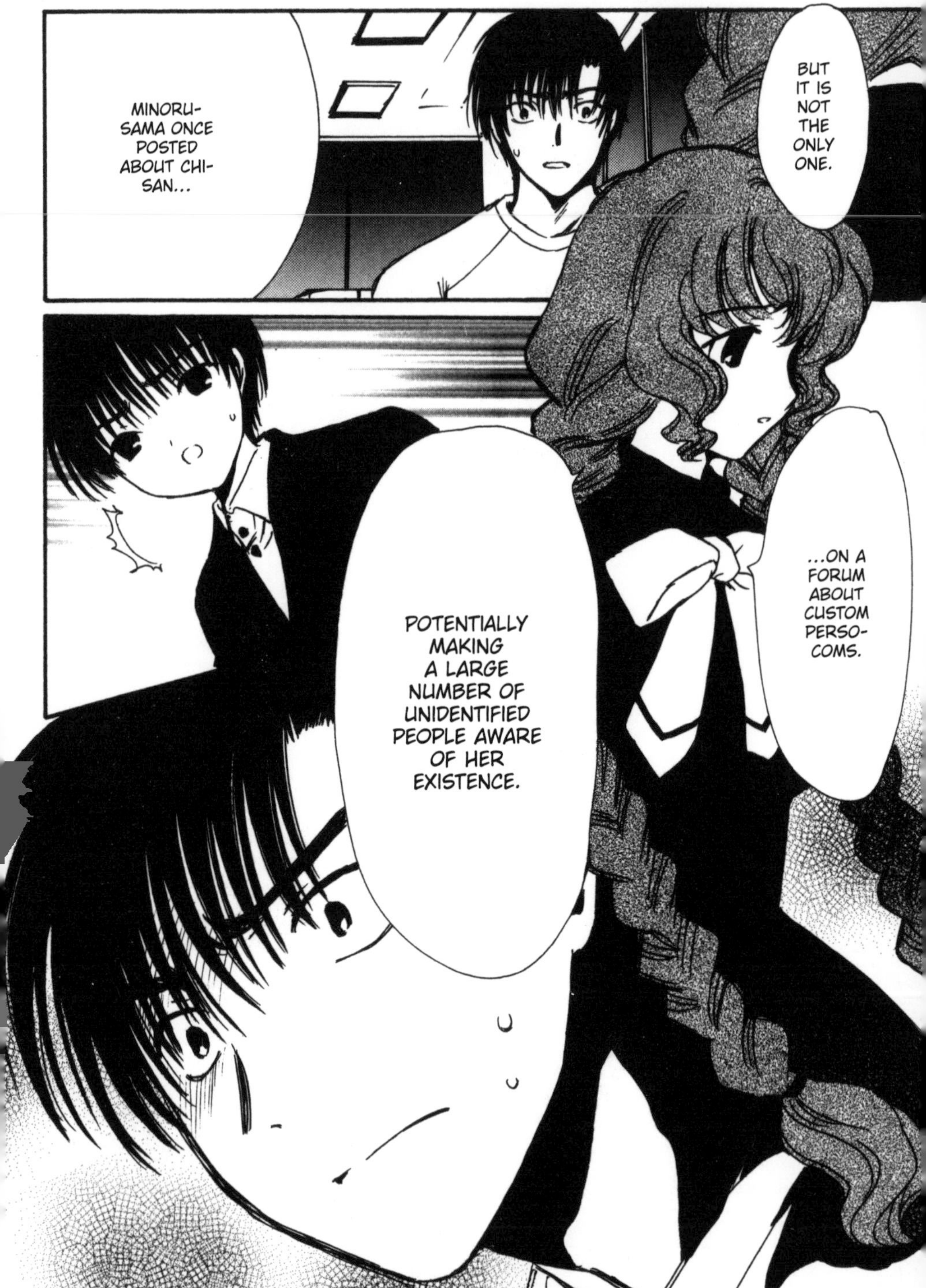
BUT IT IS NOT THE ONLY ONE.
MINORU-SAMA ONCE POSTED ABOUT CHI-SAN...
...ON A FORUM ABOUT CUSTOM PERSO-COMS.
POTENTIALLY MAKING A LARGE NUMBER OF UNIDENTIFIED PEOPLE AWARE OF HER EXISTENCE.

<chapter.42> end

Chobits

⟨chapter.43⟩

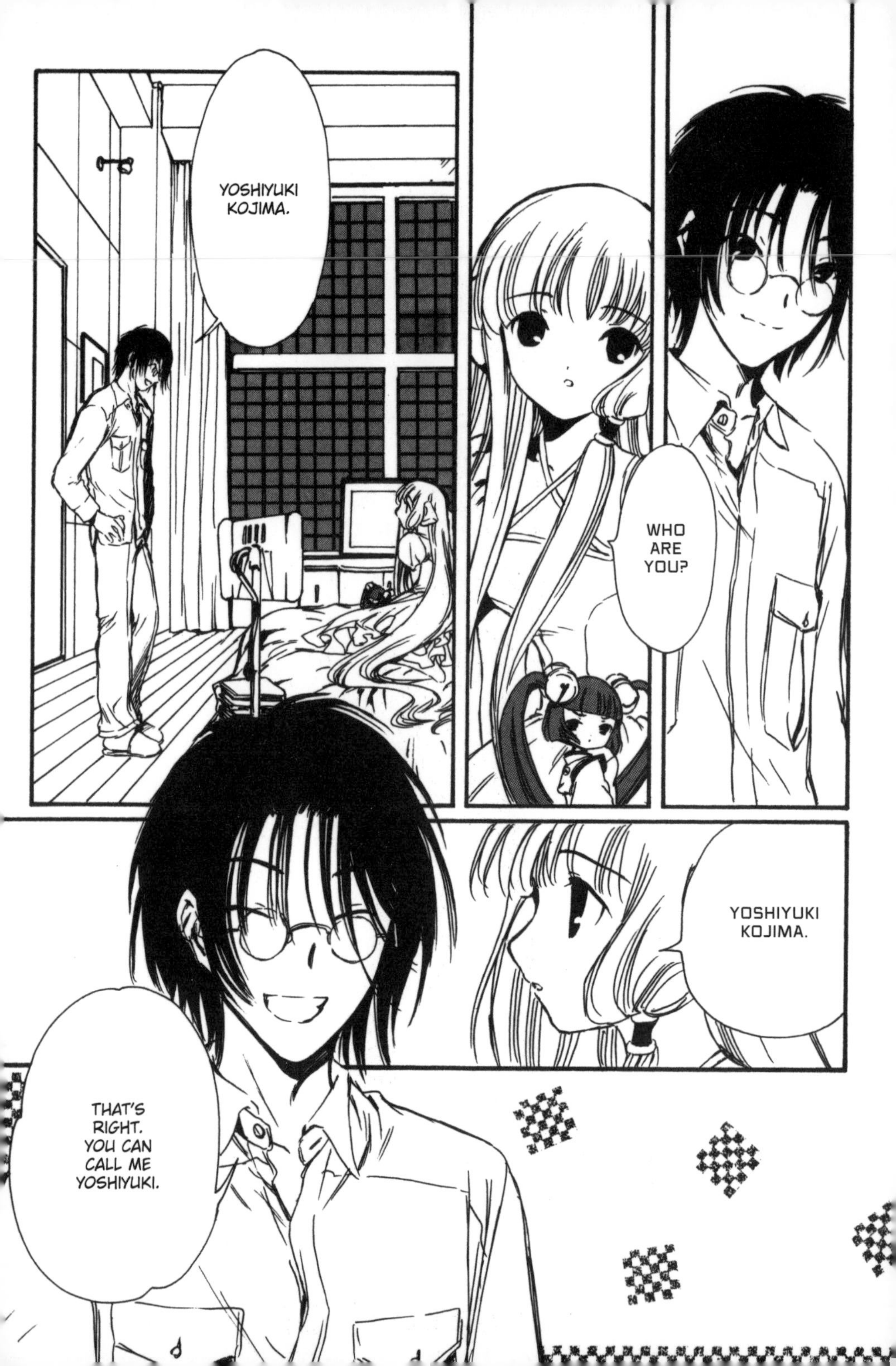
WHO ARE YOU?
YOSHIYUKI KOJIMA.
YOSHIYUKI KOJIMA.
THAT'S RIGHT. YOU CAN CALL ME YOSHIYUKI.

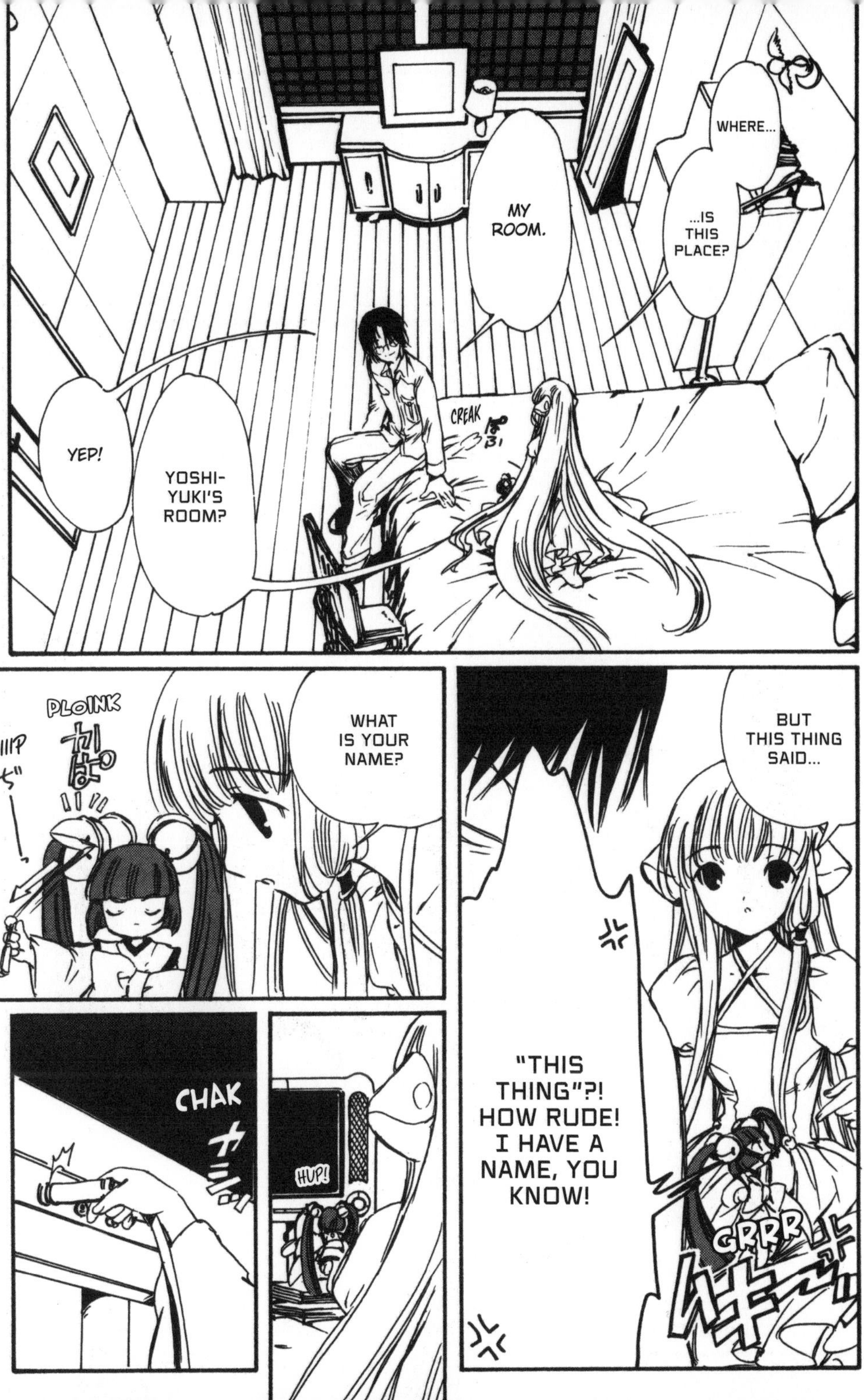
WHERE...
...IS THIS PLACE?
MY ROOM.
CREAK
YOSHI-YUKI'S ROOM?
YEP!
BUT THIS THING SAID...
"THIS THING"?! HOW RUDE! I HAVE A NAME, YOU KNOW!
GRRR
WHAT IS YOUR NAME?
PLOINK
ZIIIIP
HUP!
CHAK

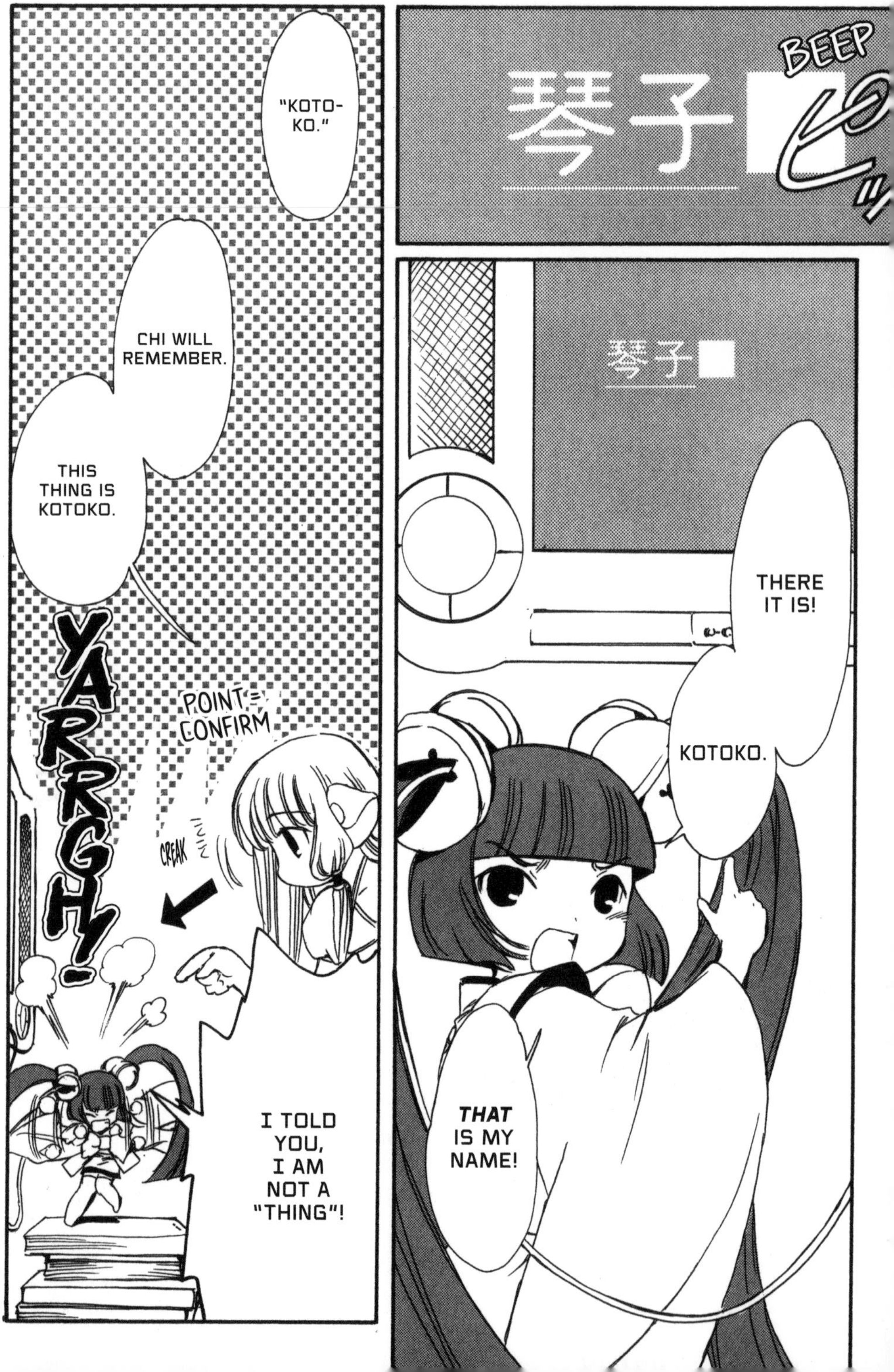
琴子■
BEEP
ピッ
琴子■
THERE IT IS!
KOTOKO.
THAT IS MY NAME!
"KOTO-KO."
CHI WILL REMEMBER.
THIS THING IS KOTOKO.
YARRGH!
POINT CONFIRM
CREAK
I TOLD YOU, I AM NOT A "THING"!

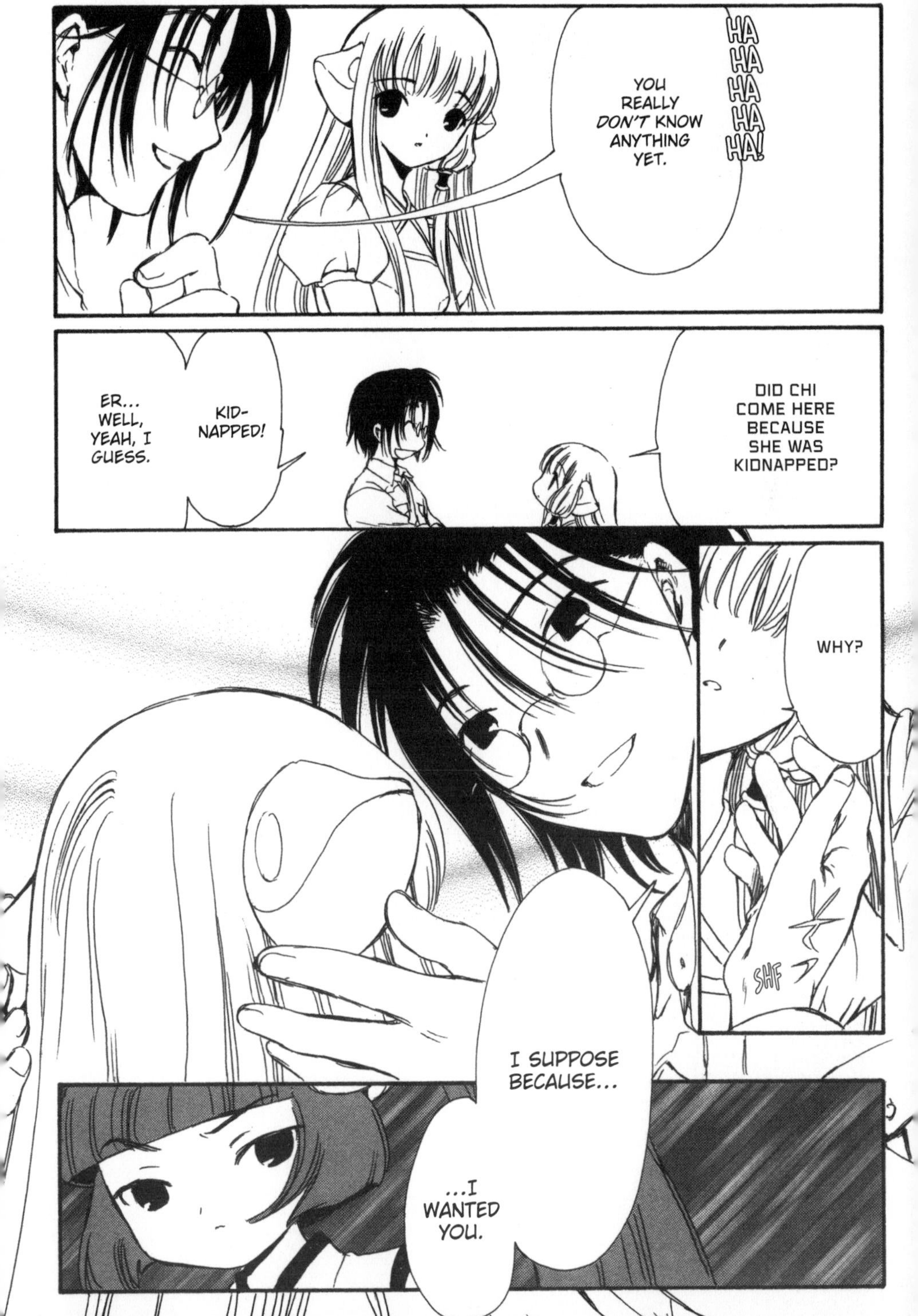
HA HA HA HA HA!
YOU REALLY *DON'T* KNOW ANYTHING YET.
DID CHI COME HERE BECAUSE SHE WAS KIDNAPPED?
KID-NAPPED!
ER... WELL, YEAH, I GUESS.
WHY?
SHF
I SUPPOSE BECAUSE...
...I WANTED YOU.

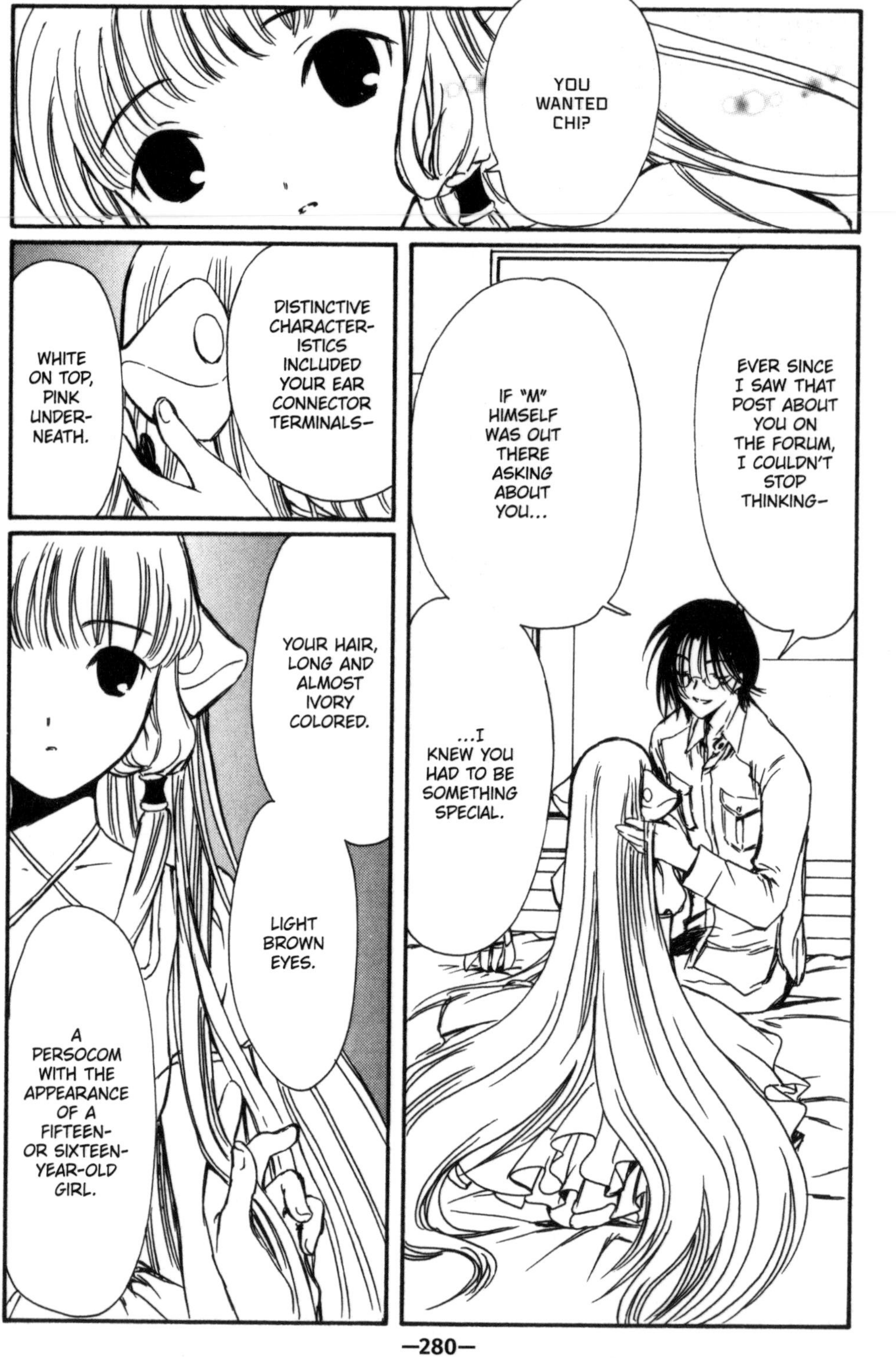
YOU WANTED CHI?
EVER SINCE I SAW THAT POST ABOUT YOU ON THE FORUM, I COULDN'T STOP THINKING–
IF "M" HIMSELF WAS OUT THERE ASKING ABOUT YOU...
...I KNEW YOU HAD TO BE SOMETHING SPECIAL.
DISTINCTIVE CHARACTER-ISTICS INCLUDED YOUR EAR CONNECTOR TERMINALS–
WHITE ON TOP, PINK UNDER-NEATH.
YOUR HAIR, LONG AND ALMOST IVORY COLORED.
LIGHT BROWN EYES.
A PERSOCOM WITH THE APPEARANCE OF A FIFTEEN- OR SIXTEEN-YEAR-OLD GIRL.

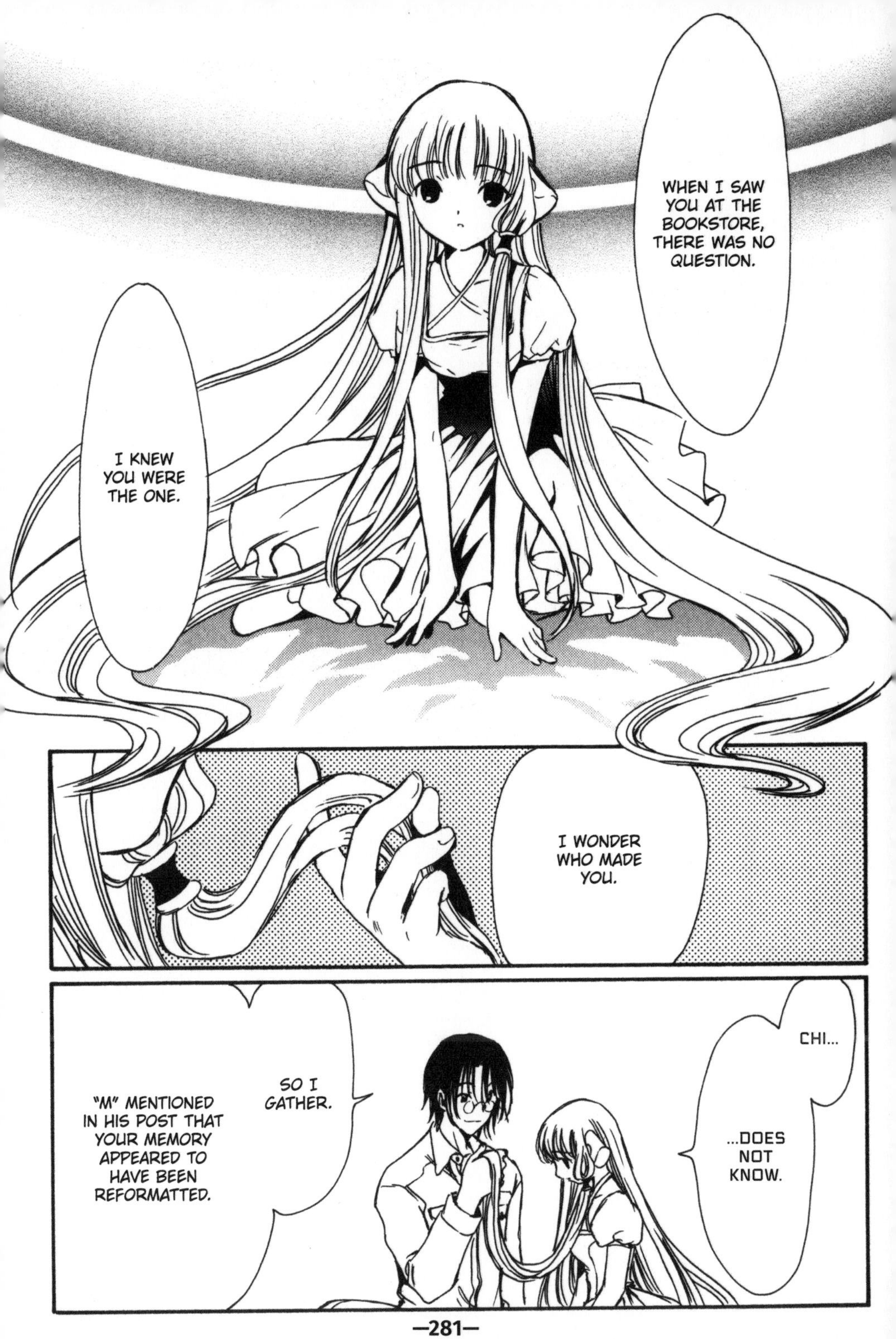
WHEN I SAW YOU AT THE BOOKSTORE, THERE WAS NO QUESTION.
I KNEW YOU WERE THE ONE.
I WONDER WHO MADE YOU.
CHI...
...DOES NOT KNOW.
SO I GATHER.
"M" MENTIONED IN HIS POST THAT YOUR MEMORY APPEARED TO HAVE BEEN REFORMATTED.

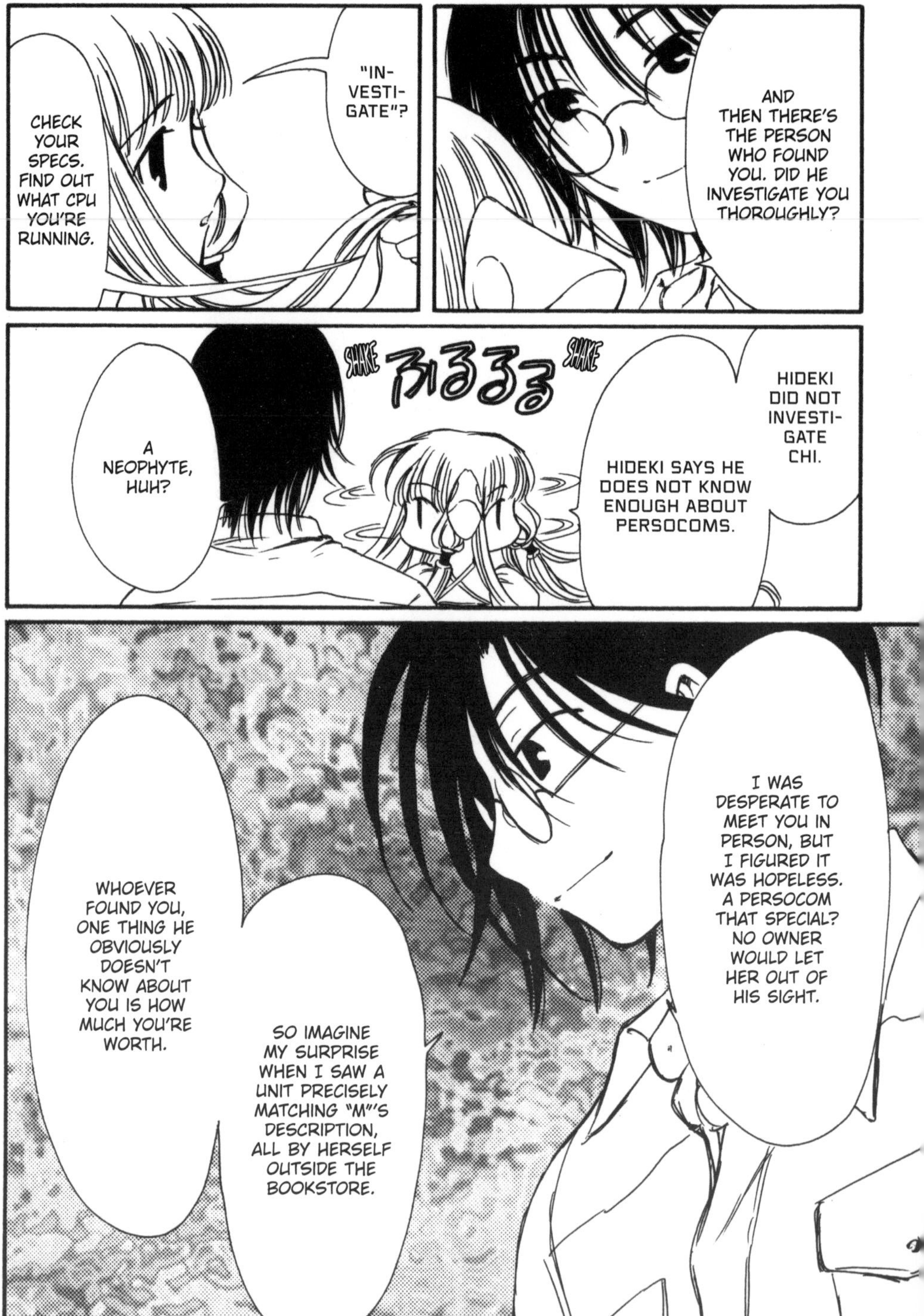
AND THEN THERE'S THE PERSON WHO FOUND YOU. DID HE INVESTIGATE YOU THOROUGHLY?
"IN-VESTI-GATE"?
CHECK YOUR SPECS. FIND OUT WHAT CPU YOU'RE RUNNING.
HIDEKI DID NOT INVESTI-GATE CHI.
SHAKE ふるるる SHAKE
HIDEKI SAYS HE DOES NOT KNOW ENOUGH ABOUT PERSOCOMS.
A NEOPHYTE, HUH?
I WAS DESPERATE TO MEET YOU IN PERSON, BUT I FIGURED IT WAS HOPELESS. A PERSOCOM THAT SPECIAL? NO OWNER WOULD LET HER OUT OF HIS SIGHT.
SO IMAGINE MY SURPRISE WHEN I SAW A UNIT PRECISELY MATCHING "M"'S DESCRIPTION, ALL BY HERSELF OUTSIDE THE BOOKSTORE.
WHOEVER FOUND YOU, ONE THING HE OBVIOUSLY DOESN'T KNOW ABOUT YOU IS HOW MUCH YOU'RE WORTH.

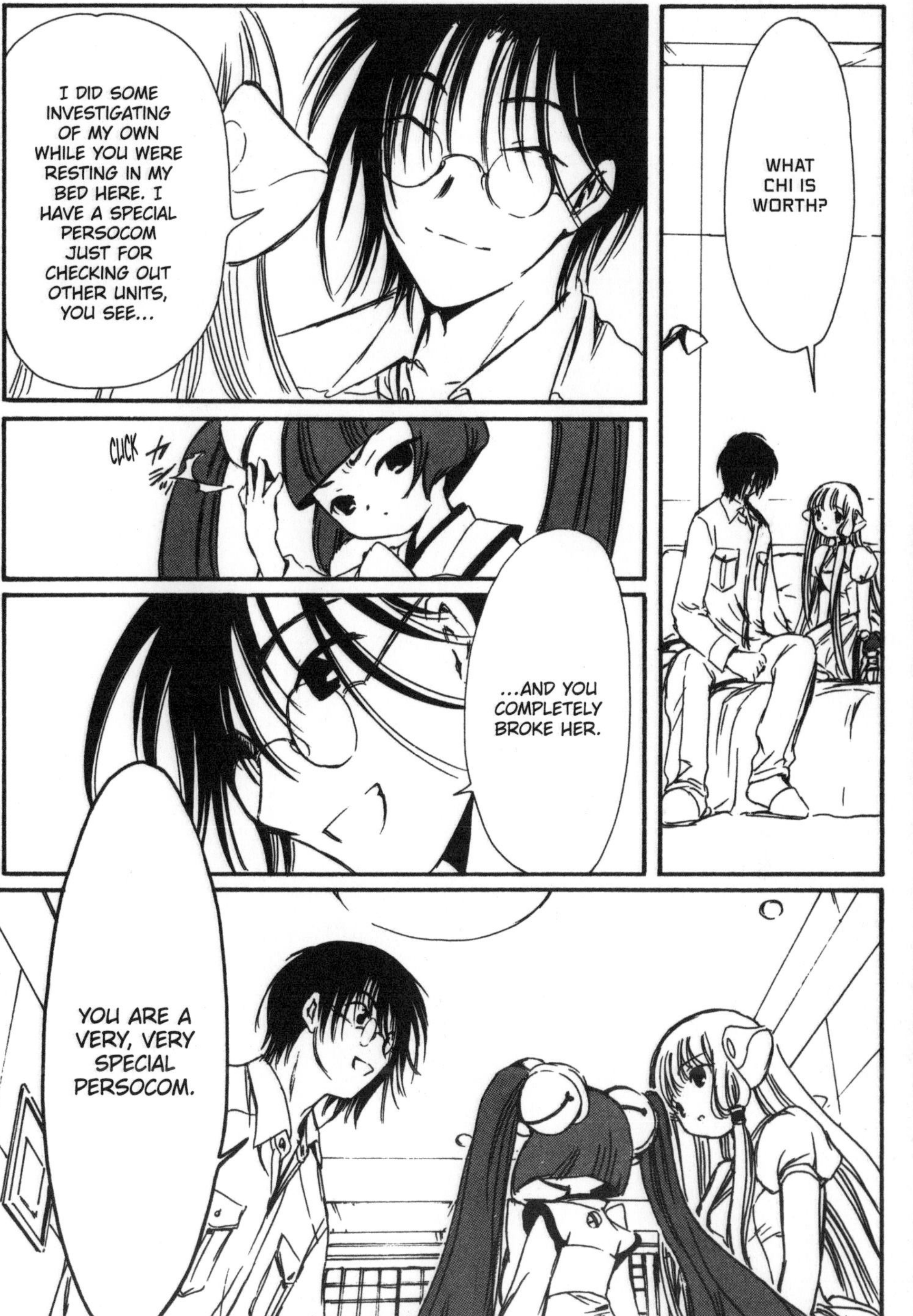
WHAT CHI IS WORTH?
I DID SOME INVESTIGATING OF MY OWN WHILE YOU WERE RESTING IN MY BED HERE. I HAVE A SPECIAL PERSOCOM JUST FOR CHECKING OUT OTHER UNITS, YOU SEE...
CLICK
...AND YOU COMPLETELY BROKE HER.
YOU ARE A VERY, VERY SPECIAL PERSOCOM.

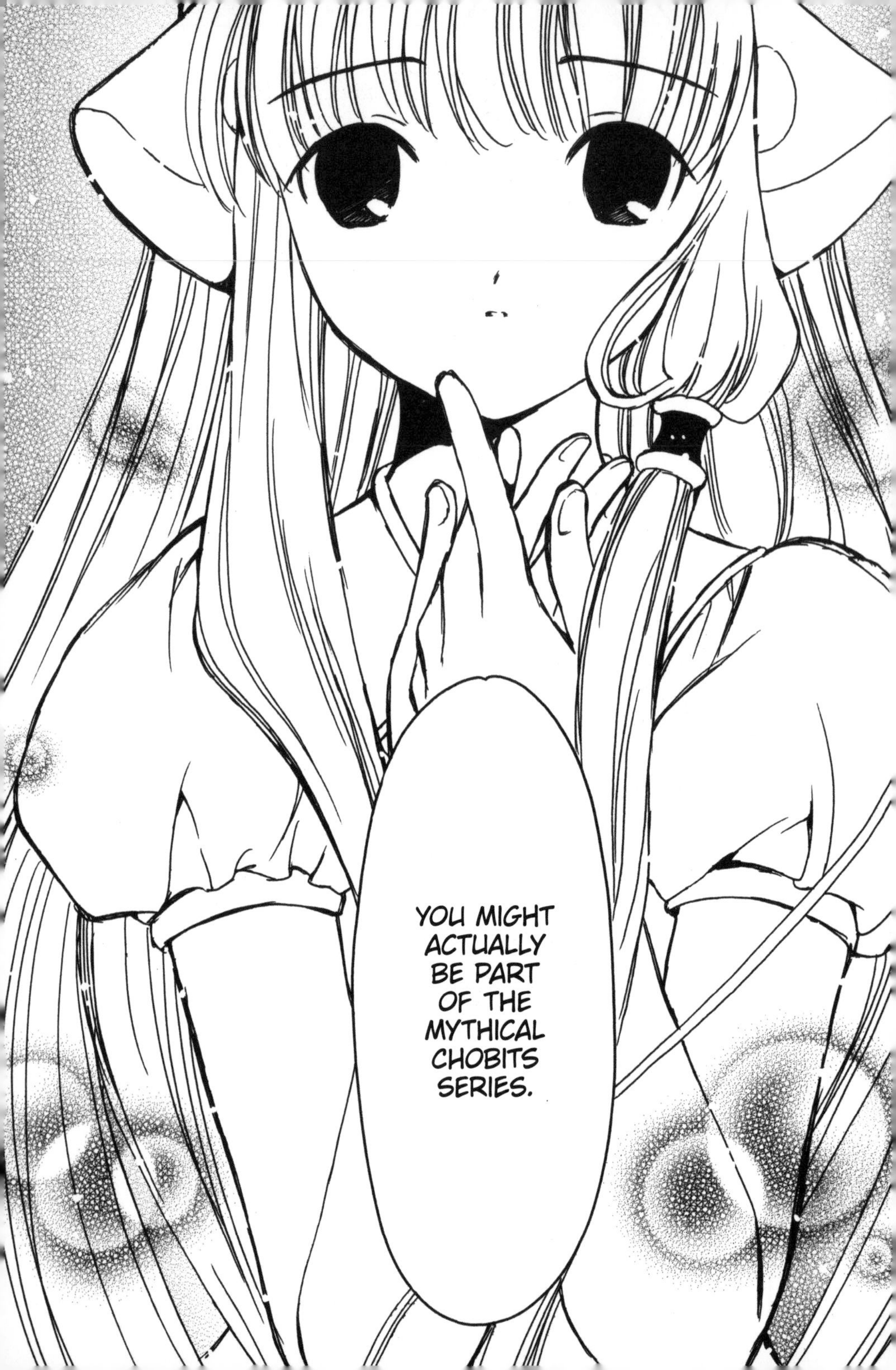
YOU MIGHT ACTUALLY BE PART OF THE MYTHICAL CHOBITS SERIES.

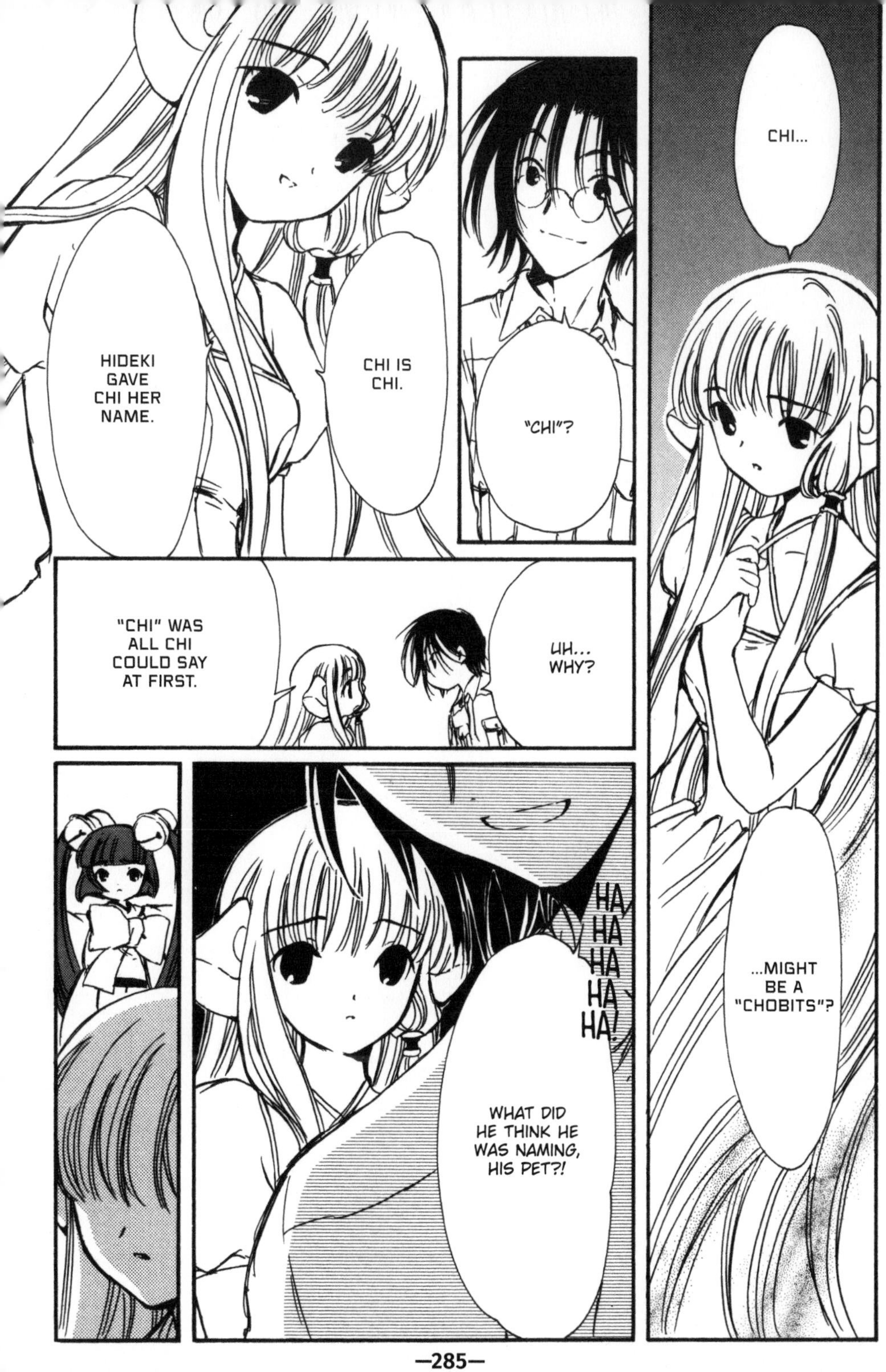
CHI...
...MIGHT BE A "CHOBITS"?
"CHI"?
CHI IS CHI.
HIDEKI GAVE CHI HER NAME.
UH... WHY?
"CHI" WAS ALL CHI COULD SAY AT FIRST.
HA HA HA HA HA!
WHAT DID HE THINK HE WAS NAMING, HIS PET?!

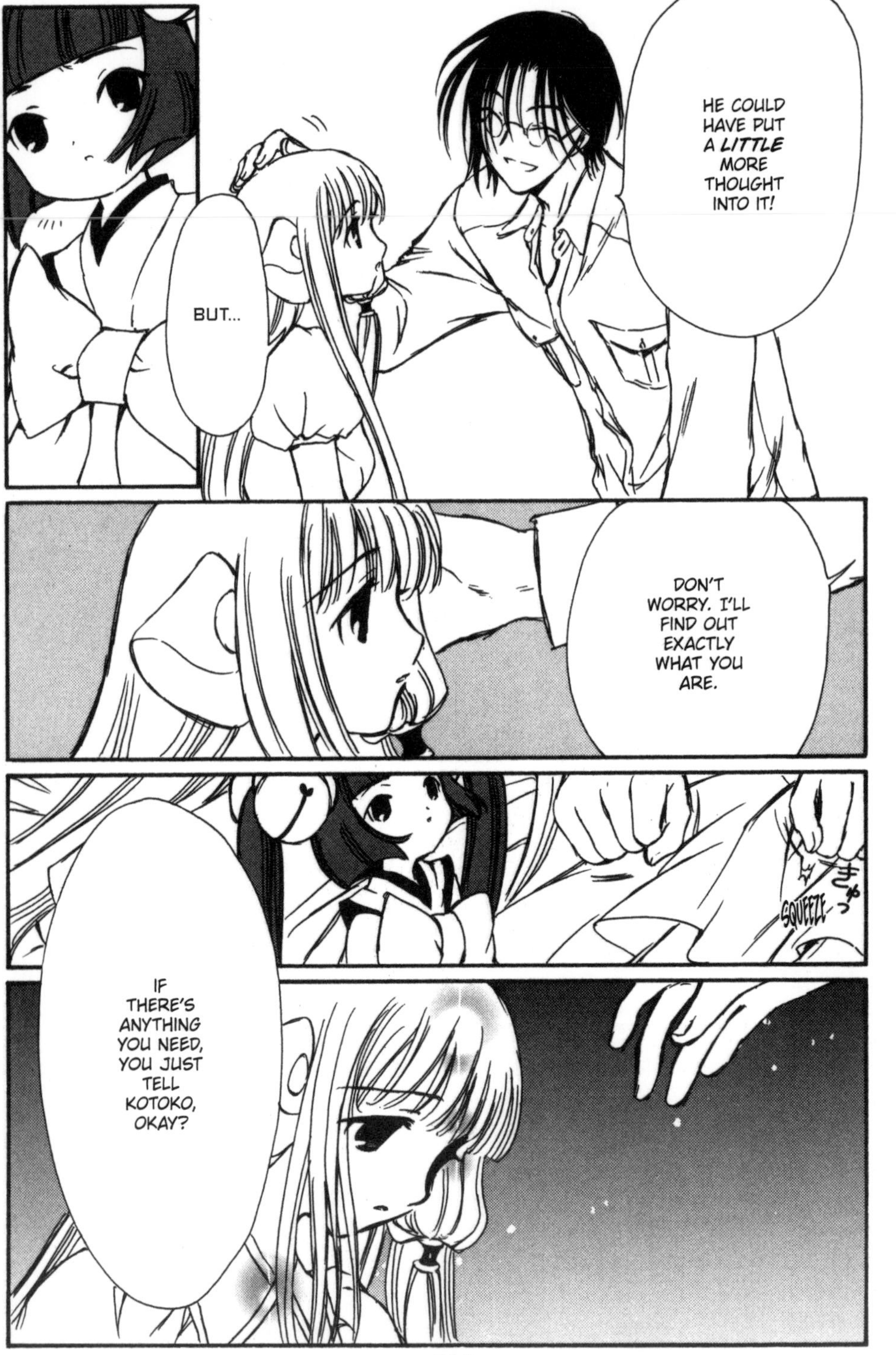
HE COULD HAVE PUT A *LITTLE* MORE THOUGHT INTO IT!
BUT...
DON'T WORRY. I'LL FIND OUT EXACTLY WHAT YOU ARE.
きゅっ
SQUEEZE
IF THERE'S ANYTHING YOU NEED, YOU JUST TELL KOTOKO, OKAY?

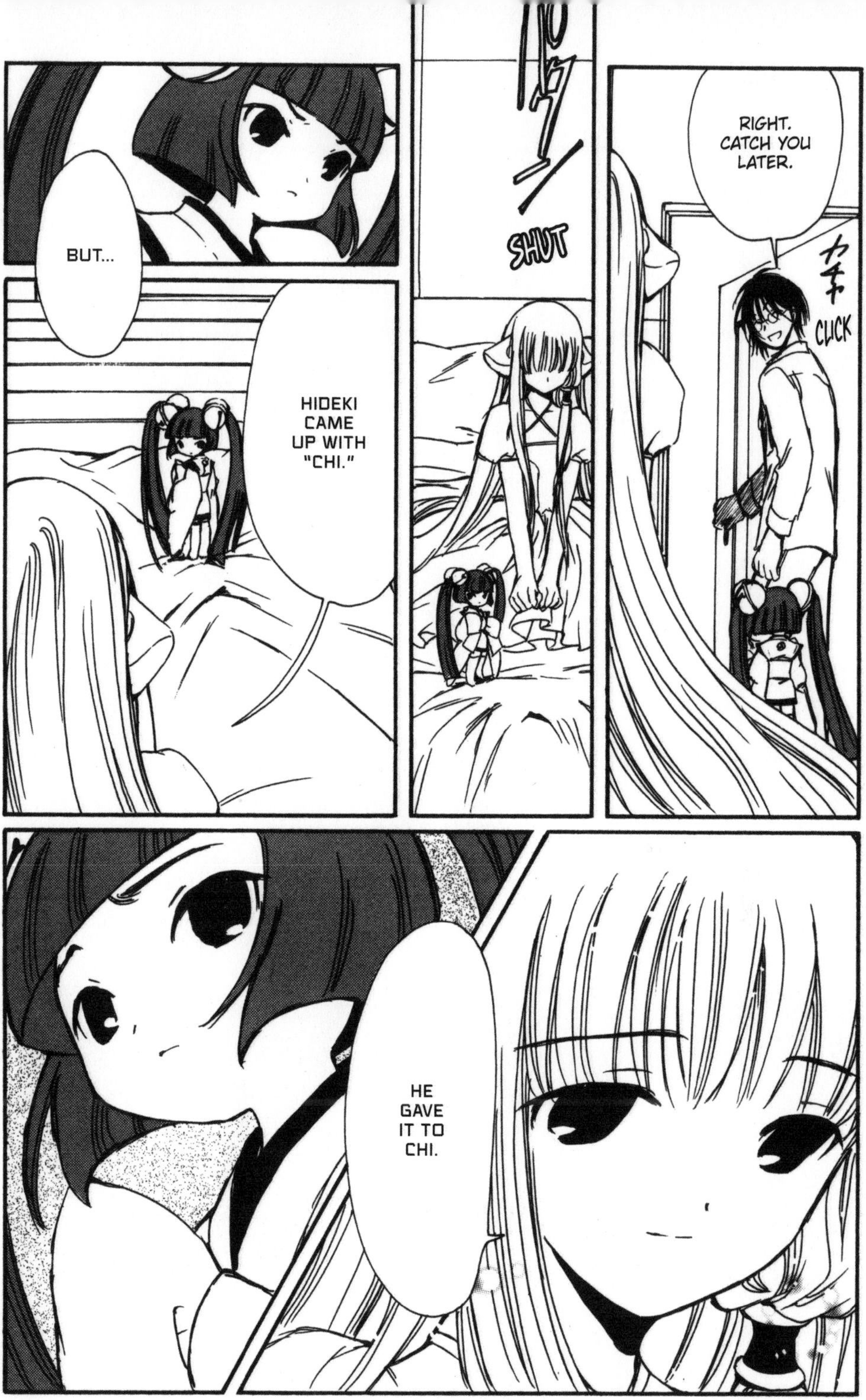
RIGHT. CATCH YOU LATER.
カチャ
CLICK
SHUT
BUT...
HIDEKI CAME UP WITH "CHI."
HE GAVE IT TO CHI.

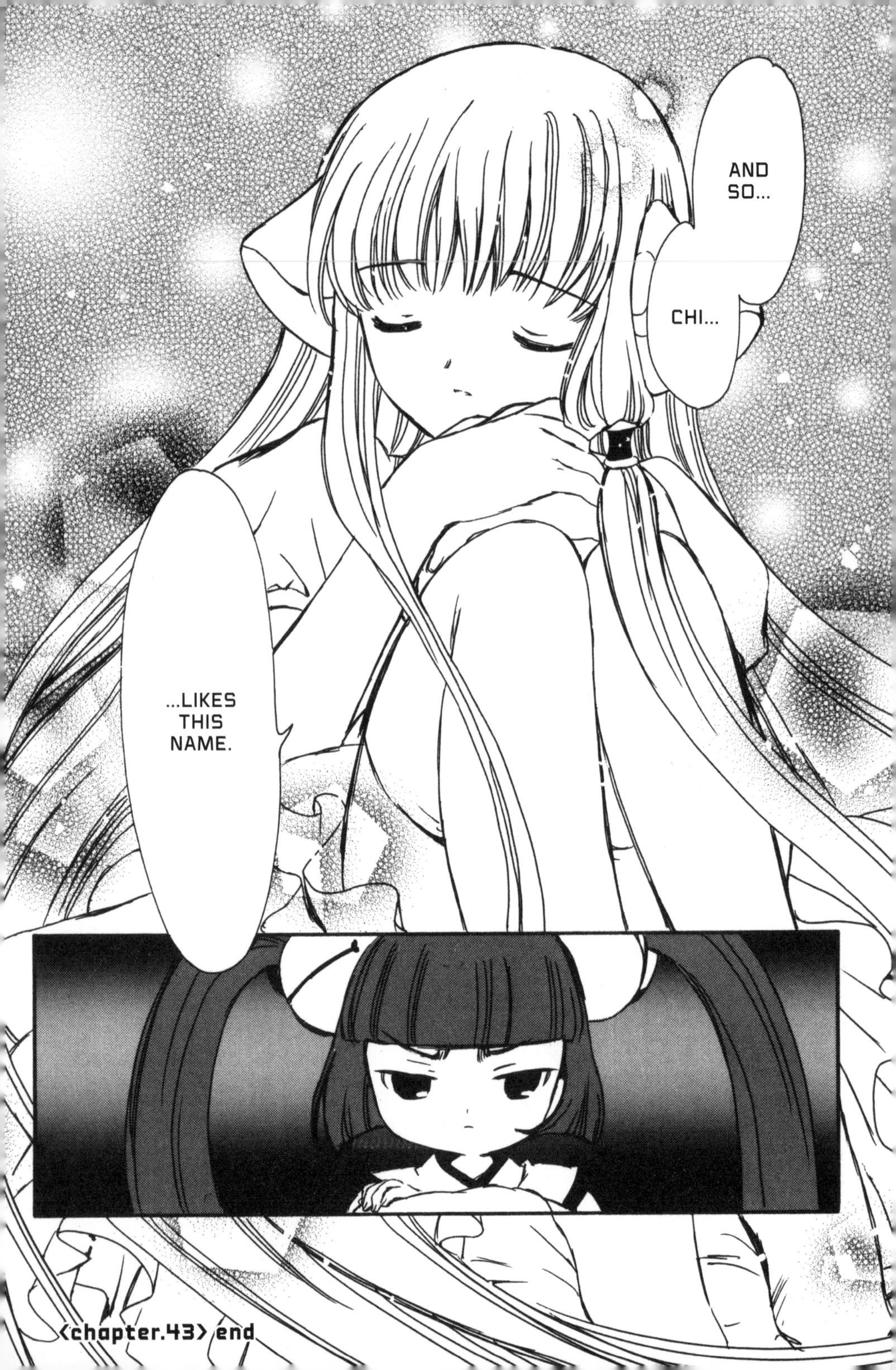
AND SO...
CHI...
...LIKES THIS NAME.
<chapter.43> end

⟨chapter.44⟩

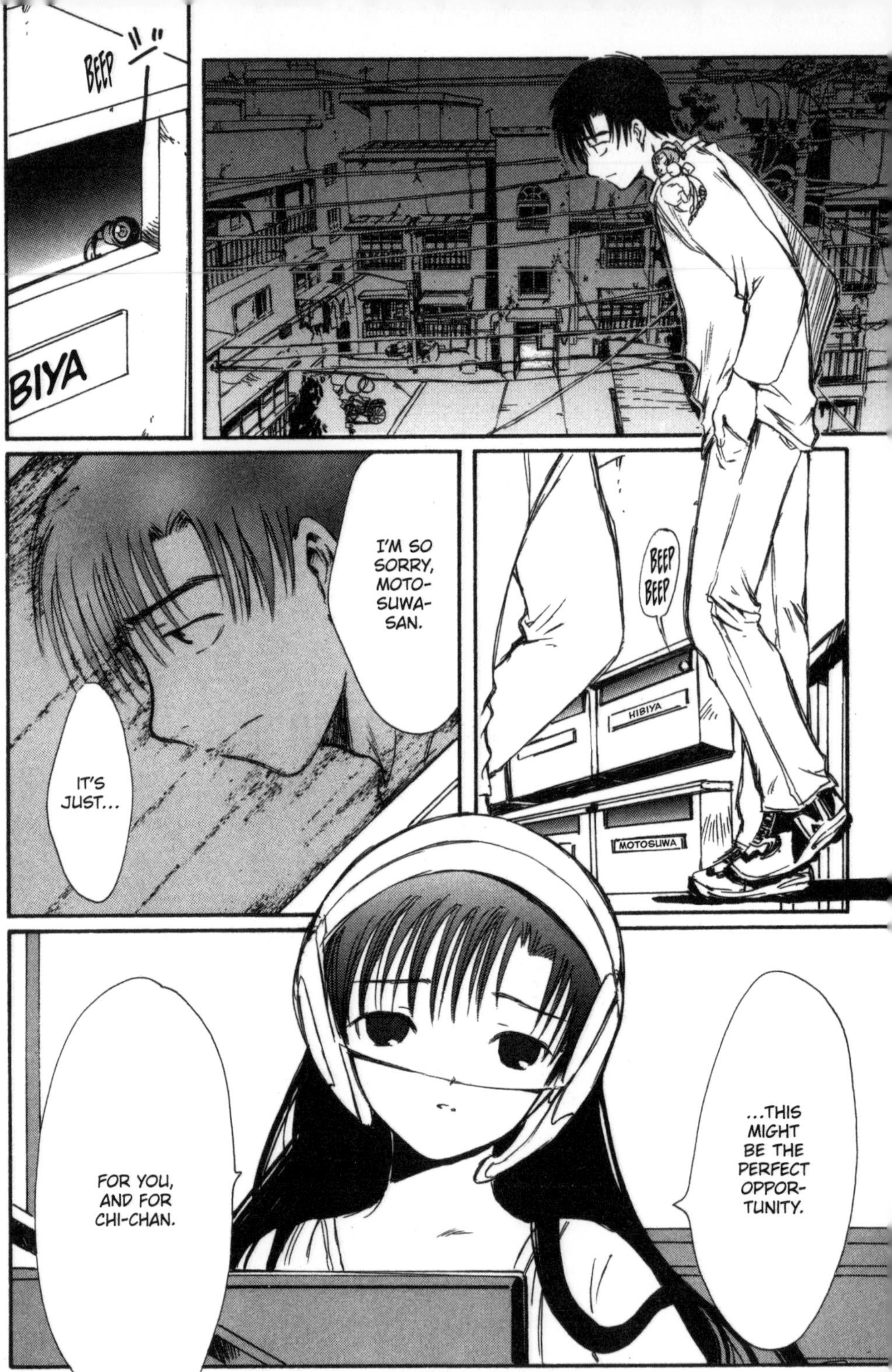

BEEP
BIYA
BEEP BEEP
HIBIYA
MOTOSUWA
I'M SO SORRY, MOTO-SUWA-SAN.
IT'S JUST...
...THIS MIGHT BE THE PERFECT OPPOR-TUNITY.
FOR YOU, AND FOR CHI-CHAN.

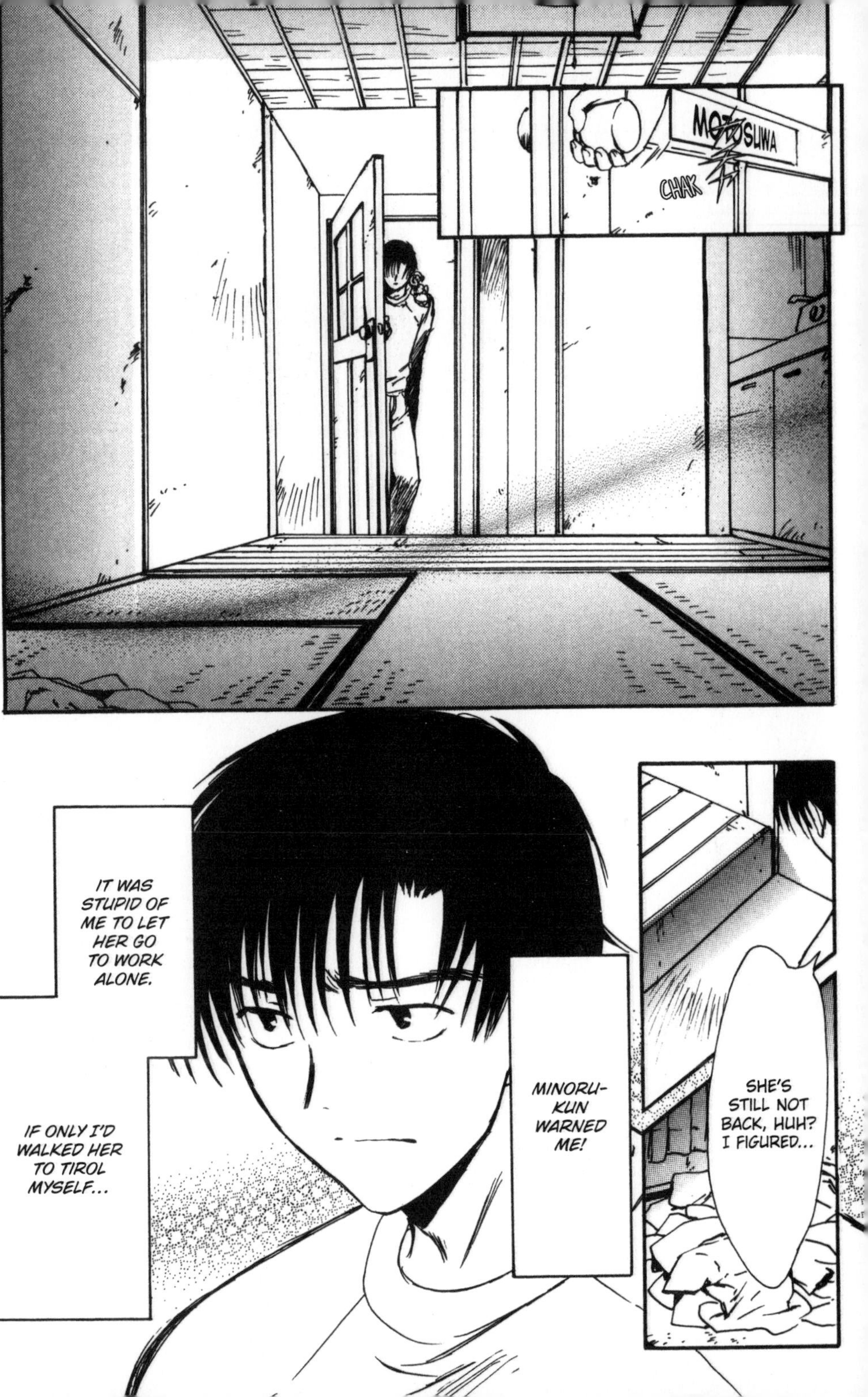
MOTOSUWA
CHAK
SHE'S STILL NOT BACK, HUH? I FIGURED...
MINORU-KUN WARNED ME!
IT WAS STUPID OF ME TO LET HER GO TO WORK ALONE.
IF ONLY I'D WALKED HER TO TIROL MYSELF...

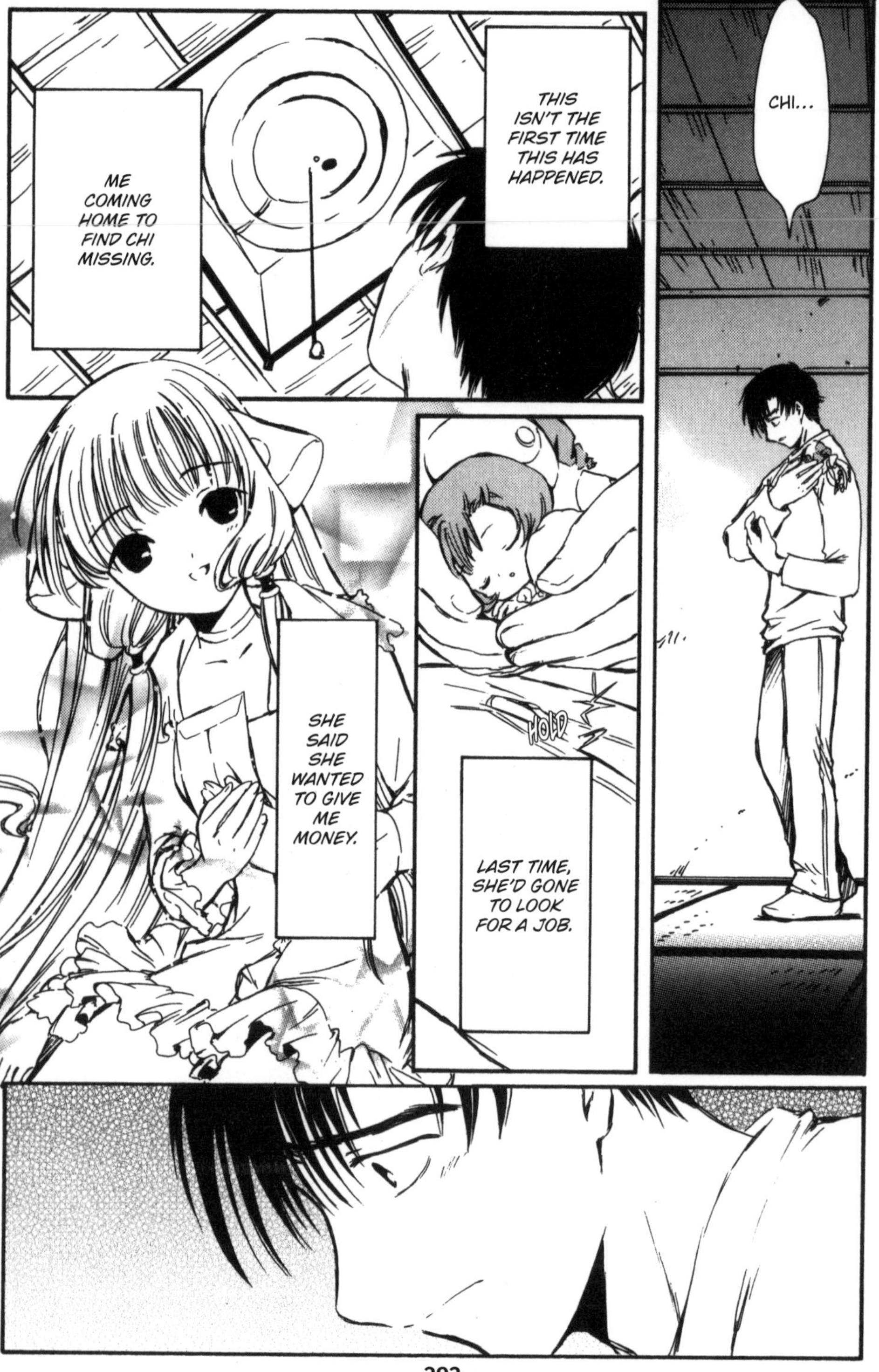
CHI...
THIS ISN'T THE FIRST TIME THIS HAS HAPPENED.
ME COMING HOME TO FIND CHI MISSING.
HOLD
LAST TIME, SHE'D GONE TO LOOK FOR A JOB.
SHE SAID SHE WANTED TO GIVE ME MONEY.

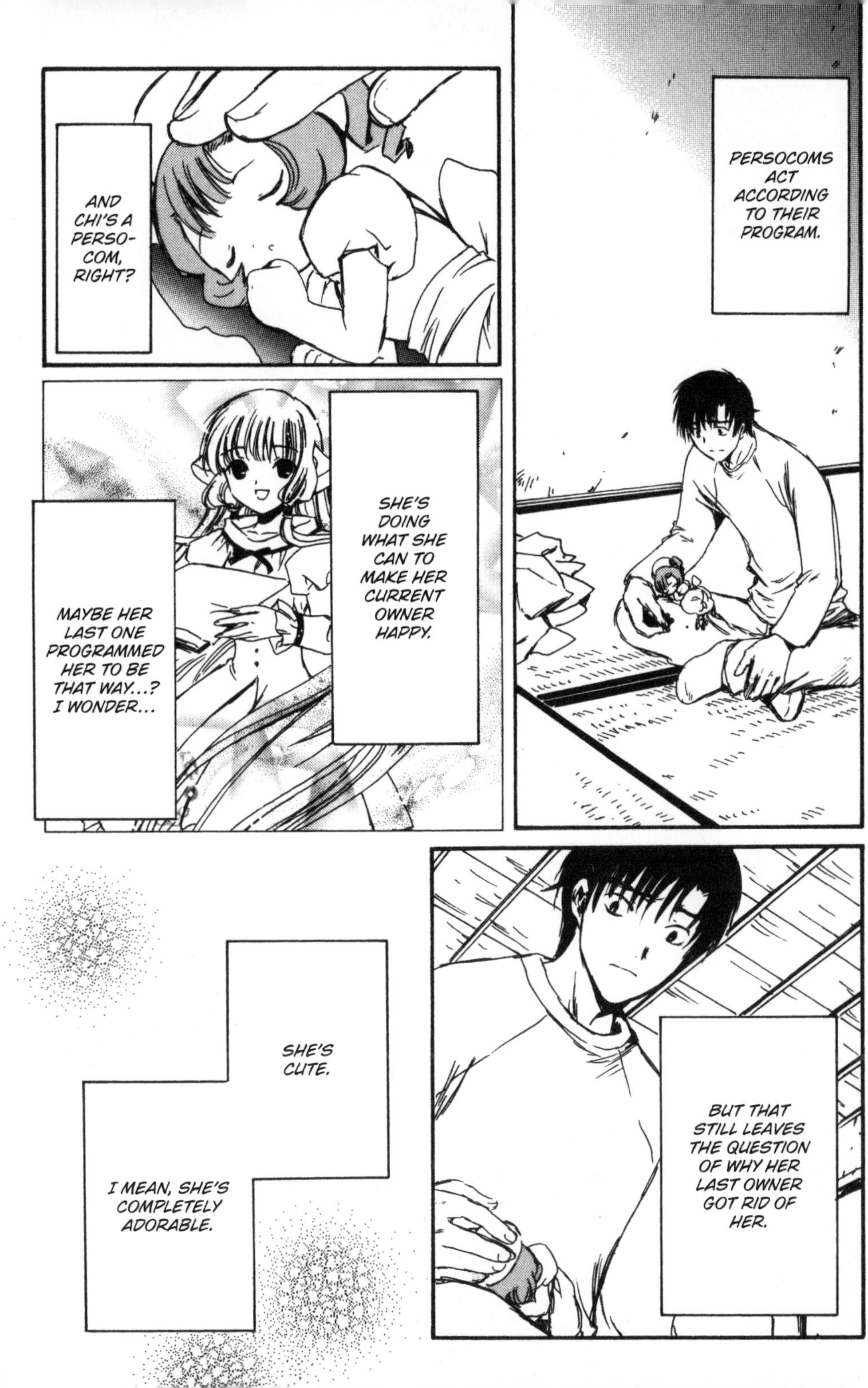
PERSOCOMS ACT ACCORDING TO THEIR PROGRAM.
AND CHI'S A PERSO-COM, RIGHT?
SHE'S DOING WHAT SHE CAN TO MAKE HER CURRENT OWNER HAPPY.
MAYBE HER LAST ONE PROGRAMMED HER TO BE THAT WAY...? I WONDER...
BUT THAT STILL LEAVES THE QUESTION OF WHY HER LAST OWNER GOT RID OF HER.
SHE'S CUTE.
I MEAN, SHE'S COMPLETELY ADORABLE.

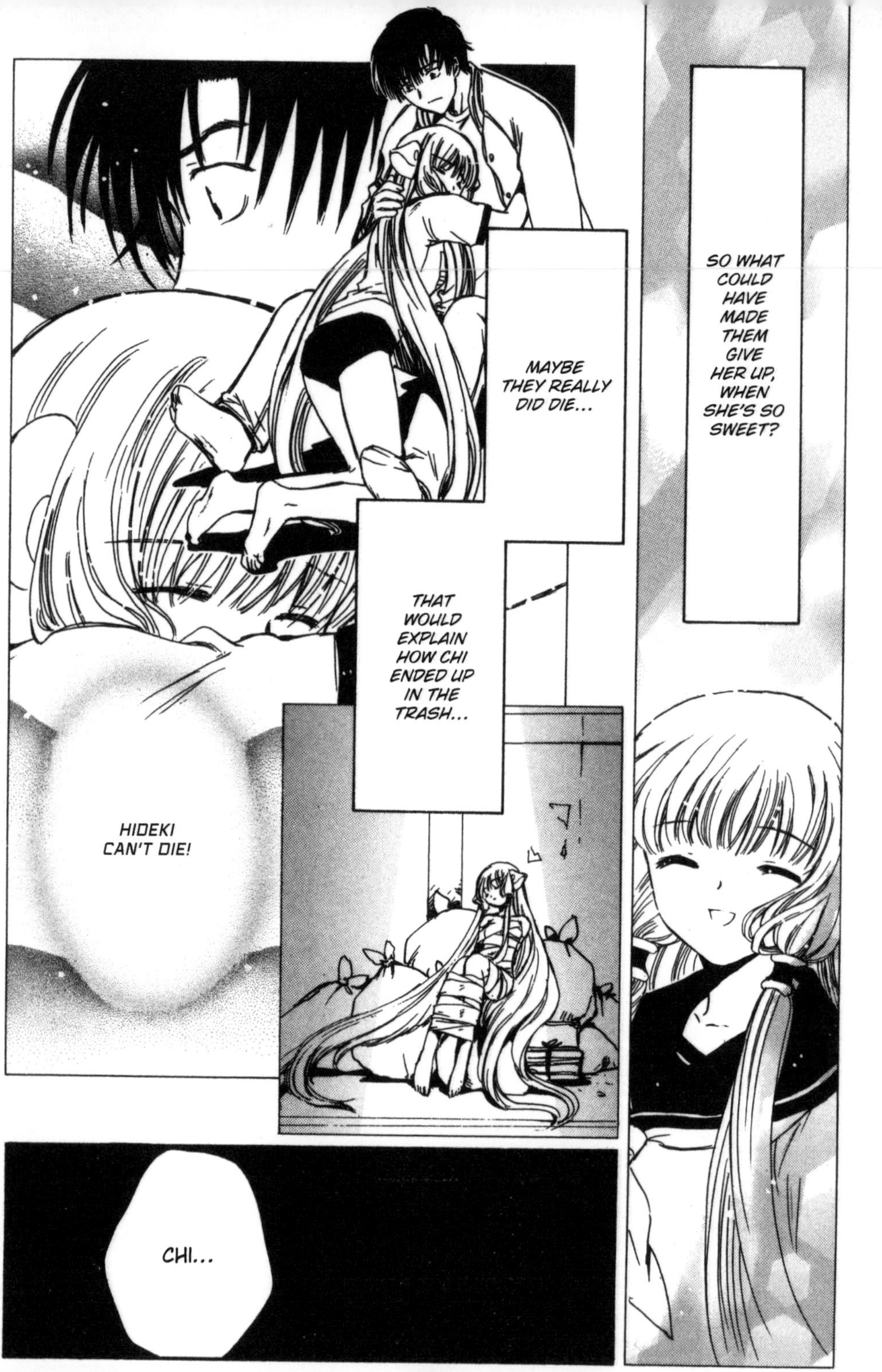
SO WHAT COULD HAVE MADE THEM GIVE HER UP, WHEN SHE'S SO SWEET?
MAYBE THEY REALLY DID DIE...
THAT WOULD EXPLAIN HOW CHI ENDED UP IN THE TRASH...
HIDEKI CAN'T DIE!
CHI...

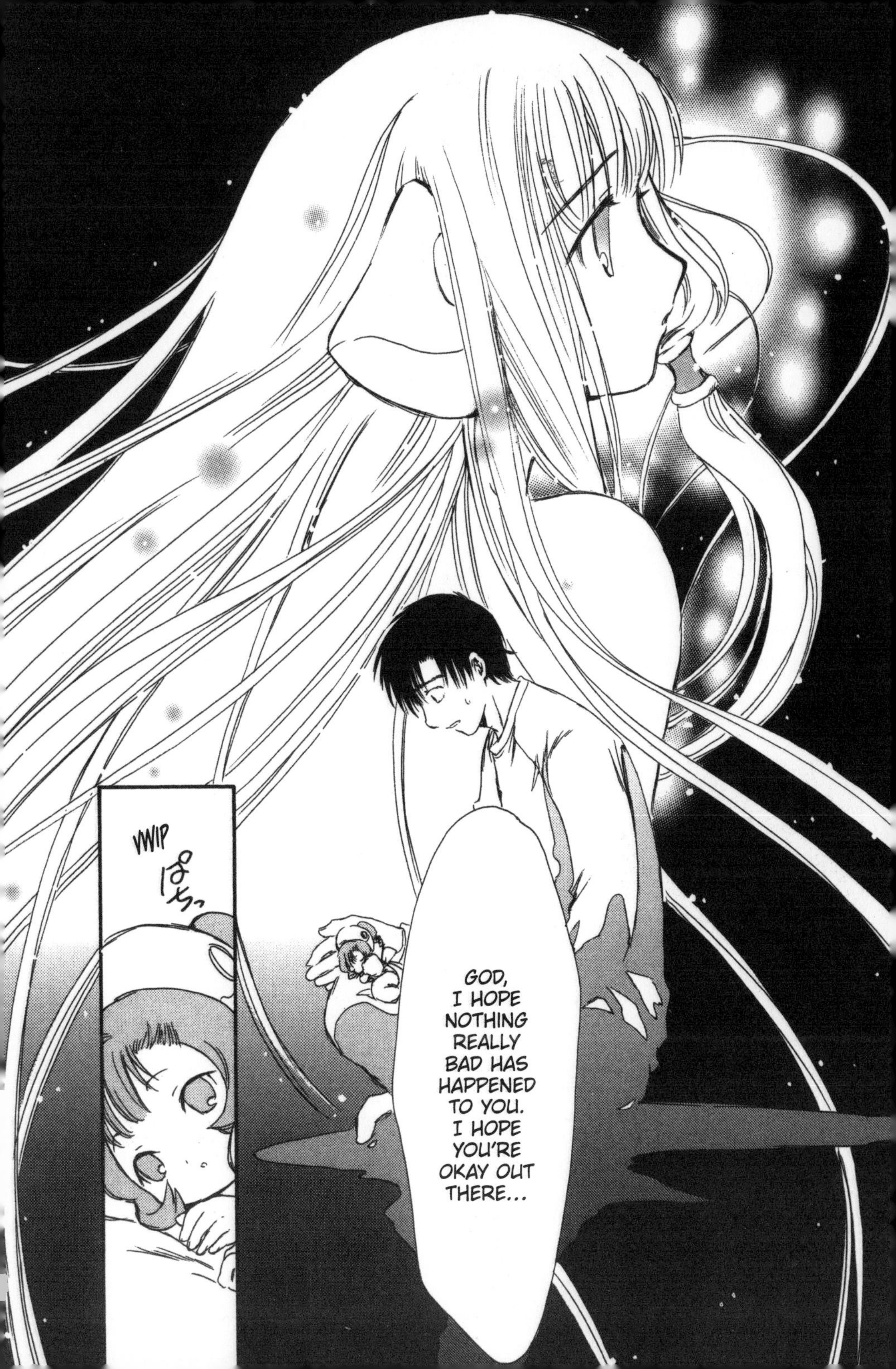
GOD, I HOPE NOTHING REALLY BAD HAS HAPPENED TO YOU. I HOPE YOU'RE OKAY OUT THERE...
VWIP
ぱちっ

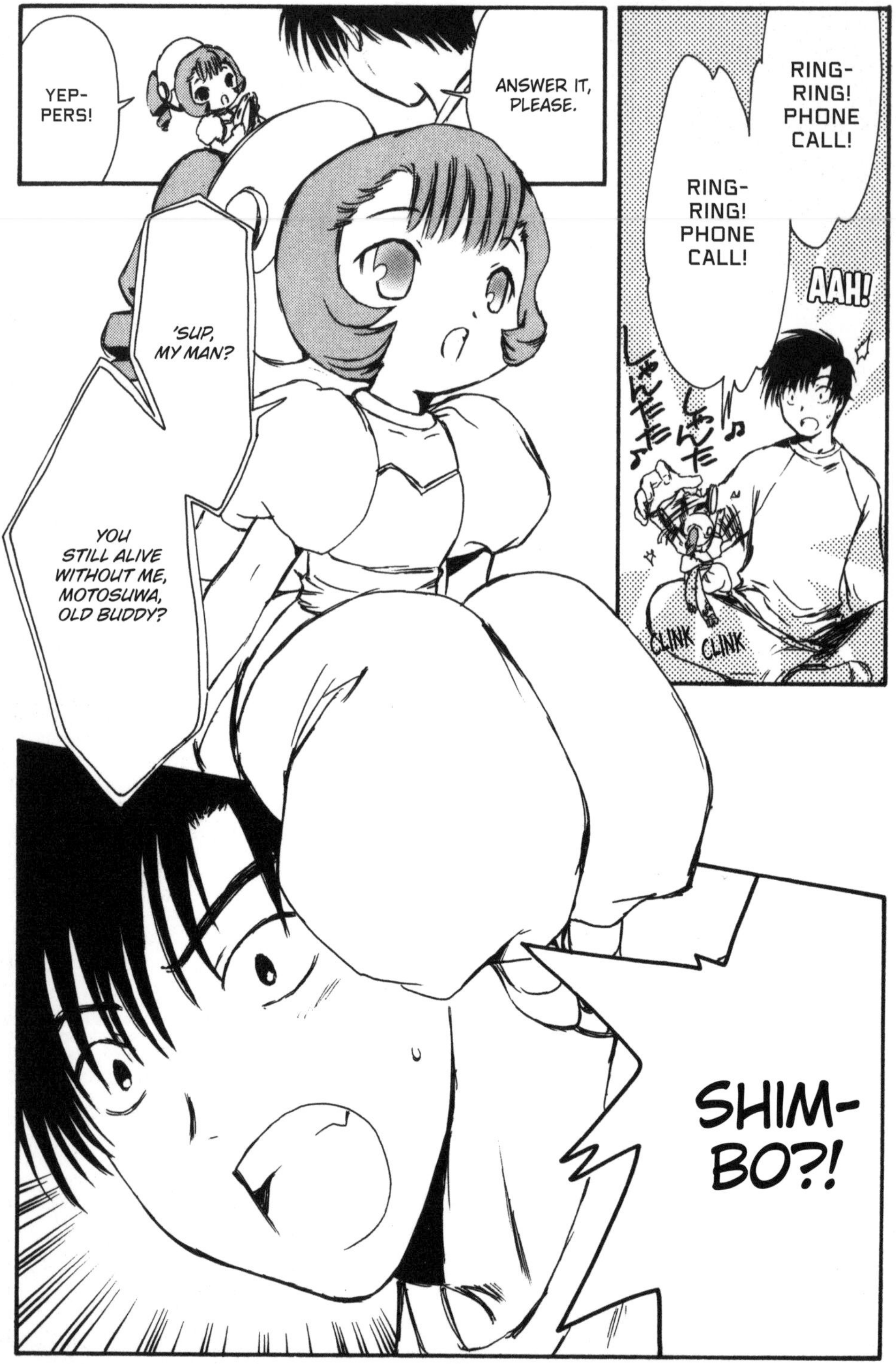
RING-RING! PHONE CALL!
RING-RING! PHONE CALL!
AAH!
しゃんた しゃんた ♪
CLINK CLINK
ANSWER IT, PLEASE.
YEP-PERS!
'SUP, MY MAN?
YOU STILL ALIVE WITHOUT ME, MOTOSUWA, OLD BUDDY?
SHIM-BO?!

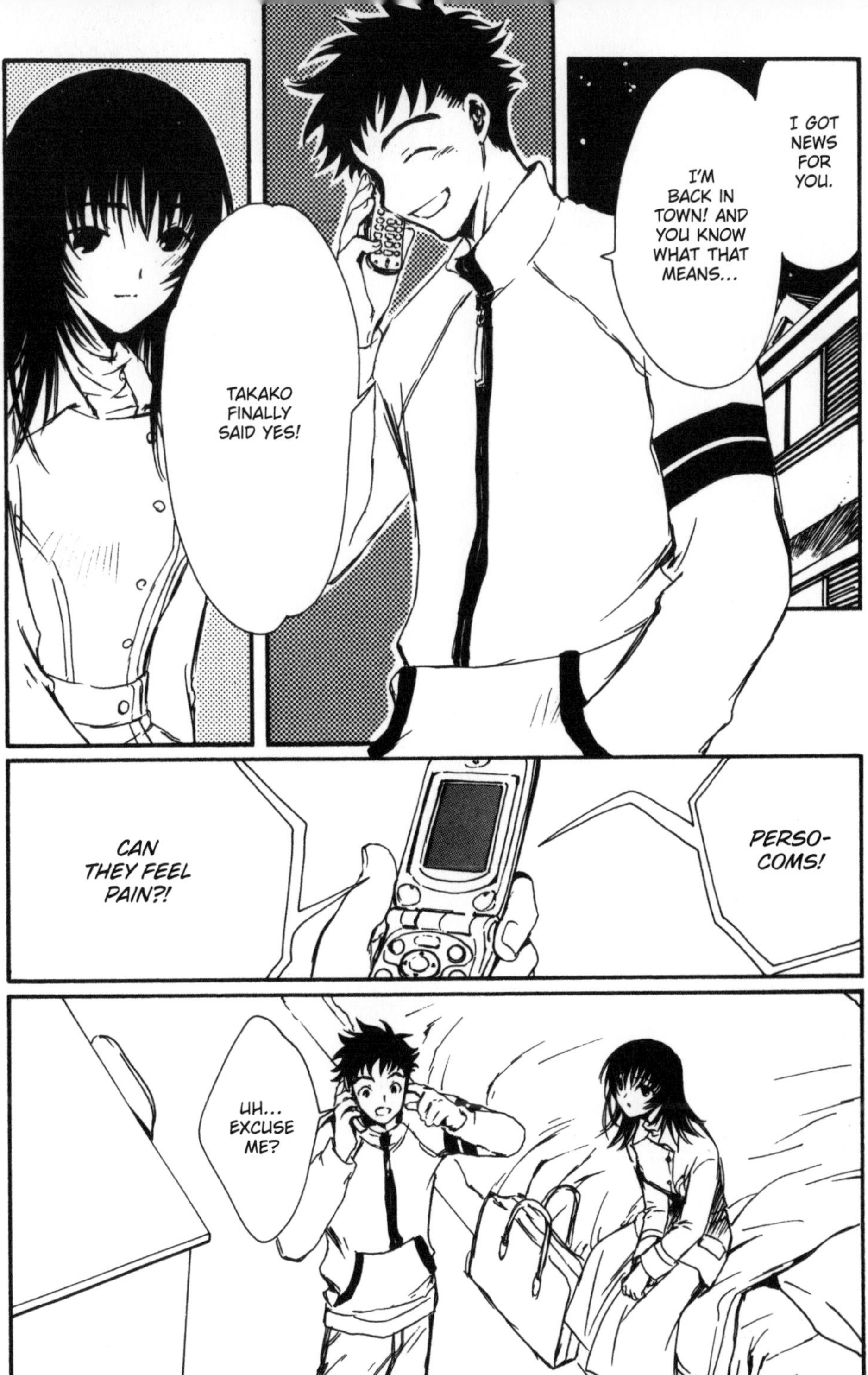
I GOT NEWS FOR YOU.
I'M BACK IN TOWN! AND YOU KNOW WHAT THAT MEANS...
TAKAKO FINALLY SAID YES!
PERSO-COMS!
CAN THEY FEEL PAIN?!
UH... EXCUSE ME?

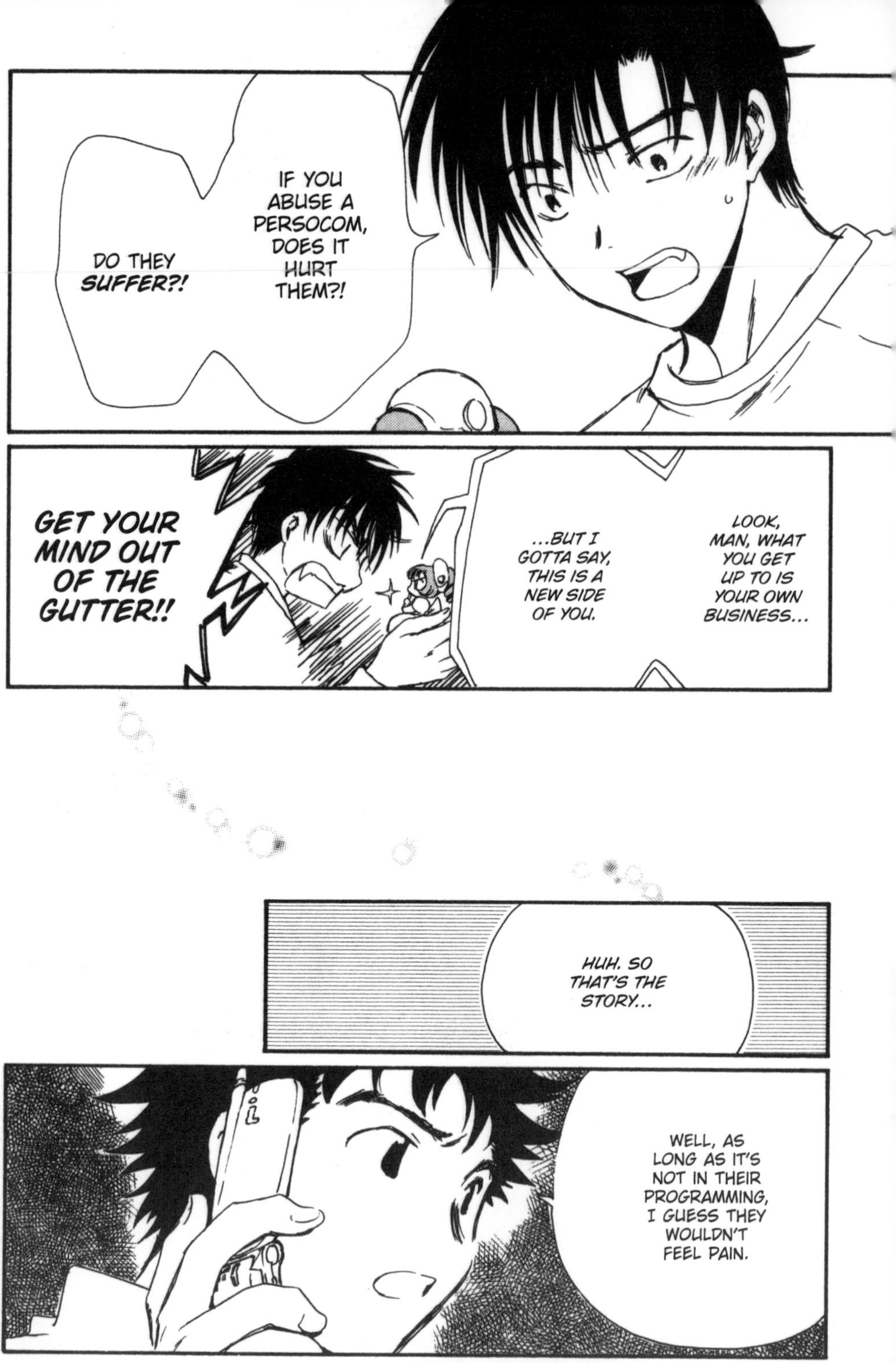
IF YOU ABUSE A PERSOCOM, DOES IT HURT THEM?!
DO THEY SUFFER?!
LOOK, MAN, WHAT YOU GET UP TO IS YOUR OWN BUSINESS...
...BUT I GOTTA SAY, THIS IS A NEW SIDE OF YOU.
GET YOUR MIND OUT OF THE GUTTER!!
HUH. SO THAT'S THE STORY...
WELL, AS LONG AS IT'S NOT IN THEIR PROGRAMMING, I GUESS THEY WOULDN'T FEEL PAIN.

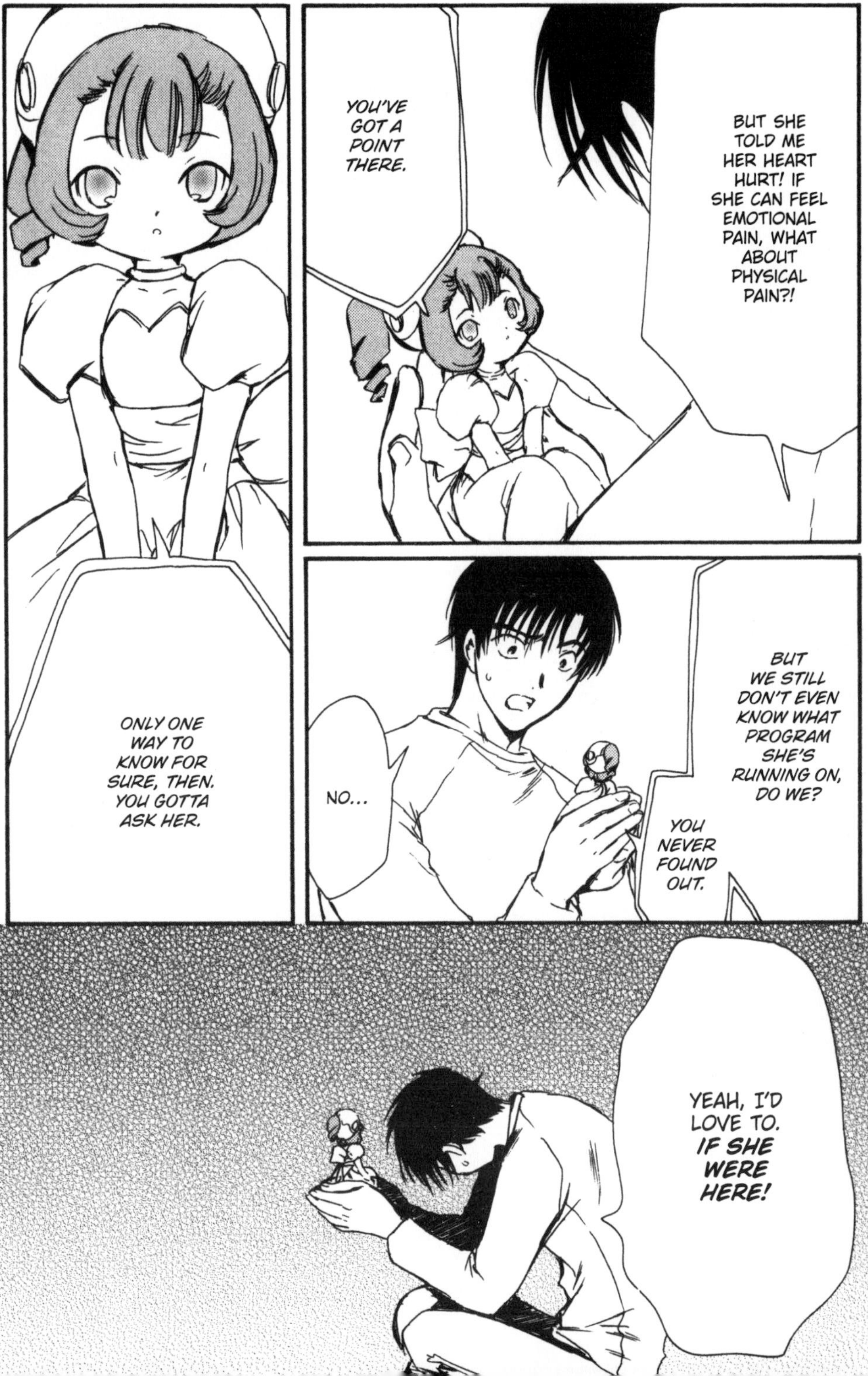
BUT SHE TOLD ME HER HEART HURT! IF SHE CAN FEEL EMOTIONAL PAIN, WHAT ABOUT PHYSICAL PAIN?!
YOU'VE GOT A POINT THERE.
BUT WE STILL DON'T EVEN KNOW WHAT PROGRAM SHE'S RUNNING ON, DO WE?
YOU NEVER FOUND OUT.
NO...
ONLY ONE WAY TO KNOW FOR SURE, THEN. YOU GOTTA ASK HER.
YEAH, I'D LOVE TO. **IF SHE WERE HERE!**

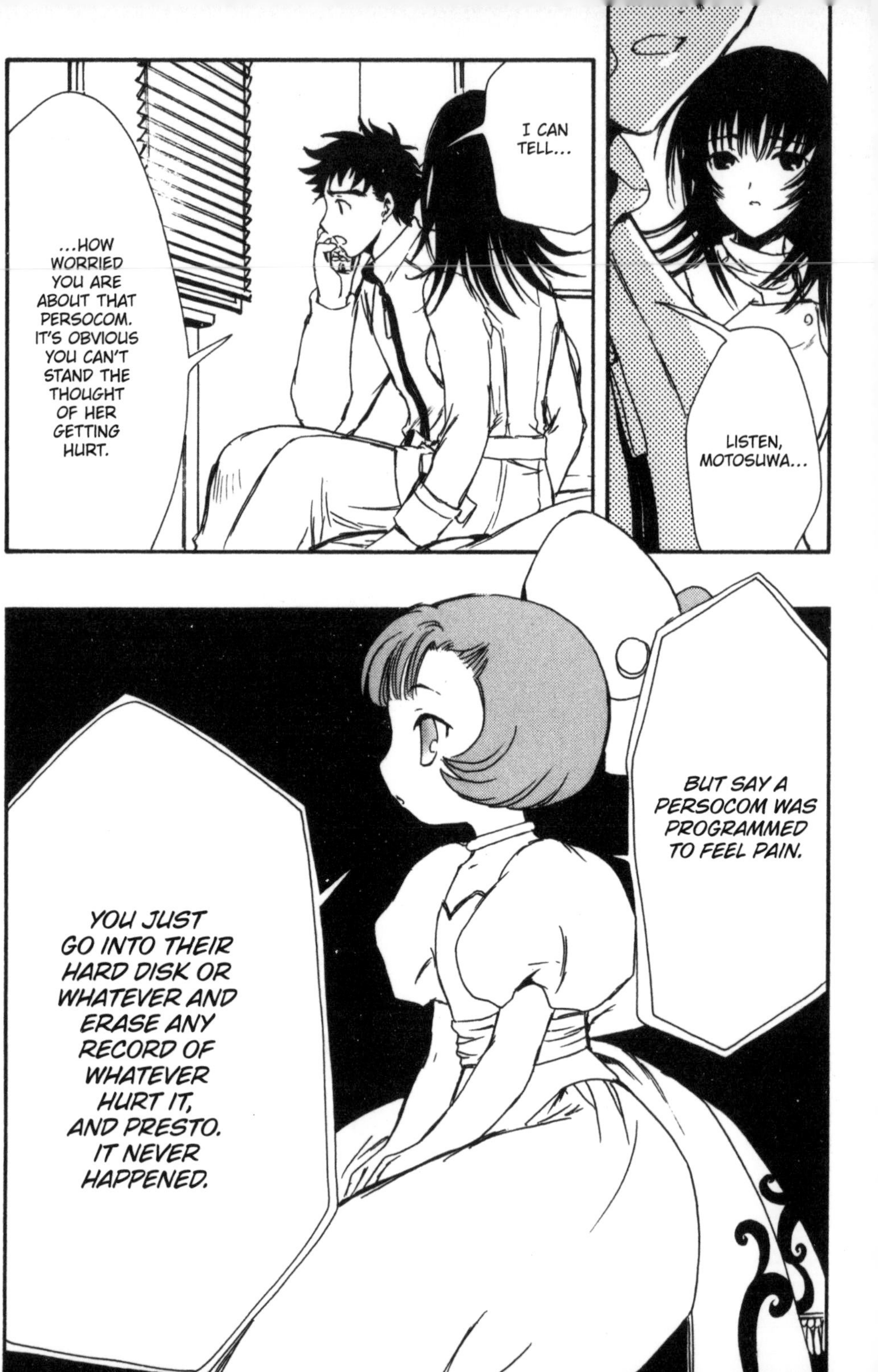
LISTEN, MOTOSUWA...
I CAN TELL...
...HOW WORRIED YOU ARE ABOUT THAT PERSOCOM. IT'S OBVIOUS YOU CAN'T STAND THE THOUGHT OF HER GETTING HURT.
BUT SAY A PERSOCOM WAS PROGRAMMED TO FEEL PAIN.
YOU JUST GO INTO THEIR HARD DISK OR WHATEVER AND ERASE ANY RECORD OF WHATEVER HURT IT, AND PRESTO. IT NEVER HAPPENED.

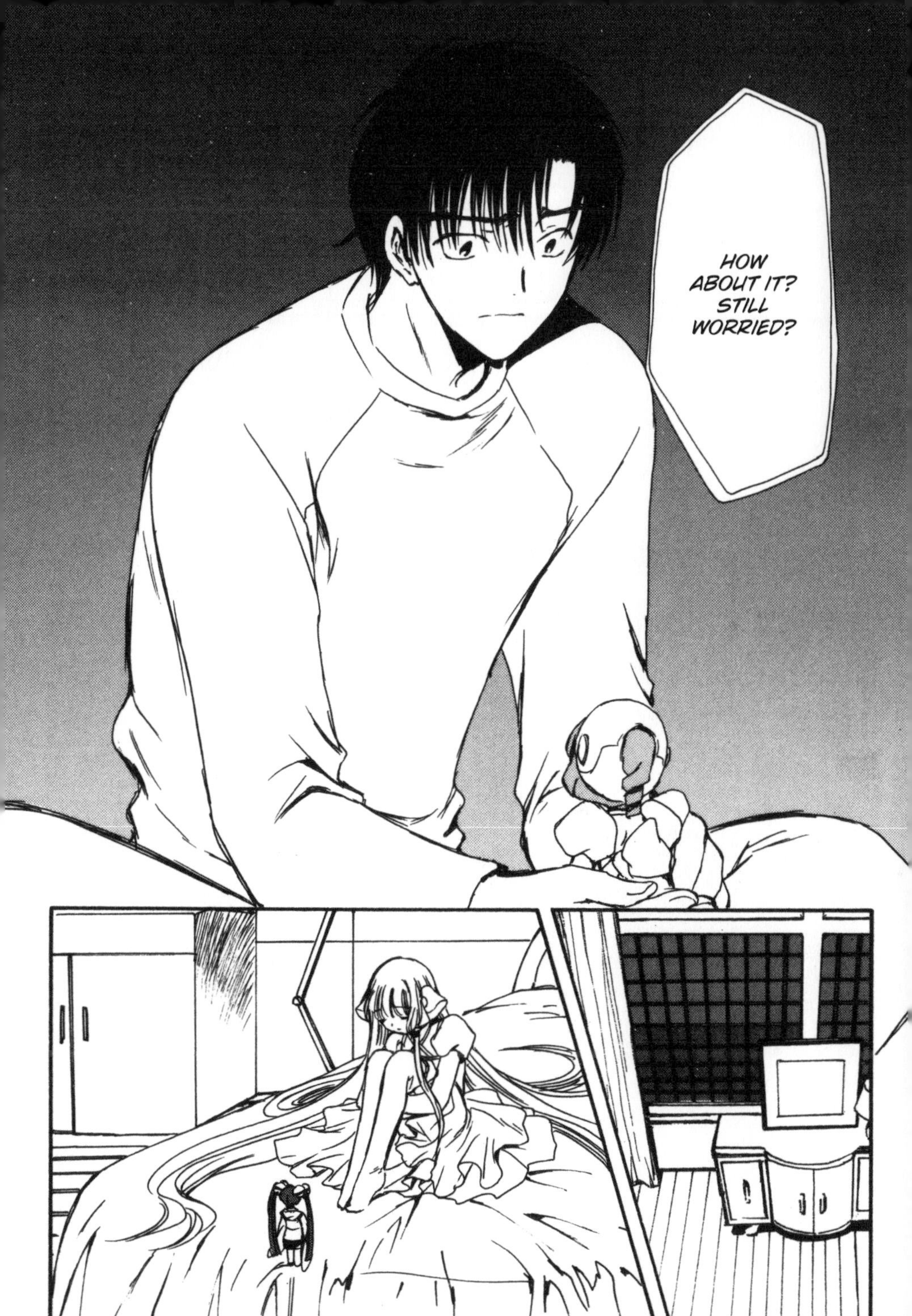
HOW ABOUT IT? STILL WORRIED?

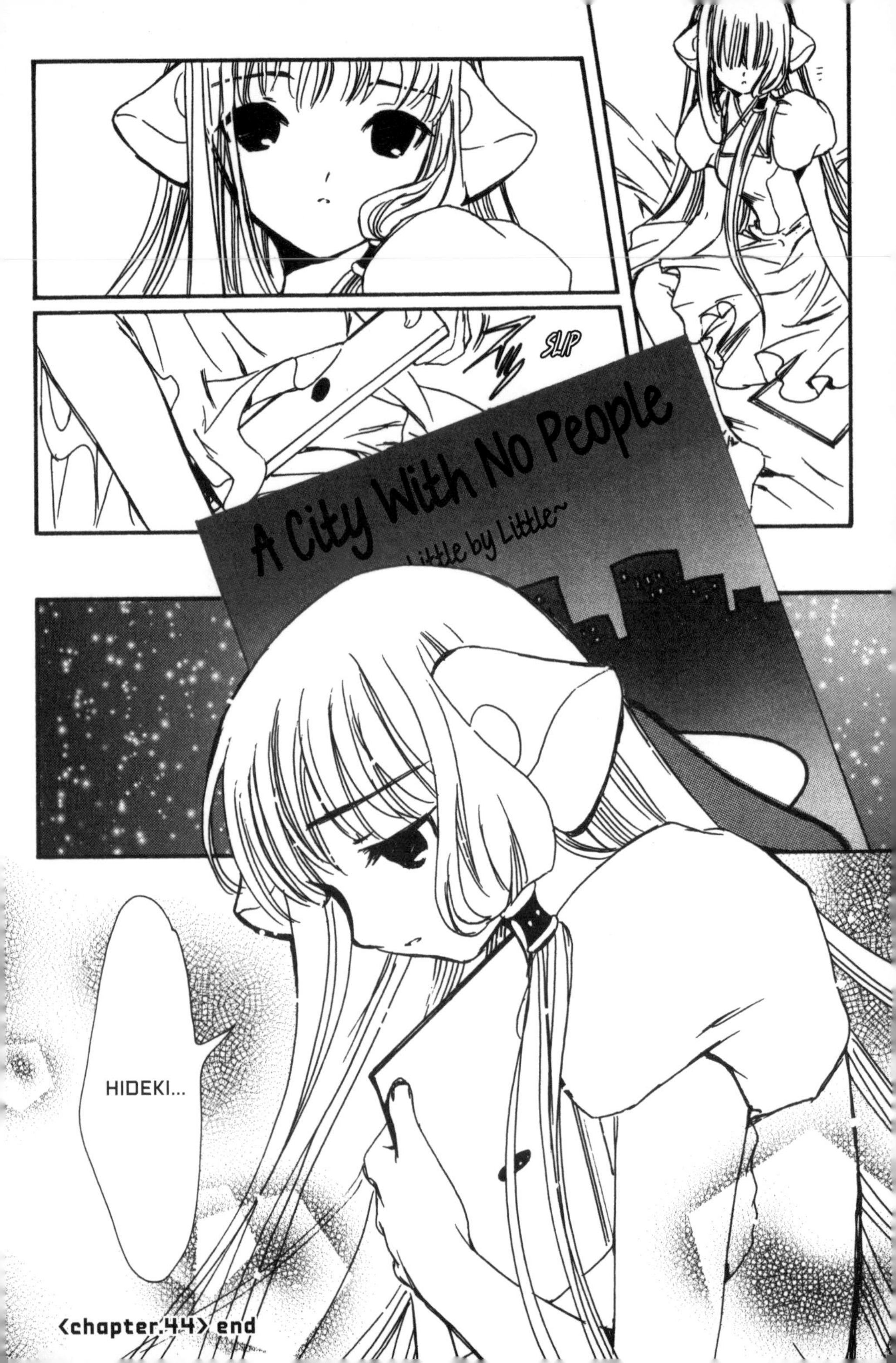
SLIP
A City With No People
~Little by Little~
HIDEKI...
<chapter.44> end

Chobits

〈chapter.45〉

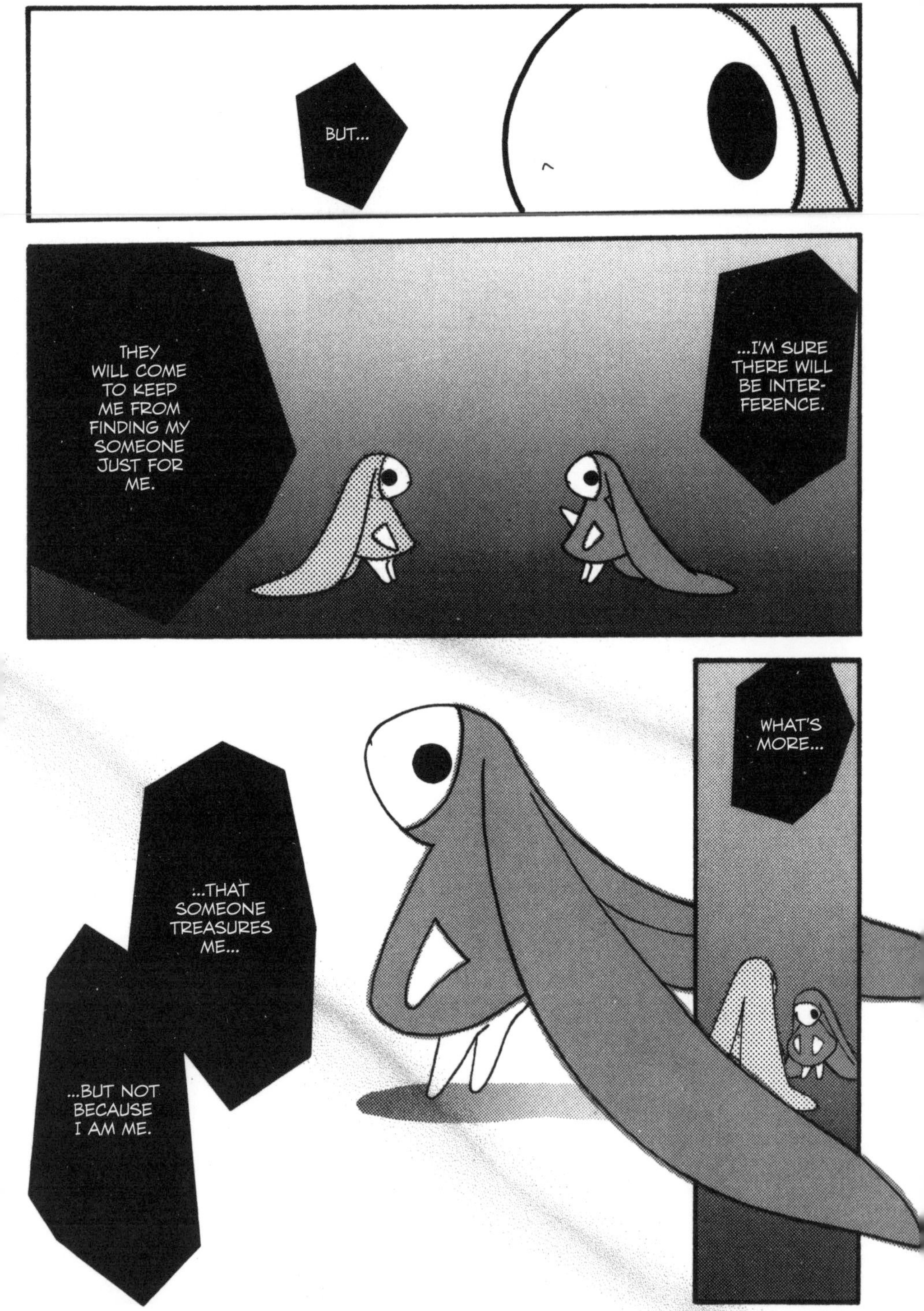
BUT...
...I'M SURE THERE WILL BE INTER-FERENCE.
THEY WILL COME TO KEEP ME FROM FINDING MY SOMEONE JUST FOR ME.
WHAT'S MORE...
...THAT SOMEONE TREASURES ME...
...BUT NOT BECAUSE I AM ME.

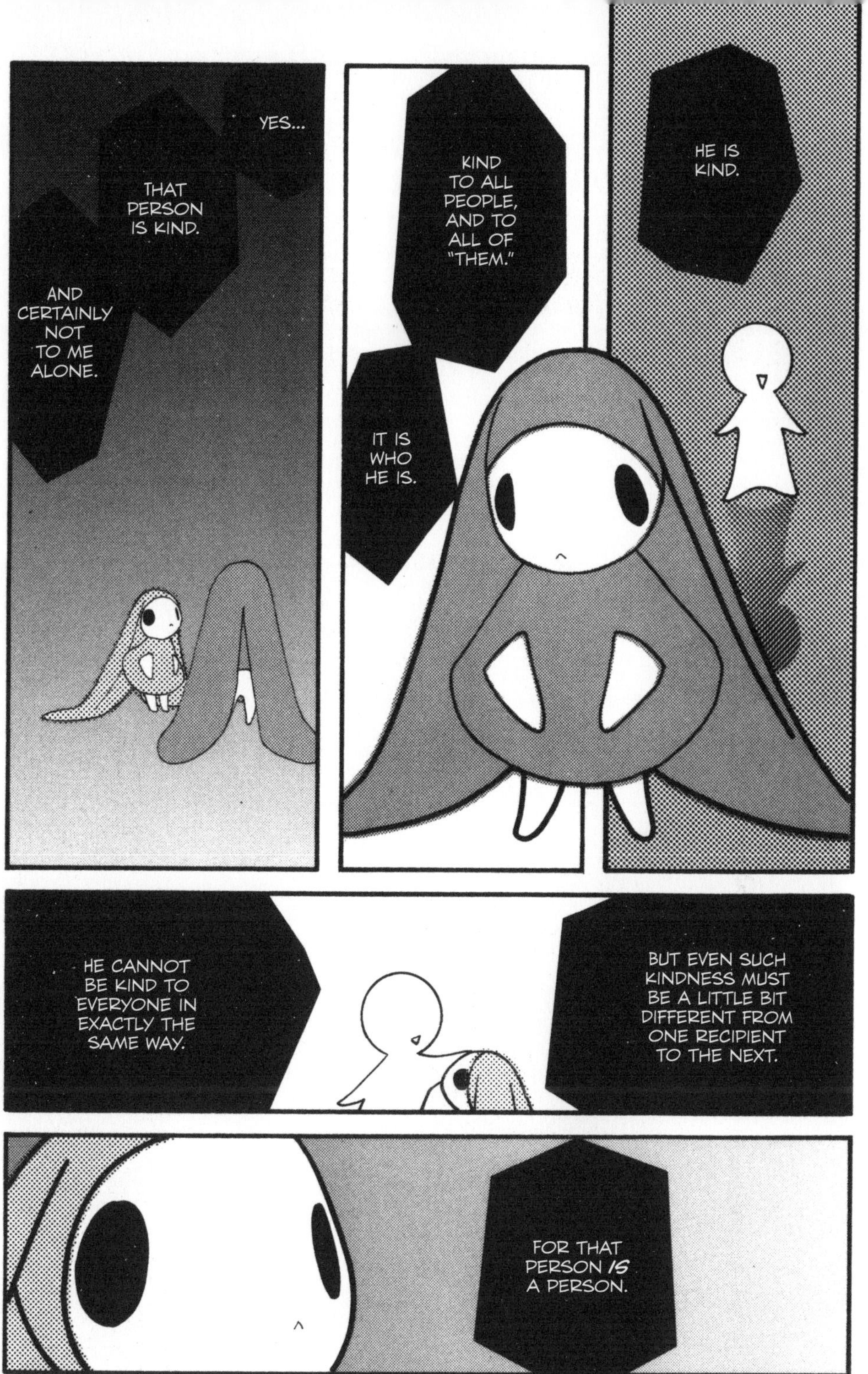
HE IS KIND.
KIND TO ALL PEOPLE, AND TO ALL OF "THEM."
IT IS WHO HE IS.
YES...
THAT PERSON IS KIND.
AND CERTAINLY NOT TO ME ALONE.
BUT EVEN SUCH KINDNESS MUST BE A LITTLE BIT DIFFERENT FROM ONE RECIPIENT TO THE NEXT.
HE CANNOT BE KIND TO EVERYONE IN EXACTLY THE SAME WAY.
FOR THAT PERSON *IS* A PERSON.

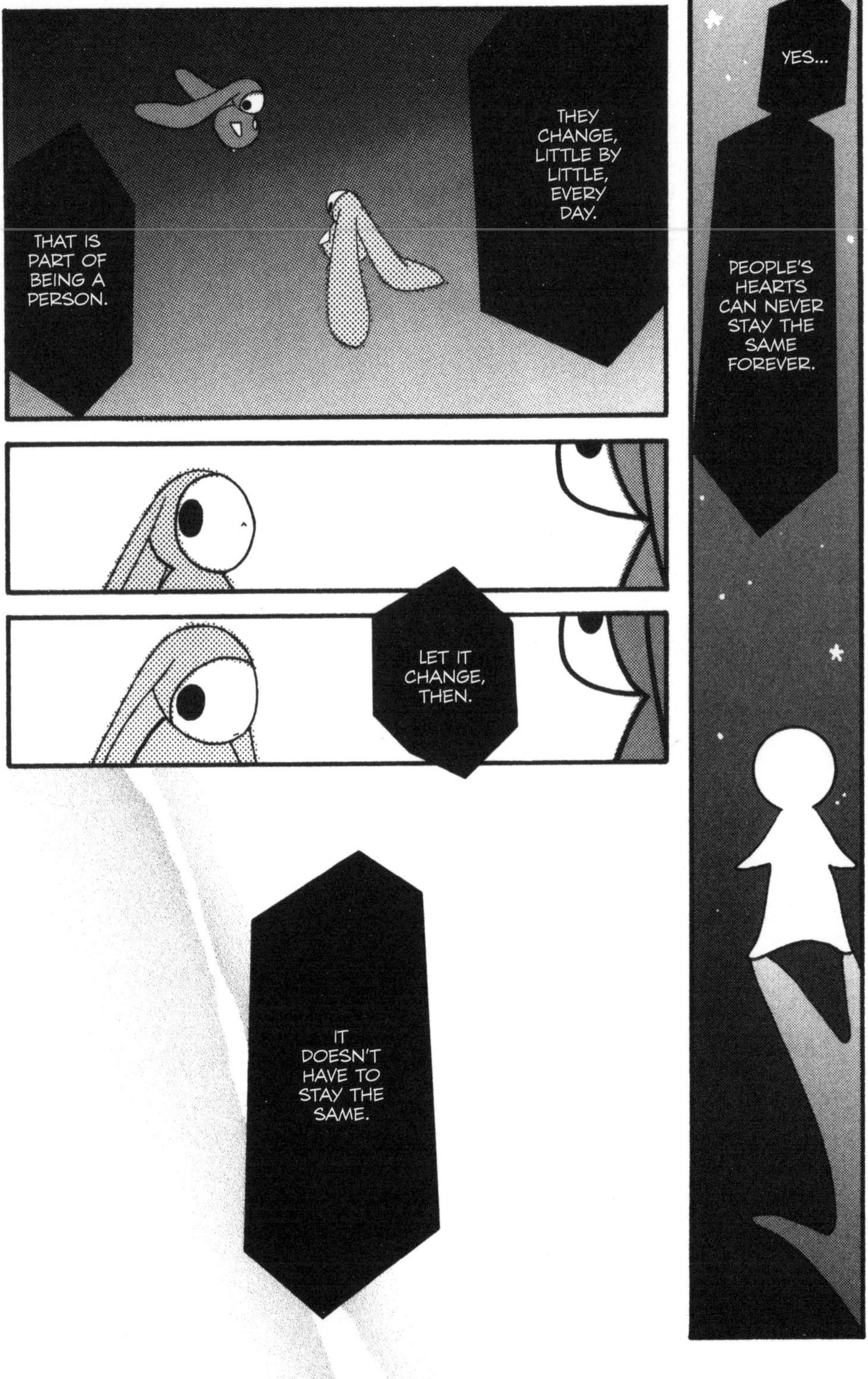
YES...
PEOPLE'S HEARTS CAN NEVER STAY THE SAME FOREVER.
THEY CHANGE, LITTLE BY LITTLE, EVERY DAY.
THAT IS PART OF BEING A PERSON.
LET IT CHANGE, THEN.
IT DOESN'T HAVE TO STAY THE SAME.

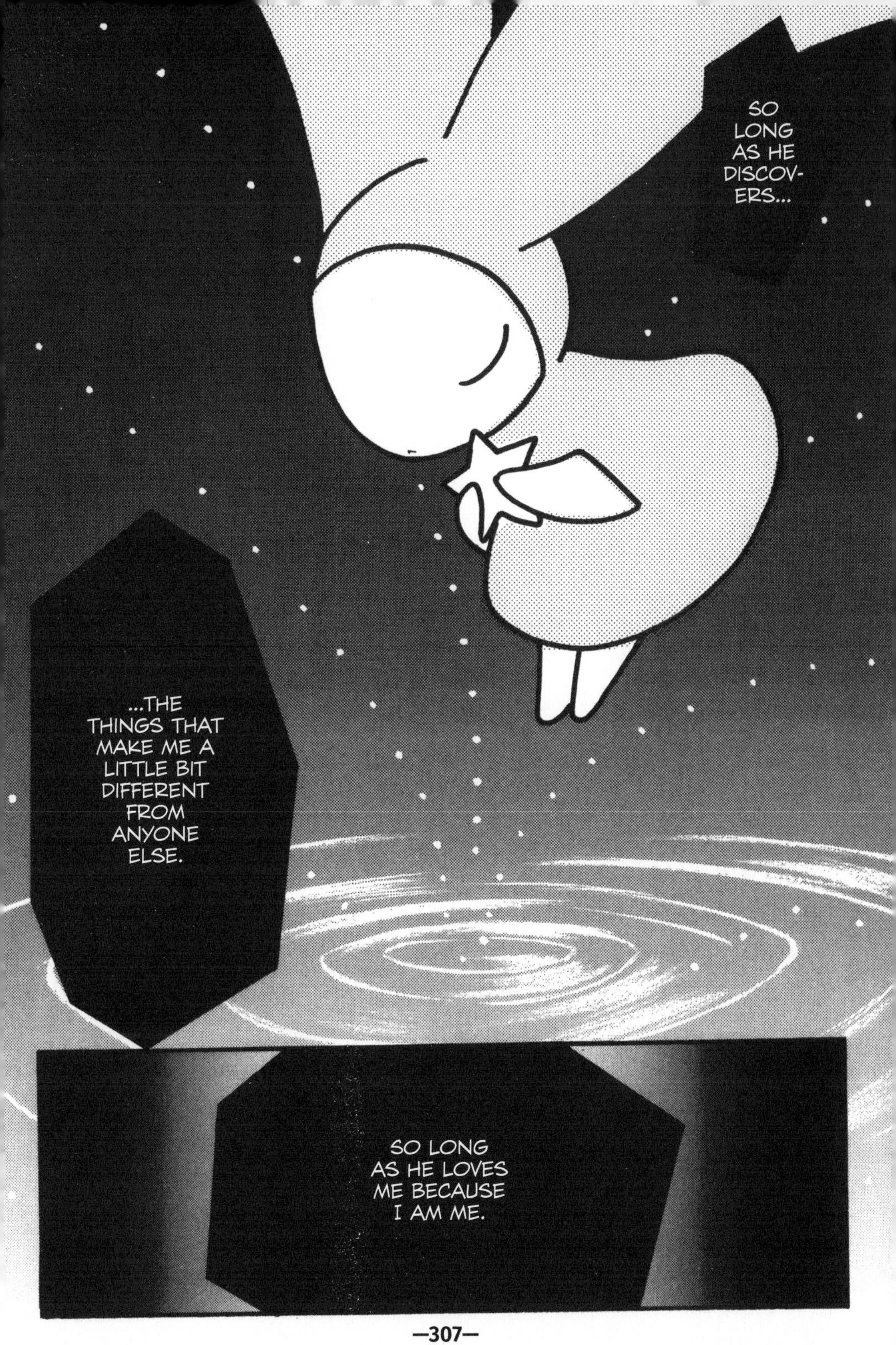
SO LONG AS HE DISCOVERS...
...THE THINGS THAT MAKE ME A LITTLE BIT DIFFERENT FROM ANYONE ELSE.
SO LONG AS HE LOVES ME BECAUSE I AM ME.

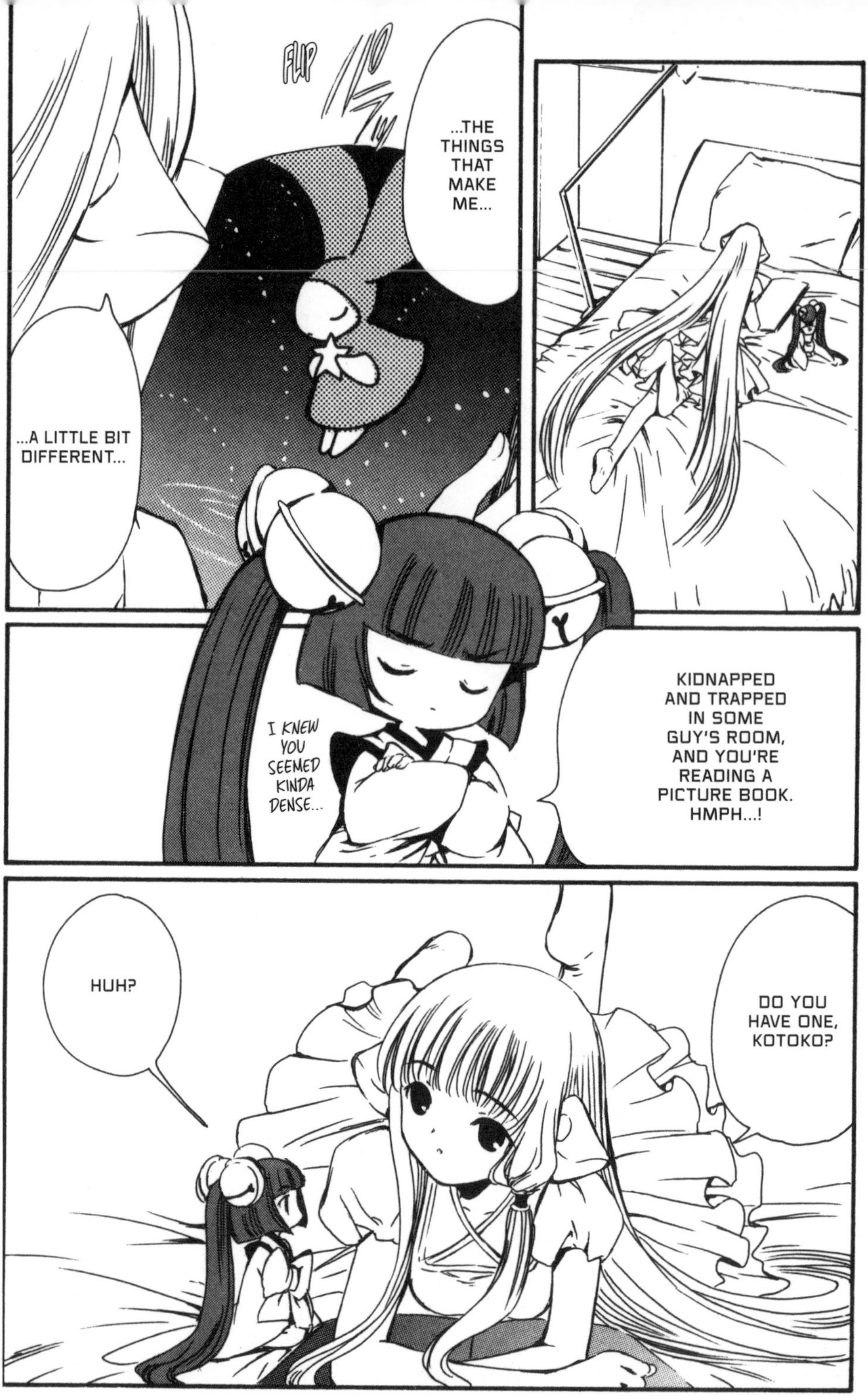
FLIP
...THE THINGS THAT MAKE ME...
...A LITTLE BIT DIFFERENT...
KIDNAPPED AND TRAPPED IN SOME GUY'S ROOM, AND YOU'RE READING A PICTURE BOOK. HMPH...!
I KNEW YOU SEEMED KINDA DENSE...
DO YOU HAVE ONE, KOTOKO?
HUH?

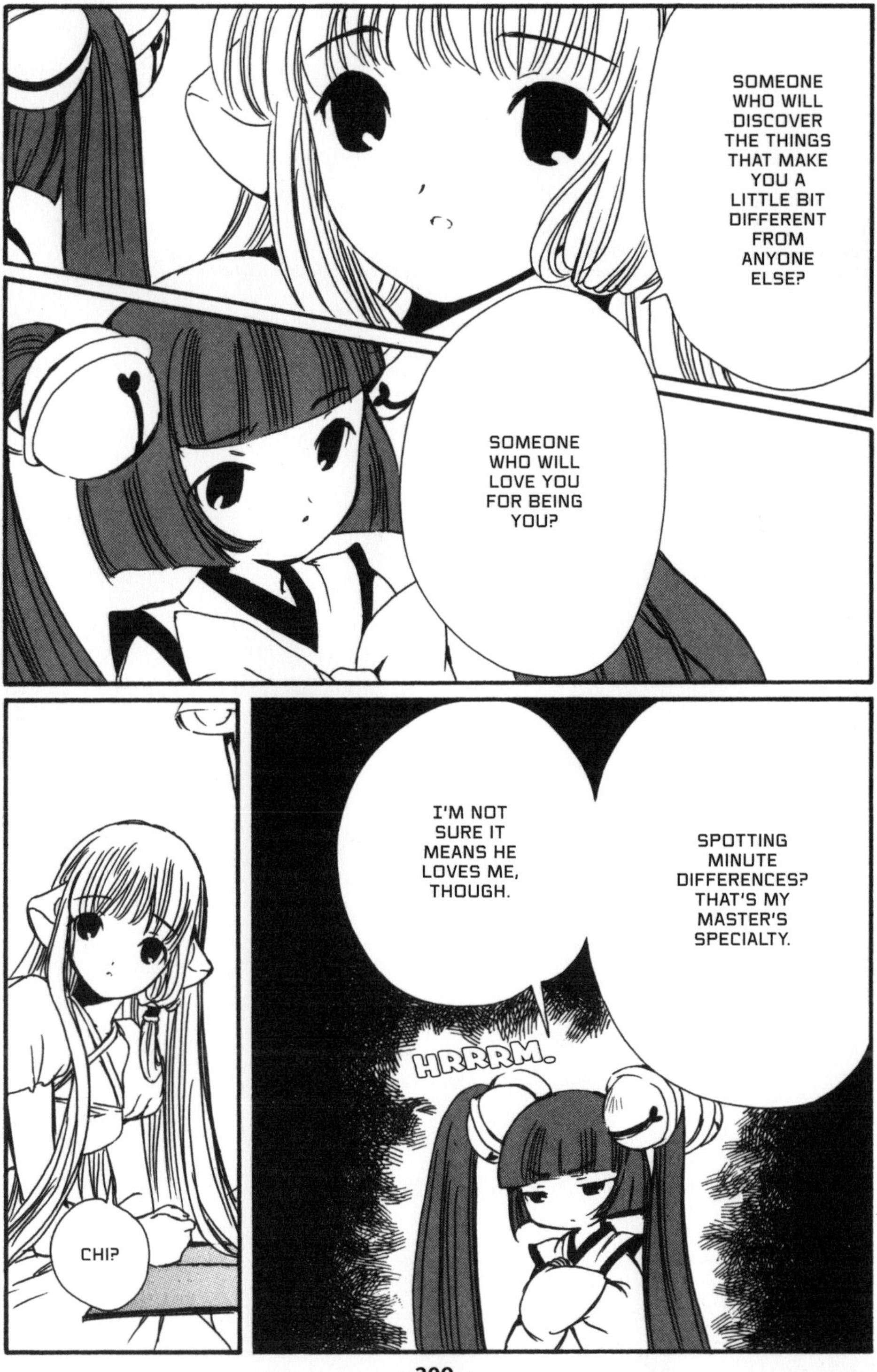
SOMEONE WHO WILL DISCOVER THE THINGS THAT MAKE YOU A LITTLE BIT DIFFERENT FROM ANYONE ELSE?
SOMEONE WHO WILL LOVE YOU FOR BEING YOU?
SPOTTING MINUTE DIFFERENCES? THAT'S MY MASTER'S SPECIALTY.
I'M NOT SURE IT MEANS HE LOVES ME, THOUGH.
HRRRM.
CHI?

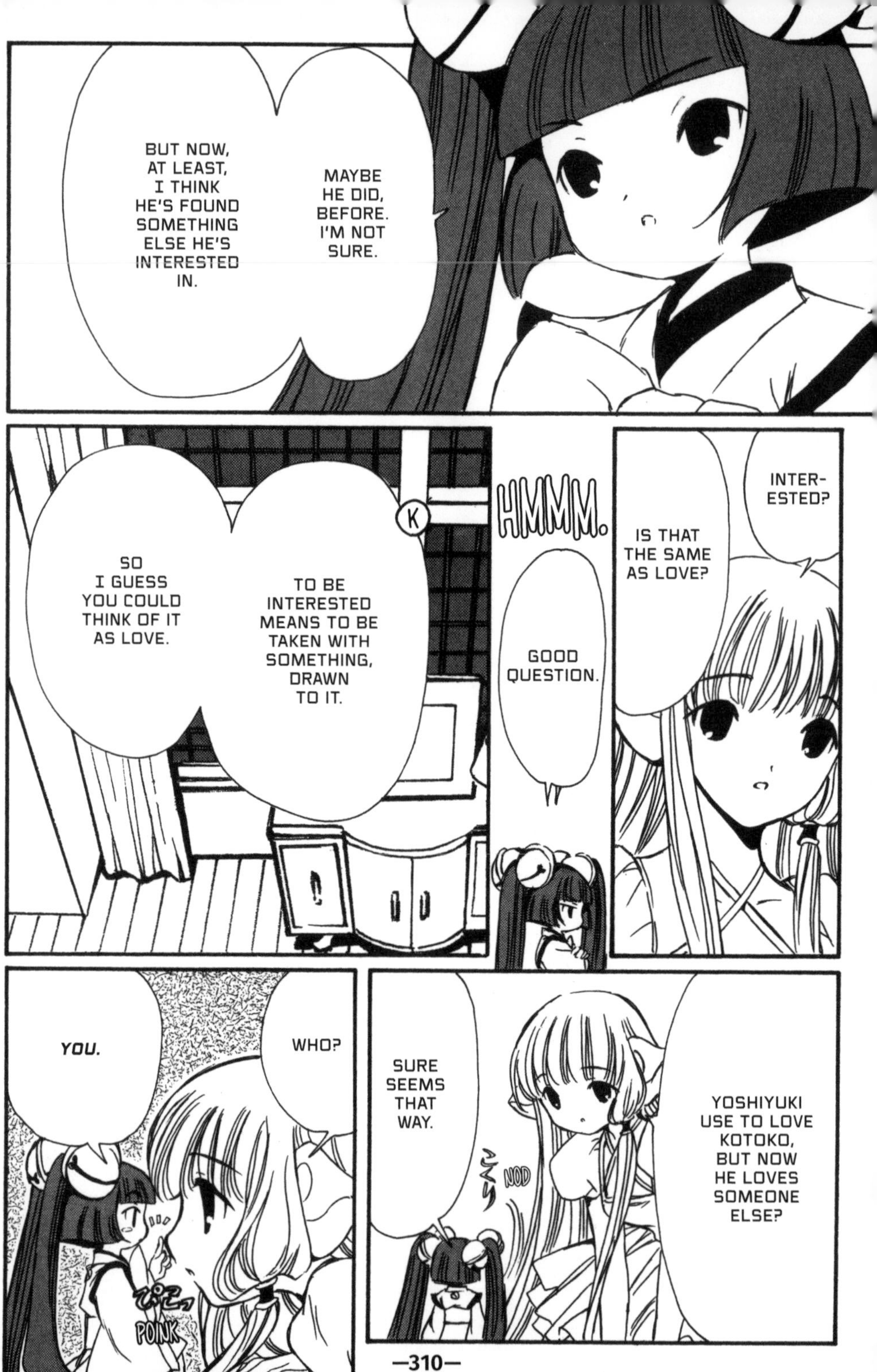
MAYBE HE DID, BEFORE. I'M NOT SURE.
BUT NOW, AT LEAST, I THINK HE'S FOUND SOMETHING ELSE HE'S INTERESTED IN.
INTER-ESTED?
IS THAT THE SAME AS LOVE?
HMMMM.
GOOD QUESTION.
TO BE INTERESTED MEANS TO BE TAKEN WITH SOMETHING, DRAWN TO IT.
SO I GUESS YOU COULD THINK OF IT AS LOVE.
YOSHIYUKI USE TO LOVE KOTOKO, BUT NOW HE LOVES SOMEONE ELSE?
SURE SEEMS THAT WAY.
NOD
WHO?
YOU.
POINK

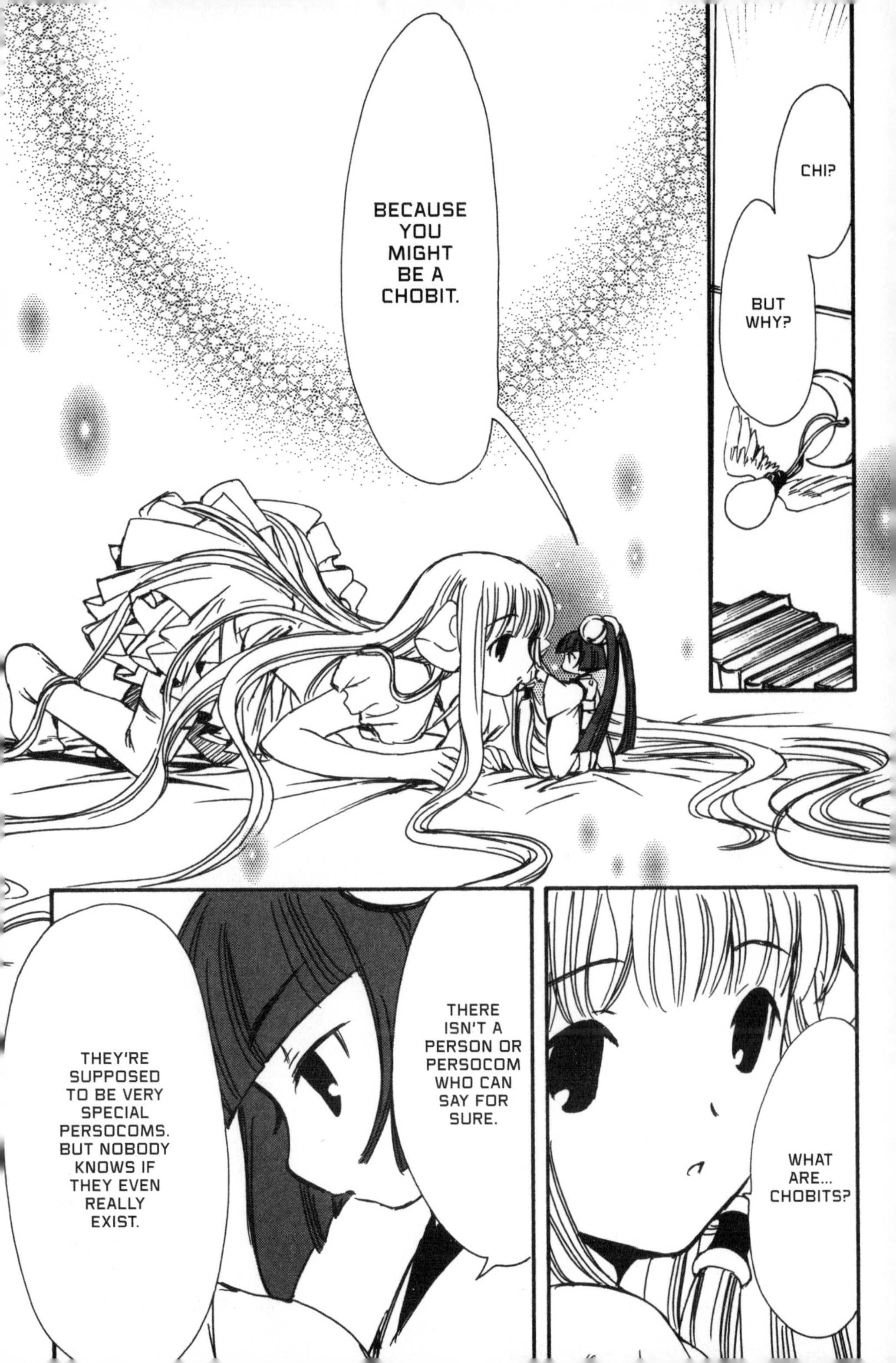
CHI?
BUT WHY?
BECAUSE YOU MIGHT BE A CHOBIT.
WHAT ARE... CHOBITS?
THERE ISN'T A PERSON OR PERSOCOM WHO CAN SAY FOR SURE.
THEY'RE SUPPOSED TO BE VERY SPECIAL PERSOCOMS. BUT NOBODY KNOWS IF THEY EVEN REALLY EXIST.

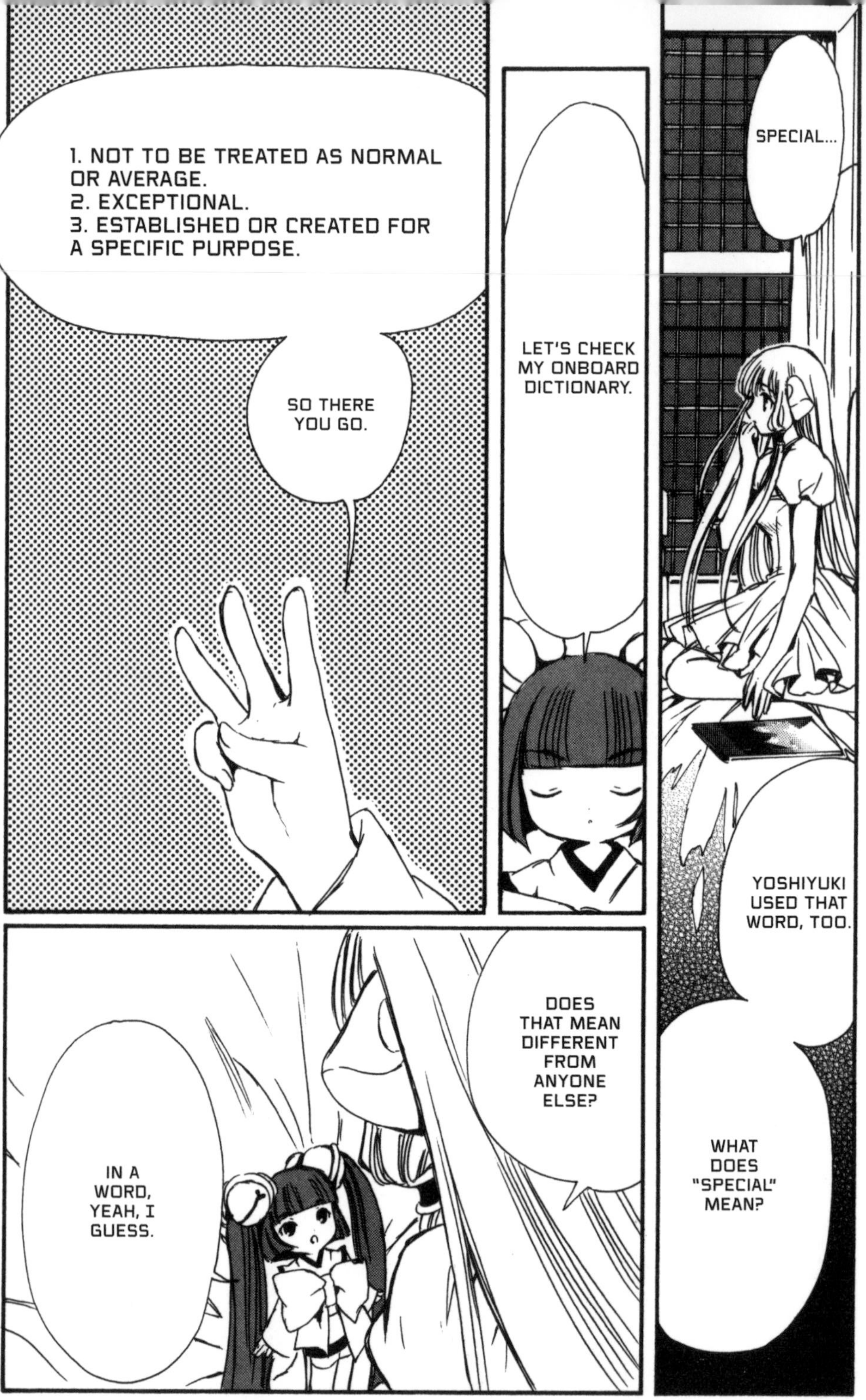
SPECIAL...
YOSHIYUKI USED THAT WORD, TOO.
WHAT DOES "SPECIAL" MEAN?
LET'S CHECK MY ONBOARD DICTIONARY.
1. NOT TO BE TREATED AS NORMAL OR AVERAGE.
2. EXCEPTIONAL.
3. ESTABLISHED OR CREATED FOR A SPECIFIC PURPOSE.
SO THERE YOU GO.
DOES THAT MEAN DIFFERENT FROM ANYONE ELSE?
IN A WORD, YEAH, I GUESS.

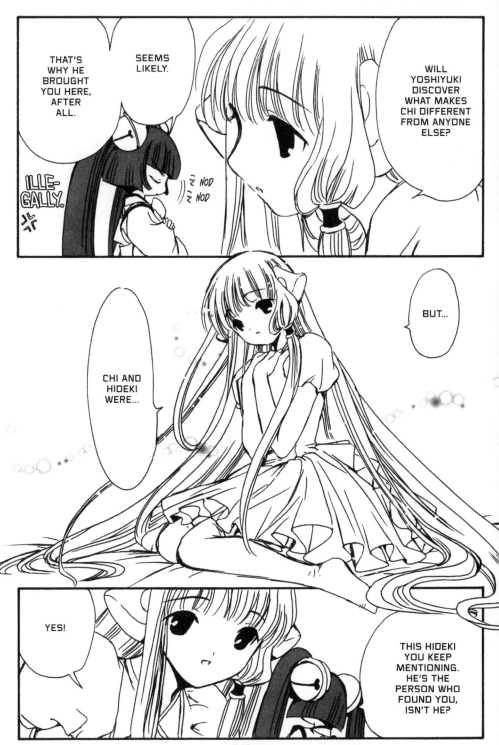

WILL YOSHIYUKI DISCOVER WHAT MAKES CHI DIFFERENT FROM ANYONE ELSE?

THAT'S WHY HE BROUGHT YOU HERE, AFTER ALL.

SEEMS LIKELY.

ILLE-GALLY.

NOD NOD

BUT...

CHI AND HIDEKI WERE...

YES!

THIS HIDEKI YOU KEEP MENTIONING. HE'S THE PERSON WHO FOUND YOU, ISN'T HE?

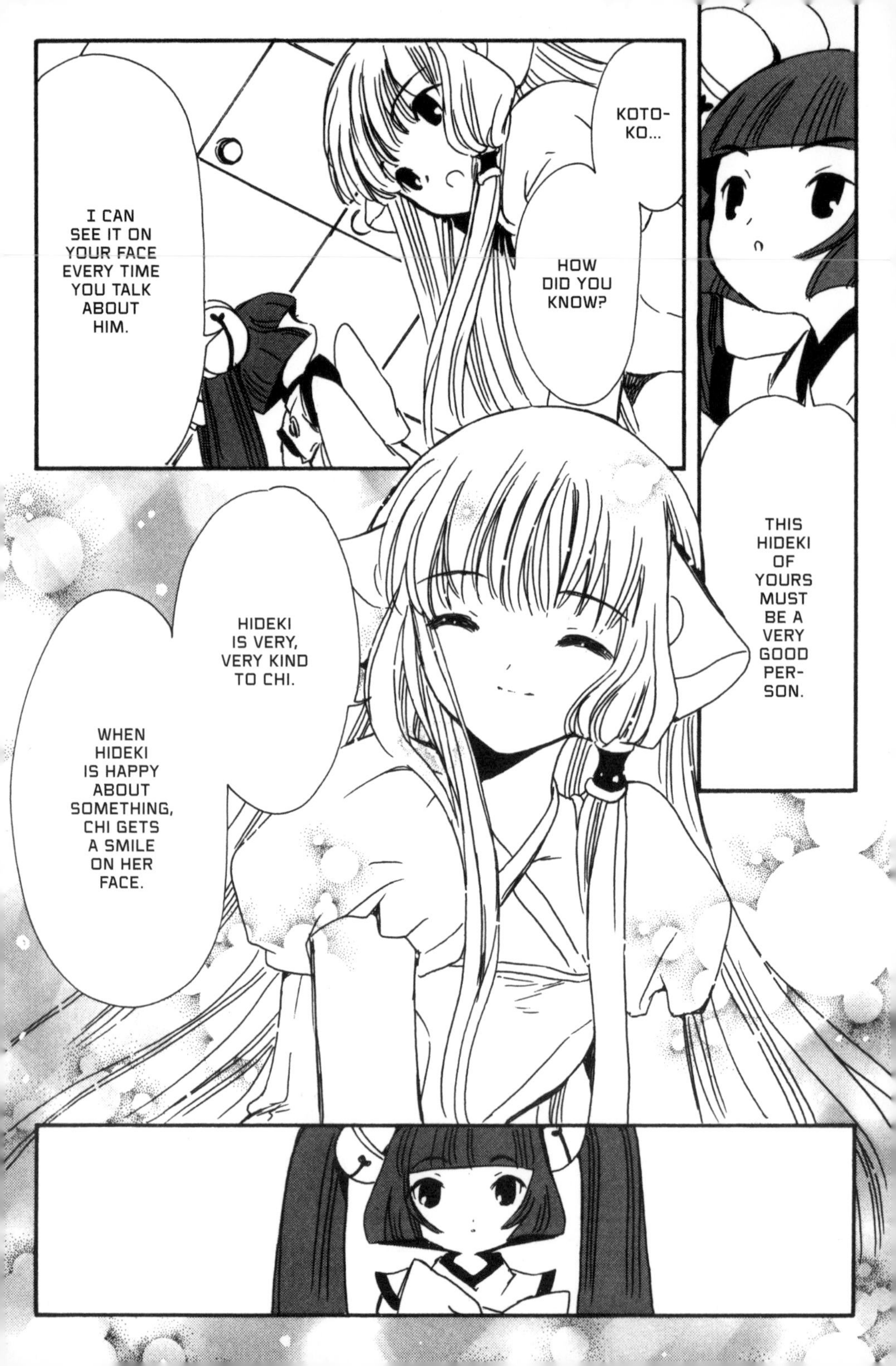
THIS HIDEKI OF YOURS MUST BE A VERY GOOD PER-SON.
KOTO-KO...
HOW DID YOU KNOW?
I CAN SEE IT ON YOUR FACE EVERY TIME YOU TALK ABOUT HIM.
HIDEKI IS VERY, VERY KIND TO CHI.
WHEN HIDEKI IS HAPPY ABOUT SOMETHING, CHI GETS A SMILE ON HER FACE.

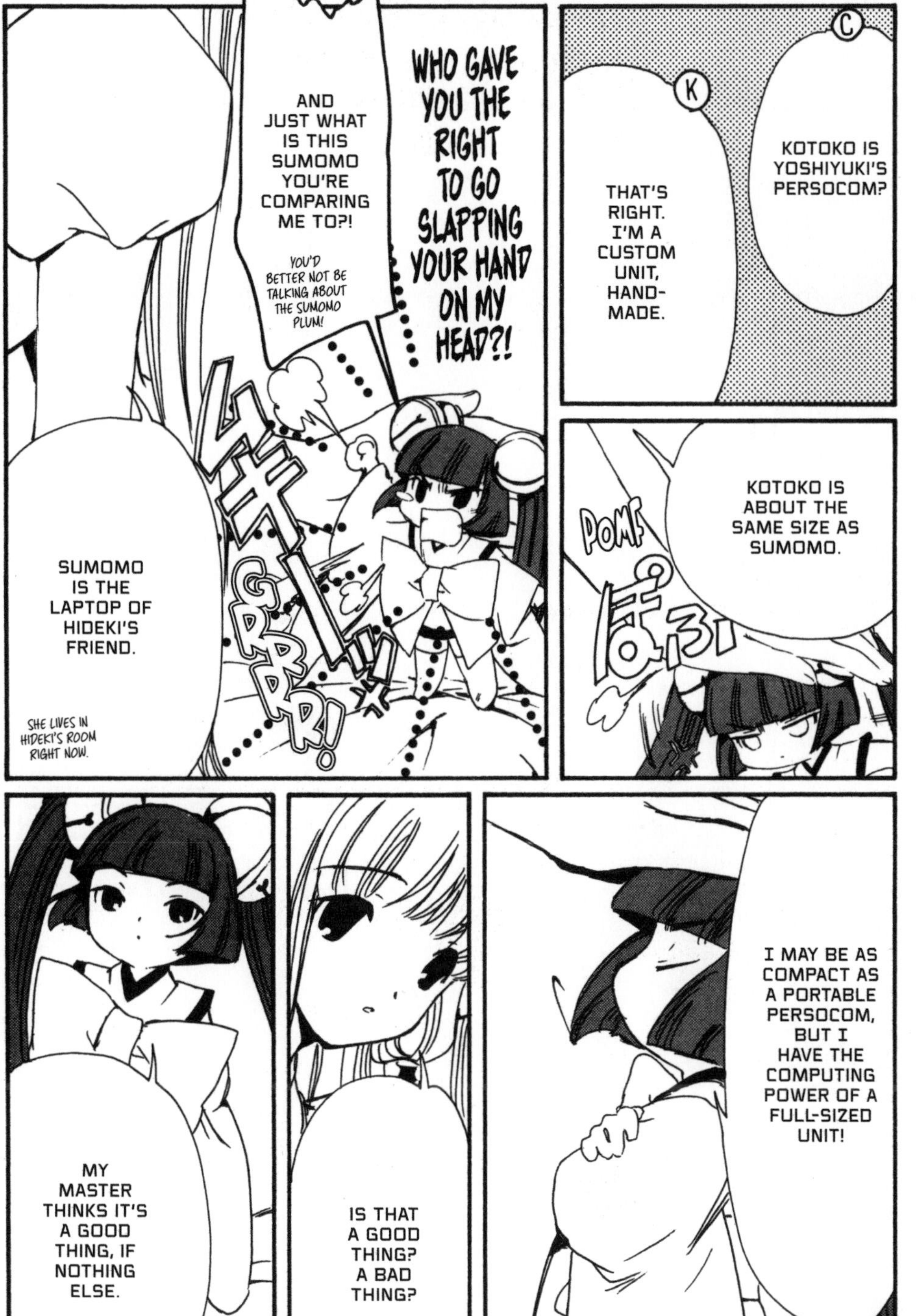
KOTOKO IS YOSHIYUKI'S PERSOCOM?
THAT'S RIGHT. I'M A CUSTOM UNIT, HAND-MADE.
POMF
ぽふ
KOTOKO IS ABOUT THE SAME SIZE AS SUMOMO.
WHO GAVE YOU THE RIGHT TO GO SLAPPING YOUR HAND ON MY HEAD?!
AND JUST WHAT IS THIS SUMOMO YOU'RE COMPARING ME TO?!
YOU'D BETTER NOT BE TALKING ABOUT THE SUMOMO PLUM!
GRRR!
SUMOMO IS THE LAPTOP OF HIDEKI'S FRIEND.
SHE LIVES IN HIDEKI'S ROOM RIGHT NOW.
I MAY BE AS COMPACT AS A PORTABLE PERSOCOM, BUT I HAVE THE COMPUTING POWER OF A FULL-SIZED UNIT!
IS THAT A GOOD THING? A BAD THING?
MY MASTER THINKS IT'S A GOOD THING, IF NOTHING ELSE.

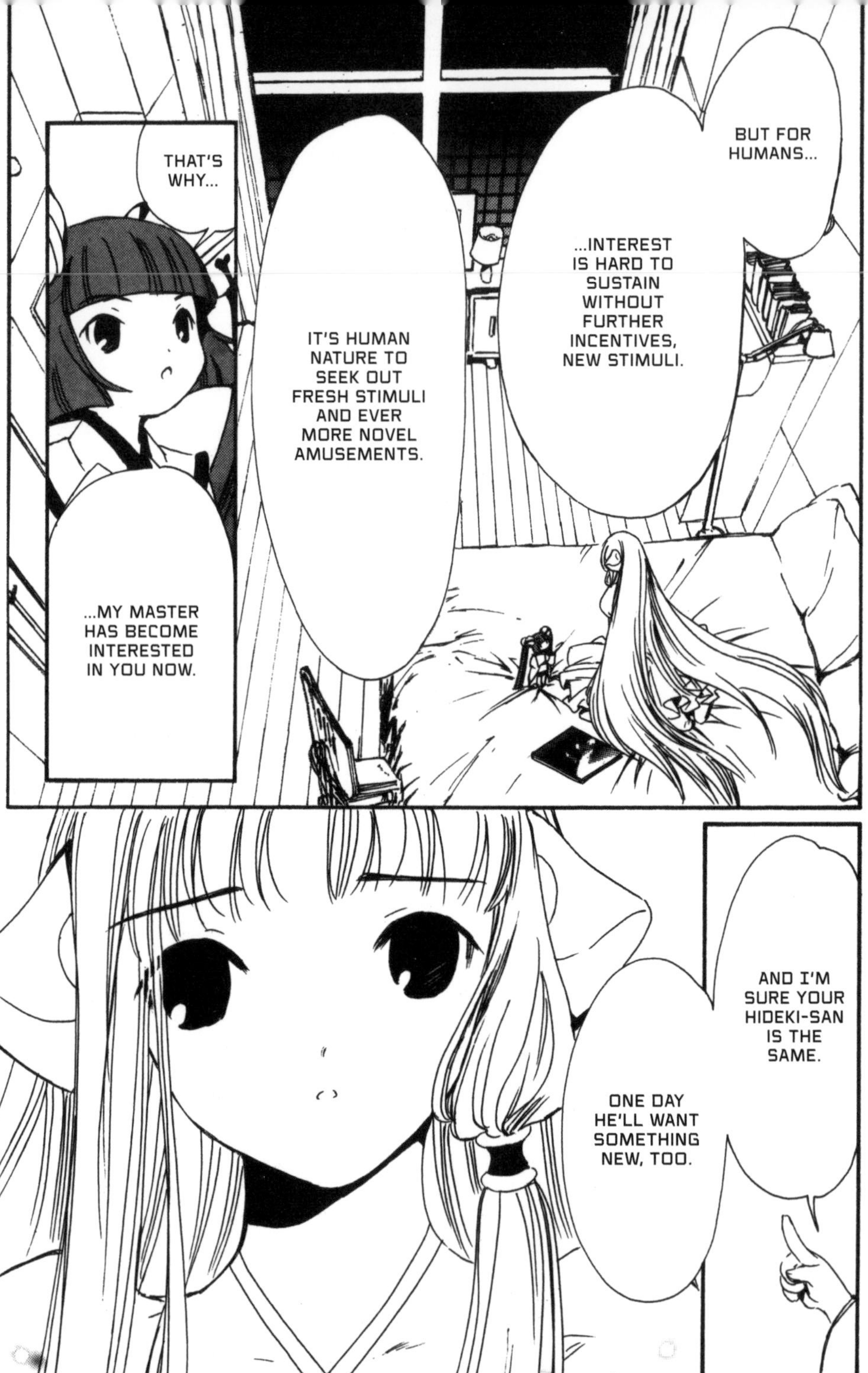
BUT FOR HUMANS...
...INTEREST IS HARD TO SUSTAIN WITHOUT FURTHER INCENTIVES, NEW STIMULI.
IT'S HUMAN NATURE TO SEEK OUT FRESH STIMULI AND EVER MORE NOVEL AMUSEMENTS.
THAT'S WHY...
...MY MASTER HAS BECOME INTERESTED IN YOU NOW.
AND I'M SURE YOUR HIDEKI-SAN IS THE SAME.
ONE DAY HE'LL WANT SOMETHING NEW, TOO.

<chapter.45> end

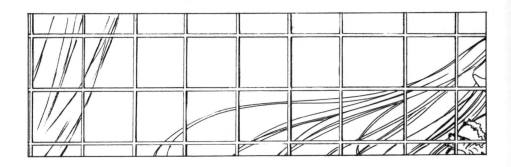

⟨chapter.46⟩

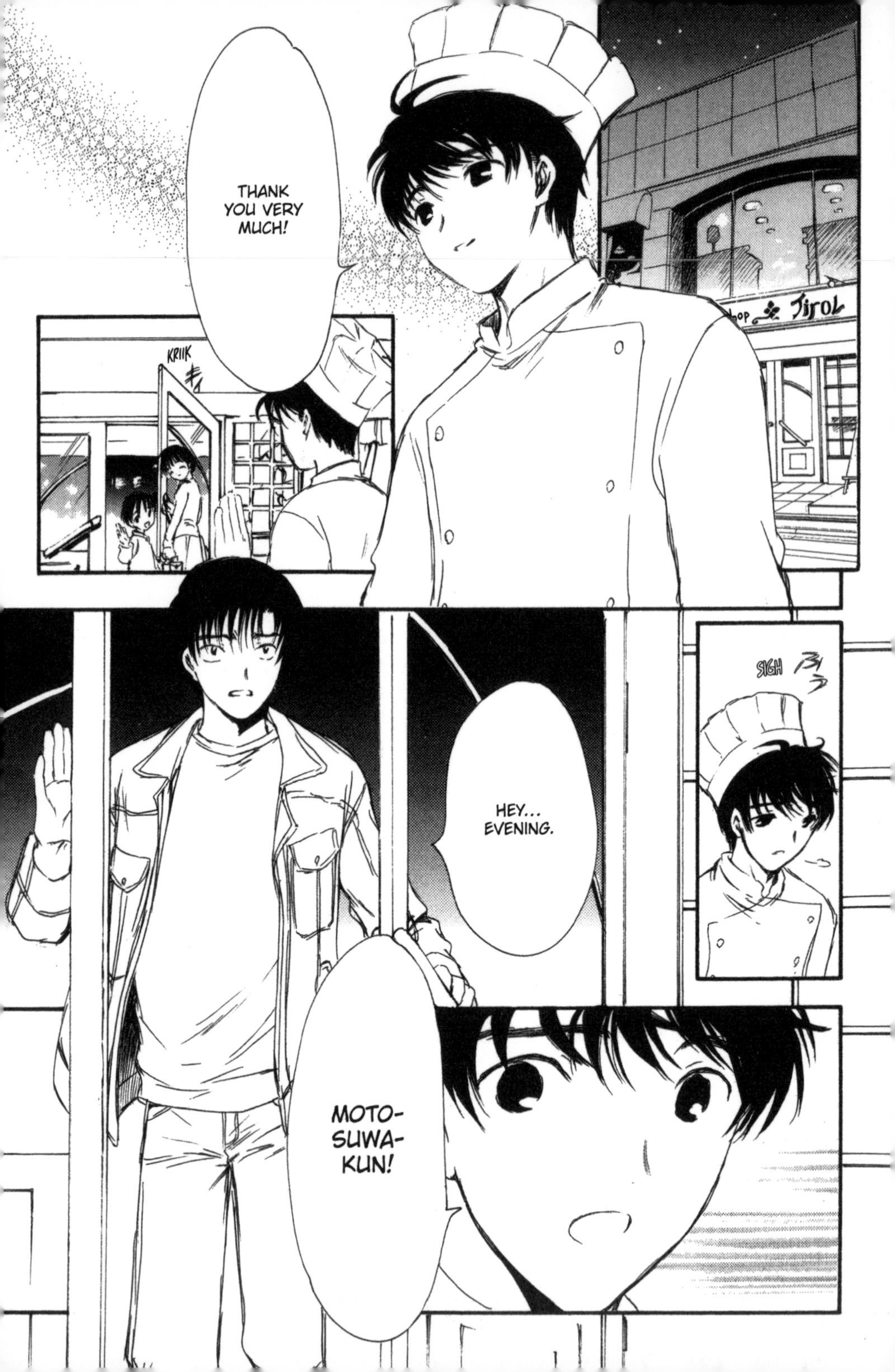
THANK YOU VERY MUCH!
Tirol
KRIIK
SIGH
HEY... EVENING.
MOTO-SUWA-KUN!

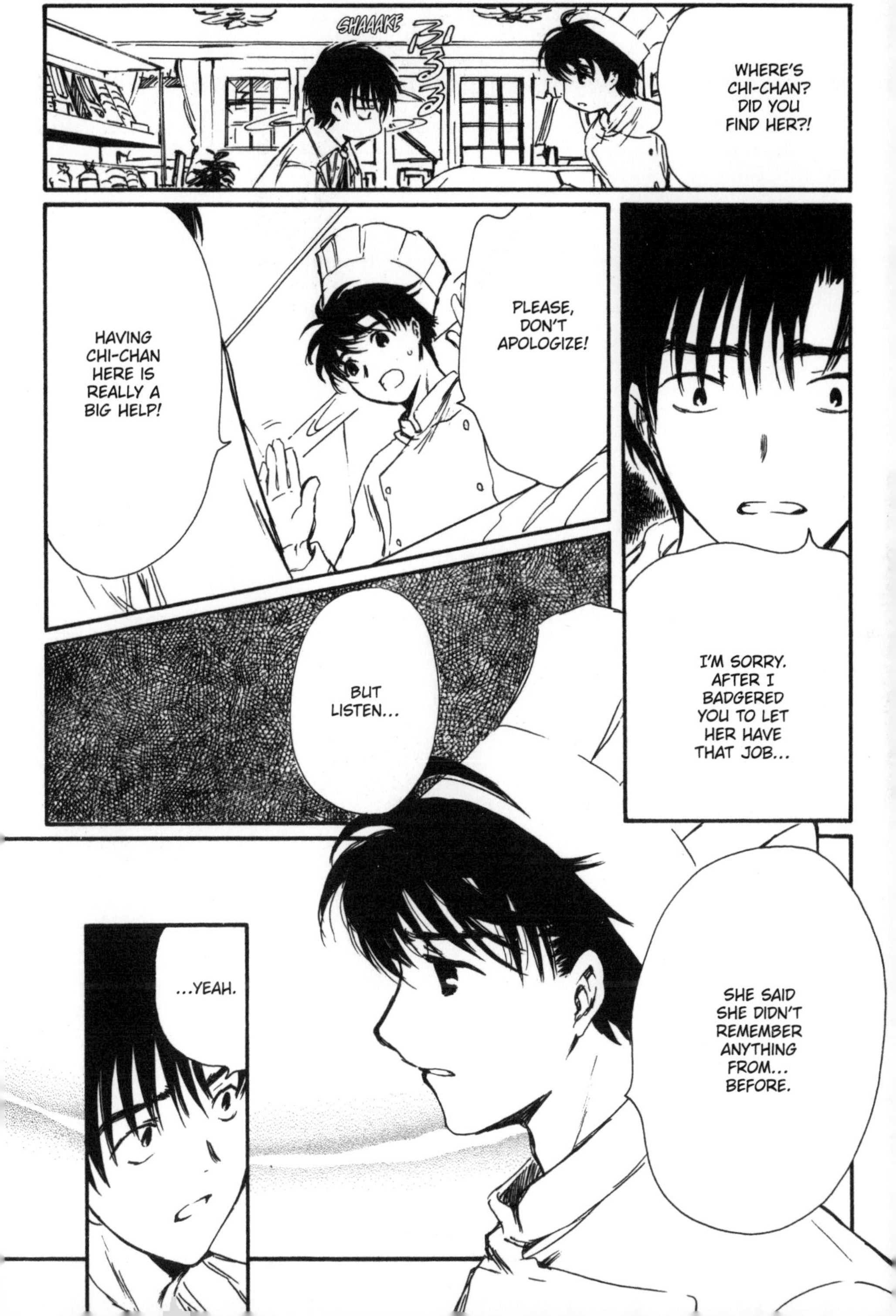
WHERE'S CHI-CHAN? DID YOU FIND HER?!
SHAAAKE
I'M SORRY. AFTER I BADGERED YOU TO LET HER HAVE THAT JOB...
PLEASE, DON'T APOLOGIZE!
HAVING CHI-CHAN HERE IS REALLY A BIG HELP!
BUT LISTEN...
SHE SAID SHE DIDN'T REMEMBER ANYTHING FROM... BEFORE.
...YEAH.

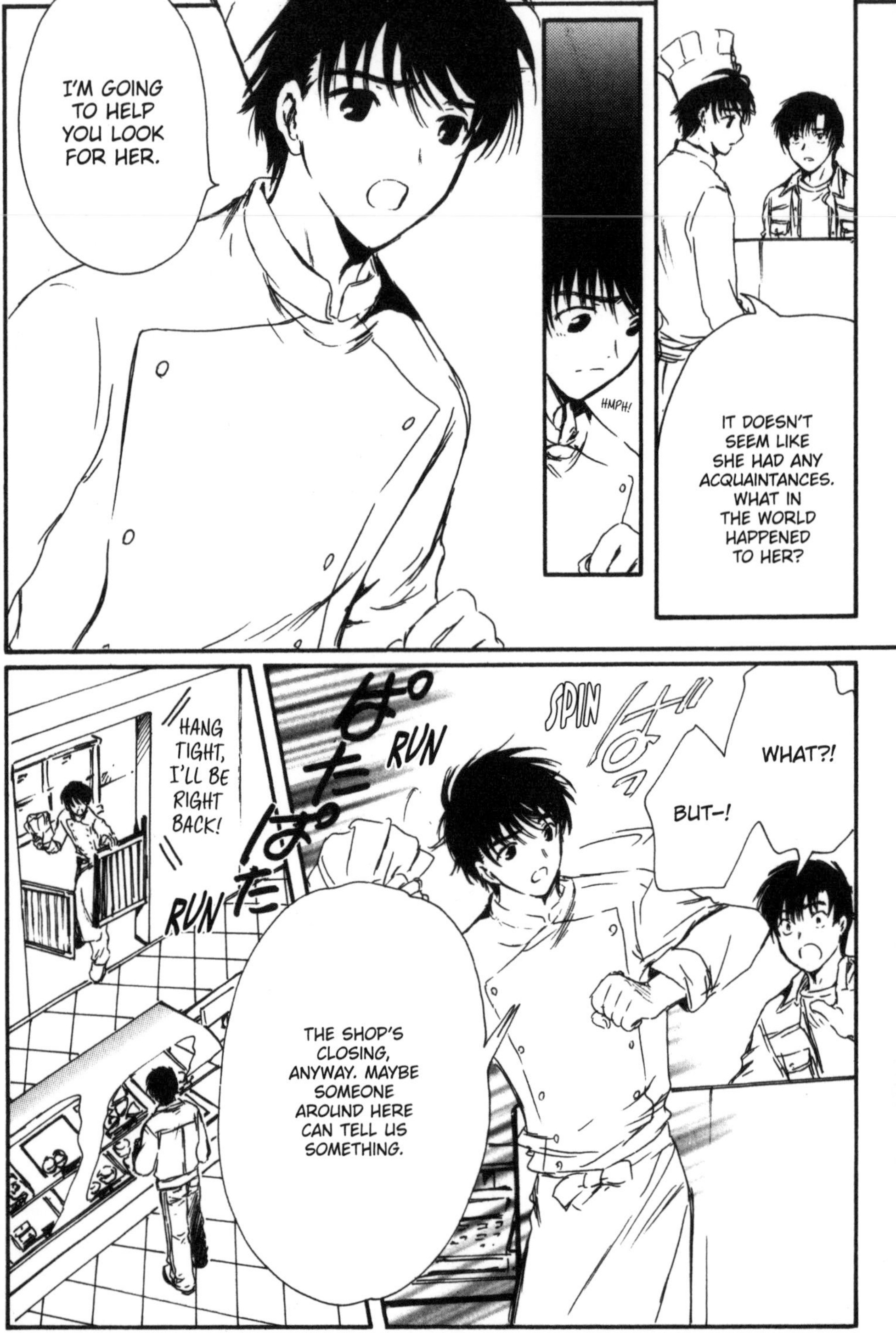
IT DOESN'T SEEM LIKE SHE HAD ANY ACQUAINTANCES. WHAT IN THE WORLD HAPPENED TO HER?
HMPH!
I'M GOING TO HELP YOU LOOK FOR HER.
WHAT?!
BUT–!
SPIN
THE SHOP'S CLOSING, ANYWAY. MAYBE SOMEONE AROUND HERE CAN TELL US SOMETHING.
ぱたぱた
RUN
RUN
HANG TIGHT, I'LL BE RIGHT BACK!

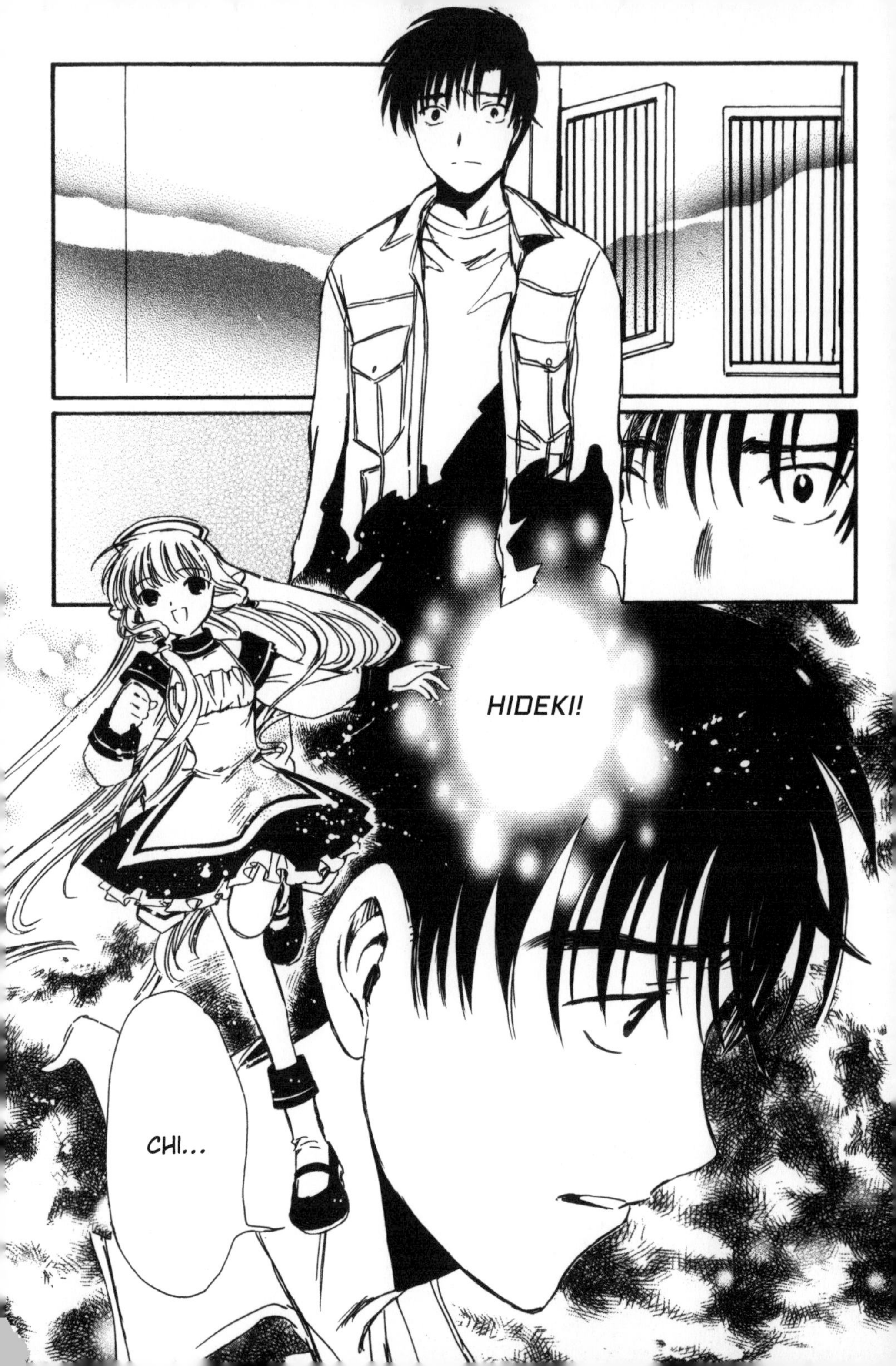
HIDEKI!
CHI...

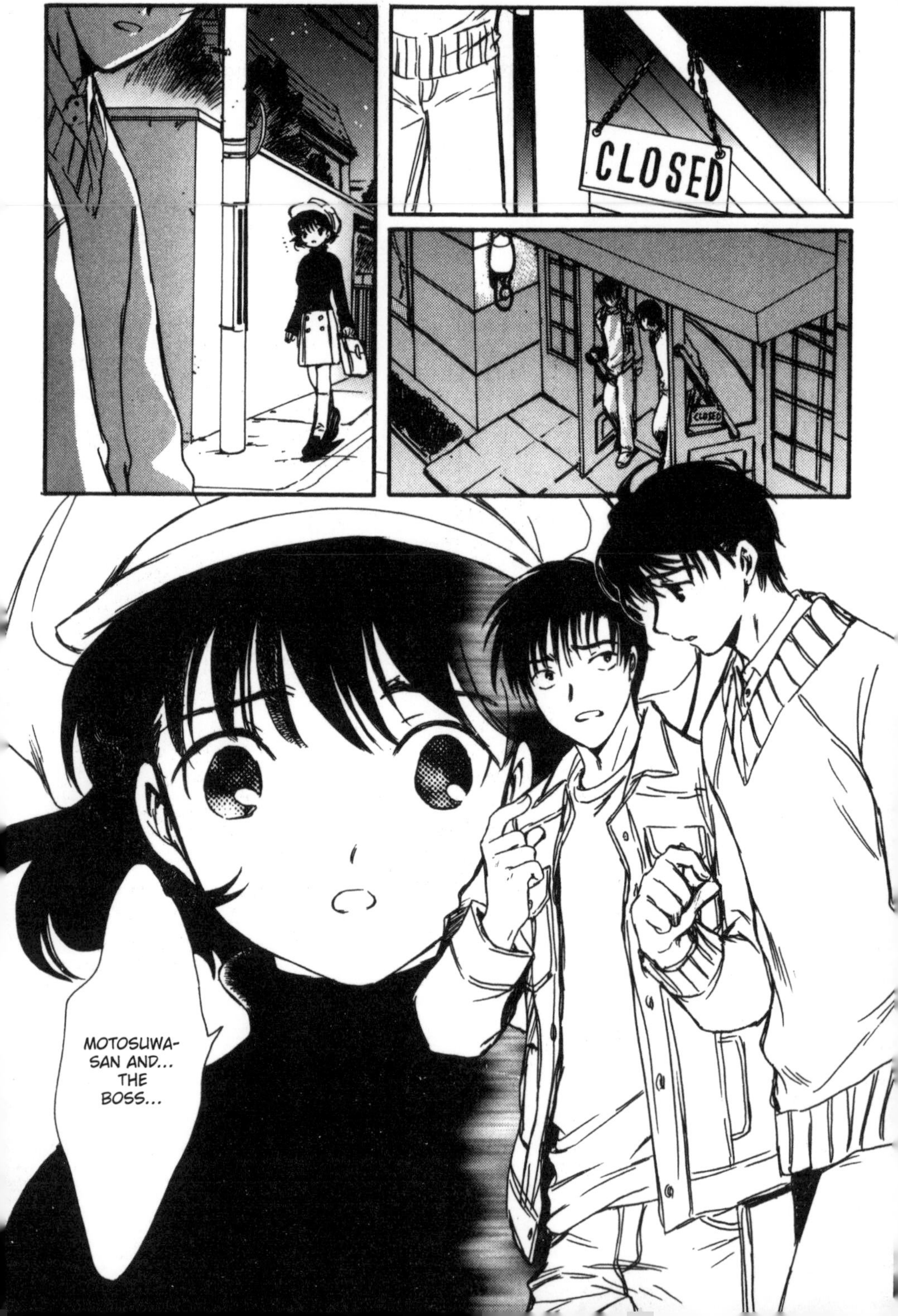
CLOSED
CLOSED
MOTOSUWA-SAN AND... THE BOSS...

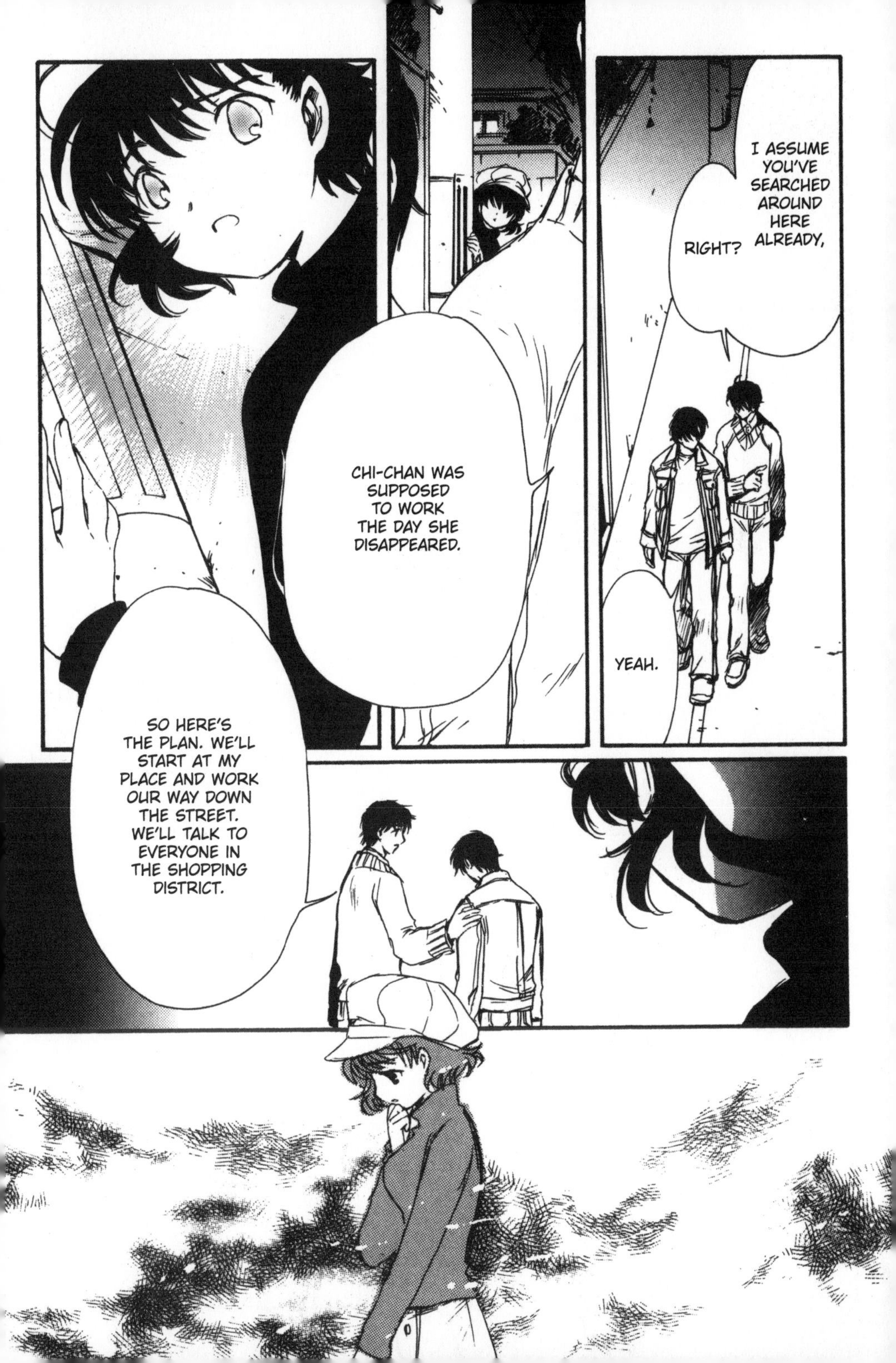
I ASSUME YOU'VE SEARCHED AROUND HERE ALREADY, RIGHT?
YEAH.
CHI-CHAN WAS SUPPOSED TO WORK THE DAY SHE DISAPPEARED.
SO HERE'S THE PLAN. WE'LL START AT MY PLACE AND WORK OUR WAY DOWN THE STREET. WE'LL TALK TO EVERYONE IN THE SHOPPING DISTRICT.

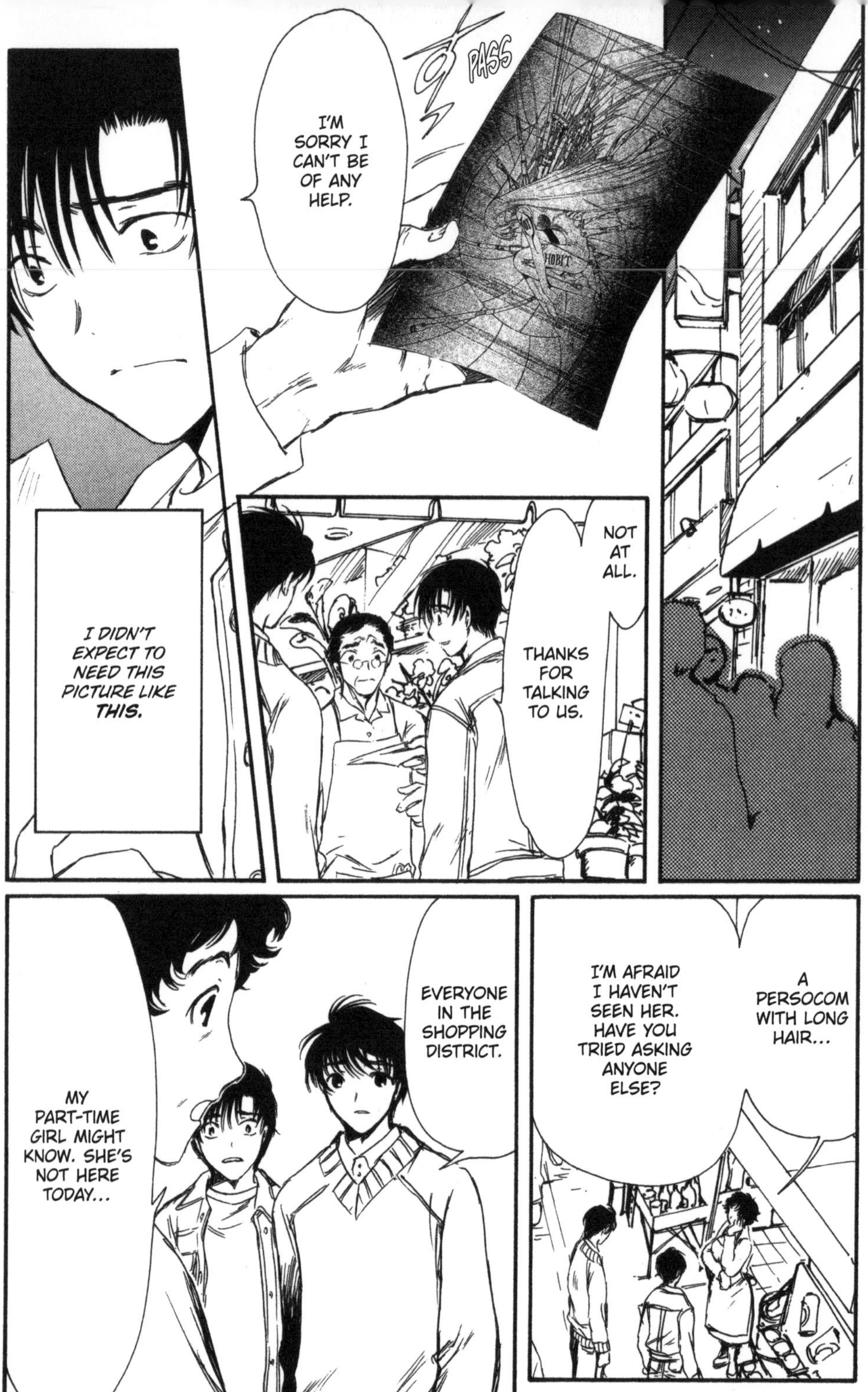
PASS
I'M SORRY I CAN'T BE OF ANY HELP.
NOT AT ALL.
THANKS FOR TALKING TO US.
I DIDN'T EXPECT TO NEED THIS PICTURE LIKE THIS.
A PERSOCOM WITH LONG HAIR...
I'M AFRAID I HAVEN'T SEEN HER. HAVE YOU TRIED ASKING ANYONE ELSE?
EVERYONE IN THE SHOPPING DISTRICT.
MY PART-TIME GIRL MIGHT KNOW. SHE'S NOT HERE TODAY...

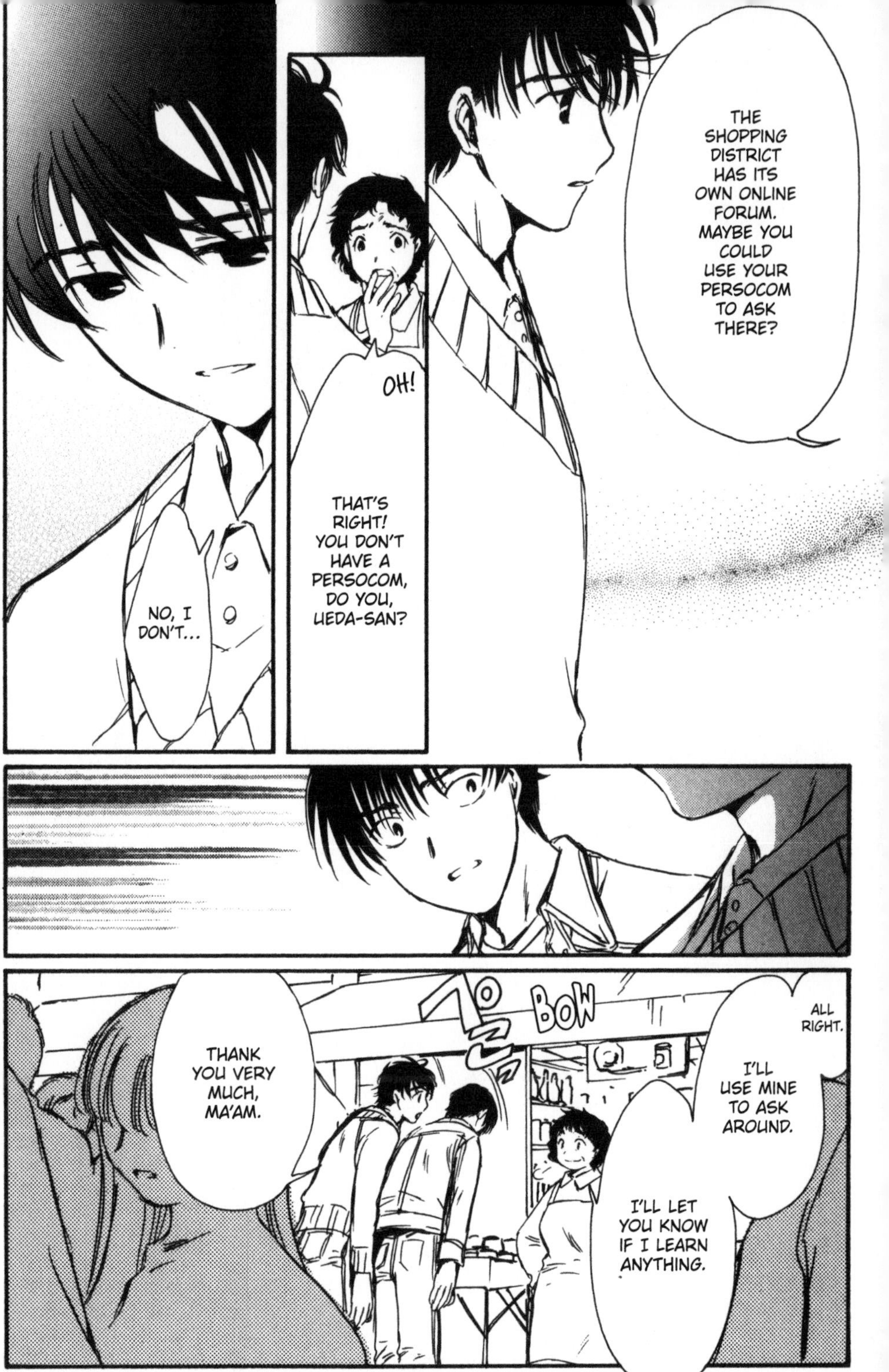
THE SHOPPING DISTRICT HAS ITS OWN ONLINE FORUM. MAYBE YOU COULD USE YOUR PERSOCOM TO ASK THERE?
OH!
THAT'S RIGHT! YOU DON'T HAVE A PERSOCOM, DO YOU, UEDA-SAN?
NO, I DON'T...
ALL RIGHT.
I'LL USE MINE TO ASK AROUND.
I'LL LET YOU KNOW IF I LEARN ANYTHING.
BOW
THANK YOU VERY MUCH, MA'AM.

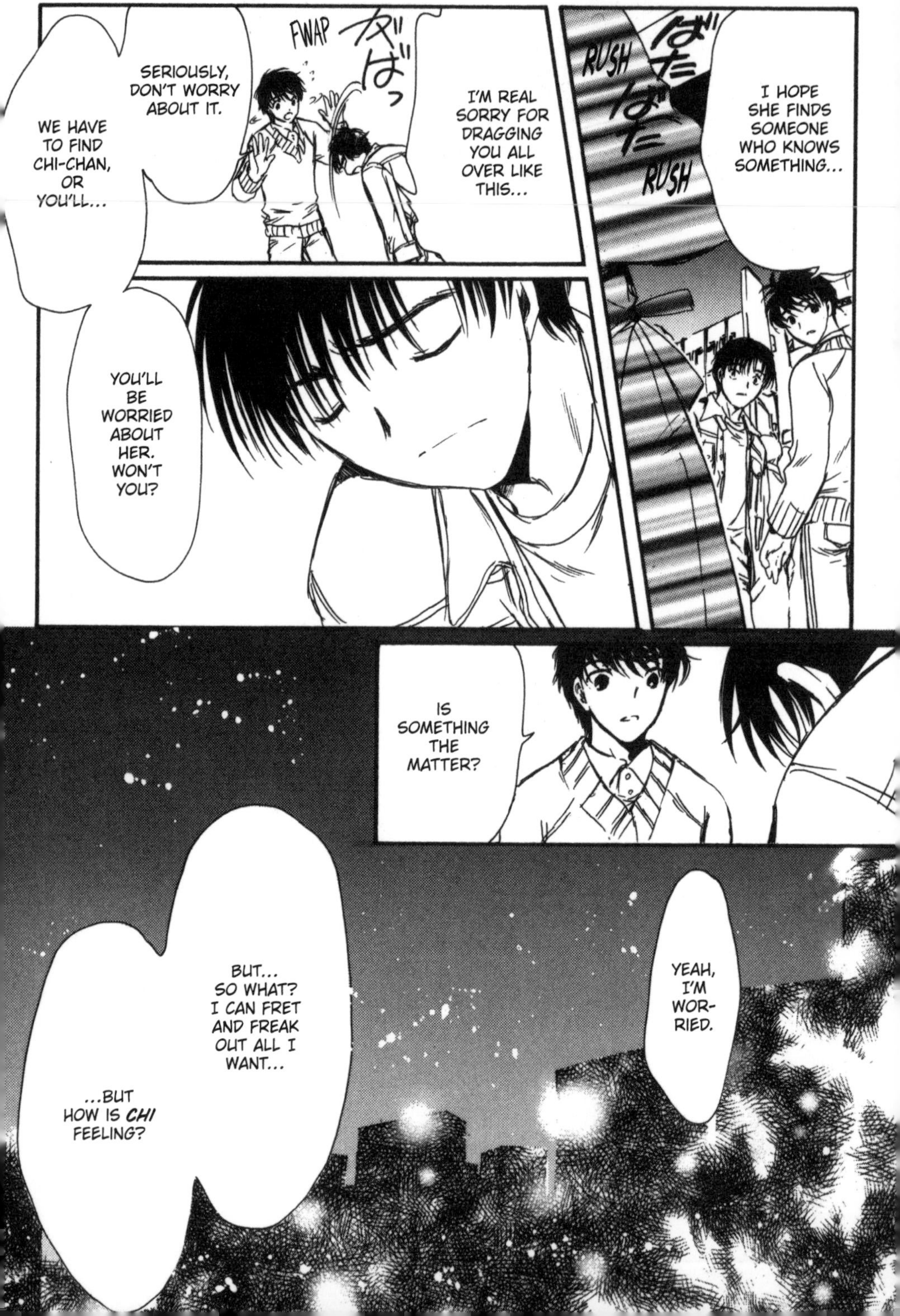
RUSH
RUSH
I HOPE SHE FINDS SOMEONE WHO KNOWS SOMETHING...
FWAP
がばっ
I'M REAL SORRY FOR DRAGGING YOU ALL OVER LIKE THIS...
SERIOUSLY, DON'T WORRY ABOUT IT.
WE HAVE TO FIND CHI-CHAN, OR YOU'LL...
YOU'LL BE WORRIED ABOUT HER. WON'T YOU?
IS SOMETHING THE MATTER?
YEAH, I'M WOR-RIED.
BUT... SO WHAT? I CAN FRET AND FREAK OUT ALL I WANT...
...BUT HOW IS *CHI* FEELING?

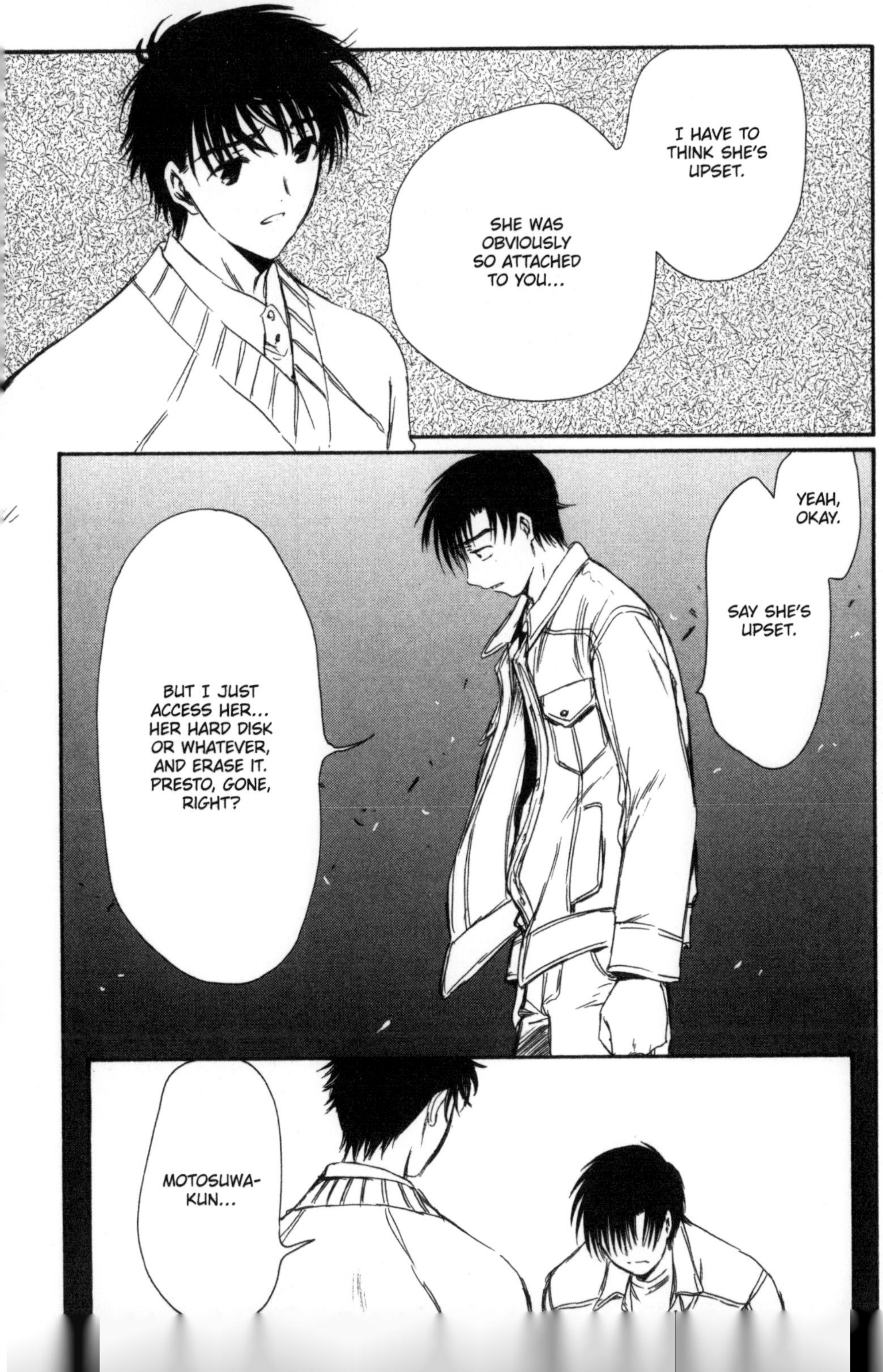
I HAVE TO THINK SHE'S UPSET.
SHE WAS OBVIOUSLY SO ATTACHED TO YOU...
YEAH, OKAY.
SAY SHE'S UPSET.
BUT I JUST ACCESS HER... HER HARD DISK OR WHATEVER, AND ERASE IT. PRESTO, GONE, RIGHT?
MOTOSUWA-KUN...

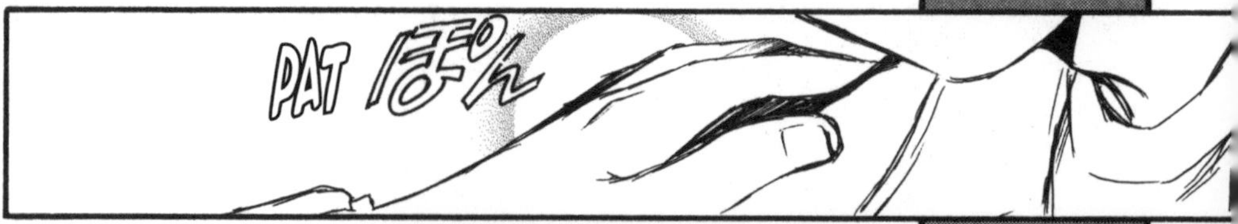
PAT ぽん

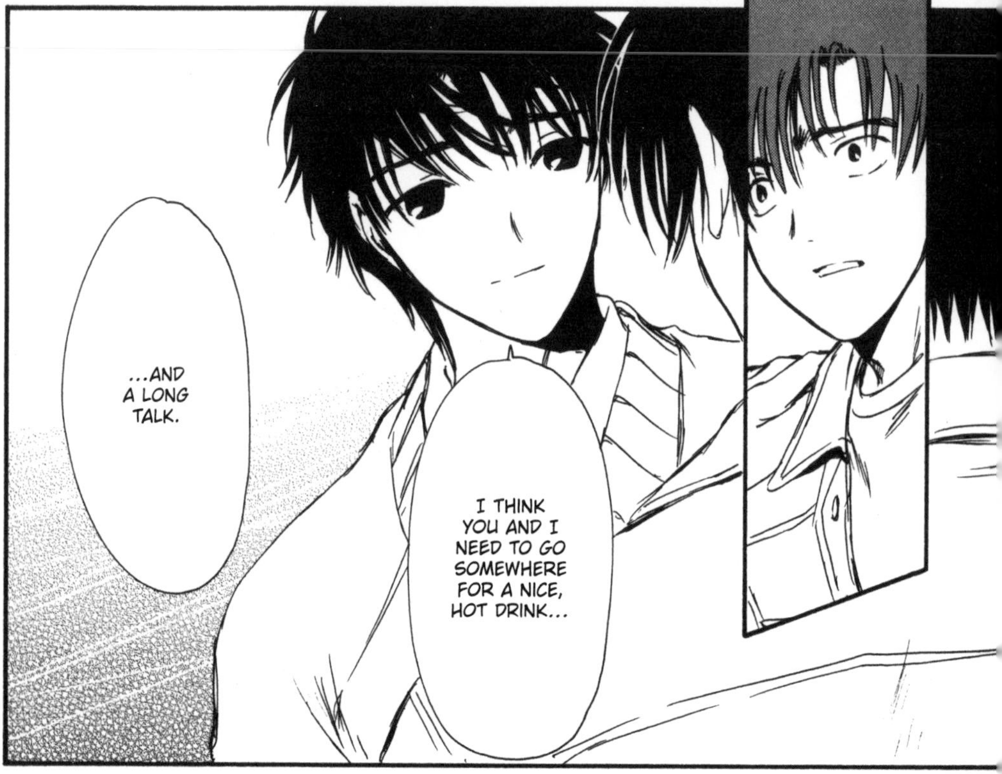
I THINK YOU AND I NEED TO GO SOMEWHERE FOR A NICE, HOT DRINK...
...AND A LONG TALK.

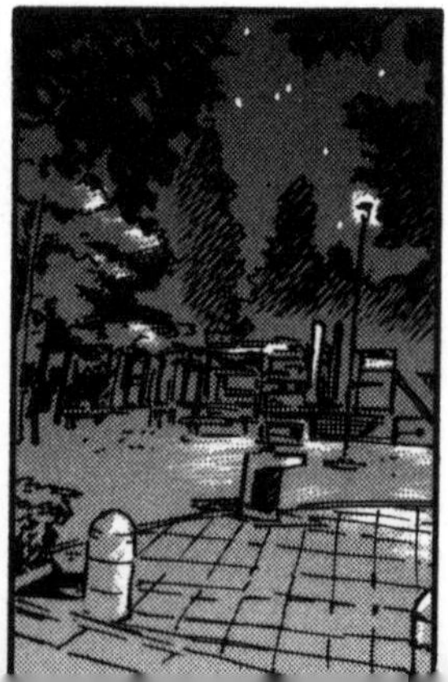

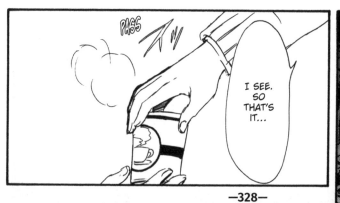

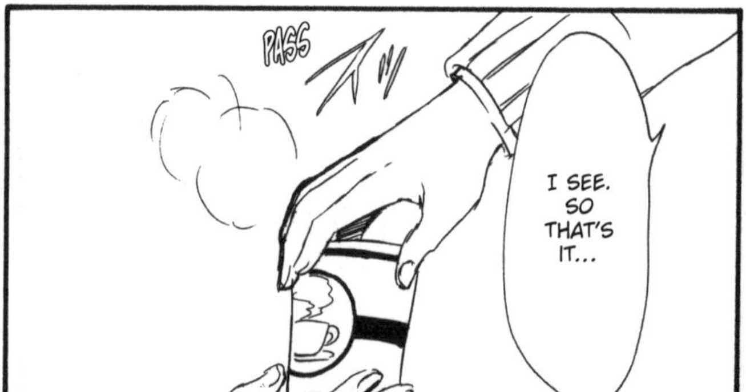
PASS
I SEE. SO THAT'S IT...

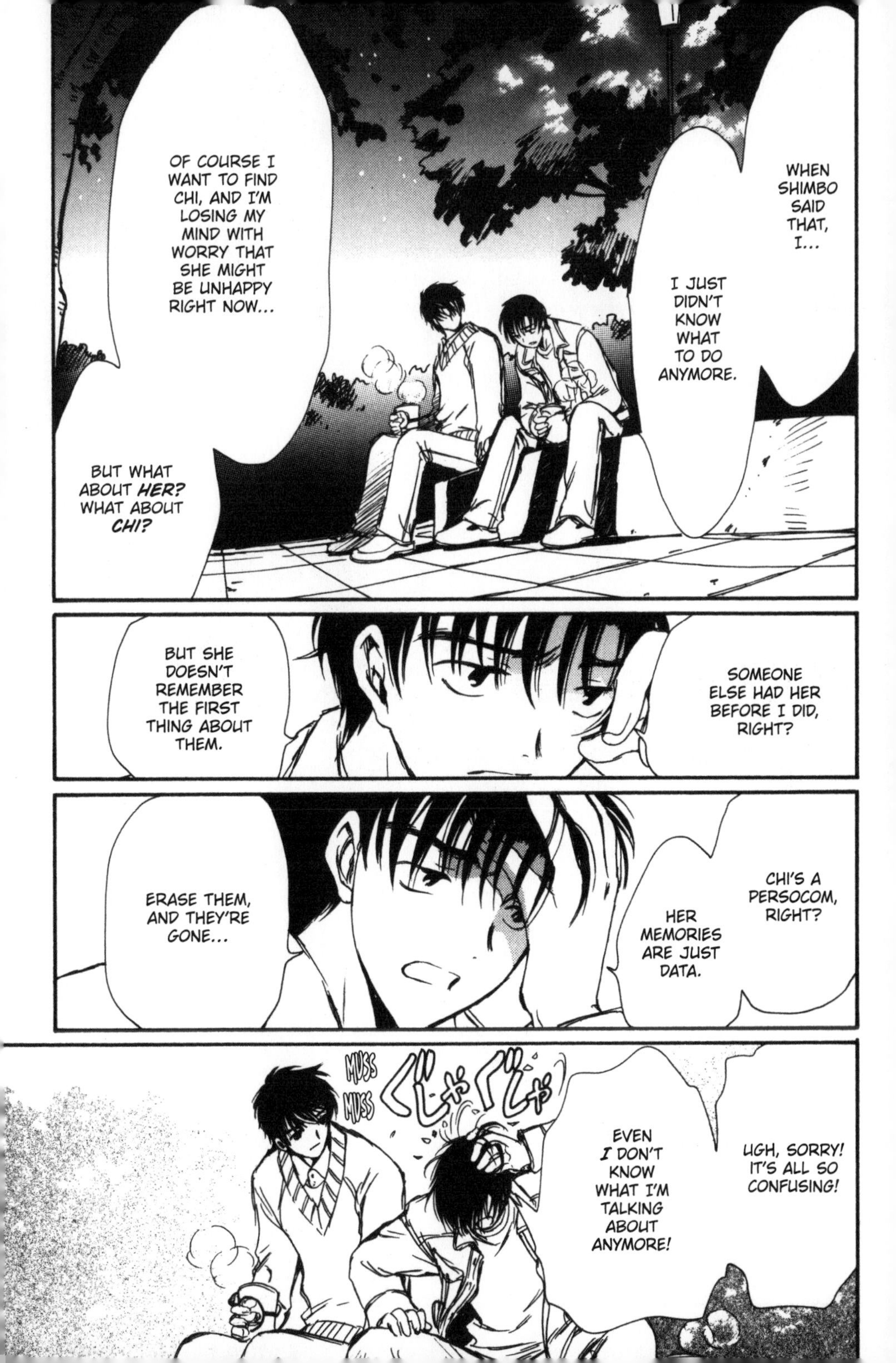
WHEN SHIMBO SAID THAT, I...
I JUST DIDN'T KNOW WHAT TO DO ANYMORE.
OF COURSE I WANT TO FIND CHI, AND I'M LOSING MY MIND WITH WORRY THAT SHE MIGHT BE UNHAPPY RIGHT NOW...
BUT WHAT ABOUT ***HER?*** WHAT ABOUT ***CHI?***
SOMEONE ELSE HAD HER BEFORE I DID, RIGHT?
BUT SHE DOESN'T REMEMBER THE FIRST THING ABOUT THEM.
CHI'S A PERSOCOM, RIGHT?
HER MEMORIES ARE JUST DATA.
ERASE THEM, AND THEY'RE GONE...
UGH, SORRY! IT'S ALL SO CONFUSING!
EVEN ***I*** DON'T KNOW WHAT I'M TALKING ABOUT ANYMORE!
ぐしゃぐしゃ
MUSS MUSS

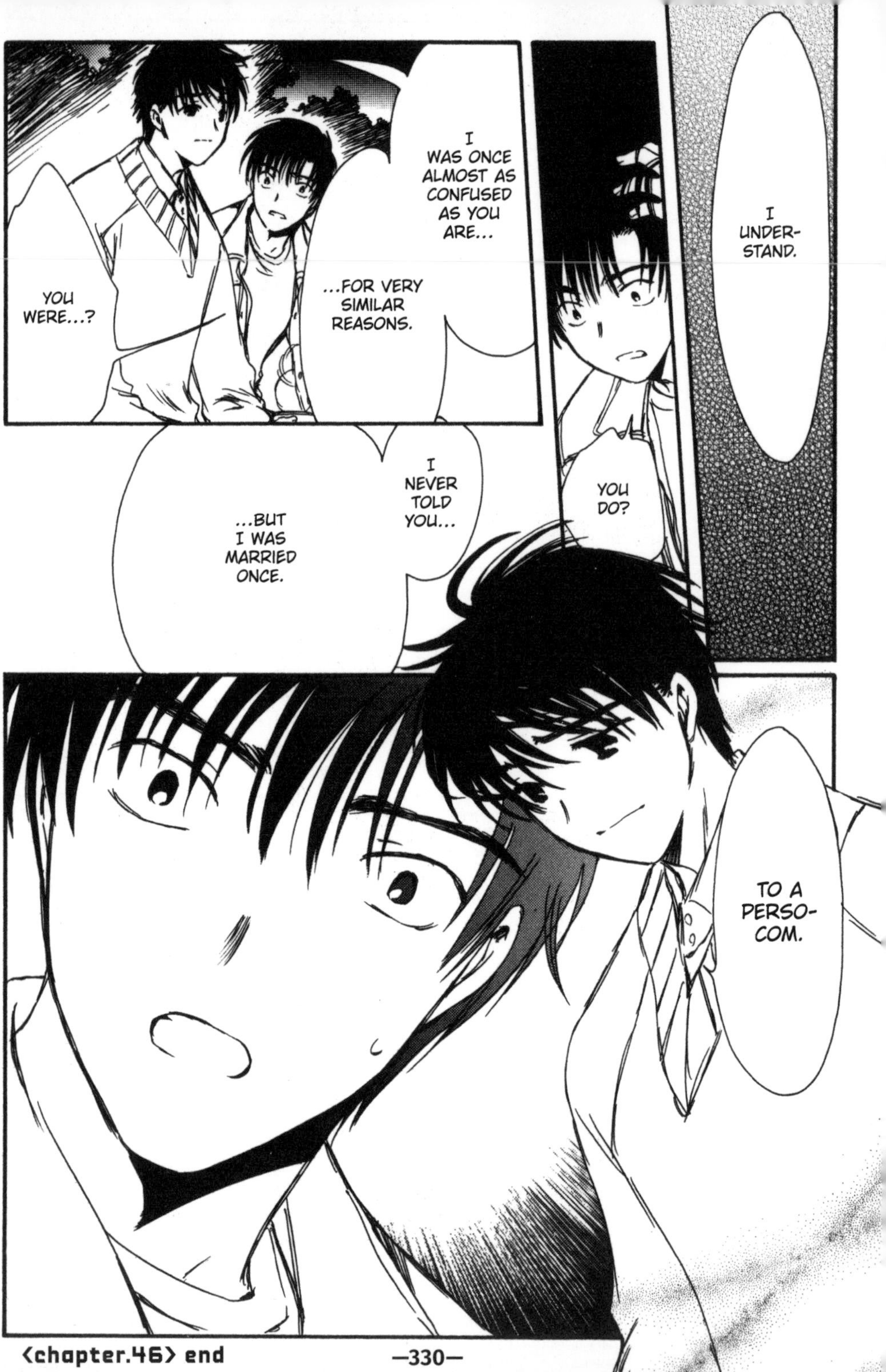
I UNDERSTAND.
YOU DO?
I WAS ONCE ALMOST AS CONFUSED AS YOU ARE...
...FOR VERY SIMILAR REASONS.
YOU WERE...?
I NEVER TOLD YOU...
...BUT I WAS MARRIED ONCE.
TO A PERSO-COM.

<chapter.46> end

BUDGET DINNERS
Easy!
FOR THE SINGLE GENTLEMAN

Chobits

<chapter.47>

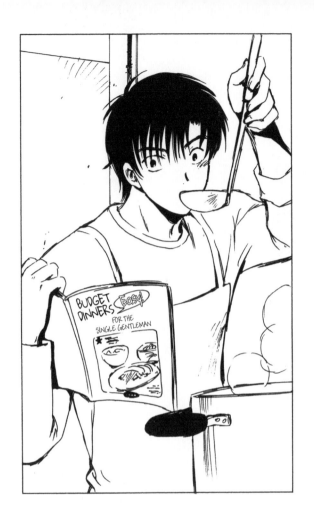

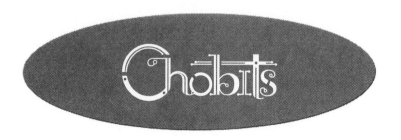

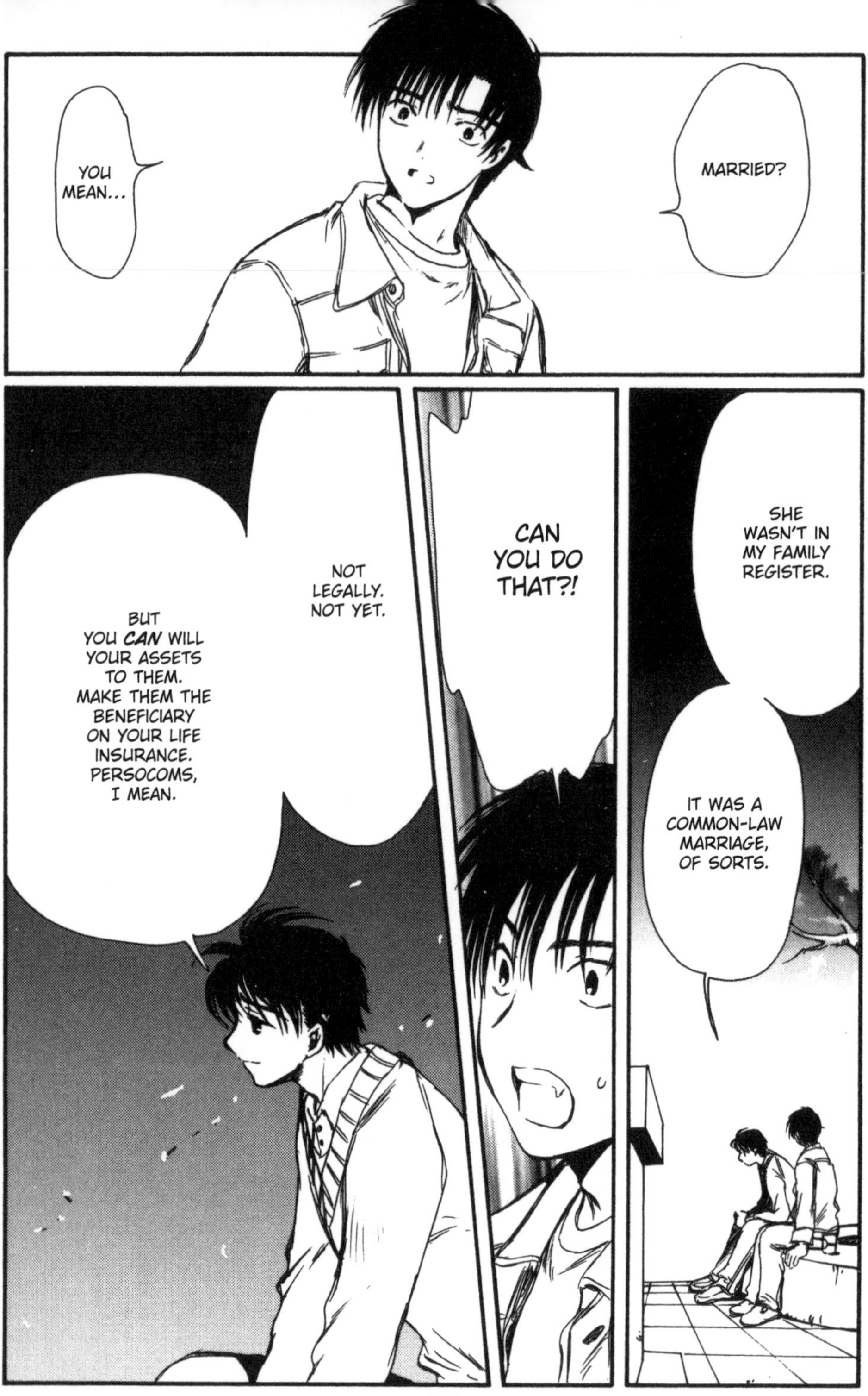
MARRIED?
YOU MEAN...
SHE WASN'T IN MY FAMILY REGISTER.
IT WAS A COMMON-LAW MARRIAGE, OF SORTS.
CAN YOU DO THAT?!
NOT LEGALLY. NOT YET.
BUT YOU **CAN** WILL YOUR ASSETS TO THEM. MAKE THEM THE BENEFICIARY ON YOUR LIFE INSURANCE. PERSOCOMS, I MEAN.

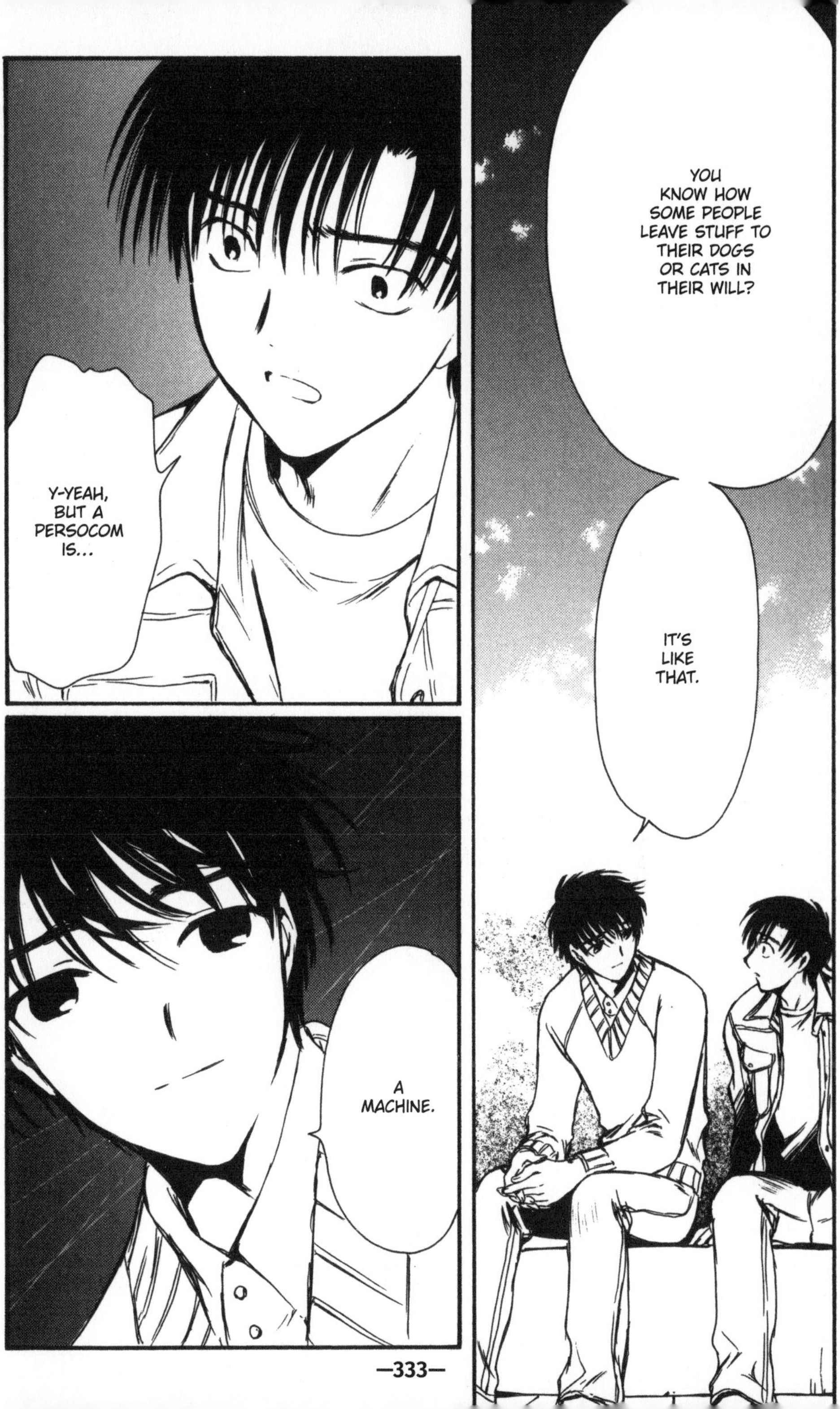
YOU KNOW HOW SOME PEOPLE LEAVE STUFF TO THEIR DOGS OR CATS IN THEIR WILL?
IT'S LIKE THAT.
Y-YEAH, BUT A PERSOCOM IS...
A MACHINE.

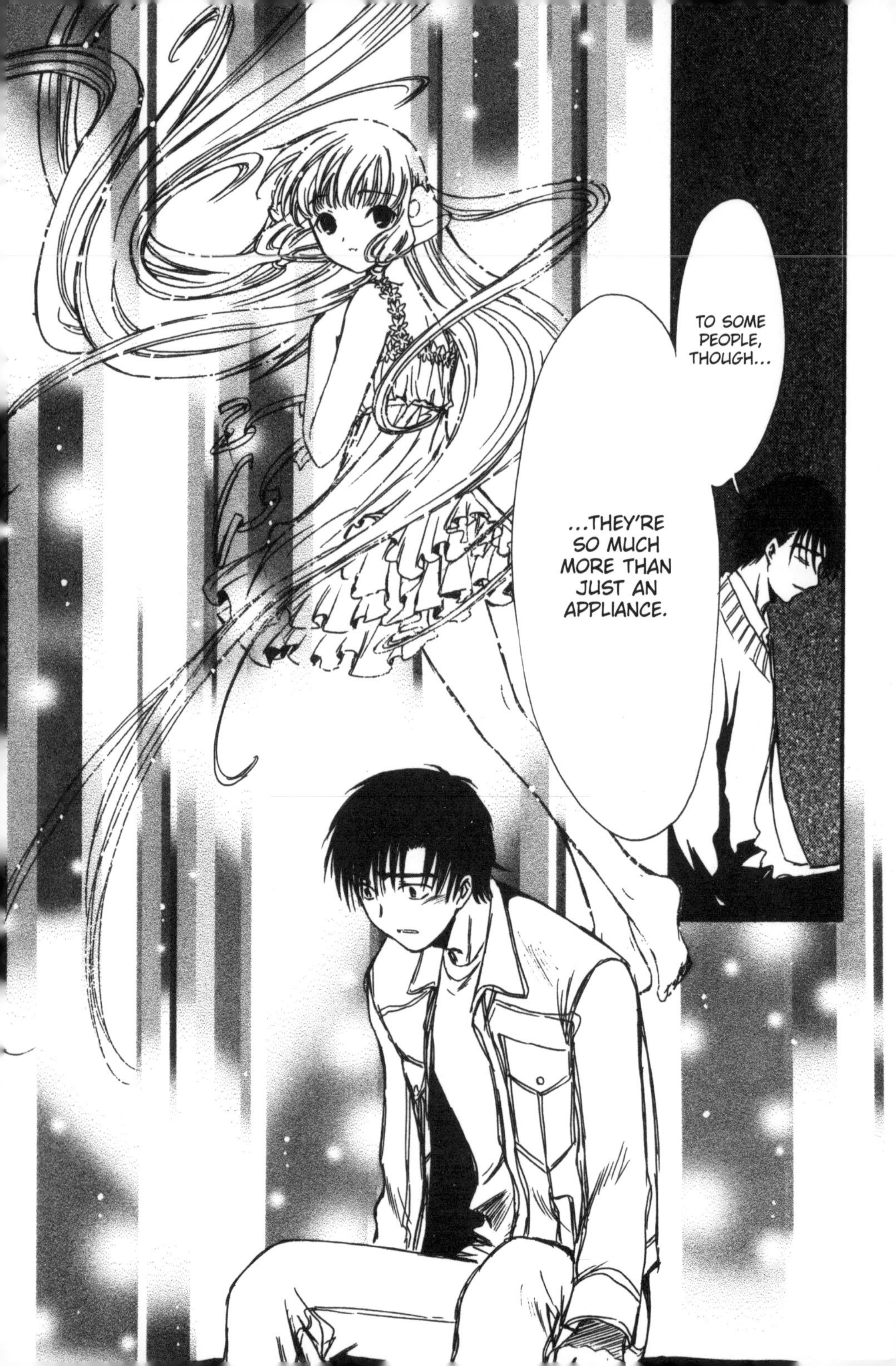
TO SOME PEOPLE, THOUGH...
...THEY'RE SO MUCH MORE THAN JUST AN APPLIANCE.

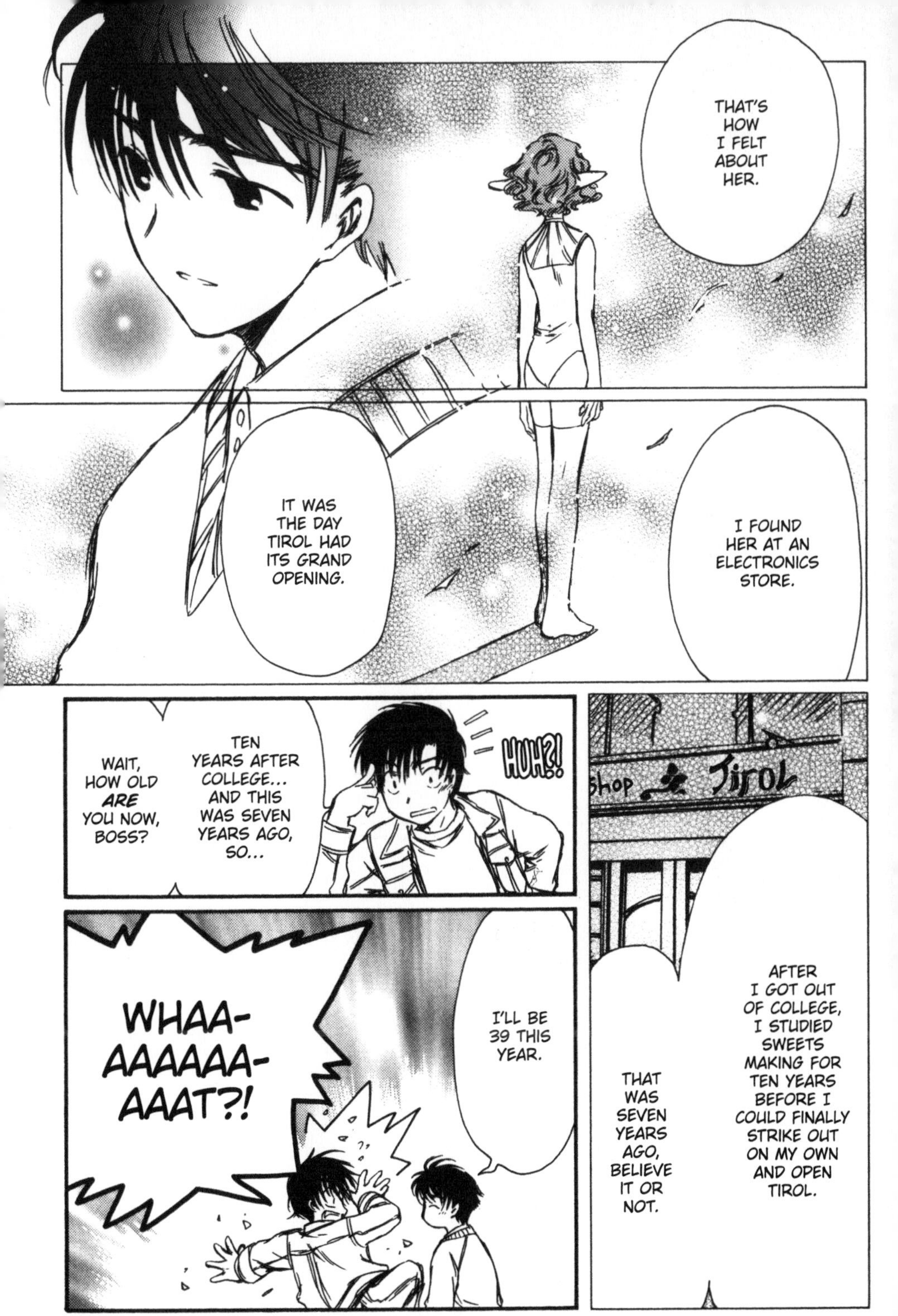
THAT'S HOW I FELT ABOUT HER.
I FOUND HER AT AN ELECTRONICS STORE.
IT WAS THE DAY TIROL HAD ITS GRAND OPENING.
Shop Tirol
AFTER I GOT OUT OF COLLEGE, I STUDIED SWEETS MAKING FOR TEN YEARS BEFORE I COULD FINALLY STRIKE OUT ON MY OWN AND OPEN TIROL.
THAT WAS SEVEN YEARS AGO, BELIEVE IT OR NOT.
HUH?!
TEN YEARS AFTER COLLEGE... AND THIS WAS SEVEN YEARS AGO, SO...
WAIT, HOW OLD *ARE* YOU NOW, BOSS?
I'LL BE 39 THIS YEAR.
WHAA-AAAAAA-AAAT?!

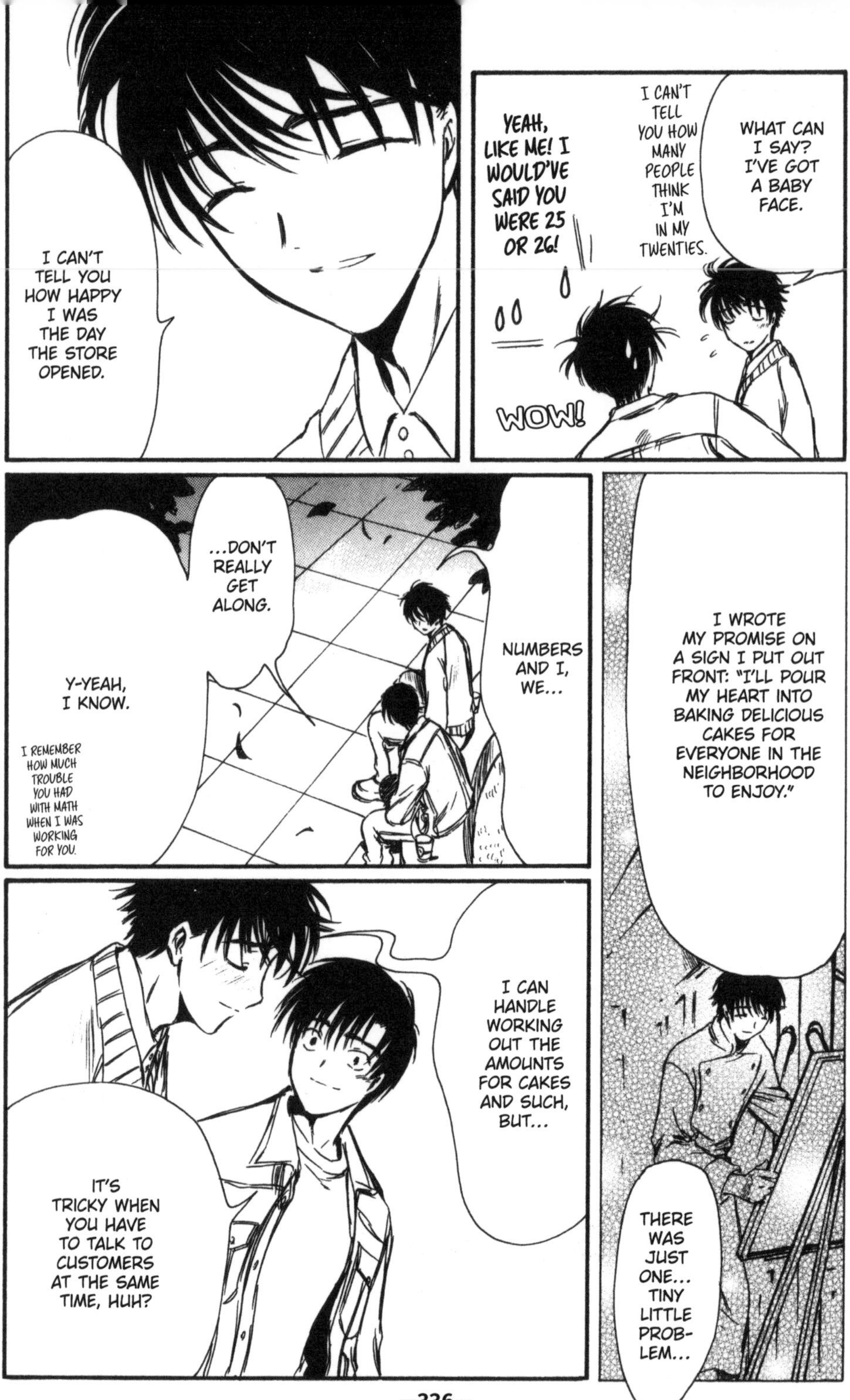
WHAT CAN I SAY? I'VE GOT A BABY FACE.
I CAN'T TELL YOU HOW MANY PEOPLE THINK I'M IN MY TWENTIES.
YEAH, LIKE ME! I WOULD'VE SAID YOU WERE 25 OR 26!
WOW!
I CAN'T TELL YOU HOW HAPPY I WAS THE DAY THE STORE OPENED.
I WROTE MY PROMISE ON A SIGN I PUT OUT FRONT: "I'LL POUR MY HEART INTO BAKING DELICIOUS CAKES FOR EVERYONE IN THE NEIGHBORHOOD TO ENJOY."
THERE WAS JUST ONE... TINY LITTLE PROB-LEM...
NUMBERS AND I, WE...
...DON'T REALLY GET ALONG.
Y-YEAH, I KNOW.
I REMEMBER HOW MUCH TROUBLE YOU HAD WITH MATH WHEN I WAS WORKING FOR YOU.
I CAN HANDLE WORKING OUT THE AMOUNTS FOR CAKES AND SUCH, BUT...
IT'S TRICKY WHEN YOU HAVE TO TALK TO CUSTOMERS AT THE SAME TIME, HUH?

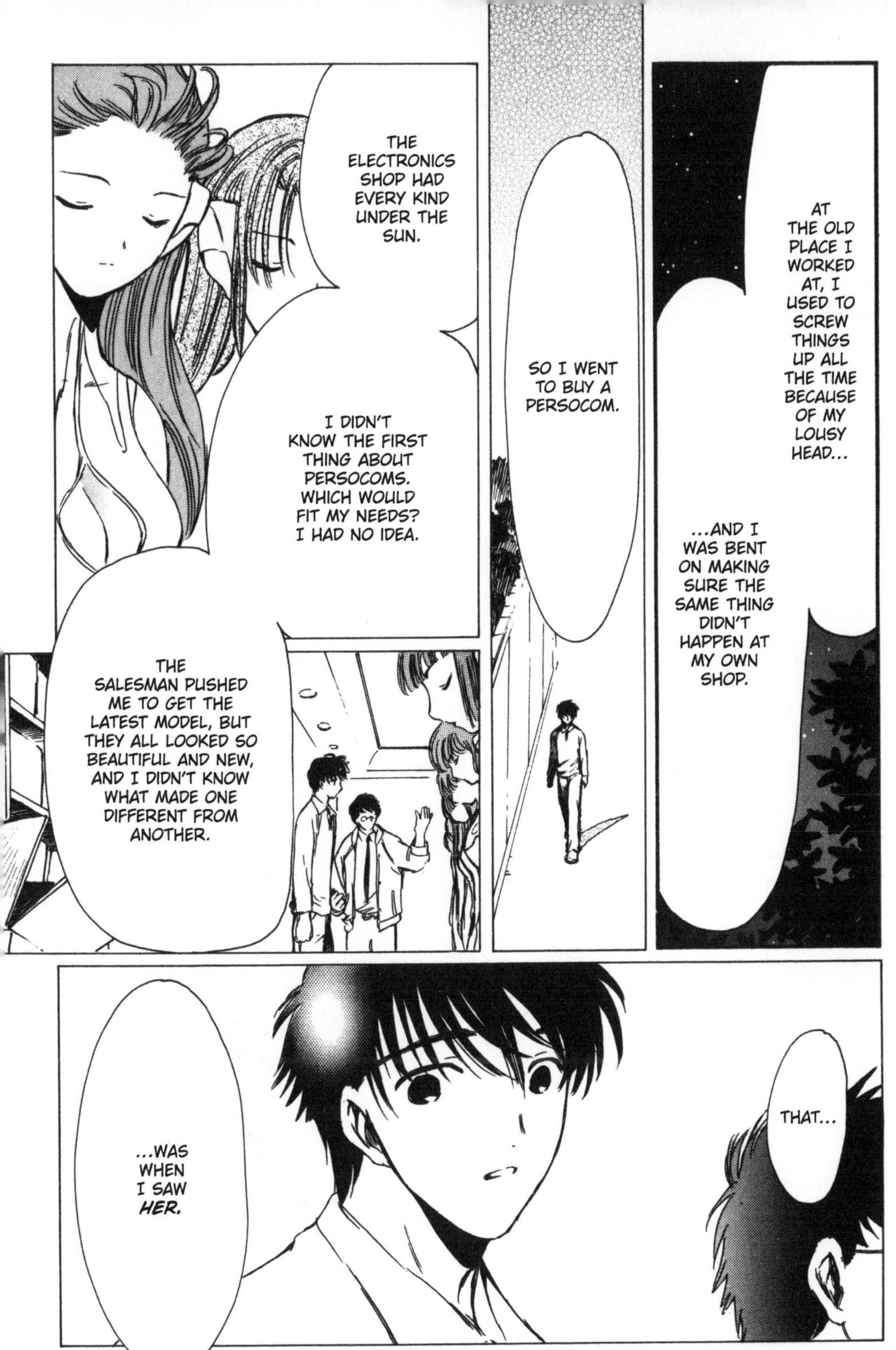
AT THE OLD PLACE I WORKED AT, I USED TO SCREW THINGS UP ALL THE TIME BECAUSE OF MY LOUSY HEAD...
...AND I WAS BENT ON MAKING SURE THE SAME THING DIDN'T HAPPEN AT MY OWN SHOP.
SO I WENT TO BUY A PERSOCOM.
THE ELECTRONICS SHOP HAD EVERY KIND UNDER THE SUN.
I DIDN'T KNOW THE FIRST THING ABOUT PERSOCOMS. WHICH WOULD FIT MY NEEDS? I HAD NO IDEA.
THE SALESMAN PUSHED ME TO GET THE LATEST MODEL, BUT THEY ALL LOOKED SO BEAUTIFUL AND NEW, AND I DIDN'T KNOW WHAT MADE ONE DIFFERENT FROM ANOTHER.
THAT...
...WAS WHEN I SAW ***HER.***

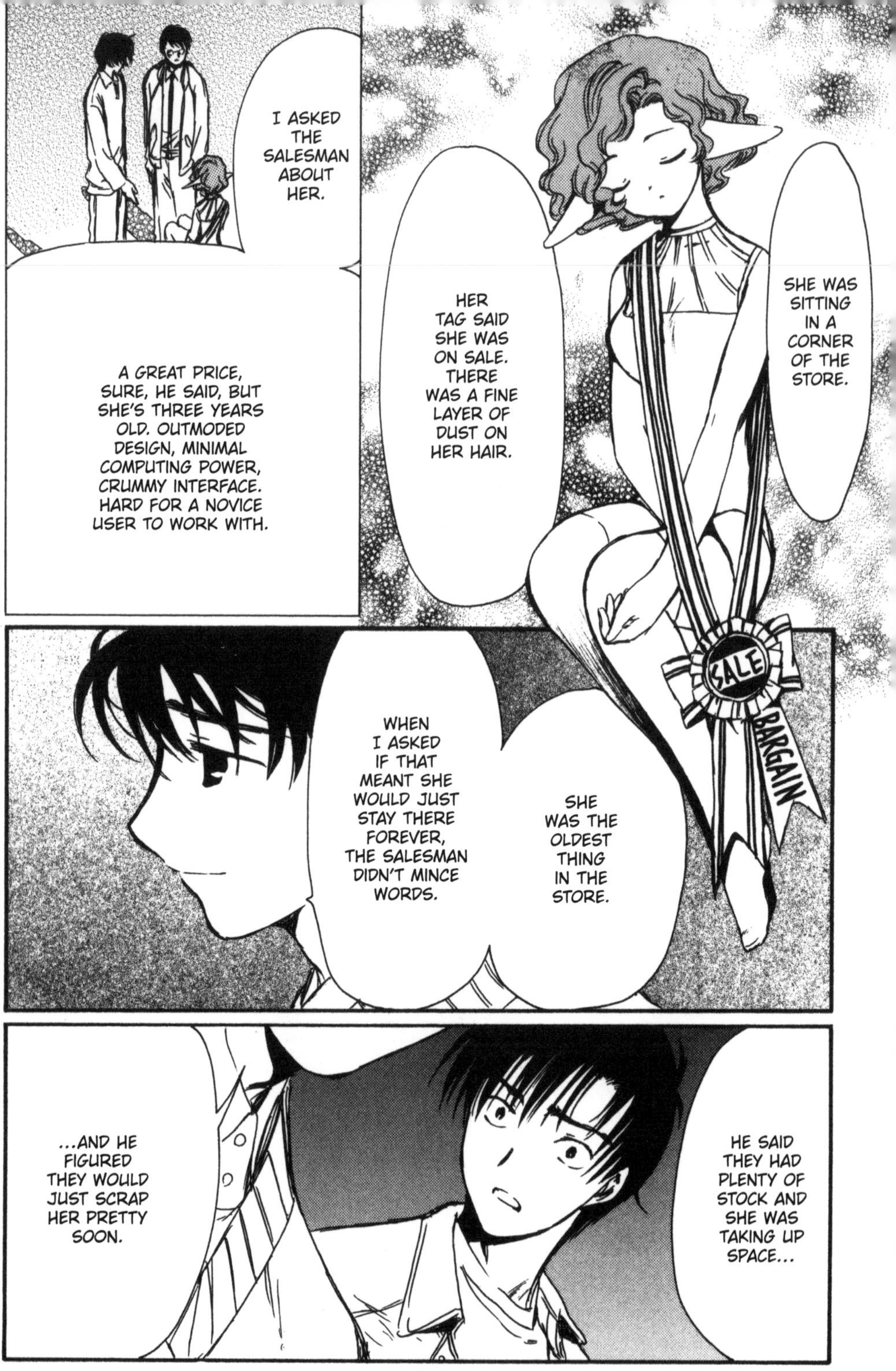
SHE WAS SITTING IN A CORNER OF THE STORE.
HER TAG SAID SHE WAS ON SALE. THERE WAS A FINE LAYER OF DUST ON HER HAIR.
SALE
BARGAIN
I ASKED THE SALESMAN ABOUT HER.
A GREAT PRICE, SURE, HE SAID, BUT SHE'S THREE YEARS OLD. OUTMODED DESIGN, MINIMAL COMPUTING POWER, CRUMMY INTERFACE. HARD FOR A NOVICE USER TO WORK WITH.
SHE WAS THE OLDEST THING IN THE STORE.
WHEN I ASKED IF THAT MEANT SHE WOULD JUST STAY THERE FOREVER, THE SALESMAN DIDN'T MINCE WORDS.
HE SAID THEY HAD PLENTY OF STOCK AND SHE WAS TAKING UP SPACE...
...AND HE FIGURED THEY WOULD JUST SCRAP HER PRETTY SOON.

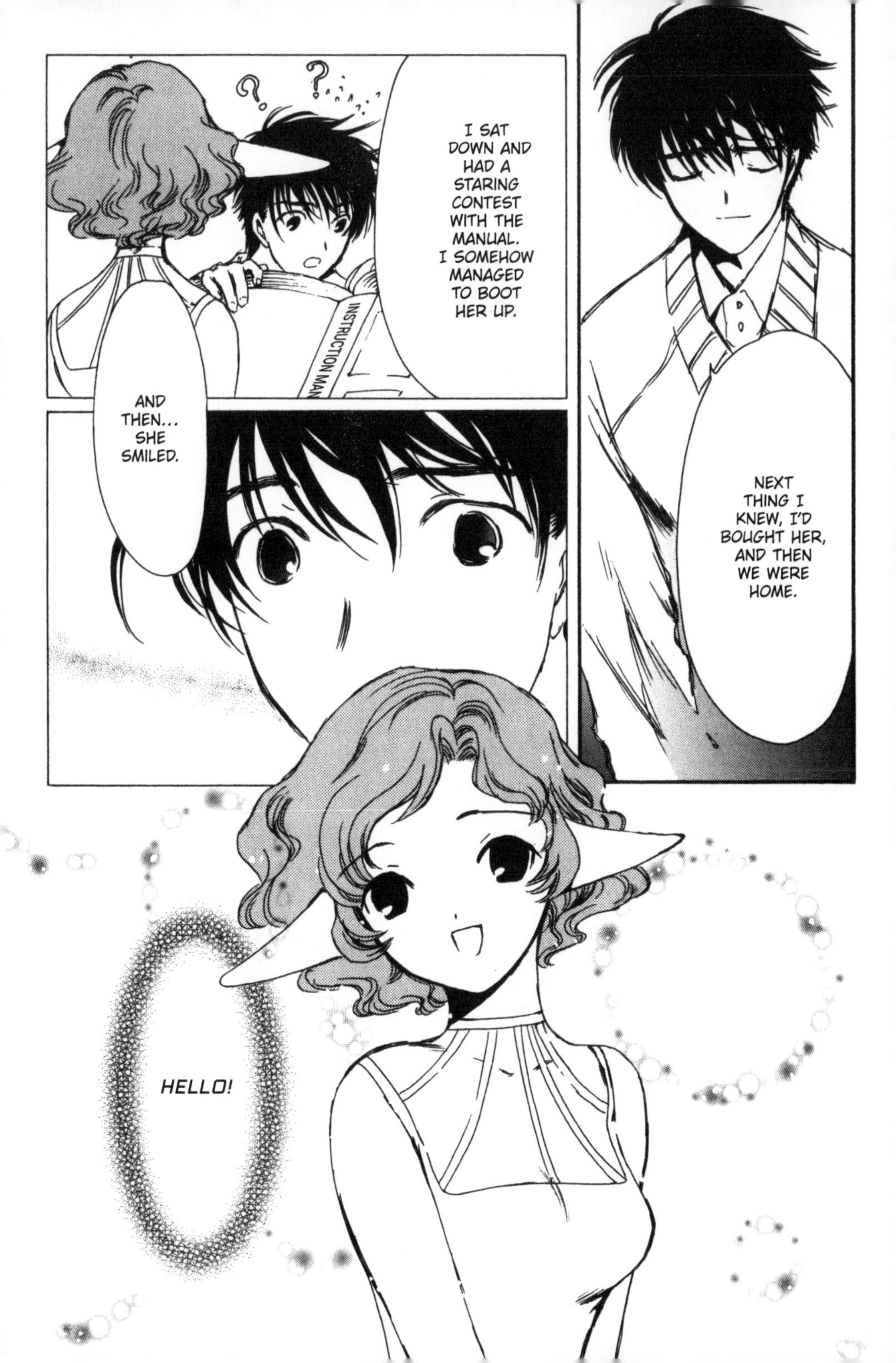
NEXT THING I KNEW, I'D BOUGHT HER, AND THEN WE WERE HOME.
I SAT DOWN AND HAD A STARING CONTEST WITH THE MANUAL. I SOMEHOW MANAGED TO BOOT HER UP.
INSTRUCTION MAN
AND THEN... SHE SMILED.
HELLO!

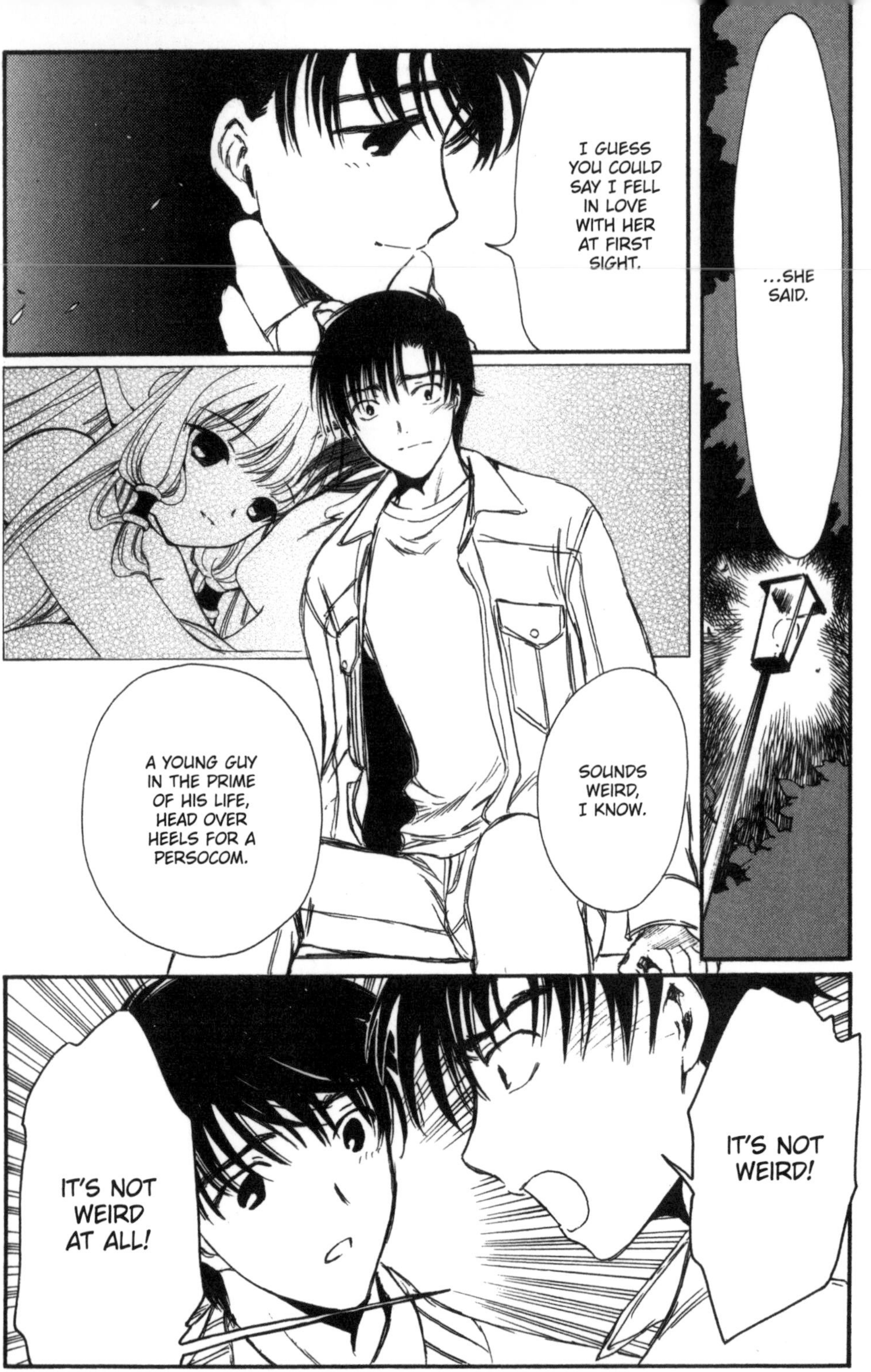
...SHE SAID.
I GUESS YOU COULD SAY I FELL IN LOVE WITH HER AT FIRST SIGHT.
SOUNDS WEIRD, I KNOW.
A YOUNG GUY IN THE PRIME OF HIS LIFE, HEAD OVER HEELS FOR A PERSOCOM.
IT'S NOT WEIRD!
IT'S NOT WEIRD AT ALL!

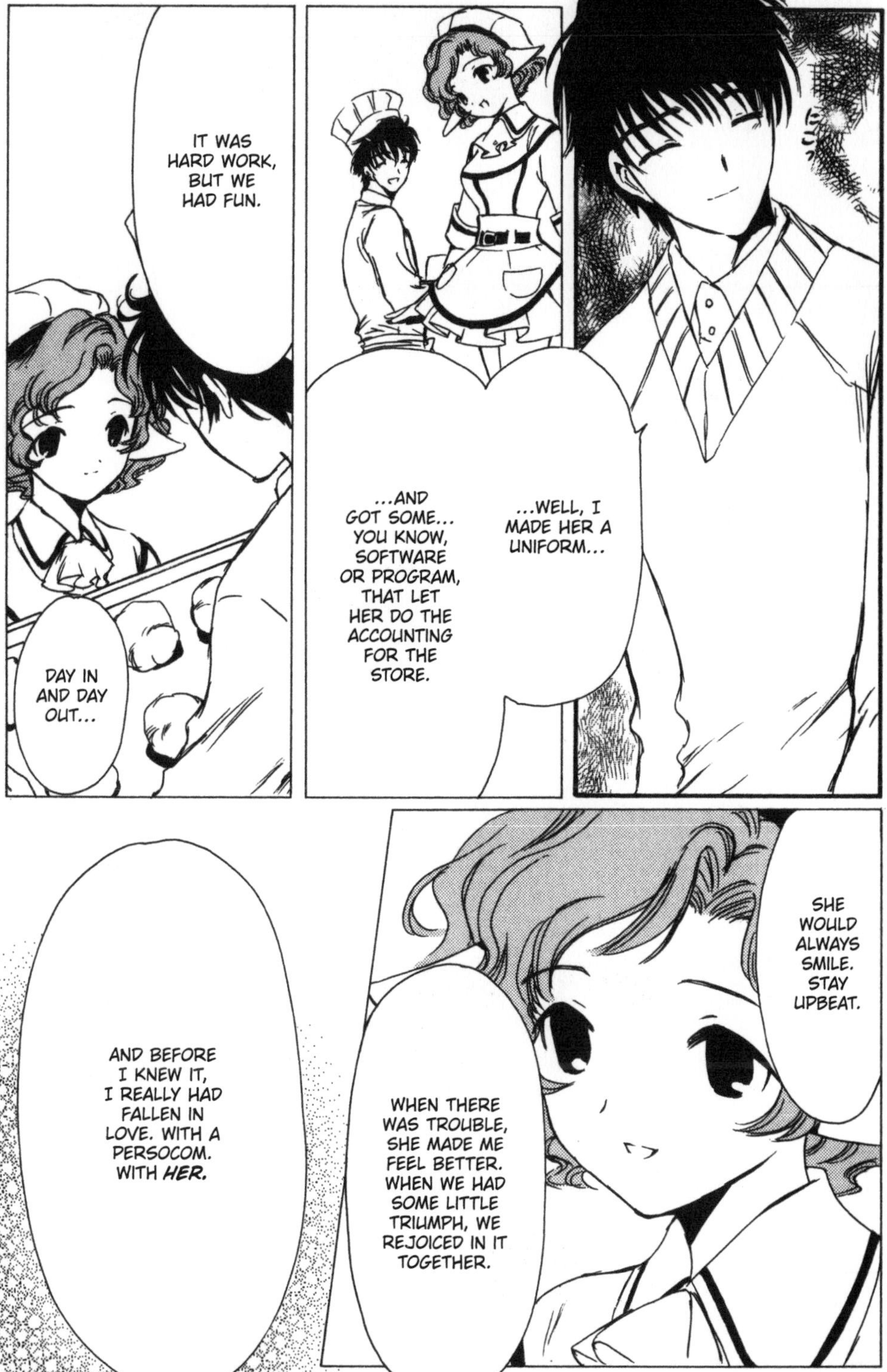
...WELL, I MADE HER A UNIFORM...
...AND GOT SOME... YOU KNOW, SOFTWARE OR PROGRAM, THAT LET HER DO THE ACCOUNTING FOR THE STORE.
IT WAS HARD WORK, BUT WE HAD FUN.
DAY IN AND DAY OUT...
SHE WOULD ALWAYS SMILE. STAY UPBEAT.
WHEN THERE WAS TROUBLE, SHE MADE ME FEEL BETTER. WHEN WE HAD SOME LITTLE TRIUMPH, WE REJOICED IN IT TOGETHER.
AND BEFORE I KNEW IT, I REALLY HAD FALLEN IN LOVE. WITH A PERSOCOM. WITH *HER.*

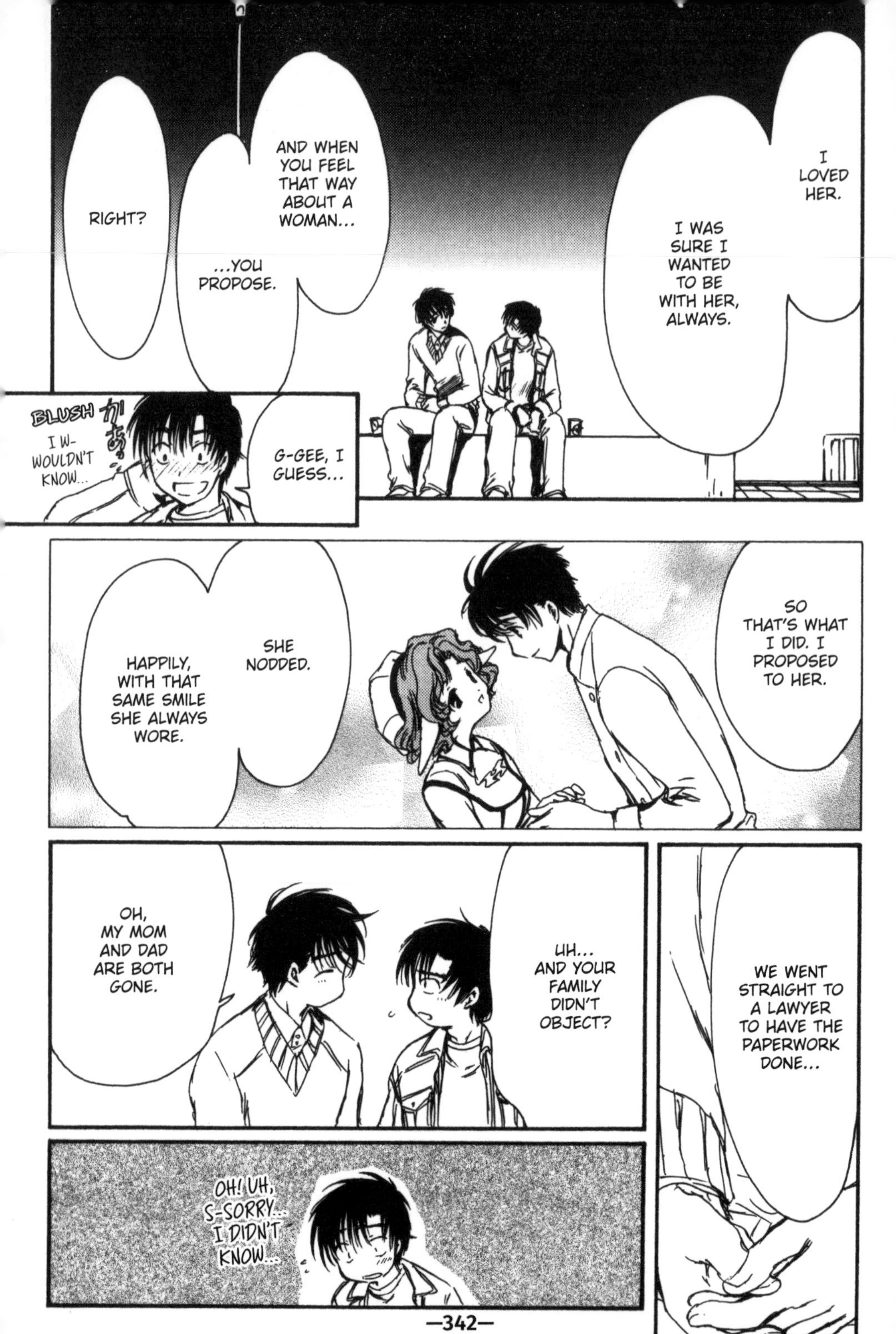
I LOVED HER.
I WAS SURE I WANTED TO BE WITH HER, ALWAYS.
AND WHEN YOU FEEL THAT WAY ABOUT A WOMAN...
...YOU PROPOSE.
RIGHT?
G-GEE, I GUESS...
BLUSH
I W-WOULDN'T KNOW...
SO THAT'S WHAT I DID. I PROPOSED TO HER.
SHE NODDED.
HAPPILY, WITH THAT SAME SMILE SHE ALWAYS WORE.
WE WENT STRAIGHT TO A LAWYER TO HAVE THE PAPERWORK DONE...
UH... AND YOUR FAMILY DIDN'T OBJECT?
OH, MY MOM AND DAD ARE BOTH GONE.
OH! UH, S-SORRY... I DIDN'T KNOW...

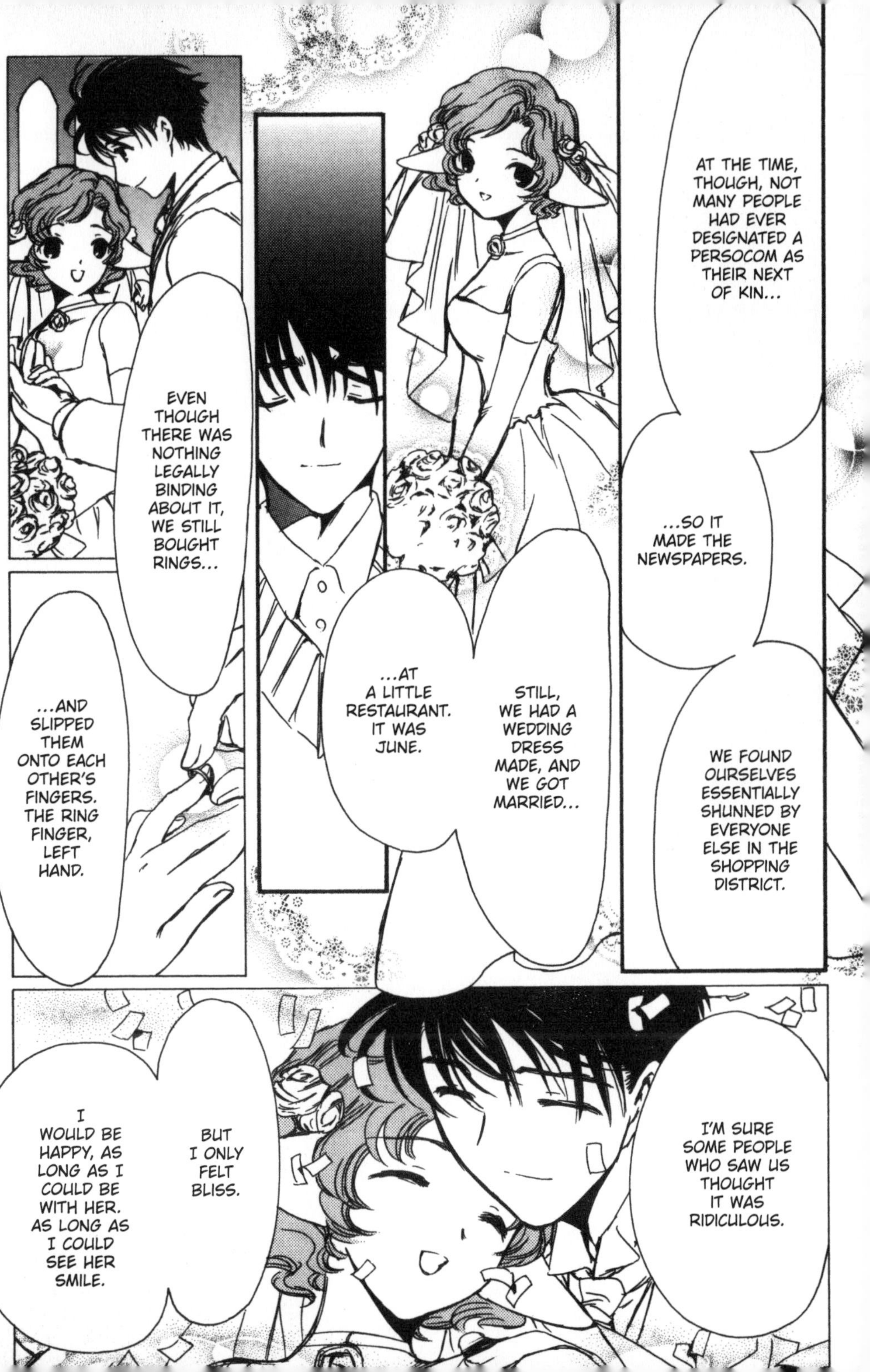
AT THE TIME, THOUGH, NOT MANY PEOPLE HAD EVER DESIGNATED A PERSOCOM AS THEIR NEXT OF KIN…
…SO IT MADE THE NEWSPAPERS.
WE FOUND OURSELVES ESSENTIALLY SHUNNED BY EVERYONE ELSE IN THE SHOPPING DISTRICT.
STILL, WE HAD A WEDDING DRESS MADE, AND WE GOT MARRIED…
…AT A LITTLE RESTAURANT. IT WAS JUNE.
EVEN THOUGH THERE WAS NOTHING LEGALLY BINDING ABOUT IT, WE STILL BOUGHT RINGS…
…AND SLIPPED THEM ONTO EACH OTHER'S FINGERS. THE RING FINGER, LEFT HAND.
I'M SURE SOME PEOPLE WHO SAW US THOUGHT IT WAS RIDICULOUS.
BUT I ONLY FELT BLISS.
I WOULD BE HAPPY, AS LONG AS I COULD BE WITH HER. AS LONG AS I COULD SEE HER SMILE.

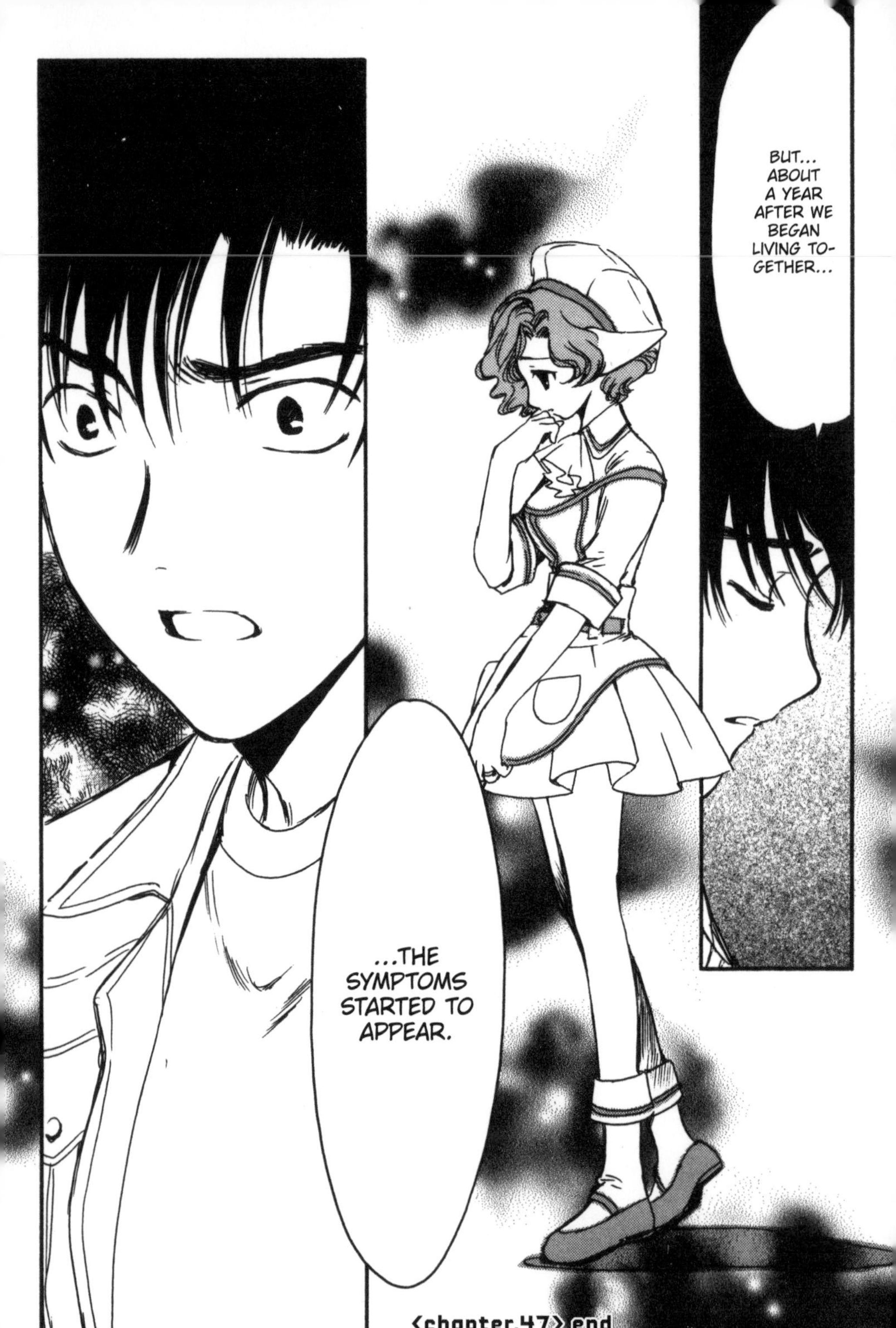

BUT... ABOUT A YEAR AFTER WE BEGAN LIVING TO-GETHER...
...THE SYMPTOMS STARTED TO APPEAR.

‹chapter.47› end

⟨chapter.48⟩

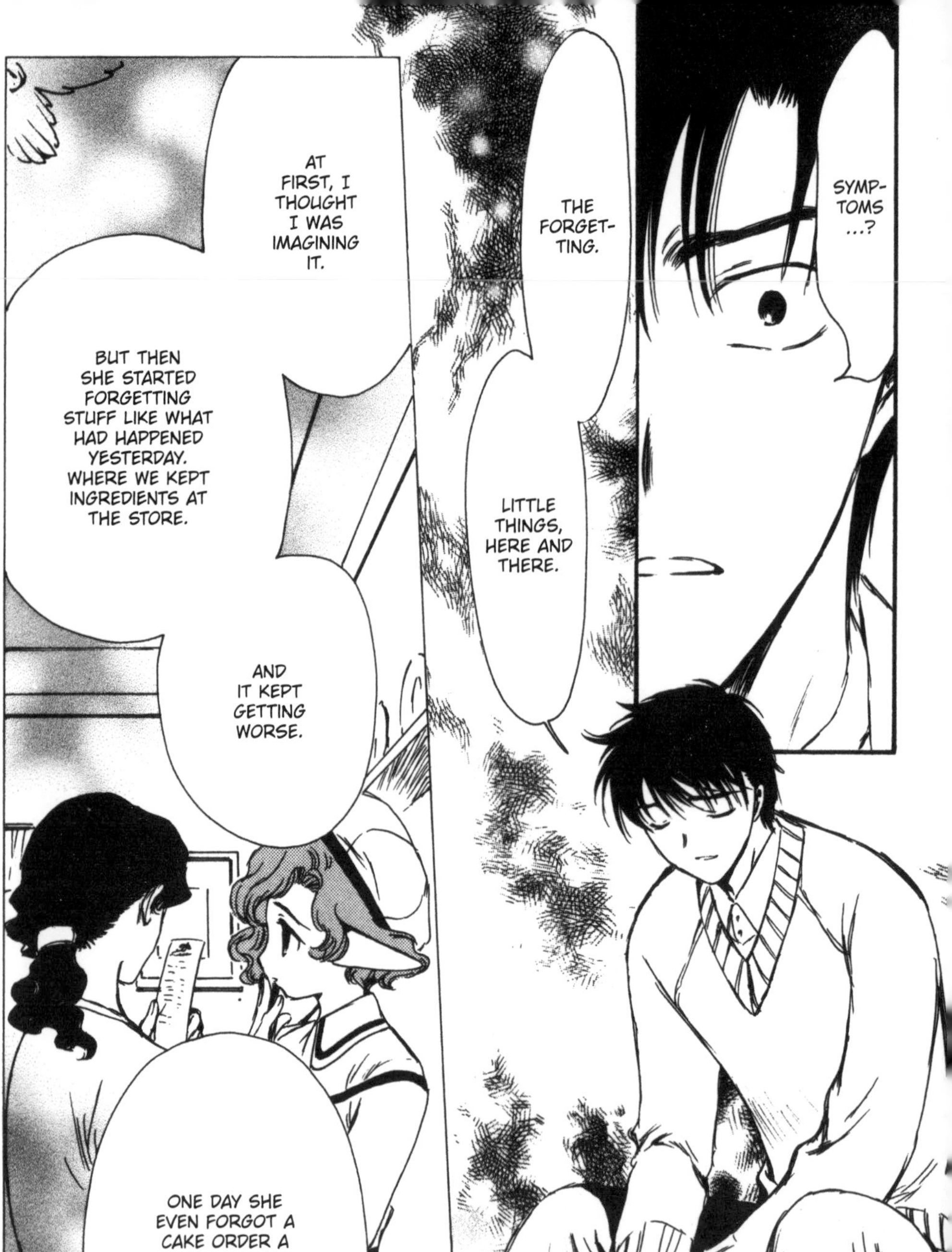
SYMP-TOMS ...?
THE FORGET-TING.
LITTLE THINGS, HERE AND THERE.
AT FIRST, I THOUGHT I WAS IMAGINING IT.
BUT THEN SHE STARTED FORGETTING STUFF LIKE WHAT HAD HAPPENED YESTERDAY. WHERE WE KEPT INGREDIENTS AT THE STORE.
AND IT KEPT GETTING WORSE.
ONE DAY SHE EVEN FORGOT A CAKE ORDER A CUSTOMER HAD PLACED JUST A FEW MINUTES EARLIER.

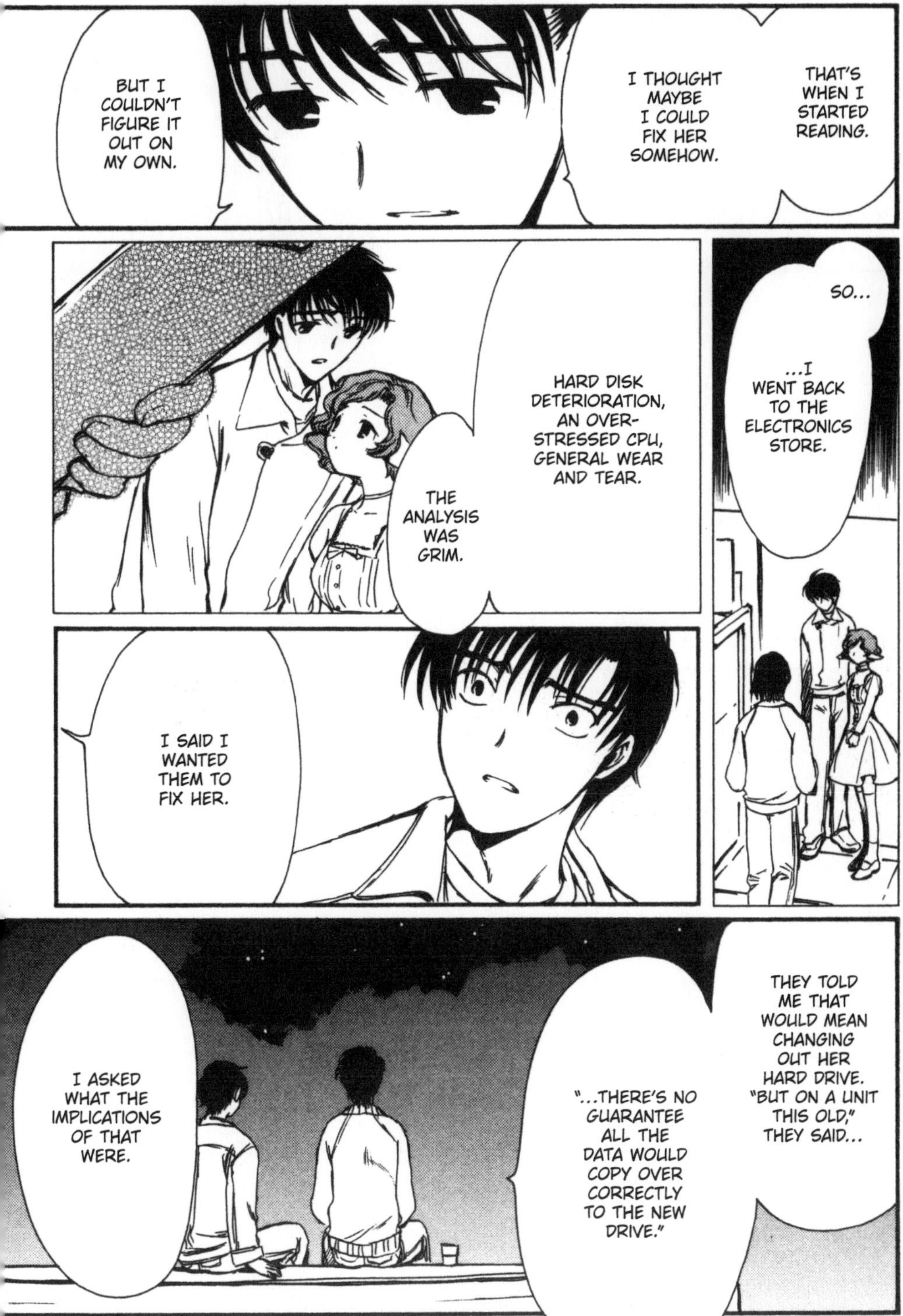
THAT'S WHEN I STARTED READING.
I THOUGHT MAYBE I COULD FIX HER SOMEHOW.
BUT I COULDN'T FIGURE IT OUT ON MY OWN.
SO...
...I WENT BACK TO THE ELECTRONICS STORE.
HARD DISK DETERIORATION, AN OVER-STRESSED CPU, GENERAL WEAR AND TEAR.
THE ANALYSIS WAS GRIM.
I SAID I WANTED THEM TO FIX HER.
THEY TOLD ME THAT WOULD MEAN CHANGING OUT HER HARD DRIVE. "BUT ON A UNIT THIS OLD," THEY SAID...
"...THERE'S NO GUARANTEE ALL THE DATA WOULD COPY OVER CORRECTLY TO THE NEW DRIVE."
I ASKED WHAT THE IMPLICATIONS OF THAT WERE.

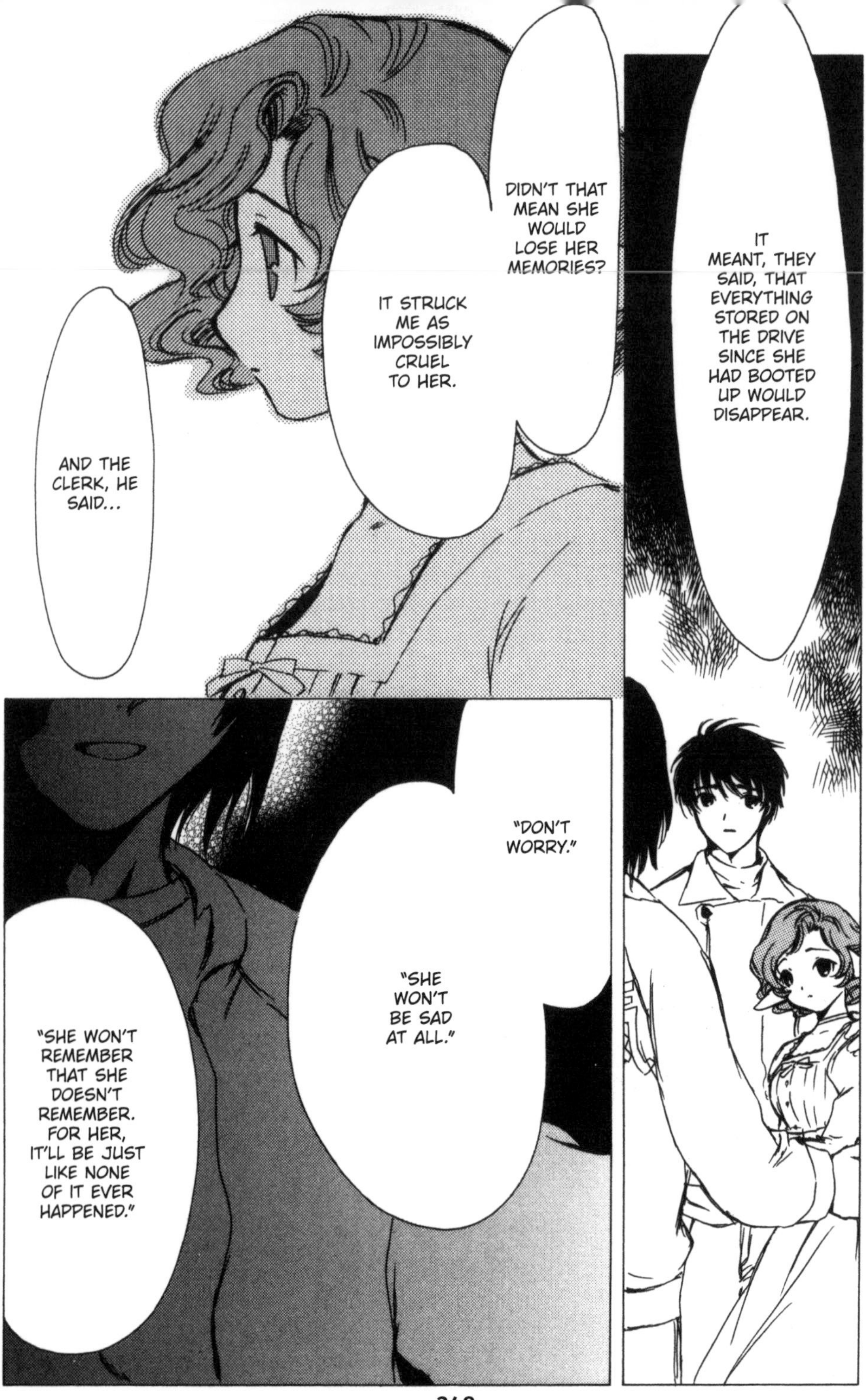
IT MEANT, THEY SAID, THAT EVERYTHING STORED ON THE DRIVE SINCE SHE HAD BOOTED UP WOULD DISAPPEAR.
DIDN'T THAT MEAN SHE WOULD LOSE HER MEMORIES?
IT STRUCK ME AS IMPOSSIBLY CRUEL TO HER.
AND THE CLERK, HE SAID...
"DON'T WORRY."
"SHE WON'T BE SAD AT ALL."
"SHE WON'T REMEMBER THAT SHE DOESN'T REMEMBER. FOR HER, IT'LL BE JUST LIKE NONE OF IT EVER HAPPENED."

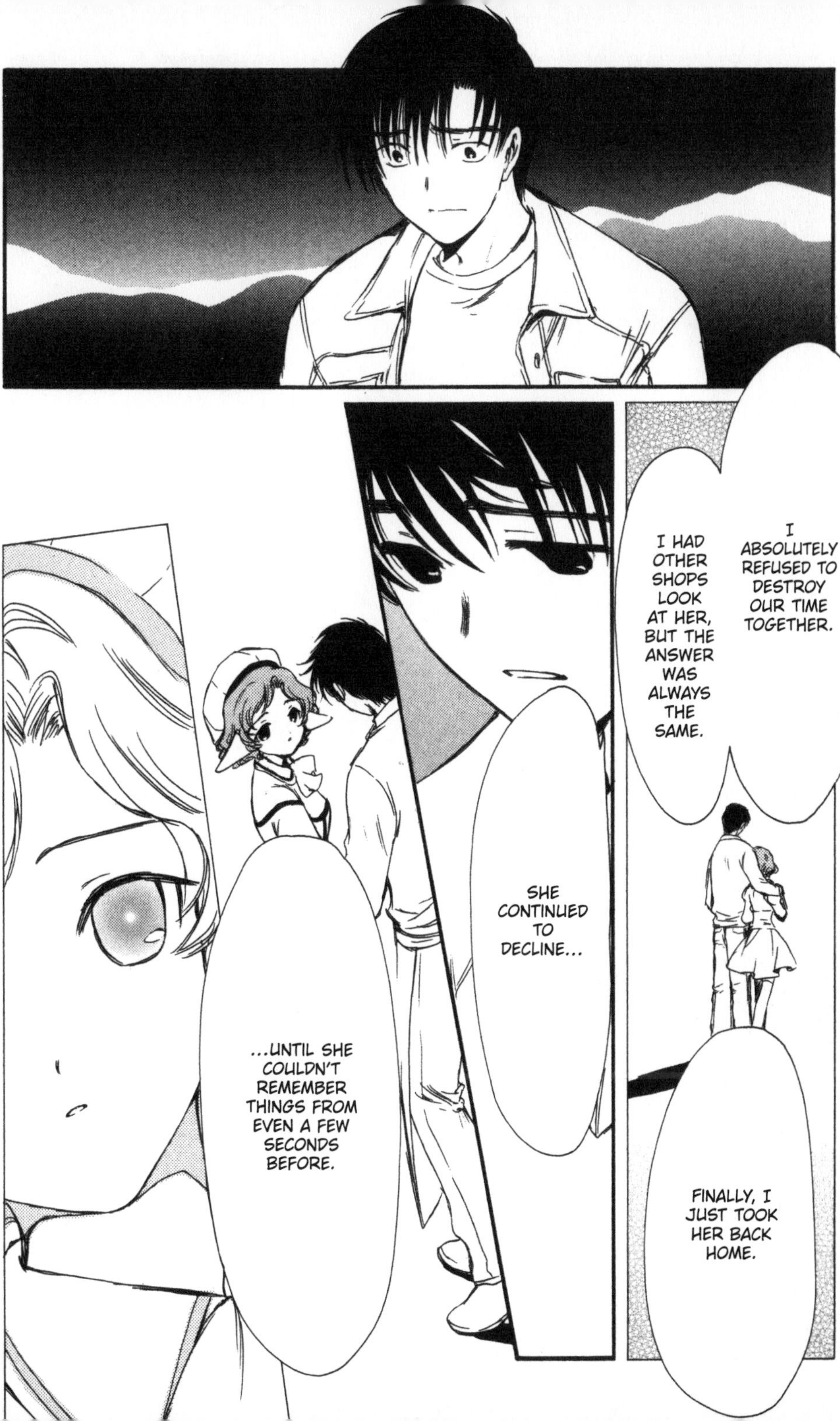
I ABSOLUTELY REFUSED TO DESTROY OUR TIME TOGETHER.
I HAD OTHER SHOPS LOOK AT HER, BUT THE ANSWER WAS ALWAYS THE SAME.
FINALLY, I JUST TOOK HER BACK HOME.
SHE CONTINUED TO DECLINE...
...UNTIL SHE COULDN'T REMEMBER THINGS FROM EVEN A FEW SECONDS BEFORE.

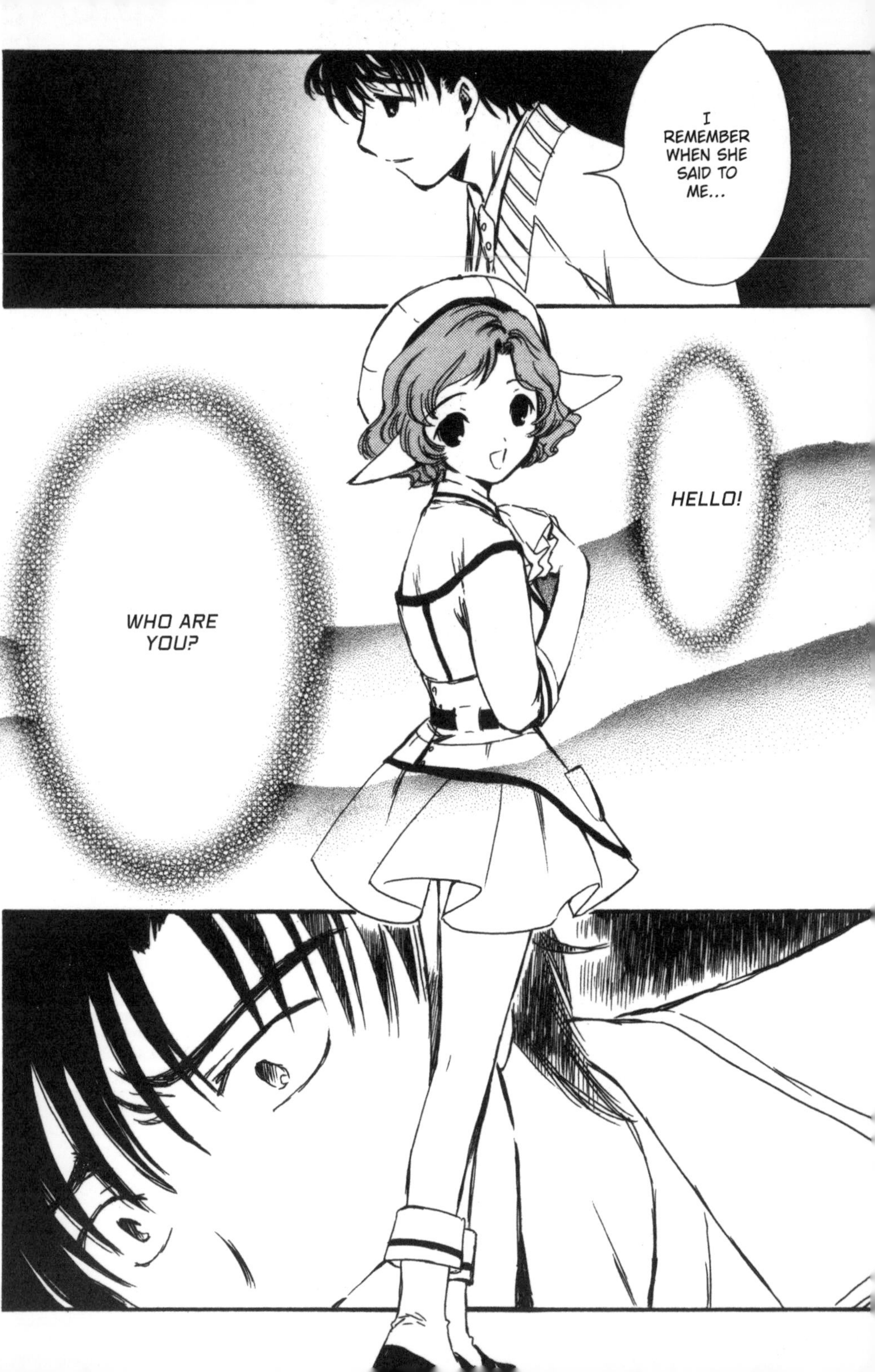
I REMEMBER WHEN SHE SAID TO ME...
HELLO!
WHO ARE YOU?

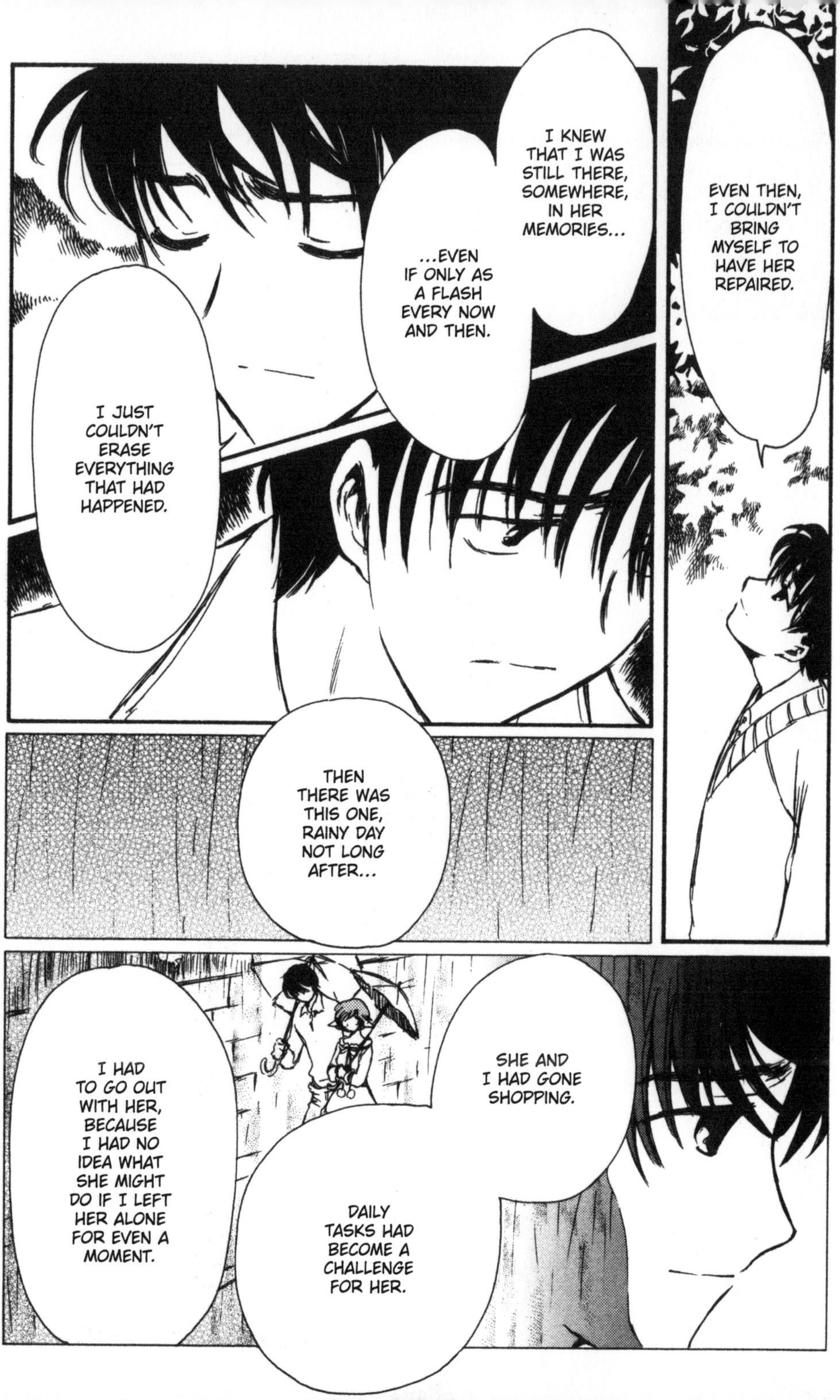
EVEN THEN, I COULDN'T BRING MYSELF TO HAVE HER REPAIRED.
I KNEW THAT I WAS STILL THERE, SOMEWHERE, IN HER MEMORIES...
...EVEN IF ONLY AS A FLASH EVERY NOW AND THEN.
I JUST COULDN'T ERASE EVERYTHING THAT HAD HAPPENED.
THEN THERE WAS THIS ONE, RAINY DAY NOT LONG AFTER...
SHE AND I HAD GONE SHOPPING.
DAILY TASKS HAD BECOME A CHALLENGE FOR HER.
I HAD TO GO OUT WITH HER, BECAUSE I HAD NO IDEA WHAT SHE MIGHT DO IF I LEFT HER ALONE FOR EVEN A MOMENT.

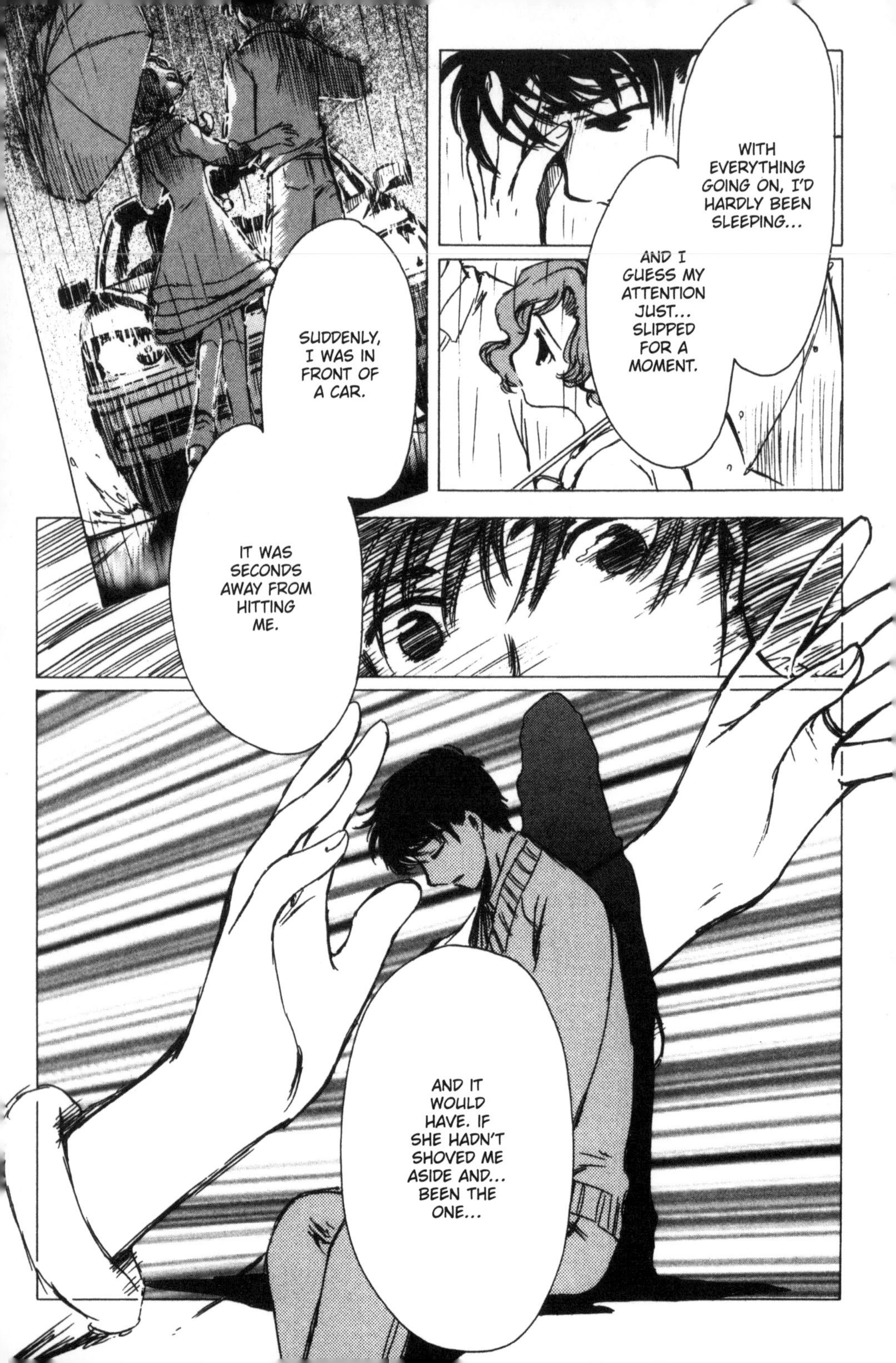

WITH EVERYTHING GOING ON, I'D HARDLY BEEN SLEEPING...
AND I GUESS MY ATTENTION JUST... SLIPPED FOR A MOMENT.
SUDDENLY, I WAS IN FRONT OF A CAR.
IT WAS SECONDS AWAY FROM HITTING ME.
AND IT WOULD HAVE. IF SHE HADN'T SHOVED ME ASIDE AND... BEEN THE ONE...

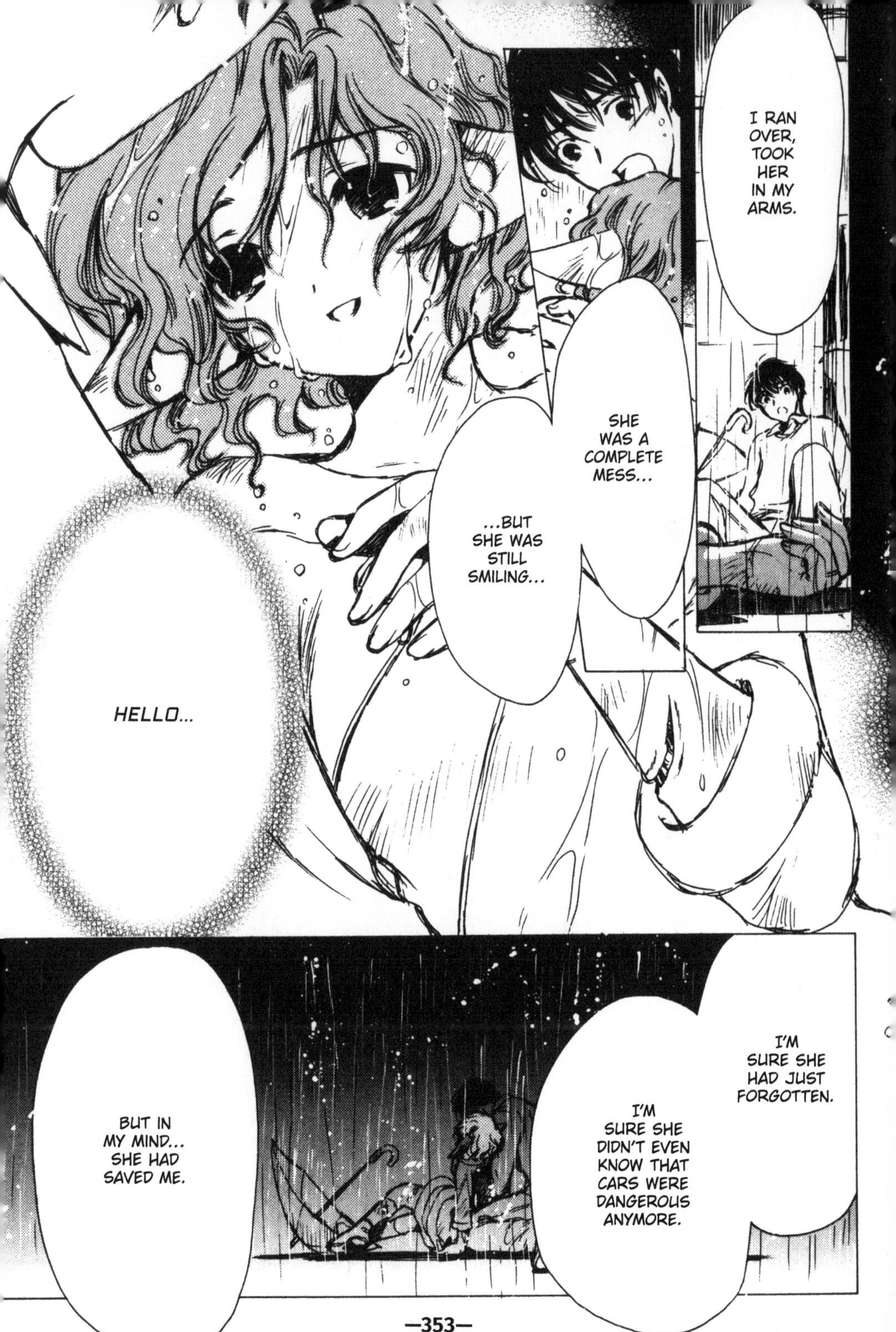
I RAN OVER, TOOK HER IN MY ARMS.
SHE WAS A COMPLETE MESS...
...BUT SHE WAS STILL SMILING...
HELLO...
I'M SURE SHE HAD JUST FORGOTTEN.
I'M SURE SHE DIDN'T EVEN KNOW THAT CARS WERE DANGEROUS ANYMORE.
BUT IN MY MIND... SHE HAD SAVED ME.

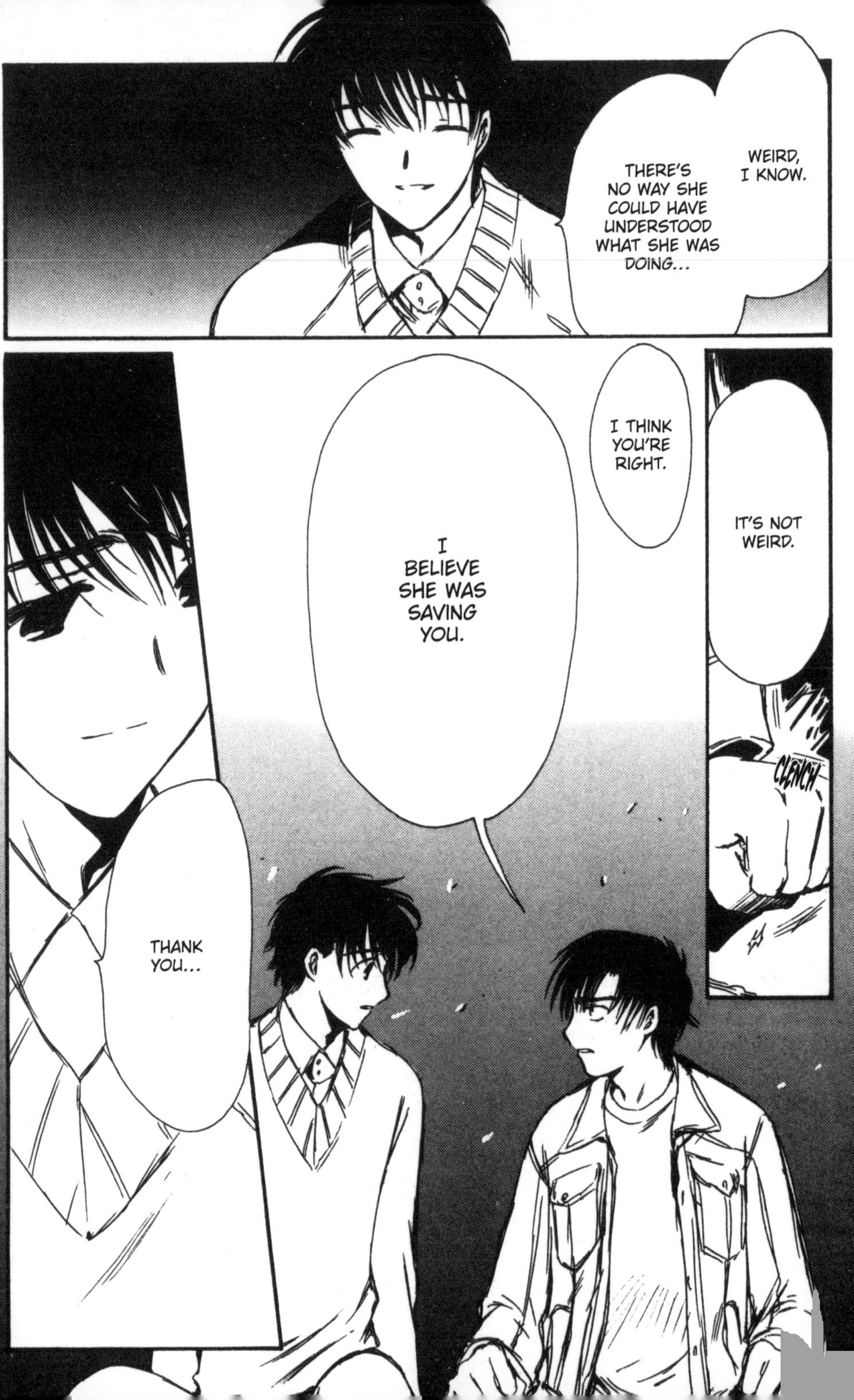

WEIRD, I KNOW.
THERE'S NO WAY SHE COULD HAVE UNDERSTOOD WHAT SHE WAS DOING...
IT'S NOT WEIRD.
CLENCH
I THINK YOU'RE RIGHT.
I BELIEVE SHE WAS SAVING YOU.
THANK YOU...

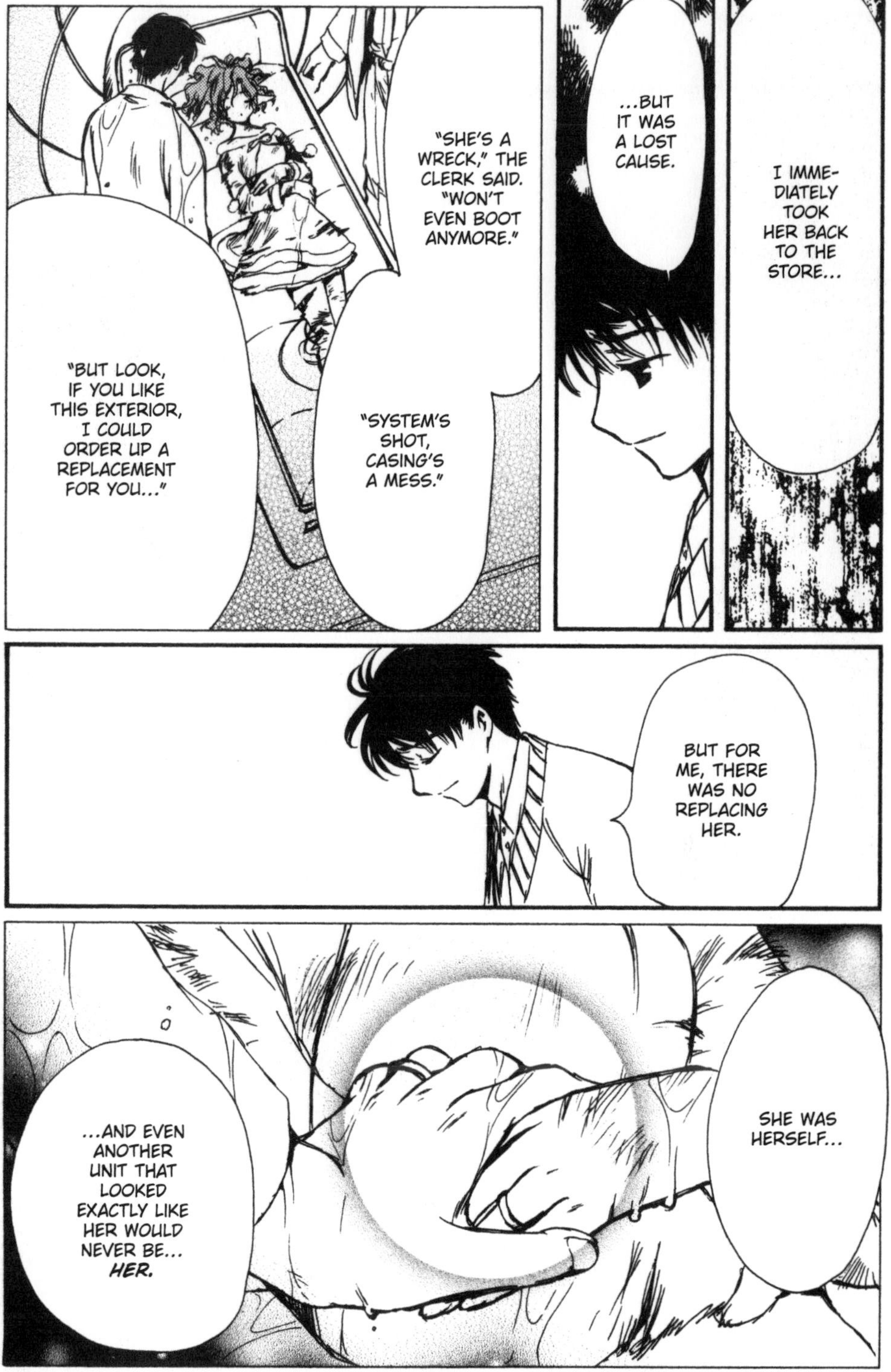
I IMME-DIATELY TOOK HER BACK TO THE STORE...
...BUT IT WAS A LOST CAUSE.
"SHE'S A WRECK," THE CLERK SAID. "WON'T EVEN BOOT ANYMORE."
"SYSTEM'S SHOT, CASING'S A MESS."
"BUT LOOK, IF YOU LIKE THIS EXTERIOR, I COULD ORDER UP A REPLACEMENT FOR YOU..."
BUT FOR ME, THERE WAS NO REPLACING HER.
SHE WAS HERSELF...
...AND EVEN ANOTHER UNIT THAT LOOKED EXACTLY LIKE HER WOULD NEVER BE... ***HER.***

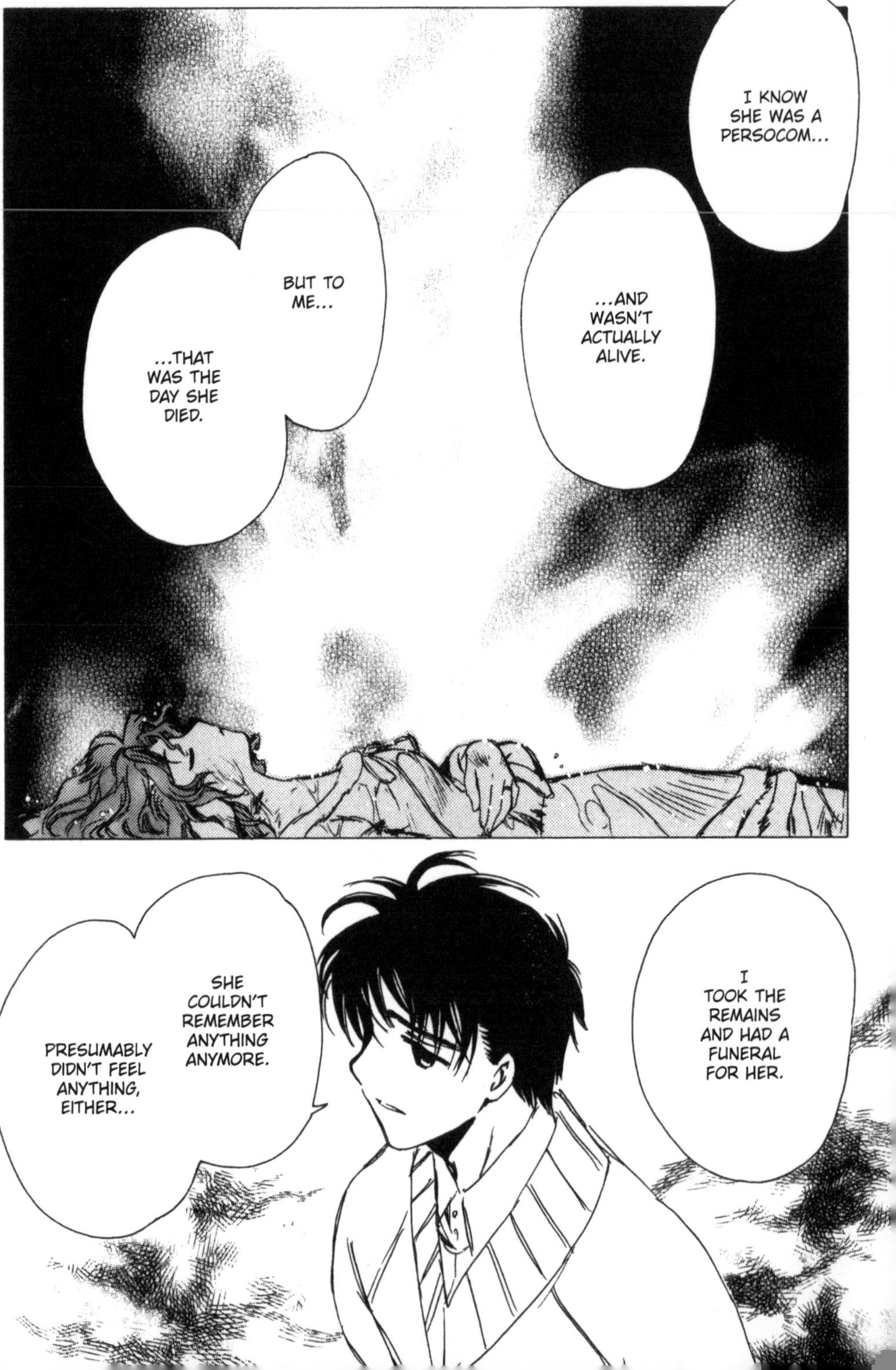
I KNOW SHE WAS A PERSOCOM...
...AND WASN'T ACTUALLY ALIVE.
BUT TO ME...
...THAT WAS THE DAY SHE DIED.
I TOOK THE REMAINS AND HAD A FUNERAL FOR HER.
SHE COULDN'T REMEMBER ANYTHING ANYMORE.
PRESUMABLY DIDN'T FEEL ANYTHING, EITHER...

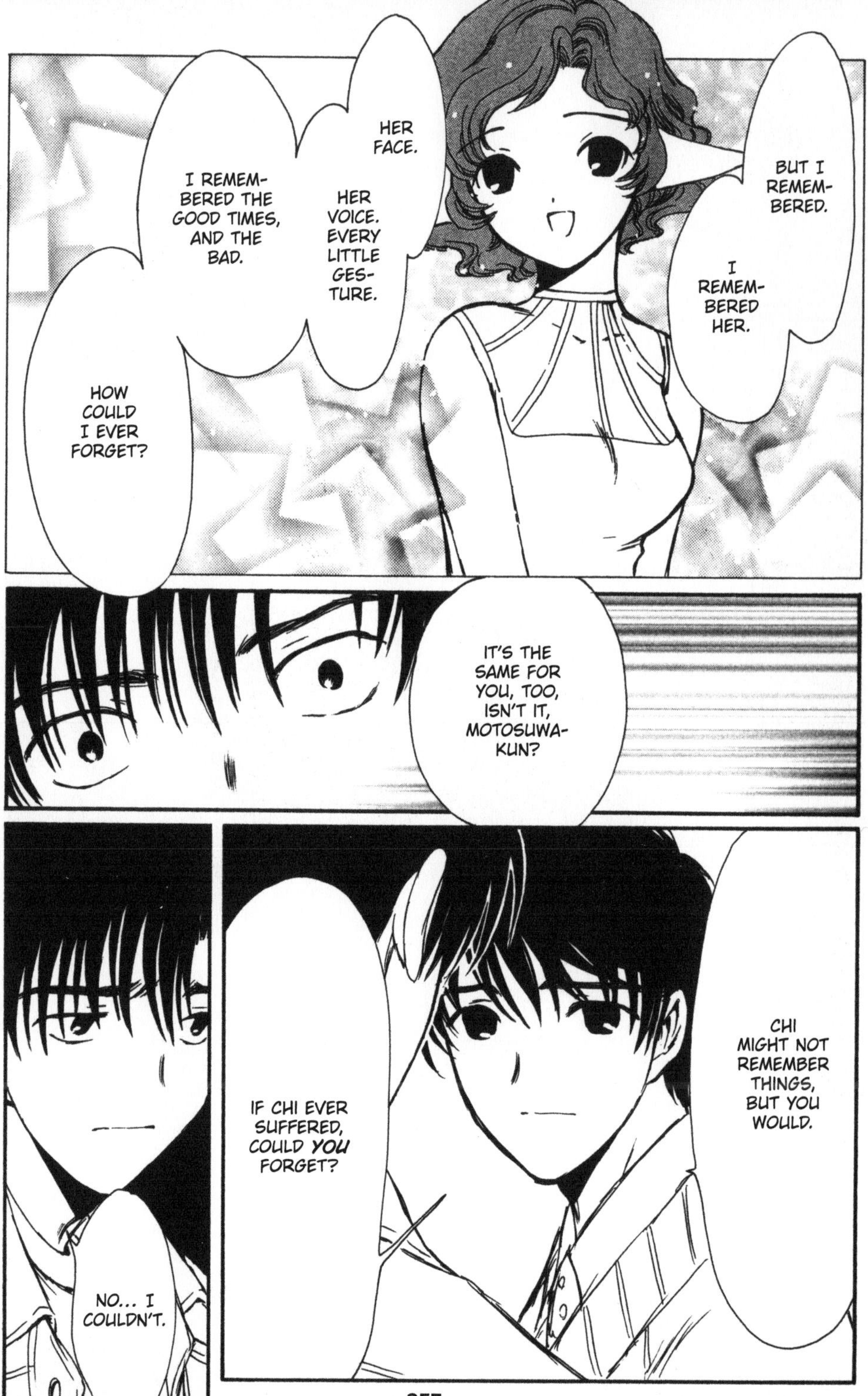
BUT I REMEMBERED.
I REMEMBERED HER.
HER FACE.
HER VOICE. EVERY LITTLE GESTURE.
I REMEMBERED THE GOOD TIMES, AND THE BAD.
HOW COULD I EVER FORGET?
IT'S THE SAME FOR YOU, TOO, ISN'T IT, MOTOSUWA-KUN?
CHI MIGHT NOT REMEMBER THINGS, BUT YOU WOULD.
IF CHI EVER SUFFERED, COULD *YOU* FORGET?
NO... I COULDN'T.

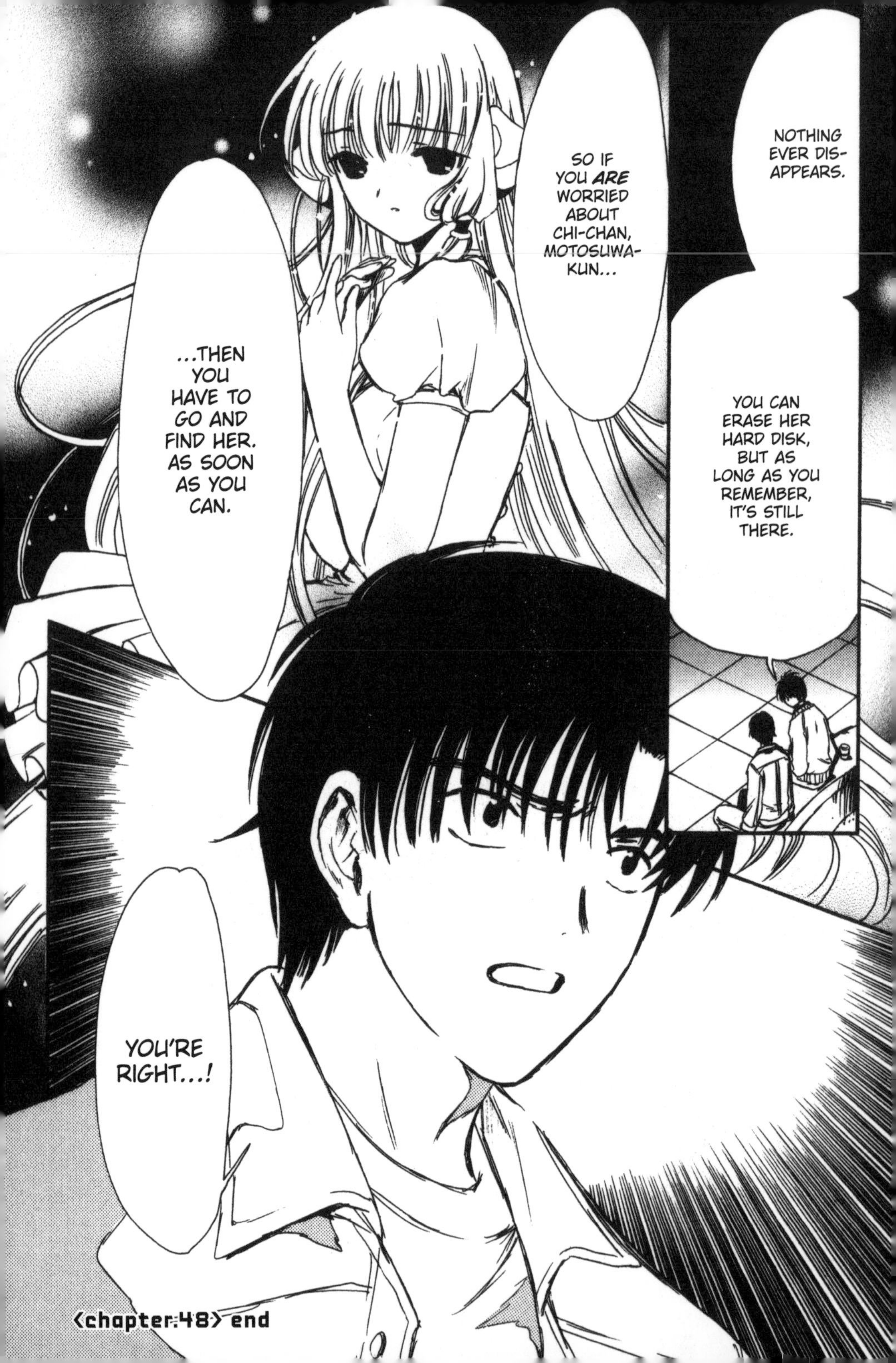
NOTHING EVER DIS-APPEARS.
YOU CAN ERASE HER HARD DISK, BUT AS LONG AS YOU REMEMBER, IT'S STILL THERE.
SO IF YOU **ARE** WORRIED ABOUT CHI-CHAN, MOTOSUWA-KUN...
...THEN YOU HAVE TO GO AND FIND HER. AS SOON AS YOU CAN.
YOU'RE RIGHT...!
<chapter.48> end

Chobits

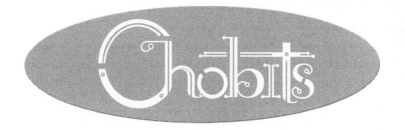

Translation Notes

Extra classes, page 170

I'M SORRY, TOO, RUSHING YOU TO MEET ME RIGHT AFTER SCHOOL.
IT'S FINE.
I DON'T GO TO EXTRA CLASSES OR ANYTHING.

Minoru says that he doesn't go to *juku*—a private school whose lessons are meant to review and expand on what students have learned at their regular school during the day, all in hopes of giving them a leg up on the incredibly intense examinations that will dictate their admittance first to high school, and then to college. *Juku* are demanding in their own right: students may stay late at night, and that's before they get home and start doing their homework. The standard translation of *juku* is "cram school," but we chose a different rendering to avoid confusion with the institution Hideki spends his days attending. That's technically a *yobi-kou*—roughly, prep school, which may be attended by high schoolers, but often caters to *ronin* like Hideki, who have failed their college entrance exams and want to study some more before trying again.

Boss, page 201

In Japan, it's common to continue to address people in terms of the most recent or most prominent social relationship you had to them, like Senpai or Sensei, even if you're no longer specifically in that position. So Hideki naturally continues to call Ueda-san 'boss' (*tenchou*), harking back to when they worked together.

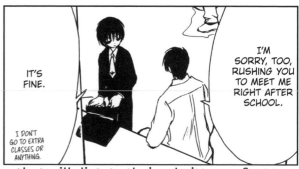

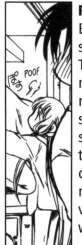

POOF

Futon storage, page 209

Because land is so expensive, Japanese houses are often smaller than their counterparts in some countries in the West. That goes double for apartments, and it goes triple for apartments in Tokyo. (And probably quadruple for the sort of apartment in Tokyo you live in when you're a broke cram school student!) For that reason, there's often a small closet to one side where the *futon* (bed-roll—it's like a mattress that goes on the floor, not a folding couch like the word evokes in the US) can be folded up and put away, giving the room's occupant the most possible usable space during the day. (A similar setup is very common in *ryokan,* traditional Japanese hotels.) That's what Chi is doing in the background of this panel.

The dupe, page 264

Traditional Japanese *manzai* (comedy duo) routines involve a straight man (*tsukkomi*) and a dupe (*boke*). The dupe says or does something ridiculous (*boke* comes from *bokeru*, meaning roughly "to be airheaded"), and the straight man makes a cutting observation in response (*tsukkomi* comes from *tsukkomu*, literally meaning "to butt in," but in practice often meaning "to deliver a sarcastic quip").

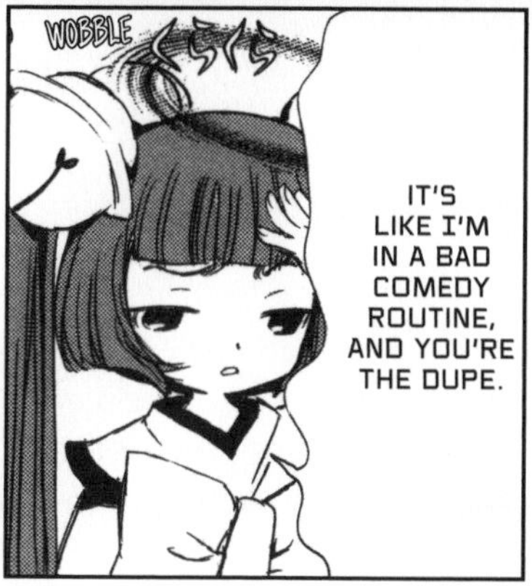
WOBBLE
IT'S LIKE I'M IN A BAD COMEDY ROUTINE, AND YOU'RE THE DUPE.

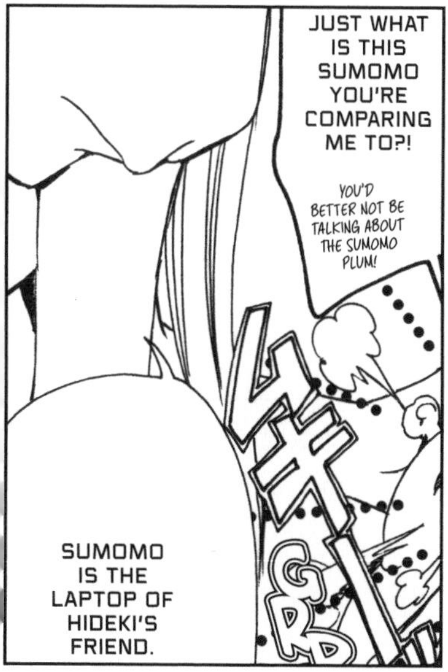
JUST WHAT IS THIS SUMOMO YOU'RE COMPARING ME TO?!
YOU'D BETTER NOT BE TALKING ABOUT THE SUMOMO PLUM!
SUMOMO IS THE LAPTOP OF HIDEKI'S FRIEND.

Sumomo, page 315

Although we chose to retain Sumomo's Japanese name in the translation, it's actually the name of a plant, *Prunus salicina*, commonly called the Japanese or Chinese plum. Confusingly, these common names are also applied to the plant known in Japanese as *ume* (*Prunus mume*), which is closely related to both the plum and the apricot, and produces the famous white "plum blossoms." By the way, just to make things extra interesting, *momo* is the Japanese word for peach (*P. persica*), and the characters *su-momo* literally mean "vinegary peach."

Family register, page 332

All Japanese families have a so-called "register," or *koseki*, that contains details about the family, including births, deaths, marriages and divorces, and, of course, the names of family members, including their spouses and offspring. The status of family members who are not Japanese citizens, however, has always been fraught: for example, foreign (*gaikokujin*) spouses are entered as essentially marginal notes to their Japanese partners. There would naturally be questions about how to handle a robot spouse in terms of the *koseki*—but a marriage whose partners are not entered in the family register is not considered valid under Japanese law.

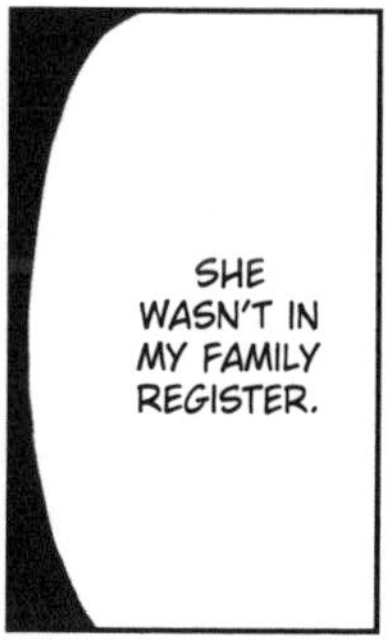
SHE WASN'T IN MY FAMILY REGISTER.

A Kodansha Comics Hardcover Original
Chobits 20th Anniversary Edition volume 2 copyright © 2001
CLAMP · Shigatsu Tsuitachi Co., Ltd. / Kodansha Ltd.
English translation copyright © 2020
CLAMP · Shigatsu Tsuitachi Co., Ltd. / Kodansha Ltd.

All rights reserved.

Published in the United States by Kodansha Comics, an imprint of Kodansha USA Publishing, LLC, New York.

Publication rights for this English edition arranged through Kodansha Ltd., Tokyo.

First published in Japan in 2001 by Kodansha Ltd., Tokyo as *Chobittsu*, volumes 3 and 4.

ISBN 978-1-64651-017-7

Printed in China.

www.kodanshacomics.com

9 8 7 6 5 4 3 2
Translation: Kevin Steinbach
Lettering: Michael Martin
Editing: Tiff Ferentini
Kodansha Comics edition cover design: Phil Balsman

Publisher: Kiichiro Sugawara
Vice president of marketing & publicity: Naho Yamada

Director of publishing services: Ben Applegate
Associate director of operations: Stephen Pakula
Publishing services managing editor: Noelle Webster
Assistant production manager: Emi Lotto, Angela Zurlo

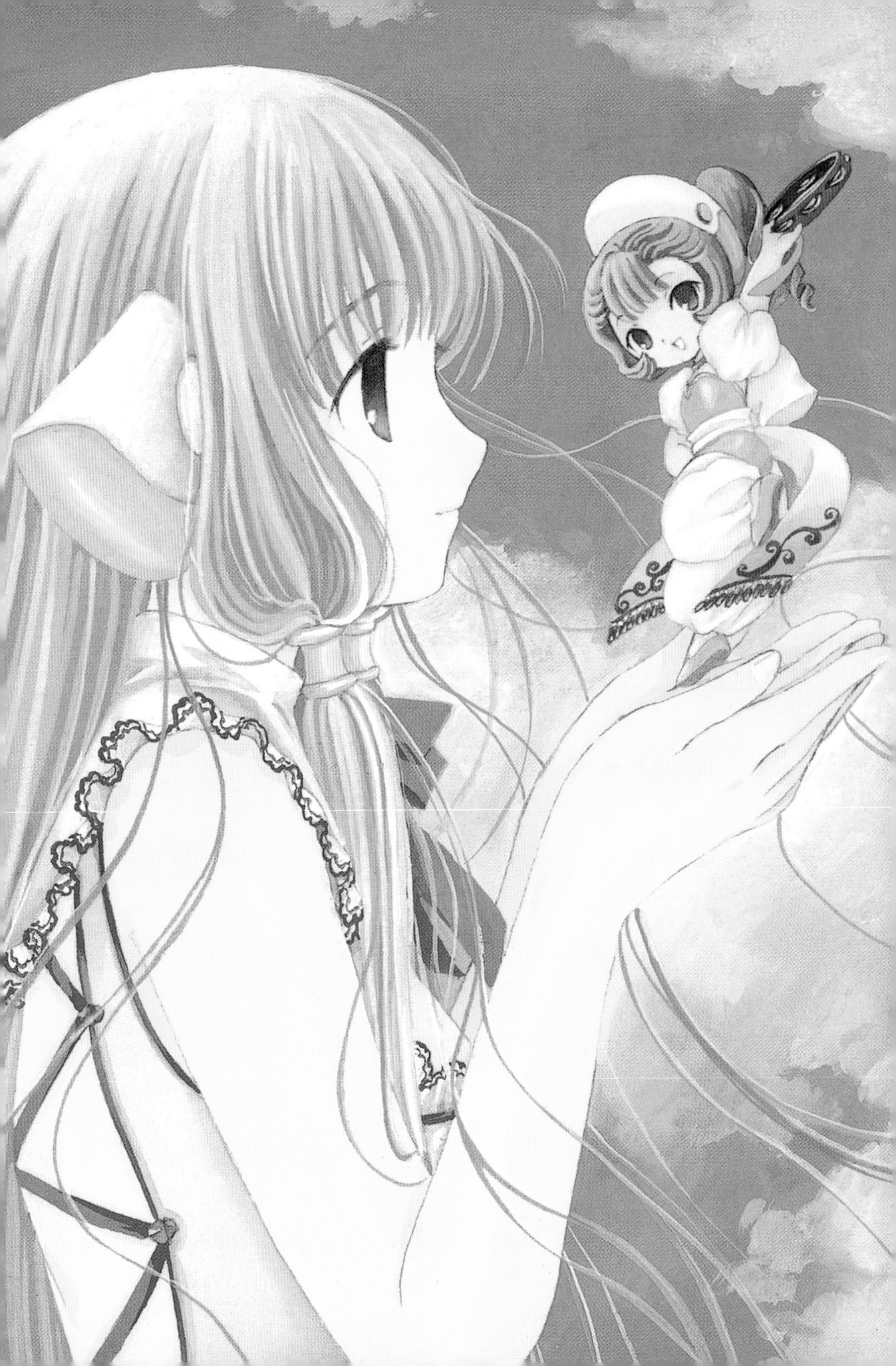

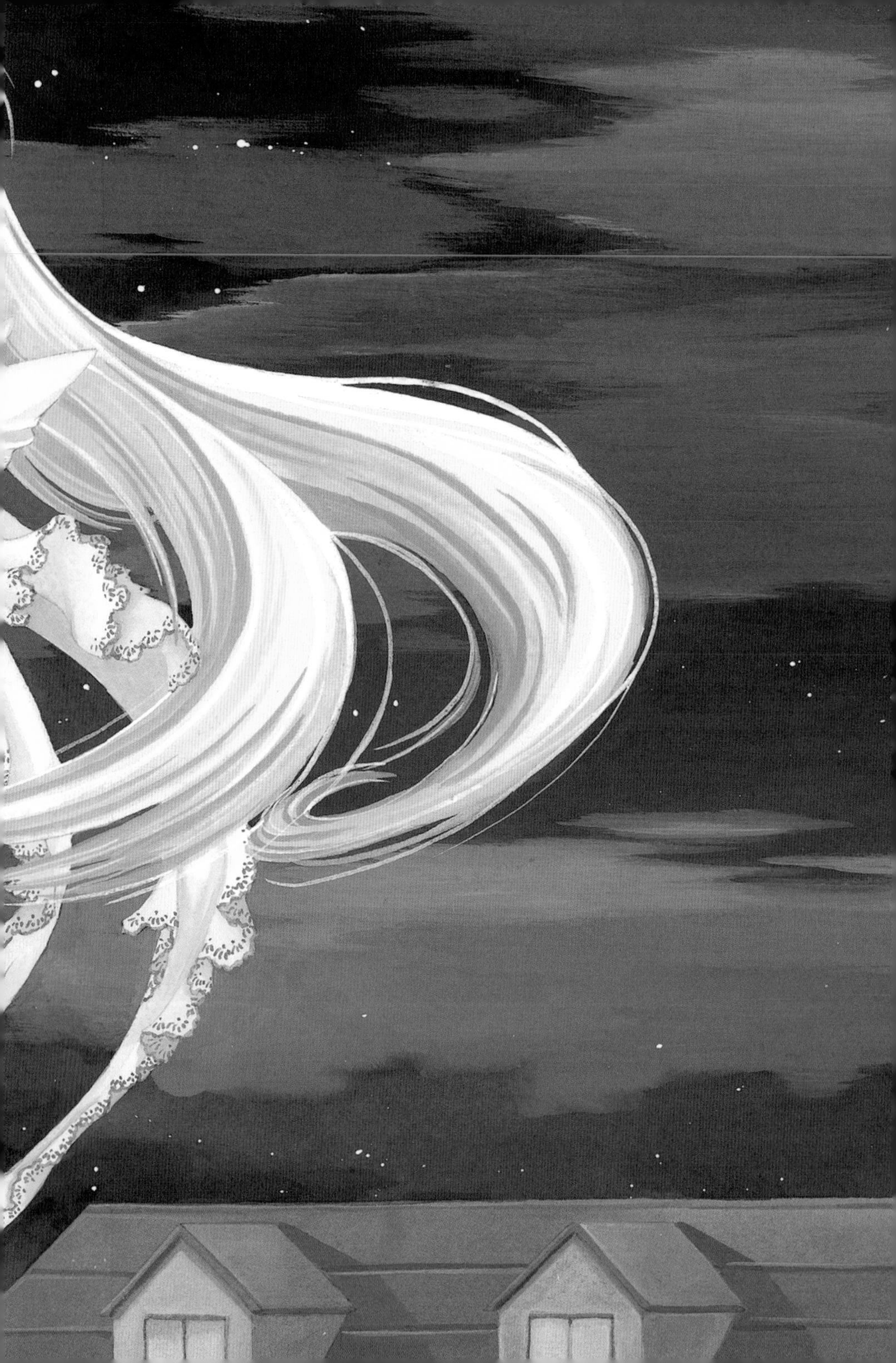

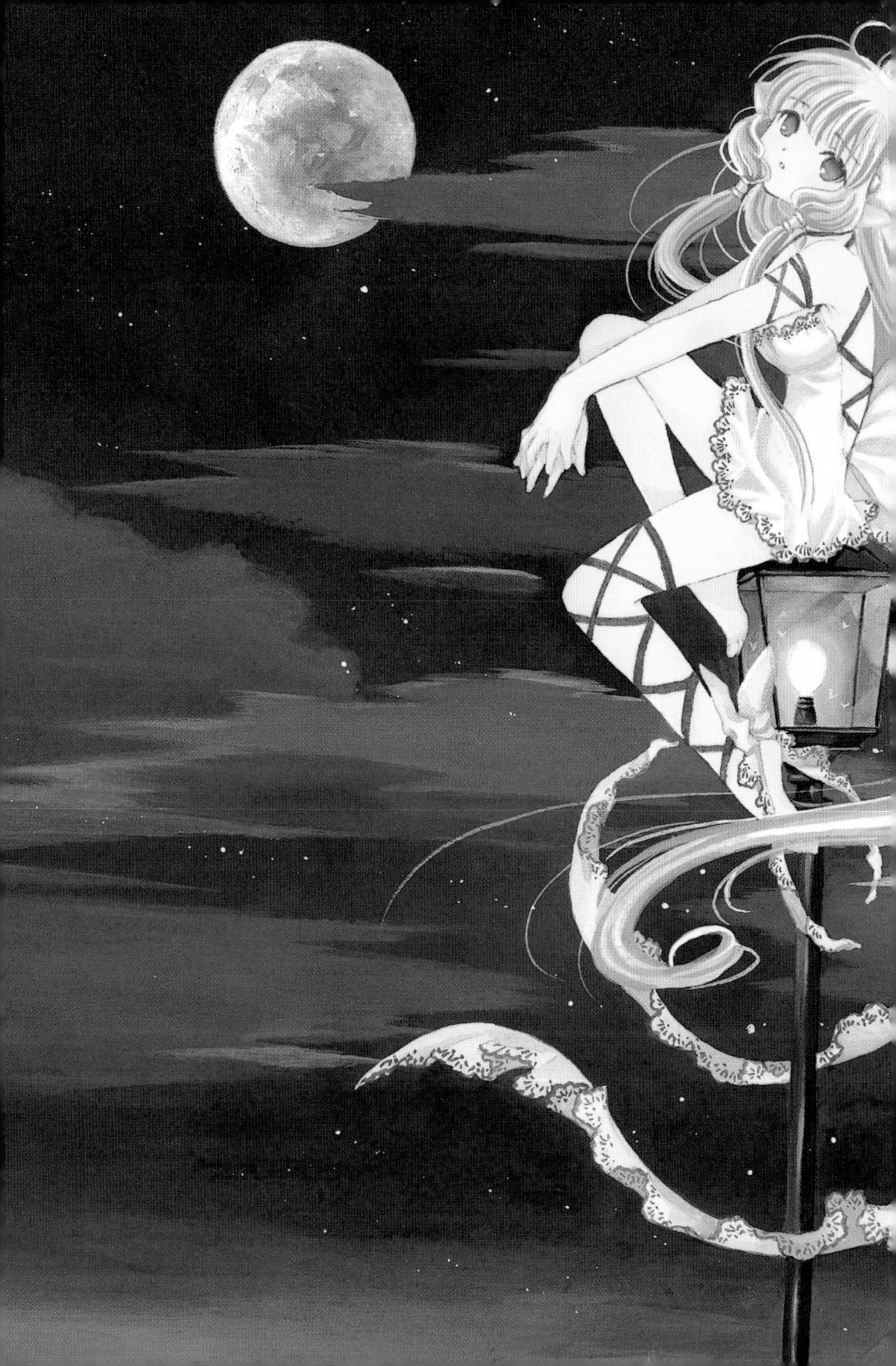

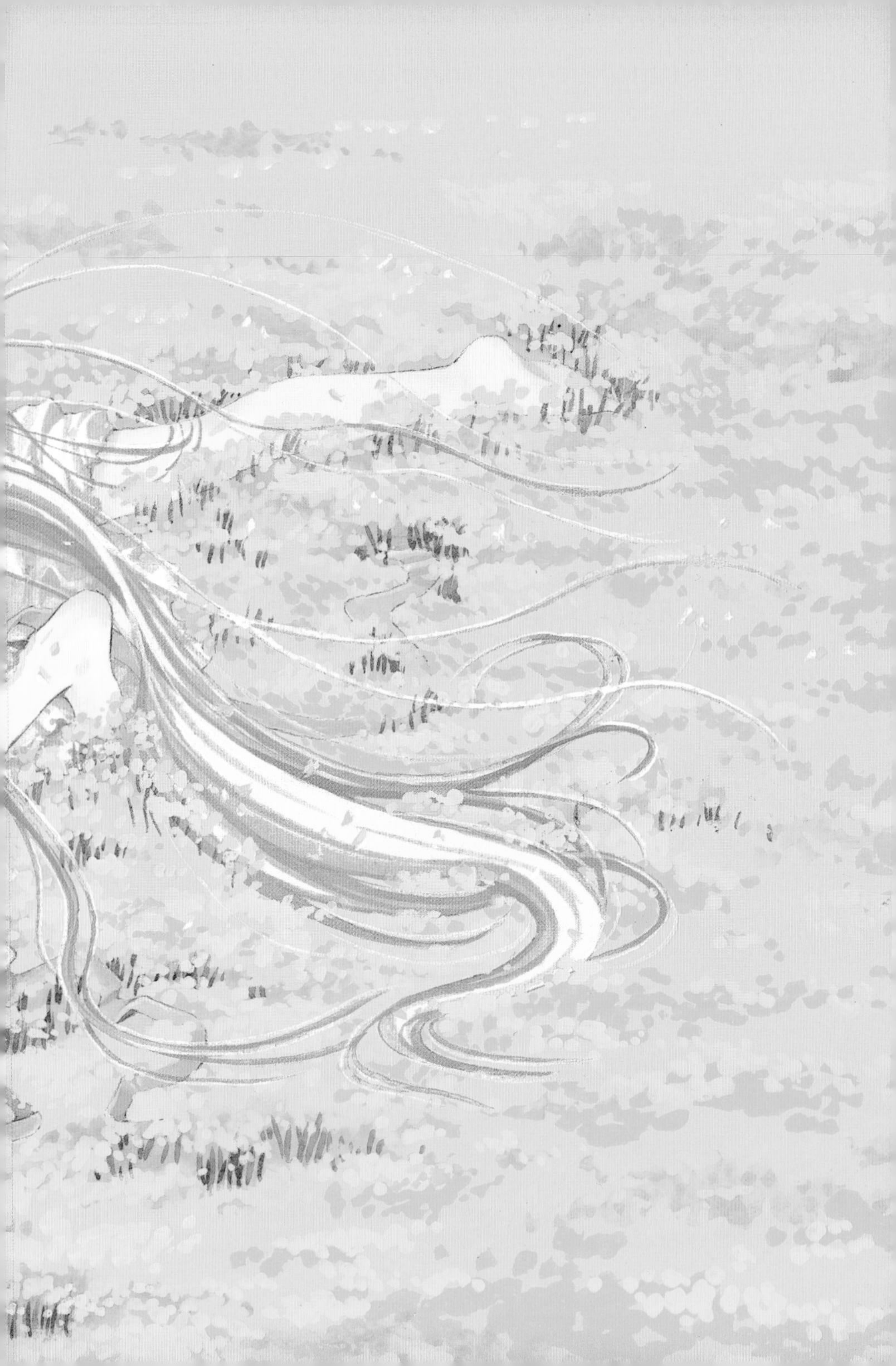

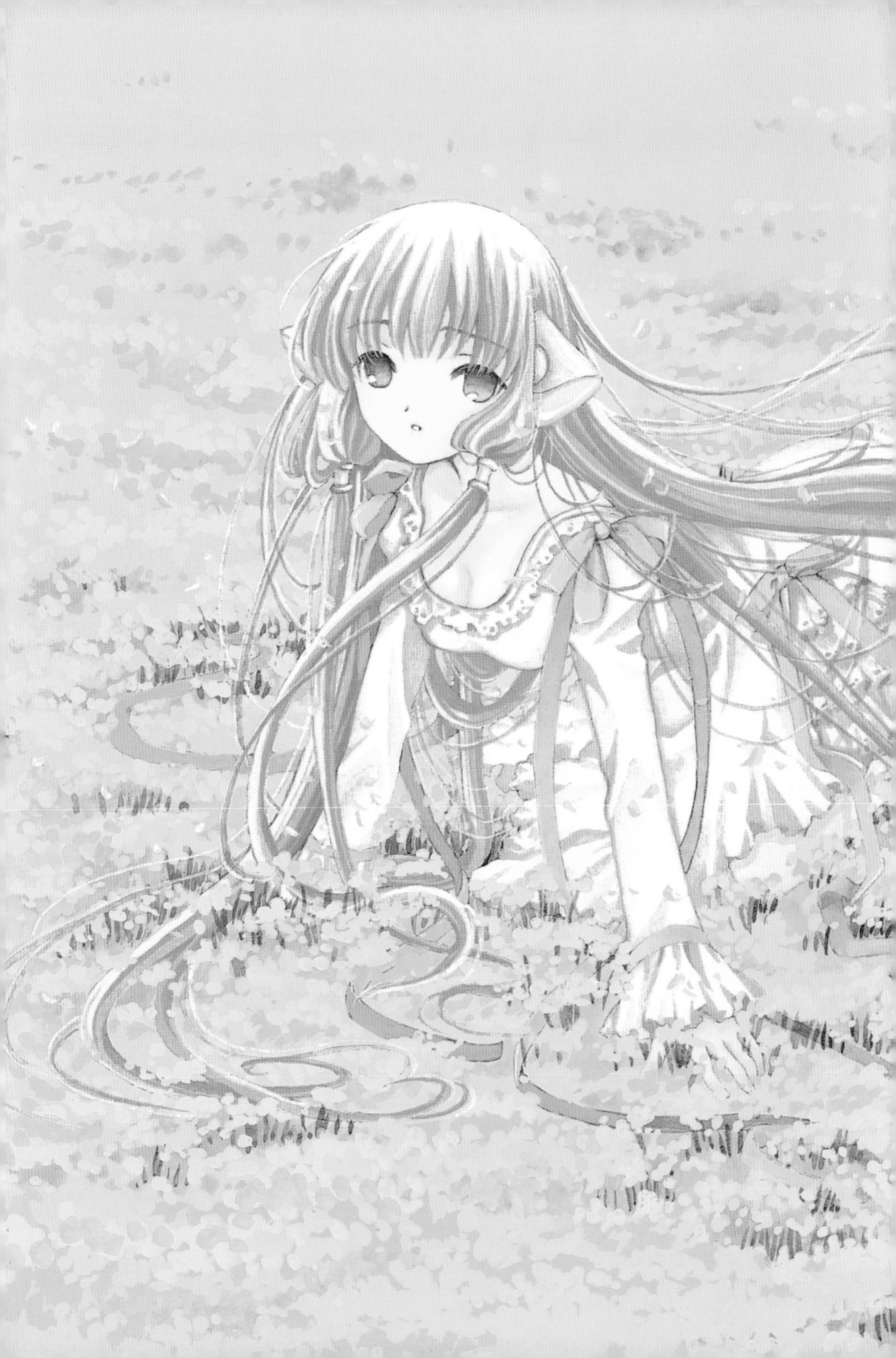

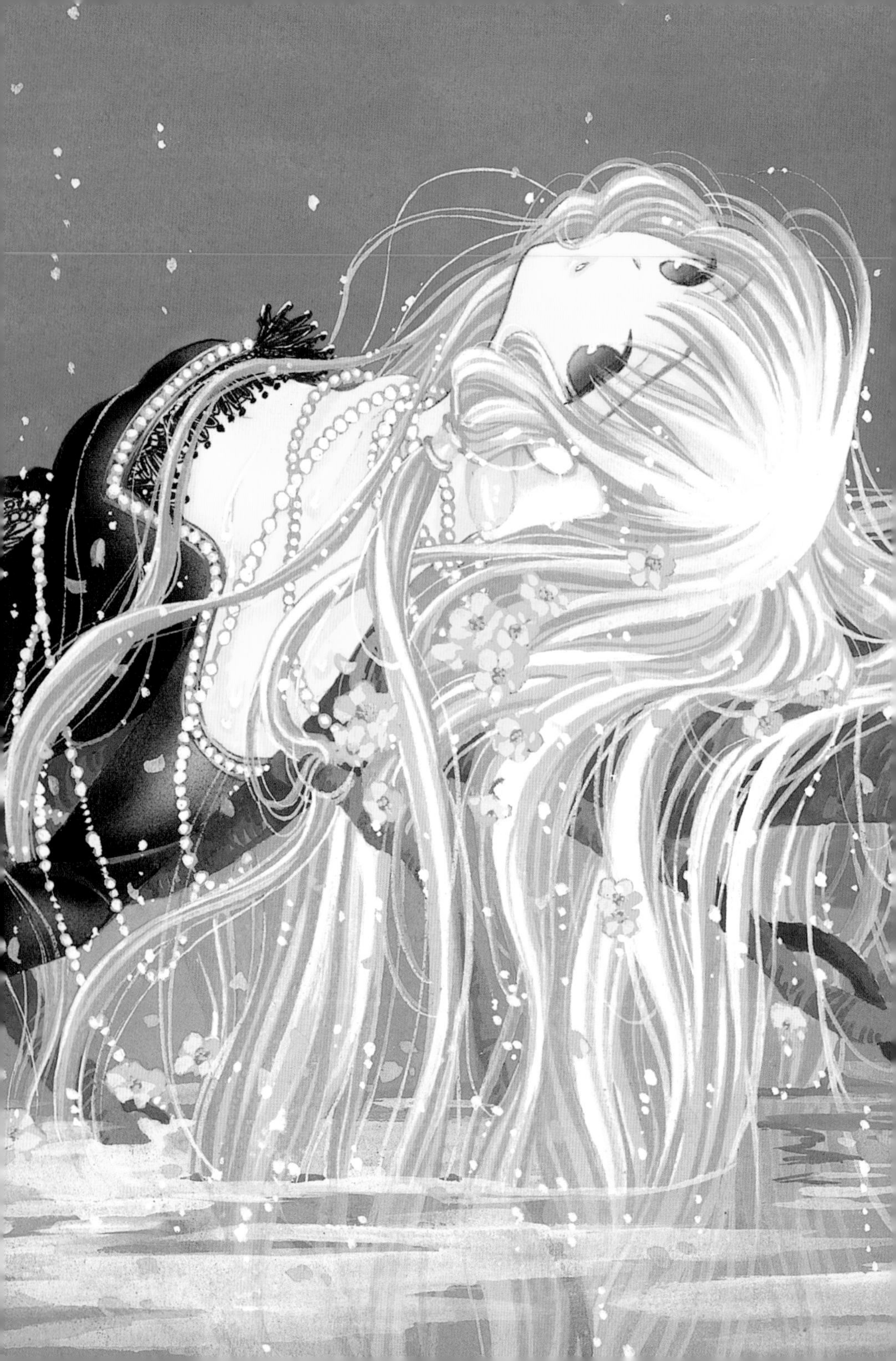

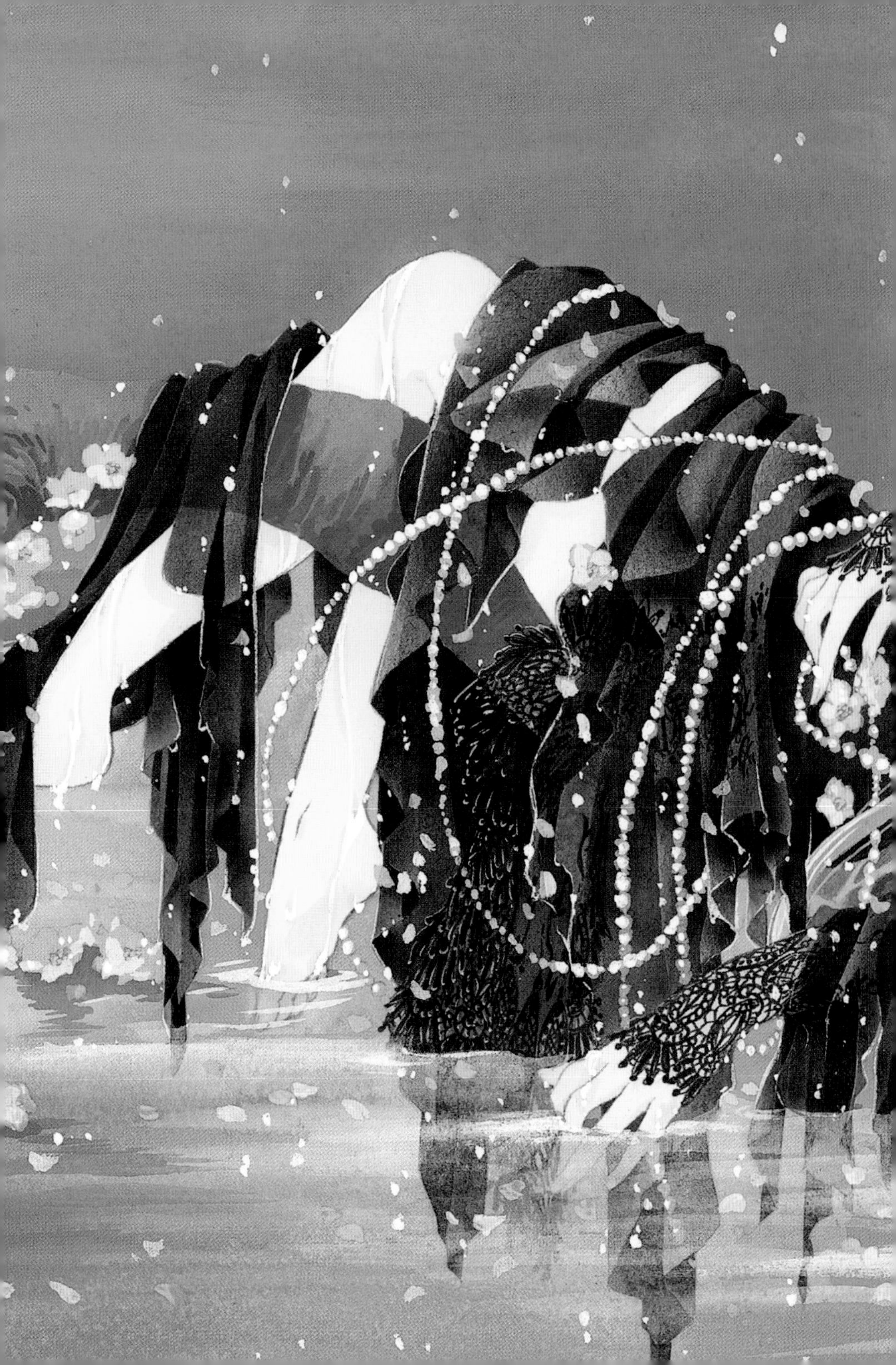

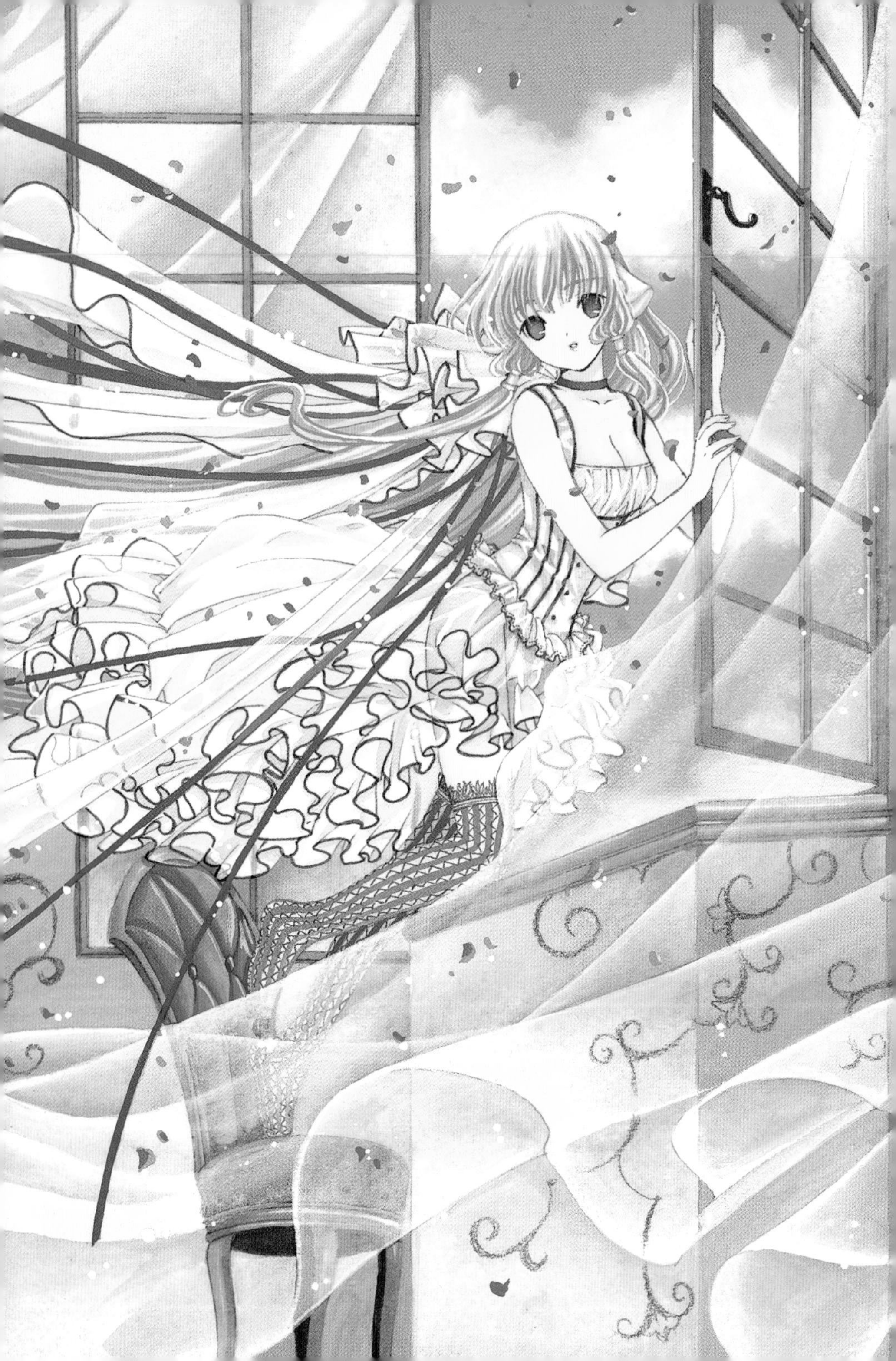

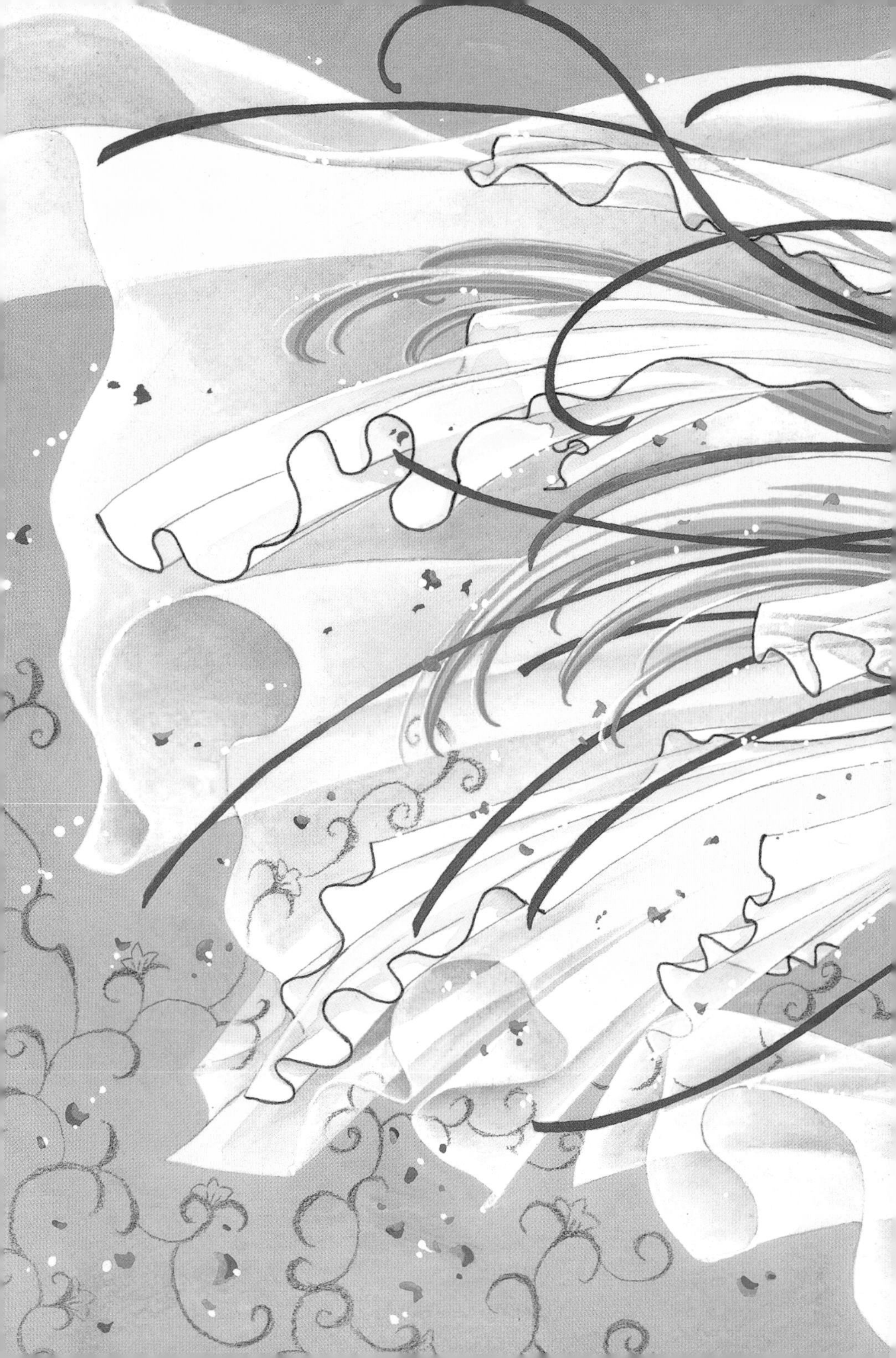

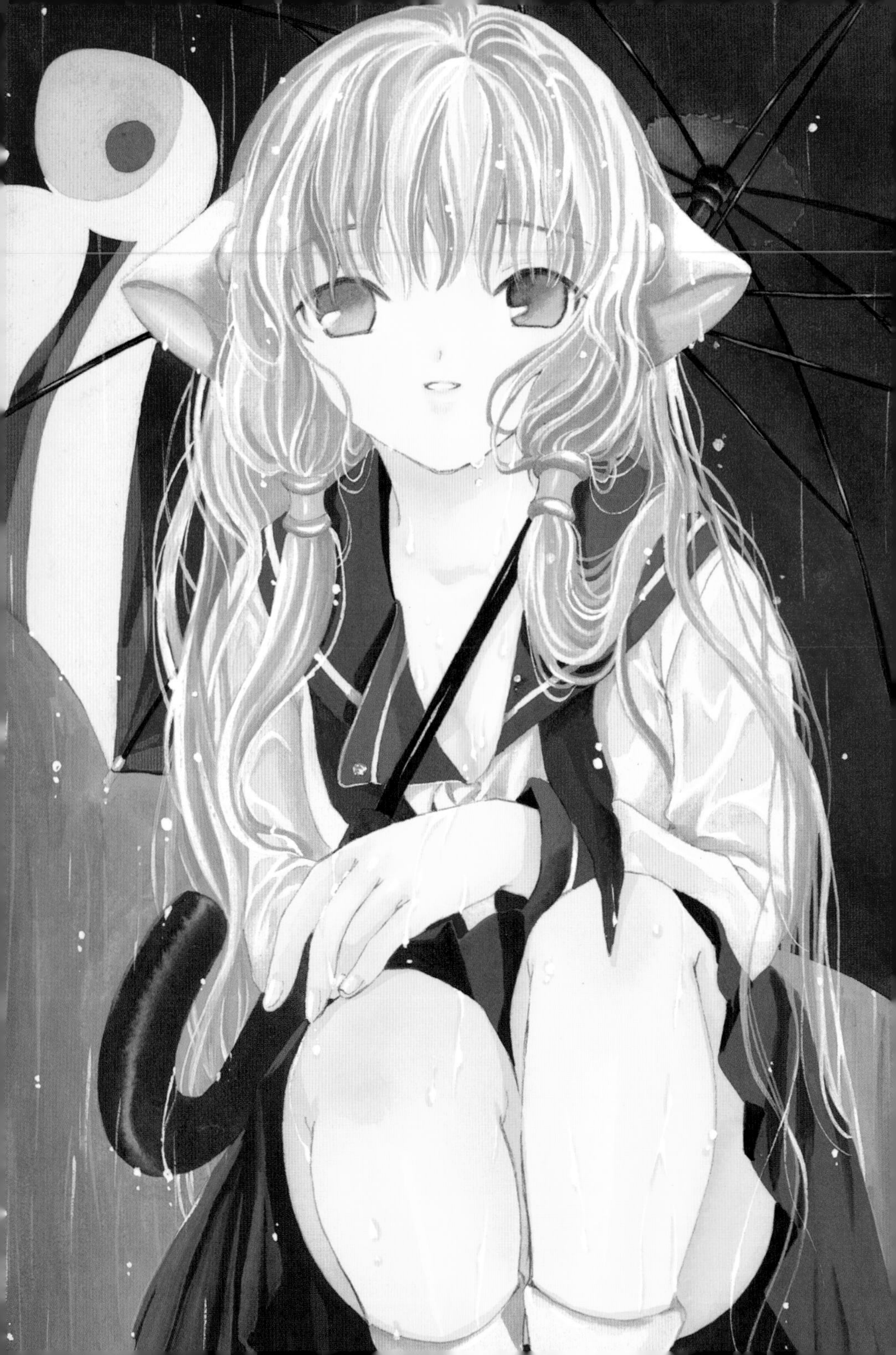

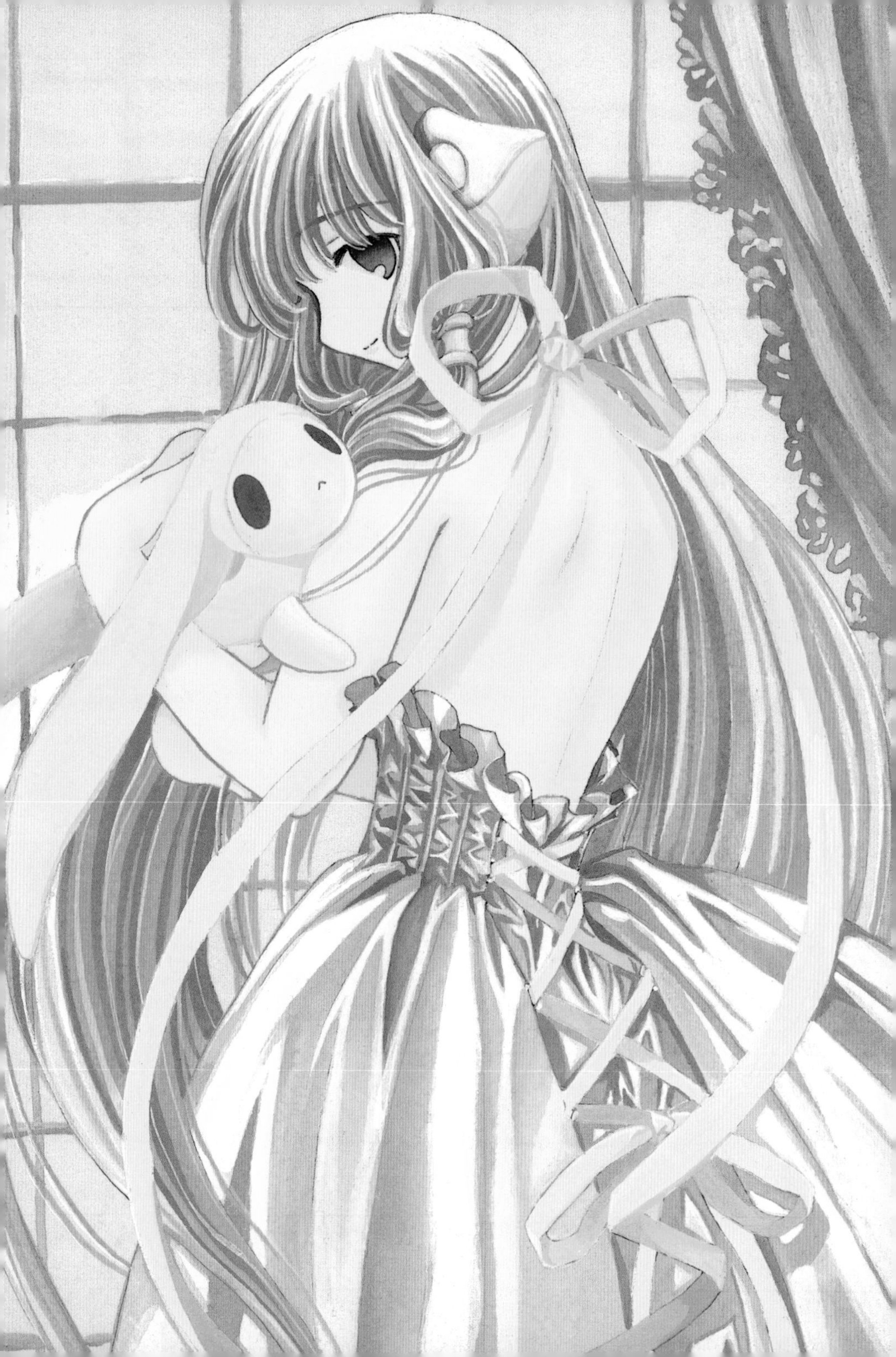

Date: 3/4/22

**GRA 741.5 CHO V.2
Chobits. 20th Anniversary
Edition /**